ENVIRONMENTAL LAW

ENVIRONMENTAL LAW

Sweet & Maxwell Textbook Series

Justine Thornton, M.A. (Cantab.)
Barrister
and
Silas Beckwith, LL.B (Lond.)
Barrister, Senior Lecturer in Law, London Guildhall University

Second Edition

SWEET & MAXWELL

Published in 2004 by Sweet & Maxwell, 100 Avenue Road, London, NW3 3PF
part of Thomson Reuters (Professional) UK Limited
(Registered in England & Wales, Company No 1679046. registered Office and address for service:
Aldgate House, 33 Aldgate High Street, London, EC3N 1DL.)
For further information on our products and services, visit
www.sweetandmaxwell.co.uk

Printed on Demand from 2013

Typeset by LBJ Typesetting Ltd of Kingsclere

Printed and bound in Great Britain by
Hobbs the Printers, Totton, Hants

No natural forests were destroyed to make this product:
only farmed timber was used and replanted

A C.I.P. Catalogue record for this book is available from the British Library

ISBN: 978-0-421-77990-7

FOREWORD TO THE FIRST EDITION

Hardly anybody would disagree with the statement that the environment needs protection; this basic rule of the game in our society seems well recognised today. Opinions only differ on the question of how much protection the environment needs, how this protection should be organised and to what part of the society the rule of the game should apply: to England, to Northern Ireland, to Gibraltar, to the European Union, to the Falklands or to the whole planet?

We are at the beginnings of our discovery of environmental law, as it is and as it should be effectively to ensure protection. We try to find appropriate rules to prevent deterioration of this planet and to leave *urbem et orbem* in a better state than they were when we took over from our fathers.

The environmental law which is presented in this book focusses on the United Kingdom: indeed, the reader cannot hope to understand European Community or international environmental law, if he does not first know and understand the provisions which affect his own neighbourhood. Of course, provisions which preserve, protect and improve the quality of the environment are technical and sometimes difficult to understand. But the authors have taken particular care to make this a transparent and readable text.

Most of the law which is presented in this book is of a very recent date, and most of it is statute law. This is not surprising: environmental problems are first and foremost problems of the affluent society, which is very complex and complicated. And the number of environmental standards is increasing, simply by the fact that the emission of pollutants into the air, the water or the soil can no longer be seen as an activity which can take place uncontrolled: pollution becomes simply too expensive for this planet. Before anybody raises concern about too many environmental standards, he should first have a look into the number of technical standards, which BSI and other national and international standardisation bodies produce annually. In the European Community, we have more than fifty thousand standards!

This book is constructed in a way that enables the reader easily to find his way through the numerous and interdependent provisions which the authors so carefully and lucidly describe and I hope that he enjoys this reading. For me, it was sometimes a pure pleasure to go through the text and rediscover the structure of the law that tries to protect the environment. I cannot but hope that the success of this book encourages the authors to write more on environmental issues.

Ludwig Kramer
European Commission
Brussels

PREFACE

Since the first edition, there have been some significant developments in environmental law. These have necessitated an expansion and restructuring of the book and the inclusion of new chapters. To take just two examples: Climate change has continued to emerge as an outstanding challenge, and the legal response to it, both international and domestic, has grown much more complex. Waste regulation has increased in detail and scope—producer responsibility for end-of-life products (an embryonic concept at the time of our first edition) will shortly become an everyday reality.

Concurrent with this growth in environmental regulation, there has been a shift in the *culture* of LAJ environmental law. The trend towards a holistic and integrated approach, apparent in the 1990s, has become even more pronounced with the adoption of the Integrated Pollution Prevention and Control regime. There is increased emphasis on public participation in environmental decision making, access to environmental information, and access to justice in environmental matters—concepts neatly embraced by Kofi Annan's phrase "environmental democracy", which we gratefully adopt in the title of Ch. 14. Environmental law-making, at least in theory, is becoming less the preserve of regulators, " scientists and specialists, and more the concern of ordinary people. This places new pressures on the law-making system, as it strives to reconcile the diverse and sometimes competing demands of science, ethics, risk management, and public accountability. Nowhere, perhaps, have these pressures been more apparent than in the regulation of Genetically Modified Organisms.

In preparing this edition, much of the burden of research has fallen on Justine. But the book remains a joint effort, and needless to say, responsibility for errors is shared. We would like to thank the following people for their assistance and support: Susan Hawker, George Barda, Owen Lomas and the Environment Group at Allen & Overy, Guy Henderson, Justin Pavry, Amy Merrill, Richard Norridge; Laura Gyte, Darren Hanwell, Annabelle Whitby-Smith, Julian Cahn, Hannah Fearn, Piers Reynolds, Suzy Lloyd, Aemelia Allen, and the document production team at Allen & Overy.

Environmental law remains in a state of constant development. We have sought to state law and policy on the basis of materials available to us in May, 2004. As in our first edition, we have tried to provide an accessible text, designed for readers approaching environmental law for the first time. Inevitably, this means we sometimes repeat ourselves. There is a mischievous and illusory line marking the distinction between a concept helpfully reinforced and a concept laboured. We can only hope that, most of the time, we have managed to draw it in the right place.

Justine Thormton
Silas Beckwith
May 2004

TABLE OF CONTENTS

TABLE OF ABBREVIATIONS

The following abbreviations are used in the text:

A-G	Attorney-General
AONB	Areas of Outstanding Natural Beauty
BAT	Best Available Techniques
BATNEEC	Best Available Techniques Not Entailing Excessive Cost
BC	Borough Council
BPEO	Best Practicable Environmental Option
BPM	Best Practicable Means
CC	City Council or County Council
CAA 1993	Clean Air Act 1993
COPA 1974	Control of Pollution Act 1974
CRWA 2000	Countryside and Rights of Way Act 2000
DC	District Council
DEFRA	Dept. of Environment Food and Rural Affairs
DETR	former Dept of Environment, Transport and the Regions
DTLR	former Dept. of Transport, Local Govt. and the Regions
EA 1995	Environment Act 1995
EEC	former European Economic Community
EC	European Community (see also EU)
ECHR	European Court of Human Rights
EJC	European Court of Justice
EIA	Environmental Impact Assessment
EMF	Electromagnetic Fields
EPA 1990	Environmental Protection Act 1990
EU	European Union (also see EC)
FOE	Friends of the Earth
HRA 1998	Human Rights Act 1998
HMIP	former Her Majesty's Inspectorate of Pollution
HSE	Health and Safety Executive
IPC	Integrated Pollution Control
IPPC	Integrated Pollution Prevention and Control
LA	Local Authority
LBC	London Borough Council
LPA	Local Planning Authority
MBC	Metropolitan Borough Council
NRA	former National Rivers Authority

ODPM	Office of Deputy Prime Minister
PCA 1991	Planning and Compensation Act 1991
PPC	Pollution Prevention and Control
PPCA 1999	Pollution Prevention and Control Act 1999
RCEP	Royal Commission for Environmental Pollution
TCPA 1990	Town and Country Planning Act 1990
TEU	Treaty of European Union
UN	United Nations
WCA 1981	Wildlife and Countryside Act 1981

TABLE OF CASES

TABLE OF STATUTES

TABLE OF STATUTORY INSTRUMENTS

Table of EC Directives

TABLE OF EC REGULATIONS

TABLE OF EC TREATIES

TABLE OF CONVENTIONS

Chapter 1

THE NATURE OF ENVIRONMENTAL LAW

"The protection and preservation of the environment is now perceived as being of crucial importance to the future of mankind." (Lord Goff, *Cambridge Water Co. v Eastern Counties Leather plc*,[1] House of Lords)

Introduction

Over the course of the last century, the relationship between human beings and the **1–001** planet on which they live changed fundamentally. At the beginning of the century, it was not possible for mankind and the technology upon which he relied to alter the environment radically. By the end of the century, huge increases in scientific knowledge had given us the power to make irrevocable changes to our planet. To appreciate the scale of what has taken place, it is instructive to consider things in this way: imagine that the hundreds of millions of years of our planet's history, during which natural resources have slowly been accumulating, is a period of one year. In other words, imagine that the world began on January 1st, and that it is now midnight, on December 31st. On this scale, the oldest known rocks appeared on February 25th, but the first plants did not begin growing until November 1st. Humans did not appear until December 29th. The industrial revolution, which has been responsible for most of mankind's exploitation of natural resources, took place only two seconds ago.[2]

The environment is the source of the energy and materials which mankind transforms into goods and services to meet his needs. It also acts as a vast sink for the wastes and polluting substances he generates. It provides a number of basic conditions needed for the existence of a successful economy—a stable climate, for example. Environmental resources form the basis of, and therefore set limits to, economic development. Many environmental problems are rooted in an increased demand for natural resources, and in the increased pollution and waste associated with current patterns of economic development.

Most people's understanding of the environment tends to be that it is ever-deteriorating. Resources are depleting. The population is increasing, which means less

---

[1] [1994] 1 All E.R. 53.
[2] *Europe's Environment: The Dobris Assessment* (eds David Stanners and Phillipe Bourdeau) (1996), The European Environment Agency.

to eat. The water and air are more polluted. Species and habitats are becoming extinct in vast numbers, and the forests are dying. On another view, however, the world is not running out of energy or natural resources, and the quality of people's lives—which ultimately reflects the quality of their environment—is getting better and better. In 1900, the average lifespan was 30 years; today it is 67 years. According to the UN, poverty has been reduced more in the last 50 years than in the preceding 500, in almost every country. Global warming is almost certainly taking place, but projections about its extent and effects may be unrealistically pessimistic. (Worryingly, the current solution, namely a reduction in the use of fossil fuels, might create a far worse problem.) Species loss in our life-time is probably 0.7 per cent, rather than the sometimes mentioned 25–50 per cent. Acid rain does not kill the forests, and the air and water around us are becoming less and less polluted.

This is the sort of optimistic view put forward by Professor Bjorn Lomborg, in his controversial book, *The Skeptical Environmentalist*.[3] The author, who is Associate Professor of Statistics at the University of Aarhus, and a former member of Greenpeace, uses the best available statistical information from internationally recognised research institutes to examine a range of major environmental problems that feature prominently in headline news across the world. He concludes that there are more reasons for optimism than pessimism, and stresses the need for clear-headed prioritisation of resources to tackle real, not imagined problems. As Lombourg suggests, however, scepticism and environmentalism are not mutually exclusive—even if an optimistic view is appropriate, this does not mean that the state of the environment is presently adequate, so that we should abandon our efforts to preserve and improve it.

How much human-induced change can the world's environment sustain? Our understanding of environmental systems is still too limited to provide any conclusive answers, which makes decisions about environmental protection difficult. Because of the subtle ways in which environmental factors inter-relate, the concepts of environmental harm and damage are not as simple as they might at first appear. Take as an example the deposit on land of toxic alkaline wastes by chemical manufacturers in Lancashire in the nineteenth century. Today, this would be regarded as a clear example of environmental harm. Nearby streams were rendered lifeless. The land on which the waste had been deposited could no longer support plant life. Gradually, however, rain and atmospheric carbon dioxide caused the calcium hydroxide on the surface of the land to disappear. This left an extremely limey soil containing few nutrients, in which a colony of beautiful orchids flourished. These sites are now protected as the most important sites in the UK for orchids.[4]

Protecting the environment is further complicated by the ability of the environment to accommodate some exposure to potentially hazardous substances without undergoing significant measurable change. This is known as the environment's "assimilative capacity". Natural processes in the environment can break down potentially hazardous substances into simple compounds that are relatively harmless. Another dimension of assimilation is the ability of various compartments of the environment to retain

---

[3] Bjorn Lomborg, *The Skeptical Environmentalist: Measuring the Real State of the World,* Cambridge University Press, 2001. (First published in Danish in 1998.)
[4] Mellanby, *Waste and Pollution—The Problem for Britain* (1992).

particular substances in "sinks" (for example, deep sediments in rivers and seas) where they are removed from circulation and either destroyed or stored, so that they no longer present an environmental hazard. This assimilative capacity of the environment must, of course, be taken into account when assessing the environmental harm likely to be caused by particular substances in particular combinations. Such assessments, therefore, are never easy, and depend on an understanding of complex scientific issues.

Environmental problems are characterised by other uncertainties in scientific knowledge. Sometimes, these result from a simple lack of data—the consequences of polluting emissions are not always clearly established, and the cumulative nature of pollutants from diverse sources means that effects may be seen only after long periods of time. Of greater complexity is uncertainty arising from the variability of natural processes. Natural systems operate by processes that are subject to chaotic fluctuations which cannot be accurately modelled, nor even understood in traditional scientific terms.

Two further factors add to the complications surrounding environmental protection:

First, our solutions to environmental problems may not always be as straightforward as we might think. It is commonly assumed, for example, that re-usable consumer products are more "environmentally friendly" than disposable ones, and that they should therefore be used in preference to disposable products. To take a particular example, the environmental problems associated with disposable nappies are well-known. Once the nappy has been used, the cotton and paper must be disposed of either by landfill (burying in the ground) or by incineration. Both of these methods of disposal cause environmental damage. Environmental damage caused at the manufacturing stage must also be considered—the use of energy, water and bleaching agents, for example—as must the damage caused by distributing the product to the consumer (for example by road, causing air and noise pollution).

The environmental problems associated with washable nappies, however, are less obvious. Clearly, fewer nappies will be disposed of, which will cause fewer environmental problems. However, washing nappies uses fresh, clean water—a valuable environmental amenity. This must be distributed to the home. Electricity may be needed to supply the fresh water and to carry away the waste water to the sewage works. Generating this electricity has adverse environmental consequences. The waste water will have to be purified so that it may be used again, which will involve removing and disposing of the detergent present in the water. The environmental consequences of manufacturing the detergent, and of distributing it to the home, must also be considered. There are adverse environmental consequences associated with the manufacture and distribution of a washing machine and with its consumption of electricity. The washing of the nappies will produce wear and tear on the machine, hastening the time when it must be disposed of, perhaps by landfill, so some way must be found of calculating the environmental consequences of this. The picture is more complicated still if a tumble dryer is used.

To take another example, we all hear about pesticides getting into groundwater. Since pesticides can cause cancer, the popular response is that they must be banned. Recent research, however, suggests that pesticides cause very little cancer. Moreover, scrapping pesticides might well result in *more* cases of cancer, because fruits and vegetables help to prevent cancer, and without pesticides fruit and vegetables would get more expensive, so people would eat fewer of them.[5]

[5] Lomborg, *The Skeptical Environmentalist*, p.10.

The second factor has to do with cultural choice. Many of the environmental problems now of most concern stem directly or indirectly from deeply-rooted and strongly-reinforced patterns of behaviour among people generally—as energy users, as travellers, or as consumers of other goods and services. (So, for example, the transport sector is a sector of the economy where emissions of carbon dioxide, which contribute to climate change, are still rising.) Protecting the environment, therefore, has a strong cultural dimension. What we choose to protect, and how we want our environment to look, are essentially cultural choices. The historian Simon Schama expresses the point well in his book, *Landscape and Memory*:

> "Although we are accustomed to separate nature and human perception into two realms, they are, in fact, indivisible. Before it can ever be a repose for the senses, landscape is the work of the mind. Its scenery is built up as much from strata of memory as from layers of rock".[6]

An example of the effect of cultural choice on legal regulation of the environment is to be found in nature conservation law, which tends to select "indicator species" to represent biodiversity, and largely offers protection only to those particular species.[7] In fact, however, the problem of loss of biodiversity is (as the word implies) a problem that relates to the entire and diverse range of creatures and plants on the planet, of which there are millions. Although the relevant law strives to offer protection to most species under serious environmental threat, there can be little doubt that the selection of "indicator species" has the potential to leave some species under-protected. The implication is that some species, through cultural choice, are treated as less important than others.

What is the "environment"?

1–002   Perhaps the simplest and most memorable definition of "environment" is that given by Albert Einstein, who once said: "The environment is everything that isn't me".

Legal definitions are more circumscribed. Whilst not expressly interpreting the term, the EC Treaty indicates that the scope of the "environment" extends to human beings, natural resources, land use, town and country planning, waste and water.[8] This includes just about all areas of the environment, in particular fauna and flora (which are part of "natural resources") and climate. The inclusion of town and country planning underlines the fact that the environment includes man-made, as well as natural elements.[9]

In the context of UK law, "environment" is usually defined very simply as consisting of land, air and water—the three "environmental media"—each of which has its own pollution control regime, discussed in this book. The various statutory regimes are

---

[6] Simon Schama, *Landscape and Memory*, Fontana Press, 1995.
[7] The species selected for protection under the Habitats Directive provide an example (see Ch. 9).
[8] Articles 174(1) and 175(2).
[9] The Treaty does, however, draw a distinction between "environment" and "working environment". Laws relating to the latter, which concern conditions in the workplace, are traditionally regarded as part of a separate discipline, sometimes called "environmental health law". As such, they are beyond the scope of this book.

designed to prevent pollution of these media from causing "harm", and the definitions of "harm" employed by each regime serve to define, and set limits to, the scope of environmental regulation—they therefore provide, in a sense, a more comprehensive definition of "environment" for the purposes of each regime. The Pollution Prevention and Control (PPC) regime, discussed in Ch. 5, uses a wider definition of "harm" than does the regime regulating contaminated land, discussed in Ch. 6. The PPC regime, in defining "pollution", refers to:

> " . . . activity which may be harmful to human health or the quality of the environment, cause offence to any human senses, result in damage to material property, or impair or interfere with amenities and other legitimate uses of the environment."[10]

A similar definition is employed for the purposes of the waste management regime. Under the contaminated land regime, however, the reference to offence to human senses is omitted from the definition of "harm". Thus, certain matters, such as ruined views and unpleasant smells caused by contaminated land, are placed beyond the scope of regulation.[11]

On an international level, approaches to defining the environment vary. Although the Stockholm Declaration (the foundation of modern international environmental law) does not include a definition of the environment, Principle 2 refers to the natural resources of the earth as including "air, water, land, flora and fauna and natural ecosystems". Those treaties which have sought to provide some form of working definition of "environment" have tended, like domestic regimes, to adopt definitions appropriate to their purpose. The 1979 Long-range Transboundary Air Pollution Convention, for example, has a definition of "environment" that includes agriculture, forestry, materials, aquatic and other natural ecosystems and visibility.[12] The Convention on Civil Liability for Environmental Damage[13] includes in its definition natural resources both "biotic" and "abiotic", thus covering not only the natural environment but the man-made environment—including man-made landscapes, buildings, and objects.

What is "environmental law"?

The labelling of certain concerns as "environmental" (and of others, by implication, as **1–003** "non-environmental") can certainly help to identify and clarify the objectives of environmental regulation. However, it can sometimes conceal the important fact that there is scarcely any area of human activity which does not impinge on the protection of environmental resources. Like many legal terms, the term "environmental law" may be seen as having a central "core of meaning" surrounded by what may be called a "penumbra of uncertainty".[14] Within the "core" are to be found those laws which relate to protection of natural resources and people's enjoyment of them. Natural

---

[10] Pollution Prevention and Control (England and Wales) Regulations 2000 (SI 2000/1973), Reg.2.
[11] Environmental Protection Act 1990, s.78A(4).
[12] 18 I.L.M. 1442 (1979).
[13] Convention on Civil Liability for Damage resulting from activities dangerous to the environment, June 21, 1993, 32 I.L.M. 1228 (1993).
[14] See Hart, *The Concept of Law* (1961).

resources include air, land, water, flora and fauna, and the climate. They are protected through variety of legal mechanisms, including integrated pollution prevention and control, the planning system, environmental impact assessment procedures, and laws guaranteeing human rights and access to environmental information, as well as by the common law and by media-specific statutory regimes. All of these mechanisms are considered in this book.

Just outside the "core" of environmental law are laws designed to protect the quality of life of particular groups of people—laws, for example, relating to sanitation in dwellings, or to the health and safety of employees. Such laws are more usually categorised by lawyers as "health and safety law" or "environmental health law". Further still outside the "core", but within the "penumbra", are laws which protect society generally, such as laws relating to road traffic or vandalism. At the very edge of the "penumbra" are laws designed to protect and enhance peoples' commercial activities, such as those relating to consumer credit, or to the carriage of goods by road, rail and sea. These, although not generally thought of in any sense as "environmental law", can have a profound impact on the protection and enjoyment of natural resources, because they affect people's perception of what is, or is not, an appropriate lifestyle, and this in turn has implications for the ways in which natural resources are managed. These laws reflect (and arguably influence) peoples' cultural choices, which, as we have seen, ultimately dictate the scope of environmental protection.

The most effective definition of "environmental law", then, is perhaps one that is all-encompassing. This idea is recognised in the concept of "sustainable development"—a concept originating in international law, which has become significant in shaping EC and UK law. The concept recognises that the natural world and human, social and economic activities are fundamentally inter-connected and inter-dependent. Legal mechanisms giving effect to this recognition include the so-called "integration principle" in Art. 6 of the EC Treaty:

> "Environmental protection requirements must be integrated into the definition and implementation of Community policies and activities . . . in particular with a view to promoting sustainable development".

The principle of sustainable development has given rise to a wide range of initiatives concerned to ensure that environmental considerations form part of all European Community policy, and are properly reflected in the Community's decision-making processes.

The philosophy behind environmental regulation

1–004 As a body of law, environmental law has come of age. It originated as a collection of rules that grew up sporadically, as a haphazard and piecemeal response to specific environmental problems, but has now achieved a certain amount of coherence, in the sense that it has a clear and unified philosophical foundation. The technical regulatory rules, discussion of which inevitably forms a large part of this book, are underpinned by a set of principles (*e.g.* the "polluter pays principle", the principle of "sustainable development", and the "precautionary principle"—each discussed in a section below). These principles are in turn underpinned by an ethical philosophy.

Current environmental law is based mainly on an anthropocentric philosophy. The basic tenet of anthropocentric thought is that mankind is inherently separate from the rest of nature, and that natural resources are to be exploited for the benefit of mankind. The welfare of mankind is therefore to be accorded primary importance in any regime for environmental protection. Conservation of natural resources and environmental amenities is justified on the basis of "stewardship", *i.e.* the idea that present generations should hold environmental assets in trust for future generations. The conservation of flora and fauna is justified on the basis of the scientific and aesthetic benefits which it brings to mankind. Lord Goff's words, which began this chapter, reveal an anthropocentric approach to environmental regulation. Whilst, occasionally, we find judges and politicians justifying regulation by saying that the "environment itself" deserves protection (for example, Smith J., in *Ex p. Duddridge*,[15] analysed the precautionary principle in these terms—see below) it is doubtful that such statements represent any significant departure from anthropocentric thought.

Alternative philosophical approaches include biocentric and ecocentric viewpoints. The biocentric viewpoint argues that, in any scheme for environmental protection, animals should have rights which are equal to those of humans. On this view, animals are not at the service of mankind. Rather, they co-exist with him in nature and are deserving of protection for their own sake. This approach is reflected in laws which protect animal welfare (see Ch. 9). The ecocentric viewpoint adopts a holistic approach to the environment and holds that humans, animals and plants have value only as part of an ecological system. Natural ecosystems are therefore seen as having an intrinsic value, irrespective of the existence of animals and mankind. Plants are thought to have an intrinsic right to protection which is independent from the uses to which they are put by animals and human beings.

The European and international dimension

Environmental law is an international, European and national response to environ- **1–005** mental problems. For European Community Member States, environmental policies and laws are now determined predominantly at a European level. Four-fifths of UK's environmental legislation now has its origin in European institutions.[16] This does not mean, however, that Member States themselves do not have responsibility for originating law and policy. The principle of subsidiarity limits EC action to situations where the objectives of the proposed action cannot be sufficiently achieved by the Member States acting individually, and can, by reason of the scale or effects of the proposed action, be better achieved by the Community. In line with this principle, recent EC Directives have divided responsibility for environmental standard-setting between EC bodies and Member States. Thus, the recent revision of the Drinking Water Directive[17] has transferred back to Member States the responsibility for setting standards in relation to aesthetic parameters which do not have a health significance (*e.g.* the colour and taste of water supplied). Modern Directives often tend to set out only a framework of obligations, leaving the specifics of implementation to the

[15] [1995] Env. L.R. 151.
[16] RCEP 21st Report: *Setting Environmental Standards* (1998) Cm 4053, p.16.
[17] Directive 98/83/EC. See Ch. 8.

Member States. One implication of this approach, for example, is that, whilst decisions about the use of certain substances (say, as pesticides) take place at EC level, decisions about the use of specific products incorporating those substances take place within Member States.

International law and policy are also increasingly relevant. Environmental problems like climate change and ozone depletion affect the whole world, and are caused by the activities of many nations. It makes obvious sense to address such problems at an international level, because they cannot be solved by any single nation acting alone. Aspects of the environment such as the high seas, the rainforests, and the Buddha statues destroyed by the Taliban in Afghanistan in 2001,[18] are increasingly regarded by the international community as being the "common concern of mankind". There are now some 200 multilateral environmental agreements (in the form of treaties or other agreements) of which the Kyoto Protocol on Climate Change (discussed in Ch. 3) is probably one of the best known. The international dimension of environmental problems is reflected in the EC Treaty, which specifically provides that Community policy should promote "measures at international level to deal with regional or worldwide environmental problems."[19] The EC has sought to protect the environment outside the territory of its Member States by measures which prevent ozone depletion, combat climate change, protect endangered species in non-EC countries, and ban the export of waste.

The history and development of environmental regulation

1–006 The development of international environmental law is discussed in Ch. 2. Although international rules on environmental concerns date from the early nineteenth century, international environmental law came of age in the 1970s, with the adoption of the Stockholm Declaration at the first international conference on the environment. The principles in that Declaration have provided the foundation for modern international environmental law. International efforts to protect the environment are now underpinned by the concept of sustainable development, which came to prominence at the 1992 Rio Conference (the first "Earth Summit"). However, discussions at the most recent Earth Summit, which took place in Johannesburg in 2002, have left it uncertain in what direction international environmental law is likely to develop. The development of EC environmental law is discussed in Ch. 4. The 1957 Treaty of Rome, which established the EC, did not contain any provisions relating to the environment. However, environmental protection is today included at the heart of the EC Treaty, and has become one of the Community's foremost objectives.

In the UK, laws to protect mankind from the environmental effects of his activities can be traced to medieval times. In 1273, Edward I, in order to protect the health of his subjects, issued a decree prohibiting the burning of sea coal. Another proclamation forbidding the use of coal (at times when Parliament was sitting) was later issued by Elizabeth I, who caused one offender to be executed! It was not until after the

---

[18] The Taliban government deliberately destroyed statues of Buddha carved into cliff-faces at Bamiyan, Afghanistan, in an effort to rid the country of un-Islamic culture. Attempts by UNESCO to avert the damage were unsuccessful. (See *www.unesco.org*).
[19] Article 174(1).

Industrial Revolution, however, in the latter half of the nineteenth century, that any significant body of environmental law developed.

The unpleasant social conditions created by pollution, overcrowding and disease provided the stimulus for legal regulation. The tort of nuisance, which had existed since medieval times, was the first legal response. Its focus on the protection of individual property rights, however, made it an inefficient and inappropriate solution for the wide-ranging social consequences of industrialisation. The need for more effective controls prompted the intervention of Parliament. The Alkali Act 1863 put in place a national system of air pollution control, and created the Alkali Inspectorate, which was the world's first national pollution control agency. Water pollution was regulated by a statute of 1861, and by more comprehensive legislation in 1876. Legislation to deal with nuisances, such as the deposit of waste, was introduced in the late 1840s and was consolidated in the Public Health Act 1875 and subsequently in the Public Health Act 1936.

Early environmental legislation was the product of ad hoc reactions to specific environmental problems, and reflected little by way of preventive policy. With the exception of the Alkali Inspectorate, control over pollution was exercised at a local level by municipal authorities. Legislation was not, as it is today, motivated by a desire to preserve the environment for future generations of mankind. Rather, it grew out of the immediate and pressing need to do something about the unsanitary living conditions of an industrialising nation. The effects of pollution were obvious, and so generally was its source. Visible dark smoke came out of factory chimneys, and such sewerage facilities as existed were unable to cope with an increased urban population.

In the nineteenth century, the dominant philosophy was one of mankind's triumph over nature by science and technology. The relatively small population, and the limits of industrial technology, meant that depletion of natural resources was not seen as a problem. Natural resources were there to be exploited. During the latter half of the century, however, a very gradual change in this attitude started to take place, reflecting an awareness that man was merely one constituent part of a global ecosystem. It was only in the latter half of the twentieth century, however, that the idea that this ecosystem might place significant limits on the activities of mankind was fully recognised.

Environmental law in the UK may be said to have come of age in the 1970s. Hitherto, legislation relevant to the environment had largely been directed towards public health and the safety of employees. In 1972, the Stockholm Declaration (mentioned above) promoted international awareness of the idea that the environment, as a global entity, required protection. 1972 was also the year in which the UK joined the European Community. These factors stimulated a legal response in the UK to wider environmental problems. Modern environmental legislation is characterised by a move away from the protection of individuals to the prevention of environmental pollution generally. Recent environmental statutes demonstrate a more coherent and integrated response to environmental degradation than did their predecessors, in particular because they address the problem of balancing the need for environmental protection against the need for economic growth. The creation of the Environment Agency, in 1996, as an amalgam of the three bodies previously responsible for separate regulation of the environmental media (see below), marked a recognition of the need for a holistic approach to environmental problems.

The nature of modern environmental regulation

1–007 In recent times, the nature of environmental regulation, at both EC and UK level, has been subject to continual change. This has been necessary in order to address the changing nature of environmental concerns, and to implement internationally agreed policy objectives. As a result of this process of change, modern environmental regulation has developed a number of defining characteristics:

(1) *Increased dependence on environmental science*

1–008 Historically, protection of the environment has been largely concerned with controlling local pollution with immediate and measurable environmental effects. However, the environmental effects that are nowadays of most concern are much broader in scope, and can be less accurately measured—either because the scientific methodology employed to measure these effects has inherent limitations, or because of the sheer enormity of the task of gathering sufficient data which is comparable and clear. Both of these difficulties apply, for example, in relation to climate change and ozone depletion.

   The need to address global and transboundary pollution is now recognised. Many pollutants migrate over very long distances, and in so doing may become concentrated, or may change when they combine with other substances. Moreover, concern about the impact of pollution on human health now often relates to possible long-term effects, perhaps occurring many decades after exposure. As can be seen with action in relation to climate change, modern regulation tries to forestall future problems, as opposed to responding to damage once it has occurred. All of this means that environmental science now plays a key role in formulating policy and law, and that much of this science is concerned with the difficult task of predicting and quantifying effects which are not certain to occur.

(2) *Increased centralisation*

1–009 The geographical expansion of environmental concerns has led to the greater influence of international and EC policy. This, and the scientific complexities of environmental policy-making, has necessitated greater centralisation of UK environmental regulation. Even where local authorities have a role—as in planning decisions, or dealing with contaminated land—they are required to follow extensive central government guidance.

(3) *A holistic approach*

1–010 Traditionally, environmental laws tended to address the need to protect a single environmental medium, such as air, from the effects of pollution. Nowadays, they increasingly focus on protecting all environment media together. Regulation is concerned to ensure that industrial processes operate in a way that causes least harm to the environment as a whole, in the light of various options that may be available for discharging pollution into different environmental media. Recently, under the PPC regime (discussed in Ch. 5) this holistic approach has been extended to encompass a consideration of the raw materials and energy used by industrial processes.

(4) *Increased participation in decision-making*

The public and environmental groups are much more involved in environmental **1–011** decision-making than they were in the past. At one time, the only parties with a recognised claim to be involved in many environmental issues were the Government, its scientific advisers, the regulator (if separate from Government) and the person causing environmental harm (*e.g.* the industry producing pollution). Nowadays, however, environmental non-governmental organisations (NGOs) often have a recognised voice in decision-making. Some are organisations with mass membership and a large staff and budget, and can often enlist widespread public support on environmental issues. Some such organisations are international, and the growth in their influence has been, perhaps, most striking at this level. Both industrial and environmental NGOs have "observer" status under some international conventions, and may wield significant influence over the positions governments adopt in international negotiations. They may even be involved in drafting conventions: the first draft of the Convention on International Trade in Endangered Species, for example, was prepared by the International Union for Conservation of Nature and Natural Resources, which has both NGO and government members.

Concurrently with the growth of NGO participation, there has been an increase in legislative measures designed to assist in environmental decision-making. These measures set out requirements and procedures for decision-making processes, but do not specify the outcomes. Examples of such requirements include environmental impact assessment and public consultation in strategic planning. The EC's Environmental Impact Assessment Directive requires Member States to adopt measures to ensure that, before development is authorised, projects likely to have significant environmental effects by virtue of their nature, size, or location are subjected to a formal assessment of those effects. At an international level, the Aarhus Convention, which came into force in 2001, makes provision for public participation and access to justice and information in environmental matters. The Secretary General to the UN has referred to its provisions as promoting "environmental democracy"—a subject that we explore in Ch. 14.

A: Principles of Environmental Law

Environmental law has developed a set of principles which underpin its rules. These **1–012** principles, which were initially developed outside the UK, are explored more fully in the chapters dealing with international and European Community law. However, their importance to an overview of environmental law is such that they are worthy of some consideration here. The principles are:

- the principle of "sustainable development";
- the "precautionary principle";
- the "polluter pays principle".

Although there is widespread agreement that these words do indeed constitute principles of environmental law, there is much less agreement on what, precisely, the words mean. As a result, the legal status and implications of the principles are unclear.

Sustainable development

1–013   The concept of "sustainable development" originated in a realisation that the world's environment, its economies, and the ways in which it treats its human and animal inhabitants, are all interlinked. The Brundtland Report, which first gave prominence to the concept, illustrated this fact by reference to the famine in Africa during the 1980s. Although its immediate cause was drought, its underlying causes were more complex. They included political unrest, rapidly rising populations, and debts owed by African countries. Inability to pay these debts forced African nations, relying on sales of agricultural commodities, to over-use their fragile soils, turning good land into desert.

It is estimated that there are over 200 definitions of "sustainable development". However, the definition offered by the Brundtland report is the one with which the concept has become most closely associated:

> ". . . development that meets the needs of the present without compromising the ability of future generations to meet their own needs."

The international community first made a substantial effort to engage with the principle at the Earth Summit in Rio de Janeiro in 1992. An agenda of action was adopted which mapped out an ambitious and wide-ranging programme needed to move towards sustainability. A key element in that programme was that individual countries should establish their own sustainable development strategies. In the UK, the Conservative Government at the time was one of the first to respond, publishing the first UK Strategy for Sustainable Development in 1994. That document provided a framework for shaping initial action towards sustainability.

In 1997, the incoming Labour government saw the need for a more wide-ranging strategy which would integrate the economic, social and environmental dimensions of policy in a more fundamental way. The new strategy was launched in 1999, under the title *A Better Quality of Life*.[20] The creation of this strategy, and the formal annual assessments of progress made in implementing it, have kept sustainability on the agenda. The annual assessments show where progress is being made and where it is lagging. The UK government is one of very few anywhere in the world to have established a monitoring process of this kind.

The language of "sustainable development" (or "sustainability") is frequently heard in discussions of environmental law and policy at every level. Indeed, such language appears in UK primary legislation.[21] That this language should have become so familiar, and so widely accepted, distinguishes the concept of sustainable development as a significant achievement of international environmental thinking. However, the effectiveness of the concept is clearly dependent, at least in part, on its being implemented through appropriate and specific laws. There remain considerable difficulties associated with doing this, because definitions of sustainable development are so abstract that they present obstacles to evaluating its legal implications. As one writer has put it:

---

[20] Cm 4345 (*www. sustainable-development.gov.uk*)
[21] Under s.4(1) of the Environment Act 1995, the Environment Agency has a statutory duty to contribute towards attaining sustainable development.

"The Brundtland report's definition is concise, simple and has symbolic value. It is an undeniable motivator, while remaining sufficiently ambiguous so as not to directly threaten vested interests."[22]

In the light of this, it may be more appropriate to regard the principle as an economic or political, rather than legal, concept. Whilst its use in a legal context is, of course, an important indication of political commitment to addressing environmental problems in a holistic and integrated way, meaningful transposition of sustainability into everyday legal rules is far from easy.

The precautionary principle

A single, precise definition of the precautionary principle does not exist. However, it is **1–014** generally accepted that the principle means that lack of full scientific evidence should not be used as a reason for postponing measures to prevent environmental degradation. Acting in accordance with the principle is justified on the basis that the damaging effects of human activities may become irreversible before the scientific community can agree about the precise nature of those effects. As will be seen in Ch. 4, the principle is expressed in the EC Treaty to be one of the guiding tenets of EC policy. It is not, however, defined in the Treaty, so the precise implications of this are unclear.[23]

In 1990, the principle was set out as part of the Conservative government's White Paper on environmental policy, *This Common Inheritance*[24]:

"Where there are significant risks of damage to the environment, the government will be prepared to take precautionary action to limit the use of potentially dangerous materials or the spread of potentially dangerous pollutants even where scientific evidence is not conclusive, if the balance of likely costs and benefits justifies it."

Subsequently, it fell to the courts to consider the meaning of the principle, as set out in the White Paper, in *R. v Secretary of State for Trade and Industry, Ex p. Duddridge*.[25] This was an action for judicial review by the parents of three children concerned that their exposure to power cables would increase the risk of leukaemia. The applicants submitted that the government had misinterpreted the precautionary principle by setting the threshold of preventive action where a *significant* risk of damage arose. They argued that the principle required action to be taken as soon as any *possible* risk was demonstrated. In rejecting this argument, Smith J. observed that the principle: "is primarily intended to avoid long term harm to the environment itself rather than damage to human health from transitory environmental conditions."

Perhaps all that can be said with certainty about the precautionary principle is that:

---

[22] Marc Pallemaerts, "International Law from Stockholm to Rio: Back to the Future?" in *Greening International Law* (ed. Sands) (1993).
[23] See Kramer, *EC Environmental Law*, 5th ed., 2003.
[24] Cm 1200.
[25] [1995] Env. L.R 151.

"[It] is a culturally framed concept that takes its cue from changing social conceptions about the appropriate role of science, economics, ethics, politics and the law in pro-active environmental protection and management. [It] is a rather shambolic concept muddled in policy advice and subject to the whims of international diplomacy and the unpredictable public mood over the true costs of sustainable living."[26]

The polluter pays principle

1–015 The polluter pays principle has been a declared policy of the European Community since its First Environmental Action Programme in 1972, although it was not introduced into the EC Treaty until 1987. In essence, the principle requires that the polluter, rather than society at large, must pay the cost of environmental clean-up required as a result of his polluting activities. In an international context, the principle appears in various forms in a number of treaties and declarations, discussed in Ch. 2.

The difficulty surrounding the principle is twofold. First, in order to make the polluter pay, it must first be ascertained whom it is appropriate to regard as a polluter. Where a car causes pollution, is the polluter the manufacturer of the car, the producer of the fuel, or the driver of the car? Secondly, if the principle is to be applied fairly, it must be ascertained to what extent the polluter has degraded the environment, and the extent of that degradation must then be given a precise monetary value. This involves the "valuing" of environmental amenities which, as discussed below, is extremely difficult to accomplish with accuracy.

B: SOURCES OF ENVIRONMENTAL LAW

1–016 Sources of international environmental law are discussed in Ch. 2. The main sources are multilateral conventions. Sources of EC environmental law are discussed in Ch. 4. Most EC environmental law is contained in Directives (as opposed to Regulations). Environmental Directives are seldom sufficiently precise to have direct effect, and so require transposition into domestic law.

The principal source of environmental law in the UK is legislation. The common law fulfils only a minor and residual role in environmental protection. Environmental law is gradually becoming distilled into a smaller number of statutes than in the past. Some of the main pieces of legislation include: the Environmental Protection Act 1990 (which regulates industrial emissions, waste management, nuisances, litter and genetically modified organisms); the Pollution Prevention and Control Act 1999 and its associated Regulations (replacing the Environmental Protection Act 1990 for the Regulation of Industrial Emissions); the Water Resources Act 1991 (which regulates pollution and management of water resources); the Water Industry Act 1991 (concerned with the supply of water and the handling of sewage); the Town and

---

[26] *Interpreting the Precautionary Principle* (eds Tim O'Riordan and James Cameron), p.23.

Country Planning Act 1990 (which contains most of the legislation relating to land development); and the Wildlife and Countryside Act 1981 (which regulates nature conservation). The Environment Act 1995 established a statutory regime for dealing with contaminated land and provides the basis for national strategies on air quality and waste management. It also established the Environment Agency as the unified administrative body for environmental matters in England and Wales.

Much of the detail of environmental obligations is set out in statutory instruments, or (as is the case with the contaminated land regime) in the form of government guidance drawn up by the Secretary of State and approved by Parliament. The advantage of delegated legislation for environmental law is that it can be made quickly by the Secretary of State, without the need for lengthy Parliamentary procedures. Such flexibility is useful in the event that environmental obligations require modification in the light of scientific knowledge. The disadvantage of secondary legislation, however, is that it reduces democratic accountability because, although statutory instruments may be scrutinised and overturned by the courts, they are made without the line-by-line scrutiny of Parliament which characterises the passing of a statute.

Environmental obligations may also be found in Circulars, Codes of Practice and Policy Guidance Notes. Compliance with the rules contained in these "quasi-legal" or "informal" documents is not directly enforceable by criminal or civil proceedings. Their precise legal status depends upon the statutory provisions that give rise to the rules which they contain, and upon judicial interpretation of those statutory provisions.[27] This will vary from case to case. A common statutory requirement, however, is for a regulatory body to "have regard to" certain matters contained in these documents. It may be said, broadly speaking, that where an administrative body makes a decision without having regard to those matters, an action for judicial review will lie to compel that body to reconsider its decision.

Sources of environmental policy

A wide range of documents are important sources of policy. At an international level, **1–017** for example, policy principles are derived from the Rio and Stockholm Declarations. At EC level, sources of environmental policy include Green Papers, "COM docs" and "Communications", the Environmental Action Programmes (which address policy in general terms) and more specific action programme documents (*e.g.* the Climate Change Programme).

At UK level, important sources of environmental policy include Command Papers (*e.g.* the Energy White Paper), and reports by the Royal Commission on Environmental Pollution. Command papers are documents prepared by the government, outlining policy on matters of general interest to Parliament and to the public. Royal Commissions perform an investigative role for the government. They undertake a serious and lengthy analysis of problems which Parliament does not have the time fully to consider. They aim to provide an expertise and an impartiality, unaffected by transient political considerations, which can be lacking in Parliamentary debates.[28]

[27] See generally the observations of R.E. Megarry in (1949) L.Q.R. Vol.60, p.125.
[28] See Clokie and Robinson, *Royal Commissions of Inquiry* (1937).

C: BODIES RESPONSIBLE FOR ENVIRONMENTAL REGULATION AND POLICY

1–018 Relevant international bodies are discussed in Ch. 2. The United Nations is the principal international body with responsibility for formulating environmental policy. Almost all recent environmental treaties have been negotiated under the auspices of the UN, with guidance being provided from its subsidiary body, the United Nations Environment Programme ("UNEP"). In addition to UN bodies, a number of other organisations play a significant environmental role on the international stage. These include the World Trade Organisation, the World Bank, and the Organisation for Economic Co-operation and Development (OECD). The development of environmental policy at European level is overseen by the Environment Directorate of the European Commission, although the Council and the Parliament are also key players. In this chapter, we concentrate on relevant bodies in the UK.

The National Assemblies

1–019 The National Assembly for Wales was established by the Government of Wales Act 1998. The Assembly can pass only secondary legislation implementing Acts of the UK Parliament in certain fields. In areas of law-making that have been devolved, which include the environment, the Assembly makes decisions on the allocation of funds made available to it by the Treasury. (For example, it can sponsor environmental protection groups and conservation bodies.)

The Scotland Act 1998 devolved the power to pass primary legislation on certain matters, including the environment, to the Scottish Parliament. In keeping with traditional divisions in the UK's legal system, Scotland has its own environment agency (the Scottish Environment Protection Agency, or "SEPA") whose functions are in most respects identical to the Environment Agency for England and Wales. Other bodies with environmental powers in Scotland include Scottish National Heritage (a government body responsible to Scottish Ministers, with duties to conserve and enhance Scotland's natural heritage) and the Scottish Organic Producers Association (SOPA), which is the certification body for organic produce grown in Scotland.

The Northern Ireland Assembly was established following the signing of the Belfast (Good Friday) Agreement on April 10, 1998, and is constituted by the Northern Ireland Act 1998. The Assembly has full executive and legislative authority for all "transferred" matters, including the environment. However, the Assembly was suspended from midnight on October 14, 2002, and remains suspended at the time of writing.

Whilst devolution clearly has some impact on the pattern of environmental regulation in the UK, it is important to note the following points:

- The power to pass any new environmental legislation is constrained by the need to comply with EC law and international obligations. As the UK is the Member State (or, for international obligations, the "contracting State"), the UK Parliament has an over-arching responsibility to ensure uniform compliance in all countries. The effect of this is that, where environmental obligations originate outside the UK (which is nowadays generally the case), the *administration* of environmental law may differ from country to country, but the *substance* of the law will be the same.

- Control over certain aspects of law-making has not been devolved. For example, most aspects of revenue-raising do not fall under the control of the National Assemblies. Thus, environmental taxes, such as the landfill tax, cannot be introduced or altered.

The Department for Environment, Food and Rural Affairs (DEFRA)

DEFRA has primary responsibility for environmental matters, although other govern- **1–020** ment departments, in particular the Department for Transport, are required as a matter of policy, and sometimes by statute (for example, if and when they give directions to the Environment Agency[29]) to take account of environmental considerations in their activities. DEFRA is concerned not only with originating environmental policy, but with clarifying and ensuring the proper implementation of existing legislation, for example by issuing Circulars and Planning Policy Guidance Notes (PPGs). The Department is headed by the Secretary of State for Environment, Food and Rural Affairs.

The Secretary of State

The Secretary of State is responsible for issuing environmental regulations, in the form **1–021** of statutory instruments, under powers granted to him by the various environmental statutes. In addition, his or her function may be seen as that of enforcing the statutory duties of those responsible for taking environmental decisions, and of ensuring that those decisions are properly taken. He or she has a general power to direct the Environment Agency in the exercise of its functions,[30] together with a number of more specific supervisory powers. Thus, for example, under the Pollution Prevention and Control regime, the Secretary of State may issue "general binding rules" relating to the operation of the regime.[31] He or she also has power to "call in" applications for planning permission and decide them personally (a task usually delegated to an inspector) or to cause a local inquiry to be held,[32] and can revoke or modify planning permission in certain circumstances.[33] Also important is the power to make Nature Conservation Orders, which impose restrictions on the rights of landowners. Under the statutes, the Secretary of State is also responsible for determining appeals by persons who are aggrieved by decisions made by the Environment Agency, or by other bodies responsible for environmental decision-making.

The Environment Agency

The creation of the Environment Agency, which came into being in April 1996, **1–022** marked the centralisation of environmental control in England and Wales. (As mentioned above, Scotland has a separate environment agency, the Scottish Environment Protection Agency.) This centralisation may be seen as a recognition of the fact

[29] EA 1995, s.7.
[30] EA 1995, s.40.
[31] Pollution Prevention and Control (England and Wales) Regulations 2000 (SI 2000/1973), Reg.14.
[32] TCPA 1990, s.77.
[33] TCPA 1990, s.100.

that the integrated nature of many environmental problems means they cannot be effectively resolved at a local level. In announcing the creation of the Agency, at the *Sunday Times* Environment Exhibition in London, in July 1991, the Prime Minister said: "It is right the integrity and indivisibility of the environment should be reflected in a unified agency." The Environment Agency constitutes an amalgam of three bodies which had previously been responsible for environmental regulation: the National Rivers Authority (previously responsible for regulating pollution of watercourses); Her Majesty's Inspectorate of Pollution (which was responsible for administering the integrated pollution control regime); and the Waste Regulation Authorities (which, operating at a local level, administered the waste management regime).

Whilst it is a centralised body, the Agency does have local offices, so that practices of local consultation and regulation are preserved. Local Environment Agency Plans are being drawn up by the Environment Agency in England and Wales. These take account of local topography, land uses, and a range of other local pressures on the environment, and set local environmental targets and standards. Some of these reflect standards set by other bodies and apply nationally or internationally, but others, for example non-statutory water quality objectives, are locally specific and are proposed by the Agency after local consultation.

The Environment Agency has a number of different functions. Its pollution control functions include:

- granting licences to deal with waste;

- granting "discharge consents" to discharge substances into waterways;

- granting "permits" to operate industrial processes regulated by the Pollution Prevention and Control regime.

The Environment Agency supervises the operation of these licensed activities. It also has some responsibility for nature conservation, flooding and land drainage. It does not, however, have a monopoly in the field of environmental regulation. Other bodies, such as local authorities, Waste Collection Authorities, the Countryside Commission and the Nature Conservancy Councils, continue to fulfil important roles.

Local authorities

1–023   Local authorities continue to have important functions in relation to the environment. In particular, they are responsible for administering local air pollution control under the Pollution Prevention and Control regime, in respect of industrial processes which have not been prescribed for integrated pollution prevention and control. In addition, they are responsible for administering the statutory nuisance regime and for making planning decisions within their areas. They have important and complex functions in relation to contaminated land. Local authorities are under a duty to establish air quality management areas under certain circumstances and, where necessary, to prepare action plans to achieve air quality standards. They are also responsible for the control of noise.

D: Techniques for Environmental Regulation

Direct regulation

Regulatory rules for environmental protection can be either preventive or remedial, or **1–024**
a combination of both. Preventive rules aim to stop pollution before it happens, for
example by setting limits on the concentrations of particular pollutants which are
permitted to enter the environment, or by curtailing certain industrial activities and
uses of land which have the potential to cause pollution. The operation of the planning
system is an example of the preventive approach. Remedial rules, on the other hand,
are aimed at cleaning up pollution after it has occurred, punishing the polluter,
ensuring that he pays the costs of clean-up and compensating people who have
suffered as a result of pollution. The use of the criminal law to protect the
environment is an example of a remedial control, with its emphasis on punishing the
polluter. The operation of the common law is also primarily remedial. All remedial
controls, however, are of course preventive in so far as they serve as a deterrent to
potential polluters. The various UK statutes which control pollution make use of both
preventive and remedial controls.

In the UK, the traditional form of environmental regulation is environmental
licensing. In other words, government agencies (regulators) grant industrial process
operators licences to pollute (variously known as "licences", "authorisations", "permits" or "consents", depending on the relevant legislation). Criminal sanctions aim to
ensure that pollution does not take place in the absence of a licence, and that the
terms of licences are complied with. Environmental licensing makes it possible to tailor
regulation to the circumstances of particular industrial processes and sites.

The strength of direct regulation (sometimes called the "command and control"
technique) is that it can impose fixed standards, based on the best available expertise
and wide consultation. These standards have an important symbolic value in that they
reflect the public interest, provide reassurance to the public that the law is being used
to protect them, and mark society's moral condemnation of environmentally harmful
behaviour. The weaknesses of the approach, however, are that the use of the criminal
law in an environmental context can be problematic, and that the existence of wide
regulator discretion as to whether and how to enforce environmental obligations can
give rise to a number of concerns.

(1) *Use of the criminal law*

Concern is growing that existing mechanisms for enforcing the criminal law may not be **1–025**
entirely appropriate in environmental matters. For example, in a prosecution in which
it is alleged that a company has failed to use the "best available techniques"[34] in order
to reduce pollution, jurors or lay magistrates, inevitably inexperienced in such matters,
will be asked to adjudicate on the merits of various competing industrial technologies.
The evidence will often be highly technical, and the decision will involve a consideration of the appropriate balance to be struck between economic and environmental
factors. It has been suggested that in such circumstances, decision-making may be

---

[34] Pollution Prevention and Control (England and Wales) Regulations 2000 (SI 2000/1973), Reg.12(10).

neither consistent nor of a high standard.[35] Upon this decision, however, may rest not only the commercial reputation of the techniques involved, but ultimately the liberty of the company's managers and directors. These concerns have led to proposals for the establishment of a specialist court for hearing environmental cases, although this idea has not yet been taken up by Government.

It may also be questioned whether the criminal law is appropriate for dealing with cases of "historic pollution" in which the accused, at the time when he set in motion the train of events which have now led to his prosecution, was acting in accordance with the law as it then stood. This type of criminal liability, which can arise under the contaminated land regime (discussed in Ch. 6), would seem to offend against the constitutional principle that the limits of the criminal law should be known in advance.

(2) Regulator discretion

1–026 Regulators have discretion as to whether and how they enforce compliance with legal environmental obligations. The Royal Commission on Environmental Pollution[36] has pointed out that the exercise of this discretion is likely to vary according to the background of regulators, the organisational culture of the regulatory body, and its legal powers. Other influential factors include the seriousness and nature of the offence (*e.g.* whether it is an offence of strict liability); limitations on resources in terms of money, people and time; the nature and speed of the prosecution process; and the range of penalties available.

The existence of discretion in enforcement brings considerable benefits, but may also create concern about the existence of "cosy relationships" between regulators and regulated industries. Regulatory bodies must tread a very fine line between, on the one hand, implementing a "compliance strategy"—designed to ensure that environmental harm is reduced through negotiation and voluntary action—and, on the other hand, implementing an "enforcement strategy"—designed to honour their obligation to society to apply the criminal law. Their position is further complicated by their obligation, in accordance with the rule of law, to treat like cases in the same way.

Some commentators argue that prosecution is often an inefficient method of enforcement compared with seeking compliance through negotiation, education and warnings, and should therefore be used only as a last resort. They favour instead an approach which concentrates on attaining the broad aims of legislation, rather than punishing individual breaches. Thus, in cases where breaches of the law are not individually very serious, but have harmful cumulative effects, or where they arise because of ignorance or genuine accident, it is argued that improving environmental management systems to prevent a repetition may lead to a better environmental and social outcome than prosecution.[37]

On the other hand, advocates of prosecution-led enforcement regard a negotiation-led approach as providing inadequate environmental protection and evidence that regulatory bodies may become the servants, rather than the masters, of those they regulate. Such criticisms were levelled at the former Her Majesty's Inspectorate of Pollution (and the Alkali Inspectorate, from which it inherited its approach). They

---

[35] See Harris, "The Environmental Protection Act 1990: Penalising the Polluter" [1992] J.P.E.L. 515.
[36] RCEP 21st Report: *Setting Environmental Standards* (1998) Cm 4053, p.16.
[37] See Woods and Macrory, *Environmental Civil Penalties: A more proportionate response to Regulatory Breach*, Centre for Law and the Environment, University College London.

were also levelled at the old Water Authorities, leading the former National Rivers Authority, from the time of its creation, to adopt a deterrence strategy of strict enforcement and prosecution of offences, in order to mark a clear break with former practice.

The Environment Agency has produced guidelines setting out the circumstances in which it will normally expect to prosecute. The intention is to take action which is proportionate to the environmental risks in question and the gravity of the offences. This approach, perhaps, can be regarded as an attempt to reconcile the two approaches of prosecution-led and negotiation-led enforcement outlined above. The guidelines promise that enforcement by prosecution will be consistent, transparent, and well-targeted.

Other techniques

The disadvantages of direct regulation, and the tensions to which it may give rise, **1–027** make it attractive to use complementary approaches which seek to incorporate environmental considerations within the decision-making procedures of potential polluters. Here, we discuss two ways in which this can be brought about:

- the use of economic instruments, designed to internalise the external environmental costs associated with the activities of either companies or individuals;

- self regulation, effected by changing cultural behaviour so as to produce voluntary action on the part of companies and individuals (for example the establishment of environmental management systems within companies, and the voluntary recycling of household waste).

Economic instruments

One way of reducing environmentally-harmful activities is to modify market prices so **1–028** as to encourage producers and consumers to choose less environmentally harmful production methods and products. This can be done either by taxing products and services which are to be discouraged on environmental grounds, or by subsidising those which are to be encouraged. One example of an environmental tax in the UK is the tax on waste disposal by landfill. Another is the Climate Change Levy, discussed in Ch. 3.

In many situations, there are unpriced, external environmental costs associated with polluting activities. Take the example of exhaust gases produced when fuel is used in motor vehicles. A tax might be imposed on fuel which reflects the "environmental cost" of motor vehicle use. It is not easy, however, to design and introduce taxes like these (or related subsidies). The value to be placed on an environmental effect may not be obvious. A pollutant emitted today may have effects for centuries to come. Another factor that has limited the use of environmental taxes is a concern to avoid "social exclusion"—a flat-rate tax on, say, fuel use, which was not graded according to income, would hit the poor, or those who live in the country, the hardest.

Valuing the environment

One of the principal difficulties for environmental policy-makers who wish to make use **1–029** of taxes and subsidies, then, has been to find a way of valuing the environment. It is clear that most people do attach some "value" to the availability of a clean environment. The precise extent to which this is so, however, is very difficult to measure; this is because people have grown accustomed to using money as a measure of their well-being. Whilst some consequences of environmental policies can be easily valued (such as the costs of installing and operating pollution abatement equipment), nearly all environmental policies have important consequences which cannot be easily valued (such as the conservation value of land).[38] These consequences do not lend themselves to being valued in monetary terms because environmental amenities (like clean air and clean water) have traditionally been regarded as "free goods" for which no-one has had to pay. Economists, however, have taken the view that it is desirable, if possible, to attach a monetary value to environmental amenities. Only when this is done, it is argued, will society, which is wedded to the idea of measuring its well-being in terms of material wealth, be able to make informed choices about sacrificing traditional indicators of prosperity for environmental benefits.

Whilst the idea of valuing environmental amenities so as to give them a market price is immensely attractive, it has, in practical terms, been virtually impossible to implement. This is because of the sheer number of different factors which need to be taken into account in calculating "environmental costs". (We noted earlier in this chapter, for example, how many factors were involved in assessing the impact of using washable nappies.) In the absence of any satisfactory mechanism for accurately valuing the environment, environmental taxes and subsidies tend to be used simply as a rough-and-ready means of discouraging environmentally harmful behaviour, rather than as a precise tool for internalising environmental costs.

Emissions trading

1–030 Emissions trading schemes are another form of economic instrument, appropriate where the cause of concern is the total emission of a substance, either globally or within a defined area, and the issue is how reductions in that total should be allocated between those producing the emissions. Emissions trading reduces pollution in a more economically efficient way than can be achieved by direct regulation alone. This can be illustrated by a simple example. Suppose that there is a national objective to halve emissions of a given substance. One way of achieving this would be to require, through direct regulation, that all companies must reduce their emissions by half. This, however, would be inefficient, because the cost of achieving the reductions may vary from company to company. (There may, for example, be differences in the cost implications of cleaner production methods, depending on what is being produced.) An alternative way to achieve the desired reduction is to issue all companies with permits to pollute—the total amount of permits issued being equal to half of existing national emissions—and then allow companies to trade these permits amongst themselves. Those who find it cost-effective to reduce emissions will then do so, selling their permits to other companies for whom the cost of emissions reduction outweighs the cost of buying permits to pollute.

The introduction of emissions trading is a key part of international and EC efforts to combat climate change. As discussed in Ch. 3, at an international level, the Koyo Protocol has made emission trading one of the "implementation mechanisms" by which nations can meet their climate change obligations. In the UK, a voluntary and

---

[38] RCEP 21st Report: *Setting Environmental Standards* (1998) Cm 4053.

experimental emissions trading scheme already exists. This is also discussed in Ch. 3, along with the European scheme that is to replace it from 2005.

Self-regulation

In the last few years there has been widespread interest in self-regulation. This term **1–031** has been applied to a wide range of things. In the case of companies, mechanisms which can be regarded as forms of self-regulation include environmental management systems, product labelling going beyond statutory requirements, negotiated agreements entered into with government or government agencies, and release of information to the public about the environmental impact of company operations. There is also great scope for individuals to limit or redirect their activities in ways that will reduce damage to the environment. Voluntary recycling initiatives are an obvious example. Other examples include lifestyle changes such as declining to fly abroad to take holidays. In the last ten years, the transport sector was the only sector of the economy to increase its emissions of global-warming gases, and there is a small but growing interest in environmentally sustainable holiday-making.

In the context of industrial pollution, the Pollution Prevention and Control regime allows for self-monitoring of emissions by industrial process operators. The results of self-monitoring are reported to the regulator. A regulatory programme is in place to test self-monitoring schemes, by making unannounced checks. Under the terms of PPC permits stipulating self-monitoring, withholding the results is a breach of the permit conditions, which means that continuing to operate without disclosing these results is a criminal offence. This approach, then, represents a compromise between self-regulation and external regulation.

E: The Environmental Law-Making Process

Here, we consider the process of making environmental policy and law in general **1–032** terms. Chapter 15 contains a case study which explores this process in greater detail in the context of Genetically Modified Organisms.

Eric Ashby, in his 1978 book, described the process in the following way:

> "In the first stage—let us call it the ignition stage—public opinion has to be raised to a temperature that stimulates action. In the second stage the hazard has to be examined objectively, to find out how genuine and how dangerous it is, and just what is at risk. In the third stage this objective information has to be combined with the pressures of advocacy and with subjective judgements to produce a formula for a political decision."[39]

This description remains apposite today, with, perhaps, one qualification: Whereas, in the past, some special factor was often necessary to ignite public concern to ensure that action was taken—for example an unexpected catastrophe, such as an explosion or

---

[39] Eric Ashby, *Reconciling Man with the Environment*, OUP, 1978.

the wreck of a tanker—there is nowadays a much greater awareness of environmental issues. Environmental groups have the ear of governments, and public debate is much wider and better informed.[40] Consequently, the "temperature that stimulates action" is now lower, and governments face less of an obstacle in obtaining popular consent for environmental regulation.

The following elements are part of the policy and law-making process:

(1) *Scientific evaluation of risk*

1–033 We have already noted that environmental science is the cornerstone of modern law and policy. One of the difficulties this creates is that there can be scientific disagreement as to the nature and extent of an environmental problem. The uncertainties of science mean it can be used by both proponents and opponents of a legislative measure to justify their stance. The work of the Intergovernmental Panel on Climate Change (IPCC) demonstrates how this difficulty may be overcome in part. The assessments of the panel have aimed to achieve maximum ownership, both by the international scientific community and by governments. Ownership by the international scientific community is achieved by involving as many scientists as possible (including the leading scientists, with the highest scientific reputations) from as many countries as possible, either as contributors, lead authors or reviewers of the assessments. Ownership by governments is achieved by subjecting the scientific assessments to a second review stage by politicians (the first review stage being a scientific peer review). "Summaries for Policymakers" are prepared, for line-by-line approval at intergovernmental meetings, at which about 100 governments have been represented. Despite these efforts, the work of the IPCC has been subject to criticism.[41]

(2) *Public involvement*

1–034 In the 1970s and 1980s, detailed knowledge of environmental matters was largely in the hands of a small group of people—mainly those employed by regulatory agencies and government bodies. Expertise about industrial technology for combating pollution was confined to the regulators and to technical consultants advising large-scale industrial enterprises. Nowadays, however, there is increased public awareness of environmental issues, and much more pollution control expertise within small-scale industry. There has been an improvement in legal rights to environmental information, and greater coverage of environmental issues in the media. These factors, coupled with a general drive for "open government" (which has made use of the internet to provide convenient access to statistics and policy documents) have resulted in placing environmental issues firmly in the public consciousness.

Public access to environmental information is a key aspect of environmental protection. If people are in possession of the relevant facts, they are well placed to make their own decisions about the importance of environmental amenities and to exert pressure for change as consumers, investors, lobbyists and electors. The solutions to environmental problems are not usually straightforward. They require decisions to be made about lifestyle. A new industrial process, for example, may create jobs and

---

[40] RCEP 21st Report: *Setting Environmental Standards* (1998) Cm 4053.
[41] See, for example, *The Economist* May 29–June 4, 2004, p.16, which refers to flaws in IPCC predictions of future greenhouse gas emissions, due to improbably high projections of economic growth in developing countries.

national wealth, but diminish the quality of the landscape or the air we breathe. Economic growth and environmental protection are both desirable, but often cannot be achieved simultaneously. In a democratic society, balancing these conflicting desires can best be resolved through public participation in the decision-making process, so that a fair balance may be struck between the interests of different parties.

All of the media-specific pollution control regimes in the UK require the enforcing authorities to maintain public registers containing detailed information about the various parties who have applied for licences to carry out polluting activities and the activities to which those licences relate. In theory, public scrutiny of these registers can provide ammunition for lay critics of the regimes. In practice, however, the registers are seldom consulted by ordinary members of the public, although the information they contain is used by environmental pressure groups, such as Greenpeace and Friends of the Earth. Another feature of the regimes is that applications for licences to pollute must be advertised in newspapers, and that representations from interested members of the public must be entertained before licences can be granted. At EC level, the right to environmental information is recognised in a number of Directives,[42] and at international level, the right is enshrined in the Aarhus Convention, discussed in Ch. 14.

Whilst it is obvious that the attitudes of an informed public can shape laws for environmental protection, what is less obvious, perhaps, is that the passing of environmental laws can shape the attitudes of the public. Environmental protection measures which necessitate small (and therefore politically acceptable) changes in lifestyle (the use of lead-free petrol, for example) serve to heighten the public's awareness of environmental problems generally with the result that, over time, society becomes conditioned into accepting ever more stringent controls on the understanding that they are of benefit. Some environmental laws, therefore, have as much to do with environmental education as they do with environmental protection. In this context, the provision of environmental information may be regarded as achieving a social-engineering purpose which facilitates the law-making process.

(3) *Economic analysis*

Finally, steps will be taken to ensure that environmental decision-making takes account **1–035** of economic considerations. An economic appraisal of proposed policies will consider their costs and benefits, so as to assist with a decision as to the most appropriate policy. An example is the study commissioned by the European Commission to investigate the costs and benefits of achieving, by 2010, the emission limit values likely to be set for concentrations of nitrogen oxides and lead.[43]

The UK Treasury has expressed the view that valuation of environmental costs and benefits has become even more important in light of the policy of sustainable development. There have, however, been relatively few formal appraisals of environmental policies which require monetary values to be ascribed to environmental effects, although the number of such appraisals is increasing. There is an ongoing debate about how useful these types of appraisal are in evaluating environmental policies, in the light of the problems associated with valuing environmental impacts. Consequently,

---

[42] *e.g.* Dir.2003/35/EC on public participation in the drawing up of environmental programmes. See Ch. 14.
[43] RCEP 21st Report: *Setting Environmental Standards* (1998) Cm 4053.

there has been more use of "cost effectiveness" appraisals. These try to identify the least costly method of implementing a particular environmental policy, but do not extend to an evaluation of environmental impacts.

In addition, the costs and benefits of environmental policies are taken into account in the following ways:

- Primary and secondary legislation in the UK must be accompanied by an assessment of the costs of compliance—this gives interested parties an idea of the costs of new legislation and identifies any unacceptable burdens before the legislation is adopted;

- Ever since the first pollution control statutes were enacted, regulators have had an obligation to take into account the costs to industry of meeting obligations imposed as a result of regulatory decisions taken in implementing environmental policy.

The implications: Challenging environmental laws

1–036 The need to reconcile economic implications, complex science and public opinion in environmental decisions casts some doubt on the appropriateness of traditional legal mechanisms for challenging those decisions. In making decisions, the Secretary of State or regulatory agency will rely on a vast amount of technical information from a variety of sources such as industry, academics, environmental groups and consumer protection groups. The final decision will inevitably represent a delicate compromise between the viewpoints held by a number of relevant groups. The institutional constraints on the courts mean that they cannot hope to have the same information available to them. Although a court has access to sources of law, in factual matters, it is often limited to consideration of a summary created by those over whom it has no control. Moreover, it has only a limited amount of time in which to get to grips with technical facts.

These factors may make it appropriate to limit judicial scrutiny of environmental decisions. The role of the court in judicial review (the principal mechanism for judicial scrutiny of environmental decisions by public authorities) is confined to ensuring that those authorities perform their functions properly—the court cannot substitute its own views on the merits of a decision for the views of the authority. In the light of the complex nature of environmental law-making outlined above, it is far from certain that the courts are well suited to assume any wider role. However, recent proposals for a specialist environmental court might reduce, to some extent at least, the impact of current limitations, and so provide greater access to environmental justice.

F: THE STRUCTURE OF THIS BOOK

1–037 Following this introductory chapter, the book begins with a chapter on international environmental law. Arguably the biggest environmental crises facing us at present (climate change, depletion of the ozone layer) are global in form. Any effective response to these problems must be an international one. The chapter offers an analysis of some of the principles which have emerged within the international environmental protection regime, for example the concept of "sustainable development", which now finds expression in UK law. The third chapter considers the issue of climate change—an international environmental problem which has been described in the EC's Sixth Environmental Action Programme as an outstanding challenge of the next 10 years and beyond. The fourth chapter outlines the principles of EC environmental law and policy. Particular consideration is given to the Directive on Civil Liability for Environmental Damage.

As we shall see throughout the book, the influence of the EC on UK environmental law has been great. It is not to be thought, however, that the flow of ideas is always one way. The UK's Integrated Pollution Control regime, for example, has been "exported" to Europe and has been responsible for shaping the EC's. Integrated Pollution Prevention and Control regime which is now replacing it. Both regimes are considered in Ch. 5. Their notable feature is that they attempt to tackle the effects of polluting substances in all three media together. As mentioned above, an integrated and holistic approach to environmental problems is increasingly becoming a dominant feature of modern regulation.

The idea of an integrated approach, however, is not yet so developed as to remove the need for media-specific environmental controls. These are examined in Chs 6, 7, 8 and 10, whilst Chs 9 and 11 deal, respectively, with the issues of nature conservation and noise pollution, both of which continue to be the subject of much passionate debate.

The bulk of environmental regulation in the UK is derived from statute. Historically, however, the common law has sometimes functioned to combat environmental problems, particularly through the tort of nuisance and through actions under the rule in *Rylands v Fletcher*, both of which are examined in Ch. 12. Chapter 13 examines the contribution made by planning law to environmental protection. The UK's planning regime is amongst the most sophisticated in the world, and, because environmental protection and land development are inextricably linked, an understanding of how the planning system works is vital to an appreciation of the specific environmental controls which it supplements. Ch. 14 considers a human rights approach to environmental protection. This chapter also looks at the concept of "environmental democracy", a term coined by the Secretary-General to the UN to encompass public participation in environmental decision-making and access to environmental information and justice. These concepts are further explored in Ch. 15, which considers regulation of Genetically Modified Organisms. The opportunity is taken to treat this subject as a case study which explores the interaction of public participation, policy formulation, and environmental decision-making procedures.

Chapter 2

International Environmental Law

"In the middle of the 20th century, we saw our planet from space for the first time. Historians may eventually find that this vision had a greater impact on thought than did the Copernican revolution of the 16th century. From space we see a small and fragile ball dominated not by human activity and edifice but by a pattern of clouds, oceans, greenery and soils."[1]

Introduction

Most people nowadays have heard about climate change and its expected impacts. The **2–001** international responses to this problem—the UN Climate Change Convention and its Kyoto Protocol—are perhaps the most publicly known and passionately debated legal documents in history. The problems of climate change, ozone depletion and loss of biological diversity have achieved great public prominence, but there are a number of other important problems which need to be tackled on a global scale. These include the scarcity and poor quality of water in certain countries, pollution of the oceans, flooding, management of biotechnology resources and management of waste. Whilst a comprehensive examination of international efforts to tackle such problems is beyond the scope of this kind of book, this chapter will give the reader some flavour of the context in which these efforts take place.

There are two reasons why solving environmental problems often requires international co-operation. In some cases (pollution of the atmosphere and oceans, for example) the territory affected by the problem is beyond the sovereign jurisdiction of any one nation. In other cases, the cause of environmental degradation originates in the sovereign territory of one nation whilst its effects are felt elsewhere. Forest cutting in Nepal, for example, has increased the severity of flooding in neighbouring India and Bangladesh. Often the effects are less direct. For example, the depletion of species through hunting or habitat destruction (*e.g.* cutting the rainforest) may cause only a local environmental problem (or may have local environmental benefits), but may be of concern to the wider international community.

"Transboundary pollution" is a significant problem. Acid rain, which causes deforestation and can destroy crops, is a classic example of this—it sometimes falls in

[1] *Report of the World Commission on the Environment and Development: "Our Common Future"* (1987) ("The Brundtland Report").

countries which are thousands of miles away from the air pollution which causes it. In recent history, two dramatic incidents, both in 1986, have concentrated the minds of the international community on the problem of transboundary pollution. In that year, an explosion at the Chernobyl nuclear power plant blasted 50 tonnes of nuclear fuel into the atmosphere and a north-westerly wind carried radioactive particles across much of Europe. Also in 1986, a fire in a warehouse in Switzerland caused the release of agricultural chemicals, solvents and mercury, which flowed into the River Rhine, killing millions of fish and threatening the safety of drinking water in Germany and the Netherlands.

International environmental law has become well established over the last ten years. However, its development is constrained by a number of factors. The most significant of these constraints is the doctrine of state sovereignty (the idea that a state can do as it pleases within its territorial borders). The concept of sovereignty has, to a limited extent, been redefined to accommodate the need for environmental protection, but it remains to be seen whether this will lead to any greater protection of the environment, and it currently remains a significant obstacle to the creation of detailed obligations.

This, together with the fact that the developed and the developing nations often have very different environmental priorities, has meant that international environmental negotiations have been fraught with compromise. Whilst these negotiations have resulted in *some* well-defined national commitments (for example, percentage reductions in emissions of greenhouse gases and ozone depleting substances), for the most part, the obligations to which states have actually committed themselves are of a very broad and general nature. They consist of acting in accordance with a set of fairly vague "principles", the detailed implications of which are undefined. Indeed, so ill-defined are these principles that many have questioned whether they can be sensibly regarded as part of international *law* at all.[2] They are, perhaps, better regarded as mere expressions of international *policy* which suggest the form that binding legal rules might (or might not) take at some unspecified future time.

The basics of international law

2–002 To understand international environmental law, it is necessary to appreciate that international law is fundamentally different from the domestic legal system of a nation state. In international law there is no supreme source of authority. The law is formed by a consensus of behaviour and of ideas between nations. These ideas are expressed either in the form of treaties—in which case they are binding only on those nations who are parties to the treaties—or in the form of internationally observed customary rules, binding on all nations. Moreover, compliance with treaties or customary rules by states is largely voluntary, because the availability of sanctions in international law is limited. Although states may impose economic sanctions or, as a last resort, wage war to ensure compliance with rules of international law, enforcement of international law depends for the most part on the persuasive powers of diplomats and on the idea that states will comply with international provisions in order to preserve their standing within the international community. In these circumstances, public opinion within a

---

[2] See, for example, Birnie and Boyle, *International Law and the Environment*, 2nd ed., 2002.

nation (and the related question of whether this opinion can be freely expressed) can be important in ensuring that nations comply with their international obligations.

A: SOURCES OF INTERNATIONAL ENVIRONMENTAL LAW

Conventions

Most international environmental law is to be found in conventions (also known as **2–003** treaties) aimed at resolving particular environmental problems. Conventions create obligations and norms of behaviour for the states which are parties to them. In principle, conventions are binding only on the signatory states, but where a large number of influential states sign a convention, their explicit acceptance of certain rules of behaviour may have a strong law-making effect. Consistent compliance with the provisions of a convention by many states for a number of years may provide evidence of customary international rules with which all states must comply.

Conventions usually become binding on states only after they have been ratified (formally adopted) by a certain specified number of states. In environmental law, conventions have tended to require only a low number of ratifications before they come into force. Once a treaty has come into force, by ratification by the required number of states, the treaty obligations become binding on *all* states who have expressly indicated, by *signing* the treaty, that they wish to be bound by it when it comes into force. The doctrine of sovereignty traditionally implies that states must expressly consent to all the details of a treaty before they become bound by it. In certain contexts, however, the doctrine is proving more flexible than this. A provision in the Montreal Protocol on Substances that Deplete the Ozone Layer, for example, provides an escape route from the requirement for full consensus. In circumstances where the parties are considering adjustments to their obligations, if two thirds of the parties that make up 50 per cent of the total consumption of the controlled substances vote for the changes, their decision will bind the remaining parties.[3]

Whilst older conventions concentrated on the territorial jurisdiction of states and on states' liability for transboundary pollution, the underlying concern in more recent treaties has been protection of the wider environment. Modern treaties have increasingly focused on global, rather than transboundary pollution, and on the conservation of entire ecosystems rather than the preservation of particular species. They have sought the conservation of common global resources (biodiversity, for example) rather than those of individual states. As a result, multilateral conventions (*i.e.* those signed by large numbers of states, as opposed to bilateral conventions signed between two states) have, since 1972, been the main source of obligations in relation to marine pollution, protection of the atmosphere, wildlife conservation and conservation of international watercourses. Multilateral treaties are almost legislative in character, in that they lay down regimes for the protection of particular aspects of the environment. Such treaties frequently follow the approach of adopting, initially, a

---

[3] See Art. 2(9)(c) of the Protocol on Substances that Deplete the Ozone Layer, Montreal, 1987. 26 I.L.M. (1987) 154.

"framework convention" which sets out the general obligations of the parties. Protocols are subsequently adopted which set out the details of those obligations. There are over 200 multilateral environmental agreements—in the form of international conventions and other agreements on environmental matters.[4]

Arguably, some of the most successful environmental treaties are those establishing the European Community and then the European Union. European Community environmental law, which is considered in Ch. 4, may be regarded as part of international law, because all EC legislation owes its validity to these treaties,[5] as do judgments of the European Court of Justice. The EC has developed a comprehensive regime of regional environmental control. Although regional regimes of international law operate in other parts of the world, they lack the detail and sophistication of their European counterpart.

Customary law

2–004 Rules of customary international law arise where there is a general recognition among states that certain practices and norms of behaviour are obligatory. In international environmental law, customary rules generally play a subordinate role to the law contained in conventions, because their existence is difficult to establish. To show that a rule of customary law is in existence, not only must the uniformity and consistency of state practice be examined, but so too must the length of time during which that practice has been adhered to.[6] Therefore, because environmental concerns are of comparatively recent origin, few rules of customary international law have yet developed in relation to them.

The most clearly established environmental rule is the so-called "no-harm rule" (discussed below). This is the rule that states have the responsibility to ensure that activities within their jurisdiction or control do not cause damage to the environment of other states, or to the environment of areas where there is no national jurisdiction.[7] Older, more traditional rules of customary international law, however, continue to provide the context within which international environmental law develops. The most important of these rules is the principle that a state is sovereign within its own borders. This principle, in its most traditional form, has the potential to undermine modern international efforts to protect the environment. For example, the "no-harm rule" is clearly inconsistent with a rule of sovereignty that implies a state may do exactly what it likes on its own territory, regardless of the consequences. The traditional doctrine of sovereignty is also under threat from emerging international principles entitling citizens to human rights and self-government.[8]

---

[4] According to the calculations of the Secretariat of the W.T.O. See also the 21st Report of the RCEP: "Environmental Standards", Cm 4053.

[5] See Hartley, "The Constitutional Foundations of the European Union" (2001) 117 L.Q.R. 225.

[6] The principle of *opinio juris* is also relevant. This principle dictates that state practice can only be taken as evidence of a rule of customary international law if the reason the states engage in the practice is that they believe they are under a legal obligation to do so.

[7] See Principle 21 of the Stockholm Declaration. Brownlie sees this as a principle of international law which stems from the more general principle of "State responsibility" for activities caused or tolerated in their sovereign territory which are a source of danger to other States. See Brownlie, *Principles of Public International Law*, 6th ed., 2003.

[8] See French, "A Reappraisal of Sovereignty in the light of Global Economic Concerns." [2001] Legal Studies 376.

Soft law

Custom and treaties make "hard law", in the sense of binding obligations. Custom, **2–005** however, as we have said, takes time to establish. Conventions also take time to negotiate, and states are often wary of signing up to very specific binding obligations. In these circumstances, the use of "soft law" is politically attractive. International declarations, which are a source of "soft law", have played a significant role in the development of international environmental law. The Stockholm Declaration,[9] arising out of a UN conference in Stockholm in 1972, may be regarded as the foundation of modern international environmental law. Its provisions have formed the basis of numerous subsequent conventions. A further example is the Rio Declaration, which arose out of the 1992 UN Conference on the Environment and Development (the "Earth Summit") in Rio de Janeiro. These two declarations are not binding on states, but have significant persuasive force. Their importance lies in their pointing to the form which formally binding treaty obligations might take in the future. In certain contexts, they have, by informally establishing acceptable norms of behaviour, changed political thinking.

Academic commentary

Academic commentary plays a much greater role in international law than it does in **2–006** many domestic legal systems. Like international declarations, academic writings are not so much sources of international law *per se* but are means by which the existence and scope of international law may be determined.

B: THE DEVELOPMENT OF INTERNATIONAL ENVIRONMENTAL LAW

International rules on environmental concerns date from the early nineteenth century. **2–007** At that time, attention centred on the exploitation of natural resources as a result of growing industrialisation. A number of bilateral treaties were signed with the aim of conserving fishing stocks,[10] but pollution and other ecological issues were not addressed. The international response to environmental issues was characterised by ad hoc reactions to immediate problems, but was significant nonetheless because it recognised that co-operation between states was necessary.

In 1893, a dispute between the US and Great Britain over the exploitation of seals for fur was submitted to international arbitration.[11] The finding of the tribunal established an important principle which is still significant today, namely that states did not have the right to assert jurisdiction over natural resources which were outside their territory in order to ensure their conservation. In 1941, the *Trail Smelter* case arose. This was a dispute between Canada and the US over the emission of sulphur fumes

[9] The Declaration of Principles for the Preservation and Enhancement of the Human Environment, June 16, 1972; (1972) 11 I.L.M. 1416.
[10] See Convention between France and Great Britain relative to Fisheries 1867; North Sea Fisheries (Overfishing) Convention, 1882.
[11] *The Pacific Fur Seals Arbitration* (1893) 1 Moore's International Arbitration Awards 755.

from a Canadian smelting works, which caused damage to crops, trees and pasture in the US. It led to what has been described as "a crystallizing moment for international environmental law".[12] The two states agreed to submit the matter to arbitration. The tribunal held that under international law:

> ". . . no state has the right to use or permit the use of its territory in such a manner as to cause injury by fumes in or to the territory of another or the properties or persons therein, when the case is of serious consequence and the injury is established by clear and convincing evidence."[13]

This principle was later to be expressed in the Stockholm Declaration.

The Stockholm Conference

2–008 By 1972, a significant body of environmental obligations had been established at both a regional and global level. International concern was no longer focused only on the conservation of flora and fauna but was addressing issues such as oil pollution and the effects on the atmosphere of nuclear tests. In 1972, the first international conference on the environment—the United Nations Conference on the Human Environment— held in Stockholm, marked a turning point in the development of international environmental law. Attended by 114 states, the conference provided an opportunity to formulate a coherent analysis of environmental problems. It placed environmental issues firmly on the international legislative agenda, and a declaration issued by the participating states proclaimed that: "a point has been reached in history when we must shape our actions through the world with a more prudent care for their environmental consequences."[14]

The Stockholm conference produced a declaration of principles (the Stockholm Declaration)[15] which, as has been said, may be regarded as the foundation of modern international environmental law. Principle 1 sets the tone:

> "Man has the fundamental right to freedom, equality and adequate conditions of life, in an environment of a quality that permits a life of dignity and well-being, and he bears a solemn responsibility to protect and improve the environment for present and future generations."

Principle 21 still represents the cornerstone of international environmental law, more than 30 years after its adoption. It states:

> "States have, in accordance with the Charter of the United Nations and the principles of environmental law, the sovereign right to exploit their own resources pursuant to their own environmental policies, and the responsibility to ensure that

[12] Sands, *Principles of International Environmental Law,* 2nd ed., 2003.
[13] *Trail Smelter Case* (1941) 3 R.I.A.A. 1905.
[14] 10 UN Doc. A/CONF. 48/14/rev.1 (UN Pub. E73, IIA (1973)), adopted June 16, 1972.
[15] The Declaration of Principles for the Preservation and Enhancement of the Human Environment, June 16, 1972; (1972) 11 I.L.M. 1416.

activities within their jurisdiction or control do not cause damage to the environment of other states or of areas beyond the limits of national jurisdiction."

Other significant provisions included the requirement for international co-operation to:

"... effectively control, prevent, reduce and eliminate adverse environmental effects resulting from activities conducted in all spheres, in such a way that due account is taken of the sovereignty and interests of all states."[16]

The declaration was intended to be a forward looking instrument, which would provide a starting point for the future development of international law. It covered most of the main global environmental issues, including sustainability (discussed below), conservation of habitats and wildlife, toxic substances, pollution of the seas, population growth and nuclear weapons. Other issues, which have since become important, were not dealt with directly. These include greenhouse gas emissions, ozone depletion (which was not known about in 1972), biological diversity and chemical and biological weapons.

The Brundtland Report

In the 1970s and 1980s, the nature and extent of the world's environmental problems **2–009** were changing rapidly, not only because the rate at which human activity was affecting the environment increased dramatically, but also because of increased scientific knowledge in relation to the global warming effects of fossil fuel emissions and mass deforestation. In 1987, a report by the World Commission on Environment and Development, known as the Brundtland Report,[17] noted that during the 1980s there had been a marked increase in the incidence of environmental crises of a "global nature", such as the drought in Africa, which put some 35 million people at risk and killed perhaps a million. The report concluded that if natural resources continued to be used at the current rate, if the plight of the poor was ignored, and if pollution and wasting of resources continued, a decline was to be expected in the quality of life of the world's population. It called upon wealthy nations to make changes in their lifestyle by recycling waste and conserving energy and land. The report raised the profile of the concept of "sustainable development" (discussed below) which has gradually come to underpin environmental law at an international, EC and UK level. The publication of the Brundtland Report led to growing pressure for further international action on the environment, and eventually to the Rio Conference.

The Rio Conference and the concept of sustainable development

In 1992, the United Nations Conference on the Environment and Development **2–010** ("Earth Summit") was held in Rio de Janeiro, Brazil. It was attended by approximately 10,000 delegates from 176 states. The conference produced the following:

---

[16] Principle 24.
[17] *Report of the World Commission on the Environment and Development: "Our Common Future"* (1987) ("The Brundtland Report").

- The Declaration on Environment and Development (the Rio Declaration),[18] which defines the rights and responsibilities of states;

- A global action plan for all states on development and the environment (Agenda 21) negotiated over a period of two years and accepted by all of the participating states;

- Two multilateral treaties, which were opened for signature: the Convention on Biological Diversity[19] and the UN Framework Convention on Climate Change.[20] These were signed by representatives of more than 150 countries.

The Rio Declaration marked a conceptual breakthrough, in that the natural world was added to the social and economic dimensions of "development" to produce the concept of "sustainable development". Principles 3 and 4 are at the heart of the Declaration:

- The right to development must be fulfilled so as to equitably meet developmental and environmental needs of present and future generations. (Principle 3)

- In order to achieve sustainable development, environmental protection shall constitute an integral part of the development process and cannot be considered in isolation from it. (Principle 4)

The Declaration is a compromise between environmental protection and development, and between the developed and developing world. Principle 3 acknowledges the right to development, which the developing countries had been arguing for, whilst Principle 4 moves environmental protection to the core of developmental policies, reflecting the wishes of the developed world.

Principle 7 introduced the concept of "common but differentiated responsibilities" of developed and developing nations (discussed below). Principle 10 has proved to be of particular importance in providing a platform for the development of procedural rights, enabling individuals and environmental groups to take action to protect the environment. It states:

"Environmental issues are best handled with the participation of all concerned citizens, at the relevant level. At the national level, each individual shall have appropriate access to information concerning the environment that is held by public authorities, including information on hazardous materials and activities in their communities, and the opportunity to participate in decision-making processes. States shall facilitate and encourage public awareness and participation by making information widely available. Effective access to judicial and administrative proceedings, including redress and remedy, shall be provided."

Some of the principles reinforce principles that appear in the Stockholm Declaration. Some of the Rio principles, however, may have marked a dilution of the Stockholm

[18] Rio de Janeiro Declaration on Environment and Development, June 16, 1992, UN Doc. A/CONF. 151/5.
[19] Convention on Biological Diversity, June 5, 1992, Rio de Janeiro, 31 I.L.M. 822 (1992).
[20] UN Framework Convention on Climate Change, May 9, 1992, New York, 31 I.L.M. 849 (1992).

principles. This is apparent, for example, in the treatment given to the concept of a human right to a healthy environment. Thus, Principle 1 of the Stockholm Declaration boldly declares:

"Man has the fundamental right to freedom, equality and adequate conditions of life, in an environment of a quality that permits a life of dignity and well-being . . ."

Principle 1 of the Rio Declaration, however, contains no clear affirmation of a human right to a healthy environment, simply stating:

"Human beings are at the centre of concerns for sustainable development. They are entitled to a healthy and productive life in harmony with nature."

Despite its initial promise, the Rio Declaration is now regarded as a less successful document than its predecessor. Its success can be judged by the disappointing extent to which it has been implemented. There has been a lack of political will to take forward many of the commitments contained in the declaration (such as the eradication of third world poverty, and the transfer of funds and technology to developing states). Save in the field of climate change, there has been little dramatic action. The declaration is perhaps best regarded as merely a mid-1992 "snapshot" of the debate over reconciling economic development with environmental protection.

To mark the 10th anniversary of the Rio Declaration, the World Summit on Sustainable Development was held in Johannesburg in September 2002. This meeting did not produce any declarations of principles. Its main focus was the eradication of poverty, and no specific actions were agreed in respect of the environment, apart from a continued commitment to sustainable development. As a result of this, there is currently no firm indication of the direction in which international environmental law is likely to develop. The most significant developments since Rio have taken place in the field of climate change, and are examined in Ch. 3.

C: RELEVANT INTERNATIONAL INSTITUTIONS

The United Nations

In 1945, the creation of a global organisation—the United Nations—after the **2–011** destruction caused by the Second World War, provided an institutional framework within which to develop international law on the environment. Although the UN Charter did not refer explicitly to environmental protection, its mandate has proved wide enough to include environmental matters. The UN is the main forum for the creation of international legal rules. The UN Charter established six "principal organs" within the UN These are: the Secretariat (concerned with administration); the General Assembly (a sort of Parliamentary forum, with limited power, which may make recommendations to member states and to the Security Council); the Security Council (concerned with "international peace and security" and comprising 15 member states, but dominated by the five "permanent members", each of which can veto its decisions); the Trusteeship Council (concerned with territories held in trust by the UN); the International Court of Justice; and the Economic and Social Committee. A number of "programmes" and "commissions" have been set up which report to the Economic and Social Committee, and some of these have an environmental role:

(1) *The United Nations Environment Programme (UNEP)*

2–012 The United Nations Environment Programme (UNEP) was created by a decision of the 1972 Stockholm Conference as a body to guide the future development of international environmental law. It comprises 58 representatives, elected to serve a three-year term. Originally, its function was perceived as the provision of general policy guidance to the UN, which would serve to co-ordinate the efforts of other UN bodies in securing environmental protection. However, in the wake of the 1992 Rio Conference its role was strengthened, so that it now takes the lead in formulating law and policy. It also collates and disseminates environmental information for the use of national governments, and provides scientific advice to the Commission on Sustainable Development.

(2) *The Commission on Sustainable Development*

2–013 This body was established in the wake of the 1992 Rio Conference. It consists of representatives of 53 states, elected to serve a three-year term. Its remit is to monitor and review the implementation of "Agenda 21"—the comprehensive international plan agreed at Rio for achieving sustainable development. The commission has few powers and resources, but serves as a permanent diplomatic forum for negotiation between governments on environmental issues.

The International Court of Justice (ICJ)[21]

2–014 The International Court of Justice was established under the UN Charter to serve as the "principal judicial organ" of the United Nations. It comprises 15 judges from member states, elected to serve nine-year terms. Although the Court normally sits with all 15 judges, some cases are referred to special chambers of fewer judges. The ICJ has two main functions: the settlement of international disputes and the delivery of "Advisory Opinions" on questions of law at the request of the General Assembly, the Security Council, or (with the permission of the General Assembly) other UN bodies. Under the UN Charter, all members of the UN undertake to comply with decisions of the court in cases to which they are a party.

Decisions of the ICJ have seldom focused directly on environmental issues. Such issues are sometimes considered incidentally, however, when the court rules on the application of other areas of international law. Environmental issues are usually addressed obliquely. Thus, the *Nuclear Tests Cases* (1973–4)[22] (brought by Australia and New Zealand against France, calling on the latter to halt its atmospheric nuclear testing in the South Pacific region) essentially used trespass, rather than environmental harm, as a cause of action. Similarly, the *Gabcikovo-Nagymaros Case*[23] (which

---

[21] See Jennings, "The role of the International Court of Justice" [1997] B.Y.I.L.1.
[22] ICJ Reports, 1974, 253.
[23] *Gabcikovo-Nagymaros (Hungary/Slovakia)* ICJ Reports, 1997, 7.

concerned a dispute between Hungry and Slovakia about the environmental impacts on the Danube of construction work) depended upon an interpretation of the obligations contained in a treaty between those two countries. The Court clearly has competence to hear environmental complaints. However, for diplomatic reasons, states do not tend to see it as appropriate to invoke the full might of the ICJ to resolve their environmental disputes. Thus, whilst in 1992 the Court established a special seven-member chamber for hearing environmental cases, not a single case has yet come before it.

The Organisation for Economic Co-operation and Development (OECD)

The OECD is not a UN agency, but a grouping of industrialised countries which aims **2–015** to promote the economic growth of its members, assist developing states, and encourage world trade. It has a membership of 24 countries, mainly from Europe, but including the US, Canada, Mexico, Japan and South Korea. The OECD has a number of committees, responsible for such matters as energy, fisheries, and scientific and technological policy. It also has an Environment Committee. This carries out assessments of member states' environmental policies and produces recommendations. It has, for example, examined methods for the disposal and transport of hazardous waste, and the environmental implications of different methods of energy production.

Much of the OECD's early environmental work concerned the problem of transboundary pollution, and in this context it was responsible for developing the well-known "polluter pays principle" (discussed below). It was the first international body to take legal action to control exports and imports of hazardous waste. The relevant Acts of the OECD Council (which are legally binding on member states) have formed the basis of the Basel Convention and an EC Regulation on the shipment of hazardous waste.[24] More recently, the OECD has produced recommendations on the management of environmental information by public bodies.

The World Bank

The World Bank supplies loans to states for "reconstruction and development" and for **2–016** projects that will enhance economic growth. The bank has 22 directors, but is primarily controlled by the developed states that contribute the most to its capital fund. Its mandate requires it to be guided exclusively by economic considerations, and this has meant that, in the past, it has financed a number of projects (such as the building of power stations, pipelines and roads) that have caused environmental damage. The World Bank has, however, committed itself to implementing the principles of the Rio Declaration. To this end, it has now established a policy of ensuring that the development which it funds is ecologically sound—borrowing states are required to submit environmental impact assessments.[25] The World Bank also supervises the

---

[24] Council Reg.259/93 on the supervision and control of shipments of waste within into and out of the European Community.
[25] For an evaluation of the World Bank's environmental role, see Fox and Brown (eds.), *The Struggle for Accountability: The World Bank, NGOs and Grassroots Movements* (Cambridge, Mass., 1998).

operation of the "Global Environmental Facility", which is fund designed to assist developing countries with the cost of implementing measures to ensure "global environmental benefits" in the fields of climate change, ozone depletion, biological diversity and marine conservation. Although under the supervision of the World Bank, the Global Environmental Facility is, in effect, a distinct entity, having its own ruling council of 32 members, half of which come from developing countries eligible to receive assistance.

The World Trade Organisation (WTO)

2–017 The World Trade Organisation was established in 1994 to serve as a forum for furthering international trade and for settling disputes arising out of the implementation of the General Agreement on Tariffs and Trade (GATT) and other trade agreements. The aim of the GATT is to facilitate world trade by reducing tariffs and other barriers to trade which may lead to discriminatory treatment between nations. To achieve this, the GATT sets out a detailed set of rules.

It is important to note the potential for conflict between the GATT rules and the rules of international environmental conventions. Approximately 20 international conventions and agreements contain trade provisions. Some of the most notable include: the Convention on International Trade in Endangered Species (CITES); the Montreal Protocol on Substances that deplete the Ozone Layer (which bans imports of substances from states which are not parties to the Protocol); and the Basel Convention on Transboundary Movements of Hazardous Wastes. There is no specific exemption in the GATT for trade restrictions required by the provisions of multilateral conventions. A problem might therefore arise if a party to a multilateral convention sought to apply a trade restriction in a convention which does not fall within one of the specific exemptions of the GATT (discrimination is acceptable if necessary to protect human, animal or plant health, or in pursuit of measures relating to the conservation of exhaustible natural resources). Although attempts have been made to resolve the situation, there is no internationally agreed set of principles to deal with the potential difficulties caused by the overlap between the GATT rules and the trade provisions of environmental conventions.

Inevitably, the resolution of trade disputes arising under the GATT rules has had an environmental dimension.[26] The best known and most controversial of these disputes have concerned the impact of methods of catching tuna on dolphins, and the impact of shrimp-catching on turtles. In neither of these contexts, however, did the World Trade Organisation's dispute settlement body feel able to restrict international trade in the name of conservation.

The issue in these cases was the application of Art. 20 of the GATT. This permits trade restrictions that are "necessary to protect human, animal or plant life or health". In the first *Tuna Dolphin* case (which was in fact decided in 1991 by a GATT dispute panel, a precursor of the WTO), the complaint was that the US had banned imports of tuna from Mexico, where the tuna had been caught in nets causing harm to dolphins.

---

[26] For further discussion of these issues, see Esty, *Greening the GATT: Trade, Environment and the Future* (1994, Institute for International Economics, Washington) and Brack (ed.), *Trade and Environment: Conflict or Compatibility?* (1998, Royal Institute of International Affairs, London.)

The issue was whether, on a proper interpretation of Art. 20, one country was allowed to impose trade sanctions on another that would, in effect, dictate the content of that other's environmental policies. The panel decided that Art. 20 could not be used in this way. The US ban was a violation of its obligation not to restrict free trade. Whilst a ban based on the *quality* of the goods might have been acceptable, a ban based on *the methods by which the goods were produced* was not. On a proper construction, Art. 20 was to be read as merely allowing a country to impose trade restrictions for the conservation of animals within its own territory. Moreover, the panel concluded that the ban was not "necessary" within the meaning of Art. 20, because the US had not exhausted other avenues to secure its conservation objectives, such as negotiating a co-operative agreement with Mexico.

The second *Tuna Dolphin* case arose in 1994, when the European Community challenged the "secondary embargo" that had also been imposed by the US. Under this "secondary embargo", the US had banned imports of tuna from all foreign countries who bought tuna from countries like Mexico, where it had been caught with nets. Again, the WTO found that the US embargo was illegal under the GATT rules. This time, however, the panel took a slightly more liberal approach. It retracted its previous ruling that Art. 20 could not be used to conserve animals in another state's jurisdiction. However, it was prepared to find against the US on the basis that Art. 20 did not allow trade restrictions in the name of conservation to be imposed *unilaterally* by one state on another. In other words, any trade restrictions based on Art. 20 would have to be agreed by the countries on whom they were imposed.

The most recent environmental dispute to have been decided by the WTO is the 1998 *Shrimp Turtle* case. Here, the issue was the legality of a US trade embargo on Thai shrimp caught in a way that endangered sea turtles. The panel reiterated their previous assertion that trade restrictions were not an appropriate means of securing conservation. The panel were at pains to point out, however, that they were not deciding that GATT members should not enter into multilateral agreements for environmental purposes, or adopt effective conservation measures. They were simply deciding that measures designed to restrict international trade were not the appropriate means for enforcing environmental policy.

The latest environmental dispute to come before the WTO relates to Genetically Modified Organisms. It is a challenge by the US, Canada and Argentina to the European Union's *de facto* moratorium on approving the use of GM products. The US is arguing that, without scientific justification, the EU has refused to authorise any GM products since 1998, and that this is inconsistent with the GATT and other agreements.[27]

D: EMERGING PRINCIPLES OF INTERNATIONAL ENVIRONMENTAL LAW

Because, as has been said, international law is formed by a consensus of ideas and **2–018** behaviour between states, it is extremely difficult to determine at what stage an obligation in a convention, or examples of state behaviour, can be said with certainty to

---

[27] See the Agreement on the Application of Sanitary and Phytosanitary Measures; the Agreement on Agriculture; and the Agreement on Technical Barriers to Trade (*www.wto.org*).

have formed a principle of international law binding on all nations. It is clear that a number of principles are emerging in the field of international environmental law, but they are at different stages of development. Probably only the "no-harm" rule and the "co-operation principle" are sufficiently established to provide the basis for a cause of action in an international court. The "precautionary principle" may have achieved this status in a European context.[28]

The "no harm" rule

2–019 This is the most fundamental rule of international environmental law, and is contained within Principle 21 of the Stockholm Declaration and Principle 2 of the Rio Declaration:

> "States have . . . the responsibility to ensure that activities within their jurisdiction or control do not cause damage to the environment of other states or of areas beyond the limits of national jurisdiction."

This no-harm rule regulates state behaviour in respect of transboundary pollution. It forms the second half of the Stockholm and Rio principle, following on immediately from the assertion that states have the sovereign right to exploit their own resources pursuant to their own environmental policies. The principle as a whole, therefore, represents a careful balance between the territorial sovereignty of a state, on the one hand, and a wider responsibility to the international community on the other.

As we have noted, state responsibility not to cause harm by transboundary pollution first appeared as a principle earlier than Stockholm, in the 1941 *Trail Smelter* case. In 1949, the *Corfu Channel Case*,[29] although not an environmental case, contributed to the development of the principle. The ICJ held that Albania was responsible in international law for failing to inform the UK about the presence of mines laid in its territorial waters. It was held that every state has a duty not to knowingly allow its territory to be used for activities that are contrary to the rights of other states.

Following its appearance in the Stockholm Declaration, the principle appeared in numerous conventions between 1972 and 1992, including the 1979 Geneva Convention on Long Range Transboundary Air Pollution,[30] the 1985 Vienna Ozone Convention,[31] and the 1989 Basel Convention on Hazardous Waste.[32] The principle is now accepted as a rule of customary international law, and its status as such has been recently recognised by the ICJ. In 1996, in the Court's *Advisory Opinion on the Legality of the Threat or Use of Nuclear Weapons*, it stated[33]:

> ". . . the environment is not an abstraction but represents the living space, the quality of life and the very health of human beings, including generations unborn.

---

[28] Sands, *Principles of International Environmental Law,* 2nd ed., 2003.
[29] *Corfu Channel Case (UK v Albania)* 1949, ICJ Reports, 4.
[30] 18 I.L.M. 1442 (1979).
[31] Convention for the Protection of the Ozone layer (Vienna) March 22, 1989. 26 I.L.M. 1529 (1989).
[32] Convention on the Control of Transboundary Movement of Hazardous Wastes and their Disposal 28 I.L.M. 657 (1989).
[33] 1996, ICJ Reports, 241–242, para.29.

The existence of the general obligation of states to ensure that activities within their jurisdiction and control respect the environment of other states or of areas beyond national control is now part of the corpus of international law relating to the environment."

The principle of state co-operation

The principle that states should co-operate in the field of environmental protection is **2–020** affirmed in virtually all international environmental agreements. The preamble to the Rio Convention on Biodiversity, for example, stresses the necessity and importance of promoting international, regional and global co-operation among states. Principle 27 of the Rio Declaration states: "States and people shall co-operate in good faith and in a spirit of partnership in the fulfilment of the principles embodied in this Declaration and in the further development of international law in the field of sustainable development." The necessity for co-operation is mentioned six times in the Rio Declaration. As has been said, the principle is probably sufficiently well established to be relied on in an international court against a state that refuses all co-operation. However, the practical requirements of the principle remain unclear.

The "precautionary principle"

The precautionary principle was developed to avoid the problem that scientific **2–021** knowledge is often not sufficiently advanced to provide concrete evidence about environmental damage likely to occur as a result of human action. The principle is to be found in a number of different forms, and so its substance cannot be stated with certainty. Broadly, however, the principle embodies the idea that states should err on the side of caution when taking steps to prevent environmental damage. The Treaty on European Union refers to the principle, but gives no definition of it. A commonly cited definition, however, is that contained in 1990 Bergen Ministerial Declaration on Sustainable Development:

"Environmental measures must anticipate, prevent and attack the causes of environmental degradation. Where there are threats of serious or irreversible damage, lack of full scientific certainty should not be used as a reason for postponing measures to prevent environmental degradation."

Principle 15 of the Rio Declaration is couched in the same terms:

"In order to protect the environment, the precautionary principle shall be widely applied by states according to their capabilities. Where there are threats of serious or irreversible damage, lack of full scientific certainty shall not be used as a reason for postponing cost-effective measures to prevent environmental degradation."

The Rio Declaration recognises that, applied without qualification, the precautionary principle may give too much weight to environmental protection at the expense of other important socio-economic principles. Hence the inclusion of provisos such as "cost effective measures", "according to their capabilities" and "serious or irreversible damage".

The principle appears not only in the Rio Declaration, but in the 1985 Vienna Ozone Convention, the Rio Climate Change Convention, and the Rio Biodiversity Convention. It is not clear, however, what level of risk is necessary before action must be taken. The Ozone Convention, in common with other international instruments, requires states to act when they have reasonable grounds for believing that activities may cause harm to the environment. One commentator argues that there is sufficient evidence of state practice to support the conclusion that the precautionary principle, as set out in Principle 15 of the Rio Declaration, reflects customary law.[34] The difficulties that have emerged in persuading the US to take action on climate change, however, indicate that there is no clear international consensus on the requirements of the principle.

The "polluter pays" principle

2–022 This principle embodies the idea that the polluter should bear the expense of carrying out measures decided upon by public authorities as necessary to ensure that the environment is in an acceptable state. One way of giving effect to this principle is to ensure that the costs of environmental protection measures are reflected in the prices of goods and services which cause pollution, through the use of economic instruments. The difficulties involved in doing this were considered in Ch. 1.

The principle is referred to in the Rio Declaration, which states:

"National authorities should endeavour to promote the internalisation of environmental costs and the use of economic instruments, taking into account the approach that the polluter should, in principle, bear the cost of pollution, with due regard to the public interest and without distorting international trade and investment."[35]

Although the principle is mentioned in a number of treaties (such as the European Community Treaty,[36] which requires that action by the Community shall be based on the principle), the precise means by which the principle is to be given effect are not clarified by international instruments.

The principle of "common but differentiated responsibility"

2–023 In essence, this principle embodies the idea that some states have different environmental concerns and responsibilities from others. Thus, Principle 7 of the Rio Declaration states:

"In view of their different contributions to global environmental degradation, states have common but differentiated responsibilities. The developed countries

[34] Sands, *op. cit.* above.
[35] Principle 16.
[36] Treaty Establishing the European Economic Community, Rome, March 25, 1957, 298 UNTS 267 as amended.

acknowledge the responsibility that they have in the international pursuit of sustainable development in view of the pressures their societies place on the global environment and of the technologies and financial resources they command."

The principle is based on the recognition that developing countries have special needs to which priority must be accorded. At Rio, developing nations made it clear that they would only participate in international environmental protection measures if they were given an incentive to do so. They took the view that it was unfair for the economically developed world, which had been able to industrialise at the expense of the environment, to deny the developing world a similar opportunity in the name of environmental protection.

Developing nations and developed nations often have very different priorities in terms of environmental problems. The environmental problems of developing nations are often directly related to poverty, whilst environmental problems in developed nations are related to excessive industrialisation and high-consumption lifestyles. A common criticism of international environmental law is that the concerns of developed nations dominate its agenda at the expense of the more immediate concerns of developing states. Thus, for example, there is much international activity and debate in relation to climate change and ozone depletion, even though their effects have yet significantly to be felt. Developing nations are faced with more pressing environmental problems. Approximately one billion third world citizens drink dirty water which fails to meet any basic safety standards. In addition, acute respiratory infection, caused by unsafe air, kills an estimated 4.3 million people in developing nations every year. As one writer has put it:

"Although global warming has yet to kill a single human being, and may not do so for centuries, it has received enormous attention and resources. At the same time silent emergencies that are killing people every day do not attract the same kind of screaming headlines and well funded action plans."[37]

As a result of the views expressed at Rio, it would seem that much of the developed world may now have accepted that it must pay a higher price than the developing world for global environmental problems. Thus, the preamble to the Rio Convention on Climate Change, which we examine in Ch. 3, notes that per capita emissions of greenhouse gases in developing countries are still relatively low, and recognises the special difficulties of developing countries, whose economies are particularly dependent on fossil fuel use. Whereas developed countries are required under the Convention to limit their greenhouse gas emissions, developing countries are required only to limit their emissions in accordance with the extent to which the developed nations fulfil their commitments to transfer finance and technology to the developing countries for that purpose. What this means, in blunt terms, is that the developed world must pay the developing world to refrain from polluting activities. This aspect of the principle of common but differentiated responsibility is one that the developed world appears a little more reluctant to accept.

[37] Dunoff, "From Green to Global: Towards the Transformation of International Environmental Law", (1995) Harvard Environmental Law Review Vol.19, No.2.

"Sustainable development"

2–024 In the early 1990s, "sustainable development" became very much the catch-phrase of international environmental law. It is now established as an international legal concept. The concept has been defined in numerous ways, but the most widely accepted definition is that given in the Brundtland Report:

> "Development that meets the needs of the present without compromising the ability of future generations to meet their own needs."

The concept recognises that protection of the environment cannot be considered in isolation from economic and development decisions. The Brundtland Report found that poverty was the cornerstone of many environmental problems. Not only were the developing nations promoting industrial growth on the scale of their more developed neighbours, which brought with it associated environmental problems, but measures to tackle poverty on the most basic level were causing environmental damage. For example, the destruction of vegetation to obtain food, or timber for fuel and building, left land unprotected so that its soil was washed away by rain. Without adequate soil, the land no longer retained water and became incapable of producing further food or timber, forcing the population to turn to new land and repeat the process of destruction. In turn, these environmental problems had a social impact. Land degradation had caused millions of "environmental refugees" to cross national borders. In Africa, for example, along the Sahel's 3,000 mile front, 10 million refugees had been displaced by barren soil.

It has been suggested that there are four elements to the concept[38]:

(1) the need to preserve natural resources for the benefit of future generations (the principle of "intergenerational equity");

(2) the aim of exploiting natural resources in a manner which is sustainable or prudent (the principle of "sustainable use");

(3) the equitable use of natural resources, implying that, in using resources, states must take account of the needs of other states (the principle of "equitable use" or "intragenerational equity");

(4) the need to ensure that environmental considerations are integrated into the economics of development plans, and that development needs are taken into account in applying environmental objectives (the principle of "integration").

The Rio Declaration placed sustainable development firmly on the international agenda. The declaration makes numerous references to it, although it does not define it. Whilst both the Brundtland Report and the Rio Declaration provide a useful analysis of sustainable development, the concept can be criticised for its vagueness. Arguably, however, the very reason the concept has become so popular is that this vagueness has made it susceptible to favourable interpretation by parties with differing

[38] Sands, *op. cit.* above.

concerns. Thus, both developing and developed states are attracted to the concept because it promotes "development", whilst hard line environmentalists can point to the fact that any development that takes place must be environmentally "sustainable".

Meeting the needs of future generations

This principle, which is also known as the principle of "intergenerational equity" is **2–025** implicit in the definition of sustainable development offered by the Brundtland Report. It asserts that states have a duty to protect the environment not only for current inhabitants of the planet, but for future generations. The idea of holding the world in trust for future generations is frequently found in international environmental instruments. We have seen, for example, that Principle 1 of the Stockholm Declaration states that man bears "a solemn responsibility to protect and improve the environment for present and future generations." Article 3 of the Rio Convention on Climate Change also refers to the principle, and Principle 3 of Rio Declaration states: "The right to development must be fulfilled so as to equitably meet developmental and environmental needs of present and future generations".

Despite the principle's apparent popularity, these international instruments contain little clarification of its practical implications. At bottom, the confusion surrounding the principle has to do with the fact that, as a matter of environmental philosophy, it is open to a number of different interpretations. On one view, the principle holds that the next generation of mankind must inherit a stock of environmental assets (green fields, clean air, etc.) no less than the stock inherited by the present generation. On another, wider view, however, the principle of intergenerational equity may be satisfied by leaving to the next generation a stock of assets which comprises environmental assets, technological assets and "know-how". This view recognises that in some respects environmental resources can be "traded-off" against technology—technology can be substituted for environmental assets, whilst still securing an appropriate standard of living for the next generation. At its most extreme, this view implies, for example, that future generations who have access to computer-generated "virtual environments" will have less need for real ones! Needless to say, a large amount of disagreement exists about the precise extent to which technological assets can properly be substituted for environmental ones.

A duty to protect the domestic environment

A principle requiring states to protect their domestic environments would, of course, **2–026** amount to a significant encroachment upon the rule that a state is sovereign over its own environmental resources. As things currently stand, it is doubtful that such a principle exists as a matter of international law. That said, modern international environmental law is developing the concept that some environmental resources might be regarded as the "common concern of mankind". This indicates an ambition to bring certain domestic environmental issues within the control of the wider international community. It indicates a change in emphasis away from the ability of states to exploit their own resources, towards the idea that states have an obligation to protect their own environment for the benefit of others.[39] The "common concern" concept was

[39] See French, "A Reappraisal of Sovereignty in the light of Global Economic Concerns." [2001] Legal Studies 376.

included within the preamble of the Rio Convention on Climate Change ("the change in the Earth's climate and its adverse effects are a common concern of mankind"). It also appears in the preamble to the Rio Convention on Biological Diversity.

One result of this emerging idea that states should protect their domestic environment for the benefit of others has been that states are increasingly willing to assume obligations of a procedural nature, which require them to notify and consult with other states before taking action with environmental consequences.

Procedural obligations

2–027 A number of environmental agreements impose obligations on states to carry out procedural steps before commencing activities that may cause environmental damage. Such obligations include duties to:

- carry out an "environmental impact assessment" as part of the decision-making procedure for projects which could impact on the environment (*e.g.* under the 1991 Convention on Environmental Impact Assessment in a Transboundary Context[40]);

- notify states potentially affected by certain activities (*e.g.* under the 1989 Basel Convention on Hazardous Waste and the 1992 Rio Convention on Biological Diversity);

- exchange information (almost all environmental treaties provide for the exchange of information on a regular basis);

- enter into consultations (*e.g.* under the 1991 Convention on Environmental Impact Assessment, the 1979 Geneva Convention on Long-range Transboundary Air Pollution, and the 1992 Industrial Accidents Convention[41]).

The purpose of these procedural obligations, in essence, is to concentrate the minds of those involved in potentially environmentally harmful activities, and give other states a chance to assist in minimising environmental impacts. Again, however, the principle of sovereignty is paramount. This means that a duty to "consult", for example, does not imply that the consent of an objecting state must be obtained before an activity goes ahead. Where transboundary pollution is the issue, however, procedural obligations clearly have a part to play in determining the scope and meaning of the "no harm" rule.

A human right to a healthy environment

2–028 We consider the relationship between human rights law and environmental law in Ch. 14. As we have already noted, Principle 1 of the 1972 Stockholm Declaration proclaims that: "Man has the fundamental right to freedom, equality and adequate

---

[40] 30 I.L.M. 802.
[41] UN/ECE Convention on the Transboundary Effects of Industrial Accidents, Helsinki, March 17, 1992. 31 I.L.M. 1330.

conditions of life in an environment of a quality that permits a life of dignity and well-being." References to the right to a healthy or decent environment have appeared in several global and regional human rights treaties. The Rio Declaration, however, avoids explicit reference to human rights, stating merely that human beings are at the centre of concerns for sustainable development.

It seems unlikely that any substantive right to a healthy environment exists as a matter of international law. To the extent that such a right *might* be said to exist, it is, perhaps, evidenced by the right to development contained in the Rio Declaration, by the elements of that declaration which deal with the procedural aspects of environmental policy within states, and by the subsequent Aarhus Convention, discussed in Ch. 14.

Chapter 3

CLIMATE CHANGE

"Climate change [is] an outstanding challenge of the next 10 years and beyond."
(sixth European Community Environmental Action Programme 2002)[1]

Introduction

A new environmental concern has become predominant over the last 10 years, **3–001** although it was barely in the consciousness of politicians or the public 20 years ago. This is climate change—the warming up of the earth. The likely physical and social consequences of climate change, and the universal nature of those consequences, have made it the single biggest global environmental concern. Compared with other environmental issues, it is high on the international political agenda. As we noted in Ch. 2, international laws on the subject, in particular the Kyoto Protocol, are perhaps some of the environmental laws best known to the general public. These laws have been hugely influential in setting the domestic agenda for the UK's responses to climate change (although the UK, in turn, is leading the agenda in international negotiations and by its domestic action).

Because, as we shall see, these international laws have in recent times sought to demand from states compliance with some quite specific and difficult obligations, climate change has become one of the most controversial and "politicised" environmental issues. At the time of writing, US policy on climate change is to focus on the development of clean technologies, whilst largely continuing with "business as usual". The US does not intend to give its support to the main piece of international climate change legislation—the Kyoto Protocol. As president George W. Bush has put it[2]:

> "The approach taken under the Kyoto Protocol would have required the United States to make deep and immediate cuts in our economy to meet an arbitrary target. I will not commit our nation to an unsound international treaty that will throw millions of our citizens out of work."

---

[1] See Decision No. 1600/2002/EC of the European Parliament and of the Council of July 22, 2001 laying down the Sixth Community Environmental Action Programme OJ L242/1.

[2] From a speech by George W. Bush, Feb. 2002, announcing the "Clear Skies and Global Climate Change Initiative": *www.whitehouse.gov/news/releases/2002/02*. President Bush goes on to say: ". . . yet we recognize our international responsibilities. So in addition to acting at home, the United States will actively help developing nations grow along a more efficient, more environmentally responsible path".

By contrast, EU policy is both to develop new technologies and to seek the reduction in emissions of greenhouse gases (the gases which cause the earth to warm up) demanded by the Kyoto Protocol. UK policy is to go much further than is required by the Kyoto Protocol in reducing domestic emissions of carbon dioxide.

The contribution of developing countries to historic and current emissions of greenhouse gases has been less than that of the developed world. Developing countries are therefore currently subject to less onerous international obligations than the developed world. However, their emissions are growing, and a decision will soon need to be taken whether to strengthen their contribution to combating climate change. Such a decision is likely to be controversial, because, as we noted in Ch. 2, they may argue that they should be entitled to the same right to develop at the environment's expense that was enjoyed by the developed states (or at least to monetary compensation for foregoing that right). Meanwhile, the impacts of climate change will be felt most in the developing states. This is not only because their arid terrain is likely to be affected more than land in the developed world, but because their poverty means they will be less able than the developed world to take measures to adapt to climate change. All of this means that drafting, passing and implementing international climate change obligations is by no means straightforward.

What is climate change?

3–002 The basic principle of climate change is simple. Several types of gas can reflect or trap heat, and so cause the world to warm up, rather as if a blanket had been wrapped around it, or as if it had been placed in a greenhouse (hence the so-called "greenhouse effect"). These gases include carbon dioxide, methane, CFC gases, ozone, water vapour and nitrous oxide (laughing gas). These are known as "greenhouse gases". Carbon dioxide is the main contributor to the greenhouse effect.

To an extent, the greenhouse effect is desirable—without it the earth would be too cold. However, the problem arises because human activity has increased the quantity of greenhouse gases, in particular carbon dioxide, in the atmosphere. About 80 per cent of this extra "man-made" carbon dioxide comes from the burning of oil, coal and gas, whilst about 20 per cent comes from deforestation and other land changes that have prevented atmospheric carbon dioxide from being naturally absorbed.[3]

Approximately 30 to 55 per cent of the carbon dioxide produced by burning fossil fuels is absorbed by the sea, forests and plants.[4] (Plant life absorbs carbon dioxide through the process of photosynthesis. Large areas of water break down carbon dioxide at their surface and carry the carbon towards the ocean floor by currents, or by means of micro-organisms that consume the dissolved carbon and then sink when they die.) The remainder is added to the atmosphere, with the effect that the concentration of atmospheric carbon dioxide has increased considerably from pre-industrial times to the present day. This in turn has led to an increase in the earth's temperature, known as the anthropogenic greenhouse effect. Over the course of the twentieth century, the earth has warmed up by about 0.6°C, largely due to increased greenhouse gas

---

[3] Lomborg, Bjorn, *The Skeptical Environmentalist: Measuring the Real State of the World*, Cambridge University Press 2001 (first published in Danish in 1998), p.258.
[4] *ibid.* p.260.

emissions from human activities. The projected increase in global temperature ranges between 1°C to 3.5°C by the end of the next century.[5] The 1990s were the warmest decade since records began.

The likely effects of a warmer climate are thought to include a rise in sea level and other changes in weather patterns. In 1999, uninhabited islands of the tiny island-state of Kiribati disappeared under the waves of the South Pacific Ocean. Other islands and low lying areas are threatened with flooding. In 1998, there were floods in Bangladesh, and around the Yangtze River in China. Other impacts may include loss of biodiversity and changes in species distribution. The effects are likely to vary from region to region. Social impacts may follow, including those arising from an increased risk of diseases like malaria (because of the increase in mosquitoes in warmer areas), hunger, lack of water, or flooding. In turn, these impacts may lead to migration by "environmental refugees" and to conflicts over scarce water resources.[6]

Energy production and use

Responding to climate change has become a central aspect of UK energy policy. **3–003** Energy production accounts for 80 per cent of the UK's greenhouse gas emissions and 95 per cent of its carbon dioxide emissions.[7] Therefore, climate change objectives must be achieved largely through changes in the way energy is supplied and consumed. Energy, of course, provides heat, light, and power for use in homes, transport and industry. It has played an important role in society throughout history and across the world. Burning wood, dung or agricultural residues provided heat for early societies, and still does so in rural areas in developing countries. The invention of steam engines that could obtain work from heat, using coal as fuel, led to the industrial revolution, although wind and water continued to be used for many years in industrialised societies to drive mills and pumps. During the twentieth century, energy use across the world has increased nine-fold. Most of this increase has taken place since 1945.[8] Today's sources of energy include gas, coal, oil, nuclear and, increasingly, renewable energy sources (although, at present, these account for only a small fraction of total energy provision).

In the UK, prior to 1950, coal was the main source of energy for industry and households, accounting for 90 per cent of the UK's primary energy needs (*i.e.* as a fuel for heating, transport and industrial processes) and generating virtually all the electricity used.[9] Following the discovery of nuclear fission in the 1930s, nuclear power plants began to be commissioned from the mid-1950s and were the first new source of electricity. In the late 1960s, natural gas was discovered in the North Sea. Gas has now become the largest source of energy for heating (both in an industrial and a domestic context) and for electricity generation. The low cost of gas, coupled with the

---

[5] Intergovernmental Panel on Climate Change, Third Assessment Report, 2001.
[6] See the press release issued by UNE.P. on World Water Day (March 22, 2000): *www.unep.org*. Discussions have already begun to assess how such conflicts could be resolved, see *http://www.worldwatercouncil.org*.
[7] Performance and Innovation Unit: *The Energy Review*, February 2002. See *http://www.number-10.gov.uk/su/energy/1.html*. (The Cabinet Office has now renamed the P.I.U. the "Strategy Unit".)
[8] See Royal Commission on Environmental Pollution, 22nd Report: *Energy—the Changing Climate*, 2000, Cm 4794, p.13.
[9] Performance and Innovation Unit: *The Energy Review*, p.21.

privatisation of the gas and electricity supply industries during the 1990s, accelerated the move from coal to gas, as did pressures to reduce acid rain. Nuclear power stations are currently being de-commissioned, as are older coal-fired stations.[10]

The so-called "dash for gas" has created considerable uncertainty in the UK about the security of its future energy supply.[11] If gas remains the favoured fuel, the UK will become heavily dependent on imports when its own North Sea supply runs out.[12] Neither coal nor oil are any longer environmentally acceptable alternatives, because they would increase emissions of carbon dioxide. Nuclear power station closures have already started, and by 2020 only one will be left.[13] Although generation of renewable energy (notably wind energy) has begun to increase, it is unlikely that renewables can be relied upon to maintain a secure supply of electricity in the event of an interruption to imported gas supplies.

Nuclear power offers a secure, zero-carbon source of electricity on a scale which, for each individual power station, is larger than any other option. Public concerns over safety, however, have to a certain extent made the re-introduction of nuclear energy an "unmentionable issue". Nevertheless, as the Vice-President of the European Commission has put it:[14]

> "Nuclear energy has made it possible to avoid around 300 million tonnes of [carbon] emissions per annum and provides 35 per cent of all electricity produced in the EU. With the current state of art, giving up the nuclear option would make it impossible to achieve the objectives of combating climate change."

Energy production, then, raises a number of interconnected issues. Not only must the supply of energy be "environmentally friendly"; it must be safe, secure and affordable. The latter concern implies ensuring continued investment in energy infrastructure, and ensuring that the energy market remains competitive. Quite apart from climate change, there are other environmental impacts associated with various kinds of energy production which must be taken into account—the extraction, processing, movement and use of different kinds of fuel may produce adverse environmental consequences. These include reductions in air quality, problems of waste disposal and impacts on the landscape. Thus, whilst this chapter focuses on climate change, it is important not to lose sight of the fact that climate change is only one factor to be balanced against others when making decisions about energy production.

The international response to climate change

3–004   Increasing scientific evidence of the impacts of human activities on the global climate, coupled with increasing public anxiety, led to climate change entering the international political agenda in the mid-1980s. In 1988 the United Nations General Assembly took

---

[10] There are currently 16 coal-powered power stations in the UK, all but one of which are more than 30 years old. See ENDS Rep.343, August 2003, p.12.

[11] The Institution of Civil Engineers, in its *State of the Nation Report (2003)*, states that "if future gas supplies were interrupted, this country would have major difficulty in keeping the lights on": *http:// www.ice.org.uk/rtfpdf/statenation_colour_full_03.pdf.*

[12] North Sea gas reserves may start to run out as early as 2015. See *The Times*, March 29, 2004.

[13] Institution of Civil Engineers, *State of the Nation Report (2003)*, p.10.

[14] European Commission Vice President—Loyola de Palacio, speaking at the World Economic Forum, Davos Switzerland (January 2001), cited in Institution of Civil Engineers, *State of the Nation Report (2003)*.

up the issue of climate change for the first time, adopting resolution 43/53 on the protection of global climate for present and future generations.[15] The preamble states that the UN is "convinced that climate change affects humanity as a whole and should be confronted within a global framework so as to take into account the vital interests of all mankind". It also states that it "recognises that climate change is a common concern of mankind, since climate is an essential condition which sustains life on earth". The resolution "determines that necessary and timely action should be taken to deal with climate change within a global framework".

Because there was little authoritative and up-to-date scientific information on the issue, the World Meteorological Organisation (WMO) and the UN Environment Programme (UNEP) established, in 1988, the Intergovernmental Panel on Climate Change (IPCC) to inform the UN's policy-making. The IPCC has published reports assessing climate change which are recognised as the most authoritative sources of information on the subject. In 1990, the IPCC issued its First Assessment Report, confirming that human-induced climate change was indeed a threat, and calling for a global treaty to address the problem. The report stated that, to stabilise atmospheric concentrations of carbon dioxide, current emissions would have to be reduced by between 60 and 80 per cent. Under a "business as usual" scenario (i.e. no changes in current policies), the panel forecast a 0.3°C per decade rise in average global temperature, and a six centimetre per decade rise in average sea level. This report, and its 1992 supplement, formed an important basis for negotiation of the UN Framework Convention on Climate Change. In 1995 the IPCC concluded that "the balance of evidence suggests a discernible human influence on global climate". Its 2001 report was much more forceful, stating: "there is new and stronger evidence that most of the warming observed over the last 50 years is attributable to human activities".[16]

The two major international legal instruments responding to climate change have been the UN Framework Convention on Climate Change and its Kyoto Protocol. These are the starting points for international efforts to cut emissions and have been very influential in setting the agenda for action at EU and national level. However, as the Royal Commission on Environmental Pollution has noted: ". . . these international agreements took a great deal of time and effort to negotiate, involving the highest levels of governments. Yet they are modest achievements when considered against the scale of the task that appears to lie ahead".[17]

A: THE CLIMATE CHANGE CONVENTION

Introduction

The UN Framework Convention on Climate Change[18] (the "Climate Change Conven- **3–005** tion") was opened for signature at the UN Conference on Environment and Development (the so-called "Earth Summit") in Rio de Janeiro, Brazil, on June 4,

---

[15] UN General Assembly Resolution, December 1988 A/RES/43/53.
[16] IPCC Second Assessment Report: *Climate Change 1995: The Science of Climate Change* (Cambridge University Press). IPCC Third Assessment Report: *Climate Change 2001* (Cambridge University Press).
[17] Report of the Royal Commission on Environmental Pollution: *Energy—The Changing Climate* p.47. Cm 4749.
[18] New York, May 9, 1992.

1992. It came into force on March 21, 1994. A decade after its adoption, 186 governments (including the European Union) are now parties to the convention. This constitutes near universal global membership.

The convention provides a framework for the stabilisation of greenhouse gas concentrations in the atmosphere "so as to prevent dangerous human interference with the climate system". Whilst the convention refers to both natural and man-made greenhouse gases, its focus is on climate change that is attributable to human activity. The objective of the convention is to *stabilise* atmospheric concentrations of greenhouse gases rather than *reduce* them. This stabilisation will require significant reductions in emissions, but will still allow some global warming to occur. The convention provides that emissions reductions must be implemented at a pace that does not threaten food production, enables sustainable economic development, and makes some allowance for ecosystems to adapt naturally to climate change. Thus, the convention adopts a pragmatic approach—whilst it would be possible immediately to stabilise atmospheric greenhouse gases, doing so would necessitate an immediate global ban on fossil fuel use. This, of course, would bring the modern world to a standstill.

To achieve its objectives, the convention set out a series of principles and commitments. More specific obligations were left to be defined in future legal instruments such as the Kyoto Protocol, discussed in a separate section below.

The convention principles

3–006   The convention incorporates a number of principles, some of which are already well known in international law:

- The convention recognises that the developed and developing world have different responsibilities in meeting the challenge set by climate change. The parties to the convention must therefore act on the basis of common but differentiated responsibilities. The convention divides countries into two main groups:

    (1) *Industrialised countries (41 countries)*. These comprise the relatively wealthy industrialised countries that were members of the Organisation for Economic Co-operation and Development (OECD) in 1992, plus countries with "economies in transition" (including the Russian Federation, the Baltic States and several Central and Eastern European States). Industrialised countries must take the lead in combating climate change, because of their greater contribution to current and historic emissions of greenhouse gases, and because they have greater financial and institutional capacity to address climate change. The OECD countries are required to take the strongest measures, whilst the states in transition to a market economy are allowed some flexibility.

    (2) *Developing countries (145 countries)*. The convention recognises that compliance by developing countries will depend on financial and technical assistance from developed countries. In addition, the needs of the least developed countries, and of those that are particularly vulnerable to

climate change for geographical reasons, are given special consideration. In particular, special consideration must be given to small island countries, countries with low-lying coastal areas, countries with arid and semi-arid areas, countries with forested areas and areas liable to forest decay, and countries with areas prone to natural disasters or to drought and desertification.

- The climate must be protected for the benefit of present and future generations.

- Where there are threats of serious or irreversible damage, lack of full scientific certainty should not be used as a reason for postponing precautionary measures.

- Economic development is essential for adopting measures to address climate change. The parties therefore have a right to, and should promote, sustainable development.

- Measures taken to combat climate change should not restrict international trade or discriminate against parties involved in it.

The parties' commitments

All parties are required, taking into account their common but differentiated **3–007** responsibilities, to:

- compile inventories of greenhouse gas emissions caused by human activities;

- compile inventories of activities which remove greenhouse gases from the atmosphere (sinks);

- develop regional programmes to mitigate climate change;

- develop and transfer technologies, practices and processes to control greenhouse gases in all relevant industrial sectors (including energy, transport, agriculture, forestry and waste management);

- promote mechanisms to remove greenhouse gases from the atmosphere (sinks). This implies the promotion of activities such as forestry and the building of lakes and reservoirs;

- co-operate in preparing to adapt to the impacts of climate change;

- take climate change considerations into account in formulating and implementing social, economic and environmental policies; and

- promote research, education and public awareness.

Industrialised countries have additional commitments:

- They must adopt national policies and take measures to mitigate climate change by limiting emissions of greenhouse gases. The aim is to reduce emissions of carbon dioxide and other greenhouse gases to 1990 levels, but this target is not binding.

● The OECD countries have a special obligation to provide finance to developing countries to enable them to comply with their obligations, and to facilitate the transfer of climate-friendly technologies.

Since its entry into force, the parties to the convention have met annually (at gatherings known as Conferences of the Parties or "COPs") to monitor its implementation and continue talks on how best to tackle climate change. The many decisions taken by the COPs at their annual sessions constitute a detailed rulebook for implementation of the convention obligations. The Marrakesh Accords, adopted at COP 7 (in November 2001), were especially important in outlining detailed rules for the implementation of the Kyoto Protocol.

B: THE KYOTO PROTOCOL

3–008 When they adopted the Climate Change Convention, the governments involved knew that their commitments would not be sufficient to have a serious impact on climate change. In 1995, therefore, the parties launched a new round of talks, aimed at producing stronger and more detailed commitments from industrialised countries. After two and a half years of intense negotiations, the Kyoto Protocol was adopted in Kyoto, Japan, on December 11, 1997. Building on the framework of the convention, the Kyoto Protocol breaks new ground. It significantly strengthens the convention by introducing legally binding constraints on greenhouse gas emissions in developed countries, and by introducing innovative mechanisms which attempt to cut the cost of curbing emissions.

The Protocol, however, is not yet in force. This means that, although a number of countries are already introducing domestic laws and policies to reflect their international commitments, the obligations in the Protocol are not yet part of international law. The rules for its entry into force require 55 Parties to the convention to ratify (or approve, accept, or accede to) the Protocol. Moreover, those parties must account for 55 per cent of the total carbon dioxide emissions (at 1990 levels) by industrialised countries that are listed in Annex I of the convention.[19] As of April 2004, over 110 countries had ratified the Protocol, but emissions from industrialised countries accounted for only 44.2 per cent of those countries' total carbon dioxide emissions. At the time of writing, only ratification by Russia or the US will bring the Protocol into force. The US is not expected to ratify.

The direct benefits from the Kyoto Protocol are likely to be modest. Emission limits are set only for developed nations, and the reductions they are required to achieve are expected to be outweighed by the increase in developing nations' emissions by 2012. Global emissions will therefore continue to rise. On one calculation, the effect of the Protocol, in the period 2008–2012, will be, at best, a reduction in global emissions of two per cent.[20] Thus, as one author has put it: "The Kyoto targets simply reflect what

[19] Article 25 of the Protocol.
[20] See: *http://www.dti.gov.uk/energy/whitepaper/ourenergyfuture.pdf*.

was politically feasible at the time and not what is appropriate from an ecological standpoint".[21]

All of this paints a rather bleak picture. It demonstrates, of course, that the Kyoto Protocol will not deliver the measures necessary to reduce the global temperature. Doing this would require much stronger commitments to reduce greenhouse gas emissions. It would also require these commitments to be made by the developing world. Such commitments may never be forthcoming. That being so, an alternative approach may be required, involving measures designed to help the world cope with a rise in temperature. This approach may imply securing economic growth in developing countries, so as to equip them with the resources and infrastructure necessary to manage global warming. As we have noted, it is these countries that are likely to experience its adverse effects the most.

The targets for industrialised countries

Under Kyoto, each industrialised country is given a target for the percentage by which **3–009** it must reduce its emissions of greenhouse gases below 1990 levels[22] in the period 2008–2012 (known as the "first commitment period"). The targets cover emissions of the six main greenhouse gases, namely: Carbon dioxide (CO_2); Methane (CH_4); Nitrous oxide (N_2O); Hydrofluorocarbons (HFCs); Perfluorcarbons (PFCs); and Sulphur hexafluoride (SF_6). The reductions, if achieved, will amount to an average reduction of 5.2 per cent from 1990 emissions levels. It will be seen that some countries, which have comparatively low emissions levels, were able to negotiate an *increase* in their emissions levels.

Country	Target
EU, Bulgaria, Czech Republic, Estonia, Latvia Liechtenstein, Lithuania, Monaco, Romania, Slovakia, Slovenia, Switzerland	− 8 per cent
US (indicated an intention not to ratify)	− 7 per cent
Canada, Hungary, Japan, Poland	− 6 per cent
Croatia	− 5 per cent
New Zealand, Russian Federation, Ukraine	0
Norway	+ 1 per cent
Australia	+ 8 per cent
Iceland	+ 10 per cent

Source: *http://unfccc.int/resource/process/components/response/respkp.html*

[21] Barret, S., "Political Review of the Kyoto Protocol" ((1998) 14 Oxford Review of Economic Policy 4, p.20).
[22] Some Central and Eastern European countries with economies in transition have a baseline other than 1990.

The EU has undertaken to reduce its emissions by eight per cent. The Protocol allows parties to fulfil their emission targets jointly, by pooling their individual emissions in a common "bubble". The EU has made use of this provision, and through a "burden-sharing agreement" has sub-divided its target of eight per cent into differentiated targets for each Member State, taking account of each Member State's national circumstances. The agreement on burden-sharing (often called the "EU Bubble") was reached in June 1998 and was made legally binding as part of the EU's instrument of ratification of the Protocol. The UK's target under the burden-sharing agreement is to reduce its emissions of greenhouse gases to 12.5 per cent below 1990 levels. It should be noted that Russia's target, which requires only that emissions are kept at their 1990 levels, will in fact exceed the actual emissions she is expected to produce. The recent collapse of the Russian economy has meant that Russia's emissions are unlikely to increase to the level that they were in 1990 by 2008. Russia is said, therefore, to have "hot air" (*i.e.* a target higher than her predicted emissions).

The Protocol provides that the parties must have made demonstrable progress in achieving their targets by 2005, and should meet their targets by 2012 at the latest. Discussions on action beyond 2012 must begin by 2005. Parties can reduce their "emissions" by increasing the amount of greenhouse gases removed from the atmosphere by use of sinks. Activities which may create such sinks include afforestation, re-forestation and preventing deforestation,[23] as well as forest management, crop-land management, grazing-land management and re-vegetation.[24]

The implementation mechanisms

3–010 Industrialised countries who negotiated the Protocol recognised that if their countries had to rely totally on domestic measures to implement their targets, the cost of complying with the targets could be very high. The Protocol therefore provides for three innovative compliance mechanisms which allow for flexibility in how countries choose to meet their targets. These mechanisms enable countries to act together, so that one country can take advantage of opportunities to reduce emissions, or create sinks, in another country where doing so will cost less.

Any industrialised country that has ratified the Protocol may use the mechanisms to help meet its emissions target. However, the use of the flexible mechanisms must be "supplemental to domestic action". The aim is that domestic action must constitute a significant element of each party's efforts in meeting its commitments. No specific limits have been set on the proportion of reductions that may be achieved through the flexible mechanisms, and this remains the subject of international debate. A particular concern is that countries might seek to meet their targets by buying up the excess emissions from countries like Russia, whose reduction target is still higher than its predicted emissions, thereby avoiding the need to make any real emissions reductions at home.

The three mechanisms are:

[23] Eligible under the Kyoto Protocol.
[24] Added to the list of eligible activities by the Marrakesh Accords.

(1) *Joint implementation*

Joint implementation[25] involves specific projects being undertaken jointly by indus- **3–011**
trialised countries to reduce greenhouse gases. An industrialised country can set up a
project to reduce emissions (*e.g.* an energy efficiency scheme, or a non-fossil fuel
power station to replace fossil fuel electricity generation) or increase removals of
greenhouse gases by creating a sink (*e.g.* a re-forestation project) in the territory of
another industrialised country. The country setting up the project can then use the
resulting reduction in emissions (known as "emission reduction units") to reach its
own target. Joint implementation projects are most likely to be set up in countries with
economies in transition, where there tends to be more scope for cutting emissions at
low cost.

(2) *The clean development mechanism*

The clean development mechanism is similar to joint implementation, but involves **3–012**
emissions reduction projects in *developing countries*, financed by industrialised nations.
The industrialised nation receives credits (known as "certified emission reductions")
which it can count towards meeting its own emissions reduction target. This practice
implements the concept of "leapfrogging", *i.e.* it enables developing countries to
develop without going through a traditional industrial revolution, with all of the
pollution which that entails.

(3) *Emissions trading*

Industrialised countries can participate in emissions trading in order to fulfil their **3–013**
commitments. This means that one industrialised country can transfer (sell) some of
the emissions allowed to it (known as "assigned amounts units") to another industrialised country that finds it more difficult to meet its emissions target. Credits
acquired through the clean-development mechanism and joint implementation
activities can also be transferred.

C: IMPLEMENTING KYOTO

The EU Climate Change Programme

Climate related initiatives by the EC date back to a 1991 strategy to limit carbon **3–014**
dioxide and improve energy efficiency. Elements of the strategy included legislation to
promote electricity from renewable energy,[26] proposed voluntary commitments by car-
makers to reduce carbon dioxide emissions, and proposals for a tax on energy.
However, the targets set by Kyoto meant that more action was required. The
European Climate Change Programme, launched in June 2000, aims to identify and
develop a strategy to implement the Kyoto Protocol.[27] Measures put forward as part of
the programme include:

---

[25] The term "joint implementation" does not appear in Art. 6 of the Protocol where this mechanism is
defined, but it is often used as convenient shorthand.
[26] Directive 2001/77/EC on the promotion of electricity produced from renewable energy sources in the
internal electricity market.
[27] Communication from the Commission to the Council and the European Parliament on EU policies and
measures to reduce greenhouse gas emissions: *Towards a European Climate Change Programme* (OM/2000)
88 final.

- An EU emissions trading scheme;

- Effective implementation of the energy efficiency requirements of the IPPC Directive (discussed in Ch. 5);

- Encouraging a move away from road and air transport to (cleaner) railways and waterways;

- Promoting "Combined Heat and Power" stations. These are stations that generate power (usually electricity) at the same time as harnessing the heat produced by the process. They are more efficient than traditional power stations, because they use heat that would otherwise be wasted[28];

- Promoting the use of "biofuels". These are fuels derived from "biomass", which is any plant or animal matter, including agricultural wastes and "energy crops" (things grown specifically to use as fuel). Biomass can be used for fuel directly, by burning, or by extraction from it of combustible oils. The Biofuels Directive[29] requires 5.75 per cent of transport fuels to be provided by zero-carbon fuels by the end of 2010.

- Vehicle taxation.

Not all of these measures have made good progress. Moreover, at the time of writing, 10 of the Member States were way off track in reaching their EU "burden-sharing" targets. For example, Ireland, which is required to limit its emission increase to 13 per cent of 1990 levels by 2012, had increased its emissions by 31 per cent by 2001. Whilst the EU as a whole has reduced its emissions, this is only because of the substantial emissions cuts made in Germany, the UK and Luxembourg.[30] The European Commission is therefore concerned to encourage Member States to adopt their own additional domestic policies, and to encourage voluntary action by citizens and companies. The Commission has acknowledged that it is difficult to be sure whether the EU is currently taking measures sufficient to meet its Kyoto target. It has also acknowledged the risk that only in 2010 or 2011 will it become clear how effective its measures have been, by which time it will be too late to adopt additional measures.[31]

In addition to the Renewables Directive and the Emissions Trading Directive (each discussed under a separate heading below), there have been other initiatives focussing on the use of renewable energy in heating applications (*e.g.* by use of solar panels),[32] on emissions from the transport sector, and on energy efficiency measures. The transport sector was the only sector of the economy where emissions of carbon dioxide grew (by 18 per cent) between 1990 and 2000. The Commission is therefore proposing a Directive on air conditioning in cars[33]—the increased use of air conditioning in cars

---

[28] Combined Heat and Power technology is used at more than 1300 sites in the UK, from small housing developments to large industrial sites. See *http://www.energyprojects.co.uk/chp.htm.*

[29] Directive 2003/30/EC on the promotion of the use of biofuels and other renewable fuels for transport.

[30] From a speech by Margot Wallström, EU Commissioner responsible for the Environment, to the 1st Brussels Climate Change Conference, Brussels, May 20, 2003.

[31] *ibid.*

[32] See *http://www.europa.eu.int/comm/energy/res/index_en.htm* and *http://www.europa.eu.int/comm/energy/res/sectors/photovoltaic_en.htm.*

[33] Proposal for a Regulation of the European Parliament and of the Council on certain fluorinated greenhouse gases COM/2003/0492 final.

is cancelling-out a significant part of the emissions reductions achieved in the transport sector by higher fuel efficiency. The Commission will also be reviewing its voluntary agreement with the auto industry concerning emissions from passenger cars. Energy efficiency measures include programmes to improve the thermal insulation of buildings, and the efficiency of gas, electrical and electronic equipment.

The UK position

The UK has managed to make substantial reductions in its greenhouse gas emissions, **3–015** and has already met its Kyoto Protocol target of a 12.5 per cent reduction of greenhouse gases from 1990 levels. This, however, is largely because of historical circumstances, namely the substitution of gas for coal as fuel in power stations, the efficiency of existing nuclear power stations, and the addition of a new large nuclear power station—Sizewell B. Projections show that action already taken in the UK is expected to cut emissions by around 15 per cent below 1990 levels by 2010. However, the amount of energy the UK uses is still increasing, and making further substantial cuts in carbon dioxide emissions after that date will become much more difficult if energy demand continues to rise. Although the energy sector is responsible for a large proportion of the UK's greenhouse gas emissions, other sectors of the economy also contribute to emissions, including the transport sector. This sector is the only sector where greenhouse gas emissions have increased since 1990, and is the focus of increasing policy-making attention.

The UK Climate Change Programme

In November 2000, the UK government produced its own "Climate Change Pro- **3–016** gramme"[34] which sets out how the UK will achieve its Kyoto target and move towards its domestic goals on carbon dioxide emission. The programme covers all sectors of the economy, including energy supply, business, transport, domestic, agriculture, forestry, land use and the public sector. The main elements of the programme are:

- a target for electricity suppliers (known as the "Renewables Obligation"), under which they must increase the proportion of electricity provided by renewable sources to 10 per cent by 2010;

- a domestic emissions trading scheme;

- a levy on commercial energy use ("the climate change levy");

- regulation of energy use under the IPPC regime (discussed in Ch. 5).

Other elements of the programme include a focus on the fuel efficiency of cars, energy efficiency in residential buildings, and a 10–year transport plan. The strategy has been criticised on the basis that, whilst energy efficiency and the promotion of renewables can obviously make a contribution to reducing emissions, the contribution

---

[34] *http://www.defra.gov.uk/environment/climatechange.*

made by renewables is likely to be quite limited—what is ultimately required is a significant reduction in energy demand, and the strategy does not go far enough in seeking to achieve this. Moreover, on the basis of current policies, the targets for renewables will not be met.[35]

The Energy White Paper

3–017 In February 2003, the UK government set out its energy policy for the next 50 years, in what has been described by Friends of the Earth as a White Paper placing climate change at the heart of energy policy.[36] The title of the White Paper, "Our Energy Future—Creating a Low Carbon Economy",[37] gives a clear indication of the government's priorities. The paper deals with the environmental impacts of energy use, and in particular climate change. It refers to the "opportunity to shift the UK decisively towards becoming a low carbon economy". The relevant policies are as follows:

- To aim for a 60 per cent reduction in carbon dioxide emissions from current levels by about 2050. This goal is much more ambitious than the UK's Kyoto Protocol commitment. The White Paper acknowledges that achieving such a reduction would require a fundamental long-term shift in the way energy is supplied and used. This objective has been described as "laudable but not realistic".[38]

- A foreign policy objective to secure international commitment to stabilising the level of greenhouse gases in the atmosphere. This is seen as necessary because the UK cannot possibly solve the problem of climate change on its own. UK emissions of carbon dioxide account for only 2 per cent of the global total.

- An ambition to increase the proportion of electricity supplied by renewables to 20 per cent of total supply by 2020.

- There are no specific proposals for building new nuclear power stations, although the White Paper does not rule out the possibility that at some point in the future new nuclear build might be necessary to meet our emissions targets.

- An emissions trading scheme. A voluntary trading scheme already exists in the UK. However, from 2005, industrial operators will be part of a much larger, Europe-wide scheme (discussed in a separate section below).

- Energy efficiency measures: A large proportion of emissions reductions are expected to come from energy efficiency measures (including better insulation of buildings, and ensuring that products like freezers waste less energy).

The scale of the challenge laid out in the White Paper is enormous. The UK appears to have taken on the role of an international leader on climate change issues. This, of course, has been made possible largely because historical circumstances have enabled

---

[35] Institution of Civil Engineers, *State of the Nation Report (2003)*.
[36] See *http://www.foe.co.uk/campaigns/climate/success_stories/thirtieth_anniversary_gift.html*.
[37] Cm 5761, February 2003.
[38] Institution of Civil Engineers, *State of the Nation Report (2003)*.

the UK to meet its Kyoto target over ten years early. However, these advantages may not repeat themselves, and reaching future targets will require dedicated policies.

The UK Climate Change Levy[39]

The Chancellor, in March 1998, indicated in his Budget speech his intention to **3–018** investigate the suitability of a tax on the industrial and commercial use of energy.[40] The subsequent report of Lord Marshall[41] suggested the introduction of an energy tax on industrial and commercial use of energy products and electricity. (It also suggested an emissions trading scheme, and this is discussed in a separate section below.) Plans for the climate change levy, which were mooted in the Chancellor's March 1999 Budget,[42] broadly followed the recommendations of the report.

The climate change levy came into effect in April 2001. It is a tax on the use of energy in business and the public sector and falls on users of energy rather than suppliers.[43] Specifically, the levy applies to the use of fuels for lighting, heating and power in industry, commerce, agriculture and public administration. It applies to all energy and fuels, including electricity, industrial gas, liquid petroleum gas, coal and coke. Oils already subject to excise duties are exempt, as is the use of renewable energy (with the exception of energy from large-scale hydro-power stations). Also exempt is energy supplied from approved Combined Heat and Power stations.

The tax is not a tax on the use of carbon. (This idea was rejected in Lord Marshall's report—because the national grid supplies electricity from a mixture of different sources, it was thought impractical to assess the relative carbon content of the various fuels used in supplying particular users.) This has led to criticism from the Royal Commission on Environmental Pollution, who wanted an "upstream" *carbon tax*, levied on *energy suppliers*, so as to directly address greenhouse gas emissions at source. There are advantages and disadvantages associated with both forms of tax (energy and carbon) with both "upstream" taxes (on energy suppliers) and "downstream" taxes (on energy consumers). The main argument for a "downstream" energy tax on consumers is that it may work better in promoting efficient energy-use technologies, by bringing home to those who use energy, in a very direct way, the financial benefits of energy

---

[39] Note that the EU has agreed a Directive on the taxation of energy products. See Council Directive 2003/96/EC of October 27, 2003 on restructuring the Community Framework for the taxation of energy products and electricity.

[40] *Hansard*, House of Commons Debates, March 17, 1998, cc 1108–1109.

[41] *Economic Instruments and the Business Use of Energy: A Report by Lord Marshall* (HM Treasury, November 1998).

[42] *Hansard*, House of Commons Debates, March 9, 1999, c 181.

[43] The Climate Change Levy is established by the Finance Act 2000, s.30. The detailed provisions are set out in sch.6 to the Act. See also SI 2003/2633 Climate Change Levy (General) (Amendment) (No.2) Regulations 2003; SI 2003/861 Climate Change Levy (Combined Heat and Power Stations) (Prescribed Conditions and Efficiency Percentages) (Amendment) Regulations 2003; SI 2003/665 Climate Change Levy (Use as Fuel) (Amendment) Regulations 2003; SI 2003/604 Climate Change Levy (General) (Amendment) Regulations 2003; SI 2002/1152 Climate Change Levy (General) (Amendment) Regulations 2002; SI 2001/1140 Climate Change Levy (Combined Heat and Power Stations) (Prescribed Conditions and Efficiency Percentages) Regulations 2001; SI 2001/1138 Climate Change Levy (Use as Fuel) Regulations 2001; SI 2001/1137 Climate Change Levy (Solid Fuel) Regulations 2001; SI 2001/1136 Climate Change Levy (Electricity and Gas) Regulations 2001; SI 2001/838 Climate Change Levy (General) Regulations 2001; SI 2001/486 Climate Change Levy (Combined Heat and Power Stations) (Exemption Certificate) Regulations 2001; SI 2001/7 Climate Change Levy (Registration and Miscellaneous Provisions) Regulations 2001.

conservation. On the other hand, an "upstream" carbon tax on suppliers involves fewer taxable entities than an energy tax. It therefore requires less fiscal supervision and lower regulatory compliance costs.[44]

The levy does not apply to domestic energy consumed in households (domestic use includes energy used by very small firms), or to energy used by the transport sector. Nor does it apply to energy used by registered charities. The exemption given to the transport sector and households is perhaps one of the weaknesses of the current approach, and may seem inappropriate at a time when the European Commission is urging Member States to respond to Kyoto by introducing policy measures that cover *all* sectors, including transport and domestic. Household consumption accounts for 29 per cent of the UK's total energy consumption (with only transport accounting for a greater share) and has increased by more than 25 per cent since the early 1970s because of population growth and changing patterns of energy use.[45]

The Royal Commission on Environmental Pollution has argued that the risk of hardship associated with increased domestic fuel prices could be adequately avoided by applying the climate change levy revenues to assist those at risk of hardship, such as pensioners and the unemployed.[46] Under current arrangements, the climate change levy is largely "revenue neutral", in the sense that revenues from the levy are returned to the business sector through a cut in the rate of all employers' National Insurance contributions of 0.3 per cent. (This does mean, however, that transport sector employers are being given something of a windfall, since they take the benefit of the reduction in National Insurance contributions without having to pay the climate change levy.) This arrangement is reflective of a general government policy of shifting taxation away from activities which create wealth and social value (employment, enterprise and investment) and placing it instead on activities which can lead to waste and pollution.

A critique of the climate change levy has suggested that the levy has been too tentative.[47] The National Insurance contribution reductions, designed to encourage employment, have not sent a strong enough signal to companies that they may be able to employ more staff if they reduce taxed energy use. One reason for this may be that many organisations have separate payroll and energy cost accounting systems, and so have not realised the relationship the levy creates between them. The authors of the critique take the view that unless there is a significant difference between the cost of "brown" and "green" energy, most industries will not make the radical changes in their operations that are necessary to create a sustainable energy system in the UK. The authors suggest that there is scope for the levy to be increased, and National Insurance contributions further reduced, in view of the recent reductions in the price of energy that have resulted from market liberalisation. In addition, they suggest that the motivation of energy suppliers to turn to renewable energy sources has come from the government-imposed "Renewables Obligation" (discussed below) rather than from consumer pressure created by the climate change levy on businesses.

---

[44] See Baranzini, Goldemberg and Speck, "A Future for Carbon Taxes", 32 Ecological Economics 3 (2000) at p.395. Under existing arrangements, the person liable to account for the levy is the person making the energy supply, but the levy is paid by those receiving the supply, via their energy bills. The energy supplier must register with the Commissioners for Customs & Excise, who administer the levy and who maintain a register of persons liable to pay it.

[45] See R.C.E.P: *Energy—The Changing Climate*, Cm 4749, at p.85 and p.97.

[46] *http://www.defra.gov.uk/environment/ccl/intro.htm*.

[47] Richardson and Chanwai, "The UK's Climate Change Levy: Is it working?" (2003) JEL Vol.15 No.1 p.54.

"Climate change agreements"

Energy intensive companies can enter into "climate change agreements". These are **3–019** voluntary agreements with the Secretary of State, under which the companies are set targets for the reduction of emissions or the improvement of energy efficiency. Companies who meet these targets benefit from an 80 per cent reduction in the climate change levy. The scheme is restricted to high energy using industries regulated under Pts A1 and A2 of the IPPC regime[48] (discussed in Ch. 5). The agreements operate until March 31, 2013.

D. RENEWABLE ENERGY

Renewable energy is energy generated from sources which occur naturally and **3–020** repeatedly in the environment. Such sources include the wind, waves, the sun, biomass (both naturally occurring and specifically grown), the tides, landfill gas and sewage treatment plant gas. Renewable energy is under-used in the EU at the moment. In the UK, its use is growing more slowly than in some other European countries, despite the availability of natural resources—the UK's lengthy coastline offers abundant opportunities to use wind and wave power, and the UK is thought to have over one third of Europe's potential for generating offshore wind energy.

Wind power is currently the most commercially viable form of renewable energy. At the time of writing, there are 82 wind farms, including 18 offshore projects, as compared with no wind farms 12 years ago. Whilst the quantity of electricity supplied by wind is still very small, wind farms are no longer the curiosity they used to be. An initial rush of land-based projects in the early 1990s produced a backlash from local populations, who objected to wind farms on amenity grounds (*e.g.* noise and visual intrusion). As a result, further projects found it difficult to get planning permission.[49] However, this position may now be changing.[50] Offshore wind farms present considerable difficulties. These include the problem of obtaining access to the electricity grid, and problems associated with the legal regimes that prevail in offshore locations beyond the UK's territorial waters.

Wave and tidal power and the use of biomass as a fuel are at a much earlier developmental stage than wind energy. The UK has one of the best wave resources in the world, being downstream of the Atlantic. As a resource, this could supply the UK with over twice its electricity demand. However the engineering problems associated

---

[48] See Finance Act 2000, s.30 and Schs 6 and 7.

[49] Generating plants of any type which have a capacity of 50 MW or more require consent from the Secretary of State for Trade and Industry in England and Wales or the Secretary of State for Scotland, under the Electricity Act 1989. The same Ministers give approval for overhead transmission lines. Before taking a decision in either context, the Minister consults local planning authorities; if the local planning authority objects, or the Minister considers it appropriate, a public inquiry may be held. If consent or approval is given under the 1989 Act, the Minister directs that planning permission is deemed to be granted.

[50] For the position in England, see PPG22: "Renewable Energy", February 1993. In Wales, the relevant advice is provided in Planning Guidance (Wales) Planning Policy First Revision April 1999, which is currently being reviewed, and Planning Guidance (Wales) Technical Advice Note (Wales) 8 "Renewable Energy". In Scotland, the equivalent guidance is National Planning Policy Guideline 6 "Renewable Energy", also under review. In Northern Ireland, there is no specific equivalent Planning Policy Statement to PPG 22.

with capturing wave power are substantial. Progress in capturing power from tides is even further behind. Tidal power is captured by means of tidal barrages, which, in effect, act in the same way as hydro-electric dams, obtaining energy from the movement of water through the barrage which occurs as the tide ebbs and flows. Installing such barrages, however, can be extremely difficult, because the forces involved are enormous and work can only take place during short periods of low tide. The use of biomass does not present the same level of technical difficulty, and is therefore currently a viable power source. Projects range from olive pips used in a power station, to small wood-fired boilers in local schools, to obtaining methane by fermenting cow slurry.[51] One of the issues with biomass, however, is price. Unlike wave, wind and tidal power, the fuel supply for many biomass projects is not free— farmers must be paid to grow biomass crops. At present, therefore, it is difficult for biomass to compete as a fuel with the low price of gas.

Renewable energy is a high priority for the EU, not only because of the need to meet the Kyoto targets, but because renewable energy provision will ensure the security of supply that comes through diversification. As has been said, UK policy with regard to renewable energy is for renewables to supply 10 per cent of UK electricity by 2010, together with an ambition that this share will double to 20 per cent by 2020. Whether the EU and the UK will meet their targets for the growth of renewable energy provision is not clear. Past experience shows that the use of renewable energy nearly always costs more than the use of fossil fuels. Regulatory and commercial arrangements in the UK have not tended to provide a level playing field for renewables and fossil fuels. Trading arrangements in the electricity sector have penalised renewable energy suppliers by requiring them to predict their output in advance (renewable power sources, such as the wind and the sun, are by their nature highly unpredictable). These arrangements have now been altered.[52] Renewable energy projects have also experienced problems in obtaining access to the electricity grid. The Renewables Directive recognises this, and requires Member States to ensure that grid operators guarantee the transmission and distribution of electricity produced from renewable sources. Member States may also allow for *priority access* to the grid system for this type electricity.

The EC Renewables Directive[53]

3–021   The Renewables Directive requires Member States to set targets for the consumption of electricity produced from renewable sources. The Directive provides guideline values for these targets. These values are set by reference to each Member State's national production of electricity from renewable sources in 1997. For the UK, production of electricity from renewable sources was 1.7 per cent of total production in 1997, and its target is to ensure that renewables account for 10 per cent of the total by 2010. This compares with the guideline target for Austria, which is 78.1 per cent by 2010. This target was set on the basis that, in 1997, 70 per cent of the total energy

---

[51] See *http://www.foe.co.uk/resource/reports/cofiring_renewables_obligation.pdf*.
[52] See the New Electricity Trading Arrangements (NETA): *http://www.ofgem.gov.uk/ofgem/index.jsp*.
[53] Directive 2001/77/EC of the European Parliament and of the Council of September 27, 2001 on the promotion of electricity produced from renewable energy sources in the internal electricity market.

produced by Austria was from renewable sources (although this represented only around 25 per cent of what it *consumed*). The target for the European Union as a whole is 22 per cent. This is part of a so-called "global indicative target" of 12 per cent of national energy being produced from renewable sources by 2010.[54] The targets in the Directive are non-binding "indicative" targets, but the Directive contains wording tentatively suggesting that binding targets will be set in the event that the European Commission considers that insufficient progress is being made.[55]

Under the Directive, energy produced from incinerating certain types of municipal and industrial waste is classified as renewable. Allowing waste incineration to count as a source of renewable energy has been controversial. Many feel that waste incineration should not be classified as a "renewable" energy source because of the high carbon content of emissions from incineration plants. It is noteworthy that energy produced in this manner has not been included within the scope of the UK's domestic renewables obligation (discussed below). However, the Directive makes clear that the incineration of waste should not be promoted where this would undermine the "waste hierarchy". The "waste hierarchy" is explained in Ch. 7. Essentially, it sets out three approaches for dealing with waste in order of preference—preventing waste from arising in the first place; recycling waste; and (only if the first two approaches cannot be used) disposing of it in the most environmentally-sensitive way. In effect, therefore, incineration of waste to produce energy should only be adopted if the waste in question could not have been prevented, could not have been recycled, *and* if such incineration is the method of disposal which causes the least harm to the environment.

Member States are required to ensure that electricity produced from renewable sources can be guaranteed as being from such sources. They must issue certificates guaranteeing the origin of such electricity to anyone requesting them. At the time of writing, the UK government has begun a period of consultation, outlining its proposals to issue Renewable Energy Guarantees of Origin (REGOs) to electricity generators. This scheme will be voluntary and the REGOs will not have any monetary value, but may prove useful in fostering trade in renewables between Member States—by holding a REGO, potential traders can demonstrate that their electricity has been produced from a renewable source.

The UK Renewables Obligation[56]

The Renewables Obligation requires electricity suppliers to supply to customers a **3–022** proportion of electricity generated from eligible renewable sources. The obligation began on April 1, 2002 and will continue until at least 2027. The setting in advance of this long time-frame during which the obligation will apply is designed to encourage investment by providing commercial certainty. Eligible renewable sources for the purpose of the obligation are defined widely, and include wind, wave, biomass, and landfill-gas sources. The percentage of supply which must be from renewable sources

[54] This was set out in the Commission's Communication *Energy for the Future: Renewable Sources of Energy*, White paper for a Community Strategy and Action Plan COM97/599 Final of November 26, 1997. See *http://europa.eu.int/comm/energy/library/599fi_en.pdf*.
[55] See Art. 3(4).
[56] See the Renewables Obligation Order 2002 (SI 2002/914) made under the authority of the Electricity Act 1982, s.32.

increases each year, building up from 3 per cent in 2002—2003 to 10 per cent in 2010. The supplier must demonstrate to the regulator—the Office of Gas and Electricity Markets ("OFGEM")—that it has supplied the requisite amount of electricity from renewable sources. OFGEM will then issue certificates (known as renewable obligation certificates, or "ROCs") to the electricity generator.[57] The certificates can be traded as an alternative means of meeting the obligation.

Instead of supplying electricity from renewable sources, a supplier can discharge its Renewables Obligation (in whole or in part) by making a payment to OFGEM. This, in effect, is the penalty price for not meeting the target. The price is known as the "buy out price" and, at the time of writing, is approximately £30 for each megawatt-hour of electricity that should have been generated from renewable sources but for which the supplier cannot produce a certificate. The money collected by OFGEM in this way is put into a "buy out fund" and is redistributed to those suppliers who have complied by producing certificates. The mechanism of the buy-out price provides a "safety net". By preventing the costs of meeting the Renewables Obligation from rising beyond a certain limit, it ensures that consumers are to some extent protected from the prospect of escalating electricity prices.

E: EMISSIONS TRADING[58]

The EC Emissions Trading Directive

3–023   Directive 2003/87 establishes an EU-wide emissions trading scheme to commence in 2005.[59] The intention is that this will assist Member States in complying with their commitments under the Kyoto Protocol. However, it is also envisaged that the scheme will operate on a "stand alone" basis if the Protocol does not come into force. An EU-wide trading scheme will minimise the potential for distortions of competition that might arise from different trading schemes in individual Member States. With the accession of ten new countries to the EU in May 2004, and more to follow in the next five to 10 years, the EU will become a major emissions trading zone. Whilst emissions trading does not, of course, of itself reduce emissions, the effect of the scheme will be that emissions reductions will be made in the EU wherever it is cheapest to make them.

The relevant industries (for which participation is mandatory) are listed in a section below. They include power generation, steel-making, glass-making and cement manufacture. Initially, the scheme will only cover carbon dioxide emissions (although the

---

[57] The relationship between REGOs, Renewable Obligation Certificates (ROCs) issued under the UK Renewables Obligation Order, and Levy Exemption Certificate (LECs) signifying exemption from the Climate Change Levy is at present complex and uncertain. The consultation paper acknowledges that this is something that needs to be addressed. See *Guarantees of Origin for renewable energy—Implementing Art. 5 of the EU Renewables Directive 2001/77/EC. http://www.dti.gov.uk/energy/consultations/regosdoc.pdf.*

[58] Rules on International Emissions Trading ("IET") under the Kyoto Protocol were largely finalised under the Marrakech Accords in November 2001. See the Marrakech Accords, Dec.18 (modalities, rules and guidelines for emissions trading under Art. 17 of the Kyoto Protocol). See *http://unfccc.int/cop7/documents/ accords_draft.pdf.*

[59] Directive 2003/87/EC of October 13, 2003 establishing a scheme for greenhouse gas emission allowance trading within the Community and amending Council Dir.96/61/EC.

Kyoto Protocol sets limits on the six greenhouse gases). This is on the basis that, in 1999, carbon dioxide accounted for over 80 per cent of the EU's greenhouse gas emissions. Moreover, levels of carbon dioxide emissions are more easily determined than levels of other greenhouse gas emissions. The intention, however, is that all the greenhouse gases will eventually be included within the scheme.

Two concepts are central to the scheme:

- greenhouse gas permits;
- greenhouse gas allowances.

The basic idea is that all participants in the scheme are given both a "permit" (placing a cap on the quantity of emissions they are allowed to discharge), and a set of "allowances" (entitling them to discharge emissions up to the level of that cap). The "allowances" can be traded. Thus, one participant, who finds it difficult to comply with the cap prescribed by the permit, might purchase "allowances" from another participant, entitling it to exceed the cap. Conversely, a participant who finds it easy to reduce its emissions to a level below the cap will have spare "allowances", which it can sell for profit. To put it another way, all participants in the scheme will have three options:

- meet their cap by reducing their own emissions;
- reduce their emissions below their cap, and sell or bank the excess allowances; or
- let their emissions remain above their cap, and buy allowances from other participants.

The best strategy for each participant will depend on the price of allowances in the market, as compared with the cost of reducing its emissions.

The permit places industrial operators under an obligation to hold allowances equal to the actual emissions of greenhouse gases from the installation. It also covers such matters as adequate monitoring, verification and reporting of emissions. Each operator must surrender, on an annual basis, sufficient allowances to match its emissions of greenhouse gases in the previous calendar year.

The level of emissions covered by the allowances initially granted to industry will be determined in accordance with "National Allocation Plans" which Member States are required to draw up. These plans will state the total quantity of allowances to be allocated amongst the various industrial sectors within the scheme, and will also specifically state the allowances to be allocated to individual industrial installations. Member States are given flexibility to allocate allowances, subject to relatively broad criteria, and allocation of allowances will not be consistent amongst Member States. In making their initial allocations, Member States will take into account their commitment under the "burden-sharing agreement" (discussed above). Environmental groups have expressed concern that initial allocation of greenhouse gas allowances may turn out to be too generous.[60] If industry is allowed to discharge too much greenhouse gas

---

[60] See Worthington, *The EU Greenhouse Gas Emissions Trading Directive and the Government's Energy White Paper* (available from Friends of the Earth, London).

initially, this will have the effect of suppressing the price of allowances on the market. A high price for allowances is required in order to provide an incentive for industry to implement technology to reduce emissions.

If installations trade allowances with other installations within the same Member State, there will, of course, be no change to the quantity of emissions which that state is entitled to emit under the "burden-sharing agreement". However, if an installation buys allowances from an installation in another Member State, there will need to be a corresponding adjustment, recorded in the national registries, to the obligations of the relevant states under the agreement. Selling an allowance to an installation in another Member State will mean that the "seller" Member State loses its entitlement to discharge the emissions covered by that allowance. Buying an allowance from another Member State, on the other hand, would entitle the "buyer" state to a higher level of emissions.

(1) *Industrial activities subject to the scheme*

3–024 Not all industrial activities are included within the scheme, but for those that do fall within the scheme, the scheme is mandatory. The industrial activities covered by the scheme are listed below. With some exceptions, these are the "heavy industry" activities regulated under the IPPC regime (discussed in Ch. 5). Approximately 4,000 to 5,000 installations will be included within the scheme. Together, these installations will account for approximately 46 per cent of estimated EU carbon dioxide emissions in 2010.[61] It is to be noted that the chemical industry and waste incineration industry are excluded. The chemical industry is excluded because its emissions of carbon dioxide are relatively low, and because the large number of chemical installations in the EU would increase the administrative complexity of the scheme. The waste incineration industry is excluded because of current difficulties in measuring the carbon content of the material burnt.

The following industrial activities are subject to the scheme[62]:

(i) *Energy activities:* combustion installations with a rated thermal input exceeding 20MW (except for hazardous or municipal waste installations); mineral oil refineries; coke ovens;

(ii) *Production and processing of ferrous metals:* metal ore (including sulphide ore) roasting or sintering installations; installations for the production of pig iron or steel with a capacity exceeding 2.5 tonnes per hour;

(iii) *Mineral activities:* installations for the production of cement clinker in rotary kilns with a production capacity exceeding 500 tonnes per day, or lime in rotary kilns with a production capacity exceeding 50 tonnes per day; or using other furnaces with a production capacity exceeding 50 tonnes per day; installations for the manufacture of glass with a melting capacity greater than 20 tonnes per day; installations for the manufacture of ceramic products by firing (tiles, bricks, porcelain and so on) with a production capacity exceeding 75 tonnes per day;

---

[61] Explanatory Memorandum to the European Commission's Proposal for a Directive of the European Parliament and of the Council establishing a scheme for greenhouse gas emission allowance trading within the Community and amending Council Dir.96/61/EC.
[62] Annex I to Dir.2003/78/EC.

(iv) *Other activities:* industrial plants for the production of pulp from timber or other fibrous materials; paper and board manufacturing plants with a production capacity exceeding 20 tonnes per day.

(2) *Timetable*

The first phase of the scheme will run from January 1, 2005 until December 31, 2007, **3–025** and will be followed by a second phase. The first phase period is prior to the first "commitment period" under the Kyoto Protocol. As there will be no international legally binding targets limiting the emissions of greenhouse gases by Member States during the first phase, there are differences between the first and second phases of the scheme. During the first phase, Member States must allocate at least 96 per cent of greenhouse gas allowances free of charge, whilst in the second phase (beginning in 2008, to coincide with the first Kyoto "commitment period") Member States must allocate at least 90 per cent of the allowances free of charge. For each phase, Member States must draw up national plans (National Allocation Plans) setting out the total quantity of allowances they propose to allocate for the period, and how they propose to allocate them.[63]

(3) *Enforcement*

From 2008, a fixed financial penalty for each tonne of carbon dioxide emitted by an **3–026** installation in excess of its permit is to be set at a tough rate of €100 per tonne, or twice the average market price per tonne, whichever is the higher. During the first phase of the scheme, this penalty will be €50 per tonne, or twice the average market price, whichever is the higher. Member States may also impose other sanctions.

(4) *Links with the Kyoto implementation mechanisms*

The European Commission recently presented a proposal[64] linking the European **3–027** emissions trading scheme with the other Kyoto Protocol flexible mechanisms of Joint Implementation and Clean Development (discussed above). The broad intention is that credits from these schemes may be converted into greenhouse gas allowances under the emissions trading scheme. Currently, under the Kyoto Protocol, credits from Joint Implementation and Clean Development can only be used by governments themselves in meeting their international obligations. The intention behind the proposal is to allow private actors to take advantage of these credits where they can show that they have put in place a relevant project. In developing this idea, it will, of course, be important to safeguard the integrity of the EU's emissions trading scheme. Allowing private industry to acquire allowances by means of Joint Implementation and Clean Development credits might reduce the incentive for technological innovation to reduce emissions within the EU.

---

[63] Article 10.
[64] Proposal for a Directive of the European Parliament and of the Council amending the Directive establishing a scheme for greenhouse gas emission allowance trading within the Community, in respect of the Kyoto Protocol's project mechanisms [SEC(2003) 785] Com/2003/0403.

(5) *Conclusions*

3–028 The Emissions Trading Directive appears to have received the support of both industry[65] and environmental groups. Friends of the Earth have described it as a "hugely significant piece of new legislation" and say that "if it works it will place a price on carbon that will rebalance the price differential between gas and non-carbon fuels, encouraging a switch to cleaner fuel and making more expensive low carbon technologies more competitive."[66] Clearly, the EU emissions trading scheme provides an effective way of shaping the market so as to favour cleaner fuels and technologies. There are, however, likely to be some difficult issues to overcome if the scheme is to succeed. The most contentious of these will be the extent of the emissions permitted to the various industrial sectors when the allowances are initially allocated.

The UK Emissions Trading Scheme

3–029 The UK's domestic Emissions Trading Scheme has been the first greenhouse gas emissions trading scheme in the world to cover all economic sectors, and has provided a valuable learning experience for the UK and other countries. The scheme is voluntary and experimental. It is not expected to last beyond 2005, when the EU trading scheme will start, because it is incompatible with that scheme. There are two types of participants in the scheme—direct and indirect. Only "direct participants" engage in true emissions *trading*. So-called "indirect participants" simply enter into Climate Change Agreements with the Secretary of State, whereby (as discussed above) they become entitled to an 80 per cent reduction in the climate change levy, in return for meeting specified targets to reduce their greenhouse gas emissions.

Whilst the EU scheme, as we have seen, starts with an initial allocation of "allowances" to industrial operators, the UK scheme started in a slightly different way—with a government auction. The government set a price per tonne for carbon dioxide emissions, and then invited companies to offer to reduce their emissions by so many tonnes, in return for payment. The 34 companies involved agreed between them to reduce their emissions by 1.1 million tonnes and were paid accordingly. It was then that the "trading" element of the scheme came into play. Companies which, in any given year, over-achieve in reducing their emissions are entitled to sell their extra achievement (in the form of "credits") for cash on the open market, or to bank those "credits" for future years. Companies who under-achieve, however, and fail to reduce their emissions by the amount they have agreed (and for which they have been paid) must either buy "credits" to the value of that under-achievement, or must withdraw from the scheme, in which case they must pay back all of the money they were given at the government auction.

In the first year's experience of trading under the scheme, 22 of the 32 direct participants had over-achieved their targets and retained 4.1 million tonnes of

---

[65] The CBI and ACBE formed the UK Emissions Trading Group that designed and oversaw the implementation of the UK Emissions Trading Scheme. The CBI is keen on emissions trading, and has recently welcomed the Linking Directive as introducing flexibility into the EU scheme. See *http://www.cbi.org.uk/home.html*.

[66] See Worthington, *The EU Greenhouse Gas Emissions Trading Directive and the Government's Energy White Paper* (available from Friends of the Earth, London).

emissions credits for trading. The remainder had failed to meet their targets and bought credits to cover their shortfall. Whilst, on the one hand, this clearly represented a successful start to the scheme, the fact that most participants were able to retain such a large number of emission credits suggests that the initial price of emissions reduction was set too low, the government having underestimated the ability of companies to reduce their emissions.

Chapter 4

EUROPEAN COMMUNITY ENVIRONMENTAL LAW

"Since 1973 EC environmental law has developed spectacularly. The amount of basic regulation has considerably increased and reached out into new areas. At the same time, the making of European environmental law becomes at present more difficult."[1]

Introduction

"Protection of the environment is one of the major challenges facing Europe. **4–001** Damage to the European environment has been growing steadily worse in recent decades. Every year, some 2 billion tonnes of waste are produced in the Member States and this figure is rising by 10 per cent annually, while CO_2 emissions from homes and vehicles are increasing, as is consumption of energy from fossil fuel sources. The European Community has been criticised for putting trade and economic development before environmental considerations. It is now recognised that the European model of development cannot be based on the depletion of natural resources and the deterioration of our environment."[2]

This statement, by the European Commission's Environment Directorate, illustrates the context in which EC environmental law is developed. EC environmental law constitutes a highly developed and sophisticated body of law which has exerted, and continues to exert, a profound influence on the content of UK law. The aims of the European Community were originally the free movement of goods, capital, services and people. However, protection of the environment is now one of its essential objectives.

EC law and policy in relation to specific aspects of environmental protection is considered in other chapters of this book, alongside relevant domestic law. The aim of

---

[1] Ludwig Kramer, Head of Unit for Governance, Environment Directorate of the European Commission, *E.C. Environmental Law*, (5th ed., 2003). (The law-making process has become more difficult, inter alia, because of the strain placed on EC institutions by the accession of the new Member States.)

[2] This statement appears on the Environment Directorate's website: *http://europa.eu.int/comm/dgs/environment.*

this chapter is to consider general principles of European Community environmental law and policy. The basic principles of European Community law are not covered in any great detail. These may be found in a number of textbooks on the subject, which the reader is encouraged to consult.[3]

The development of EC environmental law and policy

4–002 The Treaty of Rome (1957) which established the European Community, with its six original members, did not contain any provisions relating to the environment. The aims of the Community at this stage in its history were to promote harmonious development of economic activities, continuous and balanced economic expansion, increased stability, an increased standard of living, and closer relationships between Member States. The original treaty has subsequently been amended on three main occasions. Each time, the environmental profile of the European Community has been strengthened. From a position of absence in 1957, the environment today is included at the front of the treaty and environmental protection requirements must be integrated into all other policies of the EC.

In 1972, acting on the impetus generated by the UN Conference on the Human Environment, held in Stockholm, the Member States of the European Community adopted a Declaration, which stated:

> "As befits the genius of Europe, particular attention will be given to intangible values and to protecting the environment so that progress may really be put at the service of mankind."

Whilst the need to protect the environment was agreed, as was the need for a Community environmental programme, the action proposed in 1972 was to be based on inter-governmental co-operation rather than on provisions in the EC Treaty. This action, which continued throughout 1973 and 1974, included the adoption of "environmental action programmes" (discussed below).

The first legally binding measures to protect the environment were adopted in 1975 on waste and water. These areas were selected partly on the basis of the priorities set out in the environmental action programmes. As time went on, a growing emphasis on protecting the environment for its own sake began to show itself in the wording of Directives. Whilst, for example, the 1970 Directive on air pollution from cars had justified itself in terms of establishing a common market, the 1984 Directive on pollution from industrial plants referred first to the action programmes on the environment and to the importance of preventing and reducing air pollution, and only later to the necessity of avoiding the distortion of competition.[4] In 1985, the ECJ ruled that, even in the absence of an express reference to the environment in the Treaty of Rome, protection of the environment was one of the Community's "essential

---

[3] See, for example, Steiner, *Textbook on E.C. Law* (7th ed., 2000) and Kramer, *E.C. Environmental Law*, (5th ed., 2003).
[4] Council Dir.84/360/EEC of June 28, 1984 on Combating Air Pollution from Industrial Plants [1984] O.J. L188/20.

objectives" which could justify placing certain limitations on the principle of the free movement of goods.[5]

The main purpose of the Single European Act 1987[6] was to introduce a single market—an area without internal frontiers in which the free movement of goods, persons, services and capital is ensured. However, the amendments made to the treaty also gave formal recognition to the informal development of environmental policy which had taken place in preceding years. The amendments to the Treaty of Rome, inserted a chapter on the environment which outlines the environmental objectives and principles of the European Community. This gave the EC institutions, for the first time, specific law-making powers in the environmental sphere. However, measures implemented using these powers had to be adopted by Member States acting unanimously in the Council of Ministers. This was in contrast to environmental measures implemented using trade-based powers, which required only majority voting.

The 1992 Treaty on European Union (the "Maastricht Treaty")[7] introduced majority voting in the Council of Ministers for environmental matters, although some matters remained subject to unanimous decision. It also elevated the objective of environmental protection from a Community "action" to a distinct "policy". In addition, environmental protection requirements were to be integrated into the definition and implementation of other Community policies. This also marked a change from the position under the Single European Act 1987, under which environmental policy was only to be a "component" of the Community's other policies.

The Treaty of Amsterdam, which followed in 1997, introduced the co-decision procedure for environmental matters,[8] thereby aligning environmental legislative procedure more closely with that used to adopt trade-based measures. However, unanimity is still required in some environmental areas (*e.g.* land use). The profile of environmental issues was further raised by moving to the beginning of the EC Treaty the requirement that environmental protection should be integrated into the definition and implementation of other Community policies so as to promote sustainable development.[9] Hitherto, this requirement had been hidden away near the back of the treaty. The task of the Community to "respect the environment" was extended to providing "a high level of protection and improvement of the quality of the environment".

The environmental action programmes

Environmental action programmes started in 1972. The EC Treaty did not provide an **4–003** express legal basis for environmental protection measures, so action programmes developed as the alternative. Although, as we have seen, such a legal basis emerged in

---

[5] Case 240/83 *Procureur de la République v Association de Defense des Bruleurs d'Huiles Usages* [1985] E.C.R. 531.
[6] February 17, 1986, Luxembourg, and February 28, 1986, The Hague.
[7] The Treaty on European Union, February 7, 1992, Maastricht [1992] O.J. C224/1. The treaty came into force in November 1993. It made considerable amendments to the environmental Articles (Arts 130R, 130S, and 130T as then numbered).
[8] Article 175(1).
[9] For further discussion, see Stefani Bar and R. Andreas Kraemer, "European Environmental Policy after Amsterdam" [1998] 2 J.E.L. 313.

1987, the action programmes continued. These programmes set out, for a period of four to five years, the objectives, principles and priorities of EC action to protect the environment. Until 1993, their main effect was political: they created a consensus among Member States on objectives and priorities for environmental policy, and thereby often influenced environmental policy within Member States. Since 1993, adoption of the programmes by the EC has constituted a legally binding EC "decision".[10] This is significant because it means that the content of an action programme can now be seen as a source of law, and, as such, may influence interpretation of treaty articles, including those on free trade.

To date, there have been six action programmes on the environment, the last of which was published in 2002.[11] The first action programme, in 1972, covered the period from 1973–1976. It addressed urgent pollution problems and introduced the concept that the polluter should pay for environmental damage. This programme, and the following three programmes, adopted a sectoral approach to environmental issues. The third action programme, in 1983, marked a shift away from previous concerns that different national policies on pollution control might distort competition, towards a concern for the protection of health and the management of natural resources. It explicitly recognised the link between the environment and the economy, and noted that environmental resources set limits to, and therefore must form the basis of, economic and social policy. The fourth action programme, in 1987, acknowledged the contribution which protection of the environment can make to improving the economy and creating jobs, whilst the fifth action programme addressed the principle of sustainable development, as well as emphasising the need for preventive and precautionary action, and "shared responsibility" within the Community (i.e. between public and private enterprise, and between the general public and public bodies). Key objectives for Community action included climate change, air quality, noise, the conservation of biodiversity, and the management of waste, water resources and coastal zones.

The sixth action programme covers the period from July 2002 to July 2012. It begins by stating: "A number of serious environmental problems persist and new ones are emerging which require further action". Combating climate change is seen as an outstanding challenge for the next 10 years and beyond. The programme also focuses on nature and biodiversity, health and quality of life, use of natural resources, and waste. Better implementation of legislation already in place is seen as part of the solution. Public access to information and justice in environmental matters are also seen as important, as is public participation in decision-making.[12] The programme makes special reference to EU enlargement, emphasising the need to promote sustainable development in the accession countries and to secure protection of their environmental assets.

[10] Pursuant to Art. 175(3) of the amended treaty. See Dec.1600/2002 adopting the Sixth Community Environment Action Programme [2002] O.J. L242/1.
[11] First Action Programme on the Environment [1973] O.J. C1112/1; Second Action Programme on the Environment (1977–1981), [1977] O.J. C139; Third Action Programme on the Environment (1982–1986) [1983] O.J. C46; Fourth Action Programme (1987–1992), [1987] O.J. C328; Fifth Action Programme (1993) [1993] O.J. C138/1; Sixth Action Programme [2002] O.J. L242/1.
[12] See Decision No. 1600/2002/EC of the European Parliament and Council (July 22, 2002) adopting the Sixth Environmental Action Programme O.J. L242/1.

A: THE FRAMEWORK AND PRINCIPLES OF EC ENVIRONMENTAL LAW

General objectives

Protection of the environment is seen as an important objective of the Community, **4–004** which is in the Community's general interest.[13] The EC Treaty (as amended) confirms this in setting out the general objectives of the Community in Art. 2:

> "The Community shall have as its task, by establishing a common market and an economic and monetary union, to promote throughout the Community a harmonious, balanced and sustainable development of economic activities, a high level of employment and of social protection, equality between men and women, sustainable and non-inflationary growth, a high degree of competitiveness and convergence of economic performance, a high level of protection and improvement of the quality of the environment, the raising of the standard of living and quality of life, and economic and social cohesion and solidarity among Member States".

Environmental protection and the common market

The treaty does not subordinate measures to protect the environment to the free **4–005** circulation of goods. Both policy objectives are of equal weight, and, ideally, are to be achieved concurrently. In practice, however, there may be a conflict—the need to protect the environment may impede the free movement of goods, capital and services between Member States. Conflict between the two objectives is frequent, and its resolution seems to take place on a case-by-case basis.

Whilst the EC Treaty prohibits restrictions on imports and exports between Member States, it does allow a derogation from this prohibition where necessary for the "protection of health and life of humans, animals or plants", provided that the measures taken do not constitute a means of arbitrary discrimination or a disguised restriction on trade.[14] While certain environmental measures may contribute towards protecting health (*e.g.* laws limiting the presence of contaminants in drinking water) many environmental measures concerned with *enhancing* the environment are less easy to categorise in this way (*e.g.* measures concerned with environmental labelling, environmental taxes, waste prevention, and environmental liability).

The European Court of Justice has, however, provided an alternative route for securing national environmental protection measures which affect imports or exports— it has interpreted the treaty provisions on free movement of goods so as to allow for such measures. In a landmark decision known as the *Cassis de Dijon*[15] case, the court

---

[13] See Case 240/83 *Procurér de la République v Association de défense des brûleurs d'huiles usagées* [1985] E.C.R. 531; and Case 302/86 *Commission v Denmark* [1988] E.C.R. 4607.

[14] Article 30.

[15] Case 120/78 *Rewe-Zentrale A.G. v Bundesmonopolverwaltung fur Branntwein* [1979] E.C.R. I–649 (the "Cassis de Dijon" case). See also Case 125/88 *HFM Nijman* [1989] E.C.R. 3533.

declared that, in the absence of Community legislation, a national restriction on the free circulation of goods applying equally to national goods and goods from other Member States would be acceptable, provided it was proportionate and justified by a "mandatory requirement". Later, the Court recognised that environmental protection was such a "mandatory requirement". In the so-called *Danish Bottles* case,[16] the Court held that Denmark was entitled to introduce a deposit-and-return system for drink containers. This could be justified on the basis of environmental protection, even though the practical implication was that non-Danish producers and traders might find it more difficult to comply with the system. Similarly, a ban on the use of metal cans by Denmark was accepted as being justified in order to protect the Danish environment. Licensing of drinks containers, however, was considered to be a measure disproportionate to the environmental objectives it would secure.

Sustainable development

4–006 Article 2 (quoted above) places sustainable development at the centre of Europe's strategy on the environment. Article 6 (discussed below) explicitly refers to the principle. The principle is not defined in the treaty, but the commonly accepted definition for the purpose of the treaty is that given by the Brundtland report (discussed in Ch. 2), namely, "development which meets the needs of the present without compromising the ability of future generations to meet their own needs".

A high level of protection and improvement

4–007 Article 2 requires a "high level of protection and improvement of the quality of the environment". This, of course, is somewhat vague. It has been suggested, however, that the appropriate level of protection and improvement might be determined by looking at environmental standards set by Member States with a reputation for tough environmental protection measures (Denmark, the Netherlands, Sweden, Finland, Austria, Germany).[17] In addition, Art. 2 may imply that the EC cannot simply adopt "lowest common denominator" environmental standards, leaving it to individual Member States to adopt higher standards as they see fit—a high level of protection and improvement must be achieved by the Community as a whole.

Integration of environmental protection measures

4–008 Also at the front of the treaty (in Art. 6) is the so-called "integration principle":

> ". . . environmental protection requirements must be integrated into the definition and implementation of Community policies and activities in particular with a view to promoting sustainable development."

The implications of the integration principle have been significant in political, administrative and judicial terms. The principle has given rise to, or consolidated, a

---

[16] Case 302/86 *Commission v Denmark* (the "Danish Bottles" case) [1998] E.C.R. 460.
[17] Kramer, *E.C. Environmental Law*, 5th ed., 2003.

large number of measures concerned to ensure that the environmental dimension of Community activity is properly reflected in decision-making. In the context of ECJ decisions, the integration principle has been key in enabling the Court to invoke the "mandatory requirement" line of reasoning (considered above) to justify environmental protection measures which create discriminatory barriers to trade.

Environmental objectives in the treaty

Articles 174 to 176 of the treaty set out the basis of EC environmental policy. In **4–009** summary, Community policy on the environment must contribute to pursuit of the following objectives:

- preserving, protecting and improving the quality of the environment;

- protecting human health;

- prudent and rational utilisation of natural resources; and

- promoting measures at an international level to deal with regional or world-wide environmental problems.

The objectives are defined so broadly that hardly any area of environmental policy is left outside the competence of the EC. The objectives are set out in no particular order of priority, and may, of course, sometimes conflict. The objectives are not directly applicable and cannot therefore be used to challenge legislative measures by Member States. Thus, in the *Peralta Re* case, the ECJ held that they could not be used as the basis for a declaration that Italian domestic law was invalid.[18]

Environmental principles in the treaty

Article 174(2) states: **4–010**

"Community policy on the environment shall aim at a high level of protection, taking into account the diversity of situations in the various regions of the Community. It shall be based on the precautionary principle and on the principles that preventive action should be taken, that environmental damage should as a priority be rectified at source and that the polluter should pay."

Like the "objectives" referred to above, the principles referred to here represent guidance for political and legislative decision-making, but cannot be used as a basis on which to challenge Member States' actions in national courts.

(1) The precautionary principle

The "precautionary principle", which tends to be referred to synonymously with the **4–011** "prevention principle", was made part of Community policy for the first time in 1993 (by the Maastricht Treaty). It is not defined in the treaty, and the origin and content of

---

[18] Case 379/92 *Criminal Proceedings against Peralta* [1994] E.C.R. I–03453.

the principle are unclear.[19] The issue of when and how to use the principle has given rise to much debate within the EU and internationally. As we saw in Ch. 2, the principle is understood to provide a solution to the dilemma arising from the limits of current scientific knowledge: it is often impossible to understand fully the mechanisms by which the environment is damaged; the danger, therefore, is that given the uncertainty surrounding the causes of environmental deterioration, action to protect the environment may be taken too late to be of any use, or may not take place at all. The precautionary principle requires measures to be taken to protect the environment despite scientific uncertainty about the likelihood of harm, for example where there is no scientific proof of a causal link between emissions and their effects. The principle can be viewed as a mechanism to help manage risk. An example of the application of the precautionary principle is the EC's adherence to the requirements of the Kyoto Protocol, in spite of the fact that some take the view that there is uncertainty surrounding the scientific evidence about the effect of mankind's activities on climate change.

In *Pfizer Animal Health SA v Council of the European Union*,[20] the ECJ considered the interpretation and correct application of the precautionary principle. The case concerned a Directive which, because of a potential health risk, withdrew authorisation for an antibiotic formerly added in small quantities to animal feed. The court held that the principle would apply in situations where there was a risk to human health which, although not founded on mere hypothesis, was not scientifically confirmed. A scientific risk assessment by experts should be carried out before preventive measures are taken, and the scientific advice obtained must be based on the principles of excellence, independence and transparency. Such evidence must provide a sufficient indication to conclude, on an objective scientific basis, that there is a risk to human health.

(2) *The polluter pays principle*

4–012   The "polluter pays" principle has been a declared policy of the EC since its first action programme in 1972, although it was not introduced into the treaty until 1987. In essence, the principle requires that the polluter, rather than society at large, must pay the cost of environmental clean-up required as a result of his polluting activities. The treaty provides no assistance, however, in determining who, in any given situation, should be regarded as the "polluter". This, of course, is one of the fundamental problems in applying the principle—where a car causes pollution, for example, is the "polluter" the manufacturer of the car, the producer of the fuel, or the driver of the car?

(3) *Rectification of damage at source*

4–013   The principle that environmental damage[21] should be "rectified at source" is not defined further than as stated. It has been described as representing "wishful thinking rather than reality".[22] It is unclear what is meant by "rectified", and this gives the Community institutions considerable discretion in deciding how to apply the principle.

---

[19] Kramer, *E.C. Environmental Law*, (5th ed., 2003).
[20] Case T-13/99 *Pfizer Annual Health SA v Council of the European Union* [2002] E.C.R. II–3305.
[21] About half of the linguistic versions of the treaty use a word equivalent to "damage"; the other half, "impairment".
[22] Kramer, *op. cit.* above.

The most concrete application of the principle has been in the context of waste disposal, where it has been used to justify disposing of waste as close as possible to the places where it is generated.[23]

Factors to be taken into account

Article 174(3) sets out four factors which Community environmental policy, as a whole, **4–014** should take into account. In practice, these factors play only a minor and supporting role in shaping environmental policy. They do not have any particular legal effect.

In preparing its policy on the environment, the Community must take account of:

- available scientific and technical data;

- environmental conditions in the various regions of the Community;

- the potential benefits and costs of action or lack of action; and

- the economic and social development of the Community as a whole and the balanced development of its regions.

Community and Member State competence

Since protection of the environment is in the general interest of the Community, the **4–015** European Community is "competent" to legislate on environmental matters. The notion of "competence" also implies that the EC has a *responsibility* to enact such legislation. The responsibility and competence of the European Community in environmental matters is not exclusive. Competence is shared with Member States, and Community action sits alongside national, regional, local or international measures. This is made clear by the wording of Art. 174, which states that Community action shall "contribute" to achievement of the various environmental objectives. Member States retain the power to adopt environmental provisions where the Community fails to take action on a given environmental issue (so long those measures are compatible with the treaty). If the Community subsequently takes action on the issue, however, the domestic measures will no longer apply insofar as they are incompatible with Community legislation. This follows from a general rule, established by the ECJ, that where national law and Community law conflict, Community law will prevail.[24]

Where Community legislation is adopted on the basis of Art. 175, Member States are free to maintain or introduce more stringent measures, provided they are compatible with the treaty.[25] The practical effect of this is that EC legislation will always set what may be described as minimum standards (albeit affording a "high level" of protection), whilst leaving it open to Member States to impose (or maintain) stricter rules.

[23] Case C422/92 *Commission v Germany* [1995] E.C.R. I–1097.
[24] See Case 6/64 *Costa v ENEL* [1964] E.C.R. 1265; Case 106/77 *Simmenthal* [1978] E.C.R. 629; Case C213/89 *Factortame* [1990] E.C.R. I–2466; Case C184/89 *Nimz* [1991] E.C.R. I–297.
[25] Article 176.

A similar set of provisions (sometimes known as the "Green Guarantee") is to be found in Art. 95(4) (internal market measures). Under these provisions, a Member State may maintain an existing national environmental measure which provides greater environmental protection than a Community trade measure. The national measure must not, however, constitute an arbitrary discrimination or a disguised restriction on trade.

Further, a Member State may introduce a new national environmental protection measure under Art. 95(5), after a Community harmonisation measure has been adopted, based on scientific evidence relating to protection of the environment and if introduced in order to meet a problem specific to that Member State (and provided it is not an arbitrary discrimination or a disguised restriction on trade). These provisions were introduced to reassure those Member States which were concerned that the harmonisation measures adopted under Art. 95 would oblige them gradually to lower their environmental standards because of qualified majority voting.

Subsidiarity

4–016 Article 5 of the EC Treaty states:

> "The Community shall act within the limits of the powers conferred upon it by this Treaty and of the objectives assigned to it therein. In areas which do not fall within its exclusive competence, the Community shall take action, in accordance with the principle of subsidiarity, only if and in so far as the objectives of the proposed action cannot be sufficiently achieved by the Member States and can therefore, by reason of the scale or effects of the proposed action, be better achieved by the Community. Any action by the Community shall not go beyond what is necessary to achieve the objectives of this Treaty."

Environmental protection measures adopted by the Community must therefore be justified on the basis of subsidiarity. Subsidiarity is in essence a political doctrine governing Community action. The European Community must demonstrate that legislation is necessary at Community level before it can act. Such legislation must achieve objectives which cannot be achieved by domestic legislation in individual Member States. However, given that the doctrine is essentially political rather than legal in effect, it would be difficult for a Member State to challenge in the ECJ any particular piece of EC legislation as being inconsistent with the principle.

B: SOURCES OF EC ENVIRONMENTAL LAW

The legal basis for environmental legislation

4–017 As mentioned, the Treaty of Rome did not originally contain any provisions relating to the environment. As it is a basic principle of EC law that the measures which the EC adopts must have some foundation in treaty provisions, the absence of relevant treaty provisions meant, in theory, that measures to protect the environment could not be adopted. However, the fact that by the time environmental provisions were included, in 1987, there was already in place a coherent philosophy on environmental protection, together with a considerable body of legislation, bears testimony to the innovative stance towards environmental protection adopted by the institutions of the Community.

Prior to 1987, the EEC managed to introduce over 100 items of environmental legislation under provisions in the treaty which essentially related to trade, including legislation on water and air quality, waste management, and chemical use. Article 100 (as it was then numbered) permitted Directives designed to harmonise laws within Member States which directly affected the establishment or functioning of the common market. Article 235 was the other article which could be used as the basis for legislation with an environmental dimension. This article was a "catch-all" provision and gave the Council power to legislate on matters necessary to achieve the operation of the common market even where the treaty did not explicitly provide for the legislation in question. Thus, for example, the Birds Directive, which is based on Art. 235 of the treaty, was justified on the basis that:

" . . . the conservation of wild birds is necessary to attain, within the operation of the common market, the Community's objectives regarding the improvement of living conditions, a harmonious development of economic activities throughout the Community and a continuous and balanced expansion, but the necessary specific powers to act have not been provided for in the Treaty."[26]

Currently, the main legal basis for action taken by the Community with respect to the environment is Art. 175 of the treaty. However, Art. 95, which provides for measures aimed at establishing the internal market, may also be used where the main emphasis of the legislation is to ensure the free movement of goods. Community measures to protect the environment may also be based on other articles of the treaty, including those relating to transport and agriculture. Environmental measures in the energy sector, however, tend to be based on Art. 175, as there is no specific chapter on energy policy in the treaty. The "catch all" article, which provides a legal basis for legislation not specifically justified elsewhere, is now Art. 308.

Although, originally, Arts 175 and 95 required the use of a different voting procedure for the passing of legislation (with the European Parliament having greater powers under Art. 95), the current version of the treaty provides that both articles are governed by the same co-decision procedure. Under the co-decision procedure, the Council will adopt a common position on a proposal by qualified majority voting (the votes of Member States are weighted roughly in accordance with each Member State's population). Where the European Parliament indicates it intends to reject the common position by a majority (260 votes) or amends the common position by a majority in a way not acceptable to Council, a conciliation committee (composed of members of both the Council and Parliament) is set up for the Council to further explain its position. Thereafter, if the Parliament, by an absolute majority, refuses to accept the common position, the proposal is not adopted.

The co-decision procedure therefore gives the European Parliament genuine legislative power, and this, arguably, may provide for a higher level of environmental

---

[26] Sixth recital to Dir.79/409/EEC [1979] O.J. L103/1.

protection. The European Parliament has played a dominant role in initiating and increasing environmental protection since the early 1970s. In addition, the use of qualified majority voting in the Council ensures that a Member State cannot on its own veto a proposal for legislation. This can speed up the Council's decision-making procedures and make higher environmental standards easier to agree.[27] Examples of Directives adopted under the co-decision procedure include the Water Framework Directive[28] and the Waste Electrical and Electronic Equipment Directive.[29]

Some environmental measures, however, still require unanimity in the Council.[30] The Council is not legally obliged to take account of the opinions or amendments of the Parliament where the legislation in question concerns matters of land use (with the exception of waste management); planning (*e.g.* the construction of a new airport); the management of water resources; environmental taxes; or measures significantly affecting a Member State's choice between different energy sources, or the general structure of its energy supply (*e.g.* a decision to prohibit nuclear energy production on environmental grounds). The requirement for unanimity gives each Member State a veto over Community decisions which might otherwise be thought an unjustifiable intrusion into national affairs.

Areas covered by EC environmental legislation

4–018 There are over 200 items of EC environmental legislation, covering a diverse range of matters including the following:

- *AIR POLLUTION* (motor vehicles and fuels; air quality; industrial pollution; incinerators; chlorofluorocarbons (CFCs));

- *WASTE ON LAND* (waste disposal; waste oils; disposal and transfer of hazardous wastes; recycling; sewage sludge);

- *NOISE POLLUTION* (exhaust systems of motor vehicles; construction plant and equipment; aircraft noise; domestic appliances; lawnmowers);

- *NATURE CONSERVATION* (wild birds; wildlife and natural habitats; migratory wild animals; trade in endangered species; whales; seals; forests);

- *WATER POLLUTION* (river basin management; water quality for surface, drinking and bathing waters, fresh waters and shellfish waters; protection of groundwater; pollution from dangerous substances in the aquatic environment and from nitrates and detergents; urban waste water treatment; the titanium dioxide industry; the discharge of hydrocarbons at sea);

- *RADIATION* (various legislation under the *EURATOM* Treaty; control of shipments; health and safety; storage of radioactive waste);

- *PROTECTION OF THE PUBLIC AND OF WORKERS* (major accident hazards; health and safety at work, including protection from noise); and

[27] See Wilkinson, "Maastricht and the Environment: The Implications for the EC's Environmental Policy of the Treaty on European Union", (1992) J.E.L. Vol.4(2) 221.
[28] Directive 2000/60 O.J. L327 22/12/2000 p.0001–0073.
[29] Directive 2002/96 O.J. L037 13/02/2003 p.0024–0039.
[30] See Art. 175.

- *GENERAL MEASURES* (chemicals—classification, labelling, laboratory practice; pesticides; genetically modified organisms; environmental assessments and access to information; eco-labelling).

The nature of environmental Directives

Directives (as opposed to Regulations) tend to be the usual form of EC environmental **4–019** legislation. Environmental Directives are often of a framework nature, outlining general rules and basic requirements. (This is in contrast to Directives in other areas, such as agriculture, and Directives on specific products.) It is therefore exceptional for an environmental Directive to fix emission limits, or make specific provision for such matters as the frequency of environmental monitoring. The Water Directives demonstrate the tendency, in technically complicated areas, to employ "framework Directives" as the first stage in establishing a comprehensive pattern of regulation.[31] Such Directives establish the general principles which will be applied, and are then supplemented by "daughter Directives" dealing with specific issues. Another example is the Dangerous Substances Directive,[32] a framework Directive which was followed by daughter directives setting standards for individual substances.[33]

"Horizontal" Directives

So-called "horizontal" Directives do not apply to a specific area of environmental **4–020** regulation (such as water or air) but may be described as "procedural" in their nature, in that they focus on the *methods* by which environmental protection is to be achieved. Such Directives apply to a range of environmental issues and include, for example, the Directive on Environmental Impact Assessment, discussed in Ch. 13. Below, we explore one particular recent "horizontal" Directive, likely to have far-reaching implications in some Member States, namely the Directive on Liability for Environmental Damage.[34]

C: Liability for Environmental Damage

It has taken a rather long time for the EC to act decisively to make polluters directly **4–021** responsible in law for environmental damage they cause. The European Commission first published a policy paper on remedying environmental damage in 1993, and in mid-1994 the European Parliament adopted a resolution calling for a proposal on civil liability in respect of environmental damage. Parliament raised this issue again on occasion in following years, but it was not until 1997 that the Commission decided that a white paper should be prepared.

---

[31] Other framework Directives include those on Industrial Air Pollution (Dir.84/360/EEC), Construction Plant (Dir.84/532/EEC), and Waste (Dir.75/442/EEC).
[32] Directive 76/434/EEC.
[33] *e.g.* Dirs 82/176/EEC and 84/156/EEC on mercury and its compounds.
[34] Directive 2004/35/EC on environmental liability with regard to the prevention and remedying of environmental damage O.J. L143/56 30/4/2004. For further discussion, see J. Thornton, "Environmental liability—a shrinking mirage or the most realistic attempt so far?" (2003) JPEL 272.

Events would probably have continued at this slow pace had not the vexed issue of Genetically Modified Organisms (GMOs) reared its head. This issue led the European Parliament to demand that the Commission speed up its work on an environmental liability regime. In February 2000, the Commission produced a white paper, followed by a working paper, in July 2001. In January 2002, it adopted a formal proposal for a Directive, and in March 2004 the Directive was adopted.

The slow initial progress may have been due in part to the struggle between industry and environmental groups which so often characterises environmental policy-making. It may also have been due to the difficult issues that must be accommodated by any scheme of environmental liability. These include:

- balancing the ability of industry to develop and innovate against protection of the natural resources affected by its activities;

- determining how and when the complex ecosystems which make up the environment have been damaged;

- deciding how best a damaged environment may be restored, and how to accommodate the loss of its services whilst it is in a damaged state; and

- increasing the availability of insurance, which is critical to the practical success of any liability scheme.

The scheme of the Directive is set out in the diagram on page [97]. The regime has undergone significant changes from the version in earlier policy papers produced by the European Commission. These were drafted in terms of "plaintiffs", damage to health and property (as well as site contamination and biodiversity damage) and alleviating the burden of proof on plaintiffs. The current regime, however, has shed all its associations with more traditional civil liability schemes. Although imposing private liabilities, the regime is essentially now a public law regime, where damage to protected sites and species, water resources and site contamination are to be cleaned up as a matter of public interest, under the regulation of competent authorities. "Public interest" must, at least on paper, be a better protector of the environment than a regime driven by individual loss. The scope of the regime is relatively circumscribed—the effect of the regime appears, in practice, to be limited to large scale, sudden environmental accidents. It does not, for example, cover pollution of a "widespread, diffuse character where it is impossible to establish a causal link between the damage and the activities of certain individual operators."[35] This sort of pollution, however, is a significant cause of damage to the countryside in the UK. Personal injury and damage to health are excluded from the regime, which is concerned solely with damage to the environment. In addition, the Directive makes it clear that its purpose is not to give private parties a right to compensation for economic losses they suffer from environmental damage.

The regime is not applicable to oil pollution or nuclear damage, on the basis that there are already sufficient international rules covering these. The aim of the regime is to supplement, rather than provide a substitute for, existing rules. In the main, the regime will apply to activities already regulated under EC law, including:

[35] Article 3.

- the operation of IPPC installations (discussed in Ch. 5) and those operations subject to permits for discharging dangerous substances to water and groundwater;

- water abstraction and impounding;

- waste management operations (collection, transport, recovery and disposal, after-care, landfills, incineration plants);

- manufacture, storage or use of dangerous substances and preparations, plant protection products and biocidal products;

- transport of dangerous goods by road and rail; and

- contained use or deliberate release of GMOs.

"Environmental Damage"

Not all environmental damage falls within the scope of the regime. Liability is imposed **4–022** only for certain restricted categories of environmental damage, namely damage to protected species and natural habitats, damage to watercourses, and contamination of soil and sub-soil.

Common to all three categories is that the definitions of "damage" imply high thresholds, suggesting that the regime is focused on serious environmental incidents. This is re-inforced by the Directive's explanatory notes, which refer to large scale, well-known environmental disasters, including the escape of toxic dust in Seveso, the heavy pollution of the Rhine River by the Basle Sandoz plant, and the collapse of the waste retention dam near the Donana National Park, as well as to the oil spills caused by the Torrey Canyon and Amoco Cadiz. The UK Government has expressed the view that very few damaged sites will fall within the scope of the Directive.[36]

(1) *Damage to species and habitats*

(*a*) What is covered?

The preamble to the Directive indicates that loss of biodiversity, which it refers to as **4–023** having dramatically accelerated over the last two decades, is one of the motivating factors behind the Directive. Not all damage to biodiversity, however, falls within the scope of the regime. Environmental damage is defined to include damage to protected species and natural habitats listed in the relevant annexes to the Birds and Habitats Directives[37] (or, where a Member State so determines, any habitats or species not listed in the Directives which Member States designate for purposes equivalent to those laid down in the Directives). If the UK chooses to include all nationally designated sites within the scope of the regime, this will significantly extend the effect of the Directive. In the UK, Sites of Special Scientific Interest (discussed in Ch. 9) cover 300,000 hectares of land. Other nationally designated sites include, for example, National Nature Reserves and National Parks (see Ch. 9).

---

[36] DEFRA, Extended Partial Regulatory Impact Assessment on proposals for a Directive on Environmental Liability (June, 2002).
[37] Dir.79/409/EEC (the Birds Directive); Dir.92/43/EEC (the Natural Habitats Directive).

The concept of "biodiversity" is defined in the Rio Convention on Biological Diversity to mean "the variability among living organisms from all sources including, *inter alia*, terrestrial, marine and other aquatic ecosystems and the ecological complexes of which they are part." As can be seen from this definition (which was deliberately not used in the Directive) biodiversity can cover millions of creatures and plants. In practice, changes in biodiversity cannot be measured for all species, and so "indicator species" are often selected to monitor biodiversity changes. The "indicator species" selected by the Commission are those protected under the Birds and the Habitats Directive. Impacts on any other species and habitats will not be relevant, however significant the impact. The implication of this is that biodiversity as a whole may not be protected.

(*b*) What is meant by "damage"?

4–024 Damage to protected species and habitats occurs in the event of:

(1) a measurable adverse change or impairment

(2) that has significant adverse effects on reaching or maintaining

(3) the favourable conservation status of such habitats or species.

It may not be easy to assess whether damage has occurred. This is because changes to species and habitats are likely to require interpretation. Changes may show impacts in both directions on a species—a decline in one indicator may be accompanied by an increase in another. A judgment will therefore need to be made as to whether what has occurred is ecologically significant. In addition, if the measurements of change are restricted to the land on which the damage has occurred, this will give an incomplete understanding of the whole picture, because it will fail to take account of factors affecting species that tend to forage over wider areas. This is problematic. The European Commission has acknowledged that "robust indicators of the extent and significance of damage to biodiversity and the rate of biodiversity loss are still being developed".[38] Whilst it is easy to be critical of this aspect of the Directive, it should be remembered that such difficulties in measuring biodiversity changes are well known. As a recent report by the World Bank and UN has put it: ". . . our knowledge of ecosystems has increased dramatically but it simply has not kept pace with our ability to alter them".[39]

(2) *Water damage*

4–025 Waters within the scope of the regime are those regulated under the Water Framework Directive,[40] including inland surface waters, coastal waters and ground water. Waters are considered to be damaged in the event of:

(1) a measurable adverse change or impairment

(2) that significantly adversely affects

---

[38] See the explanatory memorandum to the Directive.
[39] World Resources Institute, "People and Ecosystems" (2002).
[40] Dir.2000/60/EC.

(3) the ecological, chemical and/or quantitative status, and/or ecological potential of the waters, as defined in the Water Framework Directive.[41]

(3) *Land Damage*

Land damage is defined as: **4–026**

(1) land contamination

(2) that creates a significant risk of human health being adversely affected

(3) as a result of the direct or indirect introduction in, on or under land of substances, preparations, organisms or micro-organisms.

It should be noted that land contamination is defined by reference to harm to human health (harm to the environment *per se* is not covered) and that threshold of harm is set high (there must be a "significant" risk to health).

The two obligations: Prevention and restoration

The two obligations underpinning the regime are: **4–027**

- to prevent damage to the environment or, where that is not possible,

- to remedy the damaged environment.

The Directive does not provide guidance as to what particular preventive measures might be appropriate. Remediation, however, is dealt with in more detail. Earlier proposals by the Commission recognised that valuing natural resource damage had always been controversial. For this reason, restoration of damage is favoured over measures requiring monetary compensation from the polluter—restoration costs are easier to estimate, because doing so relies less heavily on untested economic valuation methodologies.

Where environmental damage has occurred, the relevant process operator who caused it must take all practicable steps to control, contain, remove or otherwise manage the relevant contaminants. Steps must be taken to limit or prevent further environmental damage or adverse effects on human health. Thus, the remedial measures required from the operator can include any actions, or combination of actions, necessary to:

- mitigate damage, restore, rehabilitate or replace damaged natural resources and environmental amenity, and/or

- provide an equivalent alternative to those resources or that amenity.

An annex to the Directive sets out further details on remedying different types of environmental damage.

---

[41] An exception is made in the case of adverse effects to which Art. 4(7) of the Directive applies. This allows for a deterioration or failure to meet good status for reasons of overriding public interest, if no other option exists.

Remedying the environment is achieved by returning it to its "baseline condition". Baseline condition is defined as "the condition of the natural resources and services that would have existed had the damage not occurred, estimated on the basis of the best information available."[42] (The Directive uses the word "services" to refer, essentially, to environmental amenity. It defines "services" as the functions performed by a natural resource for the benefit of another natural resource or the public.) This definition of "baseline condition", of course, means that remedying damage might not, therefore, mean putting the damaged environment back into the exact same state as before if it can be said that the environment would have changed over time, irrespective of the damage. In deciding on the most suitable restorative option, the regulatory authority will consider the cost of various options and their likelihood of success. The Directive recognises that there may be cases where the most appropriate solution may not be a direct intervention at all, but simply letting nature take its course.

Whilst the clean-up is being completed, "compensatory remediation" must be undertaken. This entails making improvements to protected natural habitats, species or water (either at the damaged site or elsewhere) aimed at compensating for the interim loss of natural resources and environmental amenity pending recovery. Operators may also be required to pay "compensation for interim losses", *i.e.* compensation for loss of environmental amenity where, for example, people can no longer walk in a damaged forest during the period of recovery. The appropriate level of such compensation is likely to prove difficult to calculate.

Restoration may either be "primary restoration" (which returns the damaged site itself back to its baseline condition) or "complimentary restoration", which entails action in a different location designed to provide a similar level of natural resources and amenity elsewhere. Complimentary restoration will be appropriate where a damaged site cannot be restored to its baseline condition, or where doing so will involve a disproportionate cost. The requirement of complementary remediation aims to avoid a situation where a person who has ruined a site beyond economic recovery pays less in restoration costs than someone who has only partially damaged it.

Whilst the Directive sets out the principles for remedying environmental damage, it does not indicate how these principles should be implemented. This is perhaps not surprising, given that the Directive is intended to be a framework instrument. At the time of writing, there is no indication that these issues will be dealt with further by formally recognised Commission committees or in "daughter Directives", although there have been some indications in Council debates that some issues may be referred to Commission Working Groups. These do not have any formal constitutional status, but assist in developing common practices. In the absence of Community-led clarification, the obvious danger is that, left to themselves, Member States may adopt different approaches and standards. This, in turn, might lead to market distortion issues, as operators seek to exploit these differences.

Division of responsibility and allocation of costs

4–028 Responsibility for preventing and/or restoring environmental damage is apportioned between operators, "competent authorities" and Member States. Operators are first in the line of responsibility, in accordance with the "polluter pays" principle. An

---

[42] Article 2.

"operator" is defined widely as "any legal, private or public person who operates or controls the occupational activity, or, where this is provided for in national legislation, to whom decisive economic power over the technical functioning of the activity has been delegated." The term includes permit holders and persons registering an activity.

The primary function of the "competent authority" is to require operators themselves to take action to prevent or restore environmental damage. The authority can decide to assume responsibility itself (but is not under an obligation to do so) in circumstances where an operator fails to comply with the demands of the authority, cannot be identified, or is not required under the Directive to bear the costs. In the case of measures to *remedy* environmental damage, the power of authorities to undertake remediation themselves is expressed in the Directive to be "a means of last resort".[43] Where the authority has to step in to take action because the operator fails to do so, it can, in most circumstances, recover the costs of doing so from the operator. Unlike the position in the US, there is no financial cap on liability. However, there are certain circumstances where the costs *cannot* be recovered, namely where:

- the damage was caused by a third party, and occurred despite the fact that appropriate safety measures were put in place by the operator. (In this situation, the explanatory notes to the Directive envisage that the third party will pay the costs); or

- the damage resulted from compliance with a compulsory order of a public authority.

In addition, the operator will not be required to bear the cost of remedial actions taken pursuant to the Directive where he demonstrates that he was not at fault, and that the environmental damage was caused by:

(a) an emission or event expressly authorised by, and fully in accordance with the conditions of, a relevant environmental licence; or

(b) an emission or activity which the operator demonstrates was not considered likely to cause environmental damage according to the state of scientific and technical knowledge at the relevant time. (This is sometimes known as the "state of the art" defence).

The "compliance with an environmental licence" defence (which proved to be a controversial issue during the passage of the Directive) is based on the idea that the Community as a whole requires and benefits from industrial operations. Hence, if an operator is in full compliance with a relevant statutory licence, and nonetheless some damage occurs as a result of the operations subject to the licence, it follows that the Community should bear the cost of responding to that damage, and not the particular operator. The operator will only have done what was considered appropriate by the licensing authority before it gave its consent, and will therefore be in no way at fault. The details of the defences of "licence compliance" and "state of the art" are to be left to Member States, which may give rise to inconsistency in their application.

---

[43] Article 6(3).

There are a number of additional qualifications to operator liability in the Directive. These are fairly standard defences, including war and a "natural phenomenon of an exceptional, inevitable and irresistible character".

Roles of individuals and environmental groups

4–029 Provisions on the roles of individuals and environmental groups appear in the Directive under the heading "request for action".[44] This heading provides a good indication of their expected function within the regime. Standing is allowed to natural or legal persons who are "affected or likely to be affected" by the environmental damage, or who have a sufficient interest in environmental decision-making relating to the damage. (Member States are allowed to determine what constitutes a "sufficient interest".)

The rights allowed to both individuals and groups are procedural in character, namely the rights:

- to submit "observations" on environmental damage to the relevant regulatory authority;

- to request the authority to take action;

- to have the authority consider these observations or requests where the documents submitted show "in a plausible manner" that environmental damage exists;

- to make their views known to the authority;

- to be informed, within a reasonable time frame, of the authority's decision in respect of action to be taken, with reasons for the decision; and

- to judicial review, or some other court procedure, whereby they may challenge actions or omissions by the authority.

Financial security

4–030 Insurance and other forms of financial security are critical to the practical success of any liability regime. The issue of whether the liabilities created by the Directive can be insured has been the subject of ongoing debate. The insurance industry has made it clear that the regime is not currently insurable, on the basis that environmental liability insurance in Europe is in its infancy and the concept of insuring biodiversity damage is new. The industry cannot therefore make a realistic and reliable estimate of the amounts it might be likely to pay out, because it cannot estimate the probability of losses or their likely severity.[45]

Nevertheless, under the Directive, Member States are required to encourage the development of appropriate financial security measures by relevant "economic and

---

[44] Article 14.
[45] Evidence given to the European Parliament, in May 2002, by Tim Bell, Liability Insurance Manager, Royal Sun Alliance (see *www.europarl.eu.int/hearings*).

financial operators", with the aim of enabling operators to use financial guarantees to cover their responsibilities under the Directive.[46] Such measures are to include financial mechanisms in case of insolvency. The Commission will be required to present a report on the effectiveness of the Directive, and, in the light of its findings, may submit proposals for a system of harmonised mandatory financial security.

Diagram 1: EU Directive on Environmental Liability Scheme of Liability

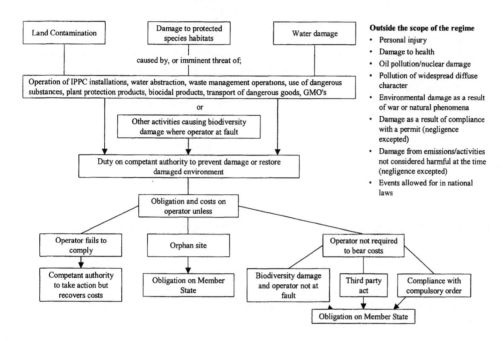

D: ENFORCEMENT OF EC ENVIRONMENTAL LAW

Failure by Member States properly to implement their obligations under environmen- **4–031** tal Directives is a serious problem throughout the Community.[47] Member States usually comply with their formal obligations to pass legislation purporting to give effect to the provisions of Directives. But this, of course, does not necessarily mean that such legislation will amount to compliance with the requirements of the Directives. Often, the discretion which a Member State has in choosing the method by which the requirements of a Directive are met is exercised in such a way as to fall short of

---

[46] Article 16.
[47] See European Commission, "Implementation of Community law—Communication to the Council and the European Parliament" COM (96) 500. See also: First annual survey on the implementation and enforcement of Community environmental law, SEC (1999) 592; Second annual survey, SEC (2000) 1219; Third annual survey, SEC (2002) 1041.

fulfilling the purpose of the Directive. There are numerous examples in UK environmental law of purported compliance with Directives which may not amount to *de facto* compliance because the legislation in question fails to make sufficient changes to the domestic regimes already in place. One such example is the Drinking Water Directive,[48] discussed in Ch. 8. Another is the Natural Habitats Directive,[49] discussed in Ch. 9.

It is the European Commission's responsibility to ensure that the provisions of the EC Treaty are applied (Art. 211). The Commission has unlimited discretion in deciding whether to bring infringement proceedings against Member States. Its policy, however, has been to focus on making sure Member States' laws conform with EC provisions and apply throughout the Member State, rather than to focus on particular instances of non-application of the domestic law implementing EC law.[50]

In the event of non-compliance, the Commission is responsible for bringing enforcement proceedings against Member States in the ECJ. It does this under Art. 226 of the EC Treaty. Between 1976 and 2002, the ECJ decided almost 300 environmental cases under Art. 226. (Whilst this figure is impressive, it should be noted that, in 2000–2001, the average time taken for each decision was 59 months—almost five years.[51]) Following the Treaty on European Union, the ECJ has the power to impose a penalty against a Member State which has failed to comply with a judgment against it.[52] It has exercised this power against Greece.[53] For a number of years, Greece had tolerated the unauthorised disposal in a river valley of the municipal and industrial waste from a whole city. It then ignored a judgement of the ECJ condemning this practice, with the result that further proceedings had to be brought. The ECJ ordered a penalty payment of €20,000 per day. Greece had to pay about €5 million before discontinuing the unauthorised landfill.

In practical terms, the Commission is faced with a number of problems in relation to enforcement. The Commission has a limited staff for investigating and dealing with infringement complaints. The pre-enlargement position was that there were 18 lawyers responsible for infringements in 15 Member States. Unlike in other areas of EC law, such as competition and customs law, there is no environmental inspectorate to investigate breaches of environmental provisions. In addition, the Commission suffers from a lack of information about infringements of Community law—and it cannot, of course, deal with infringements unless it is aware of them.

Individuals and environmental organisations have proved helpful to the Commission by acting as environmental watchdogs, but they themselves have very limited access to domestic courts and to the ECJ. It is the Commission which decides whether or not to bring proceedings against a Member State, and it does so only in a small number of cases. Individuals and pressure groups cannot compel the Commission to take proceedings, and they often lack the funds and institutional structures necessary to pursue protracted litigation themselves. Moreover, the number and nature of complaints often depends upon the particular interests of environmental organisations. For

---

[48] Directive 80/778/EEC [1989] O.J. L229/11.
[49] Directive 92/42/EEC [1992] O.J. L167/17.
[50] See Hatton, "The Implementation of EU Environmental Law" 2003 J.E.L. Vol.15(3) 273. The author suggests that, despite this policy, in practice the Commission does investigate non-application cases.
[51] See Krämer, *op. cit.* above. (Of the 59 months in total, 38 were used in pre-judicial procedure and 21 in procedure before the Court of Justice).
[52] Article 228.
[53] See Case C387/97 *Commission v Greece* [2000] E.C.R. I–369.

example, the large number of reported infringements of water pollution law in the UK has been attributed to the strength of campaigns on this issue by UK pressure groups, whilst in France the focus of similar groups has been on hunting and the protection of wild animals.

The idea of allowing individuals or organisations access to domestic courts to speak on behalf of the environment is strongly advocated by some commentators and is increasingly gaining acceptance.[54] The Aarhus Convention (discussed in Ch. 14) was signed by the European Community and its Member States in June 1998. This convention marks a growing trend of seeing effective environmental law enforcement in terms of greater public involvement. In October 2003, as a means of implementing one aspect of the Aarhus Convention, the Commission adopted a proposal for a Directive on Access to Justice in Environmental Matters. This proposal aims to establish a framework of minimum requirements for access to judicial and administrative proceedings in environmental matters, in order to achieve a better implementation of environmental law within the Community. The proposed Directive grants legal standing to members of the public, entitling them to challenge, by way of judicial or administrative proceedings, contravention of environmental law by public bodies.

E. IMPLEMENTING EC ENVIRONMENTAL LAW IN UK LAW

As a species of international law,[55] EC law is not regarded as part of our own legal **4–032** system unless it is incorporated into UK law by an Act of Parliament. By s.2(1) of the European Communities Act 1972, it is provided that EC law forms part of the law in the UK. However, in spite of this general provision, the *extent* to which individual EC environmental laws are part of the UK legal system will depend upon the particular "effect" of each individual EC legislative instrument.

Treaty provisions

The environmental provisions of the EC Treaty itself cannot be relied on directly by **4–033** individuals before UK courts in challenging action taken by the UK to fulfil its EC environmental obligations. Thus, in *R. v Secretary of State for Trade and Industry, Ex p. Duddridge and Others*,[56] it was held that the Secretary of State was not required to apply the "precautionary principle" in taking action where possible risk of harm to human health arose. According to the court, Art. 174, when examined in its context, laid down principles on which Community policy on the environment was to be based. It did not impose any immediate obligation on Member States to act in a particular way.

Directives

Most EC environmental law, as has been said, is contained in Directives. Directives are **4–034** binding on Member States as to the result to be achieved, but the actual form of domestic legislation adopted to achieve that result is left to the discretion of each

---

[54] See Kramer, "Public Interest Litigation in Environmental Matters before European Courts" (1996) J.E.L Vol.8(1).
[55] The Treaty of Rome—the basic constitutional code of the Community—was originally conceived as an international agreement between States binding in international law.
[56] The Independent, October 4, 1994, Q.B.D.

Member State. In the UK, Directives normally require the passing of an Act of Parliament or a statutory instrument before they take effect. However, the doctrine of "direct effect" allows individuals to rely upon rights or obligations conferred on them by a Directive in national courts, even though the Directive has not been transposed by the Member State within the time allowed, or has been transposed incorrectly.

(1) *Direct effect*

4–035 The doctrine of direct effect was developed by the ECJ and is justified on the basis that a Member State should not be entitled to take advantage of the fact that a Directive was not, or was not correctly or completely, transposed into national law. The doctrine is therefore conceived, in a sense, as a "sanction" against the Member State. For this reason, it is only applied in favour of individuals, never *against* individuals. The Court will not apply the doctrine in cases where two individuals are in dispute.

Opinion differs as to the extent to which Directives on the environment have direct effect. The conditions necessary for a Directive to have direct effect are that:

(1) the period for transposing the Directive into national law has expired, or the Directive has been incorrectly transposed by the Member State;

(2) the wording of the Directive is sufficiently clear and precise to be relied upon by an individual and applied by a court;

(3) the result required by the Directive is unconditional (*i.e.* there must be no room for the Member State to exercise a discretion in the method by which it is implemented); and

(4) the Directive explicitly or implicitly confers rights on an individual as against a Member State.[57]

It has been suggested that the following types of environmental Directives (or relevant parts of them) should be held to be directly effective:

- those which lay down maximum permissible levels of discharges, concentration values or emissions. These values are precise and must be adhered to unconditionally by Member States;

- those which prohibit the use or discharge of certain specified substances, or prohibit certain activities. Such prohibitions will have direct effect where they are drafted in absolute terms; and

- those which impose on Member States other clear and specific obligations to act.[58]

"Framework Directives" will not generally be construed as directly effective, nor will Directives which require Member States, in general terms, to perform certain types of

---

[57] See Case 41/74 *Yvonne van. Duyn v Home Office* [1974] I E.C.R. 1337.
[58] Kramer, "Public Interest Litigation in Environmental Matters before European Courts" (1996) J.E.L Vol.8(1).

act—for example to draw up and carry out environmental rehabilitation programmes, or programmes to reduce waste.

Such Directives do not have direct effect because the nature of the programmes will depend upon the particular extent of the environmental problems within each Member State, and upon the Member State's appropriate response to those problems. Thus, in *Comitato di Coordinamento per la Difesa della Cava v Regione Lombardia*,[59] the ECJ held that Art. 4 of the Framework Directive on Waste (Member States shall take the necessary measures to ensure that waste is disposed of without endangering human health, etc.) did not have direct effect. The Article simply set out broad objectives, and prescribed a general approach rather than the adoption of specific measures.

The UK courts have considered the doctrine of direct effect in a number of environmental cases. In *Petition of Kincardine and Deeside DC*,[60] the court considered Art. 4(2) of the Environmental Impact Assessment Directive (listed projects shall be subject to an assessment where Member States consider that their characteristics so require) and held that it was insufficiently precise and unconditional to be given direct effect. Although not asked to decide the issue, the court took the view that Art. 4(1) might have had direct effect (listed projects shall be made subject to an assessment). The Court also considered Art. 2 (Member States shall take measures to maintain the bird population, while taking account of economic and recreational requirements) and Art. 4 of the Birds Directive (certain bird species to be the subject of special conservation measures to ensure their survival) and took the view that neither could be read as being sufficiently precise and unconditional.

As has been said, because the doctrine of direct effect is essentially a sanction against Member States for failure to transpose a Directive, it will not be used against individuals, only against the state. This raises a question, however, as to what environmental bodies or organisations might be regarded as part of the state. The concept of a state in EC law is defined widely, so as to encompass local authorities and professional societies entrusted with public functions. In *Foster v British Gas plc*,[61] the ECJ held that direct effect could be relied on against:

> ". . . a body, whatever its legal form, which has been made responsible, pursuant to a measure adopted by the State for providing a public service under the control of the State and has for that purpose special powers beyond those which result from the normal rules applicable between individuals."

In the UK, this would include the Environment Agency and local authorities. It also seems wide enough to include the privatised water, sewerage, gas and electricity industries. The decision in *Commission v Ireland*[62] supports this view by suggesting that the *Foster* definition would include private bodies whose activities are subject to direct or indirect control. However, whilst South West Water Services Ltd. has been held to be an "emanation of the state" for employment law purposes,[63] the company has denied that it has obligations under the Environmental Information Regulations 1992,

---

[59] C-236/92 E.C.R. [1994] p. I–483.
[60] [1993] Env. L.R. 151.
[61] Case C188/89 [1990] I–E.C.R. 3313.
[62] Case 249/81 [1982] E.C.R. 4005.
[63] *Griffin v South West Water Services Ltd* [1995] I.R.L.R. 15.

which apply to persons with "public" responsibilities for the environment.[64] The status of waste disposal companies has not yet been tested.

(2) *Indirect effect*

4-036 The doctrine of "indirect effect" requires national courts to interpret domestic legislation so as to be consistent with, and so as to give effect to, Community law.[65] This will be so even where the national provisions in question were adopted after the Directive.[66] It follows that where domestic legislation purports to give effect to the provisions of a Directive, that legislation will not be effective in so far as it may actually be inconsistent with the Directive. The UK courts, however, have traditionally shown reluctance to apply the doctrine of indirect effect. For example, in *R. v Swale BC and Medway Ports Authority, Ex p. RSPB*,[67] the court, in reviewing a planning authority's decision to grant planning permission in the absence of an environmental impact assessment, focused exclusively on interpreting the relevant regulations, and failed to consider the wording of the Directive which they purported to implement. More recently, however, a different approach was taken in an action by Greenpeace to challenge the legality of the Secretary of State's decision to allow radioactive waste reprocessing (at the THORP complex) without a local inquiry. The Radioactive Substances Act 1993 was silent on the issue of whether such reprocessing needed to be "justified in advance", and the court was prepared to consider directly the wording of Art. 6 of Euratom Directive 80/836.[68]

F: The Future: EU Enlargement and the Environment

4-037 On May 1, 2004, 10 new countries joined the EU (Cyprus, the Czech Republic, Estonia, Hungary, Latvia, Lithuania, Malta, Poland, the Slovak Republic, and Slovenia). This enlargement of the EU has increased its size from 15 Member States and 375 million citizens to 25 Member States and 450 million citizens. Most of the new Member States are completing the transition from a centrally planned economy to a market economy, and have been undergoing far-reaching economic reforms in addition to their efforts to bring their domestic legislation into line with Community law.

Enlargement will undoubtedly have an effect on EC environmental policy, not least because it will place many of the existing institutional decision-making mechanisms under strain. As we have noted, unanimity voting is still a requirement for EC legislation relating to certain environmental issues. Clearly, the need to obtain the agreement of an additional 10 Member States could mean that progress on these environmental issues will be stalled. In the light of this problem, the expansion of the EU is likely reinforce existing Commission strategy, which is to advance policy "follow-through" and legislative coherence, rather than table new legislation.

[64] See ENDS 241, Feb 1995, p.9.
[65] Case 14/83 *Von Colson v Land Nordrhein-Westfalen* [1984] E.C.R. 1891.
[66] *Marleasing S.A. v La Commercial Internaciona de Alimentacion S.A.* [1992] 1 C.M.L.R. 305.
[67] [1991] J.P.L. 39.
[68] *R. v Secretary of State for the Environment, HMIP and MAFF, Ex p. Greenpeace* [1994] 3 All E.R. 352.

The accession states, by joining the EU, have agreed to adopt the *"acquis communautaire"*—the common body of existing European Community legislation—and have accepted that they must comply fully with this legislation. Relevant publications of the EU State that the accession countries are "for the most part well on track" to implement EC environmental legislation, although in certain areas there is a need for "enhanced efforts", and some countries will need more time to reach certain environmental targets.[69]

Whilst the accession countries may have adopted the laws necessary to give effect to EC obligations, implementing those laws may be more difficult. There is little doubt that the cost of implementing EC laws, and the accession countries' relative poverty and lack of experience with EC requirements, will make it difficult for them to "catch up" with existing European standards. This will be especially true in such contexts as waste and water management, where environmental protection is heavily dependent on effective national infrastructures. Some commentators have expressed concern that the environment has been neglected in the accession process. This concern is accentuated by the fact that, across Central and Eastern Europe, environmental issues remain at the bottom of the political agenda.

Over the last few years, there has been extensive discussion about certain reforms of the existing treaty arrangements that might be desirable in the context of an enlarged EU. In particular, these have centred around the respective competencies of the EU and Member States to deal with particular issues. The discussions have culminated in the drafting of the European Constitution, which is designed to replace the existing treaties governing the EU. At the time of writing, the Constitution is still in draft form. However, the draft constitutional text submitted to European Council in June 2003 is by no means ideal from an environmental perspective. In particular, it contains no provisions on access to justice in environmental matters. Environmentalists had hoped that the EU, in keeping with the spirit of the Aarhus Convention (discussed in Ch. 14), would take the opportunity to relax its restrictive approach to granting individuals and environmental groups access to the ECJ.[70]

---

[69] See *http://europa.eu.int/comm/enlargement/report2003*.
[70] An approach recently confirmed by the ECJ's decision in Case C50/00 *Commission v Netherlands*.

Chapter 5

INTEGRATED POLLUTION PREVENTION AND CONTROL

"Integrated Pollution Prevention and Control [sets] Member States the ambitious target of regulating almost the whole environmental impact of an installation"[1]

Introduction

Integrated Pollution Prevention and Control (IPPC) is, in essence, a philosophy of **5–001** pollution control. It is based upon a recognition that a pollutant, when emitted from an industrial process, may enter not only the air, but water or land. It recognises that solving one environmental problem may create another. Suppose, for example, that an industrial process creates dust. This might be emitted to the air, causing air pollution. Alternatively, it might be removed by the use of water sprays—but this leaves polluted water that must then be disposed of. The water may be piped into a lagoon to settle and dry out, creating solid waste. Disposing of the solid waste may create a worse problem than if the dust that had caused the original problem had been widely dispersed through a tall chimney.[2]

Another approach might be to filter the dust from the air by the use of large extractor fans—but solving the air pollution problem in this way may create a noise pollution problem. Moreover, extractor fans use a lot of power. This must be generated at a power station which, in turn, may cause atmospheric pollution. In deciding how to deal with the dust, an integrated approach to environmental protection will weigh up its different potential impacts, and select the solution that causes least harm to the environment as a whole—it will even consider whether the best solution might be to conduct the industrial process in a different way, perhaps using different raw materials, so as to prevent the dust from arising.

IPPC, then, takes a holistic approach to the management of pollution and other environmental impacts of industrial installations. This approach to pollution control marked a radical shift in regulatory technique when it was first introduced in the UK in

---

[1] DETR Consultation Paper: *UK Implementation of EC Directive 96/61 on IPPC* (July 1997).
[2] Royal Commission on Environmental Pollution Fifth Report: *Integrated Pollution Control*, Cmnd. 6371 (1976).

the form of a statutory regime that was called simply "Integrated Pollution Control" (IPC). The integrated approach promises a closer regulatory fit to the movement of pollution in the physical world than previous approaches, which were based on separate regulation of pollution of air, water and land.

Shortly after an integrated approach was introduced in the UK, the EC adopted the concept, and passed the Integrated Pollution Prevention and Control Directive.[3] This has meant that the UK must modify its existing regime to fall in line with the Directive. The European conception of IPPC is broader than that which prevails under the UK's IPC regime (hence, perhaps, the addition of the word "prevention"). We explore the differences between the two regimes later in the chapter, but here it is sufficient to note one fundamental difference: under the European regime, consideration is given to such matters raw material and energy use, and the amount of waste produced, in a way that was not possible under the UK's IPC regime. It is important to note, however, that despite these broad objectives, the European regime, in reality, is unlikely to offer much more in the near future than "end of pipe" pollution control. Nevertheless, it provides the theoretical capacity to allow regulation of almost the whole environmental impact of industrial installations.

IPPC is designed for certain types of large, complex industrial and agricultural processes that discharge significant quantities of harmful substances. It puts in place a range of organisational and legislative measures that enable regulatory bodies in Europe to deal with the connected nature of environmental problems from identifiable "point-source" pollution (as opposed to diffuse pollution, which is pollution with no discrete source). In the UK, the IPPC Directive is implemented by a regime known as Pollution Prevention and Control (PPC). This regime is governed by the Pollution Prevention and Control Act 1999 and its accompanying regulations. The UK is currently in a period of transition from IPC to PPC. The IPC regime will continue as the pollution control regime for some industrial processes until 2007. This makes it necessary to consider the operation of both regimes in this chapter. We begin by considering the history of point-source pollution control, both in the UK and at EC level, in respect of the three environmental media, and by tracing the development of the UK's IPC regime and the subsequent IPPC Directive.

Point-source pollution control in the UK

5–002   Before 1990, regulation of industrial operations in the UK was fragmented. Air and water pollution were regulated by different regulatory bodies, who had different procedures and approaches. Until 1987, air pollution had been in the hands of the Industrial Air Pollution Inspectorate (the successor to the old Alkali Inspectorate, created in 1863). This body had traditionally focussed on industrial emissions, requiring the "best practicable means" to be used to control air pollution in the most serious cases.[4] The bodies responsible for water management[5] had a different approach, based on environmental licensing, with an emphasis on the characteristics of

---

[3] Dir.96/61/EC O.J. No. L257/26.
[4] See the Clean Air Acts 1956 and 1968.
[5] The Drinking Water Inspectorate (DWI) of the Department of the Environment and the National Rivers Authority.

the water receiving the pollution. Land contamination was regulated only in a limited way which had not been designed to address the problem of contamination from industrial operations.

As far back as 1976, the Royal Commission on Environmental Pollution recognised that pollution control regimes in the UK were not properly addressing the difficulties which arose from treating the pollution of air, land and water as three separate issues, under the control of different authorities. Regulation in this manner was inefficient. Pollutants would be disposed of in a haphazard manner, without considering the best solution for the environment as a whole. Resources for pollution control would not necessarily be targeted where the pollution problems were most severe. A fragmented approach to pollution control enabled polluters to seek out the easiest and cheapest media to pollute.[6]

In the 1980s, there was growing concern, expressed both by environmental pressure groups and by politicians, that the "best practical means" principle of controlling air pollution was characterised by such flexibility and informality that "cosy relationships" between industry and regulators were a possibility, if not a reality. A fresh approach was required. The first step towards an integrated approach came with the establishment, in 1987, of a unified pollution inspectorate, Her Majesty's Inspectorate of Pollution (HMIP) to deal with the most polluting and complex industrial processes. HMIP combined the functions of the Industrial Air Pollution Inspectorate, the Hazardous Wastes Inspectorate and the water pollution staff within the Department of the Environment. The amalgamation of these bodies, however, highlighted the differences in their approaches and the need for new legislation to provide the statutory basis for regulating cross-media pollution.

In 1988, the Department of the Environment issued a consultation paper on Integrated Pollution Control. This document, based on lengthy negotiations with industry, formed the basis for the Integrated Pollution Control regime subsequently set out in Pt I of the Environmental Protection Act 1990. At the time of writing, it is this regime that remains applicable to industrial operations that have not yet been brought within the PPC regime. The operation of the IPC regime is discussed in a separate section below.

Point-source pollution control at EC level

The EC has been further behind the UK in developing an integrated approach to **5–003** industrial pollution. Directives were adopted in 1975 to address the production and management of waste,[7] in 1976 on water pollution caused by dangerous substances,[8] and in 1984 on air pollution from industrial plants.[9] These Directives, which are still in force, provide for different control regimes for the different environmental media, and each medium is subject to regulation by means of a different approach.

Under the Water Pollution by Dangerous Substances Directive, all discharges into surface waters of effluents liable to contain a dangerous substance (as defined in the

---

[6] RCEP: *Air Pollution Control: An Integrated Approach* (1976), Cmnd 6371.
[7] Directive 75/442/EEC (The "Waste Framework Directive") O.J. L194 25.7.75 (amended by Dir.91/156).
[8] Directive 76/464/EEC on pollution caused by certain dangerous substances discharged into the aquatic environment of the Community O.J. L129 18.05.76.
[9] Directive 84/360/EEC on the combating of air pollution from industrial plants O.J. L188 16.07.84.

Directive's Annex) require prior authorisation by a competent Member State authority. The scope of the Directive is not defined by reference to a specific list of industrial processes or other activities—all discharges into the aquatic environment, whatever their source, are subject to the authorisation requirements. By contrast, the Air Pollution Directive applies only to specified categories of industrial installations. The operation of these specified installations requires a prior authorisation from a competent authority. Such authorisation may be issued only if the use of the installation "will not cause significant air pollution", and if "all appropriate preventive measures against air pollution have been taken, including the application of the best available technology, provided that the application of such measures does not entail excessive costs." There is no comparable European legislation designed to address pollution of land. This factor, together with the absence of legislation to control the transboundary effects of pollution, was one of the primary reasons for proposing the IPPC Directive. In addition, several Member States, including the UK, were already developing integrated regimes, which gave rise to the possibility of inconsistent schemes within the Community.

The IPPC Directive

5–004 The IPPC Directive was adopted by the European Council in September 1996. Its provisions are derived in large measure from the UK's IPC regime, although there are some important differences. Along with the Water Framework Directive and the Waste Framework Directive, the IPPC Directive provides a comprehensive European framework for regulation of industrial activities. The European Commission has expressed its hopes for the Directive in pioneering terms, seeing the Directive as part of the EC's contribution to the development of the ten-year programme of sustainable consumption and production which was initiated at the 2002 Johannesburg Earth Summit. The Commission is particularly interested in promoting the idea of exchanging, at an international level, information on pollution-abatement techniques developed under IPPC, so that non-European countries can reap the benefits of that information.

The Directive defines its purpose as being to achieve integrated prevention and control of pollution arising from specified activities, namely some of the major causes of point-source pollution. It lays down measures designed to prevent (or where that is not practicable, reduce) emissions to air, water and land, and also to regulate waste generation and efficient use of raw materials, energy and water. The aim is to achieve a high level of protection for the environment taken as a whole. The approach prescribed by the Directive goes well beyond controlling emissions of polluting substances. It sets Member States the ambitious target of regulating almost the whole environmental impact of an installation, via conditions laid down in a single environmental licence. This regulation may extend to a diverse range of matters, from noise and vibration to the sourcing and selection of raw materials so as to ensure "the prudent management of natural resources."

The Directive abandons belief in the virtues of setting, at EC level, fixed limits for emissions from industrial installations, with those limits applying across the whole of the Community (a belief that was evident in the earlier media-specific Directives discussed above.) The preamble to the Directive stresses that it establishes a general framework of control. Accordingly, in line with the principle of subsidiarity, Member States are given considerable discretion under IPPC to regulate environmental impacts on a site-by-site basis. Variations in how the Directive is implemented can be justified on the basis that Environmental licensing decisions must take account of local environmental conditions.

Member States were given three years to transpose the Directive into national law, and are given a generous 11 years to ensure that all industrial operations within the scope of the Directive are fully compliant. The UK's experience with IPC, from which the Directive borrows heavily, has, at the time of writing, put it further ahead of other Member States in implementing the Directive's requirements. In a report on progress, published in June 2003, the European Commission identified significant shortcomings in implementation by most Member States, save for the UK.

A: THE IPC REGIME: THE PREDECESSOR TO PPC

The UK, along with the Netherlands, was ahead of its time when it introduced the IPC **5–005** regime in 1990. As has been said, this regime, though it is being superseded by the PPC regime, is still in force for some industrial operations in the UK and will remain so until 2007.

The regime was introduced by Pt I of the Environmental Protection Act 1990. The Act establishes a two-tier system of control. The most heavily polluting industrial processes are subject to central control by the Environment Agency—these are the processes "prescribed for IPC". Other, smaller and less polluting processes are subject to control by local authorities, and are regulated only in respect of air pollution—these are processes "prescribed for Local Authority Air Pollution Control (LAAPC)". The Act puts in place a system of environmental licensing for both types of industrial process.

It is the responsibility of the operator of any process which has been prescribed for IPC to prevent or, where this is not practicable, minimise, the release of "prescribed substances." The control of substances is at the heart of the IPC regime (in contrast with the PPC regime, which regulates a wider array of environmental impacts). Prescribed substances are those deemed by the Secretary of State to be potentially polluting so as to warrant control.[10] In practice, the method by which the control of prescribed substances is achieved is by regulating industrial processes which emit those substances. Regulation is by a system of prior approval by the Environment Agency (for IPC prescribed processes) or by local authorities (for LAAPC prescribed processes). An operator cannot carry on a prescribed process without consent, in the form of an environmental licence (called an "authorisation") from the Agency or local authority.[11]

In preventing or minimising the release of prescribed substances, process operators are required to use the *Best Available Techniques Not Entailing Excessive Cost* (BATNEEC). BATNEEC is essentially the means by which economic and environmental costs and benefits are compared and weighed up, so as to determine the best

[10] See the Environmental Protection (Prescribed Processes and Substances) Regulations 1991 (SI 1991/472) (as amended by SI 1992/614).
[11] EPA 1990, s.6(3).

method for controlling the prescribed substances in question. For good measure, all other (non-prescribed) substances come within a second, wider tier of control; the Act requires that non-prescribed substances must be *rendered harmless* using BATNEEC before they are released.

In applying BATNEEC to processes which are likely to discharge substances into *more than one environmental medium*, operators are further required to achieve the *Best Practicable Environmental Option* (BPEO) for the discharge of those substances. BPEO requires consideration of which environmental media will suffer the least damage in receiving the substances. BPEO is not defined in the Environmental Protection Act 1990. The accepted definition, and that which was adopted by HMIP for use in the IPC regime, was given by the Royal Commission on Environmental Pollution, in its twelfth report:

> "A BPEO is the outcome of a systematic, consultative and decision-making procedure which emphasises the protection and conservation of the environment across land, air and water. The BPEO procedure establishes for a given set of objectives the option that provides the most benefit or least damage to the environment as a whole at acceptable cost in the long term as well as in the short term."[12]

Evaluating the success of IPC

5–006 Whether IPC has been a success is a difficult question to answer. The integrated approach to pollution control has certainly produced a significant administrative and intellectual change. It has led to the unification of the regulatory authorities, and has exerted a strong influence on the development of pollution control across Europe, in the form of the IPPC Directive.

However, whether IPC has succeed "internally"—that is to say, in terms of meeting its own objectives of "preventing or minimising the release of substances into the environment" is difficult to determine. Drawing conclusions about reductions in pollution levels is problematic, because the accurate assessment of the effects of substances on environmental media is extremely difficult, if not impossible, given the limits of current scientific knowledge. The effect of a substance depends on many things, including the rate at which the substance is released, the velocity and temperature at which it is released, the propensity of the receiving medium to disperse the substance, the presence of other substances in the medium—with which the released substance may react—and the nature of those reactions. There do not appear to be any scientific studies which attempt to evaluate the success of IPC in the light of these factors. Nor, within the regime, are there any general environmental targets by which its success can be measured—there is, for example, no requirement that total emissions from certain industrial sectors should be reduced by a fixed amount. IPC does not set fixed emission limits for installations to meet. Instead, it leaves it to the regulator's discretion to regulate emissions on a site-by-site basis.

---

[12] Royal Commission on Environmental Pollution Twelfth Report: *Best Practicable Environmental Option* Cm 310 (1988).

Regulator discretion

The discretion left to regulators under IPC (and now under PPC) means that one has **5–007**
to trust the regulator to have sufficient expertise and determination to regulate
installations to an optimum environmental standard. Inevitably, the technical and
specialised nature of regulation gives rise to a concern that the relevant expertise will
be in the hands of the process operators, rather than the regulator.

We have seen that one of the motivating forces which led to the adoption of IPC
was criticism of "cosy relationships" between operators and regulators. In order to
meet such criticism, HMIP, in the early years of the IPC regime, adopted an "arm's
length" policy towards industry, designed to reassure the public that it was an objective
and independent body which would set and enforce stringent standards. This policy
was in keeping with the views of the Royal Commission, which had reported that it was
not acceptable that decisions on emissions, which affected the everyday lives of so
many people, should be taken by a small, specialist body consulting only with
industry—greater public participation and accountability were needed. The "arm's
length" approach to regulation, however, was soon abandoned, primarily because the
first applications for environmental licences under the IPC regime were of such poor
quality that HMIP found itself having to work in close co-operation with industry to
elaborate the standards to which it was expecting industry to conform, and the
methods by which this could be done.

A relationship between HMIP and industry characterised by *some* degree of co-
operation was, of course, in keeping with the Royal Commission's view that the
determination of *Best Practicable Environmental Option* should involve a consultative
and advisory role on the part of HMIP. It was felt that, in applying BPEO, HMIP
could retain a co-operative stance whilst a system of registers containing details of
applications would provide the safeguard of accountability. In practice, however, it
proved difficult for HMIP to maintain its dual role as advisor and enforcer without
sacrificing accountability. The advice given to industry by HMIP (and latterly the
Environment Agency) has undoubtedly improved the quality of licence applications,
but the unfortunate consequence has been a decline in the transparency of the
system—a register which reveals the details of an application which is the product of
consultation may tell the public little about how successful the Environment Agency
has been in curbing an operator's initial desire to pollute. Whilst the availability of
licensing information may help to elucidate public concerns about local environmental
impacts (*e.g.* noise or odour), it is unlikely to provide public accountability in relation
to the technical aspects of process regulation.

The government has recognised most of these problems during its consultation on
implementing the IPPC Directive. It has expressed a desire to issue guidance for each
industrial sector which will set out clear indicative performance standards. In addition,
it has promised to improve the transparency of the licensing process, so as to reassure
the public that they can have confidence in the regulators. Operators who apply for
permits under the PPC regime will have to justify any proposed departure from the
indicative performance standards, and the regulator, in the public register, will have to
explain why such a departure has been accepted.[13]

---

[13] See Third Consultation Paper on the Implementation of the IPPC Directive (January 1999), DEFRA.

Inherent shortcomings of the IPC regime

5–008 It is clear that there are some significant "gaps" in the IPC regime which are now to be filled by PPC. The IPC regime has a narrow focus, in the sense that it regulates only pollution by substances which emanate from regulated sites. But industrial activities can, of course, cause environmental harm in a more indirect way. A truly holistic approach must encompass consideration of the effects of energy and water consumption, raw material use and sourcing, production of waste, and the life-cycle of manufactured products. In implementing the IPC regime, a trade-off had to be made between fulfilling the vision of the Royal Commission on Environmental Pollution—which had proposed a holistic assessment of environmental impacts from industry—and the political acceptability and administrative feasibility of IPC implementation.

The Royal Commission had favoured an "imaginative response" to pollution control which involved considering an industrial process in its widest possible environmental context. Thus, the *Best Practicable Environmental Option* for a given process might be decided by reference not only to the substances released, but the environmental consequences of its use of raw materials and energy, and the methods by which any waste it produced could be disposed of. It was therefore conceivable that the BPEO for a given process might involve a higher than normal level of substance releases for the sake of using less energy or different raw materials. (To take a simplified example, the BPEO for making garden furniture might be to make it out of plastic, rather than wood, even though this might involve a much higher level of prescribed substance emission.) Under the IPC regime as implemented, however, a wide consideration of environmental effects is not possible. This is because s.7(7) of the Environmental Protection Act 1990 restricts the Environment Agency to considering substance releases only. The Agency is not given the power to adopt the truly holistic approach that had been envisaged by the Royal Commission (and which is now—in theory at least—required under the PPC regime).

B: IMPLEMENTING THE IPPC DIRECTIVE: THE PPC REGIME

5–009 Superimposing the requirements of the IPPC Directive onto an existing complex and similar UK regime was never going to be a straightforward exercise. It was estimated that approximately 4,600 industrial operations would fall within the remit of the Directive, but that a further 11,900 operations already regulated under the IPC regime (prescribed either for IPC or LAAPC) would not do so. In addition, the government wanted to make some changes to the way the existing regime regulated operations, in the light of experience gained since it was introduced. The desire was to end up with a single IPPC-style regulatory system, rather than having three different pollution control regimes running alongside each other (*i.e.* PPC, IPC and LAAPC). It was for this reason that the government chose to implement the IPPC Directive through primary legislation, rather than through regulations made under s.2(2) of the European Communities Act 1972—such regulations would only have allowed changes in respect of the installations covered by the Directive.

The Pollution Prevention and Control Act 1999 was therefore passed. The Act gave the Secretary of State authority to make regulations to provide for a new pollution control regime to implement the IPPC Directive, and for other measures to prevent or control pollution. The breadth of the power given to the Secretary of State to make such wide-ranging delegated legislation on pollution control was strongly criticised.[14] The Pollution Prevention and Control (England and Wales) Regulations 2000,[15] made under the Act, came into force on August 1, 2000. Also relevant are the Landfill (England and Wales) Regulations 2002.[16] These two sets of regulations will eventually replace all of Pt I and some of Pt II of the Environmental Protection Act 1990. Separate similar regimes have been introduced to apply the IPPC Directive in Scotland and Northern Ireland.

The main differences between IPC and PPC

The main differences between IPC and PPC are summarised below: **5–010**

- PPC has a more ambitious scope than IPC. Whereas IPC is concerned primarily with control of substances, PPC aims to regulate almost the whole environmental impact of a process—including its energy efficiency, use of waste, and use of raw materials.

- PPC covers a wider range of operations, including landfills, intensive farming and operations in the food and drink industry.

- PPC brings within its remit some large-scale waste management activities previously regulated under the waste management licensing regime.

- PPC places more industrial processes under control by an integrated approach, whereas, under the IPC regime, many processes were subject to control in respect of air pollution only (under the LAAPC part of the regime).

- PPC regulates the surrender of environmental licences (known as "permits") and the shutdown and aftercare of industrial sites. Long-term aftercare and remediation programmes may be required from former process operators.

- PPC regulates industrial *installations* rather than industrial *processes*. The practical effect of this is that only one PPC permit may be required for a site, whereas, under IPC, several authorisations might be necessary. This approach makes it easier for the regulator to consider the entire environmental impact of site operations.

- PPC requires the application of *Best Available Techniques* (BAT), as opposed to *Best Available Techniques Not Entailing Excessive Cost* (BATNEEC). The government has made it clear, however, in its first consultation paper on IPPC implementation, that "costs and advantages and economic feasibility are to be

[14] See Stephen Tromans, "Pollution Prevention, Skeletons and the Stuarts", N.L.J. April 30, 1999. The Bill allowed the Secretary of State far greater powers, leading to considerable disquiet during its passage through Parliament. Lord Peyton of Yeovil stated: "I do not believe that I have ever seen a Bill which shows more manifestly a deep and profound contempt for Parliament." (*Hansard* HL , February 15, 1999, col. 471).
[15] SI 2000/1973.
[16] SI 2002/1559.

taken into account, as in IPC."[17] That said, the government has also indicated that it intends to abandon its former approach of determining economic feasibility on an industrial sector-by-sector basis. The same criteria will now be applied to all industrial sectors, on the basis that it is unfair to shift the burden of environmental protection onto those sectors which can most afford it.

- PPC does not include the concept of *Best Practicable Environmental Option* (BPEO), which is an IPC concept. Whilst there has been a great deal of commentary analysing the implications of this, in practice the absence of BPEO is not expected to make much difference. The broad objectives of both regimes remain similar, namely to ensure site-by-site consideration of the most appropriate environmental solutions.

- PPC does not require environmental licensing arrangements to be reviewed every four years, as is the case under IPC. The PPC requirement is for "periodic" inspections of licensing arrangements, and what is appropriate will be decided on a sector-by-sector and site-by-site basis. The aim of this approach is to provide an incentive to operators to improve their performance, on the basis that this might lead to fewer inspections.

Timetable for transition from IPC to PPC

5–011   The timetable for transition varies depending upon whether an installation subject to control is "new", "substantially changed" or "existing".

- *New installations* are installations put into operation on or after October 31, 1999.

- *Substantially changed* installations are those which have undergone a change in their operations which may have a significant negative environmental impact, and have done so on or after October 31, 1999, but before January 2001.

- *Existing installations* are those in operation before October 31, 1999, or which came into operation between October 31, 1999 and October 31, 2000 in accordance with an environmental licence granted under the IPC regime before October 31, 1999.

"New" and "substantially changed" installations either came into the PPC regime on the date on which their PPC application was determined, if this was before January 2001, or, if they were in operation but had not made an application for pollution control before January 2001, on January 1, 2001. For "existing installations", the date on which they come into the new regime varies, depending upon which industrial sector they are part of. For example, some of the chemicals sector came into PPC in early 2003. However, the pharmaceutical sector does not come into the regime until 2006.

Installations which are currently regulated under the Local Authority Air Pollution Control (LAAPC) and who are transferring across to the "air only" part of PPC (*i.e.* to

[17] DETR Consultation Paper: *UK Implementation of EC Directive 96/61 on IPPC* (July 1997).

become Pt B installations—see below) do not need to make an application for a PPC permit, because the change from LAAPC will mean only a change in the terminology used to regulate them (*e.g.* they will have "permits" instead of "authorisations", and will use BAT instead of BATNEEC)—there will be no change in the substantive obligations of process operators.

Regulated installations

The installations regulated by the PPC regime include those involved in energy **5–012** production, production and processing of metals and minerals, the chemicals industry, and the waste management industry. Other installations within the scope of control include those conducting intensive farming, and those in the food and drink sectors. Some waste management installations are brought within the scope of an integrated pollution control regime for the first time, having previously been regulated under the waste management regime (discussed in Ch. 7). These include:

- installations for the disposal or recovery of hazardous waste;

- installations for the incineration of municipal waste;

- installations for the disposal of non-hazardous waste, with a capacity exceeding 50 tonnes per day; and

- landfill sites receiving more than 10 tonnes per day, or with a total capacity exceeding 25,000 tonnes.[18] Landfill sites now coming within the scope of PPC must apply for PPC permits, and will be subject to PPC application procedures (*e.g.* public consultation). However, the technical specifications to which landfill sites must adhere are not set out by the PPC regulations, but by regulations implementing the Landfill Directive.[19]

Waste management installations subject to PPC are excluded from the waste management licensing regime (discussed in Ch. 7). However, the scheme of regulation under PPC incorporates some aspects of that licensing system which have proved effective for regulating waste sites, including:

- that the operator of a waste management installation is subject to a test of being a "fit and proper person";

- that the operator of *any* installation regulated under PPC (not just waste installations) may not surrender his permit at will, but must apply to the regulator, and it will be for the regulator to accept or reject that surrender. (This gives effect to the requirement of the IPPC Directive for measures to be taken upon the closure of sites to avoid pollution risk and return the sites to a "satisfactory state";) and

- that where a waste management site requires planning permission, the planning permission must be in force before a PPC permit can be granted.

[18] Excluding landfills of inert waste.
[19] See Ch. 7.

The PPC regulators

5–013 The Directive does not specify whom the regulators of the regime should be, and leaves open the possibility that there can be a number of different regulators, acting in a co-ordinated fashion to achieve integrated regulation. In implementing the regime, various options were considered, including that of having the Environment Agency as sole regulator, and of having a joint system of supervision for all installations, with each regulator responsible for a different aspect of pollution control. However, after consultation and deliberation, the government decided to apportion responsibility for regulation between local authorities and the Environment Agency, in much the same way as it had done under the IPC regime. In its third consultation paper, the government expressed the view that local authorities had operated the LAAPC regime capably, and that a regulatory role under PPC would complement their responsibilities for local air quality management (see Ch. 10).

The principles on which regulatory responsibility was apportioned were as follows:

- Large complex installations with multi-media discharge should continue to be regulated by the Environment Agency;

- Waste management installations should continue to be regulated by the Environment Agency; and

- Installations with discharges to controlled waters, or discharges of special category effluent or other prescribed substances to sewers, should be regulated by the Environment Agency because of its greater expertise in water pollution matters.

Most of the installations which are allocated for control by local authorities are, in practice, those already regulated by local authorities under the LAAPC regime. However, regulation is extended in some cases beyond air pollution to integrated control. Local authorities must therefore develop expertise in other areas, particularly in relation to regulating water pollution. To compensate for local authorities' lack of experience in regulating water pollution, provision is made for the Environment Agency to be consulted in this regard. In addition, the Agency is responsible for the preparation of guidance for use by local authorities on discharges to water, and has the power to specify emission limit values for water to be applied by local authorities.[20]

Whilst local authorities were thought to lack expertise in water regulation, they were recognised as having expertise in noise (as a result of exercising the powers and duties discussed in Ch. 11). Since noise is more site-specific than many of the other forms of pollution regulated under PPC, there is a requirement that, where applications for permits are made to the Environment Agency, the Agency must consult local authorities, so as to enable them to provide advice on local conditions that may affect the extent of noise problems.

---

[20] Regulation 13(1).

Division of regulatory responsibility

The PPC regime divides regulated installations into three different categories, as **5–014** follows:

(1) *Part A (1) Installations*

These installations are regulated by the Environment Agency. They are the installa- **5–015** tions that have the greatest potential to impact on the environment, and tend to be large, complex installations which emit pollutants to more than one environmental medium (air, water and land). Waste management installations (where subject to PPC) are Pt A(1) Installations, on the basis that they should continue to be regulated by the Environment Agency, as they were previously under the waste management licensing regime.

(2) *Part A (2) Installations*

These installations are regulated by local authorities. Pt A (2) Installations are those **5–016** conducting activities considered to be less polluting than Pt A (1) activities, but which also have the potential to pollute more than one environmental medium, and therefore benefit from integrated regulation.

(3) *Part B Installations*

These installations are regulated by local authorities. Pt B Installations are those **5–017** carrying out generally less hazardous and complex industrial processes which tend to emit pollutants to the air only. They are therefore regulated only in respect of air pollution, in exactly the same way (except for some procedural differences) as they were formerly regulated under LAAPC. The PPC regime for Pt B Installations therefore represents a continuation of LAAPC.

Categorisation of activities

As has been said, the PPC regime focuses on the regulation of industrial *installations* **5–018** rather than *processes*. Nevertheless, under the regulations, industrial "activities" are classified as a first step in determining whether an installation falls under Pt A (1), Pt A (2) or Pt B. Sch.1 of the regulations contains an exhaustive list of activities covered by PPC. The table below sets out a few of them by way of example:

Industry	Activity	Category
Energy industry	Refining gas where this is likely to involve the use of 1,000 tonnes or more of gas in any period of 12 months.	A(1)
	Refining gas where this activity does not fall into the A(1) category.	A(2)
	The storage of petrol in stationary storage tanks at a terminal.	B

Industry	Activity	Category
Production/ Processing of Metals	Surface treating metals and plastic materials using an electrolytic or chemical process where the aggregated volume of the treatment vats is more than 30m³. There are no A(2) activities.	A(1)
	Any process for the surface treatment of metal which is likely to result in the release into air of any acid forming oxide of nitrogen and which does not fall into the A(1) category.	B

Definition of "installation"

5–019 Operations regulated by PPC can be complex, with a number of different processes and activities on a single site. For example, a combined-cycle gas turbine power station may have a number of gas turbines, heat-recovery steam generators, steam turbines and cooling systems, including cooling towers. The general rule is that an installation will be categorised according to the most harmful activities carried out there. Thus, if both "Part A (1) Activities" and "Part A (2) Activities" are carried out in an installation, it will be a "Part A (1) Installation".

An "installation" is defined in the PPC regulations as:

> "(i) a stationary technical unit where one or more [prescribed activities] are carried out; and
>
> (ii) any other location on the same site where any other directly associated activities are carried out which have a technical connection with the activities carried out in the stationary technical unit and which could have an effect on pollution."

There are therefore two limbs to the definition:

(1) *A stationary technical unit*

5–020 This is a self-contained industrial entity functioning on its own and carrying out a specified PPC activity (*e.g.* a chemical plant manufacturing chemicals). It may consist of a number of components. A site might have more than one functioning stationary technical unit (*e.g.* two combustion plants). The units will still be regarded as a single technical unit if:

(a) they carry out successive steps in one integrated industrial activity; or

(b) the activity carried out in one unit is a directly associated activity of the other unit; or

(c) both units are served by the same directly associated activity (*e.g.* they derive their fuel from the same place).

(2) *Directly associated activities with a technical connection with the unit*

Examples of such activities include feeding raw materials into the unit; processing **5–021** waste from the unit; finishing, packing and/or storing the product that is output from the unit; and storing fuel that services the unit.

The directly associated activity must serve the technical unit and not *vice versa*. So, for example, where a combined heat and power (CHP) plant provides power to small businesses not carrying out PPC regulated activities, the CHP plant will be the technical unit, but the small businesses will not be directly associated activities, because they do not serve the CHP plant; it is the CHP plant which serves them.

The practical advantage of including directly associated activities within the definition of installation is that only one permit is likely to be required for the site, as opposed to a number of different permits being required. The activities might be at different locations on the site, and whilst there will often be a physical connection, such as a conveyor-belt or pipeline, this does not have to be the case.

General principles of regulation

Control over PPC installations is exercised by a system of prior authorisation for their **5–022** operation. Any person operating an installation must apply for a PPC permit and comply with the permit. The permit will contain conditions designed to ensure that the *Best Available Techniques* (see below) are used for preventing or reducing emissions, and may contain other conditions relating to such matters as energy, raw materials and waste. A permit will not be granted if the regulator considers that the person will not ensure that the installation is operated so as to comply with the permit conditions.

As noted above, PPC attempts to regulate almost the entire environmental impact of an installation. Regulation is based on a series of principles which the regulator is required to take into account when determining the conditions of permits.[21] The regulator must ensure that all installations are operated in such a way that:

(1) pollution is prevented wherever possible, by the application of the *Best Available Techniques*;

(2) no significant pollution is caused. "Pollution" is defined widely as emissions resulting from human activity which may be harmful to health or the environment, cause offence to "any human senses", damage to property, or interference with amenities. Emissions include the direct or indirect release of substances, vibrations, heat or noise[22];

(3) production of waste is avoided. If waste is produced, it should be recovered and re-used. Disposal is to be used as a final option where recovery is technically and economically impossible, but, if necessary, should be carried out so as to avoid or reduce environmental impacts;

(4) energy is used efficiently;

---

[21] See Art. 3(f) and Reg.11.
[22] See Art. 2(5). Emissions of radioactive substances are not controlled, nor are genetically modified organisms. This is on the basis they are subject to regulation under other legislation.

(5) accidents are prevented or their consequences limited; and

(6) once activities at the site come to an end, a continuing pollution risk is avoided and the site returned to a satisfactory state.

Principles (1) and (2) apply to both Pt A (integrated pollution prevention and control) and Pt B (air pollution control) installations, but Principles 3–6 apply to Pt A installations only.

To give effect to these general principles, all PPC permits must include emission limit values (see below). In addition, Pt A permits must include conditions:

- aimed at minimising long-distance and transboundary pollution;

- ensuring the protection of soil and groundwater, and making sure the operator manages waste properly;

- protecting the environment when the installation is not operating normally— for example during start up, malfunction, or when there are temporary stoppages;

- requiring the operator to take appropriate steps before and after operation, which may include site monitoring and remediation;

- setting out how the operator should monitor emissions (*i.e.* specifying the methodology and frequency of evaluation procedures) and requiring the operator to submit reports to the regulator so that permit compliance can be checked; and

- requiring the operator to inform the regulator without delay of any accident that may cause pollution.

The regulator may also include any other conditions thought necessary to ensure a high level of protection for the environment as a whole.

The scope of conditions for Pt B permits is more limited. In addition to conditions specifying emission limit values, such other conditions are to be included that the regulator considers appropriate for preventing (or where that is not practicable, reducing) emissions into the air.[23]

Emission limit values

5–023 The Directive and the PPC Regulations[24] require all PPC permits to set a cap on levels of polluting emissions from an installation. This is done by means of "emission limit values" which specify a certain mass, concentration and/or level of a substance emitted from the installation which may not be exceeded during a specified period.

The values normally apply at the point where the emissions leave the installation, so that any subsequent dilution once the substances are in the environment is disregarded.[25] Emission limit values must be set for *all* pollutants if they are likely to be

---

[23] Regulation 12(1)(c).
[24] The PPC Regulations adopt wholesale the provisions on emission limit values laid down in the Directive.
[25] See Art. 2(6).

emitted from the installation in significant quantities, but the Directive lists pollutants of particular concern, including volatile organic compounds, metals, sulphur dioxide and asbestos.[26]

The IPPC Directive allows Member States considerable latitude in how they set emission limit values. They are set on a site-by-site basis, and Member States can replace limit values by "equivalent parameters or technical measures"[27] where appropriate. They can also lay down emission limit values for "certain groups, families or categories of substances", as opposed to individual substances.[28] To determine emission limit values, Member States must consider the *Best Available Techniques* for preventing or reducing emissions, and set the values according to what can be achieved by the application of these techniques (see below). However, the Directive leaves it open to the European Council to set emission limit values at Community level for certain categories of installations where "a need for Community action has been identified". Thus, if Member States fail to set suitable domestic emission limits, the matter may be taken out of their hands.

Best Available Techniques (BAT)

Emission limit values must be set according to what can be achieved by the application **5–024** of the *Best Available Techniques*. BAT is intended to be a dynamic, evolutionary concept which is expected to change over time as scientific knowledge and pollution abatement technology develop.[29] Member States are given considerable discretion in determining the *Best Available Techniques* for an installation, and decisions are to be made on a site-by-site basis. The PPC Regulations place regulators under a duty to follow developments in *Best Available Techniques*.[30] The Directive does not prescribe the use of any particular techniques or specific technology, and the regulators can take into account the technical characteristics of the installation concerned, its geographical location and local environmental conditions.[31] By not requiring the use of specific technology, the formula allows for the continuing development of cleaner technology and may give operators a choice of means to achieve prescribed standards.

In summary, *Best Available Techniques* is defined (in the Directive and implementing Regulations) to mean the most effective and advanced practically-available techniques which provide the basis for emission limit values designed to prevent or, where not practicable, reduce, emissions and the impact on the environment as a whole.[32] To be "available" the techniques must be developed on a scale which allows implementation in the relevant industrial sector under economically and technically viable conditions, taking into consideration the costs and advantages. In the UK, the guidance produced by DEFRA adopts a tough approach to the concept of "availability". It does not matter whether the technique originates outside the UK, or even the EU. Nor must

---

[26] Article 9(3).
[27] Article 9(3).
[28] Article 2(6).
[29] This is apparent from Annex 4, which provides that technological changes and changes in scientific knowledge are factors to take into account in determining BAT.
[30] See Reg.8(14).
[31] Article 9.
[32] See Article 2 of the Directive and Reg.2 and Sch.3 of the PPC Regulations.

the technique be in general use—a technique developed and proven as a pilot will be sufficient, provided that industry can confidently adopt it. There is no suggestion that the "availability" of a technique implies the existence of a competitive market for it.[33] "Best" means the most effective in achieving a high general level of protection of the environment as a whole. "Techniques" includes not only the technology used in the installation, but also the design, maintenance, operation and decommissioning of the installation, all of which must meet the BAT standard.

In determining BAT, the regulators must give special consideration to a list of factors.[34] The items listed indicate that selection of particular techniques may depend, amongst other things, upon current scientific knowledge; the effects of the emissions concerned; the possibility of using low-waste technology; the length of time needed to introduce the techniques; and the implications of those techniques in terms of raw-material consumption and energy efficiency. Regulators must also consider information on techniques provided by other Member States and published by the European Commission (see below)[35] or by international organisations. By this means, common practices can be established across Europe, and perhaps beyond.

The Directive provides for Member States to exchange information on BAT. The European Commission will publish the results of this exchange as "BAT Reference Documents" (shortened to "BREF notes"). These documents will describe the levels of environmental performance (emission levels, raw-materials and energy consumption) which can be achieved through the application of BAT in each industrial sector. The Directive does not make BREF notes binding on regulators or operators, but the UK government is gradually publishing domestic guidance on BAT standards for individual industrial sectors, drawing on the information contained in the BREF notes. Many important decisions concerning BAT are likely to be settled by this guidance rather than through the permit application procedure for individual sites, despite the legislative focus on a site-by-site approach.

The relevance of costs

5–025 The PPC regime makes the determination of BAT subject to the "likely costs and benefits of a measure and the principles of precaution and prevention." In addition, "available" techniques, as we have seen, are those which are economically viable. This approach ensures that the cost of any chosen technique is not excessive in relation to the environmental protection it provides. Another way to look at this, however, is that the more environmental damage a technique can prevent, the more money the regulator can justifiably require the operator to spend before the costs are considered excessive.

The particular financial circumstances of an *individual operator* are not relevant in determining what constitutes BAT for a given installation. It would clearly be unacceptable to change environmental requirements according to the success or otherwise of individual firms. To do so would be to underwrite the effects of poor management or creative accountancy. Under the UK's predecessor regime, IPC, however, the affordability of the costs involved for *all firms in the industrial sector in*

---

[33] DEFRA: *Integrated Pollution Prevention and Control—A Practical Guide* (3rd ed., February 2004) at 9.7(b).
[34] See Annex 4 of the Directive and Reg.3 and Sch.2 of the PPC Regulations.
[35] Pursuant to Art. 16(2) of the Directive.

question was a relevant consideration in determining BATNEEC. During implementation of PPC, the government began to question whether this was an acceptable approach—such an approach would inevitably either lead to a lower level of environmental protection in certain sectors, or would shift the burden of protecting the environment onto industrial sectors better able to afford it, which was thought unfair. The decision was therefore taken to phase out sectoral affordability as a factor in determining BAT.

A wide view of "costs"

Consideration of "costs" is not limited to costs to the operator. This potentially brings **5–026** into the equation a wide range of costs and benefits. Thus, for example, in addition to the cost to the operator of being required to use a particular type of fuel, it may also be necessary to take into account the wider energy-source implications of such a requirement—for example if the result would be to push an industrial sector towards exclusive reliance on a particular source of fuel.

So-called "social costs", either to a local community (redundancy, for example) or to the wider community (for instance, the social cost of reduced access to a public utility like electricity, should it become more expensive) may also be considered in the application of BAT. This differs from the position under IPC, where only the costs to the operator were relevant in determining BATNEEC. The approach now taken under the PPC regime, however, echoes the interpretation of "Best Practicable Means" (the precursor of BATNEEC) given by the Chief Inspector of the Alkali Inspectorate, nearly 30 years ago. He took the view that the economic effects of a chosen process should be considered not only in relation to the operator concerned, but in relation to the surrounding community. He justified this on the grounds that ultimately it was the public who paid for clean air, and that it was the duty of the inspectorate to see that money was wisely spent on the public's behalf.[36] The inspector's view did not find a place within the IPC regime, because of the contrary views expressed by the Royal Commission on Environmental Pollution, which, in its twelfth report, indicated that it would not endorse political reasons (*e.g.* preventing unemployment) for failing to implement environmental controls.[37] The holistic approach taken under the PPC regime means that such considerations are once again relevant, although their application is likely to prove contentious, and only in very limited circumstances, perhaps, are the regulators likely to excuse polluting emissions in the name of social advantages.

When is it "practicable" to prevent emissions?

Under the PPC Regulations, the *Best Available Techniques* must be used to *prevent* **5–027** emissions where that is "practicable". However, where this not "practicable", BAT must be used only to *reduce* emissions. What is meant by "practicable" is not expressly clarified in either the Directive or the Regulations. The meaning of the word has, however, been considered by the UK courts in other contexts. In *Adsett v K&L*

---

[36] *103rd Annual Report of the Chief Inspector* (1967, HMSO) p.3.
[37] Royal Commission on Environmental Pollution Twelfth Report: *Best Practicable Environment Option* Cm 310 (1988).

Steelfounders and Engineers,[38] Singleton LJ, in determining the meaning of "practicable" under the Factories Act 1937, referred to the definition contained in *Webster's Dictionary*, namely "possible to be accomplished with known means or known resources". Clearly, this definition allows for a consideration of financial resources. However, since the issue of financial implications is already addressed in defining BAT, it is unclear what is achieved by a requirement that the use of BAT to prevent emissions must be "practicable". In this light, the better view, perhaps, is that an assertion that it is not "practicable" to prevent emissions using BAT amounts, in reality, to saying simply that this is not "possible".

The "residual" BAT condition

5–028   There is implied into every permit a condition that the installation will use BAT to prevent or, where this is not practicable, reduce emissions.[39] This implied condition (the "residual" condition) applies to all aspects of the industrial activities which are not regulated by a *specific* condition. It is intended to cover the most detailed levels of installation design and operation, where the operator may be in a better position than the regulator to understand what is appropriate. The advantage of regulation by *specific* conditions is that it leaves an operator in no doubt as to what he must do to comply with a condition. The enforcement of specific conditions is easier than the enforcement of the residual duty to use BAT, because it is more readily apparent when specific conditions have been breached. On the other hand, the residual obligation to use BAT has the advantage of being ongoing throughout the operational life of an installation. It therefore forces operators to respond to developments in pollution control techniques and ensures that, if techniques become available in the periods between reviews of specific conditions, they will be applied.

Control over site closure and land contamination

5–029   One of the "general principles" laid down by the IPPC Directive is that that Member States, in setting permit conditions, should ensure that "upon the definitive cessation of activities, the necessary measures should be taken to avoid any pollution risk and to return the site of the installation or mobile plant to a satisfactory state".[40] Under the PPC Regulations, this Directive requirement is implemented by requiring operators to submit a report to the regulator on the state of the site as part of an application to close the site. When an installation closes, an operator cannot simply abandon his PPC permit or the site, but must apply to the regulator to surrender the permit and thereby end regulation under PPC.[41] The operator must commission a site report identifying, in particular, any changes in the condition of the site as it was described in the original site report that accompanied the application for a permit.[42] The original site report will

---

[38] [1953] 1 W.L.R. 773.
[39] Regulation 12(10) and (11).
[40] See Art. 3(f) and Reg.11(3).
[41] Reg.14.
[42] When applying for a PPC permit, operators must submit with their application a site report describing the condition of the site and identifying any substance in, on or under the land that may be a pollution risk.

therefore serve as a reference point, along with any operating records, for measuring any deterioration of the site under PPC. Any contamination that has resulted from the PPC operations must be cleaned up by the operator, and any ongoing pollution risk eliminated. The regulator will only allow the permit to be surrendered if satisfied that the operator has removed any pollution risk and restored the site to a satisfactory state.

Clean-up of contamination under PPC may be more than required under the "suitable for use" approach adopted under the contaminated land regime (discussed in Ch. 6). Under this regime, land only needs to be cleaned up so as to make it suitable for its new use. The government's view is that, whilst the "suitable for use" approach is appropriate for pre-existing contamination, its use in the PPC regime would result in operators being relieved of full responsibility for degradation of soil, land and water caused by their activities.[43] It should be noted, however, that clean-up under the contaminated land regime may be required *in addition* to clean up under PPC where, for example, a site is heavily polluted with material from pre-PPC operations and was not cleaned up before the PPC operations began.

C: Procedures under the PPC Regime

In this section, we consider briefly the procedures for applying for a PPC permit and **5–030** those which relate to applications to vary permit conditions and surrender permits.

- Before a PPC process can be carried on by any person, he or she must apply to the regulator (the Environment Agency or the local authority) for a permit. The application must be in writing and must include details of the installation and the raw materials and the energy to be used in, or generated by, the activity in question. The operator must also provide a site report describing the condition of the site.

- Members of the public have access to permit applications and related information, and are entitled to participate in the permit-application process.

- Before determining the application, the regulator is required to notify, and to receive representations from, certain other bodies (the "statutory consultees").[44]

- The regulator may refuse to grant a permit for the following three main reasons:

    (a) if the regulator is unable reasonably to "grant the permit subject to the conditions required or authorised to be imposed."[45] Thus, a permit can be refused where the activity proposed would produce an unacceptable

---

[43] DEFRA: *Integrated Pollution Prevention and Control—A Practical Guide* (3rd ed. February 2004) at 14.27.
[44] Those required to be consulted include, where appropriate, the Food Standards Agency, Health and Safety Executive, sewerage undertakers, the Environment Agency, the local authority, the relevant planning authority, English Nature and the harbour authority.
[45] Regulation 10(2).

environmental impact despite being regulated by conditions. The regulator has a general discretion to refuse to licence environmentally harmful activity;

(b) where the regulator is of the view that the operator will not comply with permit conditions; and

(c) where the application is for a permit that would authorise specified waste management activities, and the regulator is not satisfied that the specific prerequisites for this type of installation have been met.

- The Secretary of State has the power to make "general binding rules" relating to permit applications etc. for certain types of installation.[46] These are general requirements applicable to a range of installations. DEFRA guidance indicates that these rules may be applied in relation to industrial sectors where installations share similar characteristics (*e.g.* pig and poultry installations).

- Over time, regulators may vary permits to reflect changes in how installations are operated, or for other reasons. The regulator may vary permit conditions at either its own or the operator's instigation.

- An operator who has a PPC permit must advise the regulator whenever he proposes a change in the operation of the installation which may have environmental consequences. If the change could result in a breach of the existing permit conditions, or if the regulator is likely to want to review the conditions in the light of the proposal, the operator is required to apply for a variation of the permit.

- If the change is likely to amount to a substantial change with negative environmental effects, the public and the statutory consultees will be given the opportunity to comment in an enhanced public consultation procedure.

- Regulators are required periodically to reconsider, and where necessary update, permit conditions.[47] Reviewing permits enables the regulator to check whether the conditions of a permit need to be changed to reflect developments in pollution abatement technology, scientific understanding of environmental effects, or other relevant issues.[48]

- An operator must apply to surrender the permit when he stops, or intends to stop, operating the installation. The operator is required to provide details as to how the site has changed since the original application, for example through the accumulation of additional pollution. The operator is required to identify steps that have been taken to avoid a continuing pollution risk from the installation, and to return it to a satisfactory state. The regulator must then decide whether to accept or refuse the surrender. Once the regulator has accepted a surrender application, the permit ceases to have effect.[49]

- The regulator is given a wide power to revoke a permit, in whole or in part, at any time by serving a written notice on the operator (known as a "revocation

---

[46] See Art. 9(8) and Reg.14.
[47] See Art. 13 and Reg.15.
[48] See DEFRA: *Integrated Pollution Prevention and Control—A Practical Guide*.
[49] The regulator also has power to specify steps that must be taken to restore a site in cases where a permit is revoked.

notice").[50] The effect is that the permit ceases to authorise the operation of the installation (or, if a partial revocation, ceases to authorise part of that operation, *i.e.* the carrying out of specified activities).

D: COMPLIANCE AND ENFORCEMENT

Compliance

The IPPC Directive imposes three general compliance obligations, but leaves further **5–031** provisions on compliance and enforcement to Member States.[51] Under the Directive, Member States are required to take necessary measures to ensure that:

(a) conditions of the permit are complied with by the operator when operating the installation;

(b) the operator regularly informs the regulator of the results of monitoring of emissions.[52] (He must also inform the regulator without delay of any incidents or accidents significantly affecting the environment); and

(c) the operator provides all necessary assistance to the regulator to carry out inspections at the installation, take samples, and gather necessary information. (Although not specifically referred to elsewhere in the Directive, this presupposes that regulators will carry out inspections.)

The PPC Regulations give effect to these obligations by placing the regulators under a duty to take "such action as a may be necessary" to ensure that the conditions of permits are complied with.[53] Operators must monitor emissions from their installations and supply the results to the regulators on a regular basis.[54] They must also inform the regulators without delay of any incidents or accidents which are causing, or may cause, significant pollution.[55] The existence of the regulators' duty to ensure compliance provides scope for challenge by way of judicial review, for example where local residents or environmental groups consider that the regulator has not taken sufficiently firm action in respect of a company which is creating pollution problems by failing to comply with the conditions of a permit.

Enforcement

Various powers are available to assist the regulators in discharging their duty to ensure **5–032** compliance:

---

[50] Regulation 21.
[51] See Art. 14.
[52] Permit Conditions must include requirements for operators to monitor releases.
[53] Guidance issued by DEFRA provides some indication as to the content of the duty, which includes a duty to review information from the operator and carry out independent monitoring and inspections.
[54] Regulation 12(9).
[55] Regulation 12(9).

- If the regulator is of the opinion that an operator has contravened, is contravening, or is likely to contravene, any of the conditions of a permit, it may serve an "enforcement notice".[56] This will outline the matters which amount to, or are likely to amount to, a breach of the permit, and will require specific steps to be taken, within a set period, to prevent the breach from continuing or arising. Failure to comply with the requirements of an enforcement notice is a criminal offence.[57]

- Where the regulator is of the opinion that the operation of the installation involves an imminent risk of serious pollution, it is under a duty, unless it intends to take steps itself to remove the risk, to serve a "suspension notice".[58] This effectively suspends the operation of an installation or part of the installation, and may be served even though there has been no breach of the permit.[59] Failure to comply with the requirements of a suspension notice is a criminal offence.[60] Suspension notices are not necessarily intended to be used as a punitive measure. Rather, they are available to be used in the unusual event that substances are present in the environment (for example as a result of an accident at another installation) which could react with those normally released from the installation in question, thereby creating a toxic effect. Although the installation in question may be being operated in accordance with its permit, its activities may need to be suspended to prevent a serious pollution incident.

- If, in the opinion of the regulator, the operation of an installation gives rise to an imminent risk of serious pollution, or if an operator operates an installation without a permit, a regulator may arrange for steps to be taken to remove the risk, and may recover the costs of doing so from the operator.[61]

- Regulators have various powers to investigate possible offences, including the power to search premises, seize equipment, require people to answer questions, and destroy equipment or substances if they are presenting an imminent danger of serious pollution or serious harm to human health.[62]

Appeals

5–033 The following people have the right to appeal to the Secretary of State against decisions made by the regulator:

- a person who has been refused the grant of a permit;

- a person who is aggrieved about the conditions attached to a permit, or about any variation of a permit;

- a person whose application to vary the conditions of a permit has been refused;

---

[56] Regulation 24.
[57] Regulations 24 and 32.
[58] Regulation 25.
[59] A suspension notice may also be served if the regulator is of the opinion that, as respects specified waste management activities, the operator of the activities has ceased to be a "fit and proper person".
[60] Regulations 25 and 32.
[61] Regulation 26.
[62] Regulation 26.

- a person whose application to transfer a permit has been refused, or who is aggrieved by the conditions attached to any transfer;

- a person whose request to initiate the closure procedure is not approved;

- a person on whom an enforcement, suspension or closure notice has been served.

The right to appeal is restricted to operators who have in some way been hampered in their ability to operate their installations as they wish. There is no right of appeal for third parties, such as local residents affected by permit conditions, such persons are able to make representations when operators apply for permits, or apply to vary permits, and the regulator is under a duty to consider these representations.[63] Anyone who has made representations at an earlier stage is entitled to make representations in any appeal by the operator, as is anyone else who appears to the Secretary of State to have a particular interest in the subject matter of appeal. This entitlement only arises, however, when an operator appeals. In the event that the operator is happy with the regulator's decision but third parties (*e.g.* local residents) are not, there is no appeal mechanism. The only avenue available to the third parties in such circumstances will be judicial review—which will not involve a review of the merits of the case, but simply a review of the decision-making process.

On determining an appeal, the Secretary of State has the power to do the following:

- Affirm the decision;

- Where the decision was a refusal to grant a permit or to vary the conditions of a permit, direct the regulator to grant the permit or vary its conditions, as the case may be.

- Where the decision was as to the conditions attached to a permit, quash all or any of the conditions of the permit;

- Where the decision was a refusal to effect the transfer, or accept the surrender of a permit, direct the regulator to effect the transfer or accept the surrender, as appropriate;

- In an appeal against a variation, revocation, enforcement, suspension or closure notice, quash or affirm the notice, either in its original form or with appropriate modifications.

An appeal against revocation of a permit has the effect of suspending that revocation until the withdrawal or final determination of the appeal, but appeals against enforcement, suspension and variation notices do not have the effect of suspending these notices. The same principle applies in the event of an appeal in relation to the conditions attached to a permit—the conditions continue to apply whilst the appeal is pending.[64]

---

[63] See paras 6.11 and 6.12 of Sch.4, and para.4 of Sch.7.
[64] Regulation 27(6)(7) and (8). The IPC regime did not specify whether conditions of an authorisation which had already been granted were to remain in force pending the outcome of an appeal. As with other points of procedure which were not clear under IPC, the opportunity has been taken, with the advent of PPC, to make necessary amendments and clarifications.

Criminal offences[65]

5–034 It is a criminal offence for a person to:

(1) operate an installation subject to PPC regulation without a permit;

(2) contravene or fail to comply with the conditions of a permit;

(3) fail to comply with the requirements of an enforcement notice, suspension notice, or a closure notice under the Landfill Regulations;

(4) make a change to an installation without notifying the regulator;

(5) fail, without reasonable excuse, to comply with a notice served by the regulator requiring the production of information;

(6) make false or misleading statements, falsify records or forge documents; and

(7) fail to comply with an order of a court, imposed alongside a criminal conviction for an offence listed at (1) to (3) above, requiring the operator to clean up the site (see below).

A prosecution against an operator can be brought either in the magistrates' court or the Crown Court. The maximum penalty for the first three offences listed above is a fine of £20,000 and six months' imprisonment if the offence is tried by magistrates, or an unlimited fine and five years' imprisonment where the offence is tried in the Crown Court. For the other offences, the maximum fine on conviction in the magistrates court is £5,000, or, in the Crown Court, an unlimited fine and imprisonment for two years. Where an offence has been committed by a company, and it is proved that it was committed with the "consent or connivance of" any director, manager, secretary or other similar officer of the company, or where the offence is attributable to neglect on their part, the company officer, as well as the company, will be guilty of the offence.

The nature of liability varies according to the PPC offence in question. For an operator to be guilty of operating without a permit; breaching a permit; breaching an enforcement, suspension or closure notice; or making a change to an installation without notifying the regulator, it is not necessary for the commission of the offence that the operator *intended* to carry out the relevant actions. There is no "reasonable excuse" defence, and the operator will be guilty of an offence even if the problem is caused, for example, by a contractor who carries out work in a way unbeknown to the company, or if the matters giving rise to the offence are due to the actions of vandals.

For the remaining offences, however, legal responsibility is imposed on a different basis. There is a "reasonable excuse" defence available to an operator who fails to comply with a request for information from the regulator. The offences relating to misleading statements, falsifying records and forging documents are only committed if the operator acts with intent to deceive, or acts knowing the statement to be false, or recklessly as to whether it is true or false.

Injunction in the High Court

5–035 If the regulator is of the opinion that prosecution will afford an inadequate remedy, the regulator may bring proceedings in the High Court to secure compliance with an enforcement notice, a suspension notice or a closure notice.[66] There is an obvious

---

[65] The regulator has a wide discretion to decide whether and how to take enforcement action. Where prosecution is not the most appropriate course of action, the regulator may issue a formal caution or a warning. Details of a formal caution will be placed on the public register.

[66] Regulation 33.

danger that operators who breach the conditions of their permit will treat financial penalties as part of the operating costs of an installation. It may be that, whilst the sanction of imprisonment is thought too draconian, the likely level of fine in respect of a breach is not sufficient to punish or deter by adversely affecting an operator's profit. This will be especially true in the case of large organisations although, for these companies, the adverse publicity associated with an environmental offence is a significant factor in determining behaviour.

Therefore, as an alternative or in addition to prosecution, the regulator may take proceedings against an operator in the High Court for an injunction ordering compliance with the requirements of an enforcement or a suspension notice.[67] In the event that an immediate shut-down of an installation is required to prevent a serious pollution incident, an injunction may prove to be an important means of securing compliance by a reluctant operator. However, the power to seek injunctions, which is also available under the IPC regime, has seldom been used.

Power of the court to order clean-up

Where an operator has been convicted of an offence involving failure to have a permit, **5–036** breach of a permit, or failure to comply with an enforcement, suspension or closure notice, the convicting court may, instead of or as well as imposing a penalty, order the convicted person to take specified steps within his power to remedy the matters which gave rise to the commission of the offence.[68]

E: INFORMATION AND PUBLICITY

The Secretary of State has the power to require the regulators to supply information **5–037** about their PPC regulatory activities for the purpose of discharging his functions.[69] In addition, the Secretary of State and the regulators are given extremely wide information-gathering powers—they may serve a notice under the regulations requiring "any person" to supply information.[70] The power is given, not only, as might be expected, for the purposes of enabling the Secretary of State and the regulator to discharge their PPC functions, but to enable the Secretary of State to comply with an obligation of the UK under any European or international agreement "relating to the environment" (*i.e.* not only those relating to PPC). In addition, the compilation of an inventory of emissions is treated as a function of the Environment Agency, so that they may require information necessary to achieve this. The information-gathering power extends to requiring any person to provide information on emissions where this information is not in his possession, or would not otherwise come into his possession, provided that it is information which it is reasonable to require that person to compile. This provision will capture operators who fail to keep records of their activities.

---

[67] Regulation 33.
[68] Regulation 35.
[69] Regulation 28.
[70] Regulation 28(2).

Public registers

5–038 Registers enable the public, including environmental pressure groups, to obtain information in order to scrutinise the effectiveness of the PPC regime. The regulators are under a duty to maintain public registers containing details of regulated installations.[71] Information will not be included on the registers if it is, in relation to a particular individual or business, commercially confidential, and if that person or business does not consent to its inclusion. However, the Secretary of State has the power to override this protection and direct that commercially confidential information be included on the register if its inclusion is in the public interest. This might be necessary, for example, following a major pollution incident when confidential information might need to be disclosed to allay public anxiety. Further relevant provisions on information and publicity are to be found in other legislation implementing the principles of the Aarhus Convention, discussed in Ch. 14.

F: THE FUTURE: BUILDING ON IPPC

5–039 It is possible to envisage an integrated environmental regulatory system which goes much further than IPPC. Both the IPPC Directive and the UK PPC regime may be viewed within the context of a wider IPPC *philosophy*. According to such a philosophy, the idea that environmental problems should be addressed in an integrated manner is not applied solely to regulating industrial activity by environmental licensing. Such a philosophy is perhaps best set out in a Recommendation adopted by the OECD in 1991, which advises member countries to:

> ". . . practice integrated pollution prevention and control, taking into account the effects of activities and substances on the environment as a whole and the whole commercial and environmental life-cycle of substances when assessing the risks they pose and when developing and implementing controls to limit their release."[72]

Such an approach implies that the following should be achieved:

- closer co-ordination of the activities of the environmental agencies with those of government departments dealing with environmental matters (*e.g.*, transport, agriculture, land-use planning, etc.);

- greater focus on the life-cycle of products, so as to enable the regulatory system to identify and mitigate the polluting effects of substances at any point in the chain of production, marketing and use. In this context, the EC is slowly developing a policy on assessing the environmental impacts of products on a "cradle to grave" basis;

[71] Regulation 29.
[72] OECD: *Recommendation of the Council on Integrated Pollution Prevention and Control* (January 31, 1991) C (90) 164 Final, at Recommendation I.

- more extensive monitoring, so as to detect and analyse the total effect of pollutants across different environmental media, including, for example, their impact on biodiversity;

- adoption of uniform risk-based standards to optimise decisions concerning the disposal of polluting substances, and greater reliance on comparative risk to help determine environmental priorities;

- regular environmental audits by corporations, and the development of incentives for corporations to undertake long-term environmental management strategies which address pollution prevention, waste reduction, and raw material, water and energy consumption.

Chapter 6

CONTAMINATED LAND

Introduction

Land contamination can occur in a number of different ways. It can be caused when, in **6–001** the course of industrial activity, pollutants are deliberately released, either in the form of dust, which settles on land, or in the form of liquids, which permeate land. In addition, substances may be released unintentionally when they leak or are spilled on land where they are stored.

Many contaminated sites are a legacy of land-use practice that is no longer current. Such sites include old gas works (used for producing "town gas" from coal, in the days before the switch to North Sea gas), asbestos works, and sites formerly used for the disposal of certain kinds of waste, in the days before it was scientifically recognised that such wastes posed an environmental problem (one example is the dumping of electronic components containing polychlorinated biphenyls or "PCBs"). Contamination is also likely where land has been used for oil refining, sewage treatment, as a petrol station, power station, iron and steel works, chemical works, or for heavy engineering.[1] A significant cause of land contamination has been the deliberate practice of burying waste in landfill sites. Most of the solid waste the UK produces has traditionally been disposed of in this way, and this has resulted in a considerable number of contaminated sites. Contaminated landfill sites present particular environmental problems because of the danger of explosions caused by the build-up of gas from decaying matter within the site and the likelihood of water pollution occurring when rainwater drains through the contaminated soil, carrying contaminants with it into the watercourse below.

A number of incidents in recent years have served vividly to illustrate the consequences of using land as a general repository for waste materials. In 1986, for example, an explosion destroyed a bungalow in Loscoe, Derbyshire. The three occupants survived, although they were trapped in rubble for a considerable time. An

---

[1] The House of Commons Environment Committee, in its report on contaminated land, listed 19 categories of land use which were said to represent the most common contaminating uses: see Session 1989–90 First Report Vol.I para.1.2. In addition to those mentioned above, the Committee listed petroleum refineries, metal products fabrication and finishing, textile plants, leather tanning works, timber treatment works, non-ferrous metals processing, manufacture of integrated circuits and semi-conductors, docks and railway land, paper and printing works, and processing radioactive materials.

investigation found the cause of the explosion to be gas from decomposing waste in a nearby landfill site. The incident at Loscoe had been preceded by events at Lekkerkerk, in the Netherlands. Between 1972 and 1975, 268 houses were built on the site of a forgotten chemical waste dump. Toxic chemicals leaked into the domestic water supply and caused illness among the residents. In 1980 it was discovered that some 1,600 drums, containing waste chemicals from the dyestuffs industry, had been deposited illegally on the site in the past. The site was finally evacuated in 1981, when the waste was removed at a cost (in 1981) of £156,000.[2]

A further striking example comes from the US: Between 1947 and 1953, nearly 22,000 tonnes of chemical waste was dumped on a site at Love Canal, in New York State. The site was then sold, on condition that it should never be disturbed. However, in the 1950s, shortly after the sale, a 16 acre development, comprising a school and houses, was built on the site. Residents reported illness in 1976. The basements of their houses smelt of chemicals and children came home from school with holes in their shoes caused by chemical burns. In 1978, children and expectant mothers were evacuated from the site and a state-sponsored clean-up programme was initiated which involved the evacuation of some 900 families and the demolition of hundreds of homes. The site was finally declared habitable in 1988 at a cost in excess of $250 million.[3]

Pollution of land poses a special danger to the environment because it is generally of a more permanent character than pollution of the other environmental media. Small doses of air or water pollution can sometimes be blown or washed away. Natural forces work to dilute and disperse pollution in these media so that its effect is diminished. This is seldom the case with pollution on land. Although accidental events like fires, floods and explosions can cause the migration of pollutants from land, they rarely leave behind them land in an unpolluted state. Awareness of soil contamination and the need to protect land from pollution has developed comparatively recently, compared with awareness of water and air pollution. This is partly because the link between air and water quality and human health was recognised earlier. The need for clean drinking water led to water protection measures in the 19th century. Air pollution led to an increase in respiratory diseases in industrialised countries in the 1950s and 1960s, which in turn led to legislative measures. However, a comparable direct exposure of humans to contaminants in soil seldom occurs. This is perhaps why it took so long before soil protection became an issue, both in scientific research and in policy making.[4]

Pollution of land raises two main issues:

- Managing current activities on land (*e.g.* through the PPC and waste management regimes—discussed elsewhere in this book) so as to prevent new contamination from industrial processes and waste disposal;

- Cleaning-up land that has been polluted in the past (known as "historically contaminated" land).

---

[2] Tromans and Turrall-Clarke, *Contaminated Land* (1994).
[3] *ibid.*
[4] See Peter E.T. Douben (ed.), *Pollution Risk Assessment and Management* (John Wiley & Sons Ltd, 1998).

This chapter focuses on the second of these issues, and in particular on the statutory clean-up regime in Pt IIA of the Environmental Protection Act 1990 (referred to in this Chapter as Pt IIA). Part IIA creates a regime where clean-up of land and protection of waters takes place in the public interest and where public authorities regulate the regime. This may be said to represent the UK's most sophisticated liability regime, with careful thought given to the modern realities of the patterns of land ownership. The regime is, however, consequently extremely complex. The sheer volume of regulation is daunting for the newcomer, and the regime involves a number of uncertain and interrelated concepts. Time will tell whether the authors of the regime have managed to think through every eventuality.

We have sought in this chapter to provide some clarity by offering the reader a gradual and compartmentalised introduction to this complexity. Consideration of procedures and offences is left until the end of the chapter. Inevitably, the accessibility afforded by this approach comes at the expense of some repetition in the text.

What is "contaminated land"?

There are two senses in which land might be said to be "contaminated". In a wide **6–002** sense, land might be thought of as contaminated simply because it contains substances which do not naturally belong there. In a narrower sense, however, land might be regarded as contaminated only if it causes or threatens environmental harm. It is this narrower view that is adopted by the statutory regime. As we shall see, in order to qualify as "contaminated land" for the purposes of the regime, land must be causing or threatening "significant harm" or be causing or threatening water pollution. This means that land which poses only a *potential* threat—because it contains potentially harmful substances, but these are causing no problems in the context of the land's current use—is not regarded as "contaminated" for the purposes of Pt IIA. Such land may, of course, become "contaminated" if and when it is subject to a new use— because then the substances may become a source of harm. In these circumstances, however, the contamination will normally be dealt with under the planning system (rather than under Pt IIA) by means of planning conditions requiring clean-up before change of use can proceed.

The extent of the problem

One of the effects of the Pt IIA regime is to lay down a single definition of **6–003** "contaminated land", so that, as, over a period of time, land is inspected by local authorities, an accurate picture will emerge of how much land is "contaminated" in terms of that definition. The absence of a common definition prior to the regime means that existing estimates of the extent of UK land contamination vary widely. Although in quite recent times the Environment Agency has reported that as many as 100,000 sites may have been polluted by past use,[5] not all of these sites will immediately qualify as "contaminated" under the regime, because in many cases they will be contaminated only in a wider sense—the contamination in question may be

---

[5] Environment Agency report: *Dealing with Contaminated Land*, 2002, Ch. 2.1.

insignificant or dormant—and will therefore fall outside the scope of the regime.[6] The thresholds for land to be determined as contaminated under the regime are set high, as will be seen.

Liability for contaminated land

6–004   Part IIA is not the only legal mechanism for imposing liability for contaminated land. Whether land is contaminated by current or past activities, liability for contaminated land can arise in three main ways:

(1) *Clean-up requirements imposed by statute*

6–005   Here, a distinction must be drawn between land that is "historically contaminated" (*i.e.* contaminated because of a past use that is no longer its current use) and land that becomes contaminated in the course of its current use. As has been said, Pt IIA of the Environmental Protection Act 1990 regulates only the clean-up of historically contaminated land. Land which is currently subject to waste management licensing, or which is being used for a process licensed under the PPC regime, is expressly excluded from the scope of Pt IIA.[7] Contamination arising in these contexts, therefore, will be dealt with under the appropriate alternative regime. Where historically contaminated land causes or threatens water pollution, there is a degree of overlap between Pt IIA and the water pollution regime. Such water pollution, and the land causing or threatening it, may be cleaned up either under Pt IIA or by means of a "works notice" served by the Environment Agency under the Water Resources Act 1991. Guidance issued by the Environment Agency, however, makes clear that when land has been identified as contaminated, under Pt IIA, the remediation notice procedure (discussed at the end of this chapter) should, in the main, be used.[8]

(2) *Criminal sanctions*

6–006   In addition to clean-up requirements, the environmental statutes contain provisions for criminal liability. These can be invoked for failure to comply with a notice requiring clean-up of historically contaminated land, or for breaching a condition in a current environmental licence (*e.g.* a PPC permit or a waste management licence) thereby causing contamination from a current use.

(3) *Civil liability*

6–007   Where individuals wish to seek compensation for the effects of land contamination, they can bring an action at common law (*e.g.* for nuisance). The common law, however, is of limited use in dealing with contaminated land, not least because the usual remedy of damages does not prevent environmental harm. Although there exists the possibility of a mandatory injunction to order clean-up of land, the courts have been reluctant to develop the common law as a widely-used mechanism for clean-up. The rules of negligence and nuisance have developed in a way that is ill-suited to imposing the kind

---

[6] See *Contaminated Land (England) Regulations 2000* and *Statutory Guidance: Regulatory Impact Assessment*, DEFRA.
[7] EPA 1990, s.78YB.
[8] See *Environment Agency Policy and Guidance on the Use of Anti-Pollution Works Notices*.

of strict, retrospective liability (see below) that is demanded by the problem of contaminated land. In particular, there are problems relating to proof of fault and varying standards of acceptable conduct (set by such criteria as the locality of the conduct and the sensitivity of the persons affected). As noted elsewhere in this book, the House of Lords in recent times has set its face against retrospective liability for historic pollution by emphasising that foreseeability of relevant harm is a prerequisite of liability under the rule in *Rylands v Fletcher*. Delivering his opinion in *Cambridge Water Company v Eastern Counties Leather*,[9] Lord Goff summed up the general attitude of the courts when he stated:

> "I incline to the opinion that, as a general rule, it is more appropriate for strict liability in respect of operations of high risk to be imposed by Parliament than by the courts. If such liability is imposed by statute, the relevant activities can be identified and those concerned know where they stand. Furthermore, statute can, where appropriate, lay down precise criteria establishing the incidence and scope of such liability."

Retrospective liability

It is appropriate here to note how unusual the Pt IIA regime is in allowing for the **6–008** imposition of retrospective liability. The effect of the regime is that people may find themselves liable for past conduct which, at the time it was undertaken, was not unlawful and may even have been in accordance with best practice at that time. In cases where a person is informed of some newly-discovered harmful effect of substances he deposited on land, it is irrelevant to liability under the regime that contamination was not foreseeable at the time those substances were deposited. Moreover, owners or occupiers may be fixed with liability for land in circumstances where, at the time they bought the land or came into occupation, the presence of substances in the land could not have given rise to liability.

It should be noted that this element of retrospectivity makes the regime quite distinct from other forms of strict (*i.e.* "no-fault") liability created by statute. Traditionally, where statutes have created strict liability, the risks inherent in the activity from which the liability arises are well known, so that the person who engages in the activity can make an informed decision about the likely costs of assuming the risk and insure himself accordingly. Traditional strict liability arises where the legislature has thought it appropriate to allocate the risk associated with a particular activity to one party (often the party who can abate or absorb the risk at least cost) rather than to another. This often occurs in the field of employers' liability. For example, in *John Summers & Sons v Frost*[10] it was held that the statutory duty created by s.14(1) of the Factories Act 1961 required an employer to guard a grinding wheel even though to do so would render the machine unusable.

Where, however, as a matter of policy, legislation operates to shift losses in this way, the philosophical justification for shifting the liability lies in the fact that the magnitude of the risk is foreseeable (and can be given a finite monetary value in terms of an

[9] [1994] 1 All E.R. 53.
[10] [1955] A.C. 740.

insurance premium), and the employer is free to make a business decision about whether or not to accept the risk as part of the price he pays for the profits he derives from his activities. Clearly this is not possible in relation to many environmental activities, the risks of which can often be appreciated only with hindsight, in the light of advances in scientific knowledge. This raises the controversial question of whether environmental regimes that impose retrospective liability are contrary to fundamental principles of fairness and natural justice. There can be no easy answer to this question, save to state that where environmental problems exist, they must be solved in the interests of society, and that political realities mean that no government wishing to remain electable could commit to financing environmental solutions entirely through general taxation. The inevitable consequence of this is that through retrospective liability an unlucky few are made to bear the cost of resolving environmental problems which are not solely their fault.

Development of the Part IIA regime

6–009 In 1989, a report by the House of Commons Select Committee on the Environment referred to a lack of clarity in relation to both policy and liability for contaminated land. Contamination of land was only subject to legal consideration when a site was to be developed. The report noted that:

> ". . . various pieces of legislation touch on the problem but the overall effect is patchy and little or no thought has been given to the big central questions such as who should pay for contaminated land."

The Committee recommended that urgent attention should be given to creating a statutory liability regime for damage caused by contaminated land. In addition, the Committee identified a startling lack of information about the extent of contaminated sites in the UK, and recommended that a duty should be placed on local authorities to identify, and compile registers of, all land which was contaminated.[11]

In 1990, the adoption of the Environmental Protection Act provided some scope for the regulation of contaminated land under the provisions relating to statutory nuisances. Contamination of land could constitute a statutory nuisance and, if so, local authorities were empowered to require owners or occupiers to clean up the contamination. However, the provisions were rarely used for this purpose and in any event meant that contaminated land was dealt with on an ad hoc basis.

The 1990 Act also saw the Government's first real attempt to address the problem of identifying the extent of the contaminated land problem. The Act (under s.143) required registers to be compiled of land which was being used in a way which had the potential to cause contamination. The decision to adopt an approach based on "potentially contaminating uses", rather than requiring registration of land "in a contaminated state" was a response to fears on the part of industrialists and property developers that land which was labelled "contaminated" by inclusion on a register would be subject to "property blight" and might effectively be unsaleable, regardless of the extent and nature of the contamination.

---

[11] House of Commons Environment Committee, Session 1989–1990, First Report, Vol.I, p.xi.

The gentleness of the government's approach, however, was not enough to allay developers' fears of blight being caused to their land simply by its having been identified as subject to a potentially contaminating use, and, for this reason, s.143 was never implemented.[12] The fears of the property world were to some extent justified: under s.143, all land that was subject to potentially contaminating uses was to be registered, regardless of whether or not actual contamination had occurred. Moreover, the scheme was incomplete, because it made no provision for remedial action to be taken in respect of land which was in fact contaminated.

In March 1993, the government, prompted by uncertainties affecting the land market, initiated a review of the issue of contaminated land.[13] Following a protracted consultation period, the government expressed its views in 1994 as follows:

"The statutory nuisance powers have provided an essentially sound basis for dealing with contaminated land. However, in order to improve clarity and consistency, the government now considers that it is necessary to replace these powers—in respect of contaminated land only—with a modern, specific contaminated land power."[14]

The modern contaminated land power

The Environment Act 1995 put in place a comprehensive regime for dealing with **6–010** contaminated land by inserting into the Environmental Protection Act 1990 a new Pt IIA. The Pt IIA regime came into force on April 1, 2000. It has, however, made rather a slow start, because of the need to secure funding and training for the local authorities involved in its implementation, and because, initially, local authorities have had to concentrate their limited resources on developing strategies and processes for inspecting land in their areas. Thus, by March 2002, only 33 sites in England had been designated as contaminated. Now that inspection strategies are in place, however, this figure is expected to increase.

It should be emphasised here that redevelopment still provides the main opportunity to deal with contamination. Under the planning system, when land is being redeveloped, the local planning authority is required to take into account the presence of contamination when deciding whether to grant planning permission. Almost all planning permission is subject to conditions, and the planning authority may impose conditions requiring the land in question to be cleaned up, so that it becomes suitable for its proposed new use.[15] Part IIA is intended to be supplementary to, rather than a replacement for, existing powers of local authorities to clean up contaminated land through planning law. As DETR Circular 02/2000 puts it:

---

[12] DoE Press Notice 209, March 24, 1993.
[13] See "Paying for our Past: the Arrangements for Controlling Contaminated Land and Meeting the Cost of Remedying Damage to the Environment" (DoE, March 1994).
[14] See Framework for Contaminated Land (DoE, November 1994).
[15] Guidance on the relationship between planning and environmental protection is provided in Planning Policy Guidance Note 23, "Planning and Pollution Control", which sets out the general requirements for dealing with contamination where a site is subject to a change of use.

"The regeneration process is already dealing with much of our inherited legacy of contaminated land. But there will be circumstances where contamination is causing unacceptable risks on land which is either not suitable or not scheduled for redevelopment."

The statutory contaminated land regime is created by detailed legislation, accompanied by lengthy guidance, and is to be found (in England[16]) in the following:

● Part IIA Environmental Protection Act 1990;

● Contaminated Land (England) Regulations 2000[17];

● DETR Circular 02/2000 Contaminated Land;

● Statutory Guidance.

Whilst the Circular *explains* the operation of the regime, the statutory guidance (which is found in Annex 3 of the Circular) *forms part of* the regime. It has been issued by the Secretary of State in accordance with his explicit power to do so under Pt IIA, having first been laid before both Houses of Parliament, as required by the legislation.[18]

The three policy questions

6–011 We have seen that contaminated land presents a number of difficult problems. In many cases, the activity which has caused the contamination occurred at a time when its danger was not appreciated. The original polluter may have disappeared (*e.g.* gone out of business), and in this event, the question arises whether responsibility for clean-up should rest with the taxpayer, or with the owner or occupier of the land. The decision whether and how to clean up the land may be hampered by the limits of scientific knowledge about how chemicals affect land, particularly in combination with one another. In addition, little might be known about the long term effects of low level exposure to many of these chemicals. To treat as "contaminated" all land that is no longer in its natural state, and to undertake to restore it to that state, would be prohibitively expensive. Moreover, given that in a modern society land is used for various different purposes, such an approach would be unnecessary.

All of these difficulties can be expressed in the form of three essential policy questions which the government had to face in deciding how to deal with contaminated land:

● When should land to be regarded as contaminated?

---

[16] The other regional regimes are similar to the English regime. Consideration of all the regional regimes is beyond the scope of a book of this nature. The relevant local rules in the UK are the Contaminated Land (Scotland) Regulations 2000 (SI/78), the Contaminated Land (Wales) Regulations 2001, SI/2197 (w.157), and the Contaminated Land (Northern Ireland) Order 1997, SI/2778.

[17] SI 2000/227. See also: Control of Pollution (Oil Storage) (England) Regulations 2001, SI/2954; Contaminated Land (England) (Amendment) Regulations 2001, SI/663. For the rest of the UK, see Waste and Contaminated Land (Northern Ireland) Order 1997, SI/2778; Contaminated Land (Scotland) Regulations 2000, SI/178; Contaminated Land (Wales) Regulations 2001, SI/2197.

[18] EPA 1990, s.78YA.

- Who should be made responsible for cleaning up the contamination?

- To what standard should the land be cleaned up?

Each of these questions is explored in its own section below.

The "suitable for use" approach

The government's approach to the first and third policy questions, namely the **6–012** questions as to when land should be regarded as contaminated and to what standard it should be cleaned up, is based on the idea of "suitability for use". This approach recognises that hazards presented by land contamination vary greatly according to the use of the land. Take the example of a scrapyard contaminated by traces of metal. No hazard is present if the land continues to be used as a scrapyard, or if an office block is built on the site; but there would be a hazard if the land were used to grow crops. Hazards will also vary depending upon other factors such as the geology of a site. All of this means that decisions as to whether land should be regarded as "contaminated" and decisions about what, if any, clean-up measures are needed, require site-specific risk assessment.

A: WHEN SHOULD LAND BE REGARDED AS "CONTAMINATED"?

The statutory definition of "contaminated land"

As has been said, contaminated land is defined in relatively narrow terms under the **6–013** statutory regime. For the purposes of Pt IIA, contaminated land is defined as land which appears to the local authority in whose area it is situated to be in such a condition, by reason of substances in, on or under it, that either:

- it is causing significant harm, or there is a significant possibility of such harm being caused, or

- it is causing or is likely to cause pollution of controlled waters.[19]

Within each of the two categories of contamination (harm and water pollution) there are, in effect, two sub-categories ("actually causing" and "potentially causing"). Thus, we can say that land is "contaminated" for the purposes of Pt IIA if it produces any one of the following four effects:

- it is causing significant harm;

- it presents a significant possibility of significant harm being caused;

- it is causing pollution of controlled waters;

- it is likely to result in pollution of controlled waters.

[19] EPA 1990, s.78A(2).

The Act goes on to state that "in determining whether any land appears to be such land, a local authority shall . . . act in accordance with guidance issued by the Secretary of State". The guidance, as we shall see, introduces some further refinements.

"Harm-based" contamination

6–014 Harm is defined as:

> "harm to the health of living organisms or other interference with the ecological systems of which they form part and, in the case of man, includes harm to his property."[20]

Unlike the definition of harm for the PPC regime, offence to the senses of man does not constitute harm. This omission was motivated by the government's desire to prevent land from being regarded as contaminated merely because it is the source of a foul odour or is unpleasant to look at. The thresholds for harm are set high. To be contaminated, land must be causing *significant* harm or presenting a *significant possibility* of significant harm.

Water pollution

6–015 The second category of contamination occurs where land is causing or likely to cause pollution of controlled waters. Such pollution is defined as "the entry into controlled waters of any poisonous, noxious or polluting matter or any solid waste matter".[21] Controlled waters include ground water, territorial waters, coastal waters and inland waters.

The statutory guidance provides that, in order to make a determination that substances in, on or under the land are causing or likely to cause water pollution, the local authority must be satisfied that the substances are continuing to enter, or are likely to enter, controlled waters. Once a substance is already present in controlled waters, and no further entry is likely, the contaminated land regime is not the appropriate regime to deal with the problem (a "works notice" may be served under the Water Resources Act 1991[22]). Substances are to be regarded as having entered water when they are dissolved or suspended in water or, if they cannot mix with water, once they have direct contact with the water, either on or beneath it.

Perhaps as a legacy of the UK's traditional approach to water pollution (which has been to frame pollution offences very strictly, leaving enforcing authorities discretion as to whether to prosecute), the contaminated land regime draws no distinction between significant and insignificant water pollution. Land causing or likely to cause *any* water pollution, however minor, will be treated as "contaminated" under Pt IIA. This approach differs from that taken for "harm-based" contamination, which requires the impact of the contamination to be "significant". The government is proposing to

[20] *ibid.*, s.78A(4).
[21] *ibid.*, s.78A(9).
[22] Water Resources Act 1991, ss.161—161D.

amend the legislation to end this anomaly. However, the anomaly is not, perhaps, so important as it might seem, given the existence in Pt IIA of a safeguard to prevent unnecessary clean-up of insignificant water pollution, namely the provision that clean-up cannot be required where its cost would be unreasonable, having regard to the nature of the water pollution in question.[23] A further legacy of the traditional approach to water pollution is that the "suitable for use" approach does not apply where land is causing or threatening water pollution. The existence or likelihood of water pollution does not depend on the use to which the water receiving the pollution (or the land causing the pollution) is being put.[24]

The concept of a "significant pollutant linkage"

The Circular and statutory guidance clarify the circumstances in which land will be **6–016** regarded as contaminated by introducing the concept of a "significant pollutant linkage". This concept is also important in understanding how, in complex cases, liability is allocated between different persons responsible for the state of the land (discussed below).

In order for land to be classified as "contaminated", local authorities (whose job it is to identify such land) must establish the existence of at least one "pollutant linkage". This involves showing that a particular substance (referred to in the guidance as a "pollutant") is causing or threatening harm to a particular thing (a "receptor"), in a particular way (by means of a "pathway" leading from the pollutant to the receptor). It should be remembered that the term "pollutant linkage" refers to the *entire combination* of all three elements—pollutant, pathway and receptor. Only if all three elements are present can land be said to be "contaminated".

If one or more pollutant linkages have been established, what happens next will depend on whether the linkages are causing or threatening water pollution. Where this is so, the land will be classified as contaminated. However, in the absence of water pollution, the authority must go on to assess whether the pollutant linkages are *significant*. In a case where harm is actually occurring, this involves referring to the statutory guidance to see whether the harm in question is a type of harm that should be treated as "significant" in relation to the receptors being affected by it (see below). In cases where there is only the *possibility* of significant harm, the authority must consider whether this possibility amounts to a "significant possibility". This involves considering the potential presence of receptors, how susceptible the receptors might be to suffering the harm, the timescale over which harm might occur, and the seriousness of the consequences if harm does occur.

Permissible receptors

The guidance limits the scope of the regime by narrowly defining the range of **6–017** "receptors" a local authority can consider in establishing a pollutant linkage. Only the following can be regarded as receptors affected by land contamination:

- controlled waters;

---

[23] EPA 1990, s.78E(4).
[24] Note, however, that in practice s.78E(4) might be applied so as to take account of whether the pollution in question is jeopardising the relevant waters' "quality classification" as suitable for a particular use.

- human beings;

- sites protected under nature conservation law (*e.g.* SSSIs, and nature reserves);

- buildings;

- certain forms of property (namely crops, including timber; produce grown domestically or on allotments for consumption; livestock; other owned or domesticated animals; and wild animals which are the subject of shooting or fishing rights).

This means, for example, that harm to unowned, wild animals outside protected sites is to be disregarded in determining whether land is contaminated, as is harm to people's personal property. Damage to the biodiversity of farmland or gardens will also be disregarded.

Permissible types of significant harm

6–018   As has been said, where controlled waters are the receptor, the question of "harm" (and therefore of its "significance") does not arise. In relation to other receptors, however, the guidance sets out which types of harm are to be regarded as significant in relation to each receptor. In the case of man, for example, the only relevant considerations are death, disease, serious injury, genetic mutation, birth defects or impairment of reproductive functions. In the case of the relevant types of property, harm will only be significant where, for example, there is a substantial diminution in its value (*e.g.* a 20 per cent loss in the value of crops). In the case of buildings, only structural failure, or damage such as to make the building unfit for use, can be regarded as significant. In relation to protected nature conservation sites, harm will only be significant if, for example, it amounts to an irreversible adverse change in the functioning of a habitat, or in a long-term decline in the population of a species on the site.

Multiple "significant pollutant linkages"

6–019   In a simple case, there may only be one significant pollutant linkage—made up of a single substance, affecting a single type of receptor, by means of a single pathway. In other cases, however, the position can be much more complex—there may be a number of different substances, causing or threatening harm to a number of different receptors, by means of a number of pathways. In a such cases, therefore, a local authority will establish the existence of multiple significant pollutant linkages. It will be recalled that a linkage is defined as the combination of a substance (a "pollutant"), pathway and receptor. This means that, where there is more than one substance, there will, by definition, be a different linkage in relation to each substance (although the authority may treat similar substances as one substance in certain circumstances). In some cases, all these separate linkages may share a common pathway and receptor. In other cases, however, each substance, or a group of substances, may have any number of different or shared pathways or receptors. The existence of multiple linkages has important implications for determining liability for clean-up, because liability will be assessed separately in relation to each linkage. This is considered in the section below.

B: WHO SHOULD BE MADE RESPONSIBLE FOR THE CONTAMINATION?

General exemptions from the scope of the regime

Before considering the statutory scheme of responsibility, it is important to note some **6–020** general limitations on its scope. No liability can arise for contaminated land in the following situations:

- Where there is water pollution from an abandoned mine[25];

- Where the contamination in question is radioactivity[26];

- Where the person who might otherwise be made responsible for the contamination was "acting in a relevant capacity" (for example, as an insolvency practitioner or official receiver) and did nothing unreasonable while so acting[27];

- Where the contamination results from an activity subject to a waste management licence currently in force, or from any activity regulated by the IPC or PPC regimes where enforcement action may be taken under those regimes[28];

- In any case where clean-up requirements would be unreasonably costly, having regard to the seriousness of the harm or water pollution in question.[29]

Subject to these general exceptions (and a number of more specific ones, mentioned below), Pt IIA places liability on persons whom a local authority identifies as being "appropriate persons" to take responsibility for the contamination. There are two types of "appropriate persons": Class A persons and Class B persons.

Class A and Class B "appropriate persons"

Contaminated land is often the result of activities that took place many years ago. **6–021** Often, the original polluters of the land cannot be found. This creates an obvious difficulty in giving effect to the "polluter pays" principle. However, Pt IIA makes an attempt to reconcile the implementation of this principle with the practical need to identify a person on whom to place responsibility for contaminated land.

The regime adopts a hierarchical approach towards apportioning liability. In the first instance, liability will be placed on "Class A Appropriate Persons". These are persons who have "caused or knowingly permitted" the presence of the substances "by reason of which the contaminated land in question is such land".[30] As we shall see, interpreting these words involves some complexity—such persons need not necessarily

---

[25] *ibid.*, s.78J. An "abandoned mine" for these purposes is one that was abandoned on or after December 31, 1999.

[26] *ibid.*, s.78YC.

[27] *ibid.*, s.78X(3) and (4).

[28] *ibid.*, s.78YB.

[29] *ibid.*, s.78E(4).

[30] *ibid.*, s.78F(2).

be those responsible for the original *entry* of the substances. It is causing or knowingly permitting the "presence" of substances that is important. This issue is discussed in its own section below.

If, after reasonable enquiry, no "Class A Appropriate Persons" can be found, the *owners or occupiers* of the land become "appropriate persons".[31] Owners or occupiers are known as "Class B Appropriate Persons". The idea of placing liability on an owner or occupier who is not at fault in having caused or permitted the contamination was sharply criticised, during the passing of the legislation, by the Earl of Lytton, who said:

> ". . . making an economic scapegoat out of an individual for matters which in times gone by were at least partly a collective responsibility is wrong as a general principle. I have to say that I do not think it would work in practice."[32]

In some cases, it may be that nobody in either class of appropriate persons can be made responsible for a particular pollutant linkage. This might happen, for example, where no Class A persons can be found, and the linkage is causing water pollution only (for which Class B persons cannot be made responsible[33]). In such circumstances, the linkage will be an "orphan linkage", and the enforcing authority itself will have to pay if it wants the land cleaned up.

Liability of Class A appropriate persons: "causing or knowingly permitting"

6–022 Causing or knowingly permitting has been used as a basis for establishing liability in environmental legislation for more than 100 years. As well as being central to determining liability under Pt IIA, it is used in a number of other environmental regimes, most notably the water pollution regime. DETR Circular 02/2000 encourages an interpretation of the phrase for the purposes of Pt IIA based on case law decided under other legislation. Some guidance may therefore be derived from water pollution case law.

It should be remembered, however, that in the water pollution cases, the phrase has been interpreted in the context of deciding whether a defendant has committed a criminal offence (polluting controlled waters). The contaminated land regime calls for interpretation in a slightly different context. This is because being identified as a "Class A Appropriate Person" does not, of itself, imply the commission of a criminal offence (although in certain circumstances an offence may also have been committed). Under Pt IIA, criminal proceedings do not enter the picture unless and until a person identified as an appropriate person fails to comply with a formal notice requiring the land to be cleaned up (a "remediation notice"). One implication of this is that, at the stage of identifying "Class A Appropriate Persons", the relevant standard of proof is the balance of probabilities. Another may be that the phrase will be subject to a subtly different interpretation. Circular 2/2000 states:

> "It is ultimately for the courts to decide the meaning of 'caused' and 'knowingly permitted' as these terms apply to the Part IIA regime".[34]

---

[31] *ibid.*, s.78F(4).
[32] *Hansard*, H.L., Vol.559 col.1424. (December 15, 1994.)
[33] EPA, 1990, s.78J.
[34] Circular 2/2000 Annex 2, para.9.15.

It is unclear, however, at what stage in the operation of the regime it is envisaged that they will have the opportunity to do so. One such opportunity might arise where local authorities' identification of appropriate persons (and resulting appeals against remediation notices) are challenged by judicial review. Another might arise where defendants charged with failure to comply with a remediation notice plead wrongful identification as an appropriate person as a "reasonable excuse". In the latter case, there may well be a difficult issue concerning the applicable standard of proof. This is considered later in the chapter, in the context of prosecutions under the regime.

In light of all this, it is difficult to give any definitive indication of how the phrase "caused or knowingly permitted" should be construed in the context of Pt IIA. The following points, however, if treated with suitable caution, may be of some assistance:

Causing or knowingly permitting "substances" not "contamination"

The legislation imposes liability on those who have "caused or knowingly permitted the **6–023** substances, of any of the substances, by reason of which the contaminated land in question is such land to be in, on or under that land".[35]

The reference to substances, rather than *contaminants*, means that a person does not need to know that the substances are a source of contamination to be liable as an appropriate person. It is sufficient that he causes or knowingly permits the substances to be there.

"Causing"

Circular 2/2000 states that: **6–024**

> "In the Government's view the test of 'causing' will require that the person concerned was involved in some active operation or series of operations to which the presence of the pollutant is attributable. Such involvement may also take the form of a failure to act in certain circumstances."

Whether a person caused the presence of substances is a question of fact. Case law establishes that "causing" in the context of water pollution is an offence of strict liability.[36] In other words, it is sufficient that the defendant is involved in conducting an operation that gives rise to the pollution, whether or not he intended or was careless as to whether the pollution occurred. Thus, there can be liability even where the defendant has behaved impeccably and taken all reasonable steps to prevent the escape of substances.[37] Provided a defendant has a sufficient degree of involvement with an operation on land, he may be guilty of "causing", even where the escape of pollution arises because of a natural event, or the act of a trespasser.

The decision of the House of Lords in *Empress Car Company (Abertillery) Ltd v National Rivers Authority*,[38] a water pollution case, contains the most recent pronouncement on causation, and is considered in Ch. 8. In essence, "causing" is a question of

---

[35] section 78F(2).
[36] See *Alphacell v Woodward* [1972] A.C. 824.
[37] See, for example, *CPC (UK) Ltd v National Rivers Authority* [1995] Env. L. R. 131.
[38] [1997] 2 A.C. 27.

common sense and depends on whether the person in question can be said to have "done something". It need not be the case that the person in question did something which was an immediate cause of the pollution. Maintaining tanks or sewage systems is "doing something". If the immediate cause of the pollution is the act of a third party, whether that act relieves the person in question of responsibility depends on whether the act may be regarded as a normal fact of life (*e.g.* vandalism) or something extraordinary (*e.g.* terrorism).

"Knowingly permitting"

6–025 Circular 2/2000 states[39]:

> ". . . the test of "knowingly permitting" would require both knowledge that the substances in question were in, on or under the land and the possession of the power to prevent such a substance being there."

This statement requires clarification. On one view, the statement might imply a very restrictive approach. This is because it might be thought that a "power to prevent such a substance being there" can only sensibly mean a power to physically remove the substance (or—which amounts to the same thing—a power to treat the substance so as to change it into something else). It is unlikely, however, that this is what is meant. Such an approach would be inconsistent with the proposition that clean-up (discussed below) need not involve the removal or treatment of substances, but simply the removal of the contamination problem by taking action in respect of pathways or receptors—for example, erecting a fence to stop children entering a brownfield site would break the link between the pathway (access to the brownfield site) and the receptors (children). What is probably meant, therefore, is that the test is satisfied by knowledge, plus the power to prevent the land in question being "contaminated land".

Again, case law decided in other contexts can serve only as a rough guide, but yields the following indicators of how the phrase might be construed:

(1) *Knowingly*

6–026 The relevant knowledge may include:

- actual knowledge that substances are entering or are present in land; or

- constructive knowledge, *i.e.* where the court presumes the existence of knowledge because, in the circumstances, a reasonable person would be expected to have such knowledge.[40] One example of this might be where a person suspects the presence of contamination, but deliberately refrains from inquiry so as not to have his suspicion confirmed.[41]

The knowledge may relate to:

[39] citing Earl Ferrers in *Hansard*, H.L., Vol.565 col 1497 (July 11, 1995).
[40] See *Kent CC v Beaney* [1993] Env. L.R. 225.
[41] See *Westminster City Council v Croyalgrange Ltd* [1986] 1 W.L.R. 674 and *Taylor's Central Garages (Exeter) Ltd v Roper* [1951] T.L.R. 284.

- a current state of affairs by which contaminants are entering land;
- the entry of contaminants at a time in the past; or
- the presence of contaminants in land.

Corporate knowledge

Where the potential "appropriate person" is a company, the question arises: who must **6–027** know about the contamination in order for the company to knowingly permit its presence? Does the contamination need to be known about by a director or senior manager (*i.e.* a person of such seniority that their state of mind will constitute the state of mind of the company) or is it enough that site operatives know about the contamination?

In environmental cases involving corporate knowledge, there is a tendency for the courts to hold that knowledge at site level is sufficient, provided that the person who acquires the knowledge has some power to make relevant decisions. For example, in *Shanks & McEwan (Teeside) Ltd v Environment Agency*,[42] a prosecution for an illegal deposit of waste, the court held that a company in the business of accepting waste had corporate knowledge in respect of a specific illegal deposit when it was accepted by a site supervisor in the absence of the site manager.

Permitting

- A person does not "permit" what he cannot control.[43] Therefore, in order to **6–028** permit contamination he must have the ability to prevent it, for example by removing or treating the substances, blocking the pathways, or removing the receptors.

- A person need not "agree" to the presence of contamination in order to "permit" it. Thus, in a situation where contamination is present against a person's wishes, he may nevertheless "permit" its presence.[44]

- The steps it is reasonable to take to prevent contamination (*i.e.* failure to take which will result in "permitting") will depend upon all the circumstances of the case.[45]

- An owner or occupier who enters into a contract by which he allows contaminants to be placed in, on, or under land may "knowingly permit",[46] but a lender who lends money to facilitate such a use of land will not "permit" the contamination simply by reason of the loan.[47]

Knowingly permitting the "presence" of substances

Circular 2/2000 states: **6–029**

---

[42] [1997] Env. L.R. 305; [1999] Q.B. 333.
[43] See *Vehicle Inspectorate v Nuttall* [1999] 1 W.L.R. 629.
[44] See *Alphacell v Woodward* [1972] A.C. 824.
[45] *Vehicle Inspectorate v Nuttall* [1999] 1 W.L.R. 629.
[46] *Price v Cromack* [1975] 2 All E.R. 113.
[47] Circular 2/2000, citing Earl Ferrers in *Hansard*, H.L., Vol.565 col 1497 (July 11, 1995) who states that although a lender may have the power to *restrict* contaminative use (by requiring environmental covenants as conditions of the loan) he will normally have no *permissive* powers in relation to the land subject to the loan. In the light of this reasoning, it is strange that the drafters of the statutory guidance should have felt it necessary to make explicit provision for lenders to be excluded from Class A liability groups (see below).

"In the context of Part IIA, what is 'caused or knowingly permitted' is the *presence* of a pollutant in, on or under the land."[48]

This requires some clarification. The problem with extending liability to the *presence* of substances, and not limiting it to the *entry* of substances to the land, is that doing so blurs the distinction between "knowing permitters" and owners or occupiers of land (Class B Appropriate Persons). This statement in the Circular is capable of meaning that a person might knowingly permit the presence of contaminating substances simply by owning or occupying land, in circumstances where he has the power to deal with the contamination but fails to do so.

The gist of the Circular and guidance seems to be that this can only happen in certain limited circumstances, namely those in which an owner or occupier has "the ability to deal with the contamination". This, however, is conceptually unsatisfactory, because the very notions of "ownership" and "occupation" in law imply the existence of a high degree of ability to deal with what is owned or occupied. In many situations where a person is in occupation of contaminated land, that person will be able to "deal with the contamination"[49] in the sense that he could easily stop the land from being classified as "contaminated" (harmful as currently used) by the simple but drastic expedient of coming out of occupation, removing all receptors, and turning the land into a no-go area behind suitable barricades. Can it then be said that by reason of possessing this ability, he causes or knowingly permits the land to be contaminated? This is an important question, because, if the answer is "yes", he may, as a Class A Appropriate Person, have to share liability with the identifiable rogues who dumped chemicals on his land in the middle of the night. But if the answer is "no", they alone will have liability.

During the passage of the legislation, an amendment was put forward which would have made it clear that persons could only be categorised as Class A Appropriate Persons if they had caused or knowingly permitted the *original entry* of substances. In speaking against this amendment, Viscount Ullswater, for the government, stated that its effect would be to exempt too many categories of people who should be held responsible. His Lordship stated:

"We believe it would be reasonable for somebody who has had active control over contaminants on a site, for example, when redeveloping it, to become responsible for any harm to health or the environment that may result, even if he did not originally cause or knowingly permit the site to become contaminated".[50]

---

[48] Circular 2/2000 Annex 2, para.9.8 (original emphasis).
[49] The Circular, confines itself to stating that a person does not "knowingly permit" contamination simply by reason of being notified that his land is contaminated, and that the test of "knowingly permitting" will only be satisfied where a person has the "ability to deal with the contamination and has had a reasonable opportunity to do so".
[50] *Hansard*, H.L., Vol.560 col 1461. (January 31, 1995).

His Lordship's statement contains the assumption, perhaps, that in order to be made responsible for causing or knowingly permitting, a person must, by involvement with some new activity in relation to land, cause or permit the land to *change* from a state in which contamination is present but dormant, into a state whereby the land is contaminated in the statutory sense of presenting a hazard. Such an approach to interpreting the legislation would produce coherence. It would avoid blurring the distinction between Class A and Class B liability, because a person who, by undertaking new activity, causes or permits land to *become* "contaminated land" is in the same conceptual position as a person who does so by allowing the entry of substances. It is far from clear, however, that this is the approach which has been prescribed.

Arguably, much of the confusion stems from the primary legislation's preoccupation with liability for "substances". One cannot escape the feeling that the primary legislation might have been conceived without sufficient thought to how its meaning would be extended by subsequent guidance. The combination of the primary legislation and the guidance means that, in effect, a person can be made responsible in law for the "presence of a substance", even though, in common-sense terms, all he is in fact responsible for is the presence of something else, namely pathways or receptors which make that substance a problem. This approach makes for some rather convoluted statutory interpretation, which might have been avoided if the primary legislation had introduced the concept of a "significant pollutant linkage" and proceeded to create liability for causing or knowingly permitting the presence of any one of the three elements (pollutant, pathway, receptor) that go to make up that linkage. As things stand, however, we have a statute framed in terms of liability for substances, but guidance framed in terms of liability for linkages, which is unsatisfactory and needlessly complex.

In practice, the purpose of framing primary "knowing permitter" liability in such wide terms appears to be to capture former owners who have no current connection with the land, but whose past activities give rise to a responsibility for clean-up and who have the resources necessary to pay for it. Moreover, it also allows current owners or occupiers of the land to be "moved up" from secondary liability to primary knowing permitter liability if they become aware of the contamination but do nothing about it for a period of time.[51]

Liability of Class B "Appropriate Persons"

Current owners and occupiers of land will only be made responsible for contamination **6–030** if, after reasonable inquiry, no Class A Appropriate Persons can be found. The Circular indicates that "found" in this context means that a Class A person must still exist (as opposed to merely being identified). Therefore, owners or occupiers may be liable where the original polluter has died or, in the case of a company, been dissolved.[52] It is clear that local authorities will need to demonstrate that they have

---

[51] The guidance makes clear that service of a notice under Pt IIA is not enough to move the recipient into the sphere of knowing permitter liability.

[52] The guidance envisages, however, that in some circumstances it may be appropriate to make the estate of a deceased person liable, or seek annulment of an order dissolving a company.

made reasonable enquiries to identify Class A Appropriate Persons before any Class B liability can arise. Although ultimately a question for the courts, this is likely to involve land registry searches, company searches, and interviews with local residents or former employees of suspected polluting companies.

An "owner" is defined as a person who is entitled to receive a market rent for the land (as opposed to a token, or "peppercorn" rent). Mortgagees not in possession are expressly excluded from the definition.[53] The term "occupier" is not defined, but by analogy to relevant case law, its definition is likely to be associated with control of the land.[54] The term does not necessarily imply physical occupation[55] or a right to exclusive possession.[56]

It should be noted that owners and occupiers cannot be required to clean up contaminated land which is causing only water pollution.[57] Nor can they be made responsible for cleaning up other people's land in cases where contamination has escaped to their own land from other land.[58] Thus, in either of these circumstances, the enforcing authority will have to undertake remediation itself if it wants the land cleaned up.

Allocation of responsibility: "liability groups"

6–031   In a complex case, authorities may find themselves in a position where, in relation to each significant pollutant linkage identified, there is more than one potential appropriate person. There will therefore be a "liability group" in relation to each linkage. In such circumstances, the authority must determine, in accordance with the statutory guidance, whether one or more members of each liability group should be absolved from responsibility. Once these exclusion decisions have been taken, liability for clean-up in relation to each linkage is apportioned between the members of the liability group who remain. The guidance sets out a number of tests which the authority must apply, in a prescribed order, so as to decide whether certain types of persons should be excluded from a liability group. It is not possible for everyone in a liability group to be excluded—there must always be someone left in the group to take responsibility for the contamination. The idea of the exclusion provisions is that, where there are a large number of persons who might be regarded as having caused or knowingly permitted the contamination, the authority will exclude from liability those persons who might be perceived as less blameworthy. In the case of multiple owners or occupiers, the idea is to exclude persons who will derive no financial benefit from clean-up of the land.

The guidance lays down different exclusion tests for Class A and Class B liability groups. It is important to remember that in respect of each significant pollutant linkage, the authority will consider *either* the Class A liability group exclusion rules *or* the Class B liability group exclusion rules. This is because, where Class A persons are found in relation to a linkage, responsibility for clean-up must always rest with them. There is no question of excluding all the members of a Class A liability group so as to

---

[53] EPA 1990, s.78A.
[54] *Wheat v E. Lacon & Co. Ltd* [1966] A.C. 552.
[55] *Harris v Birkenhead Corp.* [1976] 1 W.L.R. 279.
[56] *Hartwell v Grayson Rollo and Clover Docks Ltd* [1947] K.B. 901.
[57] EPA 1990, s.78J.
[58] *ibid.*, s.78K.

place liability on Class B owners or occupiers. It should also be remembered that a particular person may be a member of more than one liability group, because he is responsible for the presence of more than one linkage. The guidance makes it clear that a person's exclusion from liability in respect of one linkage does not imply that he will necessarily be excluded from groups responsible for other linkages.

Class A liability groups: exclusion and apportionment

Exclusion from liability

The guidance lays down six tests which the authority must apply (in the sequence set **6–032** out below) in order to determine whether any persons who have been identified as having potentially caused or knowingly permitted the contamination should be absolved from responsibility. In certain circumstances the effect of exclusion is to extinguish a person's liability completely, whilst in other circumstances liability is transferred from one group member to another.

(*a*) Test 1: "Excluded activities"

This test excludes from liability people who could conceivably be described as having **6–033** caused or knowingly permitted the presence of the substances, but whose involvement is peripheral, for example: lenders; insurers; authorities who have granted permission for polluting activity; lawyers; scientific consultants and other advisers; and in some cases landlords and contractors.

(*b*) Test 2: "Payments made for remediation"

The guidance states: "The purpose of this test is to exclude from liability those who **6–034** have already, in effect, met their responsibilities by making certain kinds of payment to some other member of the liability group." Hence, the test excludes any member of the liability group who has paid another group member a sum sufficient to cover the cost of full clean-up. Where this test is applied, the person who has received the payment for clean-up, but failed to perform it, takes on the excluded person's share of responsibility as well as his own. It counts as a "payment" for the purposes of this test if the land has been sold to another member of the liability group at a reduced price, and the price reduction was explicitly stated to be for covering the cost of clean-up.

(*c*) Test 3: "Sold with information"

This test excludes any liability group member who has sold the land to another group **6–035** member with adequate information about the contamination. The idea here is that the buyer will have had the *chance* to negotiate a price reduction. The guidance states that large commercial organisations or public bodies buying from another group member since the beginning of 1990 will normally be presumed to have known about contamination if they were given the seller's permission to carry out site investigations (it being irrelevant whether or not they actually did so). This test can also apply where land is let on a long lease (for more than 21 years) rather than sold freehold. Where the test applies, the responsibility for contamination previously borne by the excluded person is transferred to the person who has bought the land with information.

(*d*) *Tests 4, 5 and 6: "changes to substances"; "escaped substances"; "introduction of pathways or receptors"*

6–036 These tests can be considered together, because they all have a similar effect: they operate to exclude a group member when, although he caused or knowingly permitted the presence of substances, the relevant significant pollutant linkage only exists because of the conduct of another group member.

Test 4 applies where the significant pollutant linkage only exists because of a reaction caused by later introduction of another substance. Thus, where group member A has caused or knowingly permitted the presence of substance X, but the relevant linkage only exists because of a reaction between substance X and substance Y, a substance subsequently introduced by group member B, the test works to extinguish the liability of group member A.

Test 5 applies where the only reason a person is a member of the group is that he caused or knowingly permitted substances to be on land *other than the contaminated land*, and they have escaped from that other land to the contaminated land. Such a person will be excluded from liability where another group member is responsible for the escape.

Test 6 applies where another group member has carried out development on land (including any change of use requiring planning permission) and the relevant linkage is only established because of that development. Thus, for example, the test might exclude a group member who caused or knowingly permitted the presence of substances on a vacant brownfield site, where the substances did not give rise to a significant pollutant linkage (there being no receptors or pathways present) until another group member developed the site for residential use.

Apportionment of liability

6–037 Once the exclusion tests have been applied, more than one person may remain in the liability group. If so, the authority must apply the apportionment rules set out in the statutory guidance, so as to fairly divide responsibility for clean-up. The guidance does not attempt to prescribe apportionment rules that will be fair and appropriate in all cases, but states that liability should be apportioned to reflect the relative responsibility of the group members for the risk presented by the significant pollutant linkage in question.

The guidance outlines a number of specific approaches that should be taken in particular types of case. Thus, for example, where a number of group members have caused or knowingly permitted the *entry* of a substance, account should be taken of the time periods during which each carried out contaminating operations on the land, the relative scale of those operations, and the area of the land on which each operation took place. Similarly, where a number of persons have caused or knowingly permitted the *continued presence* of substances, account should be taken of the length of time during which each person controlled the land, the area of land over which control was exercised, and the extent to which each had the means and opportunity to deal with the effects of the substances. Where no evidence is available on any of these matters, the authority is obliged to divide responsibility equally between all group members remaining after the exclusion tests have been applied.

Class B liability groups: exclusion and apportionment

The rules for excluding members from Class B liability groups are much simpler. **6–038** Where there are multiple owners or occupiers, the basic principle is that all of them are "innocent" (because otherwise they would be causers or knowing permitters). However, clean-up of the land can be expected to increase its value, so the cost of clean-up should be borne in proportion to the group members' respective interests in the value of the land. Accordingly, there is only one exclusion test, which works to exclude persons who have no share in the land's capital value, such as licensees and holders of tenancies that cannot be assigned. Again, however, this test cannot be applied so as to exclude every member of the group—at least one person must be left to pay for clean-up, even if he will derive no financial benefit from it. Once the exclusion test has been applied, if there is more than one group member remaining, the cost of clean-up is apportioned between the group members according to their respective shares in the capital value of the land.

Further rules on exclusion and apportionment

In addition to those mentioned above, there are a number of other principles the **6–039** authority must adhere to, as follows:

(1) *Companies and company officers*

Where two or more companies within a liability group are part of the same group of **6–040** companies, they are treated as a single person for the purposes of exclusion and apportionment. In certain circumstances, however, individual officers of companies (directors, managers, secretaries or similar officers) may be treated as separate persons for the purpose of the exclusion tests. When considering apportionment, the authority must initially treat the officers and the company (or group of companies) as a single unit. Then, having apportioned liability between that unit and other members of the liability group, it must, if appropriate, make an apportionment within the unit itself as between the company and its officers. In doing this, the authority must have regard to the degree of personal responsibility of the company's officers, and also to the extent to which the company, rather than its officers, will have the resources available to meet liability. This is the only exception to the general principle (discussed below) that financial circumstances are not relevant for the purposes of exclusion and apportionment.

(2) *Private agreements*

Where members of a liability group have made a private agreement about how **6–041** responsibility is to be shared between them, that agreement will determine how liability is allocated, displacing the rules on exclusion and apportionment. This might happen, for example, where one group member sells his land to another, adding a premium to the price in return for a contractual undertaking that he (the seller) will assume any future liabilities that might arise from the state of the land. In such a case, it would not be fair to exclude the seller on the basis that he had "sold with information". The guidance, however, makes provision against such private agreements being used as liability avoidance schemes by requiring the authority to disregard agreements whose effect is to transfer liability to persons who could not be required to meet the costs of clean-up because they could take advantage of the "hardship" provisions (discussed below).

(3) *Disregarding financial circumstances*

6–042 Normally, any financial problems which might be caused to a person by being made responsible for contaminated land are disregarded for the purposes of exclusion and apportionment. This prevents the operation of the rules from becoming an exercise in allocating responsibility on the basis of who is likely to have the ability to pay, ensuring instead that responsibility is determined according to relative blame (or, in the case of owners or occupiers, relative benefit from clean-up). However, although, under the rules, a person may qualify to bear all or some of the costs of clean-up, that person may not, eventually, have to pay. This is because the regime contains further provisions that prevent a person from being required to pay for clean-up where he would suffer hardship. These are discussed below.

The hardship provisions

6–043 The hardship provisions are relevant to the procedural questions of when an authority is entitled to serve a "remediation notice", and when it may recover the costs of clean-up it undertakes itself. They are considered here, however, because they go to the heart of the question of who is made responsible for contaminated land.

In simplified terms, the legislation provides that a person may not be formally required to undertake clean-up in any case where the authority considers that, for reasons of likely hardship to that person, it will not seek to recover the full costs of clean-up.[59] In these circumstances, the authority has the power to deal with the contamination itself, though no duty to do so. If the authority does take action itself, it may, in the future, recover the costs from the appropriate person if his circumstances of hardship change. As the Circular points out, however, this will seldom be the case.

Hardship is not defined in the legislation or statutory guidance. The Circular, however, makes reference to a dictionary definition of the term, namely "hardness of fate or circumstance, severe suffering or privation", and goes on to point out that, where the term has been construed in the context of other legislation, it has been held to encompass "injustice" as well as severe financial detriment. The statutory guidance notes that what amounts to hardship will vary according to the circumstances of individual cases, but instructs authorities to aim for a fair and equitable result for all those who might have to meet the costs of clean-up (including local taxpayers) and to have regard to the polluter pays principle.

The primary legislation provides that an authority must have regard both to hardship *and* any relevant statutory guidance when deciding whether or not to seek the cost of

---

[59] The statutory mechanism by which this simple premise is arrived at, however, is rather complex. The combined effect of EPA 1990, ss.78H(5), 78N 3) and 78P is that the authority must ask itself the hypothetical question: "If it were allowed to carry out the remediation itself, and did so, would it decide not to recover any of the cost, or to recover only a part of that cost?" If the answer in either case is "yes", the authority has the power to undertake remediation itself, and is therefore precluded from serving a remediation notice.

clean-up.[60] Thus, rather than clarifying the definition of "hardship", the guidance sets out various *additional considerations* to which regard must be had. It is difficult to see what advantage is gained by this approach. Given that "hardship" is capable of bearing many meanings, it might have made more sense if the legislation had provided for the guidance to assist authorities in defining it.

The additional considerations referred to in the guidance include the following:

- Where the cost of clean-up is likely to cause a small or medium-sized commercial enterprise[61] to become insolvent, the authority should consider the effect of this on the local economy, and whether to waive costs to the extent needed to prevent this from happening.

- The authority should consider whether clean-up costs might jeopardise the continuing provision of functions in the public interest, such as those performed by charities or social housing providers.

- In the case of a Class A Appropriate Person, the authority should consider waiving clean-up costs where contamination is the fault of another who cannot now be found, in circumstances where, if he had been found, the appropriate person would have benefited from the rules on exclusion and apportionment.

- In relation to a Class B Appropriate Person, it is relevant to consider whether the cost of clean-up would be more than the value of the cleaned-up land.

- Where the land in question is a dwelling, a costs waiver should be considered where its Class B owner or occupier could not reasonably have been expected to have known about the contamination when he purchased the dwelling.

It can be seen, then, that there are a number of ways in which appropriate persons who find themselves in difficulties may escape the costs of clean-up. It remains to be seen how authorities will exercise their discretion in this regard. The guidance suggests that, in order to promote transparency, fairness and consistency, local authorities may wish to prepare and adopt policy statements on the circumstances in which they will waive clean-up costs. The content of such statements may vary from area to area, depending on local circumstances.

C: TO WHAT STANDARD SHOULD LAND BE CLEANED UP?

Suitability for current use

Apart from situations involving water pollution (see below) the purpose of clean-up, in **6–044** line with the "suitable for use" approach, is simply to ensure the land is suitable for its current use. The "current use" of the land will include any likely informal recreational use (such as children playing there) whether or not this is authorised by the owners or

---

[60] EPA 1990, s.78P.
[61] Defined by reference to the European Commission's Community Guidelines on State Aid for Small and Medium-Sized Enterprises: 1996 O.J. C213, item 4.

occupiers.[62] Clean-up, therefore, is achieved by returning the land to a state in which any substances present are no longer causing or threatening significant harm in the context of the land's current use. The land will then cease to be "contaminated land" within the definition in Pt IIA.

Clean-up to the relevant standard can be achieved in a number of ways, for example by:

- removing or treating the pollutants;
- protecting or removing the receptors affected by the pollutants;
- blocking or removing the pathways by which the pollutants can reach the receptors.

What is appropriate will depend on the particular circumstances. Thus, clean-up might involve anything from a simple action of, say, putting a fence around a tar lagoon to ensure children from a nearby school cannot come into contact with it, to a complicated "pump and treat" operation. Where land is subject to a number of different uses, the clean-up operations required will take account of this. This means that different actions may be required for different parts of a site.

Water pollution

6–045   Where land is defined as "contaminated" because it is causing (or likely to cause) water pollution, the standard of clean-up cannot be measured according to the "suitable for use" approach. This is because, as has been mentioned, this approach does not apply in such circumstances. Any likelihood of the slightest entry of a polluting substance into controlled waters may cause the land to be defined as "contaminated", irrespective of the use to which the receiving waters or the land are being put, and irrespective of whether the harm or risk involved is "significant". Logically, therefore, in such cases, the relevant standard of clean-up might be to ensure that "water pollution" (defined as the entry of *any* poisonous, noxious or polluting matter or *any* solid waste matter) can no longer occur. This would mean ensuring absolute prevention of the entry of all polluting substances into the waters in question. An alternative approach, however, would be to require clean-up of the land only if and so far as is necessary to ensure that the waters in question continue to meet their "quality classification" under s.82 of the Water Resources Act 1991 (*e.g.* as suitable for bathing, or for use as drinking water). This approach would bring water pollution cases into line with "harm-based" cases, but it is not explicitly provided for in the legislation. Implementing it would require the enforcing authority to invoke the general "proportionality" provision which precludes it from requiring clean-up where the cost of this is disproportionate to the environmental benefits.[63]

A higher standard of clean-up

6–046   Part IIA does not require clean-up to any higher standard than that outlined above. It is worth noting, however, three circumstances in which (independently of Pt IIA) contaminated land might be cleaned up to a higher standard:

[62] Circular 02/2000.
[63] EPA 1990, s.78E(4).

(1) Redevelopment

Where land is subject to redevelopment requiring planning permission, planning **6–047** conditions may be imposed requiring the land to be made suitable for its proposed use. The proposed use may necessitate a higher standard of clean-up (*e.g.* residential use instead of the current car park). It should be remembered that what "suitable for use" means in this context is rather different from what it means in the context of Pt IIA, and that planning conditions may require a higher standard of clean-up than would be required under Pt IIA. This is because, in a planning context, the idea of suitability for use is not defined by reference to the absence of "significant harm", but by reference to the effect of the development on the amenity of the area. Thus, for example, planning conditions could require the clean-up of contaminants causing only an eyesore, or a foul smell.

(2) Clean-up under alternative regimes

Where land contamination results from breach of a waste management licence, or a **6–048** permit under the PPC regime, the licence holder may be required (under the relevant regime) to remove the contamination completely, as opposed to making the land suitable for its current use. The rationale for this is that to require anything less than complete clean-up would undermine these regulatory regimes, whose aim is to prevent *any* new contamination arising.

(3) Voluntary clean-up

It is always open to a person responsible for a site under Pt IIA to clean it up to a **6–049** higher standard than the regime requires. Voluntary clean-up to a higher standard might take place, for example, where a site owner plans to put the land to some alternative use in the future and it is economically efficient to undertake all necessary clean-up at a single point in time.

D: Procedures under the Regime

Part IIA lays down detailed procedures to be followed by local authorities and the **6–050** Environment Agency (either one of which may be the "enforcing authority", depending on whether the land in question is a "special site"—see below). The diagram on page [162] provides an overview of these procedures. They can be summarised in the form of twelve steps, each of which is examined below.

Step 1: Inspection and identification of contaminated land by local authorities

Local authorities (County Councils, District Councils and London Borough Councils) **6–051** are under a duty to inspect land in their area for the purpose of identifying contaminated land. In doing so, they will consider, amongst other things, any available evidence about the presence of contamination and the history, scale and nature of

Diagram 2: The "modern contaminated land power"

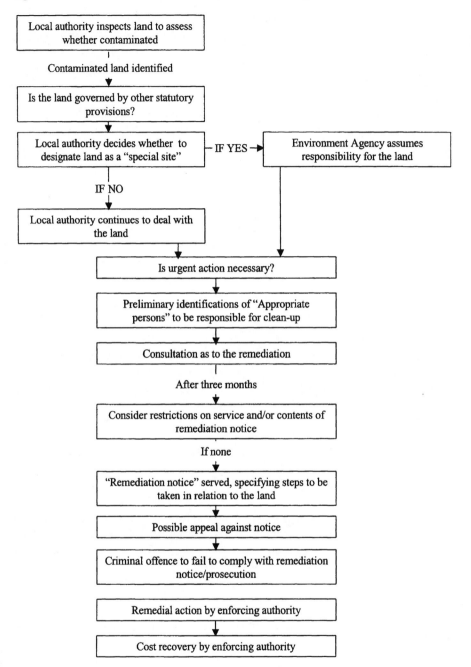

industrial activity in their area. Local authorities are required to develop strategies for performing their inspection duties. This allows them to prioritise land in their area according to the seriousness of the contamination expected to be present. The strategic approach means that local authorities need not go through their areas, metre by metre, to consider whether land is contaminated, and enables them to focus resources on key areas. Strategies will be determined by local circumstances (and will therefore vary between local authorities). Local authorities have sole responsibility for identifying and determining land as contaminated. They cannot delegate this duty to the Environment Agency. The local authority must prepare a written record of any determination that land is contaminated (although this record does not appear on a public register—see below).

As has been said, before a local authority can determine land to be contaminated, it must establish the existence of at least one "pollutant linkage". This involves carrying out investigations to obtain evidence of the actual presence of polluting substances. Historical information, or information based solely on a visual inspection of the site, will not afford sufficient grounds for the authority to conclude that such substances are present. The necessary investigation may therefore involve some form of exploratory survey (unless the relevant information is already available) which may take the form of limited sampling or a more intrusive investigation. The existence of pollutant linkages will then be considered by investigating the effects of the polluting substances on identified receptors through identified pathways. The existence of pathways and receptors will, of course, depend on the use to which the land is being put. In identifying pathways, it is sufficient for the authority to rely on general scientific knowledge about the land and substances in question (*e.g.* that the land comprises porous rock, so substances will travel through it). In identifying receptors, it will be recalled that the authority may consider only human beings and certain limited classes of animals and property, as prescribed by the guidance.

Where the contamination is "harm-based", the authority will then determine whether the identified pollutant linkages are "significant" (*i.e.* causing, or presenting a significant possibility of, significant harm). The authority must first consider whether the harm in question is "significant harm". It will be recalled that only certain types of harm (discussed above) may be regarded as "significant" in relation to each type of receptor. Where there is only a *possibility* of significant harm, the authority must consider whether this possibility amounts to a "significant possibility". Here, again, account is taken of the use to which the land is being put. Suppose, for example, that the authority identifies mercury in soil as a pollutant, and human beings as receptors. If the land in question is being used as a children's playground, significant harm (disease) may be a significant possibility, through the pathway of contact with the soil. However, if the soil in question lies beneath a concrete hardstanding and is used as a car-park, the position may be different. There may well be cracks in the hardstanding (creating a pathway through which the mercury might conceivably reach human beings), and, of course, there are likely to be human beings (receptors) in the car park. Thus, the three elements needed to establish a "pollutant linkage" will be present. However, significant harm will not arise unless, for example, children take to using the car-park as a playground. The possibility of this happening may not be regarded as a "significant possibility". Accordingly, the pollutant linkage in question will not be a "significant" pollutant linkage.

To make a determination that a substance in, on or under the land is causing or likely to cause water pollution, the local authority must be satisfied, on the balance of probabilities, that the substance in question is entering or likely to enter "controlled waters" through an identified pathway, and that the substance constitutes "poisonous, noxious or polluting matter" or solid waste matter. The relevant terms are discussed in Ch. 8.

Step 2: Are other statutory regimes appropriate?

6–052 In the course of inspecting for contaminated land, the local authority may encounter sites which are excluded from the scope of Pt IIA, because they are appropriately dealt with by other pollution control regimes:

(1) *Waste-related contamination*

6–053 If a site is governed by a waste management licence, any harm or water pollution must be dealt with under the waste licensing regime unless the contamination is unrelated to the waste management activity (*e.g.* contamination from previous use).[64] Whilst such sites cannot be identified as contaminated land by reason of their current use, local authorities remain under a duty to inspect such sites for historic contamination caused by past use, and to apply Pt IIA where appropriate. As regards contamination caused by currently licensed waste management activities, waste regulation authorities have the power to require licence holders to comply with waste management licences (which may include cleaning-up contamination) and may themselves clean-up contamination in an emergency.

Contamination arising from disposal of waste regulated under the PPC regime is excluded from Pt IIA if it can be dealt with by enforcement action (*e.g.* enforcement and suspension notices) under that regime.[65] Where contamination arises from an illegal deposit of controlled waste (often known as "fly tipping"), the local authority may designate the land as contaminated under Pt IIA, but the enforcing authority cannot require clean-up if it considers that the waste regulation or collection authority has sufficient powers to deal with the matter.[66]

(2) *Industrial process contamination*

6–054 Local authorities can designate land as contaminated where the contamination has arisen because of industrial processes regulated under the IPC or PPC regimes.[67] This means that IPC and PPC sites will be subject to inspection by local authorities. However, use of Pt IIA for clean-up is seen as an option of last resort. Thus, clean-up cannot be required under Pt IIA if the contamination can be dealt with under the IPC or PPC regime by enforcement action.

(3) *Works notices under the Water Resources Act 1991*

6–055 Sections 161 to 161D of the Water Resources Act 1991 give the Environment Agency powers to take action to prevent or remedy pollution of controlled waters. The Agency may serve a "works notice" specifying actions to be taken within certain periods of time. The notice may be served on any person who has caused or knowingly permitted

---

[64] *ibid.*, s.78YB(2).
[65] *ibid.*, s.78YB (1) (The section currently refers to IPC, but is to be amended to reflect change to PPC).
[66] *ibid.*, s.78YB(3).
[67] *ibid.*, s.78YB(1).

a pollutant to enter controlled waters, or to be in a place from which it is likely to enter controlled waters. If the pollution requires urgent action, or if there is no identifiable polluter, the Agency itself has the power to take necessary action.

Where land is contaminated because it causes or threatens water pollution, there is an overlap between the works notice powers and the powers available under Pt IIA. The Environment Agency has set out how this overlap should be dealt with.[68] In summary:

- the local authority acting under Pt IIA should consult the Environment Agency before determining that land is contaminated land because of pollution of controlled waters;

- where the local authority has identified contaminated land which is potentially affecting controlled waters, it must consult the Environment Agency and take account of any comments the Agency makes with respect to clean-up requirements;

- where the Agency itself identifies actual or potential water pollution arising from contaminated land, it will notify the relevant local authority, thus enabling the authority formally to identify the land as "contaminated land" under Pt IIA; and

- where land has been so identified, the Pt IIA enforcement mechanisms will normally be used, rather than the works notice system. This is because, once land is identified as contaminated under Pt IIA, the enforcing authority has a *duty* to require clean-up. By contrast, the Agency has only a *power* to serve a works notice. The works notice provisions remain of use, however, in cases where there is historic pollution of groundwater, but the Pt IIA regime does not apply. This may occur, for example, where the pollutants are entirely contained within the relevant body of groundwater or where the site from which the pollutants are escaping cannot be identified.

(4) *Consented discharges to controlled waters*

Part IIA cannot be used to override a consent to discharge to controlled waters **6–056** granted under the Water Resources Act 1991. Whilst the land from which the discharges are occurring can be inspected and identified as contaminated, clean-up cannot be required. It is, however, open to the Environment Agency to amend or modify the discharge consent.

(5) *Radioactivity*

Part IIA does not apply in cases of harm or water pollution attributable to the **6–057** radioactivity of substances.

Step 3: Identification and designation of "special sites"

Once a local authority has identified a site as contaminated, it must consider whether **6–058** that site is a "special site".[69] Special sites are sites in relation to which the Environment Agency, rather than the local authority, is the enforcing authority. The powers and

---

[68] See Environment Agency Policy and Guidance on the Use of Anti-Pollution Works Notices.
[69] EPA 1990, s.78C.

duties exercisable by the Environment Agency in relation to special sites are identical to those exercisable by local authorities in relation to ordinary contaminated sites. Special sites are sites where the contamination is complex, or which are otherwise thought to require the expertise of the Environment Agency. A site *must* be designated a special site if, and only if, it is of a description prescribed for designation by the Secretary of State in regulations. Under the current regulations, such sites include the following[70]:

- sites where the contamination is affecting controlled waters and may compromise the quality of drinking water, or prevent waters from meeting their "quality classification" under the Water Resources Act 1991[71];

- land contaminated by waste acid tars;

- land where activities involving explosives or petroleum have been carried on;

- land where PPC activities are being carried out;

- nuclear sites;

- military or defence sites;

- land neighbouring a special site which appears to be contaminated by virtue of substances escaping from a special site.

Step 4: Is urgent action necessary?

6–059 Where contaminated land appears to the enforcing authority to be in such a condition that there is an imminent danger of serious harm or of serious pollution of controlled waters, the authority can serve a remediation notice immediately.[72] It need not go through the usual processes of consultation and waiting for the expiry of a three month period (see step 6). Alternatively, it may take action itself in such circumstances[73] and recover the reasonable costs of so doing from the appropriate persons.[74]

Step 5: Identification and notification of potential appropriate persons

6–060 The local authority must next identify those persons it considers might potentially be "appropriate persons". Whilst some of these persons might eventually be absolved from liability by the exclusion tests (discussed above), at the stage of initial identification and notification, the authority will not apply these tests, although it must do so before requiring remediation (see below). Once it has determined those who "appear to be" appropriate persons, the local authority must notify them that it has designated the land as contaminated. It must also notify the Environment Agency, the owner of the site, and any person in apparent occupation of the site.[75] Where land is to be

---

[70] See Contaminated Land (England) Regulations 2000, SI/227.
[71] Discussed in Ch. 8.
[72] EPA 1990, s.78H(4).
[73] *ibid.*, s.78N(3)(a).
[74] *ibid.*, s.78P.
[75] *ibid.*, s.78B.

designated a "special site", similar notification requirements apply in relation to that fact, and the Environment Agency will take over the proceedings as the enforcing authority after this notification has taken place.

Step 6: Consultation on appropriate remediation

The enforcing authority is required to "reasonably endeavour to consult" before it **6–061** serves a remediation notice. It must consult the persons on whom notification has been served that the land is contaminated. It must also consult any third parties likely to be affected by things done by way of remediation, *e.g.* owners or occupiers of neighbouring land or waters, who might be required to grant rights of access. The consultation process combines with a statutory "cooling-off" period of three months, during which no remediation notice may be served. This period begins with the date on which notification identifying the contaminated land is served. It should be noted that the burden imposed on the enforcing authority is to "reasonably endeavour" to consult. Thus, where an appropriate person or neighbouring landowner is being difficult, and refusing to engage with the authority, no actual consultation need take place, and a remediation notice can be served as soon as the three month period has expired. The "cooling-off" period simply provides an opportunity to negotiate a voluntary solution to the problem.

Step 7: Consideration of remediation notices

If consultation has not produced voluntary agreement to undertake clean-up, the **6–062** enforcing authority is under a duty to serve a remediation notice. If a range of potential appropriate persons have been identified and notified, the authority will at this stage apply the exclusion and apportionment tests (discussed above) to determine (in relation to each significant pollutant linkage) which members of a liability group will be required to carry out remediation, and what each person's share of remediation will involve. The enforcing authority has a *duty* to apply these rules before serving a remediation notice.

Situations where a remediation notice cannot be served

The authority must also consider whether the circumstances are such that it is **6–063** precluded from serving a remediation notice. Owners and occupiers cannot be required to carry out remediation of land which is causing only water pollution,[76] or of other people's land where their own land is contaminated by substances that have escaped from other land.[77] In addition, a remediation notice may not be served in the following circumstances[78]:

- where the enforcing authority is satisfied that the cost of remediation would be unreasonable in the light of the environmental benefits it would secure, so that

[76] *ibid.*, s.78J.
[77] *ibid.*, s.78K.
[78] *ibid.*, s.78H(5).

nothing can reasonably be done by way of remediation.[79] In deciding this issue, the enforcing authority must prepare a costs estimate and a statement of the benefits likely to result if remediation were carried out. It must then publish a "remediation declaration" recording the reasons why the authority would, were it not for the unreasonable cost, have required particular things to be done, and the reasons why it has decided that it cannot require those things to be done.[80] It should be noted that the authority is not precluded from "changing its mind" and serving a remediation notice if advances in technology mean that remediation is no longer so costly;

- where the parties involved are voluntarily carrying out remediation. In these circumstances, the authority must prepare and publish a "remediation statement" setting out the details of the remediation being undertaken, by whom it is being undertaken, and the periods within which the things being done are expected to be done. Again, the authority may "change its mind" and serve a remediation notice if what has been agreed does not materialise;

- where the enforcing authority itself is the appropriate person and is therefore responsible for remediation. In these circumstances, it must publish a remediation statement (see above);

- where the enforcing authority has the power to carry out remediation itself (it is immaterial whether or not it actually decides to do so). The authority will have this power in a number of situations (see Step 11), including where it concludes that, if it decided to undertake remediation itself, it would decide not to recover from the appropriate person any of the costs, or it would decide to recover only a proportion of those costs. It is by this rather convoluted route that the hardship provisions and related statutory guidance fall to be considered.

Step 8: Service of remediation notices

6–064 Provided it is not precluded from doing so, the enforcing authority is under a duty to serve a remediation notice. Where, having applied the exclusion and apportionment rules, a number of appropriate persons remain in a liability group for a significant pollution linkage, a remediation notice will be served on each of these persons. The notice must state the proportion of the total cost of remediation to be borne by each of them.

What does "remediation" involve?

6–065 A remediation notice will specify what is to be done by way of clean-up, and the time periods within which these things must be accomplished. The objective of remediation is to break the significant pollutant linkage by removing or treating the pollutant, blocking or removing the pathway, or protecting or removing the receptors. "Remediation" is defined in the statutory guidance to cover three stages of work:

[79] *ibid.*, s.78E(4).
[80] *ibid.* s.78H(6).

(*a*) "Assessment action"

This is work necessary to assess the condition of the land or of polluted waters. The **6–066** effect of including this within the definition of "remediation" is that the appropriate person can be required to carry out and pay for all work necessary to determine what is the most suitable course of remedial action. The local authority's investigative duties extend as far as establishing, at its own expense, that the land is contaminated, but not to establishing an appropriate remediation strategy.

(*b*) "Remedial treatment action"

This is the clean-up itself, which may involve anything necessary to prevent the land **6–067** from continuing to be "contaminated" within the meaning of Pt IIA. As has been said, this may not necessarily involve removing or treating the substances—it may be sufficient to deal with the pathways and receptors.

(*c*) "Monitoring action"

The third stage of remediation involves carrying out subsequent inspections to review **6–068** the condition of the land once clean-up work has been carried out.

Step 9: Appeal against remediation notices

A person on whom a remediation notice has been served has 21 days in which to **6–069** appeal to a magistrates' court (if the notice was served by a local authority) or to the Secretary of State (if the notice was served by the Environment Agency).[81] The appellate authority may quash, confirm or modify the notice. In particular, it may extend the period specified in the notice for doing what is required. The grounds of appeal against a remediation notice include:

- unreasonably identifying all or any of the land to which the notice relates as contaminated;

- unreasonably identifying the recipient of the notice as responsible for remediation or unreasonably requiring something to be done by way of remediation;

- unreasonably failing to make any other person responsible for the remediation in addition to the recipient of the notice;

- unreasonably apportioning the costs between two or more appropriate persons;

- serving the notice without the appropriate consultation or during the three month "cooling off" period;

- unreasonably failing to be satisfied with voluntary remediation;

- unreasonable time limits imposed for the remediation;

- that the contamination should have been dealt with under another pollution control regime.

---

[81] *ibid.*, s.78L.

If an appeal is made, the remediation notice does not take effect pending the final determination or abandonment of the appeal.[82]

Step 10: Prosecution for failure to comply with a remediation notice

6–070 It is a criminal offence to fail, without reasonable excuse, to comply with the requirements of a remediation notice.[83] The offence is triable only in the magistrates' court, and any prosecution must be brought within six months from the date the offence was committed. Surprisingly, no provision is made for cases to be heard in the Crown Court. However, in industrial cases, there is provision for the Secretary of State, by order, to increase the maximum fine available to magistrates (which removes one of the reasons why it might be desirable to transfer a case to the Crown Court).[84] If the enforcing authority is of the opinion that prosecution would provide an ineffectual remedy, it may seek an injunction in the High Court to secure compliance with a remediation notice.

What amounts to a "reasonable excuse"?

6–071 The question of whether a person has a "reasonable excuse" is a matter of fact to be decided in the particular circumstances of each case.[85] One example of what the government considers a reasonable excuse, however, is apparent from s.78M(2). This provides that where a remediation notice requires the defendant to bear only a proportion of the cost of remediation, it is a defence if the defendant proves that the only reason why he failed to comply with the notice was that one or more of the other persons required to share the cost of remediation refused or was unable to pay. In addition, analogous case law[86] suggests that there may be a reasonable excuse where an owner who is not an occupier has difficulty in gaining access to the contaminated land, or where the appropriate person did not receive the remediation notice because he was ill or abroad. Financial difficulties are not likely to be acceptable as a "reasonable excuse". It also appears that relying on the opinion of an expert that sufficient remediation has been done to comply with the notice may not amount to a reasonable excuse in the event that the expert is wrong.[87]

Is wrongful identification as an "appropriate person" a reasonable excuse?

6–072 This is a more complex question than it might appear. At the stage of identifying appropriate persons, the relevant standard of proof is the civil standard, namely the balance of probabilities. The rather unsatisfactory result of this is that a person may find himself facing a criminal charge (failing to comply with a remediation notice) in circumstances where that charge has been brought on the basis of an identification made only on the balance of probabilities. In such a case, the difficult question will arise of whether, since the proceedings are at this stage criminal, the magistrates must revisit the local authority's identification decision, applying the criminal standard of proof (which might involve lengthy consideration of detailed evidence).

---

[82] The Contaminated Land (England) Regulations 2000, SI/227 set out the procedure for appeals.
[83] EPA 1990, s.78M.
[84] EPA 1990, s.78M. The Secretary of State's order must be laid before Parliament.
[85] Circular 2/2000, para.15.11.
[86] See, for example, *Lambert Flat Management Ltd. v Lomas* [1981] 1 W.L.R. 898.
[87] *Saddleworth UDC v Aggregate and Sand* (1970) 69 L.G.R. 103.

The issue is likely to be obscured particularly in cases where there has been an unsuccessful appeal against the remediation notice. Wrongful identification as an appropriate person is a ground of appeal against a remediation notice (see above), but if different standards of proof are applied, it may be possible to lose the appeal yet successfully defend a prosecution for failing to comply. It is surprising, perhaps, that the legislation does not explicitly refer to wrongful original identification as a reasonable excuse. There is a danger that the important question of whether the defendant is someone who ought to have received the notice in the first place might be seen as irrelevant to the specific charge. Yet this question is, in a substantive sense, fundamental to his guilt or innocence, and ought, therefore, to tested according to the criminal standard of proof.

Penalties

For non-industrial land, the maximum penalty is a Level 5 fine (currently £5,000), **6–073** together with further fines of one tenth of that sum in respect of each day after conviction on which breach of the remediation notice continues. For land used for industrial, trade or business purposes, however, the maximum penalty is a fine of £20,000 (or such sum as may be substituted by the Secretary of State) plus an additional fine of one tenth of that sum in respect of each day on which the breach of the notice continues after conviction.

Step 11: Remedial action by the enforcing authority

The enforcing authority has a power, but not a duty, to carry out remediation itself in **6–074** the following circumstances:

- it decides it needs to take urgent action to prevent imminent danger of serious harm or serious pollution of controlled waters;

- an appropriate person has failed to comply with the requirements of a remediation notice;

- it has made an agreement with a person served with a remediation notice, under which he bears the cost of the remediation, but the work is to be carried out by the enforcing authority;

- it considers that, for reasons of likely hardship to the appropriate person, it will not seek to recover any of the cost of remediation, or will seek to recover only a part of that cost;

- it is precluded from requiring remediation of controlled waters because the only appropriate person who can be found is an owner or occupier who cannot be required to undertake remediation of those waters;

- it is precluded from requiring remediation of "other land" because the only appropriate person who can be found is an owner or occupier, but his land is contaminated because substances have escaped to it, and he does not own or occupy that "other land";

- after reasonable enquiry, no appropriate person has been be found.

Clearly, whether, and to what extent local authorities or the Environment Agency will be able to carry out remediation in respect of "orphan linkages" for which no appropriate person has been found, or in cases where remediation costs will not be recovered, will depend on the financial resources advanced to them by central government for the purpose, and, in the case of local authorities, on the extent to which it is politically viable for them to secure resources through local taxation.

Step 12: Recovery of costs by the enforcing authority

6–075 The enforcing authority is entitled to recover from the appropriate person all or a proportion of the costs of remediation which it has undertaken itself. As noted above, however, in deciding whether and what proportion of those costs should be recovered, the authority must have regard to any hardship which might be caused to the appropriate person and to the statutory guidance.

Where the appropriate person from whom the enforcing authority decides to recover costs is the person who caused or knowingly permitted the contamination *and* the owner of premises on the land in question, the authority may serve him with a "charging notice".[88] This has the effect of making the recoverable costs a charge on the premises which may be enforced by the authority as if it were a mortgage. The authority may then require repayment of these costs, plus interest, by instalments over a period not exceeding 30 years. Provision is made for appeals against charging notices to a county court.

It is unclear whether Pt IIA entitles the enforcing authority to recover costs in respect of works which it considers necessary but has not yet carried out. This issue will be especially important to local authorities which may lack the funds even to commence certain complex remediation operations. The relevant provision (so far as is material) states: "Where the enforcing authority does any particular thing by way of remediation, it shall be entitled to recover the reasonable cost incurred in doing it from the appropriate person". On the face of it, the wording of the provision requires the authority at least to have commenced, and be in the process of "doing" the remediation, if not to have already done it, before costs can be recovered. The heading to the section, however, reads: "Recovery of, and security for, the cost of remediation by the enforcing authority". If the expression "security for cost" is to be construed in the sense in which it is generally understood by lawyers, it suggests that the scope of the section may be wide enough to allow the enforcing authority to start recovery proceedings in respect of remediation costs it has not yet incurred. This issue is not clarified by the guidance and may need to be settled by the courts.[89]

Public registers

6–076 Finally, it should be noted that Pt IIA requires the enforcing authorities to maintain public registers containing details of, amongst other things: all remediation notices served; all special sites; appeals against notices designating land as a special site;

---

[88] *ibid.*, s.78P.
[89] Although section headings are not, strictly speaking, part of the statute, because they have not received the scrutiny of Parliament, their use has been sanctioned by the courts as a guide to ascertaining the general purpose of the section to which they relate.

notices terminating the designation of land as a special site; and (where a remediation notice has been served) details of what is claimed to have been done by way of remediation. Authorities must also record particulars of convictions for breach of remediation notices.

Where land is identified as contaminated, and potential appropriate persons notified, these facts are the subject of written records held by local authorities, which might be used in collecting information about the extent of the UK's contaminated land problem. These facts, however, do not appear on a public register. The original legislative intention, therefore, was clearly that information about contamination should not be publicly available unless and until either the site was designated a special site, or a remediation notice was served. The absence of any requirement that a local authority maintain a register of all land in its area identified as contaminated was doubtless motivated by sensitivity to the fears of developers in relation to property blight. However, this approach is somewhat undermined by the fact that the relevant information will probably now be placed in the public domain under the Environmental Information Regulations, discussed in Ch. 14.

Registers may be kept in any form, for example as a computerised database, and must be available for public inspection at all reasonable times and free of charge. The enforcing authority is further required to provide facilities for members of the public to obtain copies of entries on the registers on payment of a reasonable fee. Information will be excluded from the registers if it is commercially confidential or prejudicial to national security. Information is commercially confidential if it would prejudice a person's commercial interests to an unreasonable degree, and it is for the enforcing authority (or, on appeal, the Secretary of State) to determine whether this is so. In deciding the matter, any prejudice to commercial interests must be disregarded so far as it relates only to the value of the land in question. Where information is excluded from the register on grounds of commercial confidentiality, a statement must be entered on the register indicating the existence of such information. Confidential information remains excluded for a period of four years, after which time the person affected may apply for it to remain excluded.

Chapter 7

WASTE MANAGEMENT

"The amount of waste generated in producing everyday products is 1.5 kg for a toothbrush, 75 kg for a mobile phone and 1,500 kg for a personal computer."[1]

Introduction

In 2000, the UK produced on average about 570kg of household waste per person, **7–001** compared to the EC average of 535kg per person. We sent the second highest amount of waste of any EC country to landfill.[2] We were in the bottom three countries when it came to recycling.[3]

Most of our waste is generated by the chemical and oil refining industries and sewerage undertakers. It also comes from construction and demolition, agriculture, mining, quarrying, and dredging.[4] Household waste is a relatively small part of the overall waste stream, but is growing. Current trends in waste generation present a mixed picture. Total waste quantities continue to increase in most European countries, but waste generation has been decoupled from economic growth in a few of these countries, with the effect that waste generation seems to be decreasing there.[5] It is, however, generally agreed that, in the absence of additional policy measures, waste generation in the EC is likely to increase for the foreseeable future.

Waste tends to be perceived in emotive terms by the public. Activities which involve the management of waste are often seen as less acceptable than those involving other types of materials. In the UK, the management of waste is mainly in the hands of private industry, whether traditional waste disposal companies or specialised businesses such as metal recyclers and those which generate energy from waste. This chapter considers the legislation which regulates this industry in England and Wales. (Inevitably, this involves a focus on EC law.) It explores the relevant EC and UK policy behind this legislation, and the history of its development.

[1] Conclusions of the Wuppertal Institute, as quoted in European Commission Communication COM (2003) 301 Final.
[2] Over 460kg *per capita*, compared to an EU average of 290kg.
[3] See *www.defra.gov.uk/environment/statistics/waste*.
[4] See *Waste Strategy 2000 (www.defra.gov.uk/environment/waste/strategy/cm4693)*.
[5] See European Environment Agency, *Europe's Environment: The Third Assessment* (2003), p.151; and *Environmental Signals 2002—Benchmarking the Millennium* (EEA) Ch. 12, pp.100–105.

As we shall see, a number of different policy approaches have been developed, giving rise to a number of different types of legislation. Some legislation (both EC and UK) attempts to control waste by setting out a broad framework of control, applicable to most types of waste and most methods of management and disposal. Other legislation is more specific, and relates to the technical details of particular waste-management and disposal operations, such as landfill. A third type of legislation attempts to control waste by identifying and regulating various "waste streams" (for example, end-of-life vehicles, batteries, or waste electronic and electrical equipment). One of the key difficulties for all of these approaches is the issue of working out just what is meant by "waste"—so this is something to which detailed consideration must also be given in this chapter.

Why does waste need regulating?

7–002   Wastes require regulation simply because they are unwanted. A waste and a raw material may have equivalent hazardous properties (*e.g.* both may be toxic or flammable). But whilst there is an economic incentive to use the raw material efficiently and carefully, there is not the same imperative with the waste. Indeed, the economic imperative is to dispose of it as cheaply and quickly as possible (*e.g.* by dumping) and without taking care to ensure that its hazardous properties do not cause harm to the environment. It is not only through disposal that waste can harm the environment. Harm can also arise when waste is stored, transported, or treated—either to reclaim useful substances within it, or to change its form so that it can be disposed of more easily. Regulation therefore needs to extend more widely than to disposal practices.

Historically, waste regulation focused only on final disposal. In the more recent past, however, the concern has been to regulate practices and standards in the *management* of waste, for the reasons given above. More recently still, attention has focused on *preventing waste from arising* by improving the efficiency of resource use. In addition to lessening the amount of waste generated, reducing the use of raw materials helps to avoid other environmental problems associated with their extraction and transformation into products.

The development of waste management in England and Wales

7–003   In pre-industrial times, the main sources of waste were such things as ash from fires, unwanted wood, bones, and vegetable waste, and, of course, human and animal excreta. Waste was often disposed of into the ground, where it would act as compost and help to improve the soil. Re-use and recycling were commonplace. Recycling included feeding vegetable wastes to livestock. Pigs were often used as an efficient method of disposing of municipal waste. (To demonstrate that recycling is not a new phenomenon, it has been astutely pointed out that, nearly 4,000 years ago, there was a recovery and re-use system for bronze scrap in operation in Europe[6]).

During the Industrial Revolution, new large-scale manufacturing processes produced increased waste and waste of a different kind. The growth of towns led to an increase

---

[6] *www.wasteonline.org.uk.*

in domestic waste, but a decrease in the space available for disposal. The need for waste management systems became necessary, and waste began to be regulated as an aspect of public health law. The Public Health Act 1875 charged local authorities with the duty to arrange the removal and disposal of waste. The Public Health Act 1936 provided that accumulation of waste which was "prejudicial to health or a nuisance" was a statutory nuisance. Authorities were given the power to prosecute for uncontrolled dumping, cesspools and scavenging. Building on contaminated land was prohibited.

During the World Wars, waste regulation became less of a priority. Despite a rise in reclamation and recycling during the wars (needed to assist the war effort), the postwar years saw the growth of huge insanitary and uncontrolled refuse tips, especially surrounding the larger cities. The practice of landfilling waste dominated the UK waste management system during the post-war years. Landfills were constructed at the most convenient and cheapest locations, with little thought given to their environmental impacts. At the same time, increases in production and consumption led to greater generation of waste, including packaging waste.

In 1947, the Town and Country Planning Act introduced more strategic and preventive regulation by requiring waste disposal sites or plants to have planning permission. The first ever legislation to control *hazardous* waste came in 1971, after the dumping of drums of cyanide waste at an abandoned brick kiln near Nuneaton. The ensuing public outcry—fuelled by press coverage of waste disposal drivers taking bribes to dump hazardous waste illegally—and a report on toxic waste by the Royal Commission on Environmental Pollution, resulted in the Deposit of Poisonous Waste Act 1972, which was drafted in 10 days and passed through Parliament within a month.

Concern about the environmental effects of waste continued, leading to the Control of Pollution Act 1974, which aimed for much wider control of waste disposal operations by introducing a system whereby waste could be disposed of only in accordance with a licence. However, the regime introduced by the Control of Pollution Act 1974 had a number of significant failings. These failings were noted by the House of Commons Environment Committee on Toxic Waste, whose second report stated:

> "Never, in any of our enquiries into environmental problems, have we experienced such consistent and universal criticism of existing legislation and of central and local government as we have done during the course of this inquiry."

The Committee found that regulatory attention was too narrowly focussed on the final disposal of waste, with little done to ensure that waste did not cause problems prior to this. Little provision was made for the aftercare of waste disposal sites once they had ceased operating—the operator of a waste disposal facility could effectively abdicate responsibility for a site by surrendering his licence after he had completed his activities, even where the activities had resulted in contaminated land which was a continuing source of pollution. Another serious deficiency was that local authorities, who were responsible for granting waste disposal licences, very often carried out waste disposal operations themselves, so that they were in effect self-regulating. This did little to engender public confidence in the operation of the regime.

Further reform came with the Environmental Protection Act 1990, which put in place the regime that applies today. The Act established a new licensing system covering commercial, industrial and household waste. It also required local authorities to consider recycling in their waste strategies. Key improvements to the previous regulatory regime included:

- a requirement that waste management licences should be granted only to people considered technically competent, with sufficient finances, and no history of waste management offences;

- more powerful enforcement procedures;

- a procedure for surrendering waste management licences, under which the consent of the regulator is required, so that operators cannot abdicate responsibility for aftercare by surrendering licences at will.

The Act also established different types of waste regulatory authorities. Further amendment by the Environment Act 1995 means that the current position is as follows:

- the Environment Agency licenses and supervises waste management activities;

- waste collection authorities (mostly District Councils in England and Wales) arrange for the collection of waste, and for its delivery to places directed by waste disposal authorities (below). They also draw up and implement waste recycling plans;

- waste disposal authorities (mostly County Councils in England and District Councils in Wales), whilst not carrying out waste disposal themselves, arrange for private companies to do so.

The development of waste management at EC level

7–004 Before the mid 1970s, waste was largely regarded as a local matter in all Member States, and the European Community had no legislation concerned with waste disposal. The adoption of the first legislation in 1975—the Waste Framework Directive—was in part a response to the introduction by some Member States of legislation intended to provide a national framework for waste policy. The Directive sought to set out a coherent programme of measures applicable in all Member States, in recognition of the need to ensure that different national requirements did not distort competition or create barriers to trade. Early measures by the EC also regulated some specific types of hazardous waste.[7]

The "waste management hierarchy"

7–005 From 1977, an early stage in the history of EC waste management, the EC started to take a broader view of waste policy than simply ensuring safe disposal of waste. Its policy extended to the ambitious goal of conserving resources. A principle for the management of waste was developed which has been part of EC waste policy ever since. Under this principle, three distinct approaches to dealing with waste are

---

[7] See *e.g.* Dir.75/439/EEC (disposal of waste oils); Dir.76/403/EEC (PCBs etc.); Dir.78/176/EEC (waste from the titanium dioxide industry).

identified, and should be adopted in order of preference. Together, these three approaches are known as the "waste management hierarchy":

(1) The priority is to prevent waste from arising;

(2) If prevention is not possible, waste should be recycled or otherwise re-incorporated into the economic cycle. This is known as "waste recovery", a term which can encompass a number of different operations. For example, it can imply that materials should be transformed into a state in which they can be used, either wholly, or for the extraction of component parts or useful substances. These operations conserve natural resources by enabling waste to serve as replacement for fresh raw materials;

(3) As a last resort, waste which cannot be recycled should be disposed of in a manner which does not cause environmental harm.

Current EC waste policy[8]

The early pieces of EC legislation have all been significantly revised or replaced, as EC **7–006** waste policy has developed. Having established a framework for waste control, the European Commission started to turn its attention to specific waste streams. Certain waste streams were prioritised for action because they had a particular environmental impact because of their volume and/or hazardous characteristics. The first waste stream to be the subject of regulatory attention was packaging waste. Other streams now regulated include end-of-life vehicles, and waste electronic and electrical equipment. One of the principles underlying the regulation of specific waste streams is the concept of "producer responsibility". This concept focuses on the role of product manufacturers in minimising and dealing with waste caused by their products.

Current EC waste policy follows, to a large extent, the early principles. Increases in waste generation must be decoupled from increases in economic growth by achieving more sustainable production and consumption patterns. The quantity of waste going to disposal must be reduced, as must the volume of hazardous waste produced. Re-use of waste should be encouraged. Waste intended for disposal should be handled and disposed of as closely as possible to the place of its generation. Methods to achieve these objectives include:

- Community-wide targets for waste reduction;
- changes in product design;
- raising public awareness of how to contribute to reducing waste;
- phasing out the use of certain substances and materials, and developing strategies for recycling others.

Current UK waste policy

Current UK waste policy, which is heavily influenced by EC policy, takes as its starting **7–007** point the principle that changes are necessary in terms of the amount of waste produced and the way that waste is managed. The UK relies too heavily on landfilling

---

[8] Current policy is set out in the European Commission Communication *Towards a thematic strategy on the prevention and recycling of waste*, COM (2003) 301 Final; and in the Sixth Environmental Action Programme, O.J. L242/1 10.9.2002.

waste, and waste is increasing.[9] Landfilling waste (simply burying it in the ground) produces methane—a gas which contributes to climate change—when biodegradable materials, such as paper and food wastes, decompose in the absence of oxygen. Landfills are increasingly scarce in some parts of England and Wales, and there are now European-wide targets to reduce the amount of waste going to landfill.[10] Landfilling does not contribute to the prudent use of natural resources and the UK's policy of sustainable development. Materials that are landfilled are valuable materials, which society cannot afford to waste. Many—particularly metals and oil-based materials such as plastic—are only available in limited quantities in the environment, or are difficult or environmentally damaging to extract.

Reducing waste generation is a primary objective of UK policy. This means putting waste to good use through an increase in recycling and composting, both of which lie at the heart of developing a more sustainable system of waste management. Re-using materials not only avoids the need for landfilling, but reduces energy consumption (because the extraction of raw materials is energy-intensive) which in turn contributes to the UK's achievement of its climate change targets. Where it does not make sense to recycle, UK policy is to give consideration to using waste as a fuel. In addition, consideration must be given to designing products that can be produced by processes that cause less waste. As with EC policy, the UK's waste policies are not new—the waste strategy set out in the 1990 White Paper *This Common Inheritance* made waste minimisation and recycling a priority.

To achieve the necessary changes in waste production, the government has set targets:

- to reduce the amount of industrial and commercial waste being landfilled to 85 per cent of 1998 levels by 2005;

- to recycle or compost at least 25 per cent household waste by 2005.

Such targets are not new concepts. Previous targets have, in fact, been missed. The 1990 White Paper *This Common Inheritance* set out a waste strategy which included an aspirational target of 25 per cent for the recycling of household waste by the year 2000. This target was confirmed in the 1996 Waste Management Strategy for England and Wales, but has not been met.

Principles of EC and UK waste management

7–008 The following principles form the basis of EC and UK waste management policy, and are reflected in waste legislation:

(*a*) The waste management hierarchy

7–009 As mentioned above, and set out first in early EC policy documents, the waste management hierarchy sets out the ways of dealing with waste in order of preference.

---

[9] See *Waste Strategy 2000*, Cm 4693.
[10] Agreed targets include reducing biodegradable municipal waste landfilled to 75 per cent of 1995 levels by 2010. See *Waste Strategy 2000*, Cm 4693.

(b) The polluter pays principle

The polluter pays principle is one of the general principles of EC policy on the **7–010**
environment, discussed in Ch. 4. The principle is set out in Art. 174(2) of the EC
Treaty. It embodies the idea that the polluter, rather than society at large, should pay
for polluting activities. In a waste context, the "polluter" is increasingly taken to mean
the producer of a product that eventually becomes waste.

(c) The principle of preventive action

The principle of preventive action is another general principle of EC environmental **7–011**
policy set out in Art. 174(2) of the EC Treaty. It tends to be referred to synonymously
with the "precautionary principle" (below) and endorses measures taken to prevent
environmental damage despite scientific uncertainty about the likelihood of harm. It is
reflected in the waste management hierarchy, where the preferred approach to dealing
with waste is to prevent it from arising.

(d) The precautionary principle

The precautionary principle requires, in this context, that waste management measures **7–012**
should be taken to protect the environment despite scientific uncertainty about the
likelihood of harm.

(e) The proximity principle

The principle that environmental damage should, as a priority, be rectified at source is **7–013**
also laid down in Art. 174(2) of the EC Treaty. It is also enunciated in the Waste
Framework Directive. In the context of waste, this principle is often referred to as the
"proximity principle"—waste should be disposed of as close as possible to the place
where it is produced, in order to limit, as far as possible, environmental effects arising
from the transport of waste.

(f) The self-sufficiency principle

The self-sufficiency principle requires the EC as a whole to become self-sufficient in **7–014**
waste disposal, and its Member States to move towards that goal individually, taking
into account geographical circumstances and the need for specialised installations for
certain types of waste. The self-sufficiency principle is referred to in the preamble to
the EC Regulation on Shipment of Waste (discussed later) as a ground on which a
Member State (of dispatch or destination) can object to shipments of waste for
disposal.

(g) The "Article 4 objectives"

The policy objectives underpinning waste disposal are set out in Art. 4 of the Waste **7–015**
Framework Directive. This states that "Member States shall take the necessary
measures to ensure that waste is disposed of without endangering human health and
without harming the environment", and in particular:

- without risk to water, air, soil, plants or animals;
- without causing a nuisance through noise or odour;
- without adversely affecting the countryside or places of special scientific
  interest.

In *Comitato di Coordinamento per la Difesa della Cava*,[11] the ECJ interpreted Art. 4 as defining a framework for action by Member States regarding the treatment of waste. The Article by itself did not, however, require the adoption of specific measures or particular methods of waste disposal. Further, it was not capable of conferring rights on which individuals could rely as against a Member State, because its requirements were not unconditional or sufficiently precise.

(*h*) Reduction in movements of waste

7–016 The Waste Framework Directive states that movements of waste are to be reduced, and that Member States should take necessary measures (in the waste management plans which they are required to draw up under Art. 7 of the Directive) to prevent movements of waste which are not in accordance with their waste management plans.

(*i*) Producer responsibility

7–017 As mentioned, one of the principles underlying the regulation of specific waste streams, like end-of-life vehicles and waste electrical equipment, is the principle of "producer responsibility". This principle was set out in the European Commission's 1989 Waste Management Strategy. Products placed on the market should "make the smallest possible contribution by their manufacture, use or final disposal, to increasing the amount of harmfulness of waste and pollution hazards".[12]

Traditionally, the cost of disposing of waste products has been borne either by the environment or the taxpayer, but this is incompatible with EC Treaty principles. Instead, producers, suppliers, consumers and public authorities must all share waste-management responsibilities for a product throughout its life. It is the product manufacturer who has the predominant role. This is because the manufacturer is the one who is able to take key decisions concerning the waste management potential of his product caused by its design, its use of specific materials, and its marketing.[13]

(*j*) "Cradle to grave" management

7–018 Waste management in the UK is based on a "cradle to grave" approach. That is to say, legal control is exercised over waste from the moment it originates to the moment when it is finally disposed of. Waste is regulated when it is being kept, transported, treated, and deposited.

(*k*) The "duty of care"

7–019 An offshoot of the UK "cradle to grave" principle is that a producer or handler of a waste material should not be able to abdicate responsibility for it entirely by passing it on to another party. This principle is given effect to by the concept of "duty of care" as respects waste,[14] which requires any person who deals with waste to:

- satisfy himself that it is being dealt with responsibly by persons further down the waste disposal chain, to whom it is passed on;

---

[11] [1994] Env. L.R. 281.

[12] See *European Commission Waste Management Strategy* SEC (89) 934 Final (1989).

[13] See *Review of the Community strategy for waste management*, Communication from the European Commission COM (96) 399.

[14] See Royal Commission on Environmental Pollution, Eleventh Report: *Managing Waste: The Duty of Care* (1985) Cmnd. 9675.

- prevent the escape of waste from his or anyone else's control;
- ensure that waste which is transferred is accompanied by a description of it which is adequate to enable the person to whom it is passed on to act responsibly.

(*l*) The "fit and proper person" principle

In the UK, only those who are "fit and proper persons" are allowed to manage waste. **7–020** Whether this is so is determined by the Environment Agency, in accordance with the Environmental Protection Act 1990. In essence, the Act provides that those managing waste must be technically competent to do so, have sufficient finances to meet their legal obligations regarding the waste, and not have any criminal convictions for waste management offences.

A: WHAT IS "WASTE"?

Introduction

The consequences of a material or substance being determined to be waste are **7–021** important. The material will be subject to regulatory controls, with accompanying costs, and will also be perceived more negatively by the public. Deciding whether a material or substance is waste is probably one of the most complex areas of environmental law.

The current definition of waste originates in the EC Waste Framework Directive, and is adopted in UK law. It is, however, too comprehensive to provide sufficient clarity for many purposes, and has therefore been the subject of much judicial debate at both EC and national level. Unfortunately, decisions of the ECJ have successively failed to provide any real degree of certainty as to when a substance or object is waste. The ECJ appears to have resisted laying down any definitive criteria. This is probably because of a desire to ensure the effectiveness of legislative control over waste, and a fear that taking anything other than a broad approach to the definition of waste might undermine that effectiveness.

The ECJ has therefore interpreted the definition of waste widely, in light of the aim and purpose of EC waste legislation—namely the protection of human health and the environment against harmful effects of waste management activities—and also in the light of general EC policy on the environment, which aims at a high level of protection, based in particular on the precautionary principle and the principle that preventive action should be taken. UK judges have not found this approach an easy one to follow. In *Castle Cement v Environment Agency*, for example, Stanley Burnton J. described the guidance given by the European Court of Justice to national courts as "less than pellucid", and as a "Delphic utterance [which] may positively mislead."[15]

The Framework Directive's definition of "waste"

The definition of "waste" set out in the Waste Framework Directive is as follows: **7–022**

---

[15] [2001] Env. L.R. 46, at paras 18 and 19.

"any substance or object in the categories set out in Annex I which the holder discards or intends or is required to discard."

The categories of waste set out in Annex I of the Directive include:

- production or consumption residues not otherwise specified below;

- off-specification products;

- residues of industrial processes;

- products for which the holder has no further use;

- any materials, substances or products which are not contained in the above categories.

As can be seen, these are extremely broad categories, which, given the existence of the last category, allow practically anything that is, or will be, discarded to qualify as "waste". The advantage of this approach is that it provides sufficiently flexibility of definition to prevent all discarded substances or objects from causing harm to the environment. The disadvantage is that considerable uncertainty can arise about when waste regulation rules should apply.

In the light of this, the European Commission has set out a detailed list of wastes considered to fall within the Annex I categories, known as the European Waste Catalogue. Here, wastes are grouped according to the industrial processes that produce them. The aim of the catalogue is to provide a uniform list which can be used across the EC to ensure a common approach in waste regulation (the catalogue attempts to clarify which wastes should be treated as hazardous). However, whilst listing by name provides clarity, it is inflexible as a regulatory technique because the list needs frequent updating to take account of technical developments. Further, inclusion of a material in the list does not necessarily mean the material is "waste"—it will only be waste if, in addition, it satisfies the general definition of waste (*i.e.* "discarding" by the holder).

Unsurprisingly, the reference in the general definition to the term "discard" has assumed great importance. The problem is that the term "discard" can cover situations where a substance or object is destined for *disposal* as well as situations where it is passed on, or set aside, for *recovery or recycling* purposes. Disposal operations are listed in Annex IIA of the Directive. They include deposit into landfill, release into a water body, and incineration on land or sea. Recovery operations are listed in Annex IIB. They include recycling, solvent reclamation, regeneration, and use principally as a fuel to generate energy. A "holder" of waste is defined as "the producer of the waste or the natural or legal person who is in possession of it". A "producer" means anyone whose activities produce waste (original producer) or anyone who carries out "pre-processing, mixing, or other operations resulting in a change in the nature or composition of the waste".

The UK definition of waste adopts wholesale the definition in the Framework Directive, by declaring that "waste" is "Directive waste", and stating, in the relevant regulations:

"Directive Waste means any substance or object in the categories set out in Part II of Schedule 4 which the producer or the person in possession of it discards or intends or is required to discard."[16]

Before embarking on an analysis of the occasionally obtuse case law on the definition of waste, it is useful to remember that in most cases it will be relatively clear whether something is waste or not. The case of ordinary disposal operations is relatively unproblematic. The difficulties arise with re-use, recovery and recycling—because in these contexts one person's "waste" can be another person's (or even the same person's) raw material. It has been pointed out that one of the key issues here is whether the definition of "waste" might be said to be too broad in situations where normal industrial processes involve more than one use of a particular substance without posing a threat to the environment.[17]

Questions before the courts

Some of the questions the courts (both the European Court of Justice and national **7–023** courts) have been asked to answer include:

- The manageress of a laundry in Italy was prosecuted for storing sludge from dry-cleaning machines in her laundry, on a temporary basis. Is the temporary storage of waste a "waste management activity" within the meaning of EC legislation, although it is not expressly mentioned in that legislation? (Held: **Yes**)

- Is acid, discarded by one person, having been used to strip metal surfaces, but very useful to another person, who transports it from one region in Italy to another region, a waste for which a waste management permit is necessary? (Held: **Yes**)

- Is left-over rock from the extraction of ore, which is stored near the ore mine, a waste? Some of the rock will remain there permanently, a small amount will be used as raw material for aggregates, some will be landscaped, and some will be used to fill in underground parts of the mine. (Held: **Yes**)

- Is a substance resulting from a manufacturing process, which is then burned as a fuel for use in the cement industry without adverse environmental effects, to be regarded as a waste or as a raw material? (Held: **A waste**)

- Are powdered wood residues from the construction and demolition industry, which are treated and then used as a fuel to generate electricity, to be regarded as waste? (Held: **Yes**)

- Does the fact that the disposal or recovery of a substance forms part of an industrial process (being carried out by the undertaking which produced the

---

[16] Waste Management Licensing Regulations 1994 (SI 1994/1056). See also the similar definition inserted into the Environmental Protection Act 1990 by Sch.22 of the Environment Act 1995. The Regulations also amend the definition of controlled waste previously used in UK legislation, so that any waste that does not fall within the definition of "Directive waste" is to all intents and purposes excluded from regulatory control. Guidance on the definition of waste is to be found in Circular 11/94.

[17] Ilona Cheyne, "The Definition of Waste in EC Law" J.E.L. Vol.14, No.1, p.61.

substance, at the place of production, as opposed to elsewhere by a specialist disposal or recovery company) remove it from the scope of the Waste Framework Directive? (Held: **No**)

- Does the concept of waste exclude objects that possess an economic value, or are dealt with as part of a continuous commercial cycle? (Held: **No**)

The approach of the European Court of Justice

7–024   Advocate-General Alber, in the *ARCO Chemie* case,[18] noted:

"There is general acknowledgement that the definition of waste in the Waste Framework Directive is too vague to provide a generally valid, comprehensive definition of waste. Instead the question of whether or not the substance concerned is to be regarded as waste has to be determined on a case-by-case basis in the particular circumstances."

The importance of the term "discard"

7–025   Whether the holder of a material intends to "discard" it is central to any decision as to whether the material is waste. The intention of the holder is to be interpreted objectively, not according to his claims as to his intention. This is on the basis that it would be very easy for a holder of waste, by declaring an intention not to discard, to circumvent the requirements imposed by the legislation.[19] As we have noted, the term "discard" covers both disposal of substances and objects, and passing them on, or keeping them, for use in recovery operations.[20]

At one stage, the ECJ tried to simplify matters, and provide greater clarity, by suggesting that, where disposal or recovery operations (listed in Annex II of the Waste Framework Directive) were to be carried out, the substance in question would always have been "discarded" and therefore waste. Later cases have rejected this view. The fact that a substance undergoes one of the waste disposal or recovery operations listed in Annex II does not necessarily mean it is to be classified as waste. Such an approach would be impractical for a number of reasons. For example, one of the listed recovery operations is spreading on land, which can involve either waste or non-waste materials (such as fertiliser). However, the fact that a substance is destined for one of the waste disposal or recovery operations may be an important indicator as to whether or not it is waste.[21]

Operations which are not listed in Annex II can still be recovery or disposal operations. Although the list is supposed to reflect operations which take place in practice, it would be inconsistent with the aim of the Directive (to protect human health and the environment) if unlisted operations were not included within its scope.[22]

---

[18] *ARCO Chemie Nederland Ltd. v Minister van Volkshuisvesting, Ruimtelijke Ordening en Milieubeheer* (C418/97) [2000] E.C.R. p.I–04475
[19] *ibid.*
[20] See Case C-129/96 *Inter-Environnement Wallonie ASBL v Région Wallonne* [1997] E.C.R. I–07411.
[21] *ARCO Chemie Nederland Ltd v Minister van Volkshuisvesting, Ruimtelijke Ordening en Milieubeheer* (C418/97) [2000] E.C.R. I-04475.
[22] *ibid. per* Advocate-General Alber.

In the joined cases of *Lirussi* and *Bizarro*,[23] the issue was the *storage* of waste prior to collection. The Directive does not expressly refer to this activity as a disposal or recovery operation. Indeed, in regulating waste management, the Directive takes as its starting point the point of collection. Nevertheless, the ECJ took a purposive approach, holding that waste awaiting collection should be regarded as Directive waste, because it was clearly a proper subject for the application of the "Art. 4 objectives" of preventing environmental harm.

Waste with a use or economic value

The central question (whether the holder discards or intends to discard the material) **7–026** becomes particularly difficult when one person's waste is another person's raw material, as tends to be the case when waste is recycled. Here, materials are transferred from a person who does not want them (and therefore might be said to have discarded them) to another person who wants them as a raw material for recycling. In such circumstances, although one person in the chain wants to be rid of the material, it might be thought that such material cannot sensibly be thought of as having been "discarded" in the normal sense of the word. This problem is compounded by the fact that some of the "disposal" and "recovery" operations listed in the Directive potentially overlap, *e.g.* incineration is listed as a disposal operation, whilst the use of waste as a fuel to generate energy is listed as a recovery operation. Similarly, soil biodegradation, listed as a disposal operation, overlaps with land treatment resulting in benefit to agriculture or ecological improvement, listed as a recovery operation.

In considering these issues, the European Court of Justice has indicated a reluctance to allow any escape from the rigorous controls of waste legislation. Thus, the Court has held that a material can still be "waste" even if it has a use or an economic value, as in *Vessoso & Zanetti*, where acid discarded after metal-stripping operations was made use of by undertakings manufacturing ferric chloride.[24] Such an approach can be explained on the basis that, from a regulatory point of view, it would be unwise to exclude materials destined for recovery, because of uncertainty as to whether a market will be available for such materials, given the volatility of recycling markets.[25]

Surplus materials and residues from production processes

Particular problems have arisen with surplus materials, residues, and by-products from **7–027** industrial processes which are usable in some way and may be of economic value. Examples include scrap metals, which can be recycled, and waste solvents, which can be blended to form industrial fuel. The difficulties here centre on deciding whether the process whereby the material is transformed into a useable product is a "waste recovery operation" (therefore dealing with "waste") or a normal industrial treatment or processing of material or substances. The courts are finding the distinction a difficult one to draw.

The fact that the collection, pre-treatment, disposal or recovery of a substance forms part of an industrial process does not automatically mean it is not a waste. The

[23] Joined Cases C–175/98 and C–177/98: *Criminal proceedings against Paolo Lirussi* (C–175/98) *and Francesca Bizzaro* (C–177/98) [1999] E.C.R. I–06881.
[24] Joined cases C–206/88 and C–207/88; [1990] E.C.R. I–1461.
[25] Ilona Cheyne, "The Definition of Waste in EC Law" J.E.L. Vol.14, No.1, p.61 at 65.

categories of waste in the Waste Framework Directive include production or consumption residues, and the list of disposal and recovery operations is sufficiently broad to cover dealings with all kinds of industrial residues, by-products and other materials resulting from production processes. Further, the Waste Framework Directive applies not only to disposal and recovery of materials by specialist undertakings, but to disposal and recovery by the undertaking which produced them, at the place of production. A substance is not therefore excluded from the definition of waste by the mere fact that it directly or indirectly forms an integral part of an industrial production process.[26]

The ECJ has taken the view that materials should only be regarded as industrial products (as opposed to waste) if re-use is a *certainty* and can be done without any further processing or treatment being necessary. Thus, left-over stone, resulting from quarrying, was held to be waste where it was stored for an indefinite length of time to await possible use. The company in question tried to argue that the left-over stone was a product which it did not intend to discard. However, the Court was only prepared to accept that this could be so if the re-use of the stone was a certainty (and not, as here, a possibility).[27]

In the *ARCO Chemie* case, the ECJ held that powdered wood-residues, resulting from construction and demolition operations, which were treated in an environmentally responsible manner and then used as a fuel to generate electricity, were to be regarded as waste. In taking this view, the Court pointed out that the danger to health and the environment typically posed by waste does not necessarily lie in the *nature of the substance itself*—it may lie simply in the fact that the holder discards the substance in question. This idea is reflected in Annex I of the Framework Directive, which classifies as "waste" products for which the holder has no further use. This classification does not refer to the danger posed by the products, but simply to the fact that the products are no longer wanted. Supervision of materials becomes necessary as soon as they cease to be used, and must take place in the interim period before they are disposed of or recovered, so as to ensure that environmentally-sound disposal or recovery takes place. The effect of this approach is that even harmless materials, such as surplus stone awaiting possible use, will be treated as "waste" requiring supervision, as will substances destined for environmentally-harmless recovery operations.

When does a material cease to be "waste"?

7–028   The courts have found similar difficulty in deciding whether and when a substance, having been waste, can cease to be waste. The issue here is that material which is not waste can be recovered from waste. One might, for example, recover from waste relatively pure metals, such as chromium, which are for all practical purposes identical to unused materials. In ordinary language, one would not describe such recovered substances as "waste".

In the *ARCO Chemie* case, the wood residues from construction and demolition were sorted and ground before being burnt to generate electricity. Sorting and grinding are recovery operations. However, the Court stated that the fact that the material was

---

[26] See Case C–129/96 *Inter-Environnement Wallonie ASBL v Région Wallonne* [1997] E.C.R. I–07411.
[27] Case C–9/00 *Palin Granit Oy v Vehmassalon kansanterveystyön kuntayhtymän hallitus* [2002] E.C.R. I–03533.

the end product of recovery operations was only *one factor* to be considered in deciding whether that material had ceased to be waste. The question had to be answered by reference to the issue of "discarding", having regard to the broad aims of the Directive. Thus, even where a substance has undergone a complete recovery operation, with the result that it has acquired the same characteristics as a raw material, that substance might nonetheless be regarded as waste if its holder intends to discard it. Such an approach is necessary to prevent a holder of waste from escaping regulatory control by simply processing it to transform it into something else for which he does not have a use.

Conclusion

We can see from the above that the ECJ has not been able to lay down any universally- **7–029** applicable definition of waste. It has declined to provide a clear test as to the meaning of "discard", which in turn means that there is no clear test for when a material will be "waste". Instead, what the judgments do is set out (in some detail) matters which do NOT determine whether a material is waste. These include:

- whether the material has been subjected to recovery operations;

- whether the material is destined for future use or recovery;

- whether the material is capable of environmentally-sound use without substantial pre-treatment;

- whether there are any adverse environmental impacts associated with the material;

- whether the view of those who deal with the material is that it is not waste.

The general approach of the ECJ has been that the question of when a material is waste should be decided on a case-by-case basis, will be heavily dependent on the particular circumstances of each case, and will be subject to a purposive approach which gives effect to the objectives of the Waste Framework Directive. The approach is summarised, in the *ARCO Chemie* case, in the words of Advocate-General Alber[28]:

"It is necessary to consider the spirit and purpose of the Waste Framework Directive to determine whether or not a substance poses a danger typical of waste such that it goes beyond the dangers posed by a comparable raw material and therefore requires regulation. That danger distinguishes between waste and primary raw materials. If a waste material is recovered or reprocessed so that a substance is obtained that no longer poses a danger typical of waste and, when used in a normal manufacturing process, does not pollute the environment any more than, but at most in the same way as, a raw material, that substance probably is no longer to be regarded as waste in the sense of being subject to control or authorisation for its further use . . . It is for the national court and the competent authorities to examine whether or not the substance in question

---

[28] *Per* Advocate General Alber in *ARCO Chemie Nederland Ltd v Minister van Volkshuisvesting, Ruimtelijke Ordening en Milieubeheer* (C418/97) [2000] E.C.R. I–04475 at para.109.

constitutes a danger typical of waste—that is to say one which goes beyond the dangers posed by a comparable primary raw material—so that supervision in accordance with the Directive must continue to be regarded as necessary."

The approach of the courts in England and Wales

7–030 Whilst the domestic courts have expressed frustration at the imprecision of the relevant ECJ decisions, they have adopted an approach based broadly on that of the ECJ, albeit occasionally with a slightly different emphasis.

In *Castle Cement v the Environment Agency*,[29] the court followed the approach of the ECJ in *ARCO Chemie*. The case arose out of the burning of Cemfuel (a fuel derived from blending waste solvents) in a cement kilns. The issue was whether this amounted to the burning of "waste" (and in particular a "hazardous waste"). Whilst accepting that Cemfuel is made from various different waste substances, Castle Cement contended that, because the process of waste recovery (blending them to make a fuel) had ceased at the time Cemfuel left its producer for delivery to Castle Cement's works, it had become a raw material akin to any other fuel. The Environment Agency, on the other hand, contended that the burning of Cemfuel in the cement kilns was part of (in fact the end of) that waste recovery process, which meant that Cemfuel remained waste until it was burnt.

The court held that Cemfuel remained waste until it was burnt in Castle Cement's kilns. In his judgment, Stanley Burnton J. took a different, more straightforward, approach to the issue that had concerned the ECJ in the *ARCO Chemie* case. His Lordship focused on the definition of the relevant recovery operation, namely "use principally as a fuel or other means to generate energy". Accordingly, the wastes used to produce the fuel could not be said to have been fully recovered until they were actually used for that purpose by Castle Cement. His Lordship acknowledged, however, that there were considerable difficulties associated with determining whether and when a substance ceases to be waste.

In *Attorney-General's Reference No.5 of 2000*,[30] the Court of Appeal, including the Lord Chief Justice, regarded it as "fortunate" that for the purposes of the reference it was not necessary for the court "to define what is meant by waste or what is meant by discard". The reasoning in *Castle Cement* was endorsed, on the basis of which it was held that a substance derived from animal rendering, and spread on agricultural fields without any intervening recovery operation, was capable of being waste.

In all of these cases where waste substances are subject to re-use, there is a difficult question of policy to be decided. On the one hand, the definition of "waste" must be drawn so as to encompass the policy objective of preventing environmental harm arising from the substances. On the other hand, given that the re-use of substances has environmental benefits, there is an argument that re-use should be encouraged by deregulation, which would imply that those substances should not be regarded as wastes.

[29] [2001] Env. L.R. 46.
[30] [2001] Env. L.R. 139.

B: WASTE MANAGEMENT LEGISLATION

As noted in the introduction to this chapter, waste legislation, at both EC and UK **7–031** level, may be divided into three main categories:

- legislation setting out a framework of control;

- legislation regulating waste treatment and disposal operations;

- legislation on specific waste streams.

Below, we consider each type of legislation in turn.

C: WASTE FRAMEWORK LEGISLATION

Three pieces of EC legislation—the Waste Framework Directive,[31] the Hazardous **7–032** Waste Directive[32] and the Waste Shipment Regulation[33]—establish a framework for the management of waste across the EC. They lay down a common set of general principles for waste management and a set of procedures for managing waste.

The Waste Framework Directive

Council Directive 75/442/EEC of July 15, 1975 on waste (as amended) (the "Waste **7–033** Framework Directive") sets out principles concerning waste management. It also attempts to provide a common definition of waste for use throughout the EC (The difficulties in applying the definition have been discussed above). The Directive was comprehensively revised in 1991[34] and again in 1996.[35] It regulates most forms of waste, although certain wastes (including agricultural waste and waste waters) are outside its scope, because they regulated by other means.

The preamble to the Directive states that the essential objective of all provisions relating to waste must be the protection of human health and the environment against harmful effects caused by the collection, transport, treatment, storage and tipping of waste. The main obligations of Member States are as follows:

- Member States must give priority to preventing waste from arising or reducing its production and its harmful effects. This can be accomplished particularly through the development and marketing of products designed to have minimal

---

[31] Directive 75/442/EEC of July 15, 1975 on waste, as amended by Dir.91/156/EEC of March 18, 1991 amending Directive 75/442/EEC on waste, O.J. L194 25.7.1975, p.39 and O.J. L78 26.3.1991, p.32.
[32] Council Dir.91/689/EEC of December 12, 1991 on hazardous waste, O.J. L377 31.12.1991, p.20.
[33] Council Regulation (EEC) No.259/93 of February 1993 on the supervision and control of shipments of waste within, into and out of the European Community, as amended, O.J. L30 6.2.1993, p.1.
[34] Council Dir.91/156/EEC of March 18, 1991 amending Dir.75/442/EEC on waste O.J. L 78 26.3.1991, p.32).
[35] Commission decision 96/350/EC of March 24, 1996 adopting Annexes IIA and IIB to Council Dir.75/442/EEC on waste (O.J. L135 6.6.1996. p.32) to update the disposal and recovery operations listed in Annexes IIA and IIB.

environmental impact. They must encourage the re-use and recovery of waste, and the use of waste as a source of energy.

- Member States must ensure that waste is recovered and disposed of without endangering human health and without using processes or methods which could harm the environment. In particular, recovery and disposal must be without risk to air, soil, plants or animals; without causing a nuisance through noise or odours; and without adversely affecting the countryside or places of special scientific interest. The abandonment, dumping or uncontrolled disposal of waste must be prohibited.

- Member States must establish an integrated and adequate network of disposal installations, taking account of the best available technology not involving excessive costs. Such a network must enable the EC to be self-sufficient in waste disposal.

- Member States are required to establish or designate a competent authority or authorities responsible for implementing the Directive. Specified tasks for the authorities include drawing up waste management plans, issuing permits and inspecting installations.

- Permits must be obtained from the competent authority by any establishment or undertaking which carries out disposal or recovery operations. Permits must regulate the types and quantities of waste handled, and the technical requirements relating to handling, such as security precautions and treatment methods.

The Hazardous Waste Directive

7–034 Whilst all wastes require regulation, simply because they are unwanted, some wastes require enhanced or specialised regulation because they pose a particular environmental threat (*e.g.* because they are explosive or toxic). Council Directive 91/689/EEC of December 12, 1991 on hazardous waste[36] builds on the Waste Framework Directive to establish a more stringent framework of control for hazardous waste. It aims to provide a precise and uniform European-wide definition of hazardous waste, and to ensure the correct management of such waste. Additional obligations, over and above the requirements of the Waste Framework Directive, include limitations on the mixing of hazardous wastes, and enhanced record keeping requirements.

"Hazardous waste" is defined as waste featuring as such in the European Waste Catalogue on the basis that the waste in question possesses one or more of the hazardous properties set out in the Directive. In Annex III of the Directive, 14 properties are listed as making a waste hazardous, including that the waste is explosive, highly flammable, irritant, toxic, carcinogenic, or infectious.

---

[36] As amended by Dir.94/311/EC.

The Waste Shipment Regulation

Council Regulation (EEC) No. 259/93 of February 1, 1993 (as amended) deals with **7–035**
cross-border shipment of waste.[37] It provides for the supervision and control of
shipments of waste within, into, and out of the EC, so as to preserve, protect and
improve the quality of the environment. It provides a harmonised set of procedures
whereby movements of waste can be limited. It is an accepted principle of EC law that,
in the context of the transport of waste, the importance of environmental concerns
fully justifies a derogation from the normal principles of free movement of goods. In
essence, the Regulation bans shipments of hazardous waste from EC countries to non-
OECD countries, in order to protect the environments of those countries.[38] In this
regard, the Regulation implements the provisions of international agreements
designed to address the concern that waste should not be exported from industrialised
countries to poorer parts of the world for disposal, where the costs may be less, but
where inadequate environmental protection measures may be in place.

For shipments within the EC, the principles of proximity and self-sufficiency allow
Member States to prohibit imports and exports of waste for disposal. However, these
principles do not apply to waste destined for recovery, so as to encourage the recovery
of waste. Therefore, such waste may move freely between Member States for
processing, provided that its transport poses no threat to the environment. The
procedures for shipments of waste for recovery vary according to whether the waste in
question is on the "Green list" of wastes—which "should not normally present a risk to
the environment if properly recovered in the country of destination"—or on the
"Amber list" or "Red list" of wastes regarded as particularly hazardous. EC
Regulations have direct effect, so the Waste Shipment Regulation applies without the
need for implementing legislation in Member States. However, in the UK, the
Transfrontier Shipment of Waste Regulations 1994[39] expand the Regulation and
ensure that it operates in practice.

Framework legislation in England and Wales

Part II of the Environmental Protection Act 1990 provides the basic framework for **7–036**
waste control in England and Wales. The provisions of the Act are supplemented by
the Waste Management Licensing Regulations 1994.[40]

(1) *Waste management licensing*

Anyone who deposits, recovers or disposes of controlled waste must do so in **7–037**
compliance with the conditions of a waste management licence.[41] This requirement is
disapplied for a number of activities,[42] but operators must still register the activity with

---

[37] Council Regulation (EEC) No.259/93 of February 1, 1993 on the supervision and control of shipments of
waste within, into and out of the European Community, O.J. L30, 6.2.1993, p.1. The Regulation implements
the EC's international obligations arising from the Basel Convention and the OECD Decision on
transboundary movements of waste.
[38] All imports of waste into the EC are prohibited except in accordance with the Basel Convention.
[39] SI 1994/1137.
[40] See also Waste Management Papers 4 and 4A (DETR); DoE Circular 11/94; Welsh Office Circular 26/94;
Scottish Office Environment Dept. Circular 10/94; DoE Circular 6/95; Welsh Office Circular 25/95; Scottish
Office Environment Dept. Circular 8/95; *Animal Remains Incineration—Guidance on Air Pollution Control*
PG5/3/95; PPG 23, *Planning and Pollution Control*.
[41] EPA 1990, s.33.
[42] Waste Management Licensing Regulations 1994, Reg.17 and Sch.3.

the Environment Agency. Such activities therefore remain within the broad ambit of regulatory control, but control is executed with a lighter regulatory touch, so as to encourage certain waste recovery activities. The exemptions cover a range of low-risk waste management activities, including the storage of waste at the place where it has been produced pending its collection.[43] The licensing regime is enforced by means of a number of criminal offences. It is an offence to:

- deposit controlled waste on land, or to knowingly cause or knowingly permit[44] controlled waste to be deposited, unless a waste management licence authorising the deposit is in force and the deposit is in accordance with the conditions of that licence;

- keep, treat or dispose of controlled waste, either on land or by means of a mobile plant, except in accordance with a licence;

- deal with controlled waste in any manner which is likely to cause pollution of the environment or harm to human health.

The last of these offences effectively means that, whilst the conditions of a waste management licence provide guidance to operators of waste disposal facilities, they can never provide an excuse for dealing with waste in an unacceptable way. Obviously, licence conditions cannot be imposed to cover every eventuality. This "residual" offence therefore ensures that environmentally acceptable standards are maintained in respect of any aspect of a waste handling operation not regulated by a specific condition.

(2) *The statutory duty of care*

7–038   The Environmental Protection (Duty of Care) Regulations 1991[45] provide further control. In essence, these regulations provide that persons handling waste have a duty to prevent other persons from committing waste management offences, and a duty to ensure that waste does not escape from their control. Thus, a holder of waste must make sure that it is dealt with responsibly by any other person, further down the waste management chain, to whom it is passed on. To achieve this, there is a requirement that, when waste is transferred, it must be accompanied by a written description such as will enable the transferee to deal with it appropriately. The duty to prevent waste from escaping implies, for example, that waste left in skips for collection should be covered if it is likely to be blown away.

(3) *Special waste*

7–039   Hazardous waste is referred to in the UK as "special waste". It is defined by reference to the Hazardous Waste Directive, the categories of hazardous properties in that Directive, and the list of hazardous wastes in the European Waste Catalogue.

---

[43] At the time of writing, certain exemptions (including land treatment, use of wastes for land reclamation, composting, storage, and spreading of sewage sludge) are under review, in the wake of allegations that they are being used for purposes other than genuine waste recovery.
[44] For discussion of "knowingly permit", see Ch. 8. Note that the defendant must "knowingly cause", as opposed to "cause".
[45] SI 1991/2839.

Regulation of special waste is more stringent than regulation of normal "controlled waste".[46] Details of consignments of special waste must normally be notified to the Environment Agency or the consignee before the waste is moved.[47] Consignment notes describing the waste must travel with the waste, and must be signed by the consignee to indicate safe receipt of the waste. During the transport or collection of special waste, it cannot be mixed with non-special waste, or with special waste of a different category.

D: LEGISLATION RELATING TO SPECIFIC WASTE OPERATIONS

Due to its general nature, framework legislation cannot take into account the **7–040** specificity of all waste management operations, nor of all waste materials. It is therefore supplemented by legislation concerning specific waste treatment and disposal operations. The main waste disposal operations subject to specific regulation are landfill and incineration.

Landfill

Landfilling waste means burying it in the ground. The environmental concerns **7–041** surrounding landfills include the production of landfill gases, including methane and carbon dioxide, formed during the decomposition of biodegradable wastes in landfill sites. These gases contribute to climate change. They also displace oxygen from soil, so that it can become unable to sustain plant growth. A particular danger associated with methane is the risk of explosion.

The UK and the EC have traditionally differed in their approaches to landfilling waste. The EC has seen landfill as a waste disposal method of last resort. In contrast, 85 per cent of waste in the UK has traditionally been disposed of by landfill. Further, the EC favours the treatment of degradable waste before it is placed in landfill sites, in order to reduce emissions of methane gas, whilst the UK has been reluctant to treat waste before it is put into landfill, arguing that this entails unnecessary expense. The UK is fortunate in having fewer problems with the emission of greenhouse gases than its continental partners, because of its large resources of natural gas, which are displacing coal for use in power generation (see Ch. 3). Unlike some of its European neighbours, therefore, the UK will be able to satisfy the timetable for the reduction of greenhouse gases set out in the Kyoto Protocol without the need for pre-treatment of landfilled waste. However, largely as a result of the EC Landfill Directive, current UK policy is to reduce the amount of waste going to landfill.[48] Another reason for this policy is a lack of space near urban centres in the UK, which makes it difficult to continue using land for waste disposal.

[46] See Special Waste Regulations 1996 (SI 1996/972).
[47] In certain cases (*e.g.* a succession of consignments) pre-notification is not required.
[48] *Waste Strategy 2000*, Cm 4693.

(1) *The Landfill Directive*

7–042   Directive 1999/31/EC of April 26, 1999 on the landfill of waste[49] was finally adopted, after an eight-year passage through the EC legislative process, in April 1999. Member States had until April 2001 to bring its provisions into force. In the UK, the Directive has had a more significant impact than in many other Member States, because of the UK's traditional reliance on landfill as the principal method of waste disposal. The main objectives and requirements of the Directive are as follows:

- To prevent or reduce as far as possible negative effects on the environment from the landfilling of waste (including pollution of surface water, groundwater, soil and air, and the emission of methane gas). To achieve this, protection of the environment should continue during the whole life-cycle of a landfill site, including when it has stopped receiving waste;

- To limit emissions of methane gas by reducing the amount of biodegradable waste going to landfill. The Directive sets reduction targets, and requires Member States to draw up an appropriate national strategy to meet them;

- To ensure that landfill sites are operated only by properly licensed persons, and that they may be closed only in accordance with specified closure and after-care procedures;

- To ban certain wastes from landfills. These include liquid wastes, tyres, and explosive, corrosive, flammable and infectious wastes;

- To ensure that waste is treated before going to landfill, in order to reduce its volume or hazardous nature, to facilitate its handling, or to facilitate recovery operations;

- To ensure that landfills are classified as landfills for "hazardous", "non-hazardous" or "inert" waste.[50] Once classified, landfill sites can only receive types of waste appropriate to their classification. The traditional UK practice of disposing of hazardous and non-hazardous wastes together must be stopped;

- To ensure that the estimated total costs of set-up, operation, closure and after-care of the site (for at least 30 years) are reflected in the price charged by landfill operators for accepting waste.

(2) *Regulation of landfill in England and Wales*

7–043   Landfills have traditionally been regulated under the waste management licensing regime (discussed above) as part of the general framework of licensing and control relating to the handling of waste. However, the Directive will introduce some key changes to UK landfilling practices—in particular, as noted above, the UK must abandon the practice of landfilling hazardous and non-hazardous wastes together. It must also pre-treat landfilled waste. Perhaps the most difficult change to accommodate will be the ban on landfilling certain types of waste (*e.g.* waste tyres).

---

[49] Council Dir.1999/31/EC of April 26, 1999 on the landfill of waste, O.J. L182, 16.7.1999, p.1.
[50] "Inert waste" is waste that does not undergo any significant physical, biological or chemical transformation once in a landfill.

The Landfill (England and Wales) Regulations 2002[51] implement the Landfill Directive. All landfills within the scope of these regulations are also regulated by the PPC Regulations (see Ch. 5). They therefore require a PPC permit to operate, although the Landfill Regulations set out the relevant regulatory controls.

A "landfill" is defined widely in the regulations as "a waste disposal site for the disposal of waste onto or into land". This normally includes "any site which is used for more than a year for the temporary storage of waste" and "any internal waste disposal site, that is to say a site where a producer of waste is carrying out its own waste disposal at the place of production". However, a site where waste is unloaded, in order to facilitate its preparation for further transport for recovery, treatment or disposal, will not be a "landfill"; nor will a site where "as a general rule" waste is sorted and kept for a period of less than three years prior to its recovery or treatment; nor any site where waste is stored for a period of less than one year prior to disposal.

The issue of defining "landfill" arose in *Blackland Park Exploration Ltd v Environment Agency*.[52] The claimant company operated an on-shore oil field. Liquid wastes, including water containing a variety of contaminants, were accepted on to the site and injected, via a borehole, into oil-bearing porous strata 1000m below the surface of the land. The company argued that this practice should be characterised as a discharge into a water environment (the oil-bearing strata being 1000m below sea level). However, the Court of Appeal took the view that the activity constituted a deposit of liquid waste into "landfill", and was therefore prohibited under the Landfill Directive and the Landfill Regulations. There was clearly a distinction to be maintained between waste disposal into land, on the one hand, and discharges into water, on the other—the latter being regulated by different legislation, and there would sometimes be cases where what was done fell somewhere near the boundary between the two. However, the fact that there was a great deal of water within the area of the site, and that the waste mixed with that water, did not prevent what was occurring from being a deposit of waste into *land*. The court was influenced by the fact that the waste was not being discharged into, say, an underground stream through which water might flow away from the place of discharge. For the company in question, the decision was disastrous—its effect is that it may have to shut down its operations because of the Landfill Directive's prohibition on the disposal of liquid waste to landfill. The decision is, perhaps, particularly draconian given that there was no suggestion in the case that the operations had had, or would be likely to have, any detrimental effect on the environment.

The landfill tax

In the UK, a tax is payable on disposals of waste made by way of landfill. This tax was **7–044** introduced by the Finance Act 1996, and is governed by a number of additional regulations.[53] The tax is not required under any provision of EC law, but is a separate domestic initiative.

[51] SI 2002/1559.
[52] CA [2003] EWCA IV 1795.
[53] See Finance Act 1996, ss.39–42. See also SI 2004/769; SI 2003/2313; SI 2003/605; SI 2002/1; SI 1999/3270; SI 1999/2075; SI 1998/61; SI 1996/2100; SI 1996/1528; SI 1996/1527.

Incineration

7–045 Directive 2000/76/EC on the incineration of waste[54] replaced three older Directives[55] and thus consolidated the EC's legal requirements concerning the incineration and co-incineration of hazardous and non-hazardous waste. The Directive establishes permit conditions for incineration plants, as well as limit values, for example in relation to emissions to air and discharges to water. A particular concern is to limit emissions of dioxins. The Directive includes requirements concerning the delivery and reception of waste, and relating to the management of incineration residues, including a requirement that, where appropriate, those residues should be recycled. It also includes requirements relating to monitoring and measurement. The Directive was implemented in the UK by regulations[56] that came into force on December 28, 2002.

E: LEGISLATION RELATING TO SPECIFIC WASTE STREAMS

7–046 Legislation to regulate specific waste streams has been motivated by the following considerations:

- Some waste streams are growing in volume or complexity, *e.g.* packaging waste, end-of-life vehicles, and waste electronic and electrical products;

- Some waste streams require specific control because they present special hazards, *e.g.* certain types of batteries, and products containing certain chemicals, such as polychlorinated biphenyls (PCBs);

- Some waste streams involve substances whose uncontrolled use can have harmful effects on human health and the environment, *e.g.* the uncontrolled spreading of sewage sludge on agricultural land.

The relevant legislation deals mainly with so-called "end-of-life products", as well as with discarded product packaging. The aim is that such materials should be recycled where possible. To achieve this, it is necessary to make provision for different types of waste to be collected separately (extracting different types of waste from a general, combined waste stream is often cost-prohibitive). It is worth noting that, when applied to household waste, separate collection requirements may have an incidental "consciousness-raising" effect, by requiring ordinary members of the public to become actively involved in environmental issues.

---

[54] Directive 2000/76/EC of the European Parliament and of the Council of December 4, 2000 on the incineration of waste, O.J. L332, 28.12.2000, p.91
[55] Council Dir.94/67/EC of December 16, 1994 on the incineration of hazardous waste (O.J. L365, 31.12.1994, p.34), Council Dir.89/369/EEC of June 8, 1989 on the prevention of air pollution from new municipal waste incineration plants (O.J. L163, 14.6.1989; p.32) and Council Dir.89/429/EEC of June 21, 1989 on the reduction of air pollution from existing municipal waste incineration plants (O.J. L203, 15.7.1989, p.50).
[56] Waste Incineration (England and Wales) Regulations 2002 (SI 2002/2980), Waste Incineration (Scotland) Regulations 2003 (SSI 2003/170); See also Pollution Prevention and Control (Designation of Waste Incineration Directive)(Scotland) Order 2003 (SSI 2003/204).

Under the relevant Directives, targets for recycling and recovery have been set in relation to a number of specific waste streams (packaging waste, end-of-life vehicles, and waste electronic and electrical equipment). These targets are necessary because separate collection and subsequent recycling of these products is not profitable under free-market conditions. Once such targets are set, the recycling industry can be confident that there will be a demand for its services in respect of particular waste products, and is thereby encouraged to invest in appropriate recycling facilities and technology. The operation of the free market is also modified by the concept of "producer responsibility", which requires manufacturers of products within specific waste streams to adopt a "cradle to grave" approach to those products. The idea is that they will pass on to consumers, in the price of new products, the costs of disposing of or recycling discarded products. This will mean, eventually, that the cost to a consumer of, say, a new hi-fi, will reflect the environmental cost associated with getting rid of an old one.

Packaging waste

Directive 94/62/EC on packaging and packaging waste[57] was one of the first pieces of **7–047** legislation to regulate a specific waste stream. The Directive has three main objectives:

- to reduce the effect of packaging on the environment;

- to co-ordinate national measures in order to prevent distortions to competition;

- to ensure the free movement of packaged goods.

Reducing the effect of packaging on the environment is to be achieved by limiting the disposal of packaging waste, and requiring, instead, that it should be re-used or recovered. Member States are required to establish "return, collection and recovery" systems. Targets are set for recovery and recycling of packaging waste. These targets are currently under review,[58] but the current draft targets are for Member States, by the end of 2008, to recover 60 per cent (by weight) of packaging waste, and to recycle between 55 and 80 per cent. Specific targets are set for the recycling of individual materials, *e.g.* glass (60 per cent), metals (50 per cent) and wood (15 per cent).

"Packaging" is defined widely to mean all products made of any material which is used for the "containment, protection, handling, delivery and presentation of goods". Packaging is subdivided into: sales or primary packaging (usually the packaging immediately surrounding the product, which the consumer unwraps); secondary packaging (generally removed by the distributor or retailer at or near the point of sale); and tertiary packaging (used for the handling and transportation of products in bulk).

Packaging which does not comply with certain "essential requirements" relating to its "composition and re-usable and recoverable nature" cannot be placed on the

[57] European Parliament and Council Dir.94/62/EC of December 20, 1994 on packaging and packaging waste, O.J. L365, 31.12.1994, p.10.
[58] A proposal has been published for a Directive amending Dir.94/62/EC on packaging and packaging waste: COM (2004) 0127.

market. Conversely, packaging which meets the "essential requirements" must be guaranteed free circulation within the European Community. Member States are required to develop national standards for the composition and re-usable nature of packaging.

The UK Packaging Regulations

7-048 The Packaging Directive is implemented by the Producer Responsibility Obligations (Packaging Waste) Regulations 1997 (as amended).[59] Although the Directive does not explicitly require *producers* to take responsibility for packaging waste, most Member States, including the UK, have chosen to implement it in this way. In the consultation paper which preceded the regulations, the government stated that: "more of the real environmental costs of waste production and disposal should be borne directly by the producers of waste and made visible to the consumer".

Under the regulations, responsibility for recovering packaging waste lies with all the various actors in the packaging chain (*e.g.* packers, retailers, and packaging manufacturers), all of whom are seen as "producers" of packaging waste.[60] Each member of the chain is given an "activity obligation", *i.e.* a percentage of packaging which must be recovered or recycled. Producers of packaging waste must take "reasonable steps" to recover and recycle specific tonnages of packaging, calculated on the basis of: (a) the tonnage of packaging handled by the producer in the previous year; (b) the "activities" that the producer performs and the percentage obligation attached to those activities; and (c) the national recovery and recycling targets.

The regulations do not require businesses to track and retrieve the actual packaging that passes through their hands. They can meet their recycling and recovery obligations by ensuring that an equivalent tonnage of *any* packaging is recycled or recovered. What this means in practice is that most businesses, rather than recover packaging themselves, will purchase from recycling companies a sufficient number of reprocessing certificates (called Packaging Recovery Notes) to demonstrate compliance. Businesses can choose to discharge their obligations by joining an industry-led scheme. The operators of the scheme take on the packaging waste obligations of businesses in return for a fee. They then contract to purchase Packaging Recovery Notes sufficient to cover the obligations all members of the scheme.

The essential requirements regulations

7-049 The Packaging (Essential Requirements) Regulations followed in 1998.[61] These limit the amount of cadmium, mercury, lead and hexavalent chromium which may be present in new packaging. In addition, the "essential requirements" are that packaging:

- must be the minimum required to ensure safety and hygiene that is also acceptable to the consumer;
- must be re-usable;

---

[59] SI 1997/648, as amended by SI 1999/1361. The Environment Act 1995 allows the Secretary of State to make regulations "imposing producer responsibility obligations" in respect of any waste stream.
[60] See *R. (on the application of Valpak) v Environment Agency* [2002] EWHC 1510 (Admin) 23 (bottles of drinks sold in a bar packaging); *Davies v Hillier Park Nurseries* [2001] Env. L.R. 42 (plant pots packaging).
[61] SI 1998/1165.

- must be manufactured so as to ensure the minimum hazardous residue after landfill or incineration;

- must be recoverable through recycling, incineration with energy recovery, composting or biodegradation.

These regulations are enforceable by the trading standards departments of local authorities. Failure to comply is a criminal offence.

End-of-life vehicles

Every year, disposal of vehicles at the end of their life generates between 8 and 9 **7–050** million tonnes of waste in the European Community.[62] Approximately 25 per cent of this waste is hazardous—amounting to around 10 per cent of the total hazardous waste generated in the EC each year. Directive 2000/53/EC on end-of-life vehicles[63] aims to reduce the amount of waste, and therefore the adverse environmental impacts, resulting from the disposal of vehicles. It aims to improve the environmental performance of operators involved at all stages of a vehicle's life, but particularly those involved in the treatment and recovery of disused vehicles.

The Directive applies to cars, vans and certain three-wheeled vehicles (*i.e.* the majority of vehicles) but does not apply to heavy goods vehicles. In line with the concept of a waste hierarchy, the Directive's priority is to ensure that waste is avoided, and then to ensure recycling and other forms of recovery. Accordingly, the focus is on reducing the use of hazardous materials in vehicle manufacture, and changing design and production techniques for new vehicles so as to make it easier for them to be dismantled, so their components can be re-used or subjected to recovery operations. This Directive was the first piece of EC legislation to make producer responsibility mandatory. The effect of the Directive is as follows:

- From July 2003, the use of lead, mercury, cadmium and hexavalent chromium in the manufacture of vehicles has been banned, except for a number of specified uses. The exceptions are expected to be narrowed in future, in accordance with technical and scientific progress;

- Member States must ensure that systems are in place to collect end-of-life vehicles, and that sufficient collection facilities are available. They must also take necessary measures to ensure that end-of-life vehicles are then transferred to authorised treatment facilities;

- Technical standards are set for the treatment of end-of-life vehicles, involving, for example, the removal of batteries, oils, metallic and plastic components, tyres and glass.

- The final owner or user of the vehicle is not expected to pay directly for the return of the end-of-life vehicle or its recovery treatment. Instead, manufacturers will be expected to bear a significant proportion of these costs (the remainder being met by government).

---

[62] See preamble to Dir.2000/53/EC. Note that figures are for the position prior to the accession of new Member States in May 2004.
[63] Directive 2000/53/EC of the European Parliament and of the Council of September 18, 2000 on end-of-life vehicles, O.J. L269 21.10.2000, p.34.

- Targets are set for the re-use of vehicle parts, or for the recovery and recycling of material where re-use is not appropriate.

Implementation of the Directive in the UK has proved controversial, mainly because of the issue of who should pay for the costs of taking back the large number of existing cars on the road that are reaching the end of their life (as opposed to the cost of eventually dealing with new cars, which might be reflected in their price). The UK failed, along with the other Member States, to meet the deadline for implementation of April 21, 2002. The Directive was eventually implemented by the End-of-Life Vehicles Regulations 2003,[64] although there is concern that these regulations effect only a partial implementation.

Waste electronic and electrical equipment

7–051 Directive 2002/96/EC on waste electronic and electrical equipment[65] (known as the "WEEE Directive") takes a similar approach to the End-of-Life Vehicles Directive. The Directive originated because of concerns that this type of waste was on the increase in the EC. Some Member States were introducing their own legislation for dealing with this type of waste, which had implications for market competition. Moreover, in order to achieve sustainable development, there needed to be significant changes in patterns of production and use of electronic and electrical equipment. The Directive took some time to be negotiated. The main areas of controversy included the questions of what should happen to "orphan waste" (products for which no producer still in existence could be found) and "historic waste" (products placed on the market before the requirements of the Directive could have been foreseen).

The purpose of the WEEE Directive is to prevent waste from arising, as well as to increase rates of re-use, recycling and recovery. It also aims to improve the environmental performance of producers, distributors and consumers involved in the life-cycle of electrical and electronic equipment. Equipment falling within the scope of the Directive includes large household appliances (*e.g.* fridges and washing machines), IT and telecommunications equipment, and electrical or electronic tools. The Directive implements producer responsibility for such equipment, *inter alia*, by setting targets for recovery of waste, requiring collection systems to be set up for the take-back of end-of-life equipment, and encouraging design and production techniques that take account of future re-use, recycling and recovery. For products placed on the market after August 13, 2005, producers will be responsible for financing the collection, treatment, recovery and environmentally-sound disposal of waste from their own products. It remains to be seen whether products will discharge this responsibility on an individual basis or by joining a collective scheme, similar to the scheme that operates in relation to packaging waste obligations (discussed above). Key requirements of the Directive are:

- The disposal of WEEE as unsorted municipal waste must be phased out, and high levels of separate collection of WEEE must be achieved;

---

[64] SI 2003/2635.
[65] Directive 2002/96/EC of the European Parliament and Council of January 27, 2003 on waste electronic and electrical equipment (WEEE) O.J. L37 13.2.2003, p.24.

- By December 31, 2006 at the latest, an average of 4kg per inhabitant per year of WEEE must be separately collected from private households. A new target will be set by December 31, 2008;

- Systems for the treatment of WEEE (which must be financed by producers) must use the best available treatment, recovery and recycling techniques. They may operated by individual companies or be set up as part of a collective scheme involving a number of producers. As a minimum, treatment is to include the removal of all fluids, plus appropriate treatment for specified forms of WEEE, *e.g.* the removal of batteries and components containing mercury.

The UK was required to comply with the Directive by August 13, 2004. At the time of writing, the government has consulted on draft regulations which would transpose most of the principal requirements of the Directive.

Other legislation on specific waste streams

(*a*) Polychlorinated biphenyls (PCBs)

Polychlorinated biphenyls (PCBs) are organo-halogen compounds which are now used **7–052** mainly as insulating fluids. They do not break down very easily in the environment and can be toxic to humans and wildlife. Directive 96/59 on the disposal of PCBs and polychlorinated terphenyls sets out a system of control for the elimination of PCBs. Member States must take steps to identify PCBs, dispose of them by a specified deadline, and decontaminate or dispose of contaminated equipment. Production of PCBs in the UK ceased in 1977. The major uses of PCBs are now in transformers and large capacitors. All new uses are now banned. Disposal of PCBs is regulated by the Environmental Protection (Disposal of Polychlorinated Biphenyls and Other Dangerous Substances) (England and Wales) Regulations 2000.[66]

(*b*) Batteries and accumulators

Directive 91/157 on batteries and accumulators containing certain dangerous sub- **7–053** stances[67] has as its purpose reducing the amount of pollution from used batteries containing lead, mercury or cadmium. It encourages recycling and the production of batteries containing lower levels of these metals, and aims to co-ordinate national measures to achieve these objectives. The European Commission has presented a proposal for a revised Directive on batteries and accumulators,[68] in line with the call for its revision contained in the preamble to the WEEE Directive. The current Directive does not require the recycling of used batteries, and does not require that Member States control or measure the disposal of used batteries, with the result that collection of used batteries remains low. Many are still disposed of by landfill or incineration. The proposal calls for a requirement of a collection rate of 160g per

---

[66] SI 2000/1043.
[67] Directive 91/157/EEC (O.J. L78 26.3.91) as amended by Dir.93/86/EEC (O.J. L264 23.10.93) (on markings) and Dir.98/101/EC (O.J. L1 5.1.99) (prohibiting certain batteries).
[68] Proposal for a Directive of the European Parliament and of the Council on batteries and accumulators and spent batteries and accumulators (COM (2003) 723 Final) of November 21, 2003.

inhabitant per year; an 80 per cent collection rate of portable nickel-cadmium batteries; separate collection targets for automotive batteries; recycling targets; and a ban on cadmium in batteries.

(*c*) Sewage sludge

7–054 Directive 86/278 is concerned with sewage sludge used in agriculture. It aims to ensure that human beings, animals, plants and the environment are protected against harmful effects from the uncontrolled spreading of sewage sludge on agricultural land. It aims to promote the appropriate use of sewage sludge in agriculture. The spreading of sewage sludge on agricultural land is banned whenever the concentration of one or more metals in the soil (resulting from the practice) exceeds specified limits. There is also a requirement that sewage sludge must normally be treated before use. The Sludge (Use in Agriculture) Regulations 1989 implement the Directive. The main burden of the regulations falls on water companies in England and Wales, and public authorities in Scotland and Northern Ireland. They are charged with analysing sewage sludge (every six months), testing soils (at first application and then every 20 years), providing farmers with information, and keeping records.

Chapter 8

WATER POLLUTION

"Water is not a commercial product like any other, but, rather a heritage, which must be protected, defended and treated as such." (EC Water Framework Directive)

Introduction

Water is vital. We drink it to stay alive; we wash in it. It is needed in agriculture for **8–001** irrigating land and for rearing livestock. Industry uses it as a raw material and as a coolant. It provides a habitat for fish and aquatic animals. It has an important psychological function in that it provides recreational areas of natural beauty. In addition, it is an important medium for processing and disposing of liquid waste.

Water pollution can occur in a number of ways. Substances such as sewage, chemical effluents and detergents are commonly released into water both accidentally and deliberately. Controlling discharges of sewage into watercourses has long been a concern of the water pollution control regime. Agriculture is a significant cause of water pollution both in terms of spills of agricultural slurry, and in terms of pesticides and fertilisers leaching into watercourses. Acidification of waterways by acid rain, which causes damage to animal and plant life, is also a problem. Water pollution can originate from easily identifiable "point" sources, such as effluent pipes from industrial sites or sewage treatment works, or from "diffuse" sources such as acid rain or surface water "run-off". Diffuse pollution is an increasing problem and cannot be as easily controlled as point source pollution.

Combating water pollution is made difficult by the fact that different types of waters (canals, ponds, lakes, tidal waters, for example) have different capacities for absorbing and dispersing pollution. River water, for example, has to some extent a natural purifying capacity by virtue of the micro-organisms present in it and the effects of sunlight and aeration. Because of this, discharges to rivers may safely be permitted up to a certain limit before pollution occurs. This makes river water a useful and effective medium for waste disposal. The problem for legislators, therefore, has been to impose sufficient controls to ensure that water does not become polluted, whilst avoiding needless over-regulation which would amount to the squandering of a valuable natural waste-removal facility.

A survey by DEFRA in 2002 found that, over the previous decade, general river quality in Great Britain had either improved or remained high. Approximately 95 per cent of rivers were of good or fair quality.[1] This may be due in part to the privatisation of the water industry which took place in 1989 and to the subsequent investment in treatment of sewage effluent. The contrast with water quality in the nineteenth century is striking. In his biography of London, Peter Ackroyd describes the Fleet River as the "insalubrious last resting place of dead dogs, corpses, human waste and noxious refuge."[2]

As in other areas of pollution control, controls over water pollution may be either preventive or remedial. Preventive controls aim to stop water pollution before it happens, for example by setting limits on the concentrations of particular pollutants which are permitted to enter certain waters, or by curtailing certain industrial activities and uses of land which have the potential to cause water pollution. Remedial controls, on the other hand, are aimed at cleaning up pollution after it has occurred, punishing the polluter, ensuring that he pays the costs of clean-up, and compensating people who have suffered as a result of the pollution. Such controls are, of course, preventive in so far as they serve as a deterrent to other potential polluters. Remedial and preventive forms of control are both found to varying degrees within the UK's water pollution regime.

The environment may suffer damage not only from the *pollution* of water, which is the focus of this chapter, but from the way in which water resources are *managed*. In times of drought, for example, an increased demand for water may, if improperly managed, lead to rivers drying up, with a consequent loss of flora and fauna, or to the intentional flooding and destruction of natural valleys to build reservoirs. Water management regulation—which focuses on such matters as land drainage, and the abstraction of water for human consumption, irrigation or industrial purposes—is beyond the scope of this book. Here, we consider the controls to be found in legislation relating specifically to water pollution. We also consider the role of the common law. European Community water law, which has had a significant influence on the development of UK water law, is considered first. This chapter is concerned with the law relating to pollution of inland and coastal waters. Pollution of the high seas is regulated by a separate legal regime and is, again, beyond the scope of this book.

A: European Community Water Law

8–002 The UK's statutory regime in relation to water has been heavily influenced by European Community water law, which is now approximately 30 years old. Water pollution was the focus of the earliest environmental policies developed by the European Community. It is now the most developed area of EC environmental law and has been successful in improving water quality throughout the Community.[3] In addition to the standards set by EC legislation, court cases brought by the European Commission against Member States like the UK for non-compliance with the Directives have, at least in the case of the UK, led to raised awareness of, and investment in, water quality.

[1] DEFRA, Statistical Release 385/03, September 23, 2003.
[2] Peter Ackroyd, *London—The Biography* (Vintage, 2001) p.537.
[3] See Ludwig Krämer, *EC Environmental Law*, 5th ed. 2003, Ch. 7.

The development of EC water policy

The "first wave" of European water legislation began in 1975 with the adoption of **8–003** standards for rivers and lakes used for the abstraction of drinking water.[4] In 1980, legally binding standards were set for drinking water.[5] This period also saw legislation setting quality objectives for fish waters, shellfish waters, bathing waters and groundwaters.[6] Emissions to water were controlled by the Dangerous Substances Directive, which prohibited discharges of certain substances into water and regulated the discharge of others.[7]

The "second wave" of legislation was introduced to make improvements and fill gaps in the existing system of regulation. Legislation adopted included:

- the Urban Waste-Water Treatment Directive, requiring the treatment of waste waters[8];

- the Nitrates Directive,[9] addressing water pollution caused by the use of nitrates in agriculture;

- a new Drinking Water Directive, reviewing the quality standards laid down in the earlier directive and, where necessary, tightening them[10]; and

- the Directive on Integrated Pollution and Prevention Control (IPPC), regulating pollution, including water pollution, from large industrial installations.[11]

This legislation made significant progress in tackling individual issues so as to improve water quality in the European Community—the Drinking Water Directive and the Urban Waste Water Directive were particularly significant. However, water policy was widely considered to be fragmented in its objectives. The legislation tended to be a piecemeal response to problems of water quality, and was becoming increasingly outdated as technical and scientific developments meant higher standards were achievable. There was little thought given to whether pollution was best reduced by fixed limits on discharges of particular substances to water, or by the use of "quality objectives" for particular stretches of water, which might vary according to the use to which that water was put.[12] Nor was there proper consideration of the relationship

---

[4] Directive 75/440 on the protection of surface waters for the abstraction of drinking water [1975] OJ L194/6.
[5] Directive 80/778 relating to the quality of water intended for human consumption [1980] OJ L229/11.
[6] Council Dir.78/659/EEC of July 18, 1978 on the quality of fresh waters needing protection or improvement in order to support fish life [1978[OJ L222/1; Council Dir.79/923/EEC of October 30, 1979 on the quality required of shellfish waters; Council Dir.76/160/EEC of December 8, 1975 concerning the Quality of Bathing Water; Council Dir.80/68/EEC of December 17, 1979 on the protection of groundwater against pollution caused by certain dangerous substances.
[7] Council Dir.76/464/EEC of May 4, 1976 on pollution caused by certain dangerous substances discharged into the aquatic environment of the Community.
[8] Council Dir.91/271/EEC of May 21, 1991 concerning urban waste-water treatment.
[9] Council Dir.91/676/EEC of December 12, 1991 concerning the protection of waters against pollution caused by nitrates from agricultural sources.
[10] Council Dir. 98/83/EC on the quality of water intended for human consumption.
[11] Directive 96/91/EC concerning integrated pollution prevention and control.
[12] Historically, Directives on water have tended to be drafted in one of two ways: they were either concerned with limiting the discharge of particular substances into waters, or they were concerned with establishing environmental quality standards (objectives) for particular stretches of water, according to the uses to which that water is put (*i.e.* the focus is on the quality of the receiving water). The Water Framework Directive accepts that both approaches are necessary.

between water use and other areas of environmental protection. In addition, it was increasingly felt that further action was required to avoid the long-term deterioration of fresh water quality and quantity.[13] These problems may, in part, have arisen because water policy is an area of mixed competence, in which both the EC and Member States take action. The Community takes action only where it is better placed to do so.

Pressure for a fundamental rethink of Community water policy came to a head in the mid-1990s. The European Council and the European Parliament called for a fundamental review of water policy in June 1995. In response, in 1996 the European Commission set out its new approach to water protection.[14] This approach was far broader in its considerations than the prevention of water pollution. Its stated objectives were:

- To provide a secure supply of drinking water throughout the Community which is safe in quality and sufficient in quantity;

- To provide a supply of water which is of sufficient quality and quantity to meet the needs of industry and agriculture;

- To maintain and enhance the ecological state of the aquatic environment; and

- To manage the water supply so as to prevent or reduce floods and drought.

The European Commission also identified the need for a single piece of framework legislation to meet these objectives. In 1997, the Commission presented a proposal for a Water Framework Directive, which was eventually adopted in October 2000.[15]

B: THE WATER FRAMEWORK DIRECTIVE

8–004 The Water Framework Directive is the most significant and ambitious piece of EC water legislation to date. The preamble sets the tone of its aspirations:

"Water is not a commercial product like any other, but, rather a heritage, which must be protected, defended and treated as such."

The Directive seeks to bring together the regulation of inland water use and quality in the Community under a single and simplified framework, consolidating the provisions of earlier, piecemeal legislation. It protects all surface and groundwaters (defined as rivers, canals, lakes, reservoirs, estuaries and coastal waters up to one mile from the shore). Previously, only water bodies specifically designated by Member States were protected by legislation. Under the Framework Directive, all water bodies are subject to quality objectives.

The Directive's objectives are wide-ranging and draw together the objectives of the earlier discrete pieces of legislation:

---

[13] See preamble to Water Framework Directive.
[14] Communication from the Commission to the Council and the European Parliament—European Community Water Policy Com/96/0059 Final.
[15] Directive 2000/60/EC of the European Parliament and of the Council establishing a framework for Community action in the field of water policy.

(1) to prevent further deterioration of the water environment and protect and enhance it;

(2) to promote sustainable water use, based on long-term protection of available water resources;

(3) to reduce, cease or phase out over time discharges and emissions of harmful substances to water;

(4) to reduce groundwater pollution; and

(5) to mitigate the effects of floods and droughts.

The Directive is likely to be hugely influential in terms of water management within the EC over the next 20 years, although it is too early to know whether its objectives will be met. Member States were required to implement the Directive into national law by December 2003, but they have until 2027 to meet some of the objectives. The Directive requires a balancing of environmental, economic and social considerations and a long programme of technical, preparatory and implementation work up until 2015.

The Directive gives effect to the principle of subsidiarity, leaving much of the detail of implementation to Member States. This is in particular contrast with previous Directives, which set emission limit values to be adhered to by all Member States. The new approach is to set common objectives for water quality at EC level, to be used by Member States in establishing measures at a local and national level to achieve the European objectives. This provides the flexibility which is necessary to accommodate the diverse range of environmental conditions found in different parts of the Community. It remains to be seen, however, whether environmental standards overall will decline if direct Community involvement in pollution control is lessened.

River basins

The Directive takes as its starting point that the best approach for the management of **8–005** water is to work with "river basins". A river basin is the natural geographical and hydrological unit of a watercourse. A good way to visualise a river basin is to liken it to a tree trunk—all the streams, surface waters and ground waters are branches which flow into the tree trunk.[16] The management of the River Rhine, by countries including Switzerland, Germany and the Netherlands, is an example of management based on a river basin rather than on national borders. Whilst some Member States have organised their water management functions in this way in the past, others, like the UK, have preferred to do so according to political and administrative boundaries.

River basin management plans

All waters are to be classified as having "high", "good", "fair", "poor" or "bad" status **8–006** according to a number of ecological, chemical and hydrological criteria. The concept of status is used for setting the main environmental objectives for river basin waters.

---

[16] A "river basin" is defined as "the area of land from which all surface run-off flows through a sequence of streams, rivers and possibly, lakes into the sea at a single river mouth, estuary or delta".

River basin management plans should be developed to achieve a "good" status for all waters within a particular "river basin district", according to specified environmental objectives (see below) designed to ensure the waters reach the requisite quality.[17] The plans should detail how the objectives set for the river basin district are to be reached within the time-scale required. They should consider the impact of human activity on the waters, and should also include an analysis of the effectiveness of full implementation of all existing water legislation. If existing legislation will ensure that the waters achieve the objectives, no additional measures need be specified, and the requirements of the Framework Directive are attained. However, if it will not, Member States must design additional measures to satisfy the Directive's objectives (*e.g.* stricter controls on pollution from industry, agriculture, or urban waste water sources). In addition, an economic analysis of water use within the river basin must be carried out, so as to enable discussion on the cost-effectiveness of the various possible measures.

Environmental objectives

8–007 **(i) Ecological Status**: One of the key objectives is general protection of the aquatic ecology. This is justified on the basis that a central requirement of the EC Treaty is that the environment be protected to a high level in its entirety. The objective of ecological protection applies to all surface waters. The concept of "good ecological status" is at the heart of the Directive, and must be achieved by all surface waters. However, it has yet to be fully defined and is complex. It relates to the quality of the biological community, and the hydrological and chemical characteristics of the water, but cannot be defined by any absolute standards which apply across the Community, because of ecological variability. The Directive lays down a set of procedures for identifying the ecological status of a given body of water, together with a system for ensuring that each Member State interprets the procedure in a consistent way (to ensure comparability). The system is complicated, but this may be expected, given the extent of ecological variability across the EC. It is too early to determine whether the approach will succeed.

(ii) Chemical Status: This objective requires all surface waters to reach a general minimum chemical standard known as "good chemical status". Good chemical status is derived from compliance with all the relevant European water quality standards relating to chemical substances.

(iii) Other objectives apply only to specific bodies of water. Thus, there are specific objectives in relation to unique and valuable habitats (which apply to rivers supporting special wetlands), drinking water resources (which apply to waters identified for drinking water abstraction), and bathing water.[18]

The Directive also provides for a higher level of protection for "protected areas". It puts an obligation on Member States to comply with any objectives that have been set for those areas. "Protected areas" include areas designated under other Community

---

[17] Member States have to establish, by 2009, programmes for each river basin district. Such programmes must be updated every six years. Furthermore, for each river basin district, a river management plan has to be produced: Art. 13(1). This obligation is, for international river basin districts, limited to the territory of each Member State.

[18] Article 4(5).

legislation, such as habitats and species protection areas designated under the Habitats Directive or Birds Directive, or areas designated to protect drinking water abstraction points.[19]

In establishing the objectives for a particular river basin district, Member States may set less stringent environmental objectives for specific bodies of water which are so strongly affected by human activity that the achievement of the normal objectives is not feasible or is disproportionately expensive.

Groundwater

Groundwater protection has previously been regulated under its own Directive, but has **8–008** now been brought under the Framework Directive, thereby integrating the management of groundwater and surface water for the first time at European level.

The approach underlying the protection of groundwater is that it should not be polluted at all, because of the low rate of renewal of waters of this type. Setting chemical quality standards is not a suitable approach, as it suggests an allowable level of pollution. Instead, the approach, which is precautionary, comprises a prohibition on direct discharges to groundwater, and (to cover indirect discharges) a requirement to monitor groundwater bodies so as to detect changes in chemical composition, and to reverse any signs of human-induced pollution. Given that groundwater is limited in quantity (because of the low rate of renewal), abstraction from groundwater is only allowed to the extent that the water abstracted is not needed to maintain the ecology of the groundwater.

The Framework Directive requires the adoption of a daughter Directive on groundwater protection, to accommodate the detail of the protection measures. At the time of writing, such a Directive is making its way through the Community decision-making processes.[20]

Reduction of harmful substances

The Framework Directive requires that a list of priority substances with harmful effects **8–009** on water should be drawn up at EC level, and action taken, again at EC level, to design measures to reduce the discharge of these substances.[21] Discharges, emissions and losses to water of these priority substances must be completely stopped within a period which "shall not exceed 20 years" after the EC has decided on the substances in question. At the end of 2001, the EC adopted a list of priority substances.[22] The list contains 33 substances or groups of substances, out of which 25 are identified as priority hazardous substances. Detailed measures for dealing with these substances have not yet been suggested.[23]

---

[19] Article 7.
[20] Commission communication COM (2003) 550 final proposal for a Directive of the European Parliament and of the Council on the protection of groundwater against pollution.
[21] Article 16.
[22] Decision 2455/2001/EC of the European Parliament and of the Council of November 20, 2001, establishing the list of priority substances in the field of water policy and amending Dir.2000/60/EC.
[23] See working document ENV/1910000/01.

Cross-border river basin management

8–010 Many river basin districts cover geographic areas that form part of a number of different countries. The Directive aims to bring together different national plans for water management, in order that such river basins can be managed comprehensively. Whilst this is clearly very important in continental Europe, where large river basins, such as the Rhine, are cross-border in nature, the cross-border issue is also important for the British Isles, because Scotland, England, and to some extent Wales, have different administrative mechanisms for regulation.[24]

Member States are only obliged to produce river basin management plans for districts that lie entirely within their territory. For international districts, Member States must co-ordinate such plans among each other and, where non-EC countries are involved, must "endeavour to produce a single river basin management plan".[25]

Transposition into Member State law

8–011 Member States were required to transpose the Directive into national law by December 2003. By 2015, at the latest, "good status" must have been achieved for all surface and groundwaters. This deadline may be extended in certain circumstances.[26] As has been noted, the Directive also provides a quality objective exception where a body of water is so affected by human activity that only a lower status is achievable.[27]

Implementation in England and Wales

8–012 The Framework Directive has been implemented largely by means of secondary legislation.[28] Nine river basin districts have been identified in England and Wales. By December 2004, the Environment Agency must have completed its preparatory work in relation to these river basins. This includes reviewing the impacts of human activity, an economic analysis, and identifying which water bodies are used for the abstraction of drinking water.

C: OTHER WATER DIRECTIVES

8–013 As part of the reform instigated by the Water Framework Directive, seven of the "first wave" of Directives have been replaced, including the Directives on surface water, freshwater fish, shellfish water and groundwater. The Framework Directive will also

---

[24] DEFRA and the Scottish Environment Protection Agency are responsible for the characterisation of river basin districts. In England, the Environment Agency will be given statutory duties to administer the rules of the Framework Directive and ensure that its objectives are met. OFWAT will deal with the consumer pricing issues that the Directive also regulates.

[25] Article 13(4).

[26] Article 4(4.c). The circumstances include technical feasibility, specific natural conditions or the disproportionate cost of achieving that status.

[27] Articles 4(5), (6), and (7).

[28] The Water Environment (Water Framework Directive) England and Wales Regulation 2003, SI 2003/3242. See also: Water Environment (Water Framework Directive) (Northumbria River Basin District) Regulations 2003; and Water Environment (Water Framework Directive) (Solway Tweed River Basin District) Regulations 2004.

replace the Directive regulating discharges of dangerous substances to water, which has been one of the most important pieces of legislation.[29] Despite this, and the comprehensive approach adopted under the Framework Directive,[30] a number of sectoral Directives continue to regulate water quality.

The Drinking Water Directive

The objective of Dir.98/83 on the quality of water intended for human consumption, **8–014** and its 1980 predecessor,[31] one of the best known EC Directives, is to safeguard human health by requiring Member States to establish strict standards for the quality of water intended for human consumption.

Drinking water, at the point of entry into the domestic distribution system, must be wholesome and clean. Drinking water is wholesome and clean when the water is free from micro-organisms, parasites and substances which may, in numbers or in concentrations, constitute a potential danger to human health; and when the requirements of some 28 parameters, (*e.g.* for lead content and pesticide content) are respected.[32] Where the parameters are exceeded, Member States have to take remedial action. Member States may derogate from these requirements in certain circumstances.

Implementation by Member States has been problematic. In particular, there have been long delays and arguments over the extent to which governments could derogate from the Directive's requirements. The UK government was found by the European Court of Justice to be in breach of the 1980 Directive for its practice of accepting undertakings from water companies who had failed to supply wholesome water. The companies undertook that they would take all appropriate steps to comply with the relevant purity requirements set out in the Directive. The UK was found to be in breach because it had relied on the water companies to decide what needed to be done, rather than passing legislation specifying that the requirements should be met.[33]

Action in the ECJ against the UK and other Member States has not always succeeded in raising standards. In a number of places in the EC, drinking water does not yet meet the requirements of the Directive. However, the 1980 Directive did set, for the first time, objective standards for drinking water, and has over time led to a considerable but slow improvement. In the UK, for example, the Directive gave rise to the first statutory standards for wholesomeness of drinking water.[34]

[29] Council Dir.76/464/EEC of May 4, 1976 on pollution caused by certain dangerous substances discharged into the aquatic environment of the Community.

[30] Directive 2000/60/EC of the European Parliament and of the Council of October 23, 2000 establishing a framework for Community action in the field of water policy.

[31] Council Dir.98/83/EC on the quality of water intended for human consumption; Council Dir.80/778/EEC of July 15, 1980 relating to the quality of water intended for human consumption.

[32] Laid down in Annex 1(A) and 1(B).

[33] *Commission v United Kingdom* C–340/96.

[34] See Water Supply (Water Quality) Regulations 1989 (SI 1989/1147); Water Supply (Water Quality) (Amendment) Regulations 1991 (SI 1991/1837); Water Supply (Water Quality) (Amendment) Regulations 1999 (SI 1999/1524); Water Supply (Water Quality) Regulations 2000 (SI 2000/3184); Water Supply (Water Quality) (Amendment) Regulations 2001 (SI 2001/2885); Water Supply (Water Quality) Regulations 2001 (SI 2001/ 3911)

The Bathing Water Directive

8–015 The Bathing Water Directive,[35] which was one of the first pieces of European environmental legislation, aims to safeguard the health of bathers by maintaining the quality of bathing water. Limits are set for total coliforms, faecal coliforms, mineral oils, surface-active substances, phenols and number of other pollutants. The Directive was transposed into national law by Member States although, again, not without some long delays and court cases for non-compliance, including Member States' failure to designate waters as bathing water, thereby avoiding the Directive's requirements.[36] The UK was held to be in breach of the Directive in relation to the standards of the waters at Southport and Blackpool.[37] The Directive has, however, led to a significant improvement in bathing-water quality. At the time of writing, a proposed new Bathing Water Directive is currently making its way through the legislative process. The proposed new Directive aims to bring the quality of Community bathing water into line with scientific advances, and into line with the Water Framework Directive.

The Nitrates Directive

8–016 The Nitrates Directive, along with the Urban Waste Water Treatment Directive (see below) tackle the problem of eutrophication. Eutrophication is the process by which water becomes enriched with plant nutrients, typically phosphorus and nitrogen, leading to a reduction in dissolved oxygen in the water. This, in turn, reduces the capacity of the water to support aquatic life. The Directives also deal with the health effects of nitrates in drinking water, and sewage in bathing water areas. These Directives regulate specific polluting activities rather than setting emissions standards or water quality objectives.

Under Directive 91/676 on protecting waters from pollution caused by nitrates from agricultural sources, Member States must designate "Nitrate Vulnerable Zones" in their territories, and establish action programmes (*e.g.* prohibiting the use of certain fertilisers during certain periods). Member States must also establish a code of good agricultural practice, with the objective of reducing nitrate pollution. Implementation of the Directive has been problematic. In 2002, agriculture continued to be responsible for between 50 and 80 per cent of nitrate inputs into EC waters.[38] Pursuant to the Directive, 55 per cent of England has been designated as a Nitrate Vulnerable Zone (see below).

The Urban Waste Water Treatment Directive

8–017 The Urban Waste Water Treatment Directive,[39] adopted in 1991, aims to reduce pollution of surface waters by certain plant nutrients and by phosphates from urban waste water (composed of industrial waste water and domestic sewage). It establishes

[35] Council Dir.76/160/EEC of December 8, 1975 concerning the quality of bathing water.
[36] On transposition and compliance: see Case C–72/81 *Commission v Belgium* [1982] E.C.R. 183; C–96/81 *Commission v Netherlands* [1982]E.C.R 1791; C–56/90 *Commission v United Kingdom* [1993] E.C.R. I–4109; C–92/96 *Commission v Spain* [1998] E.C.R I–505; C–198/97 *Commission v Germany* [1999] E.C.R I–3257.
[37] Case C–56/90 *Commission v United Kingdom* [1993] ECR I–4109.
[38] Report COM (2002) 407: The implementation of Council Dir.91/676/EEC concerning the Protection of Waters against pollution caused by nitrates from agricultural sources.
[39] Council Dir.91/ 271/EEC of May 21, 1991 concerning urban waste water treatment.

certain conditions for the discharge, collection and treatment of waste water in urban areas. Areas of more than 15,000 people had to have a sewerage system in place by the end of 2000. Sewerage systems for all areas consisting of more than 2,000 people must be in place by the end of 2005. Urban waste water must be treated in suitable water treatment plants. Member States must designate as "Sensitive Areas" areas where special treatment is required. These include areas containing eutrophic waters and waters intended for the production of drinking water.

The Urban Waste Water Treatment (England and Wales) Regulations 1994[40] implement the Directive in England and Wales. Implementation of the Directive proved to be particularly problematic, because the UK was the only Member State which had traditionally adopted the practice of discharging sewage, largely untreated, to the sea (on the "dilute and disperse" principle) and which also practised sewage sludge dumping ("sewage sludge" is solid, semi-solid or liquid residue that is produced by sewage treatment works when treating domestic sewage). Sewage sludge was licensed for dumping on the shoreline or at sea. However, dumping at sea ceased in 1998.

D: THE WATER POLLUTION REGIME IN ENGLAND AND WALES

Modern water legislation in England and Wales may be divided into two distinct **8–018** strands: legislation to regulate the conduct of the water industry—the activities of which are an important potential source of pollution—and legislation specifically concerned with pollution control.

The water industry

The water industry is concerned mainly with the supply of clean water to the public **8–019** and with the disposal of waste water and waste in liquid form, particularly sewage. Water for public supply is abstracted from groundwater and inland waters, so preventing pollution of these waters is clearly important in terms of keeping down the costs of supply—if these waters become polluted, they will have to be treated, and the cost to the public of clean water will increase.

The Water Act 1973 established the basic framework of the modern water industry by creating regional Water Authorities to supply water and arrange for the disposal of sewage. The Water Authorities had a number of general regulatory functions including the conservation of water resources, the maintenance of fisheries and the supervision of land drainage. They were also responsible for controlling pollution by granting consents for the discharge of substances into water.

The Public Utility Transfers and Water Charges Act 1988 paved the way for privatisation of the water industry by restructuring the Water Authorities so as to separate their functions into two divisions. The first of these was concerned with the exercise of the Authorities' regulatory functions, whilst the second division was

---

[40] SI 1994/2841, as amended by the Urban Waste Water Treatment (England and Wales) Amendment Regulations 2003 (SI 2003/1788).

responsible for the practical business of water supply and sewage disposal. This move was welcomed by environmentalists, who had come to see the Water Authorities, with their overarching responsibility for the water cycle, as both poacher and gamekeeper in relation to water pollution. Indeed, one of the stated aims of the government's policy of water privatisation was the achievement of greater "accountability".

The Water Act 1989 divided the functions of the Water Authorities between the newly established National Rivers Authority and the newly formed private companies which were the successors to the Water Authorities. The National Rivers Authority (later the Environment Agency) inherited the main regulatory and water management functions of the Water Authorities, whilst the functions of water supply and sewage treatment were privatised. Ten limited companies were created to provide these services. The Office of Water Services (known as "OFWAT") was set up to regulate the supply of water and provision of sewerage facilities. From an environmental perspective, privatisation appears to have been a success. Drinking water, for example, is now 99.8 per cent compliant with relevant water quality standards.[41]

Although the 1989 Act was described as "in terms of sheer bulk . . . one of the lengthiest pieces of legislation passed in recent years"[42] it did not remove the need to refer to earlier legislation, including public health legislation, which has tended to have a close association with the water industry. In 1991, various pieces of legislation (including parts of the Water Act 1989 and enactments relating to public health) were consolidated by five statutes: The Water Resources Act 1991; the Water Industry Act 1991; the Land Drainage Act 1991; the Statutory Water Companies Act 1991; and the Water Consolidation (Consequential Provisions) Act 1991. Of these, the two most important statutes are the Water Industry Act 1991 and the Water Resources Act 1991. The Water Resources Act 1991 is concerned with pollution control whilst the Water Industry Act 1991 regulates the privatised aspects of the water industry.

Under the Water Industry Act 1991, the prices charged to the public for consumption of water by water companies are regulated by the Director-General of OFWAT. In deciding on the prices that may be charged, he or she will take into account the cost of environmental measures which must be carried out by the water companies, including repairs to sewage works or measures to prevent household flooding. The public therefore pays for these measures in the cost of its water. This issue was relevant in the case of *Marcic v Thames Water Utilities Ltd*.[43] Mr Marcic brought a claim against Thames Water in relation to flooding of his home by effluent, which happened after rainfall because the sewers were overloaded. Thames Water (who were held not to be liable) had not taken action to carry out necessary repairs to prevent the flooding, as they had not sought or received, in the prices set by the Director-General, allowance for this type of repair work. They had instead prioritised money for repairs to those properties affected by internal flooding (Mr Marcic's property was effected by external flooding).

The Water Industry Act 1991 also regulates the quality of water supplied. Domestic water must be "wholesome",[44] a term introduced by the Drinking Water Directive. This concept is implemented into UK legislation by the Water Supply (Water Quality)

[41] See Drinking Water Inspectorate Report 2001 (*www.dwi.gov.uk*).
[42] See notes on Water Act 1989 in Current Law Statutes Annotated, p.15–18.
[43] [2003] UKHL 66; [2003] 3 W.L.R. 1603.
[44] See Water Industry Act 1991, s.67.

Regulations 2001.[45] The Regulations set out the parameters with which water must comply to be considered wholesome. Under the Act, it is a criminal offence to supply water that is unfit for human consumption.[46]

As well as the water companies and OFWAT, other players in the industry include the Environment Agency (which has general responsibility for water quality in England and Wales), the Drinking Water Inspectorate (which regulates public water suppliers in England and Wales and is responsible for assessing the quality of drinking water), and DEFRA (responsible for taking forward the government's water programme).[47]

History of the water pollution control regime

Legislation to control water pollution began in the fourteenth century with the passing **8–020** of the Act for Punishing Nuisances which Cause Corruption of the Air near Cities and Great Towns 1388. This made it a criminal offence to throw garbage and entrails into rivers and other waters:

> "For that so much Dung and Filth of the Garbage and Intrails as well of Beasts killed be put in Rivers and other Waters the Air there is greatly corrupt and if any do he shall be called before the Chancellor and shall be punished after the discretion of the Chancellor."

In the nineteenth century, with the passing of the Rivers Pollution Prevention Act 1876, it became a criminal offence to "cause or knowingly permit" the pollution of any British river, and it is this phraseology which appears today in the Water Resources Act 1991. The problem with the Rivers Pollution Prevention Act 1876, however, was that it sought to impose an absolute prohibition on all discharges to rivers, which proved impossible to enforce in practice. Moreover, such a prohibition was inappropriate given the ability of rivers to absorb a limited amount of pollution without harmful effect.

The Rivers (Prevention of Pollution) Act 1951 laid the foundations for the modern approach to pollution control. The River Boards, which were at that time the relevant regulatory bodies, were placed under a general duty to maintain or restore the wholesomeness of inland waters. To this end, they were granted two important powers. First, the River Boards had the power to grant consents for the discharge of trade and sewage effluent. Secondly, they had the power to make byelaws prescribing the amounts of particular substances which could be discharged. Effectively, this allowed for the imposition of uniform emission standards limiting the discharge of particular substances into waters. The River Boards' powers to set emission standards were little used, however, and were repealed in 1961.

The Control of Pollution Act 1974 consolidated the discharge consent provisions of the 1951 Act and extended them to cover underground, tidal and coastal waters. It also provided for public participation in decisions relating to water pollution and introduced measures for the provision to the public of information about discharges. The

---

[45] SI 2001/3911.
[46] Water Industry Act 1991, s.70.
[47] Other regulators include the Welsh Assembly, Scottish Executive, Scottish Environmental Protection Agency, Water Industry Commission for Scotland, and Water Customer Consultation Panels.

Water Act 1989 created the National Rivers Authority as a unified regulatory body with responsibility for pollution control. It also improved the range of controls available to curb pollution by giving the Secretary of State the power to establish "water quality objectives" for particular stretches of water. The Water Resources Act 1991 consolidated these provisions. Under the Environment Act 1995, the functions and duties of the National Rivers Authority passed to the Environment Agency.

For the sake of completeness, some mention must be made of the Water Act 2003. This is not primarily concerned with pollution control, but does have important implications for the conservation of water resources. The Act deals with the granting of licences for water abstraction. Understanding of environmental issues has developed significantly since the old framework for abstraction licensing was put in place in the 1960s, and the changes implemented by the 2003 Act are necessary to help ensure that water resources are used sustainably. Such changes include the issuing of abstraction licences for a limited time-period only, partly on the basis of current uncertainty about the effects of climate change.[48] Perhaps surprisingly, the Water Act 2003 is not part of the implementation of the Water Framework Directive.

The current pollution control framework: The Water Resources Act 1991

8–021   The current pollution control framework operates as follows: Targets, known as "water quality objectives" are set for certain stretches of water and indicate the environmental standards or quality to which water within specific designated areas is expected to conform. The objectives focus on ensuring that the water is of sufficient quality for various different purposes (*e.g.* bathing water, drinking water). Once the water quality objectives have been set, the Environment Agency, which has general responsibility for water quality in England and Wales, and the Secretary of State, are under a duty to ensure that the objectives are met so far as is practicable.[49] This is done by means of discharge consents. In general terms, no-one may discharge polluting substances to water without holding a discharge consent granted by the Agency. The Agency is thereby able to control the quality of a particular stretch of water by placing limits on the number of consents issued and by attaching conditions to those consents. Enforcement of the regime is provided for by a series of criminal offences, which prohibit discharges to controlled waters without a consent. This serves as a deterrent by imposing criminal sanctions on polluters.

The pollution control legislation is primarily concerned with discharges from point sources. Pollution from diffuse sources is very difficult to control, because it arises from a diverse range of activities which have proved difficult to restrict or prohibit. Moreover, the particular contribution of each of the many diffuse pollution sources to the overall picture of water pollution is difficult to identify. Nevertheless, the legislation seeks to prevent pollution from diffuse sources by creating "protection zones" where potentially polluting activities are curtailed. Under the Water Resources Act 1991, certain areas may be designated Water Protection Zones.[50] Areas may also

[48] See DEFRA, Review of the Water Abstraction Licensing system in England and Wales, a consultation paper, June 1998 (*www.defra.gov.uk/environment/consult/waterab*).
[49] Water Resources Act 1991, s.84
[50] *ibid.*, ss.93 and 94.

be designated Nitrate Vulnerable Zones. The idea is that agricultural and industrial activities within these zones may be restricted so as to prevent pollution from diffuse sources.

It is too soon to be able to estimate what the impact of the Water Framework Directive will be on the operation of this regime in terms of improving water quality. Much will depend on whether there is the political will to ensure that the requirements are properly implemented and enforced, and on how often the exceptions to achieving the Directive's water quality objectives are applied. The Government has been criticised for taking a minimalist approach in implementing the Directive, *i.e.* by "tweaking" the existing regime with secondary legislation, rather than enacting primary legislation. The economic implications of implementing the Directive have been extensively analysed, but the same is not true for the potential impact of the Directive on water quality, and in this regard the impact of the Directive remains to be seen.

Classification and water quality objectives

Since the late 1970s, waterways have been the subject of quality objectives. These **8–022** were set by the Water Authorities (who at the time were responsible for water supply and sewage disposal) in purported compliance with the Dangerous Substances Directive[51] and were used by the Authorities as a basis for setting discharge consents to rivers and for targeting investment in river improvement. The five basic classes of river waters were as follows:

- High quality waters suitable for all abstraction purposes with only modest treatment;

- Good quality waters usable for substantially the same purposes as high quality waters, though not as high quality;

- Fair quality waters viable as coarse fisheries and capable of use for drinking water provided the water was treated sufficiently;

- Poor quality waters polluted to the extent that fish were absent or only sporadically present, and suitable only for low grade industrial abstraction;

- Bad quality waters which are grossly polluted and likely to cause a nuisance.

(As was noted in the introduction, the survey by DEFRA in 2002 found that approximately 95 per cent of rivers were of good or fair quality according to these criteria). The classification system did not, however, have a statutory basis, which was required by EC law. The classification criteria were eventually placed on a statutory footing, in the form of "water quality objectives" by the Water Act 1989, the provisions of which are reproduced in the Water Resources Act 1991.

Under the Water Resources Act 1991,[52] the setting of water quality objectives involves a two-stage approach. First, water is classified according to a particular

[51] Council Dir.76/464/ EEC on pollution caused by certain dangerous substances discharged into the aquatic environment of the Community.
[52] WRA 1991, ss.82–84.

proposed use. Water may be classified as bathing water or drinking water, for example. The classification regulations set out the environmental standards to which waters must conform if they are to fall within a particular classification and so be deemed suitable for a particular use. The second stage in the process is the actual designation, by the Secretary of State, of particular stretches of water. The water quality objective set for each stretch of water so designated will then be for it to achieve a certain type of classification within a certain time. The water quality objective for designated stretch of water A, for example, might be for it to come within the bathing water classification within the next two years, whilst the objective for stretch of water B might be for it to achieve classification as water suitable for abstraction as drinking water.

It is clear that complete implementation of this scheme will take many years, particularly because of scientific work yet to be done in establishing the precise environmental requirements for each classification. At the time of writing, classification regulations have been made only in respect of rivers[53] and are awaited in respect of other waters such as lakes, canals, coastal waters and groundwater. After that, the setting of individual quality objectives for particular stretches of water will take further time, not only because of the sheer size of the administrative task, but because of the government's understandable reluctance to come to terms with the political implications of burdening industry, and ultimately the consumer, with the costs of bringing certain waters within their appropriate classification.

Since the classification of waters is not yet complete, no individual statutory quality objectives have been set in relation to particular stretches of water. The informal non-statutory quality objectives therefore continue to apply in relation to specific waterways, alongside the statutory "blanket" quality objectives contained in existing regulations. These blanket objectives prohibit the presence of certain dangerous substances in any waters, whatever their classification.

The provisions relating to water quality objectives in the Water Resources Act 1991 are not sufficient to implement the requirement, in the Water Framework Directive, to set European environmental objectives (*i.e.* "ecological status" objectives, "chemical status" objectives and "quantitative status" objectives). Existing provisions do not, for example, allow the setting of quantity objectives for groundwater.[54] Relevant provision has therefore been made in the Water Environment (Water Framework Directive) England and Wales Regulations 2003.[55]

Discharge consents

8–023   As has been said, the method by which statutory water quality objectives are to be met, and indeed by which the existing non-statutory objectives are currently being met, is through the regulation of discharges to water. No-one may discharge polluting substances to water without holding a discharge consent granted by the Environment Agency. The Agency is thereby able to control the quality of a particular stretch of water by placing limits on the number of consents issued and by attaching conditions to those consents. (By far the majority of consents are given for sewage effluent.)

---

[53] Surface Waters (River Ecosystem) (Classification) Regulations 1994 (SI 1994/1057).
[54] DEFRA, Water Framework Dir.2nd consultation paper, October 2002 (*www.defra.gov.uk/ environment/ consult/waterframe2*).
[55] SI 2003/3242.

Under the Water Resources Act 1991, it is an offence to cause or knowingly permit the discharge of certain substances into "controlled waters". It is also an offence to cause or knowingly permit the entry into controlled waters of "poisonous, noxious or polluting matter". The possession of a discharge consent from the Environment Agency, however, provides a defence to prosecution. The details of the various water pollution offences, which are quite complex, are examined in the appropriate section below, after consideration has been given to the procedure for obtaining a discharge consent.

Procedures

The grant, modification and revocation of discharge consents is governed by Sch.10 of **8–024** the Water Resources Act 1991. Application for a consent is made to the Environment Agency. The application must be publicised. The Environment Agency must decide whether to grant the consent unconditionally or subject to conditions, having considered any written representations and objections. Once granted, a consent attaches to the particular discharge to which it relates, rather than to the holder of the consent. It follows, therefore, that the new owner of premises in respect of which a consent is in force can take advantage of that consent. In contrast with the position in relation to waste management, there is no requirement that a holder of a discharge consent should be a "fit and proper person" to hold an environmental licence.

The Agency's power to attach conditions to a discharge consent is virtually unfettered. Under the Schedule, it may impose such conditions as it thinks fit. Conditions may relate, for example, to the places of the discharges, the temperature, volume and rate of the discharges and the times at which the discharges may be made. The power to impose conditions is, of course, subject to the normal constraints imposed by administrative law. Thus it has been suggested that, since the power to impose consent conditions is the same type of power that is exercised where conditions are imposed for planning purposes, the criteria for the validity of planning conditions, established in *Newbury DC v Secretary of State for the Environment*, applies to conditions imposed under Sch.10, *i.e.* a condition may only be imposed for a purpose to which it fairly and reasonably relates and not for an ulterior purpose. Although this argument may well succeed in an appeal against, or an application for judicial review of a consent condition, the case law suggests that it will fail if pleaded as a defence to a prosecution.

In *R. v Etterick Trout Company Ltd and William Baxter*,[56] the appellants argued, by way of a defence to a prosecution for breach of a consent condition, that the condition, which related to the volume of effluent which could be discharged, was invalid because it had not been imposed for a pollution control purpose but for an ulterior purpose, namely to limit the volume of water the appellants were permitted to discharge. Although the Court of Appeal accepted the point in principle, it took the view that, on the facts of the particular case, it was not permissible to challenge the validity of the condition by way of a defence to prosecution, since to do so was an attempt to bypass both the normal judicial review procedure and the procedure for statutory appeals.

---

[56] [1994] Env. L.R. 165.

The court stated, however, that it was unable to say that in no circumstances could such a challenge provide a defence to prosecution. The position therefore remains unclear, although it is submitted that a challenge in criminal proceedings of a condition which is blatantly irrational may very well succeed.

Revocation and modification of discharge consents

8–025 When the Agency grants a discharge consent, it will stipulate a period of time during which the consent is to be exempt from revocation and modification, and, in any event, the consent cannot be revoked or varied for at least four years from the date of issue. This provides a degree of commercial certainty to those who apply for consents.[57] Other than that, the Agency may revoke the consent, modify any of its conditions, or make an unconditional consent subject to conditions. The wide nature of this power to vary consents reflects the need to accommodate changes in the circumstances under which the consent was originally granted. It may, for example, be used to prohibit the discharge of a newly-discovered pollutant. More controversially, perhaps, it may be used to accommodate the discharge requirements of newcomers to a particular stretch of water by reducing the amount of a substance that may be discharged by existing consent holders, so as to preserve the overall quality objective for the water in question. Apart from the four-year prohibition on revocation and variation, there is nothing in the legislation which protects the right to hold a consent, or which indicates that in developing areas consents are to be held on a first come first served basis.

Enforcement notices

8–026 Where the Agency is of the opinion that the holder of a discharge consent is contravening the conditions of his consent, or that such a contravention is likely, it may serve on him an enforcement notice specifying the matters constituting the contravention (or likely contravention), the steps which must be taken to avoid it, and the time within which such steps must be taken.[58] Failure to comply with an enforcement notice is an offence, the maximum penalty for which is three months' imprisonment and a £20,000 fine in the magistrates' court or two years' imprisonment and an unlimited fine in the Crown Court. Enforcement notices, which were introduced by the Environment Act 1995, provide an alternative means to immediate prosecution, by which the Agency can ensure compliance with the conditions of a discharge consent. Their use may be appropriate, for example in cases where the Agency suspects that the person in breach of his consent conditions does not realise that this is the case.

Appeals[59]

8–027 An appeal to the Secretary of State lies where the Agency refuses to grant a consent, where it attaches conditions which are unreasonable, or where it unreasonably varies or revokes a consent. The person or company discharging water may also appeal

---

[57] WRA 1991, Sch.10 (as substituted by Environment Act 1995, Sch.22), para.8(3). Sch.10 allows for certain exceptions, including where no discharges have been made for a period of 12 months, or where it is necessary to give effect to any European Community or international obligation.

[58] WRA 1991, s.90B (inserted by Environment Act 1995).

[59] WRA 1991, s.91 (as amended by Environment Act 1995, Sch.22).

against the service of an enforcement notice. An enforcement notice remains in force pending the outcome of an appeal, but an appeal against revocation or modification of a consent has the effect of suspending the Agency's decision until the appeal is determined or withdrawn. Where the Agency is of the opinion that an immediate revocation or modification is necessary to minimise or prevent the entry of polluting matter into water or to prevent harm to human health, however, it may specify that the revocation or modification is to remain effective during the period of an appeal. Where the Agency decides to do this and that decision is, on appeal, found to have been unreasonable, the person affected is entitled to compensation.

E: Enforcing the Regime

As mentioned, water pollution legislation aims to act as a deterrent by imposing **8–028** criminal sanctions on polluters, except where they have a defence (usually in the form of a discharge consent). The Water Resources Act 1991 makes it a criminal offence, under s.85, to commit certain acts in relation to "controlled waters".

Definition of "controlled waters"[60]

Controlled waters are defined by the Act so as to include almost all inland and coastal **8–029** waters, as well as all territorial sea waters out to a distance of three miles. The Act identifies four separate categories of controlled waters:

(i) "Relevant territorial waters". The territorial sea is measured outwards from a set of internationally agreed geographical baselines which link certain points on the UK's coastline (in much the same way as a "join the dots" picture). The UK's territorial waters extend outwards for 12 miles from these baselines. Controlled waters, however, do not extend this far; they extend only to a distance of three miles.

(ii) "Coastal waters". These are estuaries and other waters landwards of the territorial sea baselines as far as the limits of the highest tides.

(iii) "Inland freshwaters". These are the waters of any lake, pond or reservoir and of rivers and watercourses (including those underground) whether natural or artificial.

(iv) "Groundwaters". These are waters which run in underground strata, including, for example, waters which serve wells and boreholes.

The definition of controlled waters also includes watercourses which have dried up. In *R. v Dovermoss Ltd*,[61] Stuart Smith L.J. held that a watercourse did not cease to be a watercourse simply because it was dry at a particular time. If, however, the watercourse

---

[60] *ibid.*, s.104.
[61] *The Times*, February 3, 1995.

was dry at the time when the poisonous, noxious or polluting matter was put into it, no offence could be committed under the Act unless and until water ran again in the watercourse. Moreover, since the Act defines inland freshwaters as "waters of any watercourse", rather than "waters *in* any watercourse", the fact that the stream in question had deviated from its normal course did not preclude it from being controlled waters.

Controlled waters include the bed of the watercourse. Although the Act is explicit that this is true even when the watercourse is temporarily dry,[62] the bottom, channel or bed of the watercourse is also part of the controlled waters when wet. This was affirmed in *National Rivers Authority v Biffa Waste*[63] where a tractor driven along the watercourse had churned up the silt and mud at the bottom, increasing the suspended particulate matter in the water flowing downstream. The defendants were found not to have caused pollution to *enter* controlled waters, because the silt and mud (which was also found not to be polluting matter) was actually *part of* the controlled waters.

Watercourses do not have to be naturally occurring to fall within the definition of controlled waters. Thus, in *Environment Agency v Brock*,[64] a man-made ditch was held to be capable of constituting a watercourse falling within the definition. The definition of relevant watercourses in s.104 (3) as including artificial watercourses was sufficient to resolve the matter if water flowed through the ditch into another watercourse, even if, as here, there was very little flow of water from the ditch into a nearby river.

The water pollution offences[65]

8–030 The Act sets out a number of inter-related water pollution offences. Under the Act, it is an offence to "cause or knowingly permit" any of the following:

(1) Any poisonous, noxious or polluting matter or any solid waste matter to enter any controlled waters[66];

(2) Any matter, other than trade or sewage effluent, to enter controlled waters by being discharged from a drain or sewer in contravention of a prohibition imposed under s.86 (see below)[67];

(3) Any trade effluent or sewage effluent to be discharged:

(a) into any controlled waters; or
(b) from land in England and Wales, through a pipe, into the sea outside the seaward limits of controlled waters[68];

(4) Any trade effluent or sewage effluent to be discharged, in contravention of any prohibition imposed by s.86 (see below), from a building or fixed plant:

---

[62] WRA 1991, s.104 (2).
[63] [1996] Env. L.R. 227.
[64] [1998] Env. L.R. 607.
[65] WRA 1991 s.85.
[66] *ibid.*, s.85(1).
[67] *ibid.*, s.85(2).
[68] *ibid.*, s.85(3).

(a) on to or into any land; or

(b) into any waters of a lake or pond which are not inland freshwaters[69];

(5) Any matter whatever to enter any inland freshwaters so as to tend (either directly or in combination with other matter) to impede the proper flow of the waters in a manner leading, or likely to lead, to a substantial aggravation of:

(a) pollution due to other causes; or

(b) the consequences of such pollution.[70]

The Act also makes it a specific offence to contravene the conditions of a discharge consent.[71]

The general offence

The first of the offences listed above (that of causing or knowingly permitting the entry of poisonous, noxious or polluting matter) may be termed the "general pollution offence", and is by far the most important in practice. It is widely drafted and prohibits the *entry* of polluting matter rather than simply its discharge. The offence of permitting the entry of matter may be committed where the offender is entirely passive, whilst permitting the *discharge* of matter may be seen as requiring acquiescence in a state of affairs which has previously been created by some positive act, *e.g.* allowing the matter to flow into the waters through a pipe. The general offence is not exclusive of the more specific offences. In other words, where an offence of discharging is committed, an offence of entry will invariably be committed as well. Thus, where the circumstances of an offence are unclear, it is common for the prosecution to charge the general offence alongside one or more of the specific offences. **8–031**

The other offences

The other offences are more narrowly defined. The offences in ss. 85(2) and (4) (set out at (2) and (4) above) are only committed where there is a prohibition in force under s.86 (see below). Where no prohibition is in force, the discharge from a drain or sewer of matter other than trade or sewage effluent (surface water run-off, for example) into controlled waters, and the discharge of trade or sewage effluent on to or into any land or into any lake or pond other than inland freshwaters (*e.g.* an industrial lagoon), will not necessarily be an offence. Such discharges, however, may give rise to the commission of an offence under s.85(1) (the general offence) if, for example, the surface water in question carries with it poisonous, noxious or polluting matter, or if trade or sewage effluent discharged on to land runs off from that land and enters controlled waters. The offence of aggravating pollution under s.85(5) is largely self-explanatory. The reference to a pipe in s.85(3), seems designed to catch the former **8–032**

[69] *ibid.*, s.85(4).
[70] *ibid.*, s.85(5).
[71] *ibid.*, s.85(6).

UK practice of discharging untreated sewage, through long outfall pipes, into the sea (*i.e.* the sea beyond the "relevant territorial waters" that are controlled waters).

Prohibitions[72]

8–033 Under s.86 of the Water Resources Act 1991, the Environment Agency may prohibit, or restrict by conditions, the discharge of substances into water. Prohibitions, which were first introduced by the Water Act 1989, are designed to cover situations where a universally applicable statutory offence is not appropriate because the matter being discharged is not of its nature harmful, but where, in certain circumstances, its discharge may pose a risk of pollution. Selective use of prohibitions enables the Environment Agency to exercise control over many different forms of discharge in only those circumstances where control is needed, and without the need to make reference to an endless list of specific statutory offences prohibiting the discharge of specific substances in specific circumstances. A prohibition may be used, for example, in relation to discharges from a drain or sewer of substances other than trade or sewage effluent (chemicals or surface water run-off, for example). A prohibition is effected by a notice served by the Environment Agency on the holder of a consent, and, save in cases of emergency, comes into force three months after the notice has been served. In addition, however, there is a standing prohibition on the discharge of certain dangerous substances prescribed by regulations, so that a discharge containing these substances gives rise to the commission of an offence automatically, without the need for the Agency to notify the discharger.

Definition of "trade or sewage effluent"[73]

8–034 "Effluent" is simply defined by the Water Resources Act 1991 to mean "any liquid". "Trade effluent" includes any effluent from trade premises (including agricultural, fish farming and research establishments), other than domestic sewage or surface water, whilst "sewage effluent" includes any effluent, other than surface water, from a sewerage works.

Definition of "poisonous, noxious or polluting matter"

8–035 The offence under s.85(1) requires "poisonous, noxious or polluting matter" to enter controlled waters. These words are not defined in the Water Resources Act 1991 and have been the subject of comparatively little judicial consideration. What is poisonous is necessarily a matter of degree. Paracelsus, who died in 1541, stated: "All substances are poisons. There is none which is not a poison. The right dose differentiates a poison and a remedy".[74] The Act contains no suggestion that "poisonous matter" should be construed merely by reference to its effect on humans. Indeed, protection of the quality of water used for rearing livestock and for fishing is of great importance. The

---

[72] *ibid.*, s.86.
[73] *ibid.*, s.221.
[74] Burnett-Hall, *UK Environmental Law*, 1995.

Act refers to the nature of the matter which enters controlled waters, and not to whether the waters themselves are thereafter rendered poisonous. It is, however, difficult to define "poisonous" in the abstract, and in most cases the word will only have meaning when considered in relation to the organisms on which a substance, ingested in a particular quantity, may have an impact. The best solution to this conundrum may be to regard as poisonous anything that may act as a poison on any organism with which it comes into contact, subject to a *de minimis* exception in cases where the amount of matter which enters the waters is so trivial as not to be a poison to anything.[75] "Noxious" is arguably somewhat broader than "poisonous", in that noxious may cover effects which are physically unpleasant without necessarily being dangerous in any respect.

The term "polluting" has been the subject of judicial consideration, notably in *National Rivers Authority v Egger UK Ltd.*[76] The case concerned a visible brown stain which extended for a length of 100 metres into the river adjoining the defendants' premises. There was no evidence that anything in the water had been harmed by the discharge, and the question arose whether mere discolouration of the river amounted to the offence of causing or knowingly permitting "polluting matter" to enter the water. Matter which merely caused discolouration of water had been expressly excluded from the definition of "poisonous, noxious or polluting matter" which had appeared in the Rivers Pollution Prevention Act 1876, and this provision had been repeated in the Rivers (Prevention of Pollution) Act 1951. No such exclusion, however, appears in the Water Resources Act 1991. The judge in *Egger* held that, in the light of this omission, mere discolouration of water could indeed amount to "pollution" under the Act. He also dealt with the more general question of whether or not matter was "polluting" was to be decided by reference simply to the nature of the matter itself, or by reference to whether its entry worsened the quality of the receiving water. Whilst the judge accepted that the word "polluting" clearly has a relationship to what is polluted, he held that it did not necessarily follow that matter could only be "polluting matter" once it had been shown that some harm had been caused by it. He went on to say that what the statute is concerned with is the nature of the material which enters the water. Therefore, the question whether matter is "polluting" should be regarded objectively in relation to a natural, unpolluted river:

> "One looks at the nature of the discharge and one says, 'is that discharge capable of causing harm to a river, in the sense of causing damage to uses to which a river might be put; damage to animal, vegetable or other—if there is such other life which might live in a river, or damaging that river aesthetically?"

If the statute is concerned only with the *potential* effect of a substance which enters controlled waters, and not with its *actual* effect, it follows that it is unnecessary to show that actual damage has been caused to the waters for an offence under s.85(1) to be made out. It also follows that adding *any* potentially polluting matter to water amounts to an offence, even where the water is already so heavily polluted, and the added matter is in so diluted a form, that the quality of the receiving water is in fact *improved*.

---

[75] *ibid.*
[76] Newcastle upon Tyne Crown Court, June 15–17, 1992, unreported.

Such a conclusion is entirely consistent with a policy of maintaining and improving the quality of waterways, even though it may appear anomalous in cases where only slightly contaminated water is discharged into a heavily polluted stream.

The meaning of "polluting" was again considered in *R. v Dovermoss Ltd.*[77] Dovermoss argued that to establish that polluting matter had entered controlled waters, it was necessary for the National Rivers Authority to show that harm had resulted to animals or plant life in those waters. The Court of Appeal, however, rejected this argument, basing its decision on the dictionary definition of "pollute", *viz.* "to make physically impure, foul or filthy; to dirty, stain, taint, befoul". The court held that actual harm need not be shown. It was sufficient to establish the offence under s.85(1) if it could be shown that the matter in question gave rise to the likelihood, or simply had the capability of, causing harm.

Definition of "causing or knowingly permitting"

8–036 Common to all of the offences under the Water Resources Act 1991 is the requirement that the offender must "cause or knowingly permit" the entry or discharge of pollutants to water. This wording involves two separate offences: first, that of "causing" and secondly that of "knowingly permitting".

"Causing" pollution

8–037 Causing polluted matter to enter or to be discharged into controlled waters is an offence of strict liability, that is to say it is not necessary for the prosecution to prove *mens rea*. In other words, so long as a causal link can be shown between the defendant's activities and the entry or discharge of the matter (the *actus reus*), liability will follow without the need to show that the defendant intended or was negligent as to the entry or discharge in question.

One of the leading judicial decisions on the matter is that of the House of Lords in *Alphacell v Woodward.*[78] Alphacell, a paper-making company, were prosecuted under the Rivers (Prevention of Pollution) Act 1951 for causing polluting matter to enter controlled waters when polluted water overflowed from their settling tanks into a river. This occurred because, without the company's knowledge, leaves and debris had prevented a pump from working. Their Lordships pointed out that the word "knowingly" applies only to the second offence of "knowingly permitting" and held that Alphacell had caused the discharge. Lord Wilberforce stated:

> "The whole complex process which might lead to this result was an operation deliberately conducted by the appellants and I fail to see how a defect in one stage of it, even if we must assume that this happened without their negligence, can enable them to say that they did not cause the pollution. In my opinion, complication of this case by the infusion of the concept of *mens rea*, and its exceptions, is unnecessary and undesirable."

[77] *The Times*, February 3, 1995.
[78] [1972] A.C. 824.

Lord Salmon, in *Alphacell*, expressed the view that an offence of strict liability was justified on grounds of public policy:

> "If no conviction could be obtained under the Act of 1951 unless the prosecution could discharge the often impossible onus of proving that the pollution was caused intentionally or negligently, a great deal of pollution would go unpunished and undeterred As a result, many rivers which are now filthy would become filthier still and many rivers which are now clean would lose their cleanliness. The legislature no doubt recognised that as a matter of public policy this would be most unfortunate."

Thus, Alphacell were found to have caused the pollution simply by having carried on the activity which gave rise to it. According to Lord Cross and Lord Wilberforce in *Alphacell*, the offence of "causing" is established only by active participation in the operation or chain of operations which result in the pollution. It therefore requires that the pollution must be the consequence (albeit unintentional or unforeseen) of a positive act on the part of the defendant, rather than of a mere passive looking on, although pollution which occurs in the latter circumstances may form the basis of a charge of "knowingly permitting".

The House of Lords has more recently considered the issue of "causing" in *Environment Agency (Formerly National Rivers Authority) v Empress Car Co. (Abertillery) Ltd*.[79] Here, Empress Car Co. maintained a diesel tank in a yard which was drained directly into a river. The tank was surrounded by a bund to contain spillage, but the company had overridden that protection by fixing an extension pipe to the outlet of the tank so as to connect it to a drum standing outside the bund. The outlet from the tank was governed by a tap which had no lock. The tap was opened by vandals and the entire contents ran into the drum, then overflowed into the yard and passed down the drain into the river. The company was charged with causing polluting matter to enter controlled waters contrary to s.85(1) of the Water Resources Act 1991. The House of Lords upheld the company's conviction for "causing" water pollution. Lord Hoffmann summarised the position as follows[80]:

(1) Justices dealing with prosecutions for "causing" pollution under s.85(1) should first require the prosecution to identify what it says the defendant did to cause the pollution. If the defendant cannot be said to have done anything at all, the prosecution must fail: the defendant may have "knowingly permitted" pollution but cannot have caused it.

(2) The prosecution need not prove that the defendant did something which was the immediate cause of the pollution: maintaining tanks, lagoons or sewage systems full of noxious liquid is doing something, even if the immediate cause of the pollution was lack of maintenance, a natural event or the act of a third party.

(3) When the prosecution has identified something which the defendant did, the justices must decide whether it caused the pollution. They should not be

---

[79] [1999] 2 A.C. 22.
[80] *ibid.*, at 35 and 36.

diverted by questions like "What was the cause of the pollution?" or "Did something else cause the pollution?" because to say that something else caused the pollution (like brambles clogging the pumps or vandalism by third parties) is not inconsistent with the defendant having caused it as well.

(4) If the defendant did something which produced a situation in which the polluting matter could escape but a necessary condition of the actual escape which happened was also the act of a third party or a natural event, the justices should consider whether that act or event should be regarded as a normal fact of life or something extraordinary. If it was in the general run of things a matter of ordinary occurrence, it will not negative the causal effect of the defendant's acts, even if it was not foreseeable that it would happen to that particular defendant or take that particular form. If it can be regarded as something extraordinary, it will be open to the justices to hold that the defendant did not cause the pollution.

(5) The distinction between ordinary and extraordinary is one of fact and degree to which the justices must apply their common sense and knowledge of what happens in the area.

Earlier in the judgement, Lord Hoffmann said that the true "common sense distinction" was between:

"... acts and events which, although not necessarily foreseeable in the particular case, are in the generality a normal and familiar fact of life, and acts or events which are abnormal and extraordinary ... There is nothing extraordinary or abnormal about leaky pipes or lagoons as such: these things happen, even if the particular defendant could not reasonably have foreseen that it would happen to him. There is nothing unusual about people putting unlawful substances into the sewage system and the same, regrettably, is true about ordinary vandalism. So when these things happen, one does not say: that was an extraordinary coincidence, which negatived the causal connection between the original act of accumulating the polluting substance and its escape. In the context of s.85(1), the defendant's accumulation has still caused the pollution. On the other hand, the example I gave of the terrorist attack would be something so unusual that one would not regard the defendant's conduct as having caused the escape at all."[81]

The imposition of strict liability, of course, can lead to some harsh decisions. In *CPC (UK) Ltd v National Rivers Authority*,[82] for example, a defectively installed pipe at a factory caused leakage into a river. The pipe had been installed about nine months before the appellants had bought the factory and a full survey at the time of purchase had not revealed the defect. Despite this, the company was held to have caused the pollution. The Court of Appeal stated that the only relevant question was whether the factory was under the control of the appellants when the leakage occurred. It was

---

[81] *ibid.*, at 34.
[82] [1995] Env. L.R. 131.

accepted, however, that the company had behaved impeccably at all times. It was therefore given an absolute discharge by way of sentence and was not required to pay the costs of cleaning up the river.

Although the sentiment behind this sentencing decision can be understood, the giving of an absolute discharge in these circumstances fails to respect the "polluter pays" principle. In subsequent cases, therefore, the courts have tended to reject attempts by companies who plead guilty to these offences to argue that their lack of culpability should be taken into account in sentencing. Thus, In *Hart v Anglian Water Services Ltd*,[83] the company pleaded guilty to causing sewage effluent to enter the River Crouch. In a hearing on the appropriate sentence, the company sought to make the point that, since the offence did not require a *mens rea*, it should be distinguished from most other acts of a criminal nature, and that lack of culpability should be an important factor in determining the level of the fine. This point was also made in another case on sentencing, *R. v Milford Haven Port Authority*[84] (discussed below), in which Lord Bingham C.J. responded as follows:

> "Parliament creates an offence of strict liability because it regards the doing or not doing of a particular thing as itself so undesirable as to merit the imposition of criminal punishment on anyone who does or does not do that thing irrespective of that party's knowledge, state of mind, belief or intention. This involves a departure from the prevailing canons of the criminal law because of the importance which is attached to achieving the result which Parliament seeks to achieve."

The Court in *Hart v Anglian Water Services* noted that sewage treatment works carried a high risk of damage to adjoining waters, and that Parliament had imposed on water companies, with responsibility for sewage treatment, a heavy burden to do everything possible to ensure that they do not cause pollution.[85]

It is possible for two or more individuals to be found guilty of "causing" a pollution incident. *In Attorney-General's Reference (No. 1 of 1994)*,[86] for example, the first respondent ran a business for the disposal of toxic industrial waste under a licence granted by the second respondents, who were sewerage undertakers. The third respondent, a local authority, performed, for a profit, the day-to-day business of the second respondents. The first respondent deposited polluting matter into the second respondents' sewerage system. The matter then flowed into controlled waters because of a failure at a pumping station run by the third respondent. The Recorder at first instance acquitted all three respondents, directing the jury that the offence of "causing" an entry of polluting matter could only be committed by one person. The Court of Appeal, however, held that this had been a misdirection and that the offence could be committed by two or more defendants, not only in the obvious case of defendants engaged in a joint enterprise, but also where each had performed different and separate acts which had contributed to the entry. Lord Taylor C.J. said that the facts of the case illustrated the impracticability of confining causation to one party,

---

[83] [2003] EWCA Crim 2243.
[84] [2000] All E.R. (D) 352.
[85] [2003] EWCA Crim 2243 at para.15, *per* Scott Baker L.J.
[86] *The Independent*, January 31, 1995.

since a jury faced with concurrent causative conduct by more than one party would experience difficulty and reluctance in choosing one culprit.

The chain of causation

8–038 In order for an offence of "causing" to be made out, a direct causal link must exist between the conduct of the defendant and the occurrence of the pollution. Therefore, where the chain of causation is broken either by the intervening act of a third party, or by an Act of God, the defendant may escape liability. The House of Lords dealt with this issue in *Environment Agency v Empress Car Co. (Abertillery) Ltd* (above). The approach in this case reflects a changed attitude towards polluting behaviour when contrasted with the 1971 case of *Impress (Worcester) Ltd v Rees*.[87] There, the court was prepared to find that the act of a vandal in opening the valve of an oil storage tank was an intervening cause of so powerful a nature that the conduct of the defendants in maintaining the tank was not a cause of the pollution at all, but merely part of the surrounding circumstances. Similarly, in *National Rivers Authority v Wright Engineering Co. Ltd*,[88] where a vandalised oil storage tank leaked oil into a brook, the Divisional Court upheld the acquittal of the defendants. Although there was evidence that minor acts of vandalism had occurred on the defendants' premises in the past, the acts were on a smaller scale and of a different type. In the light of the reasoning in *Empress Car*, however, these cases are no longer good law—whilst a defendant may escape liability because of terrorism, he will not normally do so because of vandalism.

Where the nature of an intervening act of a third party is clearly foreseeable, it will not enable the defendant to escape liability. Thus, in *National Rivers Authority v Yorkshire Water Service Ltd*[89] the defendants were responsible for a sewer into which an unidentified industrial customer of theirs had discharged solvents. The House of Lords held that there was sufficient evidence on which a court could conclude that the defendants were prima facie guilty of causing the pollution, although, in the event, Yorkshire Water Services were able to escape liability by relying on a statutory defence.

"Knowingly permitting" pollution

8–039 The offence of "knowingly permitting" an entry or discharge has been subject to less judicial consideration than has that of "causing" pollution. In essence, however, the offence is designed to catch the offender who knows that pollution is occurring, has the power to do something about it, and yet does nothing.

In *Price v Cromack*[90] the appellant was a farmer who, by the terms of a contract, had bound himself to accept on to his land effluent from a neighbouring animal by-products company of which he was a director. The effluent escaped through the defective wall of a lagoon constructed on his land and flowed into a stream. Price was convicted of having "caused" the entry of poisonous, noxious or polluting matter to

---

[87] [1971] 2 All E.R. 357.
[88] [1994] 4 All E.R. 281.
[89] [1995] 1 All E.R. 225.
[90] [1975] 1 W.L.R. 988.

enter controlled waters. On appeal, the prosecution argued, following *Alphacell*, that the defendant had undertaken a positive act by entering into an arrangement whereby effluent was received on to his land.

Lord Widgery, however, did not accept that the nature of the arrangement was sufficient to maintain a conviction for "causing" pollution. Whilst he accepted in principle the proposition that there should be no substantive difference between the case of a man who generates pollution on his own land and that of one who agrees to accept pollution generated by another, his Lordship made the point that it was not so much a question of distinguishing between the culpability of those individuals, but of ascertaining the precise nature of the offence committed. His Lordship could not accept that there was a "causing" of the entry of polluting matter "merely because the landowner stands by and watches the polluting matter cross his land into the stream, even if he has committed himself by contract to allowing the adjoining owner so to act." Lord Widgery implied what Ashworth J. had stated explicitly in the same case, namely that if the defendant had been charged instead with "knowingly permitting" the pollution, "I do not see what answer the present appellant could conceivably have had in the circumstances of this case."

The decision in *Price v Cromack* was followed in *Wychavon DC v National Rivers Authority*.[91] In that case, raw sewage escaped into the River Avon from a sewer which was operated and maintained by the district council, as agents of a water company. The council failed to remedy the situation for some hours, despite its being aware of the discharge. Quashing the conviction for "causing" the discharge, the Divisional Court held that the council should have been charged instead with "knowingly permitting", because it had not done anything positive to encourage the discharge, but had merely remained inactive.

(1) *"Knowingly"*

Knowledge that the matter in question was entering or being discharged into the water **8–040** is, of course, a necessary element of a charge of "knowingly permitting". The case of *Vehicle Inspectorate v Blakes Chilled Distribution Ltd*[92] is authority for the proposition that a party must know about a problem before it can be guilty of failing to take reasonable steps to correct it. In the absence of a confession, however, it is notoriously difficult to prove the state of a man's mind. Therefore, if the prosecution are able to establish all of the relevant surrounding facts, they are entitled to ask the magistrates or jury to infer that the accused acted with knowledge of those facts, unless there is some convincing evidence from him to the contrary.[93] Thus, in *Schulmans Incorporated Ltd v National Rivers Authority*,[94] it was held that a defendant could be fixed with constructive knowledge of facts of which he ought to have been aware in circumstances where he had deliberately turned a blind eye to the obvious, or had refrained from inquiry because he did not wish his suspicions to be confirmed.

On the question of whether or not the prosecution must establish that the defendant knows that the entry in question is poisonous, noxious or polluting, the case of *Ashcroft v Cambro Waste Products*,[95] which concerned "knowingly permitting" the deposit of

[91] [1993] 1 W.L.R. 125.
[92] [2002] EWHC 208 Admin.
[93] *per* Lord Diplock in *Sweet v Parsley* [1970] A.C. 132 at 164.
[94] [1993] Env. L.R.D. 1.
[95] [1981] 1 W.L.R. 1349.

controlled waste, suggests that this may not be necessary and that it is sufficient for the prosecution to show only knowledge of the entry.

(2) *Corporate knowledge*

8–041 Where the defendant is a company, the question arises: who must know about the pollution in order for the company to knowingly permit its presence? Does the pollution need to be known about by a director or senior manager (*i.e.* a person of such seniority that their state of mind will constitute the state of mind of the company) or is it enough that site operatives know about the contamination?

In environmental cases involving corporate knowledge, there is a tendency for the courts to hold that knowledge at site level is sufficient, provided that the person who acquires the knowledge has some power to make relevant decisions. For example, in *Shanks & McEwan (Teeside) Ltd v Environment Agency*,[96] a prosecution for an illegal deposit of waste, the court held that a company in the business of accepting waste had corporate knowledge in respect of a specific illegal deposit when it was accepted by a site supervisor in the absence of the site manager.

(3) *"Permitting"*

8–042 The definition of "permitting" was considered by the House of Lord's in *Vehicle Inspectorate v Nuttall*.[97] It was held that its meaning depended upon the context, so that (a) it could be confined to "allows" or "authorises", or (b) it could carry the wider meaning of failure to take reasonable steps to prevent the occurrence of that which should not be permitted.[98] This interpretation reflects the reasoning in a much earlier case, *Berton v Alliance Economic Investment Co. Ltd*, where it had been held that "permitting" may mean either giving leave for an act which, without that leave, could not legally be done, or to abstain from taking reasonable steps to prevent an act, where it is within a person's power to do so.[99]

There has, however, been no case law which decides whether the narrower or the wider meaning applies in the specific context of water pollution. Whilst the case of *Bromsgrove DC v Carthy*[1] (below) appears to support the wider interpretation, suggesting that, in other contexts, it is possible to be criminally liable for "permitting" by failing to take reasonable steps to prevent an occurrence, it should be remembered that the offences in relation to water pollution refer to the entry or *discharge* of pollutants. This may suggest the need for a more positive act than failing to take reasonable steps.

However, if the extended meaning of "permitting" applies, so that it can involve a failure to take *reasonable* steps to prevent pollution, it must follow that a party will not "permit" by failing to do something that was *unreasonable*. What will be reasonable will depend on the knowledge of the party and the circumstances. For example, in *Bromsgrove DC v Carthy*, a landowner had asked gypsies on his land to leave, but had stopped short of taking legal proceedings to evict them. It was held that he could not be guilty of an offence of "permitting", because he had done what was reasonable in

---

[96] [1997] Env. L.R. 305; [1999] Q.B. 333.
[97] [1999] 1 W.L.R. 629.
[98] *ibid.,* at 631.
[99] *per* Atkin L.J. in *Berton v Alliance Economic Investment Co. Ltd* [1922] 1 K.B. 742 at 759.
[1] (1975) 30 P & C R 34.

the circumstances, and it would have been unreasonable to expect him to take further steps.

Whichever meaning is ascribed, it is clear that one cannot "permit" what one does not control.[2] Thus, for example, if a freehold owner of land has transferred all powers in relation to the land to another party, and operations on the land lead to water pollution, he will not permit that pollution, because he will have given up practical control over the land. (The position may be different, however, where he has specifically let the land for a polluting use.) The idea that a person cannot "permit" an occurrence of pollution which he is powerless to prevent was applied in *Schulmans Incorporated Ltd v National Rivers Authority*. Here, convictions for "knowingly permitting" matter to enter controlled waters as a result of an oil spillage, which flowed into a brook, were overturned on appeal on the basis that there was no evidence that the appellants could have prevented the escape of fuel oil into the brook sooner than they did.

Breach of consent conditions

As has been said, s.85(6) of the Water Resources Act 1991 makes it a specific offence **8–043** to breach the conditions of a discharge consent. Two cases here are worthy of note, both of which illustrate that the courts have been prepared to adopt a tough approach and to impose strict liability in relation to this offence. In *Taylor Woodrow Property Management Ltd v National Rivers Authority*[3] the defendants held a discharge consent relating to the outflow from an industrial estate of which they were no longer the occupiers. A third party discharged oil from the outfall pipe in breach of the conditions of the consent. The defendants were convicted of an offence under s.85(6) even though they themselves had not made the discharge. Similarly, in *National Rivers Authority v Alfred McAlpine Homes (East) Ltd*[4] strict vicarious liability was imposed on the defendant company for the acts of its employees in causing a breach of the conditions of a consent, even though the employees in question could not be said to have been exercising the "controlling mind" of the company. Morland J. stated that to hold otherwise "would render important environmental legislation almost entirely nugatory."

Defences

For water pollution offences there is *no* general defence of taking all reasonable **8–044** precautions and exercising all due diligence to avoid the commission of an offence. There are, however, a number of specific statutory defences to prosecution.[5] The most obvious, of course, is that the discharge in question was made in accordance with the conditions of a consent. In addition, a discharge made in accordance with an authorisation granted under the PPC regime, or in accordance with a waste management licence, will be immune from prosecution, as will discharges made in accordance

[2] *Earl of Sefton v Tophams Limited (No. 2)* [1967] 1 A.C. 50.
[3] [1995] J.E.L. 55.
[4] [1995] J.E.L. 60.
[5] Water Resources Act 1991, s.88.

with powers granted by a statute or statutory order. A licence for dumping effluent at sea, granted under the Food and Environment Protection Act 1985, also provides a defence. Certain other kinds of defence are also afforded by the Water Resources Act 1991[6], which provides that a person will not be guilty of an offence under s.85 in any of the following situations:

(i) Where the entry or discharge is made to avoid danger to life or health provided that:

    (a) such steps as are reasonably practicable in the circumstances are taken to minimise the extent of the discharge or to mitigate its effect, and

    (b) details of the discharge or entry are furnished to the Environment Agency as soon as is reasonably practicable;

(ii) Where the discharge is of trade or sewerage effluent from a vessel. (This is regulated by byelaws);

(iii) Where a person permits (as opposed to causes) an entry of matter from an abandoned mine. (Note, however, that s.60 of the Environment Act 1995 provides that this defence does not apply after December 31, 1999 in relation to mines abandoned after that date);

(iv) Where a deposit on land of solid refuse from a mine or quarry is made with the consent of the Environment Agency, and that waste falls into inland freshwaters, provided that all reasonable steps have been taken to prevent this;

(v) Where a highway authority, or other person entitled to open a drain, causes or permits a discharge from that drain, unless that discharge contravenes a prohibition made under s.86 of the Act.

In *Express Limited (trading as Express Dairies Distribution) v Environment Agency*[7] a dairy company successfully raised the defence that entry had taken place in an emergency to avoid danger to life or health. An employee of the dairy had been driving a milk tanker along a motorway in the course of the company's business. As a result of a tyre blow-out, the delivery pipe was sheared, causing several thousand litres of milk to escape from the tank. The driver pulled onto the hard shoulder, stopping at a point where two drains fed into a brook, and allowed the milk to enter the brook. The court accepted that this action had been taken in an emergency.

Penalties

8–045 The penalty is the same for all of the offences, namely a maximum £20,000 fine and three months' imprisonment in the magistrates' court, or two years' imprisonment and an unlimited fine in the Crown Court. The fine imposed for the sinking of the Sea Empress oil tanker, in Milford Haven in 1996, is one of the best known. The Sea Empress ran aground as it was being navigated through the port of Milford Haven.

---

[6] *ibid.*, s.89
[7] [2003] EWHC 448 Admin.

Large amounts of oil were spilled. The Port Authority, who were responsible for navigating the tanker through the port, pleaded guilty to a charge of causing polluted matter to enter controlled waters contrary to s.85 of the Water Resources Act 1991. The Authority was originally sentenced in the Crown Court to a fine of £4 million, but this was reduced by the Court of Appeal to £750,000 on the basis that there had been a guilty plea, the Port Authority was a public body, and there had been a misunderstanding of the Authority's financial position.[8]

In *Hart v Anglian Water Services*,[9] Anglian Water Services appealed against a fine of £200,000 imposed for the discharge of raw sewage into the River Crouch. The sewage was discharged from a sewage treatment plant when equipment failed. The company pleaded guilty to an offence under s.85(3) of the Water Resources Act of causing sewage effluent to be discharged into the river. The Court of Appeal reduced the fine to £60,000. It took the view that each case had to be considered on its own facts. Whilst the case was a serious case of pollution—the river was polluted over two kilometres and serious damage done to fish and wildlife that lived in it—the effects were limited in time and space. The river recovered 24 hours later, due to the prompt action taken by the company, which had then pleaded guilty.

Clean-up of water pollution

Where the Environment Agency considers that polluting matter is likely to enter **8–046** controlled waters, or where such matter has already entered controlled waters, it may require the polluter to take action (or, in certain circumstances, take action itself) to prevent the matter from entering the waters or, in the latter case, to remedy pollution which has occurred. The power to require preventive measures enables the Agency, for example, to divert the course of a spillage away from controlled waters in the aftermath of a road or rail accident, whilst the power to require the effects of pollution to be remedied extends, for example, to the restocking of a river with fish. In both types of case, where the Agency has acted, it may recover the costs of its operations from the person who caused or knowingly permitted the matter to be where it was likely to enter the waters or, as the case may be, to enter the waters.

(1) Works notices[10]

The Environment Agency has the power to serve a "works notice" on the polluter, **8–047** requiring him to take specified steps to prevent polluting matter from entering controlled waters or, as the case may be, to remedy the effects of pollution which has occurred.[11] Such remediation may include the removal and disposal of the polluting matter and, so far as is reasonably practicable, the restoration of the waters in question to their former state of cleanliness. The Agency's power enables it to carry out investigations and to charge the cost of these to the suspected polluter where the investigations result in the subsequent service of a works notice.[12] The provisions

---

[8] *R. v Milford Haven Port Authority* [2000] All. E.R. (D) 352.
[9] [2003] EWCA Crim 2243.
[10] WRA 1991, s.161A (inserted by EA 1995, Sch.22, para.162).
[11] *ibid.*, ss.161A-161D.
[12] *ibid.*, s.161A(11)(b) (inserted by EA 1995, Sch.22, para.162).

relating to works notices are an important weapon in the Environment Agency's pollution control armoury. Although works notices cannot be used to prevent the making of a discharge in pursuance of a consent,[13] they may be used to prevent the occurrence of illegal discharges and, where consent conditions have been breached, to secure remediation of pollution.

Whilst the procedure for the service of works notices is broadly similar to that which obtains in relation to remediation notices served under the contaminated land regime (see Ch. 6), the Environment Agency's discretion in deciding whether to serve a works notice is much less constrained than when serving a notice under that regime. Before serving the notice, the Agency is required to endeavour to consult the person on whom it is to be served, together with others whose rights may be affected by the proposed works. Where third parties are required to grant rights to the person on whom a works notice is served to enable him to comply with it, they are entitled to recover compensation from him. In addition, where the person on whom a works notice is served fails to carry out the specified works within the specified time, the Environment Agency may carry out those works itself and recover the costs of so doing from the defaulter. Failure to comply with the requirements of a works notice is an offence punishable in the magistrates' court by three months' imprisonment and a maximum fine of £20,000, and in the Crown Court by imprisonment for two years and an unlimited fine. The advantage of works notices is that the initial costs of remediation are met directly by the polluter, thus preventing a drain on the financial resources of the Agency. The prospect of meeting the cost of cleaning-up pollution, which will usually be higher than any fine resulting from a conviction under s.85, may also act as a deterrent for industrial polluters.

The powers available to the Agency to serve works notices may, on occasion, overlap with its power (and the power of local authorities) to serve a remediation notice under the contaminated land regime,[14] for example where run-off from contaminated land pollutes water. This has caused some concern in industry, because it is far easier for the Agency to serve a works notice than to serve a remediaition notice. However, guidance issued by the Environment Agency makes it clear that, where a site could be the subject of both a remediation notice and a works notice, a remediation notice should be served.

(2) Recovery of clean-up costs[15]

8–048 Despite the above-mentioned works notice provisions, the Environment Agency may still need to take action itself to prevent or clean up pollution. The Agency is entitled to carry out preventive or remedial works only where it considers either that these are necessary "forthwith" (in the aftermath of a spillage, for example) or where, after reasonable inquiry, the person who caused or knowingly permitted the pollution (or accumulation of polluting matter) cannot be found.

---

[13] *ibid.*, s.161A(7).
[14] See Ch. 6.
[15] WRA 1991, s.161.

F: PREVENTIVE MEASURES

Cleaning up waterways which have become polluted can be very costly. This has led the **8–049**
UK, in keeping with the policy of the EC, to develop a system of controls which aim to
prevent the occurrence of pollution.

Water protection zones[16]

Under the Water Resources Act 1991, the Secretary of State may create Water **8–050**
Protection Zones with a view to preventing or restricting the entry of poisonous,
noxious or polluting matter into controlled waters. The zones are designated areas
within which certain activities likely to have this result are curtailed or prohibited. The
wording of the provisions gives the Secretary of State a large measure of discretion to
control agricultural and other activities. Alternatively, the Secretary of State may, by
adopting regulations, give the Environment Agency the power to determine which
activities should be prohibited or restricted and the manner in which this should be
done. It is not possible, however, for either the Secretary of State or the Agency to
require the carrying out of positive works. Any regulations adopted may provide a
procedure for obtaining consents from the Environment Agency to carry out restricted
activities, and may create new criminal offences for breach of those consents,
punishable on the same scale as those under s.85.

Water Protection Zones, by establishing specific regimes appropriate to the needs of
particular areas, provide a useful means of controlling diffuse sources of pollution such
as agricultural surface run-off containing pesticides. Although there is no specific
provision in the Act for paying compensation to those affected by the creation of a
Water Protection Zone, the Act provides that the Secretary of State may include in
regulations such consequential and supplemental provisions as he considers appropriate. It is conceivable that such provisions might include compensation payable to
farmers, who have so far opposed the use of Water Protection Zones for fear of the
costs which their creation might entail. To date a number of areas, including the River
Dee basin, have been designated Water Protection Zones.

Nitrate vulnerable zones

Nitrates, which are contained in agricultural fertilisers, act as a plant nutrient. On **8–051**
entering waters, they increase the numbers of some plants but cause a decline in the
growth of those plants and species which flourish in nutrient-poor waters. This leads to
a deterioration in the quality of the waters in terms of biodiversity. Nitrates can enter
water by one of three main routes: surface water run-off from agricultural land;
discharge of effluent containing sewage or animal waste; and rain. The increased use of
fertilisers has significantly increased nitrate levels in water over the last 50 years. There
have been two recent government initiatives to reduce nitrate run-off from agricultural
land into surface and groundwater.

---

[16] *ibid.*, s.93 and Sch.11.

Following enforcement action against the UK by the European Commission in the ECJ for a failure to fulfil its obligations under the Drinking Water Directive, measures were finally taken to establish what were then called "Nitrate Sensitive Areas". The aim was to reduce or stabilise high or rising nitrate levels in significant sources of public water supply, through voluntary changes to farming activity. The scheme, which encouraged farmers to take nitrate-reducing measures, was closed in 1998 following a government spending review.

Under the EC Nitrate Directive[17] (mentioned above) all known areas of land draining into nitrate-polluted water have to be designated as Nitrate Vulnerable Zones (NVZs). Following consultations, 66 NVZs, covering around 600,000 hectares, or 8 per cent of England, were designated in 1996 to protect drinking waters from nitrate pollution. However, an ECJ judgment of December 2000 ruled that the UK had failed in its obligation to designate sufficient areas to protect all surface and groundwaters (not just drinking water sources) against diffuse nitrate pollution from agriculture. As a consequence, a total of 55 per cent of England has now been designated a Nitrate Vulnerable Zone.[18] The action programme for NVZs includes measures that restrict the quantity and timing of applications of agricultural nitrogen fertilisers and livestock manures. It also requires records to be kept in relation to these substances. Failure to comply with these requirements is an offence.[19]

Other Measures

The Water Resources Act 1991 also gives the Secretary of State the power to make regulations prohibiting any person from having custody or control of any poisonous, noxious or polluting matter, unless certain prescribed works are carried out to prevent that matter from entering controlled waters.[20] The regulations may also provide that persons already in custody or control of such matter should carry out similar works. Such regulations may create new criminal offences for breach of their provisions, provided that the maximum penalty is not greater than could be imposed for an offence under s.85. To date, the only regulations which have been made under this provision are the Control of Pollution (Silage, Slurry and Agricultural Fuel Oil) Regulations 1991.[21] These impose a number of controls over silage-making operations and the design and use of stores for slurry and agricultural fuel oil.

G: WATER POLLUTION AT COMMON LAW

8–052   Whilst the statutory regime is primarily concerned with punishing the polluter, the common law provides the principal means by which those whose private rights have been interfered with may claim compensation.

[17] Directive 91/676/EEC.
[18] See *www.defra.gov.uk/environment/water/quality/nitrate/nvz.htm*.
[19] EC Nitrate Directive Action Programme for Nitrate Vulnerable Zones (Amendment) (Wales) Regulations 2003 (SI 2003/1852); Nitrate Vulnerable Zones (Additional Designations) (England) (No.2) Regulations 2002 (SI 2002/2614).
[20] WRA 1991, s.92
[21] SI 1991/324, as amended by Control of Pollution (Silage, Slurry and Agricultural Fuel Oil) (Amendment) Regulations 1997 (SI 1997/547). For Scotland, see Control of Pollution (Silage, Slurry and Agricultural Fuel Oil) (Scotland) Regulations 2003 (SI 2003/531).

The main causes of action for water pollution are nuisance and the rule in *Rylands v Fletcher*. The relevant general principles of liability are discussed in Ch. 12. Here, we concentrate on some more specific and obscure causes of action which arise from a number of miscellaneous ancient rights attaching to ownership of land. Infringement of these rights is nowadays generally regarded by the courts as the commission of a form of private nuisance. These property rights include, for example, the right to abstract water which flows through or under land, and the right—known as a "riparian" right—to use water adjacent to one's land. It is a general principle of common law that a person over or under whose land water flows is entitled to receive that water in an unpolluted state. It should be noted here that, so far as the common law is concerned, the definition of water pollution has traditionally depended upon how the rights of others to use the water are affected. For example, if the temperature of water in a stream is altered so that a person downstream is unable to use the water as before, the common law will look upon the water as "polluted", even though it may be free from harmful substances.

Riparian rights

A person who owns land adjoining a river or a stream (*i.e.* any watercourse which flows **8–053** in a defined channel) is known as the riparian owner. He normally owns the bed of the river (or owns it to a point equidistant from his neighbour on the opposite side) but he does not own the water itself. The riparian owner has, as an incident of his ownership of the land, the right to receive waters in their natural state. This means that not only has the riparian owner the right to receive water free from impurities, he is also entitled to receive water in the same quantity and of the same natural character as he has come to expect. The nature of the latter right is neatly illustrated by the decision in *Young & Co. v Bankier Distillery Co.*,[22] where discharges from a mine upstream of the plaintiffs altered the character of the water downstream from soft to hard. This in turn caused changes to the quality of the plaintiff distillers' whisky. They were able to obtain an injunction to stop the defendants' activities, even though the defendants had not made the water impure.

As has been said, riparian rights are an incident of land ownership. In other words they are a form of property right. It might be thought, then, that such rights would be unqualified and absolute, and that liability for their infringement would be strict—as is the case, for example, in relation to interference with an easement. The courts, however, have consistently tended to see riparian rights as related to the claimant's reasonable enjoyment of his land, and so have treated their infringement as analogous to the commission of a nuisance. It follows from this that such rights are not absolute, but are subject to the reasonable land-use requirements of others. Thus, it has been said that riparian owners upstream of the claimant may make "ordinary use"[23] of a watercourse in the exercise of their own riparian rights. As in an ordinary nuisance action, the courts engage in a "balancing act" to decide what is reasonable as between two riparian owners' conflicting uses of the water in question. That said, the courts have to some extent recognised the essentially proprietary character of riparian rights,

[22] [1893] A.C. 691.
[23] *per* Lord Macnaughten in *Young & Co. v Bankier Distillery Co.* [1893] A.C. 691 at 698.

in that they have been prepared to treat the interference with riparian rights as causing damage to property, rather than a mere loss of enjoyment of that property, thereby circumventing the doctrine of locality which so often stands in the way of the claimant in a traditional nuisance action.

Although the courts most commonly adopt a nuisance-based approach, liability for the infringement of riparian rights has sometimes been held to arise in trespass, which again reflects a recognition of their proprietary nature. In *Jones v Llanwrst UDC*,[24] for example, the plaintiff successfully brought an action in trespass against the defendant council, which had deposited solid waste in a river so that it came to rest on the river bed of which he was the riparian owner.

Rights in respect of groundwater

8–054 Water which percolates through or under land, as opposed to flowing in a defined channel above or beneath it, is known as "groundwater". Pollution of this is also an actionable nuisance. Thus, in *Ballard v Tomlinson*,[25] the plaintiff brewery was successful when the defendant deposited sewage in a well on his land which polluted water percolating through the plaintiffs' land, with the result that they were unable to draw fresh water from their own well.

The decision in *Ballard v Tomlinson* was considered in *Cambridge Water Company Ltd v Eastern Counties Leather plc.*[26] (discussed further in Ch. 12). The plaintiff water company abstracted water from a borehole which had become contaminated when solvents had seeped into the watercourse beneath the defendant's tannery and had percolated towards the borehole. The water company brought an action in negligence, nuisance and under the rule in *Rylands v Fletcher*. The Court of Appeal, following *Ballard v Tomlinson*, held that the right to abstract unpolluted groundwater was a proprietary one, and that, accordingly, once the water company had shown causation, liability would follow. The House of Lords, however, reversed this decision, holding that the action was properly to be categorised as an action in nuisance, of which the rule in *Rylands v Fletcher* was merely an offshoot, and that, following the *dicta* of Lord Reid in *The Wagon Mound (No.2)*,[27] foreseeability of the type of harm was a necessary ingredient in the tort of nuisance. Therefore, because the tannery had permitted the solvents to be spilled at a time when their harmful effects were not known, they escaped liability. *Ballard v Tomlinson*, in which the issue of foreseeability of harm did not arise, was distinguished.

H: PLANNING CONTROLS

8–055 Finally, it should be noted that development has the potential to affect water quality, by increasing surface run-off and, more significantly, by leading to the pollution of groundwater. The extent to which the environment is taken into account in planning

---

[24] [1911] 1 Ch. 393.
[25] [1885] 29 Ch.D. 115. Note that whilst a defendant may not pollute groundwater to the detriment of his neighbours, he may abstract it without committing a nuisance: *Bradford Corporation v Pickles* [1895] A.C. 587.
[26] [1994] 2 AC 264.
[27] [1967] 1 AC 617.

decisions is considered in Ch. 13. Planning authorities are required to take account of environmental considerations, such as potential water pollution, in preparing their development plans, and must consult with, *inter alia*, the relevant nature conservation bodies and the Environment Agency in so doing. In addition, water pollution will be a material consideration in individual planning decisions.

Chapter 9

NATURE CONSERVATION

"Whereas, in the European territory of the Member States, natural habitats are continuing to deteriorate and an increasing number of wild species are seriously threatened; whereas given that the threatened habitats and species form part of the Community's natural heritage and the threats to them are often of a transboundary nature, it is necessary to take measures at Community level in order to conserve them" (EC Natural Habitats Directive).[1]

Introduction

The term "nature conservation" encompasses the idea of maintaining the existence **9–001** and welfare of animals and plants, and, by necessary implication, the idea of preserving and enhancing their natural and man-made habitats. Arguably, it can also refer to the conservation of natural landscapes, or landscape features (such as trees, hedgerows, and limestone pavements) for the sake of the aesthetic benefits they bring to mankind irrespective of their functions as habitats. Although this latter type of conservation is more commonly known as "landscape management", there is an increasing tendency to treat both concepts as one, reflecting a holistic approach to environmental concerns. The main way in which the concepts differ is that "landscape management" concerns itself with preserving natural and man-made environments for the sake of their beauty and for public recreation, whilst "nature conservation" is concerned with these matters only in so far as they help to conserve plants, animals and geographical features of scientific importance. Despite some overlap, each type of conservation is still the subject of a distinct statutory regime.

The division between nature conservation and landscape management seems to have arisen by accident, in the days before the need for an integrated approach had become fully apparent, but it has little foundation in logic. This is because many features of the landscape which are traditionally thought of as "natural" are in fact made-made. Contrary to the romantic notion that landscapes are shaped solely by natural forces left to their own devices, what is sometimes perceived as nature in a "wild" state is very often the result of human activity. Downs, for example, would become covered with

---

[1] Preamble to Dir.92/43/EEC of May 21, 1992 on the conservation of natural habitats and of wild fauna and flora.

shrubs and trees were it not for the grazing activities of animals brought there by man. The task of nature conservation, then, is more complex than it might at first appear. It involves making difficult value-judgments about whether the effects of mankind's relationship with nature are desirable.

Even if one takes the ecocentric view that plants and animals have a right to exist independently of their use to mankind, giving effect to this idea requires a balance to be struck between the rights of plants and animals and the rights of humans. Human interest in nature is twofold: we seek aesthetic pleasure from it, but we also use it as a resource for other purposes. The purposes which conflict most heavily with conservation are agriculture and land development. Between 1932 and 1984, for example, 97 per cent of traditional hay meadows and pastures disappeared from the UK as a result of modern intensive farming,[2] and in recent times, the UK, every five years, has been losing to land development an area of countryside at least the size of Leicestershire.[3]

The interests of wildlife are not endangered principally by people acting with deliberate or malicious intent, but by those who, at least until recent times, have often been unaware of the consequences of their actions. The destruction of natural plant-covering and hedgerows in the interests of agriculture, the claiming of land for development, and the introduction of new plant and animal species (sometimes for agricultural benefit) have caused changes in nature which far exceed the results of human destruction levelled knowingly and directly against particular species or landscapes. It is this fact that makes nature conservation one of the most politically sensitive and controversial areas of environmental regulation, in which the interests of landowners have clashed dramatically with those of conservationists. The focus of the debate is the extent to which the rights of a landowner to use his land as he wishes, as the common law has traditionally allowed, should be compromised in the name of ecology. The pattern of legal regulation in the UK is one of statutory restriction of people's rights to undertake certain activities (such as cutting wild flowers or collecting birds' eggs) even on land which belongs to them. Wild animals, which belong to no-one, are also protected by statute.

Background

9–002   Concern to protect animals and plants and their habitats originated in Victorian times. It was evidenced by public reaction against such practices as cock-fighting and bear baiting, and by the establishment of zoological and botanical gardens. But it was not until the emergence of a coherent planning regime—a response to the need for land development, after the destruction caused by Second World War bombing—that nature conservation became the focus of government attention.

In 1947, a special committee of the House of Lords (the "Huxley Committee") reported on nature conservation,[4] and its recommendations still form the basis of nature conservation policy today. These recommendations were:

[2] Schoon, "Going, Going Gone: The Story of Britain's Vanishing Natural History", Bookman Projects (1996).
[3] *Hansard*, H.C., 1980–81, Vol.3 col. 548.
[4] Report of the Wildlife Conservation Special Committee: Conservation of Nature in England and Wales (1947), Cmd. 7122.

- Nature conservation should be the responsibility of central government. (It is now the responsibility of the devolved regional administrations.)

- Protection should be based on the designation of sites which are important examples of their type.

- Conservation policy should be based on scientific research into the complex relationships between animals and plants, and between plants and the soils and rocks upon which they depend.

The Huxley Committee's recommendations led to the passing of the National Parks and Access to Countryside Act 1949. This legislation introduced the practice of conserving areas of land by designating them "Sites of Special Scientific Interest" (SSSIs) or "National Nature Reserves" (NNRs). Nowadays, sites are most commonly designated as SSSIs.

The approach underlying nature conservation legislation in the UK is that it should be based upon co-operation with landowners and upon voluntary agreements made with them. This idea has in the past been expressed by central government as follows:

"The best guardians of nature are those who are closest to it. The Government remains firmly committed to the voluntary principle; helping and encouraging those who live and work in the countryside, and those who visit it, to conserve our natural heritage. Much of our wildlife and important habitats readily co-exist with man's activities, indeed in many cases rely on it. A long history of sympathetic land management has shaped the character of landscape and habitat on which the diversity of species largely depends. The Government wants to encourage management agreements with landholders which encourage positive conservation."

The legislation

The principal source of UK legislation on nature conservation is the Wildlife and **9–003** Countryside Act 1981, as amended by the Countryside and Rights of Way Act 2000. The 1981 Act strengthened the provisions relating to Sites of Special Scientific Interest which had been introduced by the National Parks and Access to Countryside Act 1949 and established a comprehensive scheme of protection for those sites. It also provided for the protection of specified animals and plants, and gave effect to the EC Birds Directive.[5] The passage of the Wildlife and Countryside Act 1981 was controversial. Over 2,000 amendments were proposed, reflecting wide divisions between conservationists and landowners. In introducing the Bill to the House of Commons, the then Secretary of State for the Environment accepted that it was a compromise between competing interests.[6]

The Countryside and Rights of Way Act 2000 introduced new sections into the 1981 Act which significantly amended the rules for designating and protecting SSSIs in England and Wales. It also contained provisions relating to "Areas of Outstanding

[5] Directive 79/409/EEC [1979] O.J. L103/1.
[6] *Hansard*, H.C., 1980–1981, Vol.3, col. 525.

Natural Beauty" and relating to public access to the English and Welsh countryside for recreational purposes (the so-called "right to roam"). The amended 1981 Act is supplemented by the Conservation (Natural Habitats etc.) Regulations 1994,[7] which implement both the Birds Directive[8] and the Habitats Directive[9] and provide for the designation of sites of European importance. The protection given to these "European sites" (which are always also designated as SSSIs) is greater than that afforded by simple designation under the 1981 Act, but there are as yet relatively few of them.

In addition to the principal legislation, there is legislation which protects particular species (for example, the Protection of Badgers Act 1992 and the Conservation of Seals Act 1970) or which ensures animal welfare generally (for example, the Protection of Animals Act 1911, and the Wild Mammals Protection Act 1996). The Countryside Act 1968 remains of importance in respect of landscape management issues.

The nature conservation bodies

9–004 Responsibility for nature conservation throughout Great Britain is divided geographically between England, Scotland and Wales. In England responsibility rests with a body called English Nature, in Wales with the Countryside Council for Wales, and in Scotland with Scottish National Heritage. In Scotland and Wales these bodies have a combined nature conservation and landscape management function, whilst in England landscape management is the function of the Countryside Agency.

The responsibilities of the nature conservation bodies include the selection of sites for designation as SSSIs and the power to enter into agreements for the management of these sites with the owners and occupiers. In addition, they are to be consulted where decisions with the potential to affect nature conservation are taken, most importantly in relation to certain applications for planning permission. Other responsibilities include the maintenance and management of National Nature Reserves and the provision of advice to Ministers on nature conservation matters.[10]

The division of the institutional framework of nature conservation into different geographical areas was accomplished by the Environmental Protection Act 1990,[11] and was a controversial move. Critics accused the Government of trying to placate worried landowners by diluting the power of the previously existing national conservation body—the Nature Conservancy Council. A House of Lords committee[12] rejected the government's view that Great Britain could be split ecologically into three distinct units, and stated that the evidence clearly supported the view that Great Britain was a biological continuum, so scientific research into nature conservation was best conducted on a national basis. The Committee, whilst accepting that nature conservation had to be delivered at a local level, also noted that dividing the administration of nature conservation in Great Britain was contrary to international trends. The

---

[7] SI 1994/2716.

[8] Directive 79/409/EEC [1992] O.J. L103/1.

[9] Directive 92/43/EEC [1992] O.J. L206.

[10] These powers and responsibilities derive originally from the Nature Conservancy Council Act 1973 (which established the Nature Conservancy Council, from which the current bodies have evolved). They have been modified and extended over the years by subsequent legislation.

[11] EPA 1990, s.128(1).

[12] House of Lords Select Committee on Science and Technology (1989–90).

government sought to meet this criticism by establishing the Joint Nature Conservation Committee. This body is effectively a mere meeting of the three regional bodies (it has no independent funding) and its remit is the maintenance of common national standards (for example, in the designation of SSSIs) and the implementation of Britain's international commitments in respect of nature conservation.

The EU influence

The European Union has justified its policy on protecting animals and plants in the **9–005** following terms:

> "Wild fauna and flora are part of mankind's common heritage. The steady decline in the number of wild species is not only in itself an impoverishment of our natural heritage, but it lessens the diversity of non-renewable genetic resources whilst at the same time affecting the ecological balance with various degrees of severity."[13]

The main effect of European legislation has been to add another layer of site designations to those provided for in UK law. The Birds Directive and the Habitats Directive constitute the main legislative activity of the European Union on nature conservation.

The Birds Directive was adopted partly because of concern over the slaughter of birds for sport in certain southern European Member States. It aimed to stem the decline in population which was occurring in a large number of species of wild birds in Europe. It applies to birds, their eggs, nests and habitats. The Directive provides for the protection, management and control of all species of all wild birds in the territory of member states, and lays down rules for their exploitation. In particular it requires the designation of "Special Protection Areas" as safe havens for birds. The Habitats Directive requires the designation of areas as "Special Areas of Conservation". This Directive was the EU's response to the continuing deterioration of natural habitats, and represented a significant advance in European policy on nature conservation, because it covered both animals and plants.

A: CONSERVATION OF SPECIES

The main provisions relating to the conservation of species are to be found in the **9–006** Wildlife and Countryside Act 1981, as amended by the Conservation (Natural Habitats etc.) Regulations 1994 and the Countryside and Rights of Way Act 2000. The Habitats Regulations do not significantly alter the operation of the 1981 Act, but do create some further offences, whilst the Countryside and Rights of Way Act 2000 strengthens considerably the protection afforded to SSSIs, not least by creating "wildlife inspectors" with powers to enter land, search and take samples.

---

[13] Resolution of the Council and of the Representatives of the Governments of the Member States meeting within the Council of May 17, 1977, on the continuation and implementation of European Community policy and action on the environment [1977] O.J. C139/26.

The Wildlife and Countryside Act 1981 uses the same methodology to protect plants, birds and other animals. Schedules identify different categories of species, and different levels of protection are afforded to each category of species according to its needs. In this way, the legislation retains a simple central structure whilst catering for the needs of many species. It imposes general prohibitions on activities which endanger the species in question, such as killing, taking, selling or attempting to sell it. Breach of these prohibitions is normally a criminal offence, although, under a licensing scheme, the holder of a licence may be granted exemption from the Act's provisions.

Wild birds

9–007   Under the Birds Directive, Member States are required to conserve the population of *all* birds naturally occurring in their territory. Certain species of bird, however, are singled out for particular protection. The schedule to the Directive lists 170 bird species which are to be the subject of special conservation measures because they are either in danger of extinction, vulnerable to changes in habitat, or are considered rare, either because they have small populations or because they are found only in certain areas.

In introducing the Wildlife and Countryside Bill to Parliament, the then Secretary of State for the Environment was of the view that little new legislation was necessary to give effect to the Birds Directive. It is certainly correct that at the time Britain had in place much greater protection for birds than any other European country. Since 1880, there had been 14 statutes passed for the protection of birds, culminating in the Protection of Birds Act 1954. Within the UK, birds have traditionally been afforded more legal protection than have other species. Indeed, the scheme of the Directive appears to have been influenced by UK legislative provisions on birds.

The Wildlife and Countryside Act 1981 follows the scheme of the Directive. Thus it is normally an offence to kill, injure, take into captivity, or be in possession or control of any wild bird (alive or dead) or its eggs. It is also an offence to destroy or damage a nest that it is being built or is in use. Extra protection is given to specified (mainly rare) birds. These are listed in a schedule to the Act and include the corncrake, golden eagle and purple heron. It is an offence intentionally or recklessly[14] to disturb such birds while they are building their nests, or while they are on or near a nest containing eggs or young, or to disturb these birds' dependent young. Licences can be obtained which grant exemption from these provisions for a number of purposes, such as research, falconry and the keeping of bird or egg collections, although certain birds must be ringed and registered with DEFRA if held in captivity.

The various offences have certain defences (*e.g.* in respect of action taken to protect crops), and some birds may be hunted for sport either at all times, or outside the close season, which is the period of the year (usually February to September) when they are rearing their young. In such cases, however, there are provisions as to the manner in

---

[14] WCA 1981, s.1(5). The term "recklessly" was introduced by CRWA 2000 and so does not apply in Scotland. The original offence, confined to intentional disturbance, proved difficult to prosecute because of the need to prove that the defendant went with the objective of causing disturbance. The lesser test of reckless disturbance merely obliges the prosecution to show that the defendant took an unacceptable risk of disturbance.

which birds may be killed[15]—they may not, for example, be shot with a bow and arrow, a crossbow, or with a semi-automatic weapon, and they may not be pursued directly in vehicles.

Other wild animals

The law relating to animals other than birds is more fragmented, with statutes such as **9–008** the Protection of Badgers Act 1992 and the Conservation of Seals Act 1970 working alongside the Wildlife and Countryside Act 1981. Under the Wildlife and Countryside Act 1981, there is no general protection for other animals as there is for all wild birds. The protection is limited to certain specified animals, in respect of which the protection is similar to that given to birds. Thus it is an offence under the Act to kill, injure, take, have possession or control of, or sell or offer for sale any wild animal (alive or dead) where that animal is listed in the relevant Schedule to the Act. This Schedule affords protection to all bats, reptiles and amphibians, but only to the rarest mammals, insects and fish. In respect of certain animals, it is also an offence intentionally or recklessly to disturb or damage, while the animals are present, any structure or place used by them as a shelter.[16]

The Habitats Regulations afford protection to those plants and animals defined by the Directive as "European protected species". These include bats, the dormouse, the great crested newt, the otter and the large blue butterfly, all of which are already protected under the 1981 Act. Under the Habitats Regulations, it is an offence deliberately to capture, kill, take, or disturb or destroy a protected species, its eggs, breeding site or its resting place. The use of the word "deliberately" is taken from the Habitats Directive and differs from "intentionally"—a word more commonly used in UK criminal law—which appears in the Wildlife and Countryside Act 1981. The meaning of "deliberate" was considered in *R. v Secretary of State for Trade and Industry Ex p. Greenpeace Ltd No.2*[17] in the context of oil exploration activities in the North East Atlantic. The High Court held that "deliberate" required a specific aim to cause the damage done to the species (in this instance whales, porpoises and dolphins) and was to be distinguished from damage arising as an incidental effect of activities. In the circumstances, although it was clear that oil exploration activities could cause harm to the species in question, the oil companies could not be said to be engaged in "deliberate" disturbance of those species. This interpretation, then, appears to equate "deliberate" with "intentional".

There is no case law of the European Court of Justice on the interpretation of "deliberate" in the context of the Habitats Directive. However, the court has considered the use of the word in Art. 5 of the Birds Directive, which requires Member States to prohibit "deliberate" killing or capture of wild birds, or destruction of their nests and eggs. In Case 412/85 *Commission v Germany*[18] the ECJ held that a provision of German law which allowed damaging activities if they occurred as part of

---

[15] WCA 1981, s.5.
[16] *ibid.*, s.9(4). In relation to certain marine species which do not have places of shelter, it is simply an offence to disturb them (for example by inappropriate use of a power boat): WCA 1981, s.9(4A).
[17] [2000] Env. L.R. 221.
[18] [1987] ECR 3503.

the "normal use of the land for agricultural, forestry or fishing purposes" did not properly implement the Directive: the destruction could be "deliberate" even though it was serving an additional purpose.[19]

Plants

9–009 Under the Wildlife and Countryside Act 1981 it is an offence intentionally to pick, uproot, destroy or offer for sale specified wild plants, which include, for example, the lady's slipper and fen orchid. Additionally, it is an offence intentionally to uproot *any* wild plant. The Habitats Regulations make similar provision in respect of "European protected species" of plants.

Introduction of new species

9–010 It is an offence under the Wildlife and Countryside Act 1981 to introduce into the wild certain species of animals and plants or any animal not normally found in Great Britain. The aim of this provision is to prevent a recurrence of such problems as those which have faced the red squirrel, which may become extinct in the UK because it is unable to compete with the larger and tougher grey squirrel introduced from North America.

Enforcement

9–011 The Countryside and Rights of Way Act 2000 has consolidated and enhanced the enforcement provisions relating to the wildlife offences discussed above. In particular, it provides that in respect of all of these offences, magistrates are able to issue search warrants to police officers where they reasonably believe that evidence of an offence will be found on premises. It also makes certain of the more serious offences "arrestable offences", so that police officers may arrest without warrant persons they believe are guilty of, or are about to commit, those offences. It provides that for all offences prosecutions may be brought within six months of the date on which sufficient evidence becomes available (ending an anomaly whereby certain offences had to be prosecuted within six months of the date they were committed). It also gives courts the power to impose custodial sentences of up to six months for most offences.

The unamended 1981 Act made some provision for authorised persons to enter premises and land to investigate offences. The Countryside and Rights of Way Act 2000 accords these authorised persons the official title of "wildlife inspectors" and extends their powers.[20] Inspectors are empowered to enter land and premises to ascertain whether offences are being or have been committed. However, they are not permitted to enter dwellings, except to investigate offences related to licensed activities where the person who holds or has applied for the licence occupies the dwelling. The amended legislation also empowers inspectors or constables to require the production of animals and to require blood or tissue samples to be taken for DNA analysis (which may be

[19] The case is noted by Jans, J.H., in J. E. L. Vol.12(3) (November 2000) at p.385.
[20] WCA 1981, s.19ZA (inserted by CRWA 2000).

necessary to establish the ancestry of animals in captivity, to determine whether or not they are wild).[21] It is an offence to obstruct an inspector or constable, or fail to assist him without reasonable cause, but this is punishable only with a fine, not imprisonment.

B: WELFARE OF SPECIES

Animal welfare is a topic at the fringe of environmental law. Traditionally, environ- **9–012** mental law has been concerned with the conservation of species and habitats, and animal welfare has only been seen as relevant in so far as it may pose a threat to that conservation. Yet there can be discerned a certain amount of overlap between environmental and welfare regulation. We have already seen, for example, how the Wildlife and Countryside Act 1981 prohibits the killing of birds for sport with crossbows—such a measure cannot be justified on purely conservationist principles, because hunting with crossbows is hardly likely to kill birds in larger numbers than hunting with shotguns. Moreover, the controversy surrounding the government's proposed foxhunting ban, which rural communities argue will threaten their economic survival and traditional way of life, has vividly illustrated the link between animal welfare issues and landscape management—which is clearly a topic at the core of environmental law. It is therefore appropriate here to give a brief overview of animal welfare regulation.

Compared with other countries, the UK has a long history of legislation to control cruelty to animals. The legislation is based on the general principle that the use of animals for food, sport and experimentation is acceptable provided it is humane. The Protection of Animals Act 1911[22] provided the foundation for welfare regulation. It protects all farm, companion, zoo and sporting animals by making it an offence to cause unnecessary suffering to any animal, and its provisions are used by, amongst others, the RSPCA, the police and local authorities when bringing prosecutions for cruelty to animals.

The 1911 Act, however, has been criticised as out of date.[23] In particular because it focuses on a relatively narrow range of practices, some of which (*e.g.* the use of dogs for carriage) are no longer current. It has also been suggested that the notion of "unnecessary suffering" should be clarified to take account of the fact that incremental, man-made changes to animal species (made either through traditional selective breeding or through genetic modification or cloning) can have welfare implications by producing animals more susceptible to suffering. The government has accepted these criticisms, and the Act is now under review. At the time of writing, there are proposals for a new Animal Welfare Bill to improve and consolidate the existing legislative framework, which is currently rather piecemeal. A number of miscellaneous statutes, some passed to remedy perceived deficiencies in the 1911 Act, protect animal welfare in various ways. One example, which shows how standards of animal welfare have moved on since 1911, is the Breeding and Sale of Dogs (Welfare) Act 1999, which sets

---

[21] *ibid.*, s.19ZB.
[22] In Scotland the Protection of Animals (Scotland) Act 1912.
[23] See "Animals and Biotechnology", a report of the Agriculture and Environment Biotechnology Commission, September 2002, available at *www.aebc.gov.uk*.

a minimum age for breeding and a limit on the number of litters that a bitch can be expected to have.

Animals used for experimentation are regulated under the Animals (Scientific Procedures) Act 1986. This requires all scientific experiments or procedures carried out on living animals to be licensed by the Home Office if they may cause pain, suffering, distress or lasting harm. Farm animals are given specific protection by the Agriculture (Miscellaneous Provisions) Act 1968, under which it is an offence to cause unnecessary pain or distress to any livestock kept on agricultural land. Under this Act, codes of practice ("welfare codes") can be introduced with the approval of both Houses of Parliament. Although these do not lay down statutory requirements, livestock farmers are required by law to be familiar with them and they can be used to interpret the legislative requirements. At European level, Dir.98/58/EC sets out general rules for the protection of animals (including fish) kept for farming purposes, and there are additional separate Directives governing laying hens, calves and pigs.[24] In addition, the Council of Europe has five Conventions covering animal welfare, including one for the protection of animals kept for farming purposes and one for the protection of pets.

Specific laws to protect wild animals from suffering have been slower to emerge than those protecting captive animals. Although wild animal welfare is dealt with incidentally by the conservation statutes, and by other miscellaneous legislation (the use of "leghold" traps is banned by the Pests Act 1954, for example) it was only in 1996 that the UK enacted legislation to deal directly with the issue. Under the Wild Mammals Protection Act 1996, it is an offence to do a variety of things to wild mammals (for example, stone, stab, drown or asphyxiate them) unless the action is perpetrated swiftly and humanely in the course of lawful sport or pest control. The offence is punishable by a separate fine and/or six month term of imprisonment in respect of each animal harmed.

C: CONSERVATION OF HABITATS

9–013 Legal regulation is necessary to protect an animal's habitat as well as the animal itself because, without appropriate habitats to provide food and shelter, animals cannot survive. Indeed, the main threat to most species is the loss of their habitats, rather than direct persecution.

Habitat protection in the UK is based upon the designation of areas of land considered worthy of a higher level of protection than is afforded by normal methods of land-use control, such as planning, anti-pollution legislation or the law of nuisance. Special statutory protection for habitats is necessary in the light of the inadequacy of the common law, which allows an owner to do as he wishes on his land. This was starkly illustrated by the fate of the RSPB's first nature reserve. The reserve, set up in 1930 at Romney Marshes in Kent, had to be abandoned when drainage activities on neighbouring land, permissible under the common law, destroyed the features that had made it worthy of protection.

---

[24] These Directives are implemented by, *inter alia*, the Welfare of Farmed Animals (England) Regulations 2000 (SI 2000/1870) and 2002 (SI 2002/1646).

Designation of sites

There are a number of different designations of land for habitat conservation **9–014** purposes, with varying objectives and legal effects. Moreover, there are a number of different methods of control which may be exercised over a designated site. For example, a statutory nature conservation organisation may acquire ownership of the land in question, it may require the owner or occupier to forbear from certain activities with respect to the land, or it may require him to manage the site in specific ways in return for payment.

The main forms of site designation are "Sites of Special Scientific Interest" (SSSIs) and "European Sites" (which are almost always also SSSIs). Other designations include "Ramsar Sites" (wetlands of international importance, designated under the Ramsar Convention), National Nature Reserves (NNRs), Local Nature Reserves, Marine Nature Reserves and areas designated under Limestone Pavement Orders. We consider the first two designations in detail and outline the remaining ones.

Sites of Special Scientific Interest

The designation of SSSIs was introduced by the National Parks and Access to **9–015** Countryside Act 1949. Under that Act, however, the provisions relating to SSSIs were relatively weak, so that designation of a site as a National Nature Reserve was seen as the better option. The Wildlife and Countryside Act 1981 significantly extended the provisions relating to the management of SSSIs, which shifted the focus of attention to SSSIs as a primary means of habitat conservation. SSSI designation is now the foundation stone for natural habitat protection in the UK. There are over 4,000 SSSIs in the UK, covering around seven per cent of its land. Nowadays, other types of site (*e.g.* Ramsar and European sites) are normally also designated as SSSIs, which provides them with a core of protection to which extra layers of protection can be added.

Failings of the old regime

Despite the improvements made by the Wildlife and Countryside Act 1981, the **9–016** protection provided by SSSI designation came to be seen as notoriously inadequate, with high levels of damage and destruction occurring to sites. The weaknesses of the regime were as follows:

- Nature conservation agencies could only suspend, not prohibit, operations with the potential to damage a site. A landowner who notified the agency, and then waited four months, could lawfully carry out damaging operations.

- Nature conservation agencies had powers which focused on preventing damage caused by specified operations. They had few powers to require positive site management (crucial for the maintenance of certain habitats which can be destroyed by neglect).

- Penalties for breach of the regime were low, and offences could only be committed by owners and occupiers, not, for example, by statutory undertakers working on a site.[25]

---

[25] See *Southern Water Authority v Nature Conservancy Council*.[1992] 3 All E.R. 481.

- Although greater protection was available,[26] this was seldom given, and was only available for sites of national importance.

A further anomaly of the system was that management agreements and compensation would usually only be offered when an owner or occupier proposed to carry out damaging operations. This meant that those who voluntarily conserved their land normally received no recognition or reward. In addition, the system made it possible for unscrupulous landowners to obtain compensation from the relevant statutory nature conservation agency by threatening to undertake unnecessary operations. Landowners complained that there was no right of appeal against designation of a site, and that the list of potentially damaging operations contained in the notification could be long and daunting, and could involve a considerable administrative burden in terms of notifying the nature conservation agency of proposed operations.

The effect of all this was that habitat conservation was only achievable where landowners co-operated with the nature conservation agencies. Critics argued that the system of voluntary control allowed too much weight to be given to the private interests of landowners at the expense of the public interest in nature conservation. As Lord Mustill put it, in *Southern Water Authority v Nature Conservancy Council*[27]:

> "It needs only a moment to see that this regime is toothless, for it demands no more from the owner or occupier of an SSSI than a little patience. . . In truth the Act does no more in the great majority of cases than give the council a breathing space within which to apply moral pressure, with a view to persuading the owner or occupier to make a voluntary agreement."

In contrast with the Town and Country Planning regime, there was no equivalent of the enforcement notice or the stop notice. Moreover, the old SSSI regime sat uneasily alongside planning—both systems placed restrictions on the use of land, but unlike the planning system, the SSSI regime offered compensation to a landowner who found he could not develop his land as he wished. This anomaly has now been resolved. Under the new regime, financial reward is given only for positive actions undertaken to maintain sites.

The new regime

9–017 Part III of the Countryside and Rights of Way Act 2000 significantly enhances the protection of SSSIs by amending the Wildlife and Countryside Act 1981. The new Act was passed against the background of a demanding government target that 95 per cent of SSSIs (by area extent) should be in a favourable condition by 2010. At the time of writing, 42 per cent of SSSIs (by area) were in an unfavourable condition. The provisions relating to SSSIs in the Countryside and Rights of Way Act 2000 only apply to England and Wales, because SSSIs are a devolved matter. (Similar legislation, however, is expected to be forthcoming in Scotland.) We deal here with the position in England and Wales, and then briefly consider the position in Scotland. For convenience, the remainder of this chapter refers to English Nature as the relevant statutory

---

[26] By the use of Nature Conservation Orders, made under WCA 1981, s.29.
[27] [1992] 3 All E.R. 481.

conservation body, but references to English Nature should be read as including a reference to the Countryside Council for Wales.

(1) *What is an SSSI?*

An SSSI is an area of land which has been notified by English Nature as being of **9–018** special interest by reason of any of its flora, fauna, or geological or physiographical features.[28] English Nature has a wide discretion in deciding whether land is worthy of protection as an SSSI—it is statutorily empowered to designate land where it is "of the opinion" that the land is of special interest.[29] In practice, designation of sites takes place on the basis of specified scientific criteria. The Joint Nature Conservation Committee has published guidelines for the selection of sites. These refer to a number of broad habitat groupings (including coastal woodland, lowland grasslands, lowland heath land and bogs) and broad species groupings (including vascular and non-vascular plants, mammals, birds, freshwater and estuarine fish).

(2) *The designation process*

Step 1: Notification of the designation

Where English Nature is of the opinion that land is worthy of protection, it is under a **9–019** duty to notify the land as an SSSI to every owner and occupier,[30] as well as to the local planning authority and the Secretary of State. It must also advertise the proposed notification in at least one local newspaper. The requirement to advertise is in part related to fact that potential criminal liability for breaches of the regime extends to persons other than owners and occupiers (see below).

The notification must contain certain information, namely:

- The flora, fauna or geological or physiographical features which make the land of special interest (the land's "features");

- English Nature's views about the management of the land and on the conservation and enhancement of its features (a "management statement"); and

- The activities which English Nature thinks might damage those features.

The requirement for a statement about management meets one of the key concerns about previously existing SSSI legislation, namely that the regime was concerned only with damaging operations, and not with positive site management. The aim is to provide a simple statement that expresses to land managers in clear and practical terms what steps are to be taken on the land.

The notification must also include the time (a minimum of three months) within which objections to the notification may be made, and notice of the procedure for making them. Although owners and occupiers are able to make representations to

[28] WCA 1981, s.52.
[29] *ibid.*, s.21(1).
[30] WCA 1981 does not contain a definition of "occupier", but s.52 (2C) states that "occupier" includes, in respect of common land, the commoners. Case law indicates that an occupier will be a person who has "a stable and continuing relationship with the land" (see *Southern Water v Nature Conservancy Council* [1992] 3 All E.R. 481). One example relevant to Scotland would be crofters.

English Nature, there is no right of appeal against a decision to designate, but there is, of course, always the possibility of judicial review. English Nature is under a duty to consider any representations or objections that are "duly made".[31] The words "duly made" imply that if the specified procedure is not followed, English Nature is not under a duty to consider the views put forward.

The notification takes effect and is registered as a local land charge, so that any subsequent purchaser or tenant will be alerted to the obligations in respect of the land when consulting the local land register.

Step 2: Confirmation of the designation

9–020   English Nature must confirm the designation within nine months of notification, and must do so by giving notice. If it does not do so, the original notification will cease to have any effect. On confirmation, English Nature may modify the original notification (*e.g.* to incorporate any technical amendments, or any matters arising out of objections or representations). However, it cannot add to the operations likely to damage the features, or extend the area of the designation.[32]

One issue likely to arise in practice is the boundaries of a designated site. *Sweet v Secretary of State for the Environment and the Nature Conservancy Council*[33] provides some guidance, although this case was concerned with the extent of land classified under a Nature Conservation Order, and the provision for making these orders has now been repealed. The applicant, Mr Sweet, challenged a Nature Conservation Order made with respect to Westhay Moor in Somerset. The order included three fields owned by Mr Sweet. His argument was that these fields were not themselves of national importance, but had been designated to act as a "buffer zone" for the purposes of conserving land of national importance. The court refused to uphold the challenge, stating that the Inspector was entitled, on the evidence before him, to conclude that while only part of the land was of national importance, the whole of the land constituted a single environment. It followed that the Secretary of State was entitled to draw the boundaries so as to treat the site as a whole as one of national importance. Interestingly, however, the judgment considers an example of rare animals grazing on vegetation which might be dependent for its continued life on an aquifer a mile away, and acknowledges that this sort of situation might present problems in deciding where to draw boundaries.

The designation and confirmation process has been the subject of a challenge under the Human Rights Act 1998. In *R. (on the application of Aggregate Industries UK Ltd) v English Nature*,[34] a decision of English Nature, whereby it had confirmed the notification of certain land as an SSSI, was challenged, *inter alia*, on the basis that English Nature's decision was made in breach of Art. 6 of the Human Rights Act—it had both issued the notification and confirmed the SSSI, and was therefore itself a party to the dispute which it had determined. The court disagreed. Whilst accepting that English Nature was not itself independent and impartial, the existence of an over-arching framework of legal control satisfied the requirements of Art. 6 by providing a number of procedural safeguards, such as the right to make representations, the preparation of a detailed

[31] WCA 1981, s.28(3).
[32] *ibid.*, s.28(7).
[33] (1989) J.E.L. vol.2, p.245.
[34] [2003] Env. L.R. 3.

report by English Nature, the confirmation meeting being in public with the opportunity for oral representations, and the possibility of judicial review.[35]

(3) *Site management after notification*

(*a*) Consents for potentially damaging operations

From the date of notification, an owner or occupier cannot carry out any of the **9–021** potentially damaging operations specified in the notification of designation without first giving English Nature notice that he proposes to do so. Commonly cited operations include ploughing, reseeding, making changes to the grazing regime of animals on the land, and the application of fertilisers. English Nature will either give written consent to the operations or require that they be carried out in accordance with a management agreement, management scheme or notice (discussed below). The important difference from the protection provided by the old regime is that under the new regime, English Nature has the power permanently to restrict damaging land use whilst the SSSI notification is in force.

Any consent by English Nature for a potentially damaging operation may be subject to conditions, and may specify that the operation may last only for a limited time.[36] Where conditions are attached, English Nature must give reasons why they have been imposed, and must provide information on the right to appeal.[37] English Nature may decide to refuse consent for the potentially damaging operation,[38] in which case it must give notice of the refusal, together with reasons for the refusal and details of the appeal mechanisms.[39] If English Nature does not respond to a notice from the landowner requesting consent for a potentially damaging operation within four months of the date on which that notice was sent, consent is deemed refused.[40] Even once granted, English Nature can withdraw the consent or modify it,[41] repeatedly if necessary. Its discretion to do so is unlimited. However, it must compensate any owner or occupier who suffers loss by reason of the withdrawal or modification.[42] Any withdrawal or modification will not take effect until the expiry of the period allowed for appeal, or, if an appeal is brought, the determination of the appeal.[43]

(*b*) Appeals[44]

As has been said, there is no right of appeal against a decision to designate a site.[45] **9–022** However, owners or occupiers may appeal against decisions relating to consents for potentially damaging operations where they are aggrieved by:

- refusal of a consent;

---

[35] See Ch. 14 for a discussion of Art. 6 and human rights.
[36] WCA 1981, s.28E(4).
[37] *ibid.*, s.28E(7).
[38] *ibid.*, s.28E(5).
[39] *ibid.*, s.28E(7).
[40] *ibid.*, s.28F(2).
[41] *ibid.*, s.28E(6).
[42] *ibid.*, s.28M.
[43] *ibid.*, s.28E(9).
[44] *ibid.*, s.28F.
[45] This has been held to be consistent with the Human Rights Act 1998. See *Aggregate Industries UK Ltd v English Nature and the Secretary of State for the Environment, Food and Rural Affairs* [2003] Env. L.R. 3.

- any conditions or time limits attached to a consent;

- modification of a consent;

- withdrawal of a consent.

Appeal is by notice to the Secretary of State, which must reach him within two months from the date of the notice from English Nature giving rise to the appeal (unless a longer time period is agreed in writing between the parties). At the time of writing, there is no guidance on appeals procedures. There is, however, a consultation paper issued by DEFRA which indicates what information should be provided with the appeal notice.[46] The Act does not prescribe the form an appeal must take, save to say that the Secretary of State may, if he thinks fit, cause a hearing to be held (which may be in private if the appellant asks and the person hearing the appeal agrees) or hold a public inquiry. If either party requests the opportunity to be heard, the Secretary of State must hold either a hearing or a public inquiry. The DEFRA consultation paper envisages that appeals will be dealt with "on paper", except where a party requests a hearing or inquiry. Regulations governing the appeals procedures will provide a framework for cases dealt with by way of written representations and/or site visits, and for cases dealt with by a hearing. The procedures for public inquiries are likely to follow those used in planning inquiries.

The Secretary of State may appoint people to act on his behalf in determining an appeal, and he or his appointee may:

- affirm English Nature's decision;

- direct English Nature to consent to a potentially damaging operation, and set the terms of that consent;

- quash any or all the terms of a consent;

- quash a decision by English Nature to withdraw or modify a consent.

The DEFRA consultation paper states that, in considering appeals, the Secretary of State must have regard to his duty to further the conservation and enhancement of SSSIs[47] as well as to the needs of agriculture, forestry and the economic and social interests of rural areas.[48] It remains to be seen how this is interpreted in regulations, but it would appear to allow consideration of social and economic issues, such as impact on jobs.

The costs of the parties and of the Secretary of State in relation to an inquiry or hearing (including where a planned hearing or inquiry does not take place) are at the discretion of the Secretary of State. The general rule is that each party will bear his own costs for appeals concluded only by written representations. However, where there is a hearing, an award of costs may be made against a party who has acted unreasonably in causing the appeal to be brought.

---

[46] "Sites of Special Scientific Interest: Appeals Regulations—a Public Consultation Paper" (June 2001), available at *www.defra.gov.uk.*
[47] Under WCA 1981, s.28G
[48] Under the Countryside Act 1968, s.37

(*c*) Management agreements

Under various statutes,[49] English Nature may enter into "management agreements" **9–023** with owners, lessees and occupiers of any land for habitat conservation purposes. Usually, but not necessarily, the land in question will have been designated as an SSSI.[50] Management agreements can also be made with owners or occupiers of other land (not necessarily within or adjacent to the site requiring conservation) for example to protect a water supply on which the conservation site is dependent.

English Nature intend to continue using management agreements as the main form of site management under the new regime. "Management schemes" (discussed below) will be used only where necessary, and are likely to be used less often. Guidance from DEFRA[51] indicates that the government's targets (*i.e.* that 95 per cent by area of SSSIs should be in a favourable condition by 2010) are expected to be met through management agreements. It also makes clear that while financial support is appropriate for SSSI management, it should be available only for "positive management" of sites, not for passive inaction:

> "Ministers are not prepared that public money should be paid out simply to prevent new operations which could destroy or damage these national assets."

This marks a clear departure from the practice of compensation for inaction which prevailed under the old SSSI regime. Examples of activities meriting payments include scrub control, changes in grazing patterns, introduction of different animals, and water level control.

A management agreement is a formal agreement, constituting a binding contract, which sets out clearly the obligations of the parties, namely the payments to be made and the management activities required. English Nature may register the management agreement as a land charge. Management agreements will normally be for a minimum term of five years, and for no longer than 10 years. Owners of land subject to a management agreement must ensure that tenants or licensees comply with the terms of the agreement. Additionally, owners and occupiers of SSSIs are required to notify English Nature if they sell, lease or licence their land or in any case where it becomes known to them that the land has a new occupier.[52]

(*d*) Management schemes[53]

As has been said, when designating an SSSI, English Nature will set out its views on **9–024** the positive steps necessary to manage the site. It will normally then conclude a management agreement with the owner or occupier to ensure that those steps are taken. However, in cases where it is satisfied that it cannot conclude a management

---

[49] See Countryside Act 1968, s.15; NPACA 1949, s.16 and WCA 1981, s.39. Under this last provision, management agreements can be made for the purpose of "conserving or enhancing the natural beauty or amenity" of land, or "promoting its enjoyment by the public". The requirement in s.39 that such land must be "in the countryside" is now repealed (as from a date to be appointed) by CRWA 2000.
[50] Section 15 of the Countryside Act 1968 refers to "areas" of special scientific interest.
[51] "Guidelines on Management Agreement Payments and other Related Matters" (February 2001), available at *www.defra.gov.uk*.
[52] WCA 1981, s.28Q.
[53] *ibid.*, s.28J.

agreement on reasonable terms (*i.e.* where the owner or occupier fails to co-operate) it is empowered under the new regime to draw up a "management scheme" and send notification of it to the owner or occupier. The scheme will set out in detail the positive steps that are required, and can be designed to restore the features of a site as well as merely conserve them. Notice of a proposed management scheme can be served at the same time as notification of proposed SSSI designation or afterwards, but it cannot be served unless the owners or occupiers have first been consulted about the scheme.

Management schemes are subject to the same two-step procedure (notification, followed by confirmation within nine months) that applies in respect of site designation. There is provision for the hearing of objections and representations (though not appeals), but there is no requirement that notification of the scheme be advertised. The scheme takes effect once a confirmation notice is served. English Nature can modify the scheme between notification and confirmation, but it must consult the owner or occupier about any changes it makes, and these cannot be such as to make the scheme more onerous. It can also cancel or modify a management scheme at any time, provided it follows the usual two-step procedure. English Nature has a discretion, but no obligation, to make payments to an owner or occupier in respect of a management scheme. The amount will be determined by English Nature in accordance with government guidance.

(*e*) Management notices[54]

9–025 Failure to comply with a voluntary management agreement, although a breach of contract, is not a criminal offence unless the failure to comply involves carrying out any specified potentially damaging operations. In other words, where a site is regulated by a management agreement, rather than a management *scheme*, the criminal law can be used to prevent damage, but it cannot be used to ensure that active steps are taken to conserve the site. In relation to management schemes, however, the new regime provides that where a scheme is in place and is not being complied with, a "management notice" requiring positive acts of compliance can be served. Failure to comply is a criminal offence.

English Nature may serve a management notice where it appears that an owner or occupier is not giving effect to a provision of a management scheme and, as a result, the site is being inadequately conserved or restored. However, it may only do so where it is satisfied that it cannot conclude on reasonable terms an agreement with the owner or occupier as to the management of the land in accordance with the management scheme. The management notice will specify the things that must be done on the site, and its requirements can be only such as are reasonable to ensure that the land is managed in accordance with the management scheme. The notice must specify time periods within which the specified things must be done. English Nature may make payment for the cost of the work required, but has no obligation to do so. If any of the things required by the management notice are not done within the specified time periods, English Nature has the power to enter the site and do the work itself, and to recover the costs from the owner or occupier.

---

[54] *ibid.*, s.28K.

(f) Appeals against management notices[55]

Any person served with a management notice may appeal against it to the Secretary of **9–026** State. The notice does not take effect until the expiry of the period for appealing against it, or, if the appeal is brought, its withdrawal or final determination. The period allowed for appeal is not specified in the Act, but is envisaged by a DEFRA consultation paper to be two months. Grounds of appeal can include that some other owner or occupier should take all or any of the specified actions, or should pay all or part of their cost. The Secretary of State can either quash the management notice or affirm it, with or without modifications. In particular, he can vary the notice so as to impose its requirements on any other person referred to in the grounds of appeal, or determine that a payment is to be made by any such person to the appellant. However, in doing so, the Secretary of State must take into account the different people's relative interests in the land and responsibilities for its being in the state which led to the serving of the management notice. He must also consider "the relative degree of benefit to be derived from carrying out the requirements of the management notice". Thus, for example, it will be relevant to consider whether one particular owner should be fixed with an obligation to do something, because doing that thing will make his particular interest in the land more valuable. The same rules regarding the form of the hearing and costs apply as with appeals against consents.

(4) *Changes to an SSSI after confirmation*

The following changes may be made to an SSSI after confirmation: **9–027**

- English Nature can add to the list of potentially damaging operations, or otherwise change the notification, provided it does so by following the usual notification and confirmation procedure (save for advertising in a local newspaper).[56]

- English Nature can enlarge an SSSI if it thinks that there are features on land extending beyond the existing SSSI which make that land of special scientific interest. The same process of notification and confirmation applies as for the original SSSI (including advertisement), except that the notices will be given to the owners or occupiers of the extra land in addition to the owners or occupiers of the original SSSI. The new notification replaces the existing notification, and a new land charge will replace the existing land charge. In most respects, then, this procedure is effectively the same as de-notifying the old SSSI and notifying a new, larger one. The only difference is that an enlargement does not affect any previously given consents for potentially damaging operations (or appeals, where consents have been refused) or any management schemes or management notices in force.[57]

- English Nature can add an additional piece of adjacent land to an SSSI if it thinks that that the addition of the adjacent land would create a combined area

---

[55] *ibid.*, s.28L. See also "Sites of Special Scientific Interest: Appeals Regulations—a Public Consultation Paper" (June 2001), available at *www.defra.gov.uk*.
[56] WCA 1981, s.28A.
[57] *ibid.*, s.28C.

of special scientific interest.[58] (This differs subtly from enlargement because here the extra land does not, of itself, need to possess features which make it of special scientific interest.) The procedures are similar to those for enlargement, except as follows: Notification is given to owners and occupiers of the extra land, as opposed to the original land. This notification will set out the contents of the notification relating to the original SSSI, and will specify the particular reasons why the combination of the original SSSI and the extra land will make the combined area of special scientific interest. Once the notification is served on the owner or occupier of "any land",[59] the original SSSI notification is treated as if it included the extra land. If, on confirmation, the new notification is modified, the original SSSI notification is also treated as having been modified. The land charge existing in relation to the original SSSI is varied so as to include the extra land.

(5) De-notification[60]

9–028 If English Nature is of the opinion that all or part of an SSSI is no longer of special scientific interest, it can "de-notify" the land, using the usual two-step procedure. Notice will be given to the same people as it is under the designation procedure, but also to the Environment Agency, and to any water or sewerage undertaker or drainage board whose activities affect the SSSI. The de-notification must be advertised in a local newspaper and must allow for objections and representations prior to its confirmation or withdrawal. The confirmation, when it is given, may relate to a smaller area of land than was originally de-notified. A de-notification takes effect only once confirmed, at which point the original notification falls away and the local land charge is discharged.

(6) Offences[61]

9–029 It is an offence:

- for an owner or occupier, without a reasonable excuse, to carry out a specified potentially damaging operation without obtaining consent from English Nature, unless the operation is carried out in accordance with a management agreement, scheme or notice;

- for public bodies (including statutory undertakers), without reasonable excuse, to carry out operations in the exercise of their functions without following certain procedures and fulfilling certain duties (discussed below);

- for any person (other than a public body), without reasonable excuse, intentionally or recklessly to destroy or damage the features of an SSSI, or disturb any fauna for which the site is designated, provided that he knew that what was destroyed, damaged or disturbed lay within the SSSI;

---

[58] *ibid.*, s.28B.
[59] It is rather odd that, where the original SSSI and the extra land have different owners, the statute does not expressly require the owner of the original SSSI to be kept informed. This would be especially important where the notification in respect of the extra land is subsequently confirmed with modifications. These modifications will also apply to the owner of the original SSSI, and whilst, in practice, he will no doubt be told, on a strict reading of the statue there is no mechanism by which this must happen.
[60] WCA 1981, s.28D.
[61] *ibid.*, s.28P.

- for an owner or occupier to fail, without reasonable excuse, to comply with a requirement of a management notice;

- for an owner or occupier to fail, without reasonable excuse, to notify English Nature within 28 days of a change in the ownership or occupation of an SSSI[62];

- for any person intentionally to obstruct any persons authorised by English Nature in the exercise of their powers of entry (discussed below).

Note that the offence of destroying, damaging or disturbing the features of an SSSI may be committed by "any person", not just by the owners or occupiers. It may not, however be committed by a public body in the exercise of its functions. This means that the regime is still to a limited extent "toothless" in respect of operations carried out by statutory undertakers such as water companies. Although such undertakers can be convicted if they fail to do what is reasonably practicable to minimise the damage, or to restore the site when they leave, they cannot be convicted simply for carrying out a damaging operation. Although there are consultation and notification procedures in respect of operations carried out by public bodies (including statutory undertakers), the ultimate decision as to whether an SSSI should be disturbed rests with the public body, not with English Nature.

Most of the offences may be tried either in the magistrates' court or the Crown Court (for more serious offences). The maximum fine in the magistrates' court for unlawfully carrying out a potentially damaging operation, or for destroying, damaging or disturbing features, is a £20,000 fine. In the Crown Court, the fine is unlimited. The maximum fine for failing to comply with a management notice is £5,000 in the magistrates' court and unlimited in the Crown Court. Prosecutions for failing to notify English Nature of a change of ownership or occupation, or for obstructing the exercise of powers of entry, are triable only in the magistrates' court, where the maximum fine is £200 for the former and £1,000 for the latter.

Where the statute provides for a "reasonable excuse", it will be a reasonable excuse if the activity forming the subject matter of the offence was authorised by planning permission, or by a public body acting in accordance with the proper procedures, or if it was carried out in an emergency and English Nature was notified as soon as practicable. There is no definition of "emergency", and it remains to be seen how this will be interpreted. Offences will usually be prosecuted by English Nature, although others may bring prosecutions with the consent of the Director of Public Prosecutions.

(7) *Powers of enforcement*

(*a*) Rights of entry[63]

One of the problems with the old SSSI regime was that it failed to give English Nature **9–030** the power to enter land to investigate whether sites should be notified, or whether they had been damaged. This was in contrast to the significant enforcement powers available to the Environment Agency under the Environment Act 1995.[64] English Nature's powers of entry are greatly increased under the new regime. Any person

---

[62] *ibid.*, s.28Q.
[63] *ibid.*, s.51.
[64] See EA 1995, s.108.

authorised by English Nature may (normally on 24 hours' notice) enter land at any reasonable time for a number of purposes, the most important of which are:

- to determine whether land should be notified;
- to assess the condition of the land's features;
- to determine whether or not to offer to enter into a management agreement;
- to ascertain whether a condition of a consent has been complied with;
- to ascertain whether an offence is being committed;
- to formulate a management scheme, decide whether a management scheme should be modified, or prepare a management notice;
- to ascertain whether a management scheme or management agreement has been complied with;
- to decide whether or not to offer payment for withdrawal or modification of a consent, or in respect of a management scheme; and
- to determine any question relating to the acquisition of the land by agreement or compulsorily (see below).

More than one authorised person can enter the land at one time, and the entrants may take a police constable with them if they reasonably believe they are likely to be obstructed. They may enter by vehicle or boat, take necessary equipment and materials, and may take samples of the land or anything on it. Land outside an SSSI may also be entered. In respect of all land, twenty-four hours' notice of the intended entry must be given to the occupier, unless the entry is for the purposes of determining whether an offence has been, or is being, committed. English Nature must compensate anyone who suffers damage from the entry, or from their failure to properly secure the land on departure where the occupier is absent. No compensation is payable, however, where the damage is attributable to the fault of the owner or occupier.

(*b*) Compulsory purchase[65]

9–031 English Nature has the power to compulsorily purchase all or part of an SSSI if satisfied that it is unable to conclude, on reasonable terms, a management agreement with the owner or occupier, or if it has entered into such an agreement but is satisfied that it has been breached in such a way that the land is not being managed satisfactorily. Having acquired the land, English nature may manage the land itself, or may dispose of it on terms designed to ensure its conservation.

(*c*) Restoration of SSSIs[66]

9–032 Where an owner or occupier has been convicted for carrying out a potentially damaging operation without consent, or a public body has acted without following the prescribed procedures, or where any person has been convicted for destroying,

---

[65] *ibid.*, s.28N. This power is additional to that in NPACA 1949, s.17 relating to Nature Reserves. It is also additional to the similar power given in the new s.15A of the Countryside Act 1968 (inserted by CRWA 2000). The s.15A power, however, is exercisable only in respect of land already subject to a management agreement.
[66] WCA 1981, s.31.

damaging or disturbing the features of a site, the court may make an order requiring the convicted party to restore the SSSI to its former condition. This is regarded by English Nature as an important new power, but it remains to be seen whether the courts will make use of it.

(*d*) Byelaws[67]

English Nature can make byelaws for the protection of an SSSI. These can prohibit or **9–033** restrict:

- the entry of persons, vehicles or boats;
- the destruction, taking or disturbance of living creatures or their eggs;
- interference with vegetation or soil;
- the shooting of birds in areas surrounding the SSSI; and
- the depositing of litter, lighting of fires, or the doing of anything likely to cause a fire.

Byelaws, however, cannot be made so as to interfere with the rights of owners or occupiers. Nor must they interfere with public rights of way, the functions of drainage authorities, or the running of telecommunications systems.

(8) *Duties of public bodies*

It is not only owners or occupiers of an SSSI who may cause damage to it. The **9–034** activities of statutory undertakers and other public bodies, engaged in such things as road building, cable laying, or repairing drains have great potential to cause harm. Despite this, under the old regime, only owners or occupiers could be prosecuted for causing damage. We have already noted how this gap in the law was illustrated by the decision in *Southern Water Authority v Nature Conservancy Council*. Southern Water Authority dredged a ditch on an SSSI, at the request of farmers who owned the SSSI. The works fell within the list of potentially damaging operations. Neither the farmers nor Southern Water notified English Nature. The House of Lords held that Southern Water could not be prosecuted under the regime, as their only connection with the SSSI was that they had entered it to carry out an operation. Lord Mustill referred to the regime as "toothless". The amendments introduced by the Countryside and Rights of Way Act 2000 go some way towards ensuring that public bodies do not cause unnecessary damage to SSSIs, in particular by requiring them (so far as is reasonably practicable) to restore sites to their former condition once operations are complete. The amendments do not, however, allow English Nature to place a ban on damaging operations.

(*a*) The general duty[68]

Certain authorities (known collectively as "s.28G authorities"), when exercising any of **9–035** their functions which are likely to affect an SSSI (including, of course, making decisions about planning permission) have a general duty to take reasonable steps to

---

[67] *ibid.*, s.28R. This section applies to SSSIs the provisions relating to Nature Reserves in NPACA 1949, s.20.
[68] WCA 1981, s.28G.

further the conservation and enhancement of its features. The authorities include Ministers, government departments, local authorities, and statutory undertakers such as water, gas, and electricity companies.

(*b*) Duties in relation to carrying out operations[69]

9–036 Any s.28G authority proposing to carry out a potentially damaging operation must notify English Nature, whereupon English Nature may either agree to the operation (with or without conditions) or refuse consent. (If English Nature does not respond to a notification within 28 days, it is taken to have refused consent.) If the authority decides to carry out the operation contrary to English Nature's wishes, it is permitted to do so (unlike owners or occupiers) provided that it notifies English Nature of the date of commencement of the operation, and also of how (if at all) it has taken account of any written advice received from English Nature about the operation. When carrying out the operation, it must do so in such a way as to give rise to as little damage as is reasonably practicable, and it must restore the site to its former condition, so far as is reasonably practicable, if any damage does occur. Failure to comply with any of these requirements is an offence punishable in the magistrates' court by a maximum fine of £20,000, or by an unlimited fine in the Crown Court.

(*c*) Duties in relation to authorising operations[70]

9–037   If a s.28G authority is in a position to authorise others to carry out a potentially damaging operation, it must, before doing so, notify English Nature of the proposed operation and wait 28 days before deciding whether to give permission. In giving permission, it must take any advice from English Nature into account, and if it decides to grant permission contrary to that advice, it must notify English Nature and must not allow the operation to start for 21 days. Failure to comply with the requirements relating to authorising operations is not an offence, but where the person carrying out the operation is prosecuted, his defence of reasonable excuse will be defective if the permission on which he relies has not been granted in accordance with the requirements.[71]

(9) *Transitional provisions*[72]

9–038 All existing SSSIs notified under the old regime are taken forward into the new regime. English Nature is required, by January 2006, to provide owners and occupiers of existing SSSIs with a statement of its views about the management of the site (a "management statement" of the type provided with notification under the new regime), to which they will be given the opportunity to make representations.

   If a consent to carry out operations on an SSSI has been given under the old regime, this will still be valid. However, English Nature has the power to withdraw or modify that consent, in which case the owner or occupier has a right of appeal and a right to compensation for any loss suffered. Where an offence took place before January 30, 2001, the provisions (and penalties) under the old regime will still apply, and the new duties of public bodies to minimise damage and restore sites will not apply in respect of operations commenced before that date.

[69] *ibid.*, s.28H.
[70] *ibid.*, s.28I.
[71] *ibid.*, s.28P(4)(a)
[72] CRWA 2000, Sch.11.

Under the old regime, an owner or occupier had the right to carry out a damaging operation without consent where a period of four months had elapsed. Where such a right has been established, it will remain alive, so that the owner or occupier may still carry out the operation, provided he commences it within three years of the legislation coming into force. In such cases, however, English Nature has the power to serve a "stop notice" to prohibit or modify the operation. The owner or occupier on whom the stop notice is served has a right of appeal to the Secretary of State, and a right to compensation if he suffers loss because of it.

(10) *The position in Scotland*

SSSIs in Scotland are currently regulated by the old regime (*i.e.* Pt II of the Wildlife **9–039** and Countryside Act 1981, without the amendments made in respect of England and Wales by the Countryside and Rights of Way Act 2000). The Scottish regime therefore differs from the English and Welsh regime in the following important ways:

- There is no requirement for Scottish National Heritage to include a management statement when notifying an SSSI, or to consider representations and objections made;

- There is no power to modify a notification, or to enlarge a SSSI;

- There is no power to de-notify an SSSI;

- Scottish National Heritage has no power to prohibit a potentially damaging operation proposed by an owner or occupier—the operation may go ahead without consent after a period of four months;

- Public bodies carrying out operations in Scotland have no duty to minimise damage to SSSIs or restore sites afterwards. Nor must they consult with Scottish National Heritage before granting permission for operations;

- Scottish National Heritage has no power to notify a management scheme, serve a management notice, or carry out works itself where the owner or occupier fails to comply with such a notice; and

- The range of enforcement powers (*e.g.* rights of entry) and penalties (*e.g.* court orders for restoration of sites) available to Scottish National Heritage is more limited than in England and Wales.

A policy statement entitled "The Nature of Scotland", issued by the Scottish Executive in March 2001, contains details of a number of proposed amendments to the SSSI regime, along the lines of those introduced by Countryside and Rights of Way Act 2000.

Proposed amendments include the following:

- Instead of notifying a long list of "potentially damaging operations", Scottish National Heritage may specify certain categories of activity which would significantly threaten the site;

- Scottish National Heritage will be able to de-notify existing SSSIs which no longer meet the selection criteria;

- Scottish National Heritage's refusal of consent to an operation will be absolute, subject to a right of appeal to an independent body;

- Compensation will no longer be paid for merely abstaining from operations—it will be available only where positive acts of land management are required by SSSI designation;

- An offence of malicious or reckless damage to an SSSI will be created; and

- The courts will have power to impose larger fines for offences in respect of SSSIs and will be able to order the carrying out of work at an offender's expense.

Diagram 3:   The New SSSI Regime

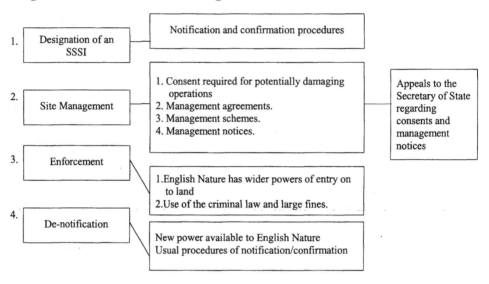

European sites

9–040   "European Sites" is the term used in UK law for certain sites whose designation has been required by EC legislation, most importantly "Special Protection Areas" (under the Birds Directive) and "Special Areas of Conservation" (under the Habitats Directive). These sites form part of a pan-European network of sites, known as "Natura 2000". The Habitats Directive requires Member States, in addition to designating sites, to contribute to this network by taking action outside designated areas "to improve the ecological coherence of Natura 2000 by maintaining, and where appropriate, developing features of the landscape which are of major importance for wild fauna and flora".[73] The European framework of protection overlaps with the UK's domestic regime—all European sites will also, in practice, be designated as SSSIs. Not all SSSIs will necessarily be European sites, although approximately 70 per cent of SSSI land has been identified by DEFRA as being of European interest.

[73] Art. 3 of the Habitats Directive.

At the time of writing, the law on European sites, whilst it may provide an appropriate level of conservation, does so through a rather unsatisfactory miscellany of legal provisions. This is because, with the strengthening of the provisions relating to SSSIs in the Wildlife and Countryside Act 1981, some of the mechanisms in place for affording enhanced protection to European sites have or may have become redundant.[74] The problem is compounded by the fact that, until the amendments to the Wildlife and Countryside Act 1981 "bed down", so that a view can be taken as to whether, in practice, they are capable of providing appropriate protection for European sites, the extent of the redundancy of other provisions cannot be properly measured. The law is currently in a state of flux, with changes likely to the Habitats Regulations, in particular to the regulation which allows for the making of "Special Nature Conservation Orders". The distinctive feature of these orders was, until recently, their unique ability to impose a permanent ban on the carrying out of potentially damaging operations. Under the new regime, however, such a ban can be imposed (except in relation to a public body) in the normal course of regulating an SSSI. For the time being, then, the law adopts a "belt and braces" approach to satisfying its European obligations. A number of provisions are available, either to English Nature, the Secretary of State, or both, to protect European sites.

It will be recalled that the Birds Directive provided general protection for wild birds, and additional protection for certain species of birds listed in the Directive as requiring special conservation measures because, for example, they may be in danger of extinction. In respect of these birds, Member States are required to find the most suitable territories in number and size, and to designate such territories as Special Protection Areas. Once an area has been so designated, Member States must take appropriate steps to avoid significant pollution, deterioration or disturbance of the habitats and birds in question. No further guidance is given in the Directive as to what this should entail. The UK chose to implement the Birds Directive by passing the Wildlife and Countryside Act 1981. In response to the Habitats Directive, extra protection was later provided by the Conservation (Natural Habitats etc.) Regulations 1994, under which Special Protection Areas for birds (as well as other types of site) could be also designated as Special Areas of Conservation.

The Habitats Directive: Special Areas of Conservation

In proposing the Habitats Directive, the European Commission commented: "The **9–041** time is now ripe for the Community and the Member States to make a major new thrust in the field of nature conservation". Although the Directive is mainly concerned with habitats, it also contains measures relating to the conservation of species *per se*. It recognises that habitats are continuing to deteriorate and that the survival of an increasing number of species is seriously threatened, and it lists various habitats and species that are to be protected. Habitats that are rare, are in danger of disappearing, or are outstanding examples of their type—for example Caledonian pine forests and blanket bogs—are to be protected. So, too, are endangered, vulnerable or rare species such as the otter and the lady's slipper orchid. Habitats and species which are found in the main only on European territory, and which are in danger of disappearing, are

[74] See "Public Consultation Paper on Technical Amendments to the Conservation (Natural Habitats) Regulations 1994", DEFRA, June 2001, available at *www.defra.gov.uk*.

given a higher level of protection than others, on the basis that the European Community has a particular responsibility to preserve them. These are referred to as "priority habitats" and "priority species". The Directive gives limited protection to countryside outside the designated habitats by requiring Member States to encourage the management of rivers, hedges, ponds and small woods.

The Directive set out a timetable and methodology for establishing Special Areas of Conservation:

- The UK was to notify the Commission of all sites within its borders which contained those habitats and species specified by the Directive as requiring protection. (This process is still ongoing, although it should have been completed by June 1995. At the time of writing, the UK has submitted 605 candidate Special Areas of Conservation to the European Commission.)[75] It appears that the selection criteria used for selecting Special Areas of Conservation are broadly similar to those used for SSSIs.[76]

- The Commission is to select, from the list provided, those sites which it considers to be of importance to the European Community, to be known as "Sites of Community Importance". (This was expected to have been done by June 1998, but has been delayed because of a lack of information from Member States.)

- The UK was then to have designated those sites as Special Areas of Conservation as soon as possible.

Once a site has been designated by the Commission as a "Site of Community Importance", Member States are under a duty to avoid the deterioration of, and not to disturb, the habitats and species within it. This duty arises even if the site has not yet been made a Special Area of Conservation. Any plan or project which is likely to affect the site significantly must be assessed to determine whether it will cause ecological damage to the site. It should be noted that such a plan or project need not be one which constitutes "development" in planning terms. A project which will cause ecological damage will be permitted only if there are overriding grounds of public interest to allow the project to proceed.

The Conservation (Natural Habitats etc.) Regulations 1994

9–042 The United Kingdom gave effect to its obligations under the Habitats Directive by the Conservation (Natural Habitats etc.) Regulations 1994. In implementing the Directive, the then Government took the view that existing legislation was sufficient to meet most of its obligations under the Directive. The purpose of the 1994 Regulations was merely to reinforce and to fill some minor gaps in that legislation.[77] The Regulations apply to Special Areas of Conservation, once designated as such by the UK on the advice of the

---

[75] See "First Report by the United Kingdom under Art. 17 on implementation of the [Habitats] Directive from June 1994 to December 2000", available at *www.jncc.gov.uk*.

[76] *ibid.*

[77] One convenient method of implementation is to impose, as the Regulations do, a duty on relevant Ministers and nature conservation bodies to exercise their functions under existing legislation in such a way as to comply with the requirements of the Directive.

Commission. However, in view of the delay in identifying and designating appropriate sites, as a matter of policy for planning and all other consent regimes, the UK Government and the devolved administrations already treat candidate Special Areas of Conservation as if they were fully designated. In England, candidate Special Areas of Conservation have additional protection in law. By an amendment to the Natural Habitats Regulations, candidate sites are legally protected from the date they are notified to the European Commission.[78]

It is difficult to assess whether the UK has successfully implemented the Directive because the approach of the Directive is to specify a particular level of protection and leave Member States to decide how best to achieve this level. The level of protection required by the Directive is left to be determined by interpretation of such vague phrases as "favourable conservation status", "adversely affecting the integrity of the site" and "overriding grounds of public interest". These broad concepts, however, provide little guidance as to the precise level of protection needed to comply. In the circumstances, it is perhaps not surprising that the Regulations tend to adopt the language of the Directive verbatim rather than risk defining its requirements in precise terms.

However, one area where it is clear that the Government has failed to implement the Directive properly is in respect of the scope of its application, in particular whether it applies outside the UK's territorial waters. This issue arose in *R. v Secretary of State for Trade and Industry and others, Ex p. Greenpeace Ltd No.2*,[79] which concerned the award of oil exploration licences by the Secretary of State in the North-East Atlantic. Greenpeace challenged the Secretary of State on the basis that the Habitats Directive (which states that it applies to the "European territory of the Member States") applied to the UK's continental shelf. The Habitats Regulations expressly state that they apply only up to the territorial limit of national waters. The Secretary of State, therefore, did not have regard to the Regulations when considering an award of exploration licences on the continental shelf. The High Court held that the Directive did apply to the continental shelf, on the basis that it was concerned to protect some habitats and species (such as reef-forming coral) which are sea-based and flourish beyond territorial waters. The Secretary of State was therefore under a duty to apply the provisions of the Directive when awarding licences. An important implication of this decision is that the UK now has an obligation to decide whether Special Areas of Conservation should be designated to protect the reef-forming coral on the continental shelf. This will not be an easy task given the limits of scientific understanding about the extent and significance of this coral, and the wide area of the North-East Atlantic which must be placed under scrutiny.[80]

Obligations in respect of European Sites

Under the Habitats Regulations, "European sites" include: **9–043**

- "Special Areas of Conservation";

---

[78] Conservation (Natural Habitats etc.) (Amendment) (England) Regulations 2000 (SI 2000/192).
[79] [2000] Env. L.R. 221.
[80] Under the Offshore Petroleum Activities (Conservation of Habitats) Regulations 2001 (SI 2001/1754), the Secretary of State must now carry out an environmental assessment before granting exploration licences, and except where there are "imperative reasons of overriding public interest" may not grant such a licence where it may adversely affect a European site.

- "Special Protection Areas" for birds;
- Candidate "Special Areas of Conservation", submitted by the UK to the European Commission; and
- "Sites of Community Importance" (*i.e.* candidate sites that the Commission has indicated should become "Special Areas of Conservation").

The Regulations allow the UK to give effect to its duty to prevent deterioration and disturbance of habitats and species (as required by Art. 6 of the Habitats Directive) through a number of mechanisms. Because all European sites are also SSSIs, all of the mechanisms discussed in the preceding section relating to SSSIs are available. We note here only the extra mechanisms provided for in the Regulations:

(*a*) Registration[81]

9–044 The Secretary of State must keep a register of "European sites" and must notify the appropriate nature conservation authority that a site has been registered. The authority will in turn notify, amongst others, the relevant landowner. The entry in the register takes effect as a local land charge which is binding on all successive owners of the land.

(*b*) Review of existing notifications and consents[82]

9–045 Where an SSSI becomes an "European site", English Nature is required to review the terms of the existing notification, and any consents it has given for operations to be carried out, to ensure they are compatible with the nature conservation objectives for European sites.

(*c*) Review of plans and projects likely to affect the site[83]

9–046 Where an SSSI consent has been sought for an operation that appears to form part of a plan or project which is not directly connected with or necessary for the management of the site, but is likely to have a significant effect on the site, English Nature is required to conduct an "appropriate assessment" to determine whether the operation will diminish the ecological value of the site. It may not give consent if the operation will "adversely affect the integrity of the site".

(*d*) Appeals[84]

9–047 Where consents are withdrawn or modified after review, there is a right of appeal to the Secretary of State, who can direct operations to go ahead if there are "imperative reasons of overriding public interest". If the site is not a "priority habitat" or does not contain "priority species", these reasons may include "reasons of a social or economic nature", for example the creation of jobs. However, if the site has been designated by the Commission as one deserving priority protection, the only considerations that the Secretary of State may have regard to are those relating to:

- public health or public safety; and

---

[81] Regulations 11 to 14.
[82] Regulation 21.
[83] Regulation 20.
[84] Regulations 24(5) and (6).

- any beneficial consequences of the operation which are of primary importance to the environment.

(e) Special Nature Conservation Orders[85]

Special Nature Conservation Orders were provided for in the Regulations to enable **9–048** the Secretary of State, in consultation with English Nature, to place a permanent ban on potentially damaging operations. Whilst, at the time of writing, the power to make such orders still exists, it is envisaged that it will be repealed, because this power is now available to English Nature under the new SSSI regime.

(f) Adaptation of planning and other controls

The Habitats Regulations introduce significant restrictions over development in **9–049** European sites in three ways:

- Local planning authorities must assess all new planning proposals to determine whether they will have a significant impact on the ecology of the site[86];

- Local planning authorities must undertake a review of planning permissions already granted and, if appropriate, where development has not yet been carried out, modify or revoke them[87];

- Existing permitted development rights in respect of European sites are restricted.

In respect of new planning permission, English Nature must be consulted and will advise planning authorities on a case-by-case basis.[88] Pressure groups had argued for an automatic call-in by the Secretary of State of all development proposals to which English Nature objected, but this was not provided for in the Regulations. A planning authority may not normally permit development if it will adversely affect the integrity of the site. However, it may decide to go ahead, despite a finding that the site will be adversely affected, if satisfied that there are "no alternative solutions" (*e.g.* an alternative site) and must obtain the consent of the Secretary of State before granting permission. Permission will only be granted if there are "imperative reasons of overriding public interest" for allowing the development to proceed. In the case of ordinary sites, these reasons may include social and economic ones, but in the case of "priority" sites, only public health and safety, or beneficial environmental consequences of primary importance may be considered (unless the European Commission, having been consulted by the Secretary of State, advises that other reasons will suffice).

Planning permissions already granted must be reviewed, and can be revoked or have new conditions imposed. However, this power cannot be exercised where the development for which the permission was granted has already been completed, or in cases where the planning permission was granted subject to a condition as to the time within

---

[85] Regulation 22. Special Nature Conservation Orders are in all material aspects identical to the Nature Conservation Orders which were formerly, but rarely, made under WCA 1981, s.29.
[86] Regulations 48, 49 and 54.
[87] Regulations 50, 51 and 55–57.
[88] Regulation 48(3).

which the development must have been started, and that time limit has not expired. A developer who has planning permission revoked or modified is entitled to compensation.

The Regulations imply a condition into all planning permission granted under a General or Special Development Order, or within a Simplified Planning Zone or an Enterprise Zone, that development likely to affect a European site cannot begin or continue without the consent of the local planning authority.[89] The onus is placed on the developer to ensure that the development does not significantly affect a designated site. If the developer considers that taking advantage of any deemed planning permission is likely to significantly affect a designated site, he must obtain the written approval of the local planning authority before proceeding. The developer is entitled to consult English Nature about any concerns, and it will give its opinion as to the likely ecological effect of the proposed development. If the planning authority concludes that the development would diminish the ecological value of the site, it cannot allow the development to proceed.

Certain development rights which arise by virtue of authorisations granted for the carrying out of works are also curtailed and must be reviewed by the Secretary of State. These authorisations include, for example, authorisations granted under the Pipelines Act 1962, consents granted under the Electricity Act 1989 and orders under the Transport and Works Act 1992. Any other planning permission deemed to have been granted by virtue of an authorisation given by a government department will be referred to that department for review if the local planning authority considers that the development in question will significantly affect a European site. IPC authorisations and Waste Management licences granted under the Environmental Protection Act 1990 are also subject to review, as are discharge consents granted under the water pollution legislation.

The Regulations require that in cases where development is allowed to proceed despite a negative assessment of the ecological implications for the site, the Secretary of State must take "compensatory measures" to ensure "the overall coherence of Natura 2000". It is not altogether clear what this means, but it may be assumed that it could involve "resettling" affected species, or, where necessary, creating new European sites in proportion to those lost or damaged through development. There are several moot points in respect of this latter issue, namely whether the alternative sites must protect the same species and habitats as those sites which have been lost, and whether sites lost in one Member State can, by agreement, be compensated by sites in other Member States.

National Nature Reserves

9–050   There are approximately 250 National Nature Reserves in the UK. The provisions relating to National Nature Reserves (NNRs) have remained substantially the same since they were introduced by the National Parks and Access to Countryside Act 1949.

In essence, the difference between NNRs and SSSIs is that the former are a means of achieving "total" conservation, whilst the latter establish "partial" conservation. A

---

[89] Regulations 60–64.

National Nature Reserve is usually purchased by the appropriate nature conversation organisation, which then takes complete control of it and actively manages it. In contrast, an SSSI continues to be controlled by the owner or occupier, subject to imposed restrictions.

Designation of a NNR performs two functions[90]:

- To preserve the flora, fauna or geological or physiographical features of the designated land; and

- To ensure that the land is managed so as to provide suitable conditions for the study and research of matters relating to the fauna and flora of Great Britain and the physical conditions in which they live, or for the study of geological and physiographical features of special interest in the area.

In contrast with designations made purely for conservation purposes, or for public enjoyment, the primary objective in designating a NNR is to facilitate the study of nature. That this is so is reflected by the fact that, in order to protect a reserve, byelaws can be made excluding all visitors from the area. The relevant nature conservation organisation (in England, English Nature) may designate a site as a NNR if it is satisfied that this is expedient in the national interest. The designation of a NNR usually requires the agreement of the landowner either to sell or to lease the land. Although English Nature has powers of compulsory purchase, they are rarely used. NNRs, however, are expensive to acquire and to run, with the result that the nature conservation organisations have tended to designate on an ad hoc basis, as and when land becomes available, rather than on the basis that a site requires protection.

Local nature reserves[91]

Local authorities may establish nature reserves if they consider it expedient to do so. **9–051** By this means protection can be given to small sites which are not of national significance but which contain important habitats.

Limestone pavements[92]

Limestone pavements possess features of great natural beauty and of botanical and **9–052** geological interest. They have, however, often been plundered to provide materials for garden rockeries. Their protection under the Wildlife and Countryside Act 1981 serves to prevent this. Where English Nature is of the opinion that any land in the countryside which comprises a limestone pavement is of special interest by reason of its flora, fauna, geological, physiographical or physiological features, it may notify the relevant local planning authority. Where it appears that the character or appearance of any land in respect of which such notification has been given would be likely to be adversely affected by the removal of the limestone, or by its disturbance in any way, the

[90] NPACA 1949, s.31.
[91] NPACA 1949, s.21.
[92] WCA 1981, s.34.

authority, the Secretary of State, or the Countryside Agency may make a Limestone Pavement Order prohibiting the removal or disturbance of the limestone. Contravention of such an order without reasonable excuse is an offence punishable by a maximum fine of £20,000.

Marine sites

9–053 The UK has many coastal areas of important nature conservation status. Indeed, of the 30 estuaries in Europe and North Africa that provide a home for approximately 20,000 wintering wading birds, over half are in Britain.

(1) *Marine Nature Reserves*

9–054 The power to designate areas as Marine Nature Reserves was first established in the Wildlife and Countryside Act 1981 in response to pressure from the House of Lords. As their Lordships made clear, international conventions such as the Berne Convention on the Conservation of European Wildlife and Natural Habitats and the Bonn Convention on the Protection of Migratory Species, to which the UK is a signatory, and which stimulated the passing of the 1981 Act, clearly placed a duty on the UK to protect the marine environment as well as habitats on land. Moreover, 40 other states, ranging from Indonesia to Ireland, already had provisions for marine reserves.[93] Such reserves are necessary because SSSIs do not extend into sub-tidal areas.

The provisions relating to Marine Nature Reserves are similar to those relating to nature reserves on land. Under the 1981 Act, the Secretary of State may order that land and waters should be managed by the relevant conservation body (*e.g.* English Nature) for the purposes of conserving marine flora or fauna or geological or physiographical features of special interest for research purposes.[94] Byelaws can be made to protect the site.[95]

Only four marine sites have been designated in the last 20 years. One of the problems has been that the agreement of all parties with an interest in the site has usually been sought before the boundaries of the site can be properly delineated. Without overcoming this basic hurdle, it has been impossible to specify what or whose operations are potentially damaging. Although more sites have been designated under EC law (see below), the relevant powers are available only for sites of European importance, as opposed to sites of mere national importance. At the time of writing, this situation may be remedied by a Bill—the Marine Wildlife Conservation Bill—which would create designation procedures similar to those which apply to SSSIs. In addition, the Bill provides for a register of marine sites and imposes duties on competent marine authorities to further the conservation of marine sites (similar to the duties of public bodies in respect of SSSIs).

(2) *European marine sites*

9–055 The Habitats Directive established a common regime for nature conservation with respect to land and sea. European sites may therefore be created which encompass, or consist entirely of, marine areas. The 1994 Regulations provide a legal framework for

---

[93] *per* Lord Melchett, *Hansard*, H.L., 1980–1981 Vol.415, col.990.
[94] WCA 1981, s.36
[95] *ibid.*, s.37.

the conservation of such sites which does not depend on their being designated as nature reserves and managed by the relevant conservation body.[96] The Regulations place a duty on the appropriate nature conservation body to formulate conservation objectives for sites and specify potentially damaging operations. Management schemes may then be drawn up by the conservation body, together with other relevant authorities, such as local authorities, the Environment Agency, and navigation and harbour authorities. The designation and management of European marine sites has been a major undertaking for the UK, because these sites lack the existing regulatory framework provided by the SSSI regime.

Ramsar sites

Under the Ramsar Convention on Wetlands of International Importance, to which the **9–056** UK is a signatory, states are required to identify, and take steps to conserve, wetlands within their territories which are important habitats for wild birds. In the UK, such sites will usually be protected by means of the SSSI regime, or as European sites. However, s.37A of the Wildlife and Countryside Act 1981 now provides a formal mechanism for the UK to fulfil its Ramsar obligations by requiring the Secretary of State to notify English Nature of the existence of such sites. English Nature must then notify the site's owners and occupiers, the Environment Agency, the local planning authorities, and certain statutory undertakers (under the Water Industry Act 1991 and the Land Drainage Act 1991) whose activities may affect the site.

Planning law and habitat conservation

Where habitats and species are not preserved by site designations, planning law may **9–057** provide more limited protection. Under the Town and Country Planning Act 1990, Unitary Development Plans, Structure Plans and Local Plans are required to include policies in relation to the conservation of the natural beauty and amenity of the land. The Habitats Regulations 1994 provide that this requirement should be taken to include policies for encouraging the management of features of the landscape which are of major importance for wild flora and fauna.[97] Nature conservation is also a material consideration in decisions whether or not to grant planning permission.[98] The protection provided by planning law, however, is limited. Agriculture is currently the biggest threat to habitats, but the use of land for agricultural purposes does not normally constitute "development" and does not therefore require planning permission.[99] Where planning permission *is* required, the decision whether to grant it is a discretionary one based on a balancing of *all* material factors in the public interest, of which ecological issues are only one.

In respect of designated sites, as noted above, there are significant controls over development within European sites. Where ordinary SSSIs are likely to be affected by planning decisions, local authorities (who are "section 28G" authorities—see above)

[96] Regulations 33–35.
[97] Regulation 37.
[98] PPG 9.
[99] TCPA 1990, s.55(2)(e).

now have greater duties than formerly to have regard to conservation issues. However, under the legislation, it is the planning authorities, and not English Nature, who have the final say as to whether development will proceed. Current Planning Policy Guidance states that where there is a risk of damage to an SSSI, the planning authority should consider overcoming that risk by attaching conditions to planning permission.[1]

Protection of wider habitats

9–058 It is increasingly being recognised that a coherent scheme of nature conservation must afford protection to areas of countryside which are wider than designated sites. Many species are dependent upon components of the environment which are found outside designated sites, and species which thrive over wide areas, such as the golden eagle, clearly cannot be protected solely by the designation of sites unless those sites are impracticably large.

To this end, there are a number of provisions relating to protection of the wider countryside. For example, a local planning authority may enter into a management agreement with any person who has an interest in land.[2] Such an agreement may restrict, for example, the method of cultivation of the land, or may impose obligations to carry out positive works. In return, the affected party may receive a grant from the Countryside Agency. A local authority, however, has no power to compel a person to enter into a management agreement, nor to impose a management scheme, so that conservation of wider habitats in this way depends on the co-operation of their human inhabitants.

The Habitats Directive also contains a provision which relates to wider habitats. Outside designated sites, Member States are under a duty to endeavour in their land-use planning and development policies to encourage the management of features of the landscape which are of major importance for wild fauna and flora. This duty, however, is perhaps rather too general to be effective. It was described by the RSPB at the time as a "pale vestige" of the stronger measures for which they had hoped.

Many habitats in the UK have been shaped by agricultural practices. The Agriculture Act 1986 aimed to reduce agricultural overproduction by environmentally harmful means and provided for the designation of "Environmentally Sensitive Areas". In these areas, farmers are encouraged to enter into voluntary agreements under which, in return for compensation, they agree to follow agricultural practices compatible with conservation. Such provisions are closely related to the general operation of the EU's Common Agricultural Policy, consideration of which is outside the scope of this book. It should be noted, however, that a review of this policy has resulted in it becoming a precondition for the receipt of a number of EU agricultural subsidies that farmers should undertake not to follow environmentally damaging practices.

Outside the agri-environment programme, a number of policies have been developed to ensure that designated sites are not isolated. A range of measures have been introduced such as the Woodland Grant Scheme. Under this scheme, the Forestry Commission provides an income for the planting of trees until the trees have grown sufficiently to yield an income.

[1] PPG 9.
[2] WCA 1981, s.39.

D: LANDSCAPE CONSERVATION

As was noted in the introduction to this chapter, protection of the landscape is **9–059** logically an aspect of nature conservation, yet has traditionally been treated separately by UK legislation, so that it has been the responsibility of different bodies. It has been said that the National Parks and Access to the Countryside Act 1949 created a "great divide" between nature and landscape conservation in Britain, which lasted until the restructuring of the agencies in 1991 and still exists in England.[3]

The approach of the bodies responsible for landscape conservation has traditionally been very different from that of nature conservation bodies. The nature conservation bodies had a strongly scientific bias and were concerned with the study of nature, whilst the Countryside Commission (now renamed the Countryside Agency),[4] responsible for protecting the landscape, approached its subject from the point of view of promoting public recreation, and forged close links with local planning authorities. During the 1980s, however, it became clear that these two approaches overlapped because, as we have noted, conserving nature "in the wild" usually involves conserving landscapes and the traditional uses which man has made of them. The anomaly of a divided regime has now been resolved in Wales, where the Countryside Council for Wales is responsible both for nature conservation and landscape conservation matters, and in Scotland, where Scottish Natural Heritage has a similar dual function. The position in England, however, is unchanged, so that English Nature has separate responsibilities from the Countryside Agency. Protection of the landscape is achieved primarily by the designation of National Parks and Areas of Outstanding Natural Beauty, as provided for under the National Parks and Access to Countryside Act 1949, and through the planning system.

National Parks

National Parks are designated by the Countryside Agency. The Agency makes a **9–060** proposal for designation to the Secretary of State which, after extensive publicity requirements have been met and a public inquiry held, he may confirm.

A National Park may be designated for two reasons:

- To conserve and enhance the natural beauty, wildlife and cultural heritage of the area; and

- To promote opportunities for the understanding and enjoyment of the special qualities of those areas by the public.[5]

There is, of course, a potential for conflict between these two objectives, the second of which relates to the pursuit of leisure activities, especially in the light of modern

---

[3] Adams, "Places for Nature Protected Areas" in *British Nature Conservation in Progress* (Eds Goldsmith and Warren) (1993).

[4] Development Commission (Transfer of Functions and Miscellaneous Provisions) Order 1999 (SI 1999/ 416).

[5] NPACA 1949, s.5 (as amended by EA 1995, s.61).

forms of outdoor leisure activity such as war games and the use of off-road vehicles. These activities can often place considerable pressure on a fragile environment. We consider in a separate section below the various ways in which such conflicts can be resolved. In relation to activities in National Parks, the position is covered by what is known as the "Sandford Principle" (discussed below) which states that where there is a conflict between the two designation purposes, greater weight should be attached to the conservation purpose.[6]

There are currently seven National Parks in England,[7] covering around 7.6 per cent of its landscape, and the Countryside Agency is in the process of designating two more.[8] The name "National Park" does not signify national ownership. Most of the designated land is owned by farmers and other private landowners. The land is managed either by its owners or by public bodies such as the Forestry Commission, English Nature, or by a National Park Authority. Each National Park has its own National Park Authority, which exercises jurisdiction over development, having regard to the objectives set out above.[9] The members of the National Park Authorities comprise a bare majority of people appointed by local authorities with land in the Park, the remainder being locally elected representatives and appointees of the Secretary of State.

Areas of Outstanding Natural Beauty

9–061 The 1949 Act also made provision for the designation of Areas of Outstanding Natural Beauty (AONBs).[10] These are in many respects similar to National Parks. The primary purpose of their designation is to conserve and enhance the natural beauty of an area, although many also fulfil a recreational purpose. There are 37 AONBs in England, covering around 15.6 per cent of the landscape.[11]

The Countryside and Rights of Way Act 2000 introduced certain measures aimed at simplifying and enhancing the management of AONBs. Formerly, AONBs were managed by the local authorities (often more than one) in whose areas they were situated. Following concern that practice differed between authorities, and because of administrative problems where an AONB was managed by several authorities, it was decided to place the management of each AONB in the hands of a unified body, to bring their management into line with that of National Parks.

To this end, the Act empowers the Secretary of State to establish "Conservation Boards" to manage AONBs, but only if a majority of the local authorities within the AONB agree. An order establishing a Conservation Board must receive an affirmative resolution from both Houses of Parliament. The membership of the Boards will comprise a combination of local authority representatives and representatives from parish meetings or parish councils, as well as a number of appointees of the Secretary of State, who will help reflect the national perspective in managing AONBs.

---

[6] NPACA 1949, s.11A (inserted by EA 1995, s.62).
[7] Dartmoor; Exmoor; Lake District; Northumberland; North Yorkshire Moors; Peak District; Yorkshire Dales. The Norfolk and Suffolk Broads, designated under separate legislation, are also very similar to National Parks, except that provision is made for such matters as navigation of their waterways.
[8] The South Downs and the New Forest.
[9] See also PPG 7.
[10] NPACA 1949 s.87.
[11] There are four in Wales.

Local authorities will be able to delegate many of their powers to the Board, but will retain jurisdiction over planning matters. All Conservation Boards will be required to prepare and publish a statutory "management plan" in respect of their AONB, or to formally adopt an informal plan which is already in place. The Act also provides that "all relevant authorities" (including statutory undertakers) now have a duty to have regard to the purpose of conserving and enhancing the natural beauty of AONBs in exercising their functions.[12]

Where a Conservation Board is established to manage an AONB, the Board will have an additional objective, besides conserving and enhancing natural beauty, namely to enhance public understanding and enjoyment of the special qualities of the area. Where there is a conflict between these two objectives, the Board (in accordance with the "Sandford principle") must attach greater weight to the objective of conservation. The Boards also have a duty to foster the economic and social well-being of local communities, provided they do not incur significant expenditure in so doing.

Planning and the landscape

The Countryside Act 1968 imposed on every Minister, government department and **9–062** public body a duty to have regard to the desirability of conserving the natural beauty and amenity of the countryside in the exercise of their functions. To this end, unitary development plans, structure plans and local plans are required to include policies in relation to these matters.[13] The effectiveness of landscape control through planning, however, is limited, principally because (with very few exceptions) the use of land for the purposes of agriculture or forestry does not constitute "development" and is therefore exempt from the need for planning permission.[14] These uses, however, are the very uses most likely to cause undesirable changes in the landscape.

E: CONSERVATION *VERSUS* ECONOMIC AND SOCIAL NEEDS

The desire to conserve species, habitats and landscapes often comes into conflict with **9–063** the social and economic needs of an area. For example, the public may wish to walk, go camping, use caravans, ride horses and bikes, rock climb, water ski, etc., or industry may wish to quarry. Such activities are of great economic value to rural communities. In this section, we consider a number of ways in which the law has attempted to strike a balance between conservation and other uses of land. We shall see that the UK's approach has sometimes brought it into conflict with the ECJ, and that it may well bring it into conflict with the European Court of Human Rights.

The right to roam

Part I of the Countryside and Rights of Way Act 2000 is designed to give the public **9–064** greater freedom to explore the open countryside. It introduces a new statutory right of access for open-air recreation to mountain, moor, heath, down and registered common

[12] CRWA 2000, s.85.
[13] TCPA 1990, ss.12 and 31.
[14] *ibid.*, s.55.

land, so that people on such land who might formerly have been trespassers, are no longer so regarded by the law. It also includes a power to extend the right to coastal land, such as beaches and cliffs, and enables landowners voluntarily to dedicate irrevocably any land to public access.

This "right to roam", however, is not a general right for members of the public to wander wherever they wish—it applies only in designated areas, which are to be mapped by the Countryside Agency. The Act seeks to balance the public interest against the interests of landowners. The right does not extend to cycling, horse riding or driving a vehicle, nor does it extend to gardens or cultivated land. The Act allows landowners to exclude or restrict access, without giving a reason, for up to 28 days a year, and to exclude dogs on grouse moors, and in small fields during lambing time, without seeking permission. Landowners are also able to seek further exclusions or restrictions on access for reasons of land management, fire prevention and to avoid danger to the public. The Countryside Agency is able to give general directions restricting access for these purposes, as well as for purposes of nature and heritage conservation.

The Countryside and Rights of Way Act 2000 did not provide for compensation to be paid to landowners who suffered economic losses, or interference with enjoyment of their land, as a result of people exercising their "right to roam". The government took the view that no economic losses would be likely to result, because the evidence suggested that increases in the number of people walking in the countryside did not usually result in an increase in such things as broken walls and fences, or damage to land. The Country Landowners' Association disagreed.

During the passage of the Bill there was some debate as to whether the government's failure to provide compensation is a violation of landowners' human rights. The European Convention on Human Rights (which is incorporated into UK law by the Human Rights Act 1998) provides that "every natural or legal person is entitled to the peaceful enjoyment of his possessions",[15] and case law in the European Court of Human Rights establishes that, where possessory rights are interfered with in the name of general national interests, a "fair balance" must be struck between those interests and private property interests. In a number of cases, striking this balance fairly has been held to entail paying compensation to the people affected.[16] Moreover, since existing legislation prior to the Countryside and Rights of Way Act 2000 provided for compensation where the value of land depreciated as a result of public access, it may be suggested that a failure to do so is unconstitutional.[17]

Article 8 of the Convention provides: "Everyone has the right to respect for his private and family life, his home and his correspondence." It is a moot point whether a landowner who is subjected to people walking across his land would suffer interference with his "home". (No access is granted under the Act to land within 20 metres of a dwelling.)[18] However, it is to be noted that in *Niemietz v Germany*[19] the Court was

[15] Art. 1 of Protocol No.1.
[16] See *Lithgow v United Kingdom* (1986) 8 E.H.R.R 329; *Hentrich v France* (1994) 18 E.H.R.R. 440 and *Holy Monasteries v Greece* (1995) 20 E.H.R.R. 1. Contrast App. No. 11763/85, *Baner v Sweden* (1989) 60 D&R. 128, a decision of the Commission which held that the addition of a right to fish with hand tackle to a scheme of general public access to land did not call for compensation for affected landowners.
[17] See NPACA 1949 (Pt V) and Highways Act 1980, ss.25–28.
[18] CRWA 2000, s.1 and Pt I of Sch.I.
[19] (1993) 16 E.H.R.R. 97.

prepared to accept that the concept of "home" could extend to business premises, and stated that it did not consider it possible to attempt an exhaustive definition of "private life". It remains to be seen whether these issues will give rise to a challenge in the European Court of Human Rights.

National Parks and the Sandford principle

The Sandford Committee, which reported in 1974, was appointed to review National **9–065** Park policies in England and Wales. It recommended that the statutory purposes of National Parks should make it clear that their enjoyment by the public was to be "in a manner and by such means as will leave their natural beauty unimpaired for the enjoyment of this and future generations." The report noted that recreation and conservation can co-exist, and that any conflict between these objectives can usually be resolved through appropriate management of a Park. However, in rare circumstances where such conflicts cannot be resolved, the report concluded that conservation should always prevail. This idea became known as the "Sandford principle" and was eventually incorporated into law by a provision of the Environment Act 1995, which inserted s.11A into the National Parks and Access to Countryside Act 1949. Section 11A makes reference to the twin purposes of conservation and promoting opportunities for understanding and enjoyment by the public, and goes on to state:

"... if it appears that there is a conflict between those purposes [the relevant bodies] shall attach greater weight to the purpose of conserving and enhancing the natural beauty, wildlife and cultural heritage of the area comprised in the National Park."

Under the Countryside and Rights of Way Act 2000, the Sandford principle now also applies in respect of Areas of Outstanding Natural Beauty. An example of the Sandford principle in action is the Lake District National Park Authority's refusal to allow caravan sites, on the shores of Lake Windermere, to open during the winter, because this would disturb wildfowl.[20]

Section 37 of the Countryside Act 1968

Section 37 of the Countryside Act 1968 provides that Ministers, the Countryside **9–066** Agency, the Countryside Council for Wales and English Nature, have a duty, when exercising their functions under the National Parks and Access to the Countryside Act 1949, and the Wildlife and Countryside Act 1981, to "have due regard to the needs of agriculture and forestry and to the economic and social interests of rural areas". A recent government consultation paper on appeals against consents and management notices under the amended SSSI regime also makes it clear that the Secretary of State should take account of s.37 when deciding appeals.[21]

---

[20] This example is taken from the Park Authority's promotional literature.
[21] "Sites of Special Scientific Interest: Appeals Regulations—a Public Consultation Paper" (June 2001), available at *www.defra.gov.uk*.

The wording of s.37 implies that the relevant bodies, in making their decisions, must perform (and be seen to perform) a balancing act, and that their decisions might be challenged by judicial review if social and economic interests appear to have been ignored or dismissed too easily. Seen in this way, the duty imposed by s.37 seems inconsistent with the Sandford principle, which, by declaring that conservation objectives always come first, dispenses with the need for such a balancing act (although bodies must still show that they have addressed their minds to the question of whether a conflict of objectives arises).

Section 37 clearly allows for decisions under the SSSI regime to be made on the basis that local economic and social considerations outweigh habitat conservation concerns. Although, in respect of "priority" European sites, this approach appears to be displaced by the Habitats Regulations (which expressly exclude consideration of economic and social interests in "priority site" decision-making), s.37 seems to require a "balancing" approach in respect of other designated sites. This approach, however, appears contrary to decisions made by the ECJ in relation to non-priority sites.

In *Commission v Germany*,[22] for example, the ECJ noted that economic and recreational reasons were not legitimate reasons for a Member State to reduce a Special Protection Area. The power of Member States to reduce the extent of Special Protection Areas could be justified only on exceptional grounds, corresponding to a general public interest which was superior to the interest represented by the conservation objective of the Birds Directive. Similarly, in *Commission v Spain*[23] the ECJ held Spain to be in breach of the Birds Directive by failing to designate an important wetland area, the Santona Marshes, as a Special Protection Area. The Court made it clear that designation should be on ornithological grounds alone, and that Member States should not take account of economic considerations when designating Special Protection Areas.

The conflict between the two approaches was summarised in evidence given by the then Department of the Environment to a House of Lords select committee in 1989[24]:

"The British government has attached considerable importance to the need to strike a balance. That is at the cornerstone of our own method of site protection. Due consideration and weighing of factors cannot imply any preconception of which way the balance must fall. That was one of the problems of the draft Directive. It was quite clear from the wording that in Special Protection Areas the interest of nature conservation would always override any other consideration. That would cause considerable difficulty not just in this country but to most other Member States."

The issue of striking a balance between conservation and economic and social needs has arisen in two UK cases concerning site designation. *R. v Secretary of State for the Environment, Ex p. Royal Society for the Protection of Birds*[25] concerned a decision by the Secretary of State to exclude an area known as Lappel Bank, in the Medway

---

[22] Case C–57/89 [1991] I E.C.R. 883.
[23] Case C–355/90 [1993] I E.C.R. 4221.
[24] House of Lords Select Committee on the European Communities (session 1988–1989), Fifteenth Report: Habitat and Species Protection (1989).
[25] *The Times*, August 2, 1996.

Estuary and Marshes, from land to be designated as a Special Protection Area. The Medway Estuary is a valuable ornithological habitat immediately adjoined by Lappel Bank. It is a wetland of international importance for a substantial number of wildfowl and water species, in particular avocets and little terns. The port of Sheerness, however, which is the fifth largest in the UK in terms of freight handling, also adjoins Lappel Bank. In order to remain competitive, the port needed to expand, and this could be done only by reclamation of Lappel Bank.

In deciding to exclude Lappel Bank from the Special Protection Area, the Secretary of State, whilst recognising the ecological importance of Lappel Bank, took the view that this was outweighed by economic and development considerations. His decision was judicially reviewed by the RSPB, which argued that at the designation stage only ornithological considerations were relevant. The matter was eventually referred to the European Court of Justice,[26] which held that, under the Birds Directive, a Member State was not authorised to take account of economic considerations when defining the boundaries of a Special Protection Area. It is worth noting that the ECJ judgment was a pyrrhic victory for the RSPB, because by the time the case was decided the port had been built—the UK court did not think it appropriate to grant an injunction to stop the building while the case was being considered by the ECJ.

In *R. (on the application of First Corporate Shipping Ltd) v Secretary of State for the Environment, Transport and the Regions.*[27] First Corporate Shipping, the statutory port authority for the port of Bristol on the Severn Estuary, challenged the Secretary of State's proposal to designate the Severn Estuary as a candidate Special Area of Conservation. It did so on the basis that Art. 2 of the Habitats Directive provides that "economic, social and cultural requirements and regional and local characteristics" should be taken into account by Member States when adopting measures pursuant to the Directive. On reference to the ECJ, the Court held that Member States could not take into account those requirements when selecting or defining the boundaries of candidate sites: under Art. 4(1) of the Directive, only factors relating to the conservation of habitats, fauna and flora were relevant considerations for the purposes of site selection and boundary definition. It was necessary for the Commission to have available to it an exhaustive list of those sites within Member States that had the requisite ecological characteristics. Only then could decisions be taken by the Commission as to whether particular sites should be designated so as to achieve a coherent European ecological network. In effect, the Court held that it was not for the UK to second guess the Commission by using economic and social considerations to exclude the possibility that a particular site would be designated.

F: INTERNATIONAL NATURE CONSERVATION

Globally, the diversity of species is being diminished by an expanding human **9–067** population requiring greater space in which to live and making greater use of environmental resources, particularly by the exploitation of species. Around 70 per

---

[26] Case C–44/95.
[27] Case C–371/98.

cent of the world's fish stocks, for example, are being harvested at levels near or beyond sustainability. It has been estimated that the destruction of the tropical rainforests in South America is causing the extinction of two species every hour.[28] In response, international policy on conserving "the variety of life in all its forms" (biological diversity) has been embraced in a number of bilateral, regional and global conventions. In its approach to conserving biological diversity (or "biodiversity"), international law has only recently moved away from the idea of protecting individual species and habitats towards a more comprehensive and global approach.

Protection of individual habitats and species

9–068 The Convention on Wetlands of International Importance[29] (the Ramsar Convention) aims to protect wetlands, which accommodate an abundant source of animal and plant life. Signatory States are required to designate and monitor certain areas of marsh, fen or peat land. (We have seen that the Countryside and Rights of Way Act 2000 now provides a mechanism for dealing with the UK's formal international obligations.) The 1979 Berne Convention on the Conservation of European Wildlife and Natural Habitats (the Berne Convention), together with the 1979 Convention on the Conservation of Migratory Species of Wild Animals (the Bonn Convention), provided the international impetus for the Habitats Directive and the Wildlife and Countryside Act 1981.

Widening the scope of protection

9–069 The Habitats Directive reflects international moves towards a more comprehensive approach to nature conservation by extending protection to all species and habitats within the EU. But the problem with conserving living creatures, of course, is that they do not often confine themselves within man-made boundaries. Therefore region-based or habitat-based protection schemes can be of only limited effectiveness. A global protection scheme is needed.

The 1973 Convention on International Trade in Endangered Species of Wild Fauna and Flora (CITES)[30] exhorts governments to regulate, and in some cases prohibit, trade in species threatened by extinction. The Convention, to which a large number of states are party, has established a permit system to regulate international trade in endangered species. In the UK, the Convention is implemented by the Control of Endangered Species (Import and Export) Act 1976, and by an EC Council Regulation of 1997,[31] which goes beyond the requirements of CITES in the controls it imposes on the import of endangered species and products made from such species.

The Convention on Biological Diversity[32]

9–070 The most sophisticated and ambitious of the nature conservation treaties is the Convention on Biological Diversity. It was signed in Rio de Janeiro by representatives of 150 states in June 1992 and came into force on December 29, 1993. Its principal

---

[28] Schoon, "Going, Going Gone: The Story of Britain's Vanishing Natural History", (Bookman Projects 1996).
[29] February 2, 1971, Ramsar, 11 I.L.M. 963 (1972).
[30] March 3, 1973, Washington, 12 I.L.M. 1085.
[31] Council Reg.338/97.
[32] June 5, 1992, Rio de Janeiro, 31 I.L.M. 822 (1992).

objectives are the conservation of biodiversity and the sustainable use of species. The Convention defines biodiversity as "the variety of life in all its forms" and recognises that the concept divides into three areas, namely the diversity of ecosystems, the diversity of species, and genetic diversity within each of those species.

Within the same species, each individual animal has unique genetic characteristics which are different from those of every other animal within that species. Protection of genetic diversity within individual species is necessary in order for species to adapt to new conditions and to develop resilience to disease. Some animals, because of their genetic make-up, will be resistant to diseases or changes in their environment which prove fatal to others of the same species. It follows, then, that the greater the number of individual animals which are conserved within a species, the greater are that species' chances of survival. It also follows that conservation of species in very small numbers, such as is occurring with pandas, for example, cannot necessarily ensure their survival.

Biological diversity is also important because it provides the raw material for the scientific application of biological organisms for the benefit of agriculture and medicine, known as "biotechnology". Little known plant species, such as the rosy periwinkle, which is used in treating some forms of cancer, have often proved invaluable in combating disease. In agriculture, often the only way effectively to ensure that crops are resilient to blight is by cross-breeding them with naturally resistant wild strains. The consequences associated with allowing the pool of species from which biotechnology may draw its material to diminish, therefore, are incalculable and potentially enormous.

There is a tendency for developed countries to rely on the availability of bio-technological resources of Third World countries without compensating those countries for providing what, in effect, amounts to a valuable service. Unsurprisingly, it is the wealthy and industrialised countries of the world which develop, and largely benefit from, new medicines and agricultural practices. Many of these are protected by patents, so that the developing world cannot afford to exploit them even though in many cases it has provided the materials which have made the technology possible. At the Rio Conference, Third World delegates sought a guarantee that their countries would be compensated for any commercially useful discoveries attributable to the conservation of biological diversity within their borders. The developed states, however, refused to agree to this.

The most important obligations deriving from the Convention on Biological Diversity are set out in Art. 6, which provides that each contracting state, "in accordance with its particular conditions and capabilities", should:

- Develop national strategies, plans or programmes for the conservation and sustainable use of biodiversity, or adapt existing strategies, and

- Integrate, as far as is possible and appropriate, the conservation and sustainable use of biodiversity into relevant plans and programmes.

The wording of the Convention is heavily qualified throughout with such phrases as "as far as possible" and "where appropriate". It is therefore questionable whether, in real terms, the contracting states have committed themselves to substantial action. The United States has still not ratified the Convention, but in the UK and at EU level, it has spawned a number of initiatives, the most important being the promotion of eco-labelling schemes for products whose use might affect biodiversity, and the raising of finance from the private sector to conserve particular species. Water UK, for example—a body representing the UK water industry—has contributed £1 million over three years for the conservation of otters. The Countryside and Rights of Way Act 2000 has put this initiative on a statutory footing by placing Ministers and government departments under a duty to take, "or promote the taking by others", of reasonably practicable steps to further the objectives of the Convention.[33]

[33] CRWA 2000, s.74.

Chapter 10

AIR POLLUTION

Introduction

Up to 24,000 people die prematurely every year in Britain because of the effects of air **10–001**
pollution. Many thousands require hospital treatment—children are particularly vulnerable. The thick smogs of the 1950s—caused by coal and wood fires in people's
homes and coal-burning power stations—which led to the deaths of thousands of
people in London, are now a thing of the past. However, a new type of smog has
replaced them—the smog caused by traffic fumes as pollution from road transport has
steadily increased. This smog is in some ways more dangerous, because it is less
visible.[1]

In addition to traffic, a wide range of activities affect the atmosphere, including
industrial emissions and smoke, as well as odours. A range of laws and policies are
therefore necessary to respond to these problems. The pollutants of primary concern
are sulphur dioxide, benzene, carbon monoxide and nitrogen dioxide, as well as
particulate matter emitted as smoke. An increasing concern is that air pollutants in
combination can form "cocktails" (ammonium sulphate, for example, particles of
which are deposited on crops) which pose a greater environmental threat than do their
constituent parts alone.

Air pollution does not remain within national boundaries. During the winter, air in
Northern Europe tends to travel eastwards from the Atlantic over the UK towards the
rest of Europe. This pattern of air movement enables the UK to "export" a significant
proportion of its own air pollution. Recent estimates suggest that more than 73 per
cent of the UK's sulphur dioxide emissions, and as much as 85 per cent of its emissions
of nitrogen oxides, are transboundary, leading to deposition in other countries or the
sea (14 per cent of sulphur dioxide and 25 per cent of nitrogen oxides may be
deposited in this way).[2] The pollutants in question are often converted through
atmospheric chemical reactions into secondary pollutants, such as sulphates and
nitrates, which are the primary cause of acid rain falling in other European countries,
especially Scandinavia. The UK also "receives" air pollution from outside its borders.

---

[1] This paragraph is extracted from the government's *Air Quality Strategy for England, Scotland, Wales and
Northern Ireland* Cm 4548, January 2000.
[2] EMEP (Co-operation programme for monitoring and evaluating the long-range transmission of air
pollutants in Europe). Figures are for 1997.

It has been estimated that around 41 per cent of the deposition (rather than ambient levels) of nitrogen oxides in the UK originate from sources outside the UK. Air pollution contributes to global warming and ozone depletion, and the international response to these issues has been a significant influence on the development of EC and UK law.

Despite these problems, there have been considerable improvements in ambient air quality over the last 30 years. Extreme air pollution is now a thing of the past. The air quality that we usually experience in the UK is generally unlikely to cause any short-term effects for the majority of the population.

The history of air pollution control in the UK

10–002   Control of air pollution has a long history. Indeed, smoke from the burning of sea coal was the first pollutant ever to be regulated in the UK, by Royal Proclamations issued in 1272 and in 1306. It was not until the Public Health Act of 1875, however, that the first general legislation to control smoke emissions was passed. The provisions on smoke abatement which that Act contained have formed the basis of modern legislation. The 1875 Act, however, was unsuccessful in securing major changes in air quality, so that Victorian cities were characterised by soot-blackened buildings and heavy smogs.

In December 1952, a very severe smog in London, caused by a combination of fog and smoke particles, which inhibited the dispersion of air pollution, resulted in the death of an estimated 4,000 people. The government appointed the Beaver Committee to look into its causes. Its recommendations led to the passing of the Clean Air Act 1956. This legislation produced a dramatic reduction in smog by imposing a prohibition on "dark smoke" from chimneys and by the creation of "smoke control areas" in which it became an offence to emit any smoke from domestic and industrial chimneys. The Clean Air Acts of 1956 and 1968 were consolidated by the Clean Air Act 1993. During the 1970s, the increased use of smokeless fuels, such as coke and gas, in preference to coal, coupled with the adoption by the electricity generating industry of taller chimney stacks aimed at dispersing air pollutants over greater distances, led to a reduction in air pollution by particulates. Particulates in the atmosphere are of special concern, because their presence can severely inhibit the dispersal of other air pollutants.

These measures, however, did little to reduce the problem of acidity in the air which, though invisible, causes considerable damage to crops and to waterways which support life. Acidity first became a real problem during the industrial revolution. "Alkali works", set up to produce soda, emitted large volumes of foul-smelling hydrogen chloride gas. This combined with atmospheric moisture to form acid rain which stripped the leaves from trees and shrubs. The recommendations of a Royal Commission, appointed to consider the problem, led to the passing of the Alkali Act 1863 and later the Alkali Act 1874. The latter Act required industry to use the "best practicable means" to minimise the emission of noxious and offensive gases. The implementation of the "best practicable means" test led to the adoption of the first emission standards in the UK, which detailed the amounts of specified substances permissible in given amounts of gas. The legislation also led to the establishment of the Alkali Inspectorate, the predecessor to HMIP and latterly to the Environment

Agency. Both of the Alkali Acts were consolidated by the Alkali etc. Works Regulation Act 1906.

Whilst the Alkali Acts exerted control over much industrial activity, problems were emerging in relation to industrial activities such as ferrous metal foundries, plants manufacturing asbestos based products, and plants producing glass and ceramics. Pollution was also arising from such sources as hospital incinerators. Control over these forms of pollution was not exercised by the Alkali Inspectorate. Rather, it rested with local authorities, in the exercise of their statutory nuisance powers under the Public Health Acts. Unlike the Alkali Inspectorate, local authorities could take action only after a nuisance had occurred and could not require plants to operate using the "best practicable means" to reduce pollution. The increasing volume of pollution produced by these activities, however, made it clear that some form of preventive control was necessary.

In 1976, the Royal Commission on Environmental Pollution recommended new and more comprehensive legislation to cover all aspects of industrial air pollution, which would give local authorities the power to exercise preventive control by making their prior consent necessary for the carrying out of certain processes.[3] The Royal Commission also recommended that a new unified pollution inspectorate be established to supervise activities which discharged pollution into more than one environmental medium. In the light of these recommendations, the government embarked on a prolonged period of review, eventually outlining its proposals in a consultation paper issued in December 1986. This document stressed the necessity of conforming to EC legislation, in particular the EC Framework Directive on combating air pollution from industrial plants.[4] This Directive required, amongst other things, that particular categories of industrial operation should be authorised before they commenced and that emissions from existing operations should be gradually improved. A few of the processes which the Directive identified as requiring prior authorisation were, in the UK, under the control of local authorities, whose powers at the time were insufficient to exert the sort of preventive controls demanded by the Directive. Therefore, the power to supervise certain industrial processes by granting or withholding licences was eventually conferred on local authorities by Pt I of the Environmental Protection Act 1990.

Part I of the Environmental Protection Act 1990 was the main mechanism for minimising air pollution from industrial sources for a number of years. This Act established two pollution control systems: the local authority air pollution control (LAAPC) system and the integrated pollution control (IPC) system, which not only took account of releases to air, but also to land and water. The IPC system resulted in some significant reductions in industrial emissions to the air. In particular, marked reductions were achieved in the amount of sulphur dioxide emitted by power stations. As discussed in Ch. 5, IPC and LAAPC are in the process of being succeeded by a new pollution prevention and control (PPC) regime.

The current pattern of regulation

Because of the varied nature of the activities which affect the atmosphere, the UK **10–003** regime of air pollution control is somewhat fragmented. PPC is the main mechanism for minimising air pollution from industrial sources. Operation of a regulated

---

[3] *Air Pollution Control: An Integrated Approach*, RCEP, Cmnd. 6371 (1976).
[4] Directive 84/360/EEC.

industrial process requires a permit from either the Environment Agency or a local authority. Industrial processes may also be controlled under the statutory nuisance regime, as may the polluting activities of private individuals.

In situations where the PPC regime does not apply, emissions of smoke, grit and dust are controlled by the Clean Air Act 1993. This Act also regulates the content of fuels used in furnaces and motor vehicles, aiming to reduce the polluting emissions to which these fuels give rise. As has been said, nowadays, vehicle emissions probably make the most significant contribution to poor air quality. They are controlled at UK level by a miscellaneous collection of statutory instruments, and at EC level by the so-called "Auto-Oil Programme".

The National Air Quality Management Strategy

10–004 The National Air Quality Management Strategy aims to provide a policy framework for an overall improvement of air quality, and for the improvement of air quality in particular geographical areas. The motivating forces behind the strategy include a marked increase in the incidence of asthma and other respiratory diseases (the publication of the draft National Air Quality Strategy, in August 1996, has been described as the clearest official acceptance yet of air pollution's impact on public health[5]) and the availability of improved scientific knowledge about the origins and effects of air pollution, which enables regulation to be more specific. The National Air Quality Management Strategy is prepared and published in accordance with a requirement of the Environment Act 1995.[6] Both the Environment Agency and local authorities are required to have regard to this strategy in exercising their pollution control functions.[7] The first strategy was published in March 1997, with a second edition in January 2000.

Protection of human health is at the heart of the strategy. Eight particular pollutants are selected for control (namely benzene, carbon monoxide, lead, nitrogen dioxide, ozone, particles, sulphur dioxide and 1,3–butadiene). Health-based standards are to be established for those pollutants, as well as "air quality objectives" for achieving these standards throughout the UK. The standards will specify acceptable concentrations of each pollutant in the atmosphere, and will be set solely on the basis of scientific assessment. For two of the pollutants, nitrogen dioxide and sulphur dioxide, standards will also be set for protecting vegetation and ecosystems. The strategy identifies what needs to be done at international, national and local level to achieve these standards. Once the standards are set, relevant air quality objectives will be set for particular areas. These will be based on an analysis of costs and benefits in the light of current technology. Methods for achieving the air quality objectives include industrial permitting under the PPC regime, land-use planning, and traffic management. Areas with particular air pollution problems can be made "air quality management areas" and subject to local air quality management "action plans" (see below).

[5] ENDS 256 (June 1996), p.15.
[6] EA 1995, s.80(1).
[7] *ibid.*, s.81(1).

Local authority air quality management areas

Under the Environment Act 1995, local authorities are required to conduct a periodic **10–005** review of air quality within their areas.[8] If the standards and objectives of the National Air Quality Management Strategy are not being achieved, or are not likely to be achieved within a particular area, the local authority must make an order designating that area as an "air quality management area". Once an area has been so designated, the local authority is under a duty to make a formal assessment of the air quality in the area, noting the respects in which the relevant standards and objectives are not being met. The authority must, within twelve months, prepare a report outlining the results of this assessment and thereafter must prepare an "action plan" to assist it in exercising its air pollution control powers. The Secretary of State has reserve powers to direct the local authority in the exercise of these functions.

A: THE POLLUTION PREVENTION AND CONTROL REGIME

Integrated Pollution Prevention and Control (IPPC)

Historically, control of industrial air pollution in the UK was divided between central **10–006** and local agencies. The Alkali Inspectorate supervised the more difficult air pollution problems, whilst local authorities controlled emissions from other industrial activities. This division of control was continued in the Environmental Protection Act 1990, under which the Environment Agency had responsibility for air pollution in the context of industry regulated by IPC, whilst local authorities were responsible for air pollution from industry regulated by the Local Authority Air Pollution Control regime ("LAAPC").

As discussed in Ch. 5, the old IPC and LAAPC regimes are currently being phased out and replaced by the PPC regime. Under the PPC regime, control of air pollution continues to be divided between the Environment Agency and local authorities. Whilst the Environment Agency has responsibility for highly polluting installations—those listed for control under Pt A(1)—local authorities have responsibility for the two other types of installation, namely those to which Pt A(2) applies (where they control air pollution alongside other environmental impacts), and those to which Pt B applies (where they control only air pollution). In relation to industry controlled under Pt A(1) and Pt A(2), an integrated regime applies, administered by the Environment Agency and local authorities respectively. This regime is examined in Ch. 5. We outline here the regime of control applying to Pt B installations, which are subject to local authority air pollution control only.

Local Authority Air Pollution Prevention and Control

The new local authority air pollution regime is in most respects the same as the old **10–007** one, which was set out in Pt I of the Environmental Protection Act 1990. However, the relevant rules are now to be found in the Pollution Prevention and Control (England

---

[8] EA 1995, s.82.

and Wales) Regulations 2000.[9] The transfer from the old regime to the new will essentially be an administrative matter. The new rules will be phased in according to a timetable, under which the transfer process will be complete by 2007. The industrial processes prescribed for control under the new regime are those whose air emissions were regulated by local authorities under the old LAAPC regime, and which do not come within the scope of the IPPC Directive. They include metal-decontamination processes, the use of cement in bulk, the use of spray paints in garages and light industry, and the operation of crematoria and hospital incinerators.

Under the regime, local authorities have the same powers in relation to the relevant installations as they have in relation to installations prescribed for integrated control, except that these powers are exercisable only for the purpose of controlling air pollution. Thus, local authorities are responsible for granting permits. It is a criminal offence to operate a prescribed installation without a permit. Permits may be made subject to conditions which regulate the industrial process in question. In particular, these conditions may require compliance with emission limits.[10] There is implied into every permit a condition that the process operator must use the best available techniques (BAT) so as to prevent the release of emissions, or, where that is not practicable, reduce emissions.[11] Local authorities can issue enforcement, suspension and revocation notices, and may appoint inspectors who have the same powers of entry, search and seizure as do those appointed by the Environment Agency.[12] They are also required to maintain public registers relating to their administration of the regime. All of these powers are examined in the context of IPPC in Ch. 5.

Case law under IPC and LAAPC

10–008   The following cases, decided under the old IPC and LAAPC regimes, will give an idea of the operation of the controls imposed under the PPC Regulations in the context of air pollution:

In *R. v Secretary of State for the Environment and R. J. Compton & Sons, Ex p. West Wiltshire DC*,[13] R.J. Compton ran a piggery and carried on a process involving animal by-products. There were numerous complaints about the smell. The local authority refused the company's application for an authorisation under the LAAPC regime. The company appealed to the Secretary of State, whose inspector allowed the appeal and granted the authorisation, subject to numerous conditions. On appeal by the local authority to the High Court, however, it was held that the inspector had failed properly to apply s.6(4) of the Environmental Protection Act 1990. This section states that an application for a process authorisation cannot be granted unless the enforcing authority considers that the applicant will be able to carry on the process so as to comply with the conditions imposed. The inspector had found that the company did not have the necessary management ability to be able to carry out the process properly, and the court held that this lack of ability could not be "cured" by the imposition of

---

[9] SI 2000/1973.
[10] *ibid.*, Reg.12(2). "Equivalent parameters or technical measures" may be prescribed instead, where appropriate: see Reg.12(8).
[11] *ibid.*, Reg.12(10).
[12] EA 1995, s.108.
[13] [1996] J.P.L. 115.

stringent conditions. The inspector had therefore failed to justify his conclusion that an authorisation should be granted.

In *R. (on the Application of United Kingdom Renderers Association Ltd) v Secretary of State for the Environment, Transport and the Regions*,[14] the animal renderers association argued that guidance which recommended the imposition of an odour condition in IPC authorisations was unlawful. The condition was recommended because rendering animal by-products has the potential to create highly offensive smells. The Court of Appeal, however, took the view that the recommendation was acceptable, given that it only required the operator to use the best available techniques not entailing excessive costs (BATNEEC) to avoid odour.

In *Dudley MBC v Henley Foundries Ltd*,[15] Henley Foundries were prosecuted for the release of orange and white fumes. The orange fumes were emitted for about two minutes, and the white fumes for about 29 minutes. One of the conditions attached to the IPC authorisation for the foundry stated that "all emissions from the prescribed process, other than steam or condensed water vapour shall be free from persistent fume, free from persistent mist and free from droplets". The court took the view that whilst the orange fumes alone would not have been "persistent", in the circumstances, they and the white fumes could be classed as persistent.

B: THE STATUTORY NUISANCE REGIME

Air pollution is controlled both by the common law of nuisance and by the law relating **10–009** to statutory nuisances contained in Pt III of the Environmental Protection Act 1990. Both of these topics are examined in Ch. 12. The operation of the statutory nuisance regime is also considered in Ch. 11, which deals with noise pollution. Statutory nuisances will not, therefore, be dealt with here in any detail. It should be remembered, however, that under s.79 of the Act, the following are statutory nuisances:

- any premises in such a state as to be prejudicial to health or a nuisance;

- smoke emitted from premises so as to be prejudicial to health or a nuisance;

- fumes or gases emitted from premises so as to be prejudicial to health or a nuisance;

- any dust, steam, smell or other effluvia arising on industrial, trade or business premises and being prejudicial to health or a nuisance.

Sewage treatment works have been held to be "premises" under the statutory nuisance legislation, which means that local authorities can use nuisance abatement notices to curb odour pollution arising from them. In *Hounslow LBC v Thames Water Utilities Ltd*,[16] Hounslow Council had served notices on Thames Water (relying on the last-mentioned category—"smell or other effluvia") ordering it to abate nuisance from

---

[14] [2003] Env. L.R. 7.
[15] [1999] Env. L.R. 895.
[16] [2004] Q.B. 212.

odours and mosquitoes emanating from its Mogden sewage treatment works. The notices had been quashed by magistrates on the ground that sewage works did not constitute "premises" subject to control under the statutory nuisance regime. The High Court, however, held that smells from sewage treatment works were within the remit of the regime.

C: THE CLEAN AIR ACT 1993

10–010 The Clean Air Act 1993 controls the emission of smoke, grit and dust. It also allows the Secretary of State to make regulations with respect to fuels. It is important to note that the provisions relating to smoke, grit and dust do not apply to industrial installations subject to the PPC regime, discussed above.[17] They are therefore of very limited use in an industrial context. They remain important, however, in the context of preventing pollution from domestic (and some commercial) premises, for example by smoke from coal fires—one of chief causes of the urban smogs so prevalent in the past.

Control of smoke

10–011 Under the Act, it is a criminal offence to emit "dark smoke" from the chimney of any building[18] or from the chimney of a furnace serving any fixed boiler or industrial plant,[19] although the Secretary of State, by regulations, may exempt the emission of certain forms of smoke, during certain periods, from control under the Act.[20] "Dark smoke" is defined by the Act as smoke which is darker than shade two on the Ringlemann Chart.[21]

There are a number of defences to prosecution,[22] namely;

- That the emission in question was due solely to the lighting of a furnace which was cold and that all practicable steps had been taken to prevent the emission;

- That the emission was due to the failure of a furnace, or of apparatus used in connection with it, where that failure could not be reasonably foreseen and provided against, and where the emission could not reasonably have been prevented by action taken after the failure;

- That the emission was due solely to the use of an unsuitable fuel, provided that suitable fuel was not obtainable, that the least unsuitable available fuel was used, and that all practicable steps were taken to prevent or minimise the emission resulting from the use of that fuel.

For commercial organisations, a "catch-all" section is provided in the Act, which makes it an offence to cause or permit the emission of dark smoke from industrial or

---

[17] CAA 1993, s.41A.
[18] CAA 1993, s.1(1).
[19] *ibid.*, s.1(2).
[20] See: Dark Smoke (Permitted Periods) Regulations 1958 (SI 1958/498).
[21] CAA 1993, s.3(1).
[22] *ibid.*, s.1(4).

trade premises (*i.e.* otherwise than by way of a chimney).[23] The Act further provides that in proceedings for an offence there shall be taken to have been an emission of dark smoke unless the defendant proves that no dark smoke was emitted. In *Sheffield CC v ADH Demolition Ltd*,[24] the court was prepared to attach a wide meaning to the phrase "trade or industrial premises", holding that it covered a demolition site. In any event, trade premises also includes farmland.[25] Under the "catch-all" provision, it is a defence for the accused to show that the emission in question was caused inadvertently and that all practicable steps were taken to minimise the emission.[26] The Act defines "practicable" so as to mean reasonably practicable, having regard, inter alia, to local conditions, the current state of technical knowledge, and to the financial implications for the defendant.[27]

In *O'Fee v Copeland BC*,[28] the defendant appealed against a conviction for emitting dark smoke, arguing that there was no evidence that the smoke went beyond the boundaries of his premises. Whilst the court was prepared to accept that an "emission" must mean a movement of the smoke above the surface of the ground within the boundaries of premises, it held that the prosecution need not prove that the smoke had travelled beyond the premises from which it had been emitted, because the purpose of the Clean Air Act 1993 was to abate air pollution *per se*, not simply air pollution which had travelled to neighbouring property.

The installation of furnaces

A furnace which has been properly built and installed should not emit smoke. **10–012** Therefore, the Act provides that no furnace may be installed in any building, or in any fixed boiler or industrial plant, unless it is, so far as is reasonably practicable, capable of being operated continuously without emitting smoke,[29] and unless notice of the proposal to install it has been given to the local authority.[30] Installing a furnace in contravention of these provisions is an offence. The provisions do not apply to domestic furnaces.

Grit and dust

The Act provides that the Secretary of State may, by regulations, prescribe limits for **10–013** the emission of grit and dust from industrial furnaces.[31] Under the regulations, where no limits have been prescribed, the occupier of the building in which the furnace is operated is placed under a general duty to minimise the emission of grit and dust. The Act also provides that industrial furnaces which burn certain types of fuel, or which operate at certain capacities, are to be fitted with grit arrestment plant.[32] In relation to

[23] *ibid.*, s.2.
[24] (1983) 82 L.G.R. 177.
[25] See *O'Fee v Copeland BC* (below).
[26] CAA 1993, s.2(4).
[27] *ibid.*, s.64(4).
[28] [1996] Env L.R. 66.
[29] CAA 1993, s.4(2).
[30] *ibid.*, s.4(1).
[31] See Clean Air (Emission of Grit and Dust From Furnaces) Regulations 1971, (SI 1971/162).
[32] CAA 1993, s.6(1) See also Clean Air (Arrestment Plant) (Exemption) Regulations 1969 (SI 1969/1262).

domestic furnaces, it is an offence to burn pulverised fuel without local authority approved grit arrestment plant fitted, and to burn any other form of solid fuel, or solid waste, at a rate of 1.02 tonnes an hour or more without such plant.[33]

The height of chimneys

10–014 The height of furnace chimneys has a direct effect on the rate at which pollutants are dispersed. The Clean Air Act 1993 therefore provides that it is an offence for the occupier of any building in which a furnace is situated knowingly to cause or permit the burning of pulverised fuel, or the burning of other fuels at certain rates, without prior approval of the furnace's chimney height by the local authority.[34] Under the Act, the local authority may not approve the height of a chimney unless it is satisfied that it is sufficient to prevent, so far as is reasonably practicable, the emission of smoke, grit, dust, gases or fumes from becoming prejudicial to health or a nuisance, having regard, *inter alia*, to the chimney's purpose, the position and description of buildings near it, and the level of neighbouring ground.[35]

Smoke control areas

10–015 The Beaver Committee, which was set up to investigate the causes of the London smog in 1952, found that half of the smoke in the UK came from domestic chimneys. It therefore recommended the establishment of "smoke control areas". This recommendation was implemented by the Clean Air Act 1956, which was consolidated by the Clean Air Act 1993. Under this Act, local authorities have the power to make an order declaring that either the whole or part of its area is a "Smoke Control Area".[36] The emission of any smoke from a chimney within such an area is an offence.[37] It is a defence to prosecution, however, for the defendant to show that the emission was not caused by the use of any fuel other than an "authorised fuel".[38] The local authority, or the Secretary of State, may limit the scope of the order so that certain types of buildings, or smoke emitted from certain types of fireplaces, are exempt from the order.[39] In addition, the local authority can compel the occupier of premises to adapt an existing fireplace so as to comply with the order (for example, by replacing a metal grate with a thicker one which can withstand the extra heat generated by the burning of smokeless fuel).[40] The local authority has a duty to make a financial grant to the occupier of any "old private dwelling" (built before August 15, 1964) to cover at least 70 per cent of the costs of such an adaptation.[41] It may also reimburse the occupiers of certain buildings used for the advancement of religion, education or social welfare for the costs of adaptation.[42] Whilst the provisions relating to smoke control areas apply to

---

[33] CAA 1993, s.8.
[34] *ibid.*, s.14. See also Clean Air (Height of Chimneys) (Exemption) Regulations 1969, (SI 1969/411).
[35] CAA 1993, s.15.
[36] *ibid.*, s.18.
[37] *ibid.*, s.20.
[38] *ibid.*, s.20(4).
[39] *ibid.*, s.18(2); Smoke Control Areas (Exempted Fireplaces) Order 1991 (SI 1991/2892).
[40] *ibid.*, s.24.
[41] *ibid.*, s.25.
[42] *ibid.*, s.26.

both commercial and domestic premises, they do not apply to industrial processes which have been prescribed for control under the PPC regime.

The composition of fuels

Under the Act, the Secretary of State may make regulations prescribing the content of **10–016** any kind of motor fuel for the purpose of reducing air pollution. Such regulations have been made prescribing limits for the content of sulphur and of lead in petrol.[43] For the same purpose, the Secretary of State can impose limits on the sulphur content of oil fuel which is used in furnaces or engines.[44]

D: OTHER FORMS OF AIR POLLUTION CONTROL

Straw and stubble burning

The burning of agricultural crop residues causes environmental problems not only for **10–017** residents in agricultural areas, but also for motorists using roads in those areas. Therefore, under the Environmental Protection Act 1990, the Secretary of State may make regulations prohibiting or restricting the practice.[45] The Crop Residues (Burning) Regulations 1993[46] have been made under this provision.

Vehicle emissions

The law on vehicle emissions, which implements emission standards set largely by the **10–018** EC, is subject to continual review. In addition to the regulations prescribing the content of motor fuel made under the Clean Air Act 1993, the Secretary of State has also made certain regulations relating to the emissions of newly produced vehicles.[47] The various Road Vehicle (Construction and Use) Regulations, made under road traffic legislation, prescribe certain emission limits for different categories of vehicles currently in use. They also regulate the use of catalytic convertors and of unleaded petrol by certain vehicles. Older vehicles, subject to annual MOT testing, must comply with emission standards in relation to smoke and carbon monoxide.

Planning controls

The planning system can also help to improve air quality. Ch. 13 considers the **10–019** planning regime and its relationship with pollution control. Air quality can be a material consideration in any decision whether to grant planning permission, as well as in preparing development plans.

---

[43] *ibid.*, s.30; Motor Fuel (Sulphur Content of Gas Oil) Regulations 1976 (SI 1976/1989) (as amended by SI 1990/1097), and Motor Fuel (Lead Content of Petrol) Regulations 1981 (SI 1981/1523) (as amended by SI 1985/1728).
[44] CAA 1993, s.31; Oil Fuel (Sulphur Content of Gas Oil) Regulations 1990 (SI 1990/1096).
[45] EPA 1990, s.152.
[46] Crop Residues (Burning) Regulations 1993 SI 1993/1366.
[47] Motor Vehicles (Type Approval) (Great Britain) Regulations 1994, (SI 1994/981).

E: EC AIR POLLUTION LAW

10–020 Air pollution has formed a significant part of EC environmental policy since the mid 1980s, when a growing awareness of the dangers posed by acid rain prompted the development of European "air quality standards" prescribing the maximum concentrations of particular substances permitted to be present in the atmosphere at ground level at given times. A number of Directives set mandatory emissions standards for sulphur dioxide and smoke,[48] and for lead[49] and nitrogen dioxide.[50]

In 1988 the Directive on emissions from large combustion plants[51] was adopted, giving effect to the aim of the EC's Fourth Environmental Action Programme to reduce emission levels at source. Rather than impose specific fixed emission limits for the release of particular substances from particular processes, the Directive imposes a general overall limit on the amount of substances which may be released from power stations and other large combustion plants such as refinery boilers and large industrial boilers. Member States are thereby given some flexibility in ensuring that these limits are complied with, since they may permit greater releases for certain processes, or in certain areas, and less in others.

The Air Quality Framework Directive

10–021 In 1994, a review of the effectiveness of the EC's air quality Directives, undertaken by the Commission, identified a number of problems. Member States were taking too long to comply with the air quality standards required by the Directives. The UK, for example, had made maximum use of the derogation provisions provided in the 1980 Directive on smoke and sulphur dioxide, so that the relevant standards were not complied with until 1993. In addition, there were large differences between Member States in the extent to which air quality was monitored. In 1992, the UK was criticised by the European Commission for having just seven nitrogen dioxide monitoring sites, some of which were situated well away from traffic. The existing Directives had failed to achieve full harmonisation of air quality measurement methods in Member States.

As a result of these findings, the Council adopted the Air Quality Framework Directive in September 1996.[52] This Directive establishes a framework under which the EC will set limit values or target values for specified pollutants. The Directive has three main goals:

- to maintain the quality of air where it is good and to improve it where it is poor;

- to establish objectives for ambient air pollution control throughout the Community;

- to move towards closer harmonisation of national air quality measurement programmes and provide monitoring information to the public.

---

[48] Directive 80/779/EEC [1980] O.J. L229/30.
[49] Directive 82/884/EEC [1982] O.J. L378/15.
[50] Directive 85/203/EEC [1985] O.J. L87/1.
[51] Directive 88/609/EEC [1988] O.J. L336/1.
[52] Council Dir.96/62/EC of September 27, 1996 on ambient air quality assessment and management.

The Directive identifies 12 pollutants for which limit or target values will be set in subsequent daughter Directives (sulphur dioxide, nitrogen dioxide, particulate matter, lead, carbon monoxide, benzene, ozone, polycyclic aromatic hydrocarbons, cadmium, arsenic, nickel and mercury).

The extent to which these broad objectives will be fulfilled depends on the content of "daughter" Directives, designed to establish specific requirements on air sampling and air quality measurement techniques, as well to prescribe new air quality standards. Under the Framework Directive, daughter Directives are to be drawn up in relation to twenty different substances (including those already covered by existing Directives, which the new daughter Directives will replace). The first air quality daughter Directive establishes legally binding limit values for sulphur dioxide, nitrogen dioxide, particles and lead, to be achieved by 2010.[53] A further daughter Directive sets limit values for benzene and carbon monoxide, and two more set target (rather than limit) values for ozone, and national emissions ceilings for various pollutants.[54] The European Commission has started work on proposals for the remaining five pollutants. The various requirements of the daughter Directives are implemented in the UK by the Air Quality Limit Values Regulations 2003.[55]

The Auto-Oil Programme

Since 1993, vehicle emissions and fuel quality standards have been tightened, with the **10–022** purpose of improving air quality. Stringent emission standards for cars and light vans (known as "Euro III standards") apply to all new vehicles sold from January 1, 2001. From January 1, 2006, further stringent standards ("Euro IV standards") will apply. In addition, tighter fuel quality specifications apply to all petrol and diesel sold from January 1, 2000 and 2005 respectively. A ban on the general marketing of leaded petrol was introduced from January 1, 2000.[56] The expectation is that by 2005, the Directives will significantly reduce emissions from road transport of particles, nitrogen dioxide, carbon monoxide, lead, benzene, hydrocarbons and volatile organic compounds (VOCs), despite forecast traffic growth.[57] Also part of the Auto-Oil Programme is a Directive establishing more stringent emission standards for heavy-duty diesel engines used in lorries, buses and refuse collection vehicles.[58]

Acidification

The Community's acidification strategy aims to further reduce emissions of sulphur **10–023** dioxide, nitrogen oxides and ammonia beyond existing commitments, thereby reducing the extent to which ecosystems within the EU are at risk from acid rain. The strategy is implemented by the following three legislative measures:

[53] Directive 99/30/EC relating to limit values for sulphur dioxide, nitrogen dioxide and oxides of nitrogen, particulate matter and lead in ambient air.
[54] Directive 2000/69/EC relating to limit values for benzene and carbon monoxide in ambient air, and Dir.2002/3/EC relating to ozone in ambient air.
[55] SI 2003/2121
[56] Directive 98/70/EC.
[57] See National Air Quality Management Strategy.
[58] Directive 2001/27/EC.

- The Directive on the sulphur content of certain liquid fuels.[59] This sets maximum levels for the sulphur content of heavy fuel oil;

- Amendments to the Directive on large combustion plant[60];

- The Directive on national emissions ceilings and ozone.[61] This is the primary means of implementing the Acidification Strategy and also of making progress on the problem of ground-level ozone. Ceilings are set for national emissions of sulphur dioxide, nitrogen dioxide, ammonia and volatile organic compounds (VOCs) to be attained by 2010.

The Solvents Directive

10–024   Directive 1999/13/EC aims to reduce emissions of volatile organic compounds (VOCs) from certain industrial installations by around 57 per cent by 2007, compared with a 1990 baseline. VOCs contribute to the formation of ozone. The Directive specifies emission limits, or the use of a reduction scheme, for each process in each of the industrial sectors covered. Member States must implement the Directive either by applying the emission limits, or through a national plan. However, certain VOCs which are carcinogenic, mutagenic or toxic to reproduction, must be controlled through emission limits. The Directive introduces to other EC Member States similar standards to those already required in the UK under the PPC regime.

The Integrated Pollution Prevention and Control (IPPC) Directive

10–025   The IPPC Directive, adopted in 1996, is, of course, the principal EC mechanism by which air pollution is controlled. To a large extent, the regime of control prescribed by the Directive mirrors the IPC regime in the UK that was put in place by Pt I of the Environmental Protection Act 1990. There are, however, some important differences. These are explored in Ch. 5. Here, it is relevant to note that a wider range of installations are covered by the Directive than were covered by the UK's IPC regime, and that, under the Directive, permit conditions must be included, where appropriate, to address transboundary pollution arising from industrial processes. The Directive, and the PPC Regulations 2000 which implement it, require individual industrial plants to take necessary measures to comply with relevant EC emission limit values set out in the air quality daughter Directives.

F: International Air Pollution Law

10–026   The movement of air does not, of course, confine itself to within national borders. Given the mobile nature of air pollution, the problems of acid rain, depletion of the ozone layer and global warming which it causes require an international response.

---

[59] Directive 1999/32/EC.
[60] Directive 2001/80/EC.
[61] Directive 2001/81/EC.

Acid rain and transboundary pollution

Acid rain is caused mainly when nitrogen dioxide and sulphur dioxide, produced by the **10–027** burning of fossil fuels in power stations and in car engines, combine with atmospheric water vapour. This vapour can often be blown thousands of miles before it falls as rain. Acid rain has caused the decline of forests in Central and Eastern Europe, and many lakes in Scandinavia and Canada are now incapable of supporting life because of acidification.[62]

The 1979 Convention on Long Range Transboundary Air Pollution[63] imposes a widely-phrased obligation on contracting states to develop policies and strategies to combat air pollution "by means of exchanges of information, consultation, research and monitoring". Protocols made under the Convention establish the substance of these obligations, including the financing of air pollution reduction programmes and reduction programmes in respect of particular pollutants including sulphur dioxide and nitrogen oxides. The 1991 Protocol on Volatile Organic Compounds is concerned with organic compounds emitted through incomplete combustion of fossil fuels, particularly in car engines. It is a more sophisticated instrument than the previous protocols and establishes specific targets and timetables for the reduction of emissions, whilst allowing contracting states to do so by methods of their own choosing.

The Persistent Organic Pollutants (POPs) Protocol, signed in June 1998, aims to control, reduce or eliminate discharges of POPs to the environment. One of these is Polycyclic Aromatic Hydrocarbon (PAH). Any future UK PAH objective, introduced under the National Air Quality Strategy, will take this Protocol into account. The Heavy Metals Protocol, also signed in June 1998, addresses atmospheric emissions of cadmium, lead and mercury. The emission limits it establishes for these metals are either already achieved or easily achievable by EC Member States. Its significance lies in its provisions for adding other metals and controls in future, if international action is required. In December 1999, the UK signed the new Protocol to abate acidification, eutrophication and ground level ozone. The Protocol covers nitrogen dioxide, VOCs, sulphur dioxide and ammonia for the wider European region (rather than the EU) and sets ceilings for these pollutants.

Depletion of the ozone layer

The ozone layer, which is defined as "the layer of atmospheric ozone above the **10–028** planetary boundary layer",[64] filters sunlight and protects the earth from ultra-violet radiation. Excessive exposure to ultra-violet radiation is dangerous to all forms of life. In humans, it increases the likelihood of skin cancer, cataracts and tumours. It can also suppress the immune system, increasing the likelihood of epidemic disease. In plant and animal life, mutations may occur, reducing crop yields and altering the ecosystem. In terms of secondary effects, depletion of the ozone layer is likely to cause an increase in acid rain and in levels of urban ozone (smog). It also contributes to global warming.

---

[62] *Europe's Environment: The Dobris Assessment* (eds David Stanners and Philippe Bourdeau) (European Environment Agency, 1995).
[63] 18 I.L.M. 1442 (1979).
[64] Convention on the Protection of the Ozone Layer, March 22, 1985, Vienna, 26 I.L.M. 1529 (1987), Art. 1.

The ozone layer is depleted by the presence in the atmosphere of carbons, chlorofluorocarbons (CFCs) and other chlorine-based substances. Evidence of ozone depletion in this way emerged in the 1980s. A "hole" in the ozone layer was identified above Antarctica and losses in ozone were also recorded in the Arctic. Unusually high levels of ultra-violet radiation have been recorded in Antarctica, Australia and in mountainous parts of Europe.

The 1985 Convention for the Protection of the Ozone Layer[65] required contracting states to formulate agreed standards with respect to ozone-depleting substances. This Convention was essentially a framework which provided scope for further action. The substantive obligations of states were set out in the Montreal Protocol on Substances that Deplete the Ozone Layer, which entered into force in January 1989. This established a timetable for reducing emissions of substances such as CFCs and set deadlines by which the consumption and production of these substances within states was to be reduced to specified levels.

The Protocol has been strengthened by a number of subsequent "adjustments", agreed at conferences of the parties (London 1990; Copenhagen 1992; Vienna 1995; and Montreal 1997). The effect of these adjustments was to impose a prohibition on the production and consumption of ozone-depleting substances in developed countries from January 1996. Developing states are subject to extended deadlines for the various substances in question. Because ozone-depleting substances persist in the environment for a very long time, however, ozone depletion is expected to continue well into this century and beyond.

Climate change

10–029 Climate change, or "global warming", is mainly caused by the presence in the atmosphere of carbon dioxide, CFCs, methane and nitrogen oxides. These pollutants trap long wave radiation emitted by the earth's surface and prevent it from escaping, causing the earth to warm up (the "greenhouse effect"). Climate change is discussed in Ch. 3.

---

[65] 26 I.L.M. 1529 (1987).

Chapter 11

POLLUTION BY NOISE

"Noise policy in the UK and Europe is undergoing a radical change. As a result of the recent Environmental Noise Directive, we and our European partners will be required to assess environmental noise exposure levels for our populations, to map local areas and to produce appropriate action plans."[1]

Introduction

Noise pollution is one of the fastest growing environmental concerns. Although, in **11–001** contrast with other pollutants, noise does not persist in the environment and seldom leaves physical scars, its consequences can be catastrophic. In September 1994, for example, a fire bomb was thrown into the home of a noisy neighbour, causing his death. In Europe, noise is estimated to affect the health and quality of life of at least 25 per cent of the EU population. It raises stress levels, disrupts sleep, and can lead to an increased risk of heart disease. Much of the problem relates to transport and construction activity—there has been an increase in rail, road and air traffic, and in the use of construction equipment.[2] In the twelve-month period ending March 31, 2001, there were over 230,000 complaints about noise nuisance in England and Wales, as compared with 111,515 between 1992 and 1993, and just over 31,000 complaints in 1980.[3] Noise pollution may be distinguished from other forms of pollution, in that its effects relate primarily to human health and comfort, as opposed to causing damage to the wider environment.

Definition of noise

Noise has been variously defined as: "sound which is undesired by the recipient",[4] and **11–002** as: "a number of tonal components disagreeable to man and more or less intolerable to him because of the discomfort, fatigue, disturbance and, in some cases, pain it

---

[1] Caroline Season, DEFRA, "UK and EU Noise Policy—An Overview", *www.defra.gov.uk/environment/ noise.*
[2] Sixth Environmental Action Programme COM/2001/0031 final.
[3] DEFRA: *www.defra.gov.uk/environment/noise.* Older statistics can be found in the report of the Neighbour Noise Working Party (DoE, March 1995).
[4] Final Report of the Parliamentary Committee on the Problem of Noise, 1963.

causes".[5] *In Hatton v United Kingdom* (discussed in Ch. 14) the dissenting judges in the European Court of Human Rights were prepared to hold that night-time aircraft noise causing sleep deprivation could be equivalent to torture and inhumane or degrading treatment.[6]

These definitions illustrate the subjectivity of noise pollution. A sound that may be acceptable in an industrial area may become "noise" if it is present in a residential area. What may be an acceptable sound during the day may become a noise at night. Music in a nightclub may exhilarate the individual who then finds it unbearable when he is trying to sleep in the house next door. A sound of small intensity, such as that from a dripping tap, may become unbearable simply by its repetition. The subjectivity of noise pollution, then, makes it very difficult to tackle by traditional legal mechanisms, which usually set objective criteria as to when and at what level pollutants should be controlled.

A: LEGAL CONTROL OF NOISE

International law

11–003 International law on noise pollution is limited—which is perhaps to be expected, given the local and limited effects of noise pollution. However, some international conventions provide for control of noise pollution in the context of their wider objectives. For example, the Working Environment (Air Pollution, Noise and Vibration) Convention 1977 of the International Labour Organisation (ILO) relates to working conditions, and therefore encompasses noise. The Convention on International Civil Aviation 1947 considers aircraft noise in an annex. The ILO Convention Concerning the Prohibition and Elimination of the Worst Forms of Child Labour, and its accompanying 1999 Recommendation, includes, within its concept of the worst forms of child labour, work which exposes children to noise levels and vibration damaging to their health.

EC law

11–004 At EC level, legislation is considerably more developed, with both a general and sectoral approach.

Directive 2002/49/EC on the assessment and management of environmental noise, which came into force on June 25, 2002, provides controls over "environmental" noise. It applies to "environmental noise to which humans are exposed in particular in built-up areas, in public parks or other quiet areas . . . near schools, hospitals and other noise-sensitive buildings". "Environmental noise" is defined as "unwanted or harmful outdoor sound created by human activities", including noise emitted by road, rail and

---

[5] Second European Community Action Programme on the Environment (1977–1981), O.J. C139.
[6] *Hatton and Others v United Kingdom* (2003) 37 E.H.R.R. 28. See also *Ireland v United Kingdom,* where the Court found that ". . . holding the detainees in a room where there was a continuous loud and hissing noise . . ." constituted a practice of inhuman and degrading treatment.

air traffic, and by large industrial sites (including those covered by the IPPC Directive). Noise created by domestic activities, by neighbours, or by military activity is expressly put beyond the scope of the Directive, as is noise in the workplace or inside means of transport.

The Directive lays down requirements for Member States to implement various measures to tackle environmental noise, and sets deadlines by which appropriate measures must have been put in place. Member States must create "noise maps" for all major roads and built-up areas by June 2007. By July 2008, action plans must have been drawn up to manage noise issues.

Directive 2000/14/EC on noise from equipment for use outdoors covers reduction of noise from outdoor equipment (such as lawnmowers) and provides sectoral control of noise from particular sources (discussed further below).

UK law

Legal controls in the UK have traditionally divided noise into various categories, such **11–005** as neighbourhood noise, noise on construction sites and transport noise. DEFRA usually classifies noise according to its sources, as follows:

- domestic premises;
- industrial and commercial premises;
- road works and construction;
- road traffic;
- aircraft.

Noise may be controlled in a number of ways: at the point of its generation, during its transmission, or at the point of its reception by the hearer. The prevention of noise at source, rather than subsequently trying to counteract its effects, is acknowledged as the best answer to the problem, but this, for technical or financial reasons, is often not possible.[7] Preventive controls can be implemented by designating geographical zones where noise cannot go above a certain level. Noise may be controlled during its transmission by sound-proofing buildings and by enclosing noisy machinery. Control of noise at the point of its reception by the hearer may be exercised through development plans designed to keep noise away from residential areas, as well as through transport policy, for example by the control of aircraft flight paths.

Legal regulation of noise in the UK is somewhat disparate. It is achieved through the common law of nuisance and by a number of statutes including the Control of Pollution Act 1974, the Civil Aviation Act 1982, the Road Traffic Act 1988, the Environmental Protection Act 1990, the Noise and Statutory Nuisance Act 1993 and the Noise Act 1996. Despite relatively recent statutory intervention in the field of noise, the opportunity has not been taken to create a comprehensive regime of noise control.

[7] See the First European Community Action Programme on the Environment [1973] O.J. C112.

Unlike other pollutants, noise does not affect areas remote from its source. For this reason, local authorities, who have knowledge of local conditions, are the main agencies involved in combating noise pollution. The traditional legal response to noise has been to employ the concept of nuisance, first in the common law, and later through the development of a simpler "statutory nuisance" procedure. Whilst nuisance remains at the heart of the legal framework, a number of preventive controls have been devised which do not rely on the concept. This chapter concentrates on *ex post facto* control of neighbourhood noise through the statutory nuisance procedure, but also examines the role of preventive measures used to control such things as construction and transport noise.

Ambient noise

11–006   "Ambient noise" is noise in the general public environment, as opposed, for example, to noise in workplaces, or noise created by neighbours. Pursuant to the Environmental Noise Directive referred to above, the UK government completed a consultation in respect of a National Ambient Noise Strategy in 2002. The strategy includes mapping and action plans. A noise map has already been completed for Birmingham as a pilot project in 1999, showing sound contours not only for road traffic, but for other sources of ambient noise, including aircraft, trains and industrial sites. The strategy proposed a national noise mapping exercise between 2002 and 2004, followed by a second phase between 2004 and 2006, designed to evaluate techniques for assessing and mitigating noise pollution. The final phase will see the preparation of the formal National Noise Strategy document, but this will not take place until 2007.

Neighbourhood noise

11–007   "Neighbourhood noise" was defined by the Noise Advisory Council in 1972 as: "the great variety of sources of noise which may cause disturbance and annoyance to the general public not including road traffic and aircraft noise and industrial noise affecting workers".[8] However, much of what was formerly regarded as "neighbourhood noise" is now included within the definition of "environmental noise" in Directive 2002/49 (above). It may therefore be convenient to think of "neighbourhood noise" more literally, as simply "noise caused by noisy neighbours". As we have seen, the Directive specifically excludes such noise from its scope. However, the extent of overlap between "environmental noise" (which the Directive covers) and "noise made by neighbours" (which it does not) is left unclear by the wording of the Directive.[9] This is because, in respect of industrial noise, the definition of "environmental noise" contained in the Directive is couched in terms of noise from "heavy industry" sites regulated by the IPPC regime. This leaves open the possibility that noise from small-scale, local industry might be regarded as "noise made by neighbours" and therefore beyond the Directive's scope.

Examples of neighbourhood noise, then, clearly include noise from domestic activities such as playing sound systems or watching television at high volumes. In

---

[8] Report of the Noise Advisory Council, 1972, p.11, paras 54 and 55.
[9] See Art. 2.

addition, examples might include local industrial noise, for example the sound of refrigeration plant emanating from butchers' shops and supermarkets, or the noise caused by use of such things as drop hammers, riveting machines and extractor fans. Neighbourhood noise is the greatest source of noise nuisance complaints in England and Wales. The National Noise Survey 2002 asked local authorities to provide information about the nature of neighbourhood noise complaints received. Amplified music was the most common cause of complaint (95 per cent of authorities listed it in the top three causes). Barking dogs was the second most common cause of complaint, followed by noise from televisions and noise from voices.

In 2002, the government launched a study into neighbourhood noise. This study was designed as the first step in developing a "Neighbour Noise Strategy" to run in parallel with the National Ambient Noise Strategy under Directive 2002/49 mentioned above. Currently, the main way of controlling these problems is by securing abatement of the noise once it has exceeded nuisance levels. This can be achieved either through a common law action or through the statutory nuisance procedure under Pt III of the Environmental Protection Act 1990. In exceptional circumstances, *prevention* of noise can also be achieved through these mechanisms, as where an injunction is sought at common law, or where an abatement order is issued under Pt III to prohibit an anticipated nuisance. In practice, the law on statutory nuisances is one of the most important legal tools for combating noise nuisance.

B: Noise as a Statutory Nuisance

Under Pt III of the Environmental Protection Act 1990, the regime of control is **11–008** activated by the occurrence, or by the likely occurrence, of a statutory nuisance. The Act sets out various heads of statutory nuisance.[10] In relation to noise, the following heads are relevant:

- noise emitted from premises so as to be prejudicial to health or a nuisance[11];
- any other matter declared by any enactment to be a statutory nuisance.[12]

The Noise Review Working Party considered that one of the main drawbacks of existing legislation was that local authorities could not control noise in the street. Therefore, by the Noise and Statutory Nuisance Act 1993, the Environmental Protection Act 1990 was amended so as to include a new category of statutory nuisance, namely noise that is prejudicial to health or a nuisance and is emitted from or caused by a vehicle, machinery or equipment in the street.[13]

Statutory definition of "noise"

The Environmental Protection Act 1990 does not define noise, except to say that it **11–009** includes vibration.[14] The Act also provides an example of noise when it states that the statutory nuisance provisions do not apply to noise caused by aircraft other than model aircraft.[15]

[10] EPA 1990, s.79(1).
[11] EPA 1990, s.79(1)(g).
[12] *ibid.*, s.79(1)(h).
[13] 1990, s.79(1)(ga). (Inserted by Noise and Statutory Nuisance Act 1993.)
[14] EPA 1990, s.79(7).
[15] *ibid.*, s.79(6).

The meaning of "statutory nuisance"

11–010 The word "nuisance" is not defined by the Act, but is traditionally thought to bear the same meaning as it has at common law. There may be some minor differences, however, between statutory and common law nuisances. In particular, in contrast to the position at common law, it may not be necessary for a statutory nuisance to emanate from premises other than those occupied and enjoyed by the person who is affected by the nuisance. In *Carr v Hackney BC*,[16] it was argued that a statutory nuisance had been created by the local council when its tenants found damp and mould in their house. Although, on the facts, the council were not liable for the damp, the court proceeded on the basis that the matters complained of could constitute a "nuisance", and failed to address the question of whether this could properly be the case even though the damp could not be said to have resulted from one person's activity on his own land which interfered with enjoyment of land by another. The approach adopted in *Carr*, then, may be an indication that the courts are prepared to attach a different, wider, meaning to the word "nuisance" as it appears in Pt III of the Environmental Protection Act 1990.

However, in *Birmingham City Council v Oakley*,[17] the House of Lords ruled that it was not a statutory nuisance for a local authority to provide housing in which the lavatory lacked a washbasin. It was held that there was nothing in the premises themselves which was prejudicial to health, and any prejudice to health would be a result of a failure to wash hands, or would result from use of the sink in the kitchen or the bathroom sink, which was accessed through the kitchen. This ruling that an arrangement of rooms was not, in itself, a statutory nuisance clearly places a limit on the scope of statutory nuisance which might be significant in a noise context.

It appears that notions of common law nuisance do not *necessarily* inform the meaning of statutory nuisance under s.79 of the EPA 1990. Indeed, it was said in *Hounslow BC v Thames Water Utilities*[18] that the definition of nuisance for the purpose of that section had been completely recast by the Act. Pitchford J. noted that the long title of the Act made it clear that Parliament's intention had been to restate the law. His Lordship added that the procedure provided by s.79 was not an exclusive procedure, and that private individuals and public authorities had other means by which to seek the cessation of common law nuisances, but that those alternative remedies did not inform the construction of s.79 of the Act.[19]

"Prejudicial to health"

11–011 Under the Act, proceedings may be brought where the act complained of is "prejudicial to health or a nuisance". It is not, therefore, necessary for the complainant to make out in every case that the act complained of is prejudicial to his health, but there will be many circumstances in which he will be able to do this. The Act defines "prejudicial to health" as "injurious or likely to cause injury, to health".[20]

[16] [1995] 93 L.G.R. 606.
[17] [2001] 1 All E.R. 385.
[18] [2004] Q.B. 212.
[19] *ibid.*, at paras 51 and 52.
[20] EPA 1990, s.79(7).

In broad terms, noise might be said to be prejudicial to health when it prevents sleep, induces stress, disturbs concentration, or interferes with communication so as to affect personal safety, for example by making it impossible for cries for help to be heard. Studies in Germany, Japan and the Netherlands suggest that the growth of the foetus may be inhibited, and the birth weight of babies reduced, by exposure to high levels of aircraft noise during pregnancy.[21]

"Premises"

"Premises" are defined by the Act to include land and any vessel,[22] except one which is **11–012** powered by steam reciprocating machinery.[23] Since "premises" include "land", noise from a rave in a field, for example, will constitute noise from premises, as will noise from roads and railways.

"Street"

As mentioned, noise emitted from or caused by a vehicle, machinery or equipment in **11–013** the street is also a statutory nuisance. "Street" is defined as meaning a highway and any other road, footway, square or court that is for the time being open to the public.[24] Because "equipment" used in the street includes musical instruments, the noise made by buskers can constitute a statutory nuisance. Other examples of street noise regulated by the Act include noise from vehicles (including car alarms) and from vehicle repairs carried out in the road, as well as noise from machinery used in road-building, such as generators and air compressors.

The duties of local authorities

Every local authority is under a duty periodically to inspect its area for the presence of **11–014** statutory nuisances, and if a complaint is made to the authority by a person living within its area, the authority must take reasonably practicable steps to investigate that complaint.[25] If the local authority fails to do this, the Secretary of State may make an order declaring the local authority to be in default, and may direct the authority to carry out its duty in a specified manner.[26] If the local authority fails to comply with the order, the Secretary of State may transfer the relevant functions of the authority to himself, or he may seek an order of mandamus (a public law remedy which compels a public body to perform its functions) from the High Court.[27]

Where the local authority is "satisfied" that a statutory nuisance exists, or is likely to occur or recur in its area, it is under a duty to serve an abatement notice. The

---

[21] Royal Commission on Environmental Pollution, Eighteenth Report: *Transport and the Environment*, 1994, Cm. 2674, p.48.

[22] EPA 1990, s.79(7).

[23] *ibid.*, s.79(12).

[24] *ibid.*, s.79(4)(c) (inserted by the Noise and Statutory Nuisance Act 1993).

[25] EPA 1990, s.79(1).

[26] *ibid.*, Sch.3, para.4.

[27] *ibid.*, Sch.3, para.4(3).

appropriate standard for the authority to apply in determining whether the nuisance exists is the civil standard, namely the balance of probabilities, because although the criminal law may be used eventually to enforce the abatement notice, at the time of its service the proceedings are civil.

The decision in *R. v Carrick DC, Ex p. Shelley and Another*[28] has made it clear that once the authority has discovered the existence of a statutory nuisance, it has no discretion as to whether or not to serve a notice. The court held that the local authority had failed in its statutory duty when, in the light of complaints about pollution on its beaches, it resolved not to take any action, but merely to monitor the situation. In granting an application for judicial review of the authority's lack of action, the court held that the authority's inaction had not been based on a decision that there was no statutory nuisance (a judgment of fact which it would have been entitled to make); rather, it had been based on a decision that serving a notice was not appropriate (a judgment based on the exercise of discretion, which it did not possess.) It is to be noted that the wording of the section allows a local authority to serve an abatement notice even before the nuisance has commenced, in order to prevent it from occurring.

The abatement notice

11–015 The local authority must serve the abatement notice on the relevant person by delivering it to him personally, by leaving it at his proper address, or by sending it to him by post at that address.[29] The notice must inform the recipient that he has the right to appeal against it to a magistrates' court within 21 days.[30] The abatement notice may require the abatement of the nuisance by imposing a complete prohibition on the activity in question, or by restricting the occurrence of the activity. It may also require the execution of works necessary to abate the nuisance, such as soundproofing in the case of noise. The notice must also specify a time limit within which its requirements are to be carried out.[31]

There are no other statutory provisions specifying what the notice must contain. In accordance with general principles of administrative law, however, the notice must tell its recipient clearly what he has done wrong and what is required of him to remedy that wrong. Just how detailed may be the steps which a local authority requires the recipient to take has been considered by the courts. In *Wivenhoe Port v Colchester BC*,[32] an abatement order, served under similar legislation which predated the Environmental Protection Act 1990, directed the company in question to use a specifically described cargo-handling system at all times. The court held that although the wording of the relevant legislation enabled a court to require the recipient of the order to undertake positive works to abate the nuisance (as does the current legislation), what was being asked for in this case went beyond "works", and that the legislation did not empower the authority to direct the company as to how it should carry out its day to day operations.

[28] *The Times*, June 15, 1996.
[29] Local Government Act 1972, s.233.
[30] EPA 1990, Sch.3, para.6.
[31] *ibid.*, s.80.
[32] [1985] J.P.L. 175

In *Network Housing Association Ltd v Westminster City Council*,[33] an abatement notice was held to be invalid when it stated that noise levels had to be reduced to a certain level of decibels, but did not say how this was to be achieved. The court held that although in some obvious cases a notice requiring little more than a reduction in noise levels might suffice, in the circumstances of this particular case, Westminster City Council should have made up their minds about the nature and extent of the works required and should have identified these in the notice. The court's decision was influenced by the fact that, whatever work was carried out, it would be practically impossible to measure or guarantee the results of that work in advance. Bearing in mind the risk of exposure to penal sanctions for non-compliance with the notice, it is essential that the appellant should be told clearly exactly what works he is required to undertake.

The notice must be served on the "person responsible for the nuisance", except in cases where he cannot be found, when it may be served on the owner or occupier of the premises on which the nuisance arises. This reflects the traditional rule that such persons are responsible for abating nuisances arising on their property. In cases where the nuisance is attributable to structural defects in premises, the notice should be served on the owner of those premises.[34] The "person responsible" for a statutory nuisance is defined by the Act as "the person to whose act, default or sufferance the nuisance is attributable".[35] Thus, the person responsible for inadequate soundproofing in a block of flats, so that tenants can hear the day to day living noises of their neighbours, is either the landlord (on the basis that the nuisance can be attributed to his default or sufferance) or the person who originally converted the building into flats (on the same basis).[36] The landlord may also receive an abatement notice simply because the nuisance arises from a structural defect in premises of which he is the owner. In *London Borough of Haringey v Jowett*,[37] however, the High Court held that the statutory nuisance provisions of the EPA 1990 can no longer be used to force landlords to provide improved sound insulation against general noise from traffic. This ruling was the result of the introduction of the Noise and Statutory Nuisance Act 1993, which inserted provisions into the EPA 1990 that excluded external traffic noise from being a potential statutory nuisance.[38]

Unattended vehicles, etc.

If the noise from a vehicle, or from machinery or equipment, which has been left **11–016** unattended in the street reaches nuisance levels, the abatement notice should be served on the person responsible for that vehicle, machinery or equipment. This will include the person in whose name a vehicle is, for the time being, registered and any other person who is for the time being the driver of the vehicle (or, where machinery or equipment are concerned, its operator).[39] The environmental health officer must

---

[33] [1995] Env. L.R. 176.
[34] EPA 1990, s.80(2).
[35] *ibid.*, s.79(7).
[36] *Network Housing Association Ltd v Westminster City Council* (1995) 93 L.G.R. 280.
[37] [2000] Env. L.R. D6.
[38] The Noise and Statutory Nuisance Act 1993 inserted s.79(1)(ga) and s.79(6)A into the EPA 1990.
[39] Noise and Statutory Nuisance Act 1993, s.2(4)(b).

spend one hour trying to trace the person responsible for the unattended vehicle, etc. so that he may be served with an abatement notice. Establishing the ownership of, or the identity of the person responsible for vehicles, machinery and equipment left unattended in the street can be difficult and time-consuming. The Noise and Statutory Nuisance Act 1993 therefore introduces an expedited procedure for the service of abatement notices in these circumstances. At the time of its introduction, the Department of the Environment (as it was then known) stated that this procedure was: "designed to balance the rights of an owner not to have his vehicle broken into, or his machinery interfered with, against the needs of those who live or work in the vicinity and who are suffering a noise nuisance".[40]

If, after an hour, the owner, driver or user of the vehicle, machinery or equipment cannot be found, the officer may affix the notice to the vehicle, etc. itself, and may then take whatever action he considers appropriate to abate the noise nuisance.[41] The environmental health officer has the power to open and enter, if necessary by force, any vehicle, machinery or equipment on the street, and to remove it to safe place if that is necessary to abate the noise.[42]

Appeal against the notice

11–017 The recipient of the notice has 21 days from the date the notice was served in which to appeal against it to a magistrates' court.[43] The grounds on which an appeal can be made to the magistrates' court include the following[44]:

- that the notice is not justified (*i.e.* that there is no nuisance);
- that there is some informality, defect or error in the notice;
- that the authority has unreasonably refused to accept an offer to comply with alternative requirements in abating the nuisance, or that the requirements set out in the abatement notice are unreasonable or unnecessary;
- that the time limit for completion of works specified in the notice is unreasonably short;
- where the nuisance consists of noise from construction works, that those works are the subject of a consent or notice issued under the Control of Pollution Act 1974;
- that the notice has been served on the wrong person.

The magistrates may either dismiss the appeal or may quash or vary the abatement notice.

Failure to comply with the notice

11–018 A person on whom an abatement notice has been served commits a criminal offence if he fails to comply with its requirements without reasonable excuse.[45] The offence is triable only in a magistrates' court, where the maximum penalty is a £5,000 fine,

[40] Guidance on the Noise and Statutory Nuisance Act 1993 (DoE, December 1993).
[41] EPA 1990, s.80A (inserted by the Noise and Statutory Nuisance Act 1993).
[42] EPA 1990, Sch.3, para.2A (inserted by Noise and Statutory Nuisance Act 1993).
[43] EPA 1990, s.80(3).
[44] See the Environmental Protection (Statutory Nuisance) (Appeals) Regulations 1990, as amended by the Statutory Nuisance (Appeals) Regulations 1995 (SI 1995/2644).
[45] EPA 1990, s.80(4).

together with further fines of £500 in respect of each day on which the defendant remains in default after conviction.[46] Although the defendant may be able to avail himself of the defence of "best practicable means" (below), it has been held that lack of finance is not a reasonable excuse for failing to comply with an abatement notice,[47] nor is the fact the nuisance constitutes music at a birthday celebration to which the neighbours have all been invited![48]

The local authority has a discretion whether or not to bring a prosecution for failure to comply with an abatement notice. Whether or not it chooses to do so, however, the local authority may itself take action to abate the nuisance and may recover the cost of so doing from the person responsible for the nuisance (or from the person who owns or occupies the premises on which the nuisance arose).[49]

The "best practicable means" defence

If the noise which constitutes a statutory nuisance is made on industrial, trade or **11–019** business premises (or, if a noise in the street, is the result of a business, trade or local industry), it is a defence for the accused to show that the "best practicable means" were used to prevent or to counteract the effects of the nuisance.[50]

"Practicable" means reasonably practicable having regard, amongst other things, to local conditions and circumstances, to the current state of technical knowledge, and to the financial implications of the means employed.[51] The "means" which may be employed to abate the nuisance include the design, installation, maintenance of plant and machinery, as well as the manner and the length of time for which it is operated. They also include the design, construction and maintenance of buildings and structures.[52] In practice, a defendant's raising the defence of best practicable means may pose serious problems for local authorities, who lack the information and investigative resources to refute the defendant's claims.

Proceedings in the High Court

If the local authority is of the view that summary conviction in the magistrates' court is **11–020** an inadequate remedy, it can seek an injunction in the High Court to abate, prohibit or restrict the statutory nuisance.[53] The idea behind this provision is to stop companies from treating a fine in the magistrates' court simply as an overhead, which they pass on to consumers in the price of their goods and services.

In City of London Corporation v Bovis Construction Ltd,[54] the Court of Appeal noted that the test for the court to apply in exercising its discretion whether or not to grant

---

[46] ibid., s.80(5).
[47] Saddleworth UDC v Aggregate and Sand (1970) 114 Sol. Jo. 931.
[48] Wellingborough BC v Gordon, [1991] JPL 874.
[49] EPA 1990, s.81(4).
[50] For the applicability of the defence to other forms of statutory nuisance, see EPA 1990, ss.80(8) and 82(10).
[51] EPA s.79(9)(a).
[52] ibid., s.79(9)(b).
[53] ibid., s.81(5).
[54] [1992] 3 All E.R. 697.

an injunction was whether it could be inferred that the defendant's unlawful operations would continue unless and until they were effectively restrained by the law, and that nothing short of an injunction would be effective to restrain those operations. The court held that, in contrast with cases concerning injunctions in planning matters, the criminal law need not have been broken for an injunction to lie. Planning cases were to be distinguished from statutory nuisance cases, where the local authority, albeit through public law, was enforcing private rather than public rights.

Action by a "person aggrieved"

11–021 An individual who suffers from a statutory nuisance can take proceedings against the person responsible for the nuisance (or, where he cannot be found, against the owner or occupier of the premises on which the nuisance has arisen) by making a complaint to a magistrates' court.[55] Before he does so, however, he must inform the person responsible of his intention to bring proceedings.[56] If the magistrates are satisfied that a nuisance exists (or, although abated at present, is likely to recur in the same premises or street) they may make an order requiring the defendant to abate the nuisance or prohibiting its recurrence and may, in that order, require the defendant to take certain specified steps to facilitate this. The magistrates can also, at the time the order is made, impose a fine up to a maximum of £5,000. Because the magistrates are imposing sanctions under the criminal law in such cases, the standard to which they must be "satisfied" of the existence of the statutory nuisance is the criminal standard, namely, beyond reasonable doubt.

If at the magistrates hearing it is proved that the alleged nuisance existed at the date on which the complaint was made, then, even if it does not exist at the time of the hearing, or by that time is not likely to recur (so that the magistrates have no power to make an abatement order), the magistrates may nevertheless order the defendant to pay the reasonable costs of the complainant in bringing the proceedings.[57] In addition, where neither the person responsible for the nuisance, nor the owner or occupier of the premises can be found, the magistrates, after giving the local authority the chance to make representations, can direct the local authority to abate the nuisance or take action to prevent it from recurring.[58]

The meaning of "person aggrieved" was examined in a general context by Lord Denning M.R. in *Attorney-General of the Gambia v N'Jie*,[59] who held that the phrase was of wide import and should not be subjected to a restricted interpretation. "Persons aggrieved" will not, of course, include mere "busybodies" interfering with matters which do not concern them, but the phrase is wide enough to cover practically anyone who has a genuine grievance. Thus, in *Sandwell MBC v Bujok*[60] it was held that anyone whose health, or the health of whose family, is affected is a person aggrieved, whilst in *Birmingham DC v McMahon*[61] it was held that a council tenant in a block of flats, who

[55] EPA 1990, s.82.
[56] *ibid.*, s.82(6).
[57] EPA 1990, s.82(12).
[58] *ibid.*, s.82(13).
[59] [1961] A.C. 617.
[60] [1990] 3 All E.R. 385.
[61] (1987) 151 J.P. 709.

complained of a nuisance affecting the block in general but not his flat in particular, was not a person aggrieved.

Failure to comply with the requirements of an abatement or prohibition order is a criminal offence for which the maximum penalty is an initial fine of £5,000, together with additional fines of £500 a day for each day on which the contravention continues after conviction. The defence of "best practicable means" is available.

It will be apparent, then, that there are certain differences between proceedings taken by a local authority and proceedings taken by a "person aggrieved". When a local authority wishes to take action to abate a statutory nuisance, it serves an abatement notice. The procedure is at this point civil. Therefore, if the recipient of the notice appeals to the magistrates, the standard of proof in any matter requiring to be proved is "the balance of probabilities". However, once the requirements of the abatement notice are disobeyed, the matter becomes criminal. By contrast, where a person aggrieved takes action by making a complaint to the magistrates, the proceedings are criminal from the outset, because the magistrates have power to fine the defendant. Accordingly, the standard of proof is the criminal standard.

The regime in practice

The inadequacies of a statutory nuisance action for problems of noise are numerous. **11–022** They include the difficulties experienced by complainants and by local authorities in establishing that a noise nuisance has occurred in the first place. Because of the degree of subjectivity involved in the concept of "noise" (and indeed in the concept of "nuisance"), it is often not easy to predict in advance whether the magistrates, on appeal against a notice, will decide that the barrier between reasonable noise and noise nuisance has been crossed. The difficulties of proving noise nuisance mean that statutory nuisance proceedings are more likely to be successful in cases of long and continuous noise emissions, as opposed to short, intermittent noise emissions. Although, in theory, proceedings can be taken to abate noise nuisances before they occur, in practice this is difficult.

Local authorities scarcely have the resources to fulfil their statutory duty of **11–023** inspecting their areas for the existence of nuisances already occurring, let alone to inspect for likely sources of future noise pollution. The right of the aggrieved individual to bring proceedings in a magistrates' court is not well publicised and is under-used. Most individuals will perceive litigation on their own as involving expense and as daunting in its complexity, and will therefore complain to the local authority in the first instance. Local authorities, however, often respond to domestic noise complaints too slowly for the complaint to be dealt with effectively. Between 1993 and 1994 there were 131, 153 complaints about noise from domestic premises alone. Abatement notices, however, were served only in a few thousand cases. 0.3 per cent of the 131,153 complaints resulted in a conviction. In the light of these statistics, the government considered that a more immediate response, and one which removed the administrative burden on noise sufferers, was needed for the problem of domestic night-time noise.

C: NIGHT-TIME NOISE: THE NOISE ACT 1996

The government's response was the Noise Act 1996. This puts in place a summary procedure for dealing with noise at night. Originally, the regime set out in the Act applied only to local authorities that chose to adopt it. However, by the Anti-Social Behaviour Act 2003, the 1996 Act was amended so that the regime now applies to all local authorities in England and Wales.[62]

The requirement of a complaint is fundamental to the operation of the regime. The aim of the regime is not that local authorities should secure the abatement of all night-time noise. Rather, it is to secure the abatement of noise which causes annoyance. Therefore a local authority only has power to act following receipt of a complaint. Under the Act, where a local authority receives a complaint from an individual who is present in a dwelling during the night that excessive noise is being emitted from another dwelling, it has a power to "arrange for an officer of the authority to take reasonable steps to investigate the complaint".[63] (Prior to the 2003 amendments, the local authority had been under a statutory *duty* to investigate the complaint. However, this duty was converted into a mere *power* when local authorities' discretion to adopt the regime was removed, in recognition of the fact that some local authorities may lack the resources to fulfil an investigative duty.) If an officer is satisfied that noise exceeding the permitted level is being emitted from the offending dwelling during night hours (11pm–7am), he may serve a "warning notice" on that dwelling. The officer need not actually measure the level of noise being emitted in order to be "satisfied" that a notice should be served. The officer of the authority has a discretion whether or not to serve a warning notice. Therefore, if the noise complained of results from a "one-off" event, such as a birthday party, the officer may decide simply to ask that the noise level be reduced.

The warning notice served by the officer must state that an officer of the authority considers that noise is being emitted from the dwelling in night hours, that the noise exceeds the permitted level, and that the person responsible for the noise may be guilty of an offence if he continues to make the noise in the period beginning 10 minutes after the time when the notice is served and ending the following morning at 7am. A "person responsible" for the noise is a person to whose act, default or sufferance the emission of noise is wholly or partly attributable. It will be appreciated that this is a very wide definition which could, conceivably, cover every guest at a party. The precise scope of the term, however, awaits judicial determination.

Where a warning notice has been served in respect of noise emitted from a dwelling, any person who is responsible for noise emitted in the period specified in the notice which exceeds the permitted level, as measured from within the complainant's dwelling, is guilty of an offence, although it is a defence for the accused to show that he had a reasonable excuse for making the noise. The defendant is liable to a fine on conviction by the magistrates, but may pay a fixed penalty instead if the officer decides it is appropriate.[64] As to the meaning of "reasonable excuse", in *A. Lambert Flat Management Ltd v Lomas*,[65] Ackner L.J., considering the matter *obiter* in the context of

---

[62] Anti-Social Behaviour Act 2003, s.42.
[63] NA 1996, s.2(1) (As amended by the Anti-Social behaviour Act 2003, s.42.)
[64] NA 1996, s.8.
[65] [1981] 1 W.L.R. 898.

the Control of Pollution Act 1974, regarded reasonable excuses as: "special reasons such as illness and non-receipt of the notice".

The permitted level of noise in a given area is determined by the Secretary of State on an area by area basis, in order to cater for the particular needs and characteristics of different areas. Parliament has suggested a base level of 35dB, reflecting World Health Organisation guidelines which, in 1980, stated that "a level of less than 35dB is necessary to preserve the restorative process of sleep". It is extremely difficult, however, to measure noise levels accurately. Walls and structures may absorb and deflect noise so that the precise angle or location at which the measurement is taken proves vital. Moreover, the variance of noise levels caused by absorption and deflection can mean, for example, that a party in house A may be very much quieter than a party in house B, but cause greater annoyance. If the person responsible for the quieter party in house A is found guilty of a criminal offence, whilst his noisier neighbour escapes prosecution, a sense of unfairness may be promoted. If the law is seen to be unfair in its application, it is unlikely to be complied with. The Act may also be criticised because it fails to deal with the problem of "cumulative noise". In many of the most serious noise pollution cases, the annoyance is caused by a repetition of incidents involving relatively small levels of noise which cannot be dealt with under the Act because they do not exceed the prescribed level, but which nevertheless cause great annoyance.

Recently, the government undertook a review of the Noise Act 1996 following the Parliamentary commitment to do so given when the Act was first introduced. The review showed that local authorities were very reluctant to adopt the legislation, and so assume a binding obligation to investigate night-time noise complaints. The main reasons given for not adopting the legislation were lack of local demand, adequacy of existing procedures, and cost. In the wake of the review, the government passed the Anti-Social Behaviour Act 2003. Section 42 of this Act amends the Noise Act 1996 so that its provisions automatically apply to every local authority in England and Wales— local authorities therefore no longer have the option of declining to adopt the regime prescribed by the Act. However, as has been said, to mitigate the financial implications of this change, the 2003 Act removes the *duty* on local authorities to investigate complaints of night-time noise, replacing it with a mere *power* to do so. In addition, the Anti-Social Behaviour Act 2003 enables local authorities to order the closure of licensed premises for up to twenty-four hours in the event that there is a "public nuisance caused by noise" coming from those premises.[66] Any person who permits premises to be open in contravention of such an order commits an offence punishable by a fine of up to £20,000, three months' imprisonment, or both.

Anti-social behaviour orders

The Crime and Disorder Act 1998 came into force on April 1, 1999. This addresses **11–024** anti-social behaviour that causes, or is likely to cause, harassment, alarm and distress. In situations where there is serious noise disturbance in the street, an order can be sought from local magistrates by the local authority and a chief constable acting together. Breach of such an order is punishable with up to five years' imprisonment.

[66] *ibid.* s.40.

D: NOISE FROM SPECIFIC SOURCES

Raves

11–025 The Criminal Justice Act 1994 contains provisions enabling the police to deal with raves which are in progress and to prevent them from being held. During the passage of the legislation, Earl Ferrers, opening the debate for the government in the House of Lords, said that raves had caused "appalling misery" to local residents and had "ripped apart the peaceful lives of rural societies".[67] The provisions of the 1994 Act were strengthened by the Anti-Social Behaviour Act 2003. Under the 1994 Act, a "rave" is now defined as a gathering of 20 or more people on land in the open air which includes the playing of amplified music. (It had formerly been defined as such a gathering of 100 people or more). In addition, the Act will apply to gatherings of 20 people or more on land which is not in the open air, where the people are trespassers.[68] Where the music, by reason of its loudness and duration and the time at which it is played, is such that it is likely to cause serious distress to the inhabitants of the locality, the police may take steps to secure that it ceases.[69] Moreover, a constable who has reasonable grounds for believing that a person is on a way to a rave may stop him and prevent him from going.[70]

Intruder alarms

11–026 Intruder alarms which are set off accidentally and sound for a considerable time have become a blight in many neighbourhoods. Therefore, the Noise and Statutory Nuisance Act 1993 provides that local authorities may, if they choose, apply the following regime to their area. Anyone installing an alarm must ensure it complies with prescribed requirements. The police must hold a list of the names, addresses and telephone numbers of those holding keys to alarms. The local authority must be notified within 48 hours that an audible alarm has been installed. Failure to comply with these requirements without reasonable excuse will constitute a criminal offence. The regime also provides that where an alarm has been sounding for an hour after it was activated and the audible operation of the alarm is giving people living or working in the vicinity reasonable cause for annoyance, the local authority may enter premises to turn it off.

Equipment used outdoors

11–027 EC Directive 2000/14 concerning noise emission in the environment by equipment for use outdoors was adopted in July 2000. Its purpose is to ensure that, at the manufacturing stage, such equipment conforms with maximum noise emission limits and labelling requirements. The legislation seeks to harmonise noise emission standards, conformity assessment procedures, product marking, technical documentation,

---

[67] *Hansard*, H.L. 1993, Vol.554, no.71, col.384–5.
[68] CJA 1994, s.63(1A). (Inserted by Anti-Social Behaviour Act 2003, s.58.)
[69] CJA 1994, s.63.
[70] *ibid.*, s.65.

and the collection of data concerning outdoor equipment. The equipment regulated includes lawnmowers, building and construction machinery, and other types of outdoor equipment that can lead to noise pollution. The Directive states that such equipment cannot be placed on the market unless it meets certain noise emission standards, bears a CE marking, and passes conformity assessment procedures.

The Directive was implemented in the UK by the Noise Emission in the Environment by Equipment for use Outdoors Regulations 2001.[71] The Regulations are enforced by the Vehicle Certification Agency. Maximum penalties for breach of the regulations are £5,000 or, for placing non-compliant equipment on the market, a prison term of up to three months.

Loudspeakers

Loudspeakers cannot normally be used in the street between the hours of 9pm and **11–028** 8am for any purpose, or at any time to advertise entertainments, trade or business.[72] If a person wishes to use loudspeakers in the street at night, he must apply to the local authority for consent.[73] The police and the fire brigade are exempt from these provisions, as are loudspeakers used in public transport systems for making announcements to passengers.

Construction noise

Construction and demolition works pose special noise problems compared with most **11–029** other types of industrial activity. They are mainly carried on in the open air, they are of temporary duration, and the noise involved emanates from a wide variety of different activities such as the use of pneumatic concrete breakers and the operation of excavators. The intensity and character of construction noise may vary greatly depending on the phase of the work which is being undertaken. Unlike other sources of noise pollution, construction sites cannot be kept away from areas which are sensitive to noise through the operation of planning law. The statutory nuisance procedure is often too slow to abate construction noise, which may last only for a few weeks before a contractor moves elsewhere.

Control over construction noise is exercised by local authorities under the provisions of Pt III of the Control of Pollution Act 1974, in particular, ss.60 and 61. The emphasis is on preventive action rather than on action to secure abatement. Construction noise is widely defined under the Act as noise resulting from the "erection, construction, alteration, repair or maintenance of buildings, structures and roads, or from breaking up, opening or boring under any road or adjacent land in connection with the construction, inspection, maintenance or removal of works, demolition or dredging work and any work of engineering construction".

Where such works are in progress or are to be carried out in the future, the local authority has a discretion to serve a notice imposing requirements in relation to the

---

[71] SI 2001/1701. (As amended by SI 2001/1803.)
[72] Control of Pollution Act 1974, s.62(1).
[73] Noise and Statutory Nuisance Act 1993, s.8 and Sch.2.

way in which the works are carried out.[74] The conditions which a local authority may specify include those governing the type of plant and machinery which can be used, the hours during which the works may be carried out, and the level of noise that may be emitted.[75] In practice, most notices served under s.60 prohibit work outside specified hours where that work is audible beyond the boundary of the construction site. In this way, the local authority exercises stringent control over construction operations.

It is a criminal offence to contravene a requirement of the notice without reasonable excuse, but it is a defence to prosecution that the works are carried out in accordance with a consent issued under s.61.[76] In *City of London Corporation v Bovis Construction Ltd*,[77] Bovis Construction were prosecuted when they breached a notice served under s.60 of the Control of Pollution Act 1974 requiring them to restrict operations which caused noise outside the boundaries of the site to the hours between 8am and 6pm on weekdays, between 8am and 1pm on Saturdays, and entirely on Sundays and bank holidays.

Prior consent for construction work

11–030 If a developer wishes to carry out construction work, he may apply in advance to the local authority for a consent to allow the works to be carried out at the particular noise level which he proposes. The advantage of applying for a consent in advance, of course, is that the contractor obviates the risk that a local authority will serve a notice under s.60 requiring a change in working methods and hours of work which might cause the developer expense. Once a consent is granted, it becomes a criminal offence knowingly to carry out works or knowingly to permit works to be carried out in contravention of the conditions of a consent.[78]

The consent procedure under s.61 of the Act is rarely used. It has been suggested that industry may well be reluctant to seek prior consent for noise levels because of a fear that the local authority will impose too many restrictions on working practices,[79] the implication being that many contractors prefer to "take their chances" with a local authority and see what level of noise they can get away with. However, where discussions have been held between local authorities and representatives from industry, there have been few concerns over the conditions of consents or the contents of notices.

Transport noise

11–031 In its eighteenth report on transport and the environment, in 1994, the Royal Commission on Environmental Pollution concluded that present levels of exposure to noise from transport were causing serious damage to people's quality of life and were therefore incompatible with the notion of sustainable development. The Commission's

---

[74] COPA 1974, s.60(2).
[75] *ibid.*, s.60(3).
[76] *ibid.*, s.61(8).
[77] [1992] 3 All E.R. 697.
[78] COPA 1974 s.61(5).
[79] See Report of the Noise Review Working Party 1990.

follow-up report, in 1997, found few signs that this position had changed. For the majority of people in the UK, transport is the most pervasive source of noise in the environment. In a survey carried out over a 24 hour period in 1990, noise from roads was recorded outside 92 per cent of a sample of dwellings in England and Wales. This section focuses on the two main problems: road traffic noise and aircraft noise.

(1) *Road traffic noise*

In terms of the number of people affected, road traffic noise is the most serious of all **11–032** transport noise problems. Roads are everywhere and there are few restrictions on the vehicles which may use them. Noise is emitted from vehicles because of bad maintenance, accidental damage or, occasionally, because of deliberate interference to silencing systems. Certain types of silencers deteriorate in use before finally failing with the result that the vehicle may emit more noise than when it was new. A significant proportion of noise from road traffic is produced by tyres and can therefore be influenced by the nature of the road surface.[80]

Preventive control over road noise is exercised through secondary legislation which governs the construction of vehicles and the way in which they may be driven.[81] For example, horns must not be sounded between 11.30 at night and 7.00 in the morning. It is a criminal offence to contravene these regulations. Domestic and EC-based noise standards for vehicles have been laid down in the Motor Vehicles (Type Approval) (Great Britain) Regulations 1984[82] and the Motor Vehicles (EC Type Approval) Regulations 1998.[83]

A more long-sighted preventive approach can be taken through the planning system. Vehicles produce their maximum noise when they are accelerating in low gear. Traffic noise can therefore be substantially reduced by minimising the number of occasions on which vehicles start and stop. This can be achieved by constructing by-passes and outer ring-roads so as to reduce through-traffic in town centres.[84] Noise from roads can also be reduced by using earth banks or barriers made of timber, metal, or plastic. These are much less widely used in the UK than in France, Germany and Japan, partly because of their cost, but also because they are considered unsightly.[85]

So far as remedial provisions are concerned, the Highways Noise Payments and Moveable Homes (England) Regulations 2000[86] provide that persons living in mobile homes (including boats) that are subjected to excessive traffic noise as a result of works to roads are entitled to compensation from local authorities of up to £1,650.

(2) *Aircraft noise*

The International Civil Aviation organisation has noted: **11–033**

"The ability to travel safely, comfortably and quickly across vast distances has given human beings greater access to distant places and a heightened awareness of

---

[80] Royal Commission on Environmental Pollution, Eighteenth Report: *Transport and the Environment,* 1994, Cm 2674.
[81] See The Road Vehicles (Construction and Use) Regulations 1986 (SI 1986/1078), as amended.
[82] SI 1984/81.
[83] SI 1998/2051.
[84] RCEP, Eighteenth Report (above).
[85] *ibid.*
[86] SI 2000/2887.

their own cultural and social diversity. However it must be recognised that—like many other human activities—civil aviation can sometimes have adverse environmental consequences."[87]

Air transport is the most rapidly growing mode of transport, both in the UK and globally. Between 1982 and 1992 the number of passengers on international scheduled services to and from UK airports more than doubled.[88] At the time of writing, the most recent published forecast (June, 2000) predicts that UK demand for air travel will double by 2020.[89] Because of its geographical position and historical links with other nations, the UK has a disproportionately large share of international air traffic.

Aircraft noise is regulated by the Civil Aviation Act 1982, under which the Secretary of State has set maximum noise levels for aircraft serving Heathrow, Gatwick and Stansted. By s.78 of the Act, the Secretary of State has the power, if he considers it necessary to reduce or avoid noise, to specify the maximum number of occasions on which aircraft may be permitted to take off or land at an airport, or even to prohibit take-off during a specified period. Under s.79 of the Act, schemes may be established which require designated aerodromes to make grants towards the cost of insulating certain buildings in the vicinity which require protection from noise. Aircraft taking off from or landing at UK airports are now required, under the Air Navigation (Environmental Standards) Order 2002[90] and the Aeroplane Noise regulations 1999,[91] to hold a noise certificate indicating the maximum total weight at which the aircraft is permitted to take off in compliance with noise certification standards.

As discussed in Ch. 14, aircraft noise has been the subject matter of recent legal challenges under the European Convention on Human Rights and the Human Rights Act 1998. In *Dennis v Ministry of Defence*[92] the claimant, who owned an estate neighbouring an RAF airfield, alleged that noise from jet fighters flying training missions amounted to a nuisance and a breach of the European Convention on Human Rights. The court upheld this claim, but was not prepared to grant an injunction requiring the flights to stop, because RAF training was in the national interest. The solution was to allow the flights to continue, but award substantial damages. In *Hatton v United Kingdom*,[93] the claimants, who lived in the vicinity of Heathrow Airport, claimed that increased noise levels created by night flights were disturbing their sleep, and were therefore a breach of their human rights. The European Court of Human Rights held that the night flights did not, in themselves, result in a human rights breach, but was prepared to uphold the claim that judicial review had not been an adequate remedy in relation to the claimants' grievances.

---

[87] International Civil Aviation Organisation Environmental Technical Manual on the Use of Procedures in the Noise Certification of Aircraft (2nd ed., 1995).
[88] RCEP Eighteenth Report, p.63.
[89] Source: DETR. See *www. aef.org.uk.*
[90] SI 2002/798.
[91] SI 1999/1452.
[92] [2003] EWHC 793; 153 N.L.J. 634.
[93] [2003] All E.R. (D) 122.

E: PREVENTIVE CONTROL OF NOISE

Noise abatement zones

The concept of nuisance provides limited control over noise. The law of nuisance **11–034** comes into play when an unjustified noise is emanating from an identifiable "point" source, but it is of little use where the general level of noise in an area, from often unidentifiable and arguably justifiable sources, gradually rises over time. Moreover, nuisance procedures are concerned largely with abating excessive noise once it has occurred. Even though a local authority may serve an abatement notice where a nuisance is likely to occur, in order for the problem to have come to the authority's attention, there must have been some indication that a nuisance was likely. Thus, the nuisance procedure is not truly a form of preventive control, because it does not allow for controls to be instigated before noise has caused at least some problems.[94]

We have seen that the question of "ambient noise" from diffuse sources is currently being addressed in the context of the EC Environmental Noise Directive. Under existing law, general noise from diffuse sources may be controlled by a local authority, which may designate certain areas or the whole of its area as a "noise abatement zone". Within such zones, target levels are set for noise emissions in order to reduce (or prevent an increase in) the ambient noise level. The statutory framework for noise abatement zones is to be found in Pt III of the Control of Pollution Act 1974.

Noise reduction notices

If, having set target noise levels in a noise abatement zone, the local authority decides **11–035** that in order to hold steady or to reduce ambient noise levels there should be a reduction in the level of noise from certain sources, it may issue a noise reduction notice on the person responsible for the noise. The notice may require any reduction which is reasonably practicable and would secure public benefit. It may specify particular times or days during which the noise level is to be reduced and may require noise to be reduced to different levels at different times or on different days.[95]

Building regulations

Building regulations are designed to ensure that buildings are constructed to an **11–036** adequate standard. Part E of Sch.1 to the Building Regulations 2000[96] is designed to prevent undue noise being transmitted between separately occupied units of the same building (*e.g.* blocks of flats) or between individual buildings in a group of contiguous buildings (*e.g.* terraced or semi-detached houses). Carrying out work in contravention of the building regulations is an offence. Moreover, the local authority may require the removal or alteration of the offending work.

---

[94] See *Neighbourhood Noise* (The Noise Advisory Council, 1971.)
[95] COPA 1974, s.66(4).
[96] SI 2000/2531.

Highways

11–037 Highway authorities must either carry out noise insulation works or provide grants to insulate certain buildings against the effects of traffic noise where those effects increase as a result of the construction or alteration of a highway.

Protecting workers

11–038 The Noise at Work Regulations 1989[97] directly regulated for the first time what had become a well established risk to workers' health and safety. Under Reg.6, every employer (with certain limited exceptions) is required to reduce the risk of damage to the hearing of employees and others to the lowest level reasonably practicable.

Planning and noise pollution

11–039 The planning system can be very effective in preventing or reducing noise pollution. Noise levels are a material consideration for planning authorities in determining planning applications. Because noise decreases with distance, noise from local industry can sometimes be reduced by the imposition of planning conditions which require the noisiest parts of factories to be located in the middle of sites, as far as possible from the site boundary.

Government guidance makes the somewhat obvious point that noise sensitive developments (such as housing, hospitals and schools) should be separated from major sources of noise (road, rail and air transport, and certain types of industrial development). It suggests that development plans should give developers and local communities a degree of certainty about the areas in which particular types of development would be acceptable and those in which special measures may be required in order to mitigate the impact of noise.

Noise and the Pollution Prevention Control (PPC) regime

11–040 The PPC regime (discussed in Ch. 5) regulates noise pollution from industrial sites. PPC requires noise to be controlled in much the same way as any other pollutant, with the Environment Agency exercising control over noise regulation at premises covered by the regime. Operators are required to use the "best available techniques" to prevent or minimise noise nuisance. Moreover, under Environment Agency guidance, it is clear that companies are expected to control noise under PPC by including, in their applications for PPC licensing, an assessment of the risk of noise affecting sensitive receptors. The Environment Agency has adopted the standard that "noise should not be loud enough to give reasonable cause for annoyance to persons in the vicinity". Sites with a noise problem will be expected to submit a noise management plan with their PPC permit applications, and conforming with this plan will form part of the conditions of any permit issued.

[97] SI 1989/1790.

Chapter 12

THE COMMON LAW AND THE ENVIRONMENT

"public bodies, both national and international, are taking significant steps towards the establishment of legislation which will promote the protection of the environment . . . given that so much well informed and carefully structured legislation is now being put in place for this purpose, there is less need for the courts to develop a common law principle to achieve the same end and indeed it may well be undesirable that they should do so."[1]

Introduction

Although the modern trend in environmental law is for regulatory agencies to control **12–001** the environment under authority derived from statute, the common law may also be used to control environmental damage. The primary function of the common law, however, is to protect the private rights of individuals, and there are a number of ways in which this overriding concern of the common law can operate to the detriment of environmental amenities.

The common law tends to reward the exploitation of natural resources by man. Wild animals, for example, may be killed or taken into ownership under the common law, subject only to the prior claims of the owner of the land on which they are found. Similarly, a public right to fish in tidal waters is enshrined in the common law, as are the private fishing rights of the owner of land adjacent to non-tidal waters. The common law regards fish simply as profits of the land, and cares nothing for their protection. A further example is the distinction drawn in the common law, absurd in ecological terms, between water which percolates beneath the ground and water which flows in defined channels. Percolating groundwater cannot be owned until it is abstracted. It follows that a landowner has an absolute right to abstract percolating water from beneath his land, irrespective of the consequences to his neighbours or to the surrounding community, who have no recognised interest in the water.[2]

Many environmental amenities are "public property", in the sense that they are not owned by ascertained individuals. The common law can operate only where harm has been caused to an ascertained individual, rather than to the environment *per se*, so its

---

[1] *per* Lord Goff in *Cambridge Water Company v Eastern Counties Leather Co. plc* [1994] 1 All E.R. 53 at 76.
[2] *Bradford Corporation v Pickles* [1895] A.C. 587.

effectiveness is limited to the resolution of what may be termed "neighbourhood" environmental problems (*e.g.* the migration of landfill gas to neighbouring property). Therefore, the extent to which common law rules can provide protection for the environment is limited. Moreover, the manner in which the common law develops—by decisions in individual cases—is ill-suited to the process of developing rules for environmental protection, which requires the balancing of a wide range of competing interests. The only interests that can be considered in an adversarial courtroom battle are those of the individual litigants. Nevertheless, the common law retains an important, albeit ancillary, function in environmental law.

The predominant method of common-law environmental control is the nuisance action. Closely related to this is the action for the escape of noxious things from land, brought under what is known as "the rule in *Rylands v Fletcher*".[3] Following the decisions of the House of Lords in *Cambridge Water Company v Eastern Counties Leather*,[4] and *Transco plc v Stockport MBC*[5] this rule is nowadays to be regarded as an aspect of the tort of nuisance rather than as a distinct cause of action. Consideration of the law of nuisance, then, forms the bulk of this chapter.

Also related to common law nuisance is the "statutory nuisance" regime under Pt III of the Environmental Protection Act 1990. The operation of this regime has been considered in Ch. 11 in relation to noise—the remaining statutory nuisances are considered here. In addition, the torts of trespass and negligence, which have some limited utility in protecting the environment, are briefly considered. A detailed examination of the law of tort is beyond the scope of this book. This chapter aims to give the reader an overview of the relevant rules as they relate to environmental protection.

A: NUISANCE

12–002 In summary, there are three types of nuisance:

- Private nuisance;
- Public nuisance; and
- Statutory nuisance.

In recent times, there have been a number of cases in which it has been alleged that the nuisance in question has also constituted a breach of the European Convention on Human Rights. The two most notable cases are *Dennis v Ministry of Defence*[6] and *Marcic v Thames Water Utilities Ltd*.[7] These cases are considered in Ch. 14.

B: PRIVATE NUISANCE

12–003 Private nuisance may be defined as unlawful interference with a person's use or enjoyment of land. It is an important mechanism for the protection of the individual's private right to freedom from pollution. Typical situations which may give rise to

[3] (1868) L.R. 3, H.L. 330.
[4] [1994] 1 All E.R. 53.
[5] [2003] 3 W.L.R. 1467.
[6] [2003] EWHC 793; (2003) 153 N.L.J. 634.
[7] [2003] 3 W.L.R. 1603 (HL); [2002] Q.B. 929 (CA).

liability in nuisance include incursions on to the plaintiff's property, or interference with his enjoyment of that property, by water, smoke, smell, fumes, gas, noise, heat, vibrations, electricity, animals and vegetation.[8] There is authority to suggest that disease or germs brought onto property by the act of another can also found an action in nuisance.[9]

The range of interests protected by the law of nuisance, however, is limited. In contrast with other legal systems, English law has persistently refused to condemn aesthetic nuisances. Thus, ruining a view can create no cause of action, for it is a matter only of "delight" not of "necessity".[10] Similarly, the right to clear television reception will not be protected where it is interfered with by the presence of a new building. Expressing a sentiment subsequently affirmed by the House of Lords in the leading case of *Hunter and Others v Canary Wharf Ltd*,[11] Pill L. J., in the Court of Appeal, said:

> "I accept the importance of television in the lives of very many people. However, in my judgment the erection or presence of a building in the line of sight between a TV transmitter and other properties is not actionable as an interference with the use and enjoyment of land."

The law of private nuisance, then, protects a person's freedom to use land. Long before planning and environmental legislation placed limits on this freedom, it was recognised that the very exercise of a freedom to enjoy land creates, as its corollary, an obligation of non-interference with the freedoms enjoyed by owners of neighbouring land. In other words, the freedom to use land can never be absolute, but must be exercised so that it does not unreasonably prevent a neighbouring landowner from enjoying *his* freedom. Therefore, in an action for private nuisance, the court strives to strike an appropriate balance between the rights landowners and the rights of their neighbours. To assist them in performing this "balancing act", the courts have developed and applied a number of general principles which are examined below.

Who can sue?

In contrast with the position in relation to public nuisance and statutory nuisance, it **12–004** has traditionally been necessary for a claimant who wishes to bring an action in private nuisance to show that he has a legal interest in the land affected by the nuisance. This is because, historically, the tort of private nuisance arose as an offshoot of land law, so that a plaintiff's lack of a legal right to occupy or enjoy his land was fatal to a nuisance claim. In 1993, however, the decision of the Court of Appeal in *Khorasandjian v Bush*[12] appeared to sweep this requirement aside. In *Khorasandjian*, a daughter living in the parental home was granted standing to sue in respect of harassing telephone calls. The Court of Appeal thought that occupation of land as a home should be sufficient to allow the occupier to sue in nuisance.

[8] Salmond and Heuston, *Law of Torts*, p.57.
[9] *per* Viscount Maugham in *Sedleigh-Denfield v O'Callaghan* [1940] A.C. 880 at 888, H.L.
[10] *per* Wray C.J. in *Aldred's* case (1610) 9 Co.Rep.57.
[11] [1996] 2 W.L.R. 348. Affirmed H.L. [1997] A.C. 677.
[12] (1993) 137 Sol. Jo. LB 88.

This decision seemed to transform the tort of private nuisance from a tort protecting only land into a tort which also protected wider, personal, interests. In *Hunter and Others v Canary Wharf Ltd*,[13] however, the House of Lords indicated that it was not prepared to allow the tort of nuisance to develop in this way. Here, the plaintiffs included wives, husbands, partners, children and other relatives who shared a home with householders affected by a nuisance. Relying on *Khorasandjian*, they sought damages for interference with their television reception and for the effects of dust caused by the construction of a link road. The Court of Appeal allowed them standing to sue. The House of Lords, however, reversing the decision of the Court of Appeal and overruling the decision in *Khorasandjian*, reasserted the traditional view that only those who have exclusive possession of the land affected by the nuisance are entitled to sue in private nuisance.[14]

Who can be sued?

12–005   A person will be liable in nuisance if he bears "some degree of personal responsibility" for the nuisance.[15] Thus, the potential defendants in a nuisance action include the creator of the nuisance and the person who, being an occupier of land on which a nuisance has arisen, fails to take reasonable steps to remedy the state of affairs giving rise to the nuisance. As was noted by Veale J. in *Halsey v Esso Petroleum Company*,[16] there appears to be no requirement that the acts complained of must emanate from land belonging to the defendant.

Authorising a nuisance

12–006   In certain circumstances, a defendant may be liable for authorising a nuisance committed by another person. However, the courts have made it clear that merely furnishing another with the means to commit a nuisance will not suffice in this context. For public policy reasons, the courts have been very reluctant to make local authority landlords liable in nuisance for the activities of their unruly tenants (whom local authorities have a statutory duty to house).[17] Thus, in *Hussain v Lancaster City Council*[18] the local authority was not liable for the activities of its racist tenants which amounted to a nuisance.

In order for liability to arise in respect of authorising a nuisance, it has to be established that the nuisance is the *inevitable* consequence of the defendant's conduct in (for example) letting his premises be used by another. Thus, in *Tetley v Chitty*[19] a local authority was liable for nuisance that was the inevitable result of its having granted permission for premises to be used for the purpose of go-karting.

---

[13] [1997] A.C. 677. (Note that the House of Lords preserved the rule that a reversioner may sue if he can establish that the nuisance is sufficient to damage his reversionary interest.)

[14] Note that the exclusive possession need not necessarily be lawful. See *Foster v Warblington UDC* [1906] 1 K.B. 648. For the position of a "tolerated trespasser", see *Pemberton v Southwark LBC* [2000] 1 W.L.R. 1672.

[15] *per* Lord Atkin in *Sedleigh-Denfield v O'Callaghan* [1940] A.C. 880 at 897.

[16] [1961] 1 W.L.R. 683.

[17] *Smith v Scott* [1972] 3 All E.R. 645.

[18] [2000] Q.B. 1. Contrast *Lippiat v South Gloucester Council* [2000] Q.B. 51, where travellers were using the council's land as a "launch pad" for their nuisance-creating activities.

[19] [1986] 1 All E.R. 663.

Naturally occurring nuisances

A defendant can be liable for failing to take reasonable steps to abate a nuisance **12–007** occurring naturally on his land.[20] In deciding what steps are reasonable in this context, the courts apply a subjective test which takes account of the financial resources and physical capabilities of the landowner. This means that the question of liability will vary from case to case. In *Leakey v National Trust*[21], for example, the defendants were liable when, following an exceptionally dry summer, land forming part of an ancient earthwork began to fall onto the plaintiffs' cottages—the defendants had been aware of this risk, had had the resources to address the problem, but had declined to act. In *Holbeck Hall Hotel Ltd v Scarborough BC (No. 2)*,[22] however, there was no liability on the part of a local authority for a landslide that meant that the claimants' hotel, situated on top of a cliff, had to be demolished. In view of the expense of the work involved in preventing such a landslide, the Court of Appeal was prepared to hold that the scope of the local authority's duty might have been limited to warning the claimants, and sharing such information as they possessed about the likelihood of a landslide. In the event, it was not strictly necessary to decide the scope the local authority's duty, because the case turned on the fact that the type and extent of the claimants' loss was not foreseeable—the council could not be liable for having failed to take steps that only an expert geologist could have identified as necessary.

Physical damage to land

The courts have distinguished two types of act which may constitute a private nuisance: **12–008**

- An act which causes unreasonable interference with a person's enjoyment of his land, for example by the ingress on to the land of fumes or noise; and

- An act which causes physical damage to a person's land.

The distinction between these two types of private nuisance is important for this reason: in cases of interference with enjoyment, such as by noise or smell, the claimant must show that the defendant's activities constituted an unreasonable use of his land *given the characteristics of the locality in which the land is situated*, whilst in cases of physical damage to property, so long as the damage is more than trivial, liability follows automatically on proof of the damage, the character of the neighbourhood being irrelevant.[23] This distinction, which originated during the Industrial Revolution, when noises or smells were trivial problems compared with thick black soot from factories which destroyed crops, is, perhaps, less easy to justify today.

---

[20] *Goldman v Hargrave* [1966] 1 A.C. 645.
[21] [1980] 1 All E.R. 17.
[22] [2000] Q.B. 836.
[23] *St Helen's Smelting Co. v Tipping* (1865) 11 H.L. Cas.642.

Interference with the enjoyment of land

12–009 Where the act complained of causes an interference with the claimant's enjoyment of his land, but does not damage the land, it becomes relevant for the court to consider whether or not the defendant is making reasonable use of his own land *vis-à-vis* the claimant. In answering this question, the courts have recognised that a certain level of inconvenience is to be tolerated as part and parcel of modern life, and have held that the interference complained of must be substantial if it is to amount to an actionable nuisance. Thus, according to Knight-Bruce V.C. in *Walter v Selfe*,[24] the question for the court is:

> "ought this inconvenience to be considered in fact as more than fanciful, more than one of mere delicacy and fastidiousness, as an inconvenience materially interfering with the ordinary comfort physically of human existence, not merely according to elegant and dainty modes or habits of living, but according to the plain and sober and simple notions among the English people?"

A trivial interference with enjoyment, then, cannot be a nuisance. However, the loss of just one night's sleep because of excessive noise has been held to constitute a nuisance,[25] as has the use of adjoining premises as a sex shop.[26] By contrast, in *Southwark BC v Mills*[27], where the claimant complained about noise from adjoining flats which could be heard because of poor sound insulation, the House of Lords held that the ordinary use of residential premises was not capable of amounting to an actionable nuisance.

There is no precise test for deciding whether the defendant's use of his land is unreasonable, the matter being dependent on the facts of each particular case. However, the extent and nature of the harm alleged, the duration of the nuisance, the utility of the defendant's activities, the abnormal sensitivity of the claimant, malice on the part of the defendant, and the character of the neighbourhood in which the activity is carried on, have all been identified as relevant considerations.

The character of the neighbourhood

12–010 As has been said, where the nuisance complained of constitutes mere interference with the claimant's enjoyment of his land, the character of the neighbourhood in which the defendant's activities are undertaken is a relevant consideration. It follows that certain forms of activity are permissible in industrial areas which would constitute a nuisance if carried on in a residential area. As Thesiger L.J. put it in *Sturges v Bridgman*[28]: "What would be a nuisance in Belgrave Square would not necessarily be so in Bermondsey."

Case law suggests that a grant of planning permission may change the character of the neighbourhood, and thereby permit certain activities which, prior to that change,

[24] (1851) 4 De G. & Sm. 315.
[25] *Andreae v Selfridge & Co. Ltd* [1938] Ch. 1.
[26] *Laws v Florinplace Ltd* [1981] 1 All E.R. 659.
[27] [1999] 4 All E.R. 449.
[28] (1879) 11 Ch.D. 852.

would have been actionable nuisances. In *Gillingham BC v Medway (Chatham) Dock Co. Ltd*,[29] the defendants were granted planning permission to change a little-used naval dock into a commercial port, with the result that levels of noise and disturbance to local residents increased dramatically. The council, on behalf of the local residents, brought an action in nuisance and sought an injunction to restrict the movement of vehicles at night. Buckley J. held that the grant of planning permission had changed the character of the neighbourhood so that 24 hour access to the dock was permissible. It followed that, since the question of the reasonableness of the defendants' activities fell to be decided by reference to the character of the neighbourhood, there could be no actionable nuisance. Buckley J. was influenced by the fact that, before granting planning permission, a local planning authority would balance the interests of the community against those of individuals. His Lordship took the view that, this having been done, the environmental controls imposed through planning law must prevail over those available in private law. The learned judge put the matter in the following terms:

> "planning permission is not a licence to commit a nuisance and a planning authority has no jurisdiction to authorise nuisance. However, a planning authority can through its development plans and decisions, alter the character of a neighbourhood. This may have the effect of rendering innocent activities which, prior to the change, would have been an actionable nuisance."

In *Gillingham*, Buckley J. clearly saw the grant of planning permission as determinative of the character of the neighbourhood. His Lordship's reasoning seems to have been based on an analogy between planning permission and statutory authority, which may operate as a defence to a nuisance action (see below). The validity of this analogy, however, has subsequently been firmly rejected by the Court of Appeal in *Wheeler v J.J. Saunders Ltd*.[30] The plaintiffs brought an action in nuisance when the smell from the defendants' neighbouring pig farm interfered with their enjoyment of their property. The units housing the pigs had been erected in accordance with planning permission. The court held that the existence of the planning permission could not operate as a defence to the nuisance claim because, in contrast with the position in *Gillingham*, the planning permission had not sufficiently altered the character of the neighbourhood. It was held that the analogy between the grant of planning permission and the defence of statutory authority could not be justified because, whilst Parliament may be entitled to authorise the commission of nuisances under statute, a local planning authority has no such power. Although this suggests that the *dictum* of Buckley J. in Gillingham should be treated with caution, it should be remembered that the key finding in *Wheeler* was that the planning permission for the housing of pigs was insufficient to alter the character of the neighbourhood. Therefore, the possibility remains that where, as in *Gillingham*, the planning permission in question is of a strategic character and is designed to promote the regeneration of a large area, it may in practical terms extinguish residents' claims in private nuisance.

[29] [1993] Q.B. 343.
[30] [1995] 2 All E.R. 697.

The utility of the defendant's activities

12–011   Clearly, because in a nuisance action the courts are concerned with what is reasonable as between the claimant and the defendant, the purpose to be served by the defendant's activities is a relevant consideration. This is, of course, apparent in the decision in *Gillingham* (above), where the activities in question were of general benefit to the community in terms of urban regeneration and job creation.

Similarly, in *Harrison v Southwark and Vauxhall Water Co.*[31] it was said that for a man to pull down a house for the purposes of rebuilding on his land would be a reasonable use of the land, and therefore not an actionable nuisance, provided that he took all reasonable care to avoid causing inconvenience to his neighbours. This would be so even where considerable inconvenience was caused and the operation lasted for several months, for progress would be unduly hampered if the law of nuisance were to prevent the development of land. However, where serious damage is being done to the claimant's property or livelihood, the court will not accept the argument that the claimant alone should bear the burden of the activity from which the community as a whole will benefit. Nor will a court grant damages instead of an injunction, since this would amount to expropriation of rights without the sanction of Parliament. Thus, in *Bellew v Cement Co.*[32] an Irish court granted the plaintiff an injunction which had the effect of closing for three months the only cement factory in Ireland at a time when building was an urgent public necessity.

Malice

12–012   It follows that if the utility of the defendant's activities is relevant, then where the act in question is maliciously perpetrated and therefore has no social utility, the court will more readily presume that it constitutes an actionable nuisance. Thus in *Christie v Davey,*[33] North J. was prepared to grant an injunction restraining the defendant from annoying the plaintiff by banging on a party-wall, beating tea-trays, whistling and shrieking. The defendant had taken these actions in protest at noise from music lessons given by the plaintiff next door. North J. stated that, " if what has taken place had occurred between two sets of persons both perfectly innocent, I should have taken an entirely different view of the case."

Similarly, in *Hollywood Silver Fox Farm Ltd v Emmett,*[34] where the defendant, motivated by spite, caused guns to be fired on the boundary of his land in order to frighten the plaintiff's foxes and prevent them from breeding, Macnaghten J. considered that the intention of the defendant was relevant in determining liability for nuisance and awarded damages together with an injunction.

In both of these cases, the courts were concerned to protect a recognised legal right to the enjoyment of property. Where no such right exists, however, the position is different. Thus, in *Bradford (Mayor of) v Pickles,*[35] where the defendant deliberately

---

[31] [1891] 2 Ch. 409.
[32] [1984] Ir.R. 61.
[33] [1893] 1 Ch. 316.
[34] [1936] 2 K.B. 468.
[35] [1895] A.C. 587.

abstracted groundwater from his land, which diminished the plaintiff's water supply, in order to induce the plaintiff to purchase his land, the House of Lords stated that a malicious motive could not make unlawful an act which was otherwise lawful. Because it had previously been established by case law that no legal interest can exist in percolating groundwaters before those waters have been abstracted, no recognised interest of the plaintiff had been infringed and the motive of the defendant was therefore irrelevant.

"One-off" events

There is some authority for the proposition that an isolated incident cannot found an **12–013** action in nuisance. In *Bolton v Stone*[36] the plaintiff, who was standing on the highway, was injured by a cricket ball which had been hit from the defendant's land. Oliver J., at first instance, stated that a nuisance must be: " a state of affairs, however temporary, and not merely an isolated happening." In the Court of Appeal, however, the nuisance was regarded not as the isolated hitting of the ball on to the highway, but as the carrying on of a cricket game adjacent to the highway.

This illustrates the tendency of the courts, where the event complained of is a "one-off", to hold that the essence of the nuisance is the state of affairs which gives rise to the event rather than the event itself. Thus, in *Spicer v Smee*,[37] where defective electrical wiring installed in the defendant's bungalow caused a fire which damaged the plaintiff's adjacent bungalow, Atkinson J. held that the defendant was liable in nuisance because he had permitted a dangerous state of affairs to exist on his land. Where, however, the isolated event falls within the rule in *Rylands v Fletcher* (below), there is no need to show that the event is referable to a "state of affairs".

Abnormal sensitivity of the claimant

If the claimant, or his use of his land, is abnormally sensitive to the interference of **12–014** which he complains, he will not be granted relief. The principle is illustrated by the decision in *Robinson v Kilvert*.[38] The defendant carried on a business in the lower part of a building which required certain hot and dry air conditions and he heated the basement accordingly. This had the effect of heating the plaintiff's premises above, where the plaintiff stored a quantity of brown paper. As a result of the heat, the brown paper dried and diminished in value. There was no evidence that the levels of heat inconvenienced the plaintiff's workmen, or that it would cause damage to paper generally. Refusing to grant an injunction, the court held that: "a man who carries on an exceptionally delicate trade cannot complain because it is injured by his neighbour doing something which would not injure anything but an exceptionally delicate trade."[39]

However, where it can be shown that the activity of the defendant is such as would inconvenience a claimant who is not abnormally sensitive, the fact that the claimant's

[36] [1951] A.C. 850.
[37] [1946] 1 All E.R. 498.
[38] (1884) 41 Ch.D. 88.
[39] *per* Lopes L.J. at 97.

activity is particularly sensitive will not prevent him from recovering losses which result from its interruption. Thus, in *McKinnon Industries Ltd v Walker*,[40] the plaintiff recovered in respect of his inability to grow orchids in circumstances where the defendant's interference with his enjoyment of his land was substantial.

C: PUBLIC NUISANCE

12–015   Unlike private nuisance, which is only a tort, the commission of a public nuisance is also a criminal offence. A nuisance is said to be a public nuisance when it "materially affects the reasonable comfort and convenience of the life of a class of Her Majesty's subjects".[41] The number of people required to establish that a "class" of people has been affected is a question of fact in each case. In *Attorney-General v P.Y.A. Quarries Ltd*, Denning L.J. held that the correct approach was not specifically to count the numbers of people affected, but to assess whether the nuisance was so widespread and indiscriminate in its effect that it would not be reasonable to expect one person, rather than the community at large, to take action to put a stop to it. Denning L.J. gave as an example the non-repair or blocking of a public footpath used by few people. The obstruction nevertheless affects indiscriminately everyone who may wish to walk along it.

Special damage

12–016   A public nuisance only becomes actionable at the suit of an individual where he can show that he has suffered some special damage over and above that which has been suffered by the other members of the public whom the nuisance affects. Thus, if a public highway is obstructed, the claimant will not succeed in public nuisance if he can prove no damage beyond being occasionally delayed or having to make a detour, because every other user of the highway has incurred a similar inconvenience.[42] If, however, the claimant falls over the obstruction and sustains injury, then he has suffered some particular or special damage not suffered by all users of the highway and will therefore be entitled to bring an action.

The difference between public and private nuisance

12–017   The key difference between an action in private nuisance and an action by a person suffering special damage because of a public nuisance is that the claimant in a private nuisance action has to show that his interest in land is affected, whilst the claimant in public nuisance has standing to sue irrespective of whether or not this is so. Although in many cases what is a public nuisance will also amount to a private nuisance, this is not always the case. The distinction between the two forms of nuisance is illustrated by the decision in *Tate & Lyle Industries Ltd v G.L.C.*[43] Ferry terminals constructed by the

[40] [1951] 3 D.L.R. 577.
[41] *per* Romer L.J. in *Attorney-General v P.Y.A. Quarries Ltd* [1957] 2 Q.B. 169 at 184.
[42] *Winterbottom v Lord Derby* (1867) L.R. 2 Ex. 316.
[43] [1983] 2 A.C. 509.

defendants in the Thames caused silting of the river bed which prevented large vessels from accessing the plaintiffs' jetty. The plaintiffs' claim in private nuisance was dismissed because the jetty itself had not been affected and they had no proprietary interest in the bed of the river. The silting, however, had caused an interference with a public right of navigation. It was held that because the plaintiffs had incurred considerable expense in dredging the river in order to carry on with their business, they had suffered special damage and were therefore entitled to recover in public nuisance.

The relevance of public nuisance today

Public nuisance at common law once had a useful role in safeguarding the local **12–018** environment. However, over the last hundred years or more, virtually the entire area which was traditionally the province of public nuisance has been covered by statute. Although the common law of public nuisance still fulfils a residual role, particularly in relation to matters concerning pollution of the highways, it will often be cheaper and more convenient for an individual affected by a public nuisance to complain to the local environmental health officer, who may bring an action to abate the nuisance under the provisions relating to statutory nuisances (below). However, because the remedy for a statutory nuisance is abatement of the nuisance, the law of statutory nuisance can do little to compensate a person who has been the victim of a nuisance. The common law action for public nuisance therefore remains an effective tool for those determined to seek compensation in addition to a cessation of the defendant's activities.

D: DEFENCES TO A COMMON LAW NUISANCE ACTION

Prescription

Under the doctrine of prescription, if an activity which constitutes a private nuisance **12–019** continues for a period of 20 years it will become immune from suit. Commission of a public nuisance, however, cannot be made legal in this way. In practice, it is extremely difficult to prove a prescriptive right to commit a nuisance. This is because the 20 year time period does not commence until there is an actionable nuisance in existence. The point is illustrated by the facts of *Sturges v Bridgman*.[44] For more than 20 years a confectioner had used a large mortar and pestle on his property which adjoined the garden of the plaintiff doctor. This was not a nuisance to the doctor until he built a consulting room at the end of his garden when he found, for the first time, that the noise and vibration interfered with the running of his practice. In granting an injunction to restrain the defendant from using the mortar and pestle, the court held that the defendant had not acquired a prescriptive right to commit the nuisance because there had not been in existence an actionable nuisance for a continuous period of 20 years.

[44] (1879) 11 Ch.D. 852.

Statutory authority

12–020 In practice, statutory authority is the most important defence to an action in nuisance. Many activities which might constitute a nuisance are carried out by private and public bodies authorised by Parliament to undertake those activities. Broadly speaking, where the statute places the body under a *duty* to do the act which is complained of and it is unavoidable that the act must be done in the particular place where it causes a nuisance, the body will be immune from suit.

Where, however, on a proper construction of the statute, the body is given a discretion as to where to do the act in question, the body may be liable in nuisance if it could reasonably have undertaken the activity in another location where no nuisance would be caused. Similarly, where the statute confers a *power* to act, rather than a duty, the power must normally be exercised in such a way as not to interfere with private rights.[45]

Where a nuisance is the "inevitable" result of an activity authorised by statute, then, the body responsible for the activity will be immune from suit. It is a matter of statutory interpretation in each particular case whether or not the nuisance is "inevitable". In *Allen v Gulf Oil Refining Ltd*,[46] for example, the defendant company was authorised by statute compulsorily to acquire land for the purpose of constructing an oil refinery. The defendants built the refinery and then operated it in such a way as to cause a nuisance to the plaintiffs. The court held that the statutory authority to construct a refinery impliedly carried with it the authority to operate the refinery when it was constructed. It followed that the company enjoyed immunity with respect to nuisances that were the inevitable result of an oil refinery being built. Lord Wilberforce stated that the establishment of an oil refinery was bound to involve some alteration of the environment, and so of the standard of amenity and comfort which neighbouring occupiers might expect. Therefore, to the extent that the environment had been changed from peaceful unpolluted countryside to an industrial complex, to which different standards apply, Parliament must be taken to have authorised the nuisances.

Other defences

12–021 The claimant's consent to the existence of a nuisance is a defence. Act of God, or act of an unidentified third party, may also provide a defence. Moreover, where negligence is the essence of liability, the defendant may sometimes escape liability through absence of fault, although it is not altogether clear when this will be so.[47] The Law Reform (Contributory Negligence) Act 1945 is applicable to nuisance and can therefore operate to reduce an award of damages where the claimant, through carelessness, has contributed to his own loss. In certain cases, it seems that ignorance of the circumstances in which the nuisance arises can also provide a defence. Thus, in *Noble v Harrison*,[48] a branch of a tree which overhung the highway fell on to the

---

[45] *Metropolitan Asylum District Managers v Hill* (1881) 6 App.Cas.193, H.L.
[46] [1981] A.C. 1001.
[47] See *Dymond v Pearce* [1972] 1 All E.R. 1142.
[48] [1926] 2 K.B. 332.

plaintiff's car. The branch fell because of a "secret and unobservable operation of nature" for which the defendant could not be held responsible.

The following are NOT defences to an action in nuisance:

(1) *That the claimant "comes to the nuisance"*

It is not a defence to a claim in nuisance for the defendant to argue that "he got there **12–022** first", or in other words that the claimant "came to the nuisance". Thus, in *Bliss v Hall*,[49] where the defendant set up a tallow-chandlery which emitted noise and offensive smells to the annoyance of the plaintiff, it was held to be no defence for the defendant to argue that the factory had been in existence for three years before the plaintiff's arrival. When the plaintiff moved into his house, he "came to the house with all the rights which the common law affords, and one of them is a right to wholesome air."[50] Similarly, the defendant in *Sturges v Bridgeman* (above) was not permitted to defend the doctor's claim on the basis that the doctor should not have built his consulting room at the end of his garden knowing of the likelihood of noise and vibration from the defendant's business.

(2) *That the nuisance is due to many*

It is no defence that the nuisance complained of is due to the actions of other people **12–023** acting together with the defendant and that the defendant's act, considered in isolation, would not have amounted to a nuisance. In assessing what is reasonable conduct on the part of the defendant, the court will take account of all the surrounding circumstances, including the conduct of others.[51]

(3) *That the defendant's activity is socially useful*

Whilst the utility of the defendant's conduct is relevant in determining whether his **12–024** activities are reasonable, it is not, of itself, a defence for a defendant to show that his activities are socially worthwhile. Thus in *Adams v Ursell*,[52] the defendant opened a fish and chip shop in what had hitherto been a "well to do" residential area. In resisting the grant of an injunction to stop a nuisance caused by smells from the shop, the defendant argued that, in effect, he was providing a social service and that closing the shop would cause hardship to the "less well off" in the area, who were his customers. This argument was rejected, the court holding that the defendant should have located his shop in the area where his customers lived, presumably because, being of a lower class, they would not be offended by the smell of fish and chips!

E: REMEDIES

The principal remedies available to the claimant in an action for nuisance are an award **12–025** of damages and/or an injunction. In addition, the claimant has the "self-help" remedy of abatement.

---

[49] (1838) 4 Bing. N.C. 183.
[50] *per* Tindal C.J., *ibid.* at 186. See also *Holbeck Hotel Ltd. v Scarborough BC* (above).
[51] *Lambton v Mellish* [1894] 3 Ch. 163.
[52] [1913] 1 Ch. 269.

Damages

12–026 An award of damages aims to evaluate the loss to the claimant which results from the defendant's activities and to put the claimant in the position he would have been in had the nuisance not occurred. The traditional method of quantifying damages is to assess the diminution in the market value of the claimant's property. Whilst this method has the advantage of relative simplicity, it may be criticised as often underestimating the subjective value of the property to the resident owner. The diminution in value test assumes that the property is worth no more to the claimant than its market value and fails to take account of the emotional and psychological damage which can flow from a disturbance in the home.

Injunction

12–027 An injunction has the effect of preventing the defendant from carrying out the activity that is being complained of, or of restricting the scope of that activity. Exceptionally, an injunction may be mandatory in its terms, requiring the defendant to perform some positive act rather than to forbear from doing the act complained of. Unlike an award of damages, an injunction is an equitable remedy, so that the claimant is not entitled to it as of right, but must have the discretion of the court exercised in his favour. In exercising this discretion, the courts take the view that injunctive relief is generally preferable to an award of damages but that in certain circumstances damages in lieu of an injunction are appropriate. Thus, where the claimant has acted maliciously in retaliation against the nuisance, as in *Christie v Davey* (above), he may be deprived of injunctive relief.

In deciding whether or not to grant the claimant damages instead of an injunction, the traditional approach of the courts has been to grant an injunction without having regard to the social and economic effects on third parties of doing so. Thus, in *Shelfer v City of London Electric Co.*[53] the court refused to award the plaintiff damages instead of an injunction, despite the defendants' argument that the public at large derived a benefit from their supplying electricity. Traditionally, then, the courts will not grant damages instead of an injunction where this would amount to allowing the defendant to "buy" the right to continue the nuisance. However, in a number of cases concerning the activities of clubs, the courts have taken account of the social utility of the defendant's activities in either refusing to grant an injunction (as in the well-known case of *Miller v Jackson*[54] where cricket was played on a village green, causing damage to local houses) or in granting a limited injunction (as in *Kennaway v Thompson*[55] where the activities of a power-boat racing club were curtailed but not stopped.)

Abatement

12–028 Traditionally, where a claimant is affected by a nuisance he is entitled in law to take steps himself to abate the nuisance without recourse to legal proceedings. Thus in *Lemon v Webb*[56] the plaintiff was held to have acted legally when he trimmed the

[53] [1895] 1 Ch. 287.
[54] [1977] Q.B. 966.
[55] [1981] Q.B. 88.
[56] [1895] A.C. 1.

branch of a tree which overhung his land. The remedy of abatement, however, must be exercised within narrow confines. In particular, notice must be given to the defendant by the plaintiff prior to his taking action unless he can abate the nuisance without going on to the defendant's land; the abator must not do unnecessary damage to the defendant's land in abating the nuisance; and, where there is more than one method of abating the nuisance, the abator must select the course of action which causes least harm to the defendant financially, except where this would have a detrimental effect on innocent third parties or on the public.

F: Statutory Nuisances

As has been noted above, most of the activities which once constituted public **12–029** nuisances at common law are now statutory nuisances. The law in relation to statutory nuisances has its origin in legislation dating from 1848 and was consolidated by the Public Health Act 1936. The law was further consolidated in Pt III of the Environmental Protection Act 1990. The statutory nuisance regime provides a fast and cheap remedy by comparison with common law public nuisance, and although proceedings for statutory nuisance will normally be brought by a local authority, aggrieved individuals have a statutory right to apply to a magistrates' court for the abatement of a nuisance.[57]

Under the Environmental Protection Act 1990, district councils and London borough councils are under a duty to inspect their areas for statutory nuisances.[58] Although the duty is to carry out inspections periodically, it has been suggested that if a member of the public complains of a statutory nuisance and the authority fails or refuses to inspect, an action for judicial review will lie to compel the authority to do so.[59] The Act lists a number of activities which are statutory nuisances. In addition, it provides that certain other activities specified in other legislation as constituting a statutory nuisance are to be governed by the provisions of the Act. These activities include, for example, those prescribed under the Noise and Statutory Nuisance Act 1993 (considered in Ch. 11). Under the Environmental Protection Act 1990, the principal criterion for establishing that an activity is a statutory nuisance is whether or not it is "prejudicial to health or a nuisance".

The meaning of "prejudicial to health or a nuisance"

For the purposes of the statutory regime, the word "nuisance" his traditionally thought **12–030** to have the same meaning as attached to it by the common law.[60] "Prejudicial to health" is defined by the Environmental Protection Act 1990 as "injurious, or likely to cause injury, to health".[61] In *Coventry City Council v Cartwright*,[62] a resident complained of a statutory nuisance (under the Public Health Act 1936) emanating from a

---

[57] EPA 1990, s.82.
[58] EPA 1990, s.79.
[59] Bell and McGillivray, *Environmental Law* (5th ed., 2000), p.433.
[60] *National Coal Board v Thorne* [1976] 1 W.L.R. 543. But see the remarks of Pitchford J. in *Hounslow BC v Thames Water Utilities* [2004] Q.B. 212, discussed in Ch. 11.
[61] EPA 1990, s.79(7).
[62] [1975] 1 W.L.R. 845.

nearby refuse tip owned by the council. The Divisional Court held that because the rubbish accumulated on the site was inert rather than putrescible, so that there was no likelihood that vermin or disease would emanate from the site, the site could not be said to be "prejudicial to health". The chance that people might be caused injury by walking on the site was not sufficient to make the site prejudicial to their health.

Categories of statutory nuisance

12–031 The following categories of statutory nuisance are set out in the Environmental Protection Act 1990. Some of these relate to problems of noise, and were considered in Ch. 11, whilst others, relating to air pollution, were considered in Ch. 10.

- Any premises in such a state as to be prejudicial to health or a nuisance;
- Smoke emitted from premises so as to be prejudicial to health or a nuisance;
- Fumes or gases emitted from premises so as to be prejudicial to health or a nuisance;
- Dust, steam, smell or other effluvia arising on industrial, trade or business premises and being prejudicial to health or a nuisance;
- Any accumulation or deposit which is prejudicial to health or a nuisance;
- Any animal kept in such a place or manner as to be prejudicial to health or a nuisance;
- Noise emitted from premises so as to be prejudicial to health or a nuisance; and
- Any other matter declared by any enactment to be a statutory nuisance.

Abatement notices

12–032 If the authority is satisfied that a statutory nuisance exists, it is under a duty to serve an abatement notice on the person responsible for the nuisance or, in cases where he cannot be found, the owner or occupier of the premises on which the nuisance arises.[63] The local authority has no discretion whether to take action. It is under a duty to do so. In *R. v Carrick DC, ex p. Shelley and Another*[64] the Divisional Court held, on an application for judicial review, that a local authority had not discharged its duty under s.80 of the Environmental Protection Act 1990, when, having discovered the existence of a statutory nuisance, it resolved that it was not appropriate to serve a notice but that it would continue to monitor the situation.

The notice will require the recipient to stop the nuisance altogether, or to restrict its occurrence. In addition, it may require him to take certain specified steps (including the carrying out of positive works) in order to comply with the notice. Failure to comply with the requirements of an abatement notice without reasonable excuse is an

[63] EPA 1990, s.80.
[64] [1996] Env. L.R. 273.

offence. The recipient of an abatement notice may appeal against it to a magistrates' court on the grounds that the notice is not justified, that there has been an error in the service of the notice, that the authority has unreasonably refused to accept alternative methods of complying with the notice, that its requirements are unreasonable or unnecessary, that the period for compliance is unreasonably short, or that the best practicable means were used to abate the nuisance.

Defences

A number of defences are available to a person prosecuted for statutory nuisance. In **12–033** particular, the defences of reasonable excuse and best practicable means. In determining whether or not a person has a reasonable excuse to commit the nuisance, an objective test is appropriate, the question for the court being "would a reasonable person think that the excuse given was consistent with a reasonable standard of conduct?"[65] Thus, in *Wellingborough BC v Gordon*,[66] the defendant was held not to have a reasonable excuse when he argued that there had been a three year delay between the service of the abatement notice and its breach and that no-one had complained about the breach because the inconvenience caused was minimal.

Where the nuisance emanates from trade or industrial premises, it will be a defence for the accused to show that he used the best practicable means to prevent the occurrence of a nuisance.[67] In deciding whether or not this is the case, the court must take into account local conditions, the current state of technical knowledge and the design and operation of the defendant's plant and machinery, as well as the financial implications for the defendant of compliance with the abatement notice.[68] In addition, certain special defences are available where the nuisance consists of noise.[69]

G: THE RULE IN *RYLANDS V FLETCHER*

The "rule in *Rylands v Fletcher*" is an aspect of the tort of nuisance which applies **12–034** where the defendant carries on an unusual activity on his land, which, through no fault of his, results in damage to the property of another.[70] In the recent case of *Transco v Stockport MBC*,[71] the House of Lords was invited to abolish the rule and hold (as the High Court of Australia has done) that it has nowadays been "absorbed" into the law of negligence. Their Lordships, however, thought it right to preserve the rule, although

---

[65] Bell and McGillivray, *Environmental Law* (5th ed., 2000), p.441. As those authors point out, "reasonable excuse" is not technically a "defence". Rather, "without reasonable excuse" is a component of the offence. This means that the onus is on the prosecution to show that the excuse is not reasonable.

[66] [1993] Env. L.R. 218.

[67] EPA 1990, s.70.

[68] *ibid.*, s.79(9).

[69] *ibid.*, s.80(9).

[70] In *Transco v Stockport MBC* [2003] 3 W.L.R. 1467, the House of Lords asserted that, despite previous authority to the contrary, the rule has no application to claims for personal injury. Note also that, in the light of *Hunter and Others v Canary Wharf* [1997] A.C. 655 it is doubtful that such claims are covered by the tort of nuisance generally.

[71] [2003] 3 W.L.R 1467

they made it clear that it would nowadays only apply in limited circumstances. Accordingly, the rule remains part of the law of England and Wales. It has no application in the law of Scotland.[72]

The rule

12–035   The *Rylands v Fletcher* rule has its origins in a case of that name.[73] The defendants were owners of a mill who wanted to improve their water supply. To this end, they engaged a firm of independent contractors to construct a reservoir on their land. During the course of the works, the contractors discovered a number of disused mines and passages under the land on which the reservoir was to be built. They failed to seal off these passages, with the result that, when the reservoir was filled with water, the water ran through the passages and flooded the plaintiff's mine.

The defendants could not be liable under the usual rules of nuisance, which at the time did not allow for liability for a "one-off" event. Nor was it clear that the contractors should have foreseen that their activities would cause harm to the plaintiff, so it was unlikely that the plaintiff would have succeeded in negligence. An action in trespass may have failed because the damage caused to the plaintiff was not a direct and immediate consequence of the defendants' activities. Therefore, according to one view of the case, Blackburn J. in the Court of Exchequer created a new principle on which liability could be founded. However, as has been emphasised by the House of Lords in the recent cases of *Cambridge Water Co. v Eastern Counties Leather plc*[74] and *Transco v Stockport MBC*,[75] Blackburn J., in *Rylands v Fletcher*, was not, in fact, enunciating any new principle of law. Indeed, the terms in which his famous *dictum* is phrased indicate that he thought he was stating an established principle of law, rather than creating a new one, when he said:

> "We think that the true rule of law is, that the person who for his own purposes brings on to his lands and collects and keeps there anything likely to do mischief if it escapes, must keep it in at his peril, and, if he does not do so, he is prima facie answerable for all the damage which is the natural consequence of its escape."

This statement of principle by Blackburn J. was explicitly approved by Lord Cairns L.C. on appeal to the House of Lords. His Lordship, however, added the requirement that the defendant must be making a "non-natural use" of his land in order for liability to follow under the principle. The rule, therefore, has a number of elements, each of which is examined below.

Accumulation of things on land

12–036   Blackburn J. referred to the defendant "bringing" things on to his land. Thus, where the escape causing the damage is of something which arises naturally on the land or has accumulated there by natural forces, no liability will follow under the rule

---

[72] See *R.HM Bakeries (Scotland) Ltd. v Strathclyde Regional Council* 1985 SLT 214, where Lord Fraser (at 217) described the suggestion that the rule had any place in Scots law as a "heresy".
[73] (1868) L.R. 3 H.L. 330.
[74] [1994] 1 All E.R. 53. This view was subsequently endorsed by the House of Lords in *Transco v Stockport MBC* [2003] 3 W.L.R. 1467.
[75] [2003] 3 W.L.R. 1467.

(although it may, of course, follow in nuisance where the defendant fails to deal with the accumulation). In *Giles v Walker*,[76] for example, an escape of thistle seeds was not covered by the rule, nor, in *Smith v Kenrick*[77] was the escape of a natural accumulation of rain water.

"For his own purposes"

As formulated by Blackburn J., the rule appears to apply only to things which the **12–037** defendant has accumulated on land for his own purposes, so that if the things are brought on to the land by the defendant for the purposes of another he cannot be liable. The position in this regard is unclear. However, in *Rainham Chemical Works v Belvedere Fish Guano Co.*,[78] where two parties engaged in the manufacture of explosives had, in breach of the terms of their lease, assigned their tenancy of a factory to a company which they had formed, the House of Lords held that the parties were liable when an explosion occurred because they could not have, under their lease, (and therefore had not) effectively divested to the company their occupation of the premises. Lord Parmoor, however, was of the opinion that if the company had become the tenant and had entered into exclusive occupation of the premises, the materials brought on to the premises could not be said to have been for the purposes of the two individuals, but for the purposes of the company, so that it would be the company, and not they, who were liable.

"Likely to do mischief"

It is clear from the recent decision of the House of Lords in *Transco v Stockport MBC*[79] **12–038** (discussed below) that the rule will only apply where the defendant has done something which gives rise to an "exceptionally high risk of danger or mischief if there should be an escape".[80] This decision has done much to settle the question of whether it is a requirement of the rule that the thing which escapes from the defendant's land must be inherently dangerous. Although, not surprisingly, much of the relevant case law in the past had made reference to the "dangerousness" of the various things which had given rise to liability, in *Read v Lyons Ltd* (below), Lord Macmillan had stated that it would be impractical for the law to draw a distinction between "dangerous" and "non-dangerous" things, and the Law Commission had come to a similar conclusion.[81] The more straightforward approach taken by their Lordships in *Transco*, however, was to point out that the question whether a thing was "likely to do mischief" could not be sensibly considered in isolation from the requirement that the defendant was making a "non-natural" use of his land (see below). In other words, if a "non-natural" use of land means a use entailing exceptional risk, it follows that, where there is such a use, there must be something on the land that produces that risk in the sense that it is "likely to do mischief" if it escapes.

---

[76] (1890) 24 Q.B.D. 656.
[77] (1849) 7 C.B. 515.
[78] [1921] 2 A.C. 465.
[79] [2003] 3 W.L.R. 1467.
[80] *ibid.*, *per* Lord Bingham at 1474.
[81] *Civil Liability for Dangerous Things and Activities* (1970) (Law Com. 32).

"Escape"

12–039 For liability to arise, the thing which the defendant has on his land must "escape". Thus, in *Read v Lyons Ltd*,[82] where the plaintiff was injured by the explosion of a shell inside the defendants' war-time munitions factory, the defendants were not liable under the rule because the explosion was confined to within their premises.

Non-natural use of the land

12–040 The requirement that the defendant's use of his land be "non-natural" has led to particular difficulties. An examination of the use of the words "natural" and "naturally", as they appear in the judgments in *Rylands v Fletcher*, reveals that for both Blackburn J. and Lord Cairns L.C., the word "natural" meant "in accordance with nature". The original function of the "non-natural use" requirement, therefore, was to draw a distinction between a naturally occurring event (such as a natural flood) and an event which occurred because of something artificial (such as the flooding of a reservoir). However, in a line of cases, culminating with the famous decision in *Rickards v Lothian*,[83] the sense in which Blackburn J. and Lord Cairns had used these words was altered by the courts, so that a "natural" use of land came to mean a use of land which was "ordinary" or "usual".

In *Rickards v Lothian*, the plaintiff's offices were flooded when water flowed into them from the defendants' premises two floors above. The flooding was caused by the blocking of a lavatory basin which had overflowed because a "malicious person" had left a tap running into it. The Privy Council held that the defendants were not liable under the principle in *Rylands v Fletcher*. Lord Moulton stated:

> "It is not every use to which land is put that brings into play that principle. It must be some special use bringing with it increased danger to others, and must not merely be the ordinary use of the land or such a use as is proper for the general benefit of the community."

By adopting an expansive interpretation of "non-natural use", then, the courts narrowed the scope of *Rylands v Fletcher* liability—such liability could never arise if the defendant was making a usual and ordinary use of his land.[84] It is, of course, difficult to say, in any given set of circumstances, whether the defendant's use of his land might be regarded as "usual" or "ordinary", and despite the recent attempts in *Transco* to define the concept of "non-natural use" more closely, the concept remains rather vague, which means that it is impossible to state with certainty when the rule in *Rylands v Fletcher* will apply.

In *Cambridge Water Co. v Eastern Counties Leather plc*, where the defendants, in the course of their business, had stored chemicals on their land, Lord Goff expressly rejected the trial judge's finding that the activities of the defendants constituted a "natural" use of the land in the sense that they were proper for the general benefit of

---

[82] [1947] A.C. 156.
[83] [1913] A.C. 263.
[84] See Newark, "Non-Natural User and *Rylands v Fletcher*" (1961) 24 M.L.R. 557.

the community because they created employment. His Lordship stated that: "the storage of substantial quantities of chemicals on industrial premises should be regarded as an almost classic case of non-natural use." The facts of *Cambridge Water* may be contrasted with those of *Transco*. Here, the House of Lords regarded the laying of a three-inch pipe to supply water to a block of flats as a "natural" use of the land, because such a use was a commonplace and ordinary use of land.[85]

Strict liability

Liability under the rule in *Rylands v Fletcher* is often described as "strict liability". **12–041** "Strict liability" can mean a number of things in different contexts. In the context of *Rylands v Fletcher* liability, however, it simply means that absence of negligence is no defence. In other words, where there is an "escape" from the defendant's land, he will be liable for the consequences even where he shows that he took all reasonable care to prevent that escape. This follows from Blackburn J.'s insistence that the defendant must "keep [the thing] in at his peril". (There are, however, a number of defences to an action under the rule in *Rylands v Fletcher* which serve to undermine this principle—see below.)

A further meaning of the phrase "strict liability" implies that the defendant will be liable *even where he cannot foresee that the escape of the thing in question will cause damage to the defendant.* This type of "strict liability" is the sort of liability which arises under certain environmental statutory provisions which give effect to the "polluter pays" principle, for example those related to liability for contaminated land.[86] For some time it was thought that the rule in *Rylands v Fletcher* could also give rise to this form of "strict liability", and this was what the plaintiffs contended for, unsuccessfully, in *Cambridge Water Company v Eastern Counties Leather plc.*[87]

The decision in *Cambridge Water*

The defendants, Eastern Counties Leather, had operated a tannery in Sawston near **12–042** Cambridge for over 100 years. Until 1976, solvents for use in their business had been delivered to them in 40 gallon drums and transported for storage using fork-lift trucks. Over the years there had been a considerable number of spillages on the site. The spilled solvents had leached into the soil beneath the defendants' premises and had permeated the watercourse below. They had then travelled through the underground watercourse and percolated towards a borehole some 1.3 miles away, which the plaintiffs were using to abstract domestic drinking water for their customers. Cambridge Water Company began to use the borehole in 1979 and, before doing so, had established that the water was "wholesome" in accordance with the standards of water quality which were then current. In 1980, however, a new EC Directive relating to the particular solvents in question meant that the water could not be lawfully supplied as drinking water. The plaintiffs, who sought to recover their expenses in

---

[85] Their Lordships, however, approved Lord Goff's suggestion in *Cambridge Water* that it was unhelpful to consider whether the use in question was "proper for the benefit of the community".
[86] See Ch. 6.
[87] [1994] 1 All E.R. 53.

locating a new source of groundwater, brought an action in negligence, nuisance and under the rule in *Rylands v Fletcher*.

At first instance, the trial judge, finding that it could not be foreseen in 1976 that the spillages which had occurred would give rise to contamination of the watercourse in this way, dismissed the plaintiffs' claims. The Court of Appeal, overturning the decision of the trial judge, followed *Ballard v Tomlinson*,[88] and held that since what was complained of was interference with a right akin to a property right (the right to abstract water), then liability would follow without foreseeability, the only issue being whether the defendants had caused the interference. On appeal to the House of Lords, their Lordships allowed the appeal by Eastern Counties Leather on the basis that foreseeability of the relevant damage was necessary to found liability in nuisance, negligence *and* under the rule in *Rylands v Fletcher*.

As a matter of policy, the House of Lords was reluctant to impose liability for pollution without foreseeability of the relevant harm because to do so would, in effect, impose retrospective liability on a defendant. The idea of retrospective liability is generally alien to the UK legal system, although it is now provided for in relation to contaminated land (see Ch. 6). Their Lordships took the view, therefore, that liability for "historic pollution" (*i.e.* pollution which occurs at a time when it is not known that the substance being released into the environment is a pollutant) is a matter for Parliament rather than for the courts. As Lord Goff put it:

> "I incline to the opinion that, as a general rule, it is more appropriate for strict liability in respect of operations of high risk to be imposed by Parliament than by the courts. It is of particular relevance that the present case is concerned with environmental pollution. The protection and preservation of the environment is now perceived as being of crucial importance to the future of mankind, and public bodies, both national and international, are taking significant steps towards the establishment of legislation which will promote the protection of the environment and make the polluter pay for damage to the environment for which he is responsible. But it does not follow from these developments that a common law principle such as the rule in *Rylands v Fletcher* should be developed or rendered more strict to provide for liability in respect of such pollution. On the contrary, given that so much well-informed and carefully structured legislation is now being put in place for this purpose, there is less need for the courts to develop a common law principle to achieve the same end and indeed it may well be undesirable that they should do so."

The decision in *Transco*

12–043   In *Transco v Stockport MBC*[89] the defendants, Stockport Council, were the owners of a three-inch pipe which supplied water to a block of flats. The claimants (formerly British Gas plc) were the owners of a gas main on neighbouring land. Without fault on the part of the council, a leak developed in the pipe which went unnoticed for some time. The water saturated the land beneath the block of flats and then percolated

[88] (1885) 29 Ch.D. 115.
[89] [2003] 3 W.L.R. 1467.

towards the land on which the gas main was situated. Eventually, the presence of the water caused a landslide, which resulted in the gas main being left unsupported. In these circumstances, there was a serious risk that the gas main would fracture with disastrous consequences. Transco therefore acted promptly to remedy the situation, incurring expense. They sought to recover this expense from the council under the rule in *Rylands v Fletcher*.

In denying Transco's claim, the House of Lords took the opportunity to consider and refine the role of the *Rylands v Fletcher* rule in modern law. In particular, their Lordships made the following observations:

- The rule protects a claimant's interest in *land*. Therefore, only parties with exclusive possession of the affected land may bring a *Rylands v Fletcher* claim;

- The rule cannot be used to recover damages for personal injury; and

- The rule applies only to activities on land that are exceptionally hazardous. It has no application where land is being used for a commonplace purpose which presents no extraordinary risk—such use of land is to be regarded as a "natural" use of the land for the purposes of the rule.

Their Lordships in *Transco* did not think that the supply of water to a block of flats through a pipe constituted an exceptionally hazardous activity which presented an extraordinary risk. Accordingly, Stockport Council could not be liable under the rule.

Defences to an action under *Rylands v Fletcher*

As has been said, liability under *Rylands v Fletcher* is "strict" in the sense that it is no **12–044** defence for the defendant to show that he took all reasonable care to prevent the escape. It therefore differs from common law liability in negligence. However, although absence of negligence is not generally a defence, there are certain circumstances in which it will be:

(1) *Statutory authority*

If the dangerous thing is operated under statutory authority, the defendant will not be **12–045** liable unless he is shown to have been negligent. Thus, in *Green v Chelsea Waterworks*,[90] where a water main burst without any negligence on the part of the defendants, it was held that since statute had authorised the defendants to lay the water main and to maintain a continuous supply of water, the statute had also impliedly exempted them from liability in the absence of negligence. (Note that, in *Transco*, Lord Hoffmann pointed out that it was ironic that, had the *Transco* case been about a burst water main—the maintaining of which would be "a much more plausible high-risk activity" than maintaining a three-inch pipe—liability under *Rylands v Fletcher* would have been excluded by statute.[91])

---

[90] (1894) 70 L.T. 547.
[91] *Transco v Stockport MBC* [2003] 3 W.L.R. 1467, *per* Lord Hoffmann at para.42.

(2) *Act of stranger*

12–046 This defence provides that where the damage is caused by the actions of a third party which were not foreseeable by the defendant, he will not be liable. Thus, in *Perry v Kendrick Transport Ltd*,[92] where two boys ignited the fuel tank of a bus, injuring the plaintiff, the Court of Appeal held that the plaintiff had failed to show that the removal of the petrol cap by a third party was the type of act which the defendants ought reasonably to have foreseen and taken precautions against. Obviously, the operation of this defence somewhat dilutes the idea that the defendant must keep in the dangerous thing at his peril and, where the actions of third parties are involved, approximates liability under *Rylands v Fletcher* to liability in negligence.

(3) *Act of God*

12–047 As in a nuisance action, the defendant will escape liability if he can show that the damage has been caused by an Act of God. According to Lord Westbury in *Tennant v Earl of Glasgow*,[93] the defence will operate in circumstances which are:

> "circumstances which no human foresight can provide against, and of which human prudence is not bound to recognise the possibility, and which when they do occur, therefore, are calamities that do not involve the obligation of paying for the consequences that may result from them."

H: TRESPASS

12–048 In essence, the tort of trespass requires that the defendant's conduct be intentional rather than careless (as in the tort of negligence)[94] or unreasonable (as in nuisance). Moreover, for trespass to be established, the damage which results to the claimant must be a direct, rather than indirect, consequence of the defendant's activities. The point was illustrated by Fortescue J. in *Reynolds v Clarke*[95]:

> " if a man throws a log into the highway and it hits me I may maintain trespass because it is an immediate wrong; but if, as it lies there, I tumble over it and receive an injury, I must bring an action upon the case [*i.e.* an action in negligence] because it is only prejudicial in consequence."

For these reasons, the tort of trespass is of limited utility in environmental protection. The requirement of "directness" is particularly difficult to overcome because, where substances are released into the environment and may affect any number of persons in a number of different ways, the damage is inevitably "consequential" in nature.

Despite these difficulties, an action in trespass may have a number of advantages. For example, in *Jones v Llanrwst UDC*,[96] where faecal matter deposited by the council

---

[92] [1956] 1 W.L.R. 85.
[93] (1864) 2 M. (H.L.) 22.
[94] *Letang v Cooper* [1965] 1 Q.B. 232.
[95] (1725) 1 Stra. 643.
[96] [1911] 1 Ch. 393.

came to rest on the plaintiff's river bed, the court refused to allow a defence of statutory authority to succeed, holding that a private individual was entitled to an injunction to restrain the council from allowing sewage to escape from a sewer, notwithstanding that the council was under a statutory duty to accept and dispose of the sewage. A further advantage of trespass is that, unlike nuisance, it is actionable without the claimant's needing to show that he has suffered, or is likely to suffer, any damage. This makes it easy for the claimant to obtain an injunction in cases where the gathering of evidence to prove that damage has occurred would be time-consuming or costly.

I: NEGLIGENCE

An action in negligence, which requires the claimant to show that the defendant owes **12–049** him a duty of care, that he has breached that duty (in that his conduct has fallen below the standard required of the "reasonable person"), and that the damage caused by the breach is of a kind which is reasonably foreseeable, is also of limited use in environmental matters. There have, however, been cases in which it has succeeded. In *Tutton v A.D. Walter Ltd*,[97] for example, a farmer who, contrary to the advice of the manufacturers and of government, sprayed his land with insecticide when oil seed rape was in flower, was held to have been negligent when he caused the death of a number of the plaintiff's bees. More controversially, perhaps, in *Scott-Whitehead v National Coal Board*,[98] a regional water authority was held liable in negligence for failing to advise a farmer that the water which he was abstracting for irrigation purposes was contaminated.

J: RIPARIAN RIGHTS

The owner of land adjacent to water has certain common law rights of a quasi- **12–050** proprietary nature in the soil beneath the water. These are important in the context of water pollution and are therefore considered in Ch. 8.

[97] [1985] 3 W.L.R. 797.
[98] (1987) 53 P.&C.R. 263.

Chapter 13

PLANNING LAW AND THE ENVIRONMENT

"Planning control is primarily concerned with the type and location of new development and changes of use. Once broad land uses have been sanctioned by the planning process, it is the job of pollution control to limit the adverse effects that operations may have on the environment. But in practice there is common ground."[1]

Introduction

Land is needed for homes, transport, industrial activity and the production of food. **13–001** The aesthetic qualities of landscapes are also of benefit to mankind. The amount of land used in the UK has increased dramatically over the last century or so, in line with the expansion of the population. The ways in which land has been used have profoundly affected the environment. In many cases they have changed the nature of land irrevocably, so that future generations are deprived of the choices enjoyed by present generations about the uses to which land can be put. In deciding whether and how to develop land, the advantages of development must be balanced against the advantages of conserving land in its undeveloped state. The principal legal mechanism for striking this balance is the planning system. Approximately 500,000 applications for planning permission are made each year.

Planning law is a vast subject. To cover it in its entirety is beyond the scope of this book. This chapter, however, aims to explain the basic principles of planning law and to consider the ways in which the operation of the planning system is related to the operation of the various pollution control regimes and environmental protection principles examined elsewhere in the book.

Planning decisions and environmental protection are intricately linked, and it is sometimes unclear where the dividing line is to be drawn between "planning" and "environmental" controls. As we can see from the quotation that begins this chapter, the two regimes of control have slightly different purposes. What is clear, however, is that very often the purposes of the two regimes converge, so that "environmental" issues must form part of planning policy and procedure: A proposed motorway may cut across the habitat of a rare bird. Environmental problems can be aggravated by bad planning decisions, but can often be avoided by sensitive location of new development.

[1] *This Common Inheritance—Britain's Environmental Strategy* (Cm 1200, September 1990).

Despite the far-reaching statutory provisions in relation to contaminated land (see Ch. 6), problems of contamination are to be tackled primarily through the planning system.[2]

In some situations, the purposes of the two forms of control have the potential to conflict—environmental "initiatives" may be at odds with more traditional planning concerns. One classic example of this conflict arises over the location of wind farms, which have sometimes been refused planning permission on grounds of noise and visual impact. Another example arises in the context of waste management. Before a waste management licence can be granted, planning permission for the waste disposal site must be obtained. The "proximity principle" (see Ch. 7) requires that new waste management and disposal facilities should be located near to the source of the waste—but this will not always be easy to reconcile with the traditional objectives of urban planning law, which might suggest that out-of-town locations would be preferable.

History and development of planning law

13–002   In the aftermath of the Second World War, the UK was left with ruined towns and cities which needed to be redeveloped. Industry, which needed to adapt to serve the peacetime market, also required land for development. There was perceived an opportunity, and indeed a need, to create a new and comprehensive planning regime which could impose some coherence on development. To this end, the Town and Country Planning Act 1947 was passed. This repealed all previous planning legislation and provided the basis for the modern planning system. At this time, the emphasis was on development, so as to rebuild the country. There was little concern for environmental protection, and indeed very little environmental protection legislation. Today, the physical and regulatory landscape is very different—and whether the modern planning regime has adequately adapted to the changes is a matter of debate.

A series of Acts subsequent to the 1947 Act completed the modern system. In 1962 and 1971 there were certain repeals of previous legislation. A further repeal and consolidation took place in 1990 with the passing of the Town and Country Planning Act 1990, the Planning (Listed Buildings and Conservation Areas) Act 1990 and the Planning (Hazardous Substances) Act 1990. The provisions of these Acts, however, were swiftly amended by the Planning and Compensation Act 1991, which made a number of amendments and additions to the new system. The Town and Country Planning Act 1990 (as amended) is the most important statute.

Features of the modern planning system

13–003   The following may be identified as the most significant features of the modern planning system:

(1) Ownership of land entails merely the right to go on using it for its existing purposes or for very similar purposes. An owner has no *right* to "develop" his

---

[2] See DETR Circular 02/2000 Contaminated Land: Implementation of Pt IIA of the Environmental Protection Act 1990.

land. That is to say he has no right to build on the land or change the use to which it is put. However, if he wishes to do so, he does not have to demonstrate a "need" for development, and once planning permission is granted, it effectively confers a right to develop—planning permission, once granted, cannot normally be varied or revoked except on the payment of compensation.

(2) Almost all development requires planning permission before it can proceed (for some types of development, however, as we shall see, permission is automatically granted, or is not needed). However, there may be said to be a presumption in favour of granting permission—approximately 90 per cent of planning applications made each year are granted.[3] There are suggestions that this approach may provide inadequate control over development in the light of environmental concerns. Whilst there is a right of appeal against a *refusal* to grant planning permission, there is *no* right of appeal by third parties (*e.g.* objectors) where planning permission has been *granted*.

(3) Control of development is achieved by means of flexible "development plans", drawn up by the planning authority, which afford the planning authority some discretion in whether or not to grant planning permission. Such a system is to be contrasted with a rigid "zoning" system, under which, once the development plan has marked out an area of land for a particular purpose, development within that area which does not fulfil that purpose will be prohibited absolutely.

(4) Decisions on applications for planning permission are taken in accordance with the development plan for an area, unless there are "material considerations" which indicate otherwise. The planning authorities must have regard to policies contained in various documents, including Planning Policy Guidance (PPGs), National Planning Guidance (NPGs), Regional Planning Guidance (RPGs) (in England), County Structure Plans (in England), Unitary Development Plans and Local Plans (in England), White Papers and Circulars. PPGs and RPGs are the principal source of guidance on general planning *policy*, whilst Circulars are the main source of guidance on the interpretation of legislation and on procedural matters.

(5) The planning regime is administered at a local level by planning authorities. However, strong control over planning matters is retained by central and regional government[4] by the publication of guidance (above) and by the Secretary of State's power to "call-in" plans and planning applications for approval.

(6) Decisions on planning applications result from an essentially political decision-making process. They are taken by elected local planning authorities, or by the Secretary of State, who must balance political, social, economic and environmental factors. The courts have always been careful to recognise this political dimension of planning control, and have therefore allowed planning decision-makers considerable autonomy.

[3] Development Control Statistics: England 2002–2003: *www.odpm.gov.uk/stellent/groups/odm-planning/documents/page/odm_plan_027304.pdf.*
[4] Following devolution, planning matters in Wales, Scotland and Northern Ireland are the responsibility of the devolved administrations.

Planning and other environmental controls

13–004 In formulating policy and determining planning applications, a planning authority's terms of reference are to consider the effect of development on the "amenity of the locality". As PPG 1 puts it:

> "The purpose of the planning system is to regulate the development and use of land in the public interest. The material question is not whether the occupiers of neighbouring properties would suffer financial or other loss from a particular development, but whether the proposal would affect the locality generally and unacceptably affect amenities that ought in the public interest to be protected."[5]

This focus on "locality", then, means that, *prima facie*, the remit of the planning system does not include consideration of the impacts of development on the wider environment. The system is primarily designed to control the local built environment.

Although protection of the wider environment sometimes has a place in the planning system, it is clear that it is only *one factor* amongst many which must be balanced in formulating policy and making decisions whether to grant planning permission. The planning system has to take account of a wide range of other considerations. Given that planning decisions are ultimately *political* decisions, there is scope for environmental considerations to be given less weight than other considerations—thus, for example, PPG 9 states that local planning authorities should not refuse planning permission if other factors are sufficient to override nature conservation considerations.

Because of its heavy reliance on discretionary decision-making, planning policy is rarely capable of affording land absolute immunity from development for the protection of the wider environment. This is usually only possible by designation of a site as a National Nature Reserve and by appropriation of the site by a nature conservancy council (see Ch. 9). Sometimes, the planning system simply has no opportunity to consider the wider environment. For example, the use of land for the purposes of agriculture or forestry is exempt from the need for planning permission, because it is statutorily declared not to constitute development.[6] Thus, although intensive farming is one of the main causes of habitat destruction, it cannot be regulated from within the planning system.

Administratively, there are some key differences between the planning system and the various pollution control regimes, and these differences place limits on what the planning system can achieve in terms of environmental protection. One such difference is that planning control takes place essentially on a "one off" basis. Although there are various enforcement measures available to prevent the use of land in a way that has not been authorised, planning control lacks the sort of active and continuing supervision which characterises environmental licensing. Environmental licences tend to be periodically reviewed once granted, through formal procedures, often with the onus on the licence holder to show compliance. By contrast, compliance with planning control is monitored by a system of relatively informal observation, and by considering

[5] PPG 1.
[6] TCPA 1990, s.55.

complaints from the public. The onus is on the planning authority to show non-compliance.

Another key difference is that environmental licensing is often a *personal* matter, in the sense that the likelihood of compliance or non-compliance by the licence holder is taken into account in licensing decisions—the holder of a waste management licence, for example, must be a "fit and proper person" (see Ch. 7). By contrast, the focus of planning decisions is solely on the *land being developed*. Planning permission, once granted, attaches to the land, not the person to whom it is granted. This means that if the land is sold, permission to use that land as authorised is transferred to the buyer, regardless of any likelihood that he will exceed the terms of the permission.

The relationship between planning and the various pollution control regimes was described in the 1990 White Paper *This Common Inheritance*,[7] the first comprehensive government statement of environmental strategy:

> "Planning control is primarily concerned with the type and location of new development and changes of use. Once broad land uses have been sanctioned by the planning process, it is the job of pollution control to limit the adverse effects that operations may have on the environment. But in practice there is common ground. In considering whether to grant planning permission for a particular development, a local authority must consider all the effects, including potential pollution; permission should not be granted if that might expose people to danger. And a change in an industrial process may require planning permission as well as approval under the environmental protection legislation."

This makes it clear that pollution concerns have a place in planning decisions, but two aspects of this statement are noteworthy. First, planning authorities are not explicitly exhorted to consider the *general* effect of pollution on the *wide* environment. Secondly, a restricted anthropocentric view is taken towards pollution problems—they might "expose people to danger". This suggests that consideration of the effects of pollution on, say, habitats and ecosystems, might be less relevant. That said, it is clear that an increasing number of environmental obligations (most of EC origin), such as those relating to air quality, environmental impact assessment, and habitat conservation, are placing wider environmental considerations at the heart of the planning system and are placing new boundaries on the discretion of decision-makers.

Current government guidance on the overlap between planning and pollution control[8] states that the role of the planning system is to focus on whether the development is an acceptable use of the land, rather than to make development decisions in every case by reference to the development's likely impact on the wider environment.[9] In making decisions, the planning authority must assume that the risk and impact of pollution from the proposed development will be dealt with fully by the relevant pollution control authority. Under the UK pollution control regimes, almost all operations on land with the potential to cause pollution—such as the use of land as a landfill site, or for an industrial activity prescribed under the IPC or PPC regimes

---

[7] *This Common Inheritance—Britain's Environmental Strategy* (Cm 1200, September 1990).
[8] PPG22 : Planning and Pollution Control (1994) and PPG10: Planning and Waste Management (1999).
[9] PPG 23.

(see Ch. 5)—require a licence, either from the Environment Agency or from the local authority. A grant of planning permission will not exempt the operator of an industrial or waste management process from the need to obtain such a licence, and the fact that planning permission has been granted does not mean that such a licence will be forthcoming—the planning authority and the pollution control authority will have regard to different considerations.

The relationship between planning and other environmental controls was considered in *Gateshead MBC v Secretary of State for the Environment*.[10] The case concerned an application for planning permission to build a clinical waste incinerator. The Secretary of State had granted outline planning permission for the project, on the basis that the controls available under the Environmental Protection Act 1990 could and would address any environmental concerns. In upholding the grant of planning permission, Glidewell L.J., in the Court of Appeal, referred to government guidance on the relationship between pollution control and planning control, and stated: "It is not the job of the planning system to duplicate controls which are the statutory responsibility of other bodies."

It followed that issues concerning air quality policy, which were raised during the appeal, were properly to be considered by the relevant environmental authorities, rather than by the Secretary of State in the exercise of planning control. It might, of course, be appropriate to refuse planning permission in cases where it became clear, when considering a planning application, that the environmental impacts were so unacceptable that the pollution control authorities would *inevitably* refuse an environmental licence. However, where, as here, environmental issues were raised, but there was no clear evidence as to the environmental effects in question, matters should be left to the pollution control authorities. As his Lordship put it:

> "The dividing line between planning and pollution control considerations is therefore not always clear-cut. In such cases close consultation between planning and pollution control authorities will be important at all stages, in particular because it would not be sensible to grant planning permission for a development for which a necessary pollution control authorisation is unlikely to be forthcoming."

A: THE REGULATORY AUTHORITIES

Local planning authorities

13–005   The decision whether planning permission should be granted is normally made by a local planning authority. Local planning authorities are differently constituted in different parts of the country. At the time of writing, in the six metropolitan counties in England (Greater Manchester, Merseyside, South Yorkshire, Tyne and Wear, West Midlands and West Yorkshire), the local planning authority is the metropolitan district council. In Greater London the local planning authority is the borough council for

[10] [1995] Env. L.R. 37.

each of the 32 boroughs. In the rest of the country, that is to say in the 47 non-metropolitan counties (or "shire" counties), the traditional position is that the county council is the planning authority for the whole county, whilst the district council is the planning authority for each district. However, 24 shire counties (plus the Isle of Wight) have been re-organised under a one-tier unitary council, which is the sole planning authority. In certain special areas[11] (e.g. National Parks and Enterprise Zones) planning matters have been taken out of the hands of the usual planning authorities. These areas have their own specially-constituted planning authorities (e.g. National Park Authorities). In Wales, the system of local government is unitary—the county council or county borough council for an area is the local planning authority.[12]

The Secretary of State

The Secretary of State has a series of wide-ranging supervisory powers, including the **13–006** power to "call in" development plans for approval. He may also "call in" individual planning applications.[13] "Call in" of planning applications for determination tends to occur with applications that the Secretary of State believes should be more closely scrutinised before permission is granted. They will usually involve planning issues of more than local importance—i.e. issues which have effects beyond the immediate locality; issues which give rise to substantial regional or national controversy; or issues which conflict with national policy on important matters. The functions of the Secretary of State are in England vested in the Secretary of State for Transport, Local Government and the Regions, and in Wales in the National Assembly for Wales.

The Planning Inspectorate

The Planning Inspectorate is an executive agency of the Office of the Deputy Prime **13–007** Minister in England and the National Assembly in Wales. It serves the Secretary of State, and the First Minister of the National Assembly for Wales, in matters relating to plan-making, planning decisions, and enforcement. Members of the inspectorate (planning inspectors) chair planning inquiries, which may be held in relation to the drafting of plans or the determination of planning applications. The inspector is required to hear all the evidence presented at the inquiry and then produce a considered report for the Secretary of State.

Planning in Scotland and Northern Ireland

In Scotland, planning legislation was consolidated in the Town and Country Planning **13–008** (Scotland) Act 1997, which is in most respects similar to the Town and Country Planning Act 1990. The "call in" powers are exercised by the Scottish Ministers. Planning matters in Northern Ireland are also governed by legislation which mirrors

---

[11] National Parks, the Norfolk and Suffolk Broads, Urban Development Areas, Enterprise Zones, Housing Action Trust Areas and Urban Regeneration Areas.
[12] See Local Government (Wales) Act 1994.
[13] TCPA 1990, s.77.

the Town and Country Planning Act 1990,[14] although there are important differences (including the absence of a legal presumption in favour of following the development plan). Responsibility for planning lies with the Department of the Environment (Northern Ireland), which determines planning applications through a "planning service", there being no local planning authorities (although local authorities have a consultative role).

B: The Meaning of "Development"

13–009 The planning system regulates the "development" of land. The statutory definition of "development" has been described as "the very essence of the Town and Country Planning Act 1990—the pivot on which the whole system of day-to-day control of land development under the 1990 Act turns and depends."[15] An understanding of this definition, then, is vital in order to appreciate the scope of planning law. "Development" is defined in the Act[16] as:

(1) The carrying out of building operations, engineering operations, mining operations or other operations in, on, over, or under land; or

(2) The making of any material change in the use of any buildings or other land.

The Act provides that "development" can occur even where the land in question is not physically altered. In addition, the following four matters are specifically mentioned as constituting development:

(1) The use of a single dwelling-house for the purpose of two or more separate dwellings[17];

(2) The deposit of refuse or waste materials on an existing dump if either:

(a) The superficial area of the dump is extended, or
(b) The height of the dump is extended and exceeds the level of the land adjoining the dump;

(3) The placing or assembly of a tank in any inland waters for the purpose of fish farming;

(4) The display of an advertisement on the external part of a building not normally used for such display.[18]

"Building operations"

13–010 Building operations include the demolition of buildings, rebuilding, structural alterations or additions to buildings, and any other operations normally undertaken by a person carrying on business as a builder.[19] Internal works in a house, however, do not

---

[14] Planning (Northern Ireland) Order 1991.
[15] Heap, *An Outline of Planning Law.*
[16] TCPA 1990, s.55 and s.336(1).
[17] *ibid.*, s.55(3)(a).
[18] *ibid.*, s.55(5) and s.222.
[19] *ibid.*, s.55(2).

constitute "building operations".[20] The courts have taken the view that an object attached to land can be a "building" even if it is very small (*e.g.* a model village).

"Engineering operations"

The 1990 Act gives little guidance on the meaning of "engineering operations". They **13–011** have been broadly defined by the courts as "operations of the kind usually undertaken by engineers"[21], which takes us little further, but would exclude, for example, the removal of turf or top-soil from land, such as might be undertaken by a landscape gardener.

"Mining operations"

The Act defines "mining operations" so as to include the removal of material of any **13–012** description from a mineral working deposit; or from a deposit of pulverised fuel ash or other furnace ash; the removal of clinker from a deposit of iron, steel or other metallic slags; and the extraction of minerals from a disused railway embankment.[22]

"Material change of use"

A change of use occurs when there is a change in the use to which the land, building or **13–013** structure is currently put. The courts have taken the view that the question whether or not a change of use is "material" is a matter of fact and degree for the local planning authority to decide. They will only interfere with a decision if it is one to which no reasonable authority could have come.[23] The Use Classes Order (discussed below) provides a useful indication as to when land will be considered to have changed its use. Changes of use will include, for example, changes from commercial to residential use, and *vice versa*, as where a residential house is used for offices. Certain changes of use, however, are statutorily declared not to constitute development and are therefore exempt from the need for planning permission (see below).

C: Exemptions From the Need to Apply for Planning Permission

Some forms of activity do not require an application for planning permission. This will **13–014** be for one of two reasons:

- Some activities are exempt from the requirement because they *do not constitute development*.

---

[20] *ibid.*, s.55(2)(a).
[21] *Fayrewood Fish Farms Ltd v Secretary of State for the Environment* [1984] J.P.L. 267.
[22] TCPA, s.55(4).
[23] *Bendles Motors Ltd v Bristol Corporation* [1963] 1 W.L.R. 247.

- Other activities are exempt because, although they constitute development, permission is *granted* for those activities by legislation.

Matters which do not constitute development

13–015 The following seven matters do not constitute development[24]:

(1) Internal or external improvements, alterations or maintenance works none of which materially affects the external appearance of the building so treated;

(2) Maintenance or improvement works carried out by a local highway authority to, and within the boundaries of, a road;

(3) The breaking open of streets etc. for the inspection, repair or renewal of sewers, mains, pipes, cables etc. by a local authority or a statutory undertaker;

(4) The use of any buildings or other land within the curtilage of a dwelling house for any purpose incidental to the enjoyment of the dwelling house;

(5) The use of land for agriculture or forestry and the use for those purposes of any building occupied in connection with land so used;

(6) The demolition of any description of building specified in a direction given by the Secretary of State to local planning authorities generally or to a particular local planning authority; and

(7) In the case of buildings or other land used for a purpose of any class specified in an Order made by the Secretary of State, the use thereof for any purpose within the same class.

(1) Agriculture and forestry

13–016 Agriculture and forestry have long been exempt from most development controls. This may have been appropriate in 1947, after the Second World War, when the production of food was a priority. However, the exemption is questionable nowadays, given the significant environmental impacts of agriculture which might be controlled through planning law. Impacts of farming on the environment include pesticide run-off into waters, over-abstraction of water, reduction in biodiversity, and erosion of soil. In 2002, farming was responsible for 12 per cent of the most serious pollution incidents in the UK.[25]

(2) The Use Classes Order

13–017 The Use Classes Order[26], made by the Secretary of State, provides that certain changes in the use of land do not constitute development. The aim of the Order is to reduce the need for planning permission where it is unnecessary because the change of use

---

[24] TCPA 1990, s.55.
[25] See Spotlight 2002 Environment Agency report in the environment performance of farming: *www.environment-agency.gov.uk*.
[26] Town and Country Planning (Use Classes) Order 1987 (SI 1987/764) (as amended by SI 1995/297). The content of the order in England is currently under review.

will not damage the amenity of the area. In this way, property owners are given greater freedom, and the burden of planning control is lifted in relation to a variety of commercial activities.

The Use Classes Order divides uses of land into different "classes", according to their potential to affect the amenity of the area. Changes of use within the same class are permitted, as is a change from within a "bad for local amenity" use-class to a "better for local amenity" use-class. Thus, for example, where a post office is changed to become a travel agency, this will not constitute development, so no planning permission will be required. If, however, the post office were to change into a take-away selling hot food, a change of use not permitted by the Use Classes Order would have taken place, so planning permission would be necessary. Unlike a post office, a take-away might be open late at night; people might congregate outside; litter might be deposited; so it would not be appropriate to permit such a change without regulatory control.

Matters for which planning permission is granted by legislation

Some operations are exempt from control by planning authorities because planning **13–018** permission is granted for them by regulations or by primary legislation. This is sometimes referred to as "deemed" planning permission. These operations include:

(1) *Development permitted under a Development Order*

Under the Town and Country Planning Act 1990, the Secretary of State may make **13–019** "Development Orders" which grant planning permission for certain types of development.[27] Eighty-four classes of development are permitted. These include:

(a) Marginal development, such as enlarging a dwelling house or erecting a gate;

(b) Development by certain types of developers, such as local authorities, highways authorities and water authorities; and

(c) Development connected with development allowed under other statutory provisions.

(2) *Development in an Enterprise Zone*

Enterprise zones are areas designated by the government in order to encourage **13–020** industrial and commercial activity.[28] In such zones, developers do not have to go to the trouble and expense of applying for planning permission for every kind of development.

(3) *Development in a Simplified Planning Zone*

Any development in a Simplified Planning Zone that conforms with the terms of the **13–021** scheme laid down for that area does not require planning permission. The planning regime in such a zone is similar to that in an Enterprise Zone, but whilst Enterprise

[27] TCPA 1990, s.59. The orders currently in force include the Town and Country Planning (General Permitted Development) Order 1995 (SI 1995/418) and the Town and Country Planning (General Development Procedure) Order 1995 (SI 1995/419).
[28] Local Government Planning and Land Act 1980, Sch.32 para.17(1).

Zones have other advantages, Simplified Planning Zones relate solely to planning freedom.

D: DEVELOPMENT PLANS

13–022 Development plans set out the planning policies, aims and objectives of each local planning authority. In preparing their plans, local planning authorities must have regard, *inter alia*, to guidance issued by the Secretary of State and to national policies. In the "shire" counties, two different plans are prepared—a "structure" plan and a "local" plan—whilst in other areas of the country there is only one "unitary" plan. The plans are important because there is a legal presumption (discussed below) that plans should be followed when determining planning applications. During their preparation, plans are subject to extensive public consultation. The Secretary of State has the power to supervise the making of all development plans. He is a statutory consultee at the preparation stage, where he can object to the plan and make a direction that it should be modified. Exceptionally, he can "call in" all or part of the plan for approval or rejection.[29] Although these powers are rarely used, their purpose is to ensure that development plans do not become greatly out of step with government policy.

Structure plans

13–023 Structure plans are prepared in relation to a substantial region, such as a whole county. The policies in structure plans deal only with the major uses of land in the region, and set out broad policies in relation to future development. The Act requires structure plans to include policies with respect to the conservation of the natural beauty and amenity of the land, the improvement of the physical environment, and the management of traffic.[30] In addition, structure plans will include policies on housing, Green Belts, conservation of the built environment, urban and rural economies, transport, waste management, tourism, leisure and energy generation (including the use of renewable energy).[31]

Local plans

13–024 Local plans translate the broad strategic issues dealt with in the structure plan into specific detailed policies and proposals. Each local plan will comprise a map, designating particular areas of land for the implementation of particular policies, together with a written statement detailing those policies. The local plan forms the basis for determining planning applications. If a developer wishes to see what he can do with his land, he can easily consult the local plan to find out what policy restrictions attach to his land and the purpose for which it has been designated. These matters will usually determine whether or not his application for planning permission will succeed,

[29] TCPA 1990, s.35A (structure plans) and s.44 (local plans).
[30] TCPA 1990, ss.12(3A) and 31(3).
[31] See PPG 12, para.5.9.

although they are not conclusive. The difference between structure plans and local plans can be illustrated by looking at the way in which they deal with housing policy. The structure plan will allocate a specific number of houses to each district, whilst the local plan will allocate these to specific sites.

Unitary development plans

For areas that have unitary authorities, there is only one plan which covers both broad **13–025** policy and specific details. This is known as a "unitary development plan". It consists of a Pt 1 and a Pt 2, which have the same functions as a structure plan and a local plan respectively.

Environmental considerations in development plans

Government guidance on the drawing up of development plans is contained in PPG **13–026** 12, which states:

> "Local planning authorities should take account of the environment in the widest sense in plan preparation. They are familiar with the "traditional" issues of Green Belt, concern for landscape quality and nature conservation, the built heritage and conservation areas. They are familiar too with pollution control planning for healthier cities. The challenge is to ensure that newer environmental concerns such as global warming and the consumption of non-renewable resources are also reflected in the analysis of policies that forms part of plan preparation."

Most policies and proposals, in all types of plan, will have environmental implications which should be appraised as part of the plan-preparation process. However, PPG 12 does not currently require planning authorities to conduct a full environmental impact assessment in relation to its policies.[32] The Strategic Assessment Directive,[33] adopted in June 2001, plugs this gap by requiring environmental impact assessment of a range of plans and programmes that is broad enough to cover development plans. The Directive must be implemented in Member States by July 21, 2004. At the time of writing, the Office of the Deputy Prime Minister is consulting on implementation.

Planning authorities are also required to have regard to other government guidance in preparing their development plans. Such guidance requires, for example, that a planning authority should take account of any designations affecting land (*e.g.* for nature conservation purposes), and weigh up the need to encourage rural enterprise with the need to protect the landscape, wildlife habitats, and historic features. Plans must include policies encouraging the management of features of the landscape which are of major importance for wild fauna and flora. These are defined as those features essential for migration, dispersal and genetic exchange of wild species—reflecting the wording of the Conservation (Natural Habitats) Regulations 1994,[34] which implement

[32] PPG 12, para.5.2.
[33] Directive 2001/42/EC.
[34] See Conservation (Natural Habitats, etc.) Regulations 1994 (SI 1994/2716), reg.37.

the Habitats Directive (discussed in Ch. 9). The structure plan should indicate how the balance between development and conservation has been struck.

Development plans should also include policies for the clean-up and re-use of contaminated land, for the protection of groundwater resources, for the environmental effects of new water services, and for the siting of hazardous installations and mineral extraction operations. They should also contain policies in relation to waste. When drawing up development plans, planning authorities are required to have regard to the principles set out in the Waste Framework Directive, including that waste should be recovered or disposed of without harming human health, and without using methods which could harm the environment.

Consultation on development plans

13–027 In drawing up the plans, a statutory process of public consultation and debate takes place.[35] This is the primary means of reconciling conflicts between the need for development and the need to protect the environment. The reality is that this is the most important point for integrating environmental considerations into the planning process, because, once the plan is in place, decisions whether or not to grant planning permission, and decisions about planning conditions, will depend upon the content of the plan.

Planning authorities are required to consult, *inter alia*, the Environment Agency and the relevant nature conservancy council when drawing up development plans. Once a plan has been prepared, it will be "deposited" for a time. During this time, interested parties are able to object to policies in the plan. For local plans, objectors have the right to have their objections considered at a local plan inquiry held by an inspector appointed by the Secretary of State. The inspector can recommend modifications to any of the plan's policies, and his recommendations will be considered by the planning authority. If modifications to the plan are made, there is a further period of consultation. If new issues are raised during this period, a further inquiry can be held. For structure plans, the process is similar, except that objections to the plan are considered at an examination in public (EIP) presided over by a panel. No person has the *right* to be heard at an EIP, so representations can only be made by those who are invited to speak.

E: ENVIRONMENTAL CONSIDERATIONS IN PLANNING POLICY

Sustainable development

13–028 Sustainable development (discussed in Ch. 2) has become a central theme of planning guidance. PPG 1 states that government policy is that development should be sustainable and "should not deny future generations the best of today's environment."[36] To this end, planning authorities are required to include specific policies on

---

[35] TCPA 1990, ss.13 and 33.
[36] PPG 1, para.3.

sustainable development in their development plans.[37] PPG 1 sets out a vision of a sustainable planning framework, which should:

- provide for the nation's needs for commercial and industrial development, food production, minerals extraction, new homes and other buildings, while respecting environmental objectives;
- use already developed areas in the most efficient way, while making them more attractive places in which to live and work;
- conserve both the cultural heritage and natural resources (including wildlife, landscape, water, soil and air quality) taking particular care to safeguard designations of national and international importance; and
- shape new development patterns in a way which minimises the need to travel.

There is some debate as to whether the concept of sustainability is a new concept for planning. The commonly accepted definition of sustainable development, namely "development that meets the needs of the present without compromising the ability of future generations to meet their own needs"[38] contains two elements:

- a temporal element: consideration of the long-term impact of our actions upon future generations;
- a spatial element: a concern to protect the wider environment.

Some commentators take the view that "sustainable development" is just a new label for these two elements, which have been concerns of planning law and policy for a long time.[39] The planning system has, from its early roots in the public health legislation of Victorian England, always looked beyond the present day, and has always been concerned to protect environmental amenity. What is perhaps new about sustainable development is that the environmental amenity to be considered is now global, as opposed to local. (An example of the way in which the planning system is required to take account of the global environment is through complying with EC legislation concerned to protect habitats, and thereby global biodiversity.) Other commentators take the view that the position is not so clear-cut, arguing, for example, that a planning system which continues to favour development—by not requiring a developer to demonstrate a need for a development, and placing the burden on the planning authority to justify a refusal of planning permission—cannot be said to reflect the principle of sustainability.[40]

Transport

Transport policy is at the centre of the government's objective of making development **13–029** more sustainable.[41] Its principal aims are to reduce the number and length of motorised journeys, and to encourage alternative means of travel which are more

[37] PPG 12 , para.4.2.
[38] This is the definition offered in the Report of the World Commission on the Environment and Development: *Our Common Future* (1987) (The Brundtland Report), discussed in Ch. 2.
[39] See Denzil Millichap, "Sustainability: A Long Established Concern of Planning" [1993] J.P.L. 11.
[40] See Tim Jewell. "Planning Regulation and Environmental Consciousness: Some Lessons from Minerals" [1995] J.P.L. 482.
[41] See PPG 13.

environmentally friendly, so as to reduce people's reliance on private cars. This will reduce the need for fuel, which will in turn reduce emissions of greenhouse gases and other pollutants. Transport policy is to be implemented by ensuring, where possible, that housing, employment, retail, leisure and education should be located close to public transport, and as close as possible to one another, so as to avoid the need for travel. Parking is to be controlled, cyclists and pedestrians provided for, and local authorities are to assist in public transport provision. Journeys can also to be reduced by encouraging development in town centres, as well as development which mixes residential and business uses. Thus, a revival of the former trend for people to live above shops is to be encouraged. This idea marks a change in policy—formerly it had been thought that out-of-town locations had a distinctive role to play in providing for new retail development in a way which could relieve congestion in high streets.

Renewable energy

13–030 Renewable energy sources are sources of energy which occur naturally and repeatedly in the environment. They include energy from the sun, the wind, the sea and the fall of water. They offer the possibility of increased diversity and security of energy supply, as well as of reducing the greenhouse gas emissions which occur with traditional methods of energy generation in large and centralised power stations burning fossil fuel. Government policy is set out in PPG 22:

- Sites proposed for the development of renewable energy sources will often be in rural areas or on the coast, and such development will almost always have some local environmental effects. The government's policies for developing renewable energy sources must be weighed carefully with its continuing commitment to policies for protecting the environment. It will always be important that a particular proposal should cause the minimum harm to the countryside or the coast.

- Renewable energy resources can usually only be developed where they occur, and each authority should consider the contribution their area can make to meeting need on a local, regional and national basis. Planning authorities should also bear in mind that investment in renewable energy development can make an important contribution to the national economy, and can help to meet our international commitments on limiting greenhouse gas emissions.

The effect of PPG 22 was considered in *West Coast Wind Farms Limited v Secretary of State for the Environment and Another*.[42] Planning permission for two wind farms in an attractive location in North Devon was refused. In upholding the refusal, the court took to view that PPG 22 as a whole, whilst according great importance to the provision of energy from renewable sources, did not provide a presumption in favour of development for that purpose. A proper balance had to be struck between renewable energy needs and other environmental concerns. In these circumstances, the inspector had been entitled to conclude that the environmental harm likely to result

[42] [1996] Env. L.R. 29.

from noise and visual impact from the wind farm was not outweighed by the benefits of exploiting renewable energy.

Nature and landscape conservation

Nature conservation designations can significantly restrict new development. The **13–031** Conservation (Natural Habitats etc.) Regulations 1994,[43] which implement the Natural Habitats Directive (discussed in Ch. 9), make significant alterations to the planning system with respect to the Special Areas of Conservation (SACs) designated under the regulations. The regulations require that where an SAC has been designated, planning permission which has been granted for projects within the area must be reconsidered, and, where development has not yet taken place, may be revoked unless there are reasons of overriding public interest for not doing so, or unless conditions can be imposed to prevent ecological damage. The regulations also effectively extinguish rights of permitted development within such areas, so that an application for planning permission becomes necessary for development to proceed.

Preservation of the countryside is discussed more fully in Ch. 9. For present purposes, it should be noted that the guiding principle of government policy is that development in the countryside should benefit the rural economy, as well as maintaining or enhancing the environment. Any development in open countryside away from existing developed areas should be strictly controlled. In areas which have been designated for special protection, special rules apply. Sites of Special Scientific Interest (SSSIs), National Nature Reserves (NNRs), Marine Nature Reserves, and sites designated under Limestone Pavement Orders are discussed in Ch. 9. Some other forms of site designation which also have an impact on planning law are briefly considered below.

(1) *National Parks*

National Parks are designated under the National Parks and Access to Countryside **13–032** Act 1949. Their statutory purpose is the conservation and enhancement of natural beauty, wildlife and cultural heritage and the promotion of opportunities for public understanding and enjoyment of their special qualities. National Park land covers eight per cent of the land area of England. Responsibility for the detailed running of the parks rests with a National Park Authority, which must prepare local plans covering the whole of its area. Government policy is that major development should not take place in the National Parks save in very exceptional circumstances. Because of the serious impact that major developments may have, applications for such developments must be subject to rigorous examination.

(2) *Areas of Outstanding Natural Beauty*

Areas of Outstanding Natural Beauty (AONBs) are designated to conserve the natural **13–033** beauty of the landscape. These form 16 per cent of the total land area in England. They are different from National Parks in that promotion of recreation is not an objective of designation. In general, policy and development control decisions affecting

---

[43] SI 1994/2716.

AONBs should favour conservation of the natural beauty of the landscape. Thus it would normally be inconsistent with the aims of designation to permit the siting of major industrial or commercial development within such an area.

(3) *Green Belts*

13–034 The purpose of a Green Belt is to act as a "buffer zone" between the countryside and large built-up areas, so as to stop the outward expansion of those built-up areas from encroaching on the countryside. In this way, Green Belts can assist in preserving the special character of historic towns. Within Green Belts, there is a general presumption that inappropriate development will not be permitted.[44]

(4) *Listed buildings*

13–035 Historic or otherwise culturally important buildings are subject to strict planning controls. The case law has made clear that the preservation of listed buildings is a "paramount consideration" in planning decisions.[45] The protection given to listed buildings may be seen as an example of the application of sustainable development, in that it is motivated by a concern for the interests of future generations. Protection is afforded by the Town and Country Planning (Listed Buildings and Conservation Areas) Act 1990. It is criminal offence to carry out works to a listed building without the necessary listed building consent (in addition to any planning permission required).[46]

(5) *Waste management*

13–036 Waste management facilities are the only area where legislation makes a specific link between the need to have planning permission and the grant of an environmental licence. Under Part II of the Environmental Protection Act 1990, if planning permission is required for a waste management site, it must be obtained before an application is made for a licence.[47] As has been said, in drawing up plans and determining planning applications, planning authorities are required to have regard to the principles set out in the Waste Framework Directive, including that waste should be recovered or disposed of without harming human health, close to the place where it is generated, and without using methods which harm the environment.

In *R. v Bolton MBC, Ex p. Kirkman*,[48] a local waste disposal company submitted a planning application to the local planning authority for works to upgrade an obsolete waste incinerator. The applicant was a local resident concerned about air pollution and noise which would be emitted from the proposed plant. Following public consultation, planning permission was granted. In upholding the grant of planning permission, the Court of Appeal endorsed the approach taken in *Gateshead* (above). It indicated that, in the case of waste management facilities, the planning authority should consider the objectives set out in the Waste Framework Directive and UK regulations. However, it was acceptable for the planning authority to allow the details of environmental control to be dealt with by the Environment Agency. By way of passing reference, the court

---

[44] See PPG 2.
[45] *Trustees of the Bristol Meeting Room Trust v Secretary of State for the Environment* [1991] J.P.L. 152.
[46] See PPG 15: Planning and the Historic Environment.
[47] EPA 1990, s.36(2).
[48] [1998] J.P.L. 787.

observed that in decisions on waste facilities, the planning authority was entitled to exercise greater control, and to conduct a greater degree of investigation, than would be permitted or expected in other, non-waste cases, although it had no legal duty to do so.

Contaminated land

Government policy is that redevelopment should be the primary mechanism for **13–037** restoring contaminated land. Thus, under the statutory contaminated land regime (discussed in Ch. 6), where a developer is prepared to undertake voluntary clean-up of a contaminated a site, controls under the regime cannot be imposed.[49] Policy guidance on the development of contaminated land is contained in PPG 23. Development plans should consider the possible effects on health and the environment from contaminated land. The existence of contamination will be a "material consideration" in determining planning applications (see below), and proposed remediation works should deal with any unacceptable risks to health or the environment, judged in the light of the site's actual or intended use. There is also a policy preference expressed for developing "brownfield sites" (sites that are contaminated or have been previously developed) instead of "greenfield"(never developed) sites, where possible. Detailed planning conditions (see below) can be required where permission is granted to develop contaminated land.[50]

F: The Grant of Planning Permission

Once an application for planning permission has been made, the local planning **13–038** authority has eight weeks in which to notify the applicant of its decision. The application can be decided by a committee or by an officer of the local planning authority.[51] The local planning authority can grant planning permission unconditionally, grant it with conditions, or refuse it.

When deciding an application for planning permission, the local planning authority must have regard to the development plan, so far as material to the application, and to "any other material considerations".[52] Section 54A of the Town and Country Planning Act 1990 (discussed below) requires that determination of the planning application *shall be in accordance with the plan unless material considerations indicate otherwise.* Material considerations will include local and national planning policies, as expressed in PPGs and other guidance (see above). The authority must also consider any representations or objections which have been made to the development proposal. In certain cases, it has a duty to consult with another body, such as the Environment Agency or one of the nature conservancy councils. Such bodies are known as "statutory

---

[49] EPA 1990, s.78H(5)(b).
[50] Model conditions on further investigations and required are set out in Circular 11/95 (see paras 73–76). See also [1995] J.P.L. 759 for a detailed example of the conditions placed on a permission for residential development on a former tannery site.
[51] Local Government Act 1972, s.101.
[52] TCPA 1990, s.70(2).

consultees". The very general nature of all these duties, however, enables the local planning authority to exercise a considerable amount of discretion in determining planning applications.

The presumption in favour of development in accordance with the development plan

13–039 Section 54A of the Town and Country Planning Act 1990[53] states:

> "Where, in making any determination under the planning Acts, regard is to be had to the development plan, the determination shall be made in accordance with the development plan unless material considerations indicate otherwise."

The effect of this section is that the development plan is the most important factor in any decision about planning permission. The presumption is that developments proposed in accordance with the development plan will be granted planning permission. The presumption in favour of following the plan can be rebutted, however, if the applicant produces convincing reasons why a development at odds with the plan should go ahead. Material considerations indicating that such development should go ahead must be weighed against the development plan in making the decision. (One such consideration is how up-to-date are the policies contained in the development plan.) A consequence of the presumption in favour of the plan is that the process of reviewing development plans, which takes place every ten years or so, has become a key forum for developers, landowners and environmental campaigners to express their views, in the hope of influencing the content of the plan.

Material considerations

13–040 As has been said, the planning authority is required to have regard to the development plan and to "any other material considerations". The Act offers no guidance as to what considerations might be regarded as "material". It has therefore fallen to the courts to determine this matter. Cooke J., in *Stringer v Minister of Housing and Local Government*,[54] stated:

> "In principle any consideration which relates to the use and development of land is capable of being a planning consideration. Whether a particular consideration falling within that broad class is material in any given case will depend on the circumstances."

Material considerations must be genuine planning considerations, that is to say they must be related to the purpose of planning legislation, which is to regulate the development of land in the public interest. For a consideration to be "material", it must also "fairly and reasonably relate to the proposed development" (*i.e.* not relate

---

[53] Inserted into the Act by the Planning and Compensation Act 1991.
[54] [1971] 1 All E.R. 65 at 77.

principally to something other than the development in question).[55] Material considerations, then, will include the number of buildings to be constructed, their size, their layout, where they are situated, how they are designed, and the means by which they are to be accessed. Consideration of their impact on the neighbourhood and their effects on supporting infrastructure (*e.g.* the sewerage system and the transport system) will also be material. Planning guidance sets out a number of environmental factors which will constitute material considerations (see below). The question of whether a development is economically worthwhile, however, is not a material consideration.[56]

Environmental considerations as material considerations

Some environmental material considerations (*e.g.* waste policy) have already been **13–041** discussed, in the section above on planning policy. Here, it should be noted that the environmental impact of emissions is also a material consideration, as is the impact from noise, and the need to preserve ancient monuments.[57] The fact that a site is designated a World Heritage Site (as are Blenheim Palace and Stonehenge, for example) is a key material consideration in any decision whether or not to grant planning permission.[58]

All PPGs and other forms of guidance which refer to protection of the wider environment are, of course, important material considerations. The problem, however, is to determine how much weight should be attached to the broad policy statements in such documents, in the light of the evidential problems relating to environmental degradation. In *Bolton MBC v Secretary of State for the Environment*,[59] for example, the court recognised the enormous evidential problems of determining the amount of carbon dioxide which would be generated by traffic because of a proposed new shopping centre, so that it might be compared with the amount generated by shoppers using existing shops. It is clear from PPG 23 that a mere *perception* of risk cannot be a material consideration unless there is evidence to justify concern.[60] Thus, planning authorities cannot refuse permission for developments such as mobile telephone masts or chemical factories simply because such developments are "controversial". However, in the case of certain proposed projects, they must conduct a formal environmental impact assessment, and the resulting "environmental statement" is a material consideration to which they must have regard.

Environmental impact assessment

Assessment of the environmental effects of major proposed developments before **13–042** planning permission is granted is now a central part of the decision-making process for planning authorities. Environmental Impact Assessment is of EC origin. The Directive on Environmental Impact Assessment[61] requires the environmental effect of development to be considered before planning permission is granted for projects such as oil

[55] *R. v Westminster County Council, Ex p. Monahan* [1989] 3 W.L.R. 408.
[56] *Walters v Secretary of State for Wales* [1979] J.P.L. 171.
[57] *Hoveringham Gravels Ltd v Secretary of State for the Environment* [1975] Q.B. 754.
[58] PPG 15.
[59] [1994] J.P.L. B37.
[60] See PPG 23 , para.3.17.
[61] Directive 85/337/EEC on the Assessment of the Effects of Certain Public and Private Projects on the Environment O.J. L175 July 5, 1985, p.40, as amended by Dir.97/11/EC O.J. L73 March 14, 1997, p.5, which came into force March 14, 1999.

refineries, large power stations and motorways. For projects like roads, intensive livestock farming and mineral extraction, an impact assessment will be required if the project is likely to have significant effects on the environment by virtue of its size or location. The purpose of the assessment is to ensure that the environmental effects of projects are considered as early as possible in the planning process. It is important to note that the Directive merely puts in place procedures for taking environmental effects into account in the decision-making process. It does not seek to influence the substantive outcome of the decision by, for example, requiring environmental considerations to take precedence over other considerations.

Public involvement is an important aspect of the environmental impact assessment process. Development consent for the project cannot be given without taking the views of the public (including environmental groups) into account. The public must be informed of the decision eventually taken about whether development is permitted, and also of the main reasons for that decision.[62] Much importance is attached to the provision of clear information in the "environmental statement". As government guidance puts it:

> "The general public's interest in a major project is often expressed as concern about the possibility of unknown or unforeseen effects. By providing a full analysis of the project's effects, an environmental statement can help to allay fears created by lack of information. At the same time it can help to inform the public on the substantive issues which the local planning authority will have to consider in reaching a decision. It is a requirement of the Regulations that the environmental statement must include a description of the project and its likely effects together with a summary in non-technical language. One of the aims of a good environmental statement should be to enable readers to understand for themselves how its conclusions have been reached, and to form their own judgments on the significance of the environmental issues raised by the project."[63]

The Directive is implemented in England and Wales by a number of statutory instruments, the main regulations being set out in the Town and Country Planning (Environmental Impact Assessment) (England and Wales) Regulations 1999.[64] The regulations, which in essence repeat the contents of the Directive, establish two classes of project for which a formal environmental impact assessment is appropriate. For projects listed in Sch.1 of the regulations, a formal assessment is mandatory (subject to certain thresholds being met), whilst for those listed in Sch.2, a formal assessment may be undertaken at the discretion of the planning authority. Projects listed in Sch.1 include crude oil refineries, thermal power stations, installations dealing with asbestos, installations for the intensive rearing of poultry or pigs, and the construction of motorways. Those listed in Sch.2 include such activities as glass making and paper manufacturing. Thresholds are set for some of these projects, below which an impact assessment will not be necessary. However, for any Sch.1 or Sch.2 project proposed in

---

[62] See Arts 6(2) and (3).

[63] Environmental Assessment: A Guide to the Procedures (HMSO, 1989), p 4.

[64] SI 1999/293. Projects for which an application for planning permission was submitted before the March 14, 1999 will be subject to the requirements of the less strict 1985 EIA Directive and its implementing regulations: the Town and Country Planning (Assessment of Environmental Effects) Regulations 1988.

a sensitive area (such as an SSSI or Candidate Special Area of Conservation—see Ch. 9); an assessment is required irrespective of thresholds.

The regulations on environmental impact assessment have given rise to a considerable amount of case law. This is probably because the costs of environmental impact assessment are significant, and assessment causes delays to projects. Case law has arisen on such matters as the scope of a "project" (*e.g.* is the construction of side roads to a main link road part of a "project"?,[65]) whether projects pre-date the EC Directive and therefore do not require an impact assessment,[66] and whether a proposed development falls within the relevant Schedules.[67]

In *Berkeley v Secretary of State for the Environment*,[68] the House of Lords quashed a decision to allow the redevelopment of Fulham Football Club, on the basis that an environmental impact assessment had not been prepared. Their Lordships held that, pursuant to the Directive and regulations, it was not open to the court to dispense retrospectively with the assessment requirement on the ground that the outcome would have been the same without an assessment. Normally, the courts have a discretion, in judicial review proceedings, whether to quash a decision that is procedurally flawed, and will not usually do so where the procedural flaw has made no difference to the outcome. However, their Lordships in *Berkeley* held that where the flaw is a failure to conduct an environmental impact assessment, the court ought not to exercise this discretion—to do so would be to uphold a planning permission granted contrary to the provisions of the Directive, and would be inconsistent with the court's obligations to enforce EC law. The effect of this decision is that, where there has been a breach of the Directive's requirements, courts will quash planning decisions as a matter of course.

Consultation

There are statutory requirements on a local planning authority to consult with a **13–043** number of expert bodies in the making of a planning decision.[69] Some examples of the duty to consult include the following:

- If development is likely to affect land in a National Park, the National Park Authority must be consulted;

- If the development is likely to affect the site of a scheduled ancient monument, the Historic Buildings and Monuments Commission must be consulted;

- If the development is in, or likely to affect, a Site of Special Scientific Interest (SSSI) of which notification has been given to the local planning authority, or is in a notified area within two kilometres of an SSSI, the relevant nature conservancy council must be consulted;

[65] *Lewin v Secretary of State for the Environment* [1991] J.P.L. 342.
[66] Projects like the Twyford Down M3 extension and the A41 Newbury Bypass have not required an assessment because the application for development consent was submitted before the Directive came into force on July 3, 1988.
[67] *R. v Swale BC*, Ex p. *RSPB* [1991] J.P.L. 39.
[68] [2001] 2 A.C. 603.
[69] General Development Procedure Order 1995.

• The Environment Agency is a statutory consultee for certain classes of development with a high water pollution potential.

If the local planning authority decides not to follow the advice of the specialist bodies it has consulted, it must have reasons for doing so. In *R v Newbury DC Ex p. Blackwell*[70] and in *R v Warwickshire County Council Ex p. Powergen*[71] local planning authorities were held to have acted unreasonably when they failed to show reasons for not following a highway authority's advice.

Planning conditions

13–044 Almost all planning permission granted is subject to conditions. The issue is often not whether the development should be permitted, but on what terms it may be permitted. Conditions may be used by a planning authority to keep the nature of the development under tight control. The government's policy in relation to planning conditions is that, if used properly, they can enhance the quality of development and enable many development proposals to proceed where it would otherwise have been necessary to refuse planning permission.[72]

The planning authority has the power to attach to planning permission whatever conditions it thinks fit.[73] It is also given a specific power to attach conditions to land under the control of the applicant which is not part of the land which he proposes to develop.[74] A condition may also be imposed to the effect that planning permission will last only for a limited period, so that the development must commence, or must be completed, within a specified time.[75] In exceptional cases, a condition may be imposed which limits the duration of the time for which the development can remain in existence. The advantage of this approach is that where objections are made to a particular development, a "trial run" of the development may be permitted to see whether the objections are well founded. Thus, where a developer wished to attach a large fibreglass fish to the exterior of his house, and concerns were expressed that this might prejudice road safety by surprising passing drivers, the planning inspector granted planning permission for the fish to remain for three years!

Although the local planning authority has wide discretion in deciding what conditions to impose, its discretion is not totally unfettered. The following limits to the discretion were identified in *Newbury DC v Secretary of State for the Environment*[76]:

(1) The condition may only be imposed for a "planning" purpose and not for any ulterior purpose;

(2) The condition must fairly and reasonably relate to the development permitted by the planning permission;

[70] [1998] J.P.L. 680.
[71] [1998] J.P.L. 131.
[72] Circular 11/95: The Use of Conditions in Planning Permission (1995).
[73] TCPA 1990, s.70.
[74] *ibid.*, s.72(1)(a).
[75] *ibid.*, s.72(1)(b).
[76] [1981] A.C. 578.

(3) The condition must not be so unreasonable that no reasonable planning authority could have imposed it.

In *R v Hillingdon LBC, Ex p. Royco Homes Ltd*,[77] for example, a condition of planning permission which required a proposed residential development to be occupied by people on a local authority's housing waiting list was held to be *ultra vires* because it had been imposed for an improper purpose. It represented an attempt by the local authority to use its planning powers to shift the burden of the duty to house people in need on to the developer. This was not permissible, because the duty was imposed by law on the local authority. Similarly, in *Hall & Co Ltd v Shoreham-by-Sea UDC*,[78] a condition which had the effect of requiring the developer to construct a public road at his own expense was held to be unreasonable. In *Newbury DC v Secretary of State for the Environment*,[79] a condition attached to a planning permission to use aircraft hangars to store rubble for 10 years, which required that the hangars be demolished after that time, was held to be invalid because it did not relate to the development permitted, which was the *use* of the hangars.

Appeals

If the local planning authority refuses to grant planning permission, or grants it subject **13–045** to conditions, the applicant can appeal to the Secretary of State within 28 days of the decision.[80] The Secretary of State (on the recommendations of a planning inspector whom he appoints to hear the appeal) may allow or dismiss the appeal or may vary the decision by imposing different conditions. An appeal takes the form of a rehearing[81] which can be conducted either by way of an oral hearing before a planning inspector, known as a local inquiry, or by way of written representations by the parties, which produces a faster result. As mentioned above, third parties—*i.e.* parties other than the applicant—do not have a right of appeal (though they may make representations in appeals by the applicant). This means that a challenge by third parties who are unhappy about a grant of planning permission can only be made on the limited grounds available under judicial review.

If an applicant is dissatisfied with the Secretary of State's decision, he may appeal to the courts, exercising statutory rights of appeal under ss.288 and 289 of the Town and Country Planning Act 1990. The general principles of review are similar to those of judicial review, and include that the Secretary of State acted perversely; failed to take account of relevant material; took into account irrelevant material; failed to abide by statutory procedures; and that, where, on the basis of new evidence, the Secretary of State has departed from the inspector's recommendations, he has failed to allow the parties the opportunity to make further representations.[82] An appeal before the courts does not take the form of a rehearing of the application, because, as has been mentioned, the courts will not review the political substance of a planning decision,

---

[77] [1974] Q.B. 720.
[78] [1964] 1 W.L.R. 240.
[79] [1981] A.C. 578.
[80] TCPA 1990, s.78.
[81] *ibid.*, s.79.
[82] *Seddon Properties v Secretary of State for the Environment* [1978] J.P.L. 835.

which will have been made by elected officials. As Lord Hoffmann put it, in *Tesco Stores Ltd. v Secretary of State for the Environment*[83]: "If there is one principle of planning law more firmly settled than any other, it is that matters of planning judgement are within the exclusive province of the local planning authority or the Secretary of State."

Planning by agreement

13–046 By s.106 of the Town and Country Planning Act 1990, an applicant for planning permission may enter into an agreement with the planning authority to carry out, or refrain from, certain activities on his land, or to pay money to the planning authority. Thus, for example, a developer may agree to provide a community centre, a crèche, or sewerage facilities, or to make a contribution to the cost of widening a road where his development will increase the amount of traffic on the road. Where the developer offers to do such things, he is said to be offering the planning authority a "planning gain" in return for permitting his development to proceed.

In contrast to the position in relation to imposing planning conditions, the planning authority has a virtually unregulated discretion to enter into planning agreements. This means that such agreements may be made for purposes which would be unlawful if pursued by way of planning conditions, as for example where the developer agrees to provide housing for people on the local authority's waiting-list. Where planning gain is offered, the authority is able to grant the permission on the basis that the benefits associated with the proposed development are material considerations which outweigh its adverse effects. This means, of course, that the nature of the planning gain must be capable of being a material consideration—it cannot simply be a "bribe" to the planning authority.

The practice of accepting planning gain, which is followed by different local planning authorities in different parts of the country operating under widely different rules, has the potential to become, in effect, a system of local taxation on development. Although planning gain cannot be *demanded* by the planning authority, in real terms, where a developer offers it, he will often know that it is a precondition to his proposals being accepted. A government circular has attempted to address this problem by providing that planning gain should be sought only where it is necessary for the development to proceed, and relevant to the proposed development. The circular states that unacceptable development should never be permitted because of unrelated benefits offered by the applicant.[84]

The House of Lords, in *Tesco Stores Ltd v Secretary of State for the Environment*,[85] has effectively drawn a distinction between planning obligations which are *required* by the planning authority, and planning obligations *offered* by developers. As regards the former, the clear limits outlined in the circular apply. As regards the latter, the circular is less relevant. In reality, however, where a formal application for planning permission in relation to a large development is preceded by lengthy preliminary negotiations with the planning authority, and by the submission of outline proposals, it will often be very

---

[83] [1995] 1 W.L.R. 759.
[84] Circular 16/91.
[85] [1995] 1 W.L.R. 759.

difficult to draw the distinction which their Lordships have suggested between situations where planning gain is "offered" and situations where it is "required". Planning gain remains a very controversial topic, because, although it has the potential significantly to affect the environment, it remains virtually unregulated by statute.

G: ENFORCEMENT OF PLANNING CONTROL

Enforcement of planning control is primarily designed to prevent breaches of planning **13–047** control rather than to punish the wrongdoer. Carrying out development without planning permission, or failing to comply with a condition imposed on planning permission, is a breach of planning control. It is not, however, a criminal offence. The occurrence of a breach enables the planning authority to serve a variety of notices designed to remedy the breach. It is failure to comply with the requirements of such notices which constitutes a criminal offence.

Planning contravention notices

Where it appears to the local planning authority that there may have been a breach of **13–048** planning control, it may serve a "planning contravention notice" requiring information about the operations which are being carried out on the land. The aim of such notices is to enable planning authorities to obtain information so as to resolve the matter by co-operation without further recourse to enforcement procedures. Failure to provide the information can result in a fine.

Breach of condition notices

If planning permission is granted subject to conditions and any of those conditions are **13–049** not complied with, the planning authority may serve a "breach of condition notice" requiring compliance with the conditions. This notice will specify a time within which certain steps necessary to comply with the conditions must be carried out, after which time the person responsible for the breach will be guilty of an offence.

Enforcement notices

If the local planning authority decides not to use either of the above procedures, or **13–050** uses them but without success in remedying the breach, it may serve an "enforcement notice". This will outline the matters constituting the breach of planning control and steps that must be taken to remedy the breach. The notice will specify a time limit within which the required steps must be taken. After this time, the planning authority may enter the land and carry out the specified steps itself, and recover the expense of so doing. It is a criminal offence to fail to comply with an enforcement notice. The maximum fine in the magistrates court is £20,000, whilst the fine in the Crown Court is unlimited. In determining the amount of the fine, the court can take into account any financial benefit which has accrued or appears likely to accrue to the developer in consequence of the offence. The service of an enforcement notice may be appealed against by any person having an interest in the land to which it relates, or by the occupier of the land. The appeal is to the Secretary of State. Once an appeal is brought, the enforcement notice is of no effect until the appeal has been decided or is withdrawn.

Stop notices

13–051 If a serious breach of planning control is being committed and the planning authority considers that it should be stopped immediately, it can issue a "stop notice" at the same time as the enforcement notice, or at any time afterwards.

Injunctions

13–052 The local planning authority has an express power to obtain an injunction to restrain an actual or threatened breach of planning control. This power was given to planning authorities for the first time by the Planning and Compensation Act 1991. Prior to this Act, injunctions could only be sought in exceptional cases, and as a last resort, under s.222 of the Local Government Act 1972, to restrain breaches of the criminal law. The courts have held that the new powers are much wider than those under s.222 and that their exercise is not subject to the same restrictions.

Limitations on enforcement

13–053 It is a significant restriction on the ability to enforce planning control that there are time limits on the taking of enforcement action:

(a) If operations have been carried out on land without planning permission, no enforcement action can be taken four years after the operations were substantially completed.[86]

(b) If a change of use is made to a building to convert it to a single dwelling house, in breach of planning control, no enforcement action can be taken after the end of four years from the date on which the breach occurred.[87]

(c) No enforcement action can be taken for any other breach of planning control after the end of 10 years following the date of the breach.[88]

H: Problems With the Planning System

13–054 The planning system is widely regarded as too flexible and bureaucratic. Problems include the following:

[86] TCPA 1990, s.171B.
[87] *ibid.*, s.171B(2).
[88] *ibid.*, s.171B (3).

- The plethora of plans and guidance at regional, county, and local level. This can result in inconsistency and uncertainty.

- The process of updating plans is expensive and slow. Ten years after the current "plan-led" system was put into place, 45 local authorities in England (13 per cent) had still to adopt their first plan, and 214 current plans were becoming out of date, with little sign of review being completed.[89] This means that planning policy can become outdated even before it is implemented.

- At the moment, it takes too long for planning decisions to be reached about major projects. The decision-making process is lengthy, unwieldy, and expensive for all concerned. For example, the planning inquiry for the building of Terminal 5 at Heathrow Airport lasted almost 4 years, and cost over £83.5m.[90]

The Planning and Compulsory Purchase Bill, which at the time of writing is making its way through Parliament, attempts to resolve these problems. The Bill includes a series of reforms to speed up the planning system, including proposals designed to simplify the current hierarchy of development plans and enable planning inquiries to be completed more swiftly. It aims to improve the predictability of planning decisions, and to make the planning system more effective as a mechanism for achieving sustainable development.

---

[89] See Planning and Compulsory Purchase Bill: Full Regulatory Impact Assessment (*www. odpm.gov.uk*).
[90] See *www. planning. odpm.gov.uk/callins/terminal5*.

Chapter 14

HUMAN RIGHTS AND ENVIRONMENTAL DEMOCRACY[1]

> "The Court recognises for its part that in today's society the protection of the environment is an increasingly important consideration." (European Court of Human Rights, 1991.[2])

> "The Aarhus Convention ... is the most ambitious venture in the area of 'environmental democracy' so far taken under the auspices of the United Nations."[3]

Introduction

Many natural resources which are necessary for economic development, such as oil and **14–001** timber, are located on land that is inhabited by communities which depend on that land for survival. Exploitation of that land can often lead to conflicts about environmental priorities, the allocation of resources, and the manner in which those who harvest the resources interact with local communities. The conflict between Shell International and the Ogoni people of Nigeria, which began in 1958, is an example.[4] The Ogoni people occupy a fertile area of the Niger Delta which is also rich in oil. Extraction of oil by Shell led to a number of oil spills. Protests by the Ogoni people led to Shell leaving the area, and to the execution, by the Nigerian Government, of eight members of the Ogoni people's protest movement. These issues (sometimes referred to as issues of "environmental justice") can be seen in terms of a link between human rights and environmental protection. Violations of human rights (*e.g.* the rights to life, health, family and possessions, for example) can often result from environmental damage. Human rights and environmental protection are also linked in the concept of sustainable development (discussed in Ch. 2), in the sense that development that

---

[1] This chapter is based in part on an article appearing in the *Journal of Environmental Law* (1999, Vol.11 No.1, p.3) entitled "Human Rights and Environmental Wrongs" by Justine Thornton and Stephen Tromans. The authors are grateful to Oxford University Press for their permission to use the material in this article.
[2] *Fredin v Sweden* (1990) 13 EHRR 784.
[3] Kofi Annan, Secretary-General to the UN, *www.unece. org/env/pp*.
[4] Other examples include the Huaorani tribe in Ecuador who reside in the area of one of Ecuador's biggest oil deposits, and the Yanomami, living on the borders of Brazil and Venezuela, whose lands have been subject to environmental degradation by excessive agriculture, logging and mining.

infringes human rights cannot sensibly be said to be meeting the needs of the present generation.[5]

International human rights instruments, however, have typically accorded minimal attention to the environment. The three primary international human rights instruments (the International Covenant on Civil and Political Rights; the International Covenant on Economic, Social and Cultural Rights; and the Universal Declaration of Human Rights) barely mention the relationship between the environment and human rights. The main European instrument (the European Convention on Human Rights) does not specifically guarantee a right to a decent environment. Sometimes, however, as we shall see, use may be made of other human rights under that Convention to secure environmental protection.

Case law and academic writing on the issue has been hesitant to recognise the link between human rights and the environment. The hesitancy may be explained, in part, by the inherent limitations in a human rights-based approach to environmental protection[6]:

- Human rights protect individuals. This means that it is a necessary precondition for invoking human rights that the environmental damage in question has a substantial and direct impact on particular individuals. This will not always be the case. For example, emissions from factories and cars cause forests to die, but this will not necessarily result in any immediate and direct interference with an individual's rights.

- The interests of the environment and of individuals do not necessarily coincide. Indeed, the exercise of human rights may in fact cause environmental damage. Thus, the rights of the Amazonian Indians not to go hungry (and therefore to cut down the rainforest to provide farmland) are not compatible with long-term ecological integrity.

- Human rights only protect the present generation. They cannot easily be used to give full effect to the principle of sustainable development, which requires us to preserve the environment for future generations.

All of this, however, does not mean that the link between human rights and environmental protection should be discounted. The language and framework of human rights law can provide a useful set of tools for environmental protection. This is becoming particularly apparent in the context of "procedural obligations" of states and public authorities, designed to ensure that environmental protection measures are properly implemented. Such obligations include: the provision of environmental information; the provision of access to effective dispute resolution; and the provision of mechanisms to facilitate public participation in environmental decision-making. These obligations are now enshrined in the Aarhus Convention and other instruments, which we examine at the end of this chapter. The phrase "environmental democracy" has been used by Kofi Annan as shorthand for the three obligations.

---

[5] See, for example, the views expressed by Mary Robinson, High Commissioner for Human Rights, in a speech delivered at the World Summit on Sustainable Development, Johannesburg, in September 2002 (available at *www.un.org/events/wssd/statements/unhchrE.htm*.
[6] For a full discussion, see C. Miller, *Environmental Rights—Critical Perspectives* (Routledge, 1998).

"Environmental justice"

Environmental problems may also be associated with issues of social justice, such as **14–002** race discrimination. This approach points out that, in many situations, oppressed minorities can be regarded as "environmental victims".[7] In the US, this approach has become more than a field for academic research, and has manifested itself in a number of administrative and legal measures aimed at giving effect to the concerns of what is sometimes styled the "Environmental Justice Movement".[8]

This movement has focused in particular on perceived injustices in the siting of waste management facilities and other potentially harmful facilities in predominantly poor or ethnic minority neighbourhoods.[9] A Presidential Executive Order[10] has declared that establishing environmental justice for minority and low income communities should be a national priority, and that all communities should generally live in a safe and healthy environment. Subsequent case-law, and administrative guidance issued by the US Environmental Protection Agency, has focused on the existence of individuals' rights to challenge the licensing of such facilities, partly on the basis that licensing decisions may violate civil rights to freedom from discrimination on grounds of race, colour or national origin.

In the UK, as in the US, industrial or waste-related facilities will more often be found in poor, urban areas than more prosperous suburban or rural communities. Article 14 of the European Convention on Human Rights (and now, of course, the Human Rights Act 1998) requires that the Convention's rights and freedoms should be enjoyed without discrimination on grounds of sex, race, colour, language, religion, political or other opinion, national or social origin, association with a national minority, property, birth or status. It is conceivable that this provision could be used to attack the decisions of a planning authority which appears to be applying differential standards of amenity as between different areas. Even more fundamentally, could this Convention right be said to be at odds with the famous judicial statement that what would be a nuisance in Belgrave Square would not necessarily be so in Bermondsey?[11] Later in this chapter, we explore the extent to which the UK courts have been prepared to embrace the concept of "environmental justice" by examining environmental case law that has arisen under the Human Rights Act 1998.

Environmental rights in international law

The link between human rights and the environment in international law was first **14–003** made in 1972, in the Stockholm Declaration. Principle 1 of the The Declaration stated:

> "Man has a fundamental right to freedom, equality and adequate conditions of life, in an environment of a quality that permits a life of dignity and well-being, and he bears a solemn responsibility to protect and improve the environment for present and future generations."

[7] See "Environmental Victims", (1996) Social Justice Journal 23 (4).
[8] See Davy, *Essential Injustice* (Springer, 1997).
[9] See Gerrard, *Whose Backyard, Whose Risk?* (Cambridge, Ma, MIT Press, 1995).
[10] Presidential Executive Order 12898, of February 11, 1994.
[11] *Sturges v Bridgman* (1879) 11 Ch D 852.

A number of non-binding but widely accepted declarations supporting the individual's right to a clean environment were subsequently adopted. At a regional level, the 1981 African Charter on Human and Peoples' Rights stated that: "All peoples shall have the right to a generally satisfactory environment favourable to their development".[12] The 1989 San Salvador Protocol to the 1969 American Convention on Human Rights went further, establishing positive obligations on the part of the state to protect the environment. Some human rights treaties addressed the issue by including the value of the human environment in their scheme of rights protection (see, for example, the 1989 International Labour Organisation Convention concerning Indigenous and Tribal Peoples in Independent Countries,[13] and the UN Convention on the Rights of the Child[14]). The 1992 Rio Declaration, however, rather than repeating the direct approach that had been taken in the Stockholm Declaration, shifted the vocabulary away from human rights towards the theme of sustainable development, stating that:

> "Human beings are at the centre of concerns for sustainable development. They are entitled to a healthy and productive life in harmony with nature."

The impact of the Rio Declaration, with its emphasis on "sustainable development", has been that, whilst the link between development and environmental protection has tended to receive wide recognition, the link between human rights and environmental protection has found less acceptance. The shift of emphasis apparent in the Rio Declaration continued at the 2002 UN World Summit on Sustainable Development in Johannesburg, convened to assess progress made since the 1992 Rio Conference. The Johannesburg Declaration on Sustainable Development makes some oblique references to "human dignity", but otherwise focuses on sustainable development.

It seems unlikely, therefore, that a substantive right to a healthy and decent environment exists as a matter of international law. To the extent that such a right *might* be said to exist, it is, perhaps, evidenced by the elements of the Rio Declaration which deal with the procedural aspects of environmental protection.

Principle 10 of the Rio Declaration has, proved to be of particular importance in enabling concerned individuals and groups to take action for environmental protection. It states:

> "Environmental issues are best handled with participation of all concerned citizens, at the relevant level. At the national level, each individual shall have appropriate access to information concerning the environment that is held by public authorities, including information on hazardous materials and activities in their communities, and the opportunity to participate in decision-making process. States shall facilitate and encourage public awareness and participation by making information widely available. Effective access to judicial and administrative proceedings, including redress and remedy, shall be provided."

This Principle has provided the impetus for establishing detailed mechanisms, in the domestic law of states, for the exercise of procedural rights relating to environmental

---

[12] Adopted June 27, 1981 in Nairobi, Kenya: 21 I.L.M. 58 (1982).
[13] June 7, 1989. (ILO No. 169), 72 ILO Official Bull. 59.
[14] Adopted November 20, 1989 in New York: 28 I.L.M. 1448 (1989), corrected at 29 I.L.M. 1340 (1990).

information and participation in decision-making. The Aarhus Convention (discussed below) makes a further important contribution in this regard.

Environmental rights in national constitutions

Since 1992, the right to a healthy environment has been formally incorporated in the **14–004** national constitutions of over 90 countries. In other countries, especially those in South Asia and Latin America, constitutional provisions guaranteeing rights to life, health and family have been interpreted as embracing environmental factors. The treaties establishing the EU create a number of rights for citizens of the EU (for example, the right to move and to reside freely). They do not, however, create a right to a healthy environment or to quality of life. Despite this, the EU has acknowledged the significance of human rights as an element of the Community's legal order. Thus, Art. 2 of the Maastricht Treaty states: "The Union shall respect fundamental rights as guaranteed by the European Convention for the Protection of Human Rights."[15] The European Court of Justice has also evolved its own "rights-based" jurisprudence, inspired by constitutional traditions common to Member States.[16]

In constitutional arrangements, states must, of course, often strike a balance between competing rights. An examination of the South African constitution highlights some of the issues involved in balancing environmental rights against other considerations. Section 24 of the 1994 Constitution of the Republic of South Africa sets out the following provisions:

> "Everyone has the right:
>
> (a) to an environment that is not harmful to their health or well-being; and
> (b) to have the environment protected, for the benefit of present and future generations, through reasonable legislative and other measures that:
>
>> (i) prevent pollution and ecological degradation;
>> (ii) promote conservation; and
>> (iii) secure ecologically sustainable development and use of natural resources while promoting justifiable economic and social development."

The way in which these rights have been formulated has attracted criticism[17] on the basis that the list of measures at para.(b) is incomplete and is qualified by the concepts of "reasonableness" and "justifiable economic and social development". Such concerns illustrate the inherent difficulty that rights concerning the environment generally cannot be accorded absolute status—the questions of whether and when such rights can be enjoyed will inevitably involve questions of balance and reasonableness. The use of the somewhat vague term "well-being", in para.(a), illustrates another problem: if "environmental rights" are taken to guarantee health and physical welfare, to what

---

[15] See Macrory, "Environmental Citizenship and the Law: Repairing the European Road" (1996) JEL 8 (2) 219.

[16] See, for example, *Internationle Handelsgesellschaft mbH*, Case 11/27, [1970] ECR 1125; *Hauer v Rhineland Pfalz*, Case 44/79, [1979] ECR 3727; *Johnston v Chief Constable of RUC*, Case 222/84, [1987] QB 129; [1986] ECR 1651; *ERT*, Case C–260/89, [1991] ECR I–2925.

[17] See Winstanley, "Entrenching Environmental Protection in the New Constitution" (1995) 2 SAJELP 85.

extent does this imply that they can be taken to guarantee aesthetic and spiritual welfare?[18]

A: ENVIRONMENTAL RIGHTS UNDER THE EUROPEAN CONVENTION ON HUMAN RIGHTS

14–005 The European Convention on Human Rights came into being through the efforts of the Council of Europe, a pan-European body that is wider in membership than the EU. The Convention was signed in 1950, only five years after the end of the Second World War. With the existence of totalitarian regimes in Eastern Europe, environmental considerations were, understandably, not at the forefront of the signatories' minds—they had more immediate human freedoms to be concerned about. The Convention therefore contains no explicit reference to environmental rights. Although, in 1999, the Council of Europe recommended that the Convention should be amended to include a right to a healthy and viable environment, this amendment has yet to take place.

The Convention is divided into two main parts. The first part lists the substantive rights that are to be protected, whilst the second part covers procedural matters, such as the composition of the European Court of Human Rights. A number of protocols add new rights to the Convention or make procedural amendments. The European Court of Human Rights ensures observance of the Convention. The Court investigates complaints and rejects inadmissible ones.[19] Grounds for inadmissibility include non-exhaustion of domestic remedies, that the complaint is made out of time, that it falls outside the ambit of the Convention, and that it is manifestly ill-founded. The Court makes a final and binding decision as to whether a violation of the Convention has occurred and, if it has, may order the payment of compensation.

Complaints under the Convention must be brought by a person, group of persons, or non-governmental organisation (NGO) claiming to be the "victim" of a human rights violation. The term "victim" refers to a person directly affected by the contentious act or omission. It does not, therefore, on the face of it, allow an individual or organisation to bring an action on behalf of the "environment itself" in cases of environmental damage. A further hurdle for would-be environmental complainants, of course, is that they must point to the infringement of a specific right guaranteed by the Convention. Thus, in 1976, faced with a complaint from members of an environmental organisation over the use of marshland for military purposes, the European Court of Human Rights dismissed the case because the Convention does not guarantee a right to nature conservation.[20]

Complainants in a number of cases, however, have managed to overcome these hurdles, and have brought environmental cases before the Court. These cases have

---

[18] See Glazewski, "The Environment, Human Rights and a New South African Constitution" (1991) 7 SAJHR 167; and "The Environment and the New Interim Constitution" (1994) 1 SAJELP 1.

[19] This was formerly the role of the European Commission on Human Rights, but is now a function of the Court: See Protocol 11, which came into force on November 1, 1998. See also Bratza and O'Boyle, "Opinion—The Legacy of the Commission to the New Court under the Eleventh Protocol" (1997) EHRKR, 2111.

[20] *X and Y v Federal Republic of Germany*, 5 Eur Com HR Dec & Rep (1976).

ranged from complaints about noise from Heathrow Airport to a complaint about the decision of a licensing authority to allow a company to dump waste. Faced with an absence of explicit environmental rights, applicants have sought to rely on other Convention rights, in particular their rights to life, respect for private and family life, peaceful enjoyment of possessions, a fair hearing, and freedom of expression. Only two cases have succeeded: *Lopez Ostra v Spain* (which concerned the environmental effects of a waste treatment plant) and *Guerra v Italy* (which concerned failure to inform residents about the risks from a chemical factory). The circumstances of these cases were extreme. However, as we shall see, the way in which the Court has interpreted the Convention marks a growing recognition of the importance of environmental protection.

Article 8: The right to respect for private and family life

The right to respect for private and family life is the right which has tended to feature **14–006** most prominently in the developing jurisprudence on environmental protection.

Article 8 of the Convention states:

> "Everyone has the right to respect for his private life and family life, his home and his correspondence.
>
> There shall be no interference by a public authority with the exercise of this right except such as is in accordance with the law and is necessary in a democratic society in the interests of national security, public safety or the economic well-being of the country, for the prevention of disorder or crime, for the protection of health or morals, or for the protection of rights and freedoms of others."

The Article follows the structure of the other Convention rights. In other words, the first paragraph guarantees the right, and the second paragraph outlines the circumstances when interference with the right may be justified.

Environmental issues considered under Art. 8 have included:

- Fumes, smells and contamination caused by a waste treatment plant in Spain, which caused health problems and nuisance to local people (*López Ostra v Spain*)[21];

- Noise from an airport affecting local residents (*Arrondelle v United Kingdom*; *Rayner v United Kingdom*; *Powell and Rayner v United Kingdom*; *Hatton v United Kingdom*)[22];

- Erection of a nuclear power station close to a family home[23];

---

[21] *López Ostra v Spain* 41/1993/436/515.

[22] *Arrondelle v UK* App 7889/77; 23 Y.B. Eur. Con. H.R. 166 (1980). *Rayner v United Kingdom* 9310/81 47 Eur. Com. H.R. Dec. & Rep. 5 (1986). *Powell and Rayner v United Kingdom*, 172 Eur. Court. H.R. Ser. A (1990); *Hatton v United Kingdom* App.36022/97 (2003) 37 E.H.R.R. 28.

[23] App.13728/88 (May 1990), reprinted in 3 RUDH 236 (1991). The applicant alleged that the erection of a nuclear power station 300m from her house had transformed the previously rural surroundings and impinged on her family life.

- Dust emitted during construction works affecting local residents (*Khatun v United Kingdom*);[24]

- Failure by a government to release details to local residents of pollution risks from a chemical factory. (*Guerra v Italy*).[25]

The European Court of Human Rights has accepted that environmental pollution can affect home and family life. In *López Ostra v Spain* (the case concerning the waste treatment plant) it stated:

> "Severe environmental pollution may affect individuals' well-being and prevent them from enjoying their homes in such a way as to affect their private and family life adversely, without, however, seriously endangering their health."

In *Powell and Rayner v United Kingdom* (one of the Heathrow Airport cases) the Court was prepared to find a breach of Art. 8 because:

> ". . . the quality of the applicant's private life and the scope for enjoying the amenities of his home had been adversely affected by the noise generated by aircraft using Heathrow Airport".

Article 8, therefore, is wide enough to cover not only direct measures taken against a person's home but also "indirect intrusions which were unavoidable consequences of measures not at all directed against private individuals"[26] such as noise from aircraft. States can be made to account for pollution caused by private sector companies, as well as for defaults by state agencies.[27]

The scope of Art. 8 extends to include failure by a government to release details of pollution risks. In *Guerra v Italy*,[28] decided in February 1998, the Court was prepared to find a breach of Art. 8 where the Italian authorities had failed to provide the local population with information about the risks associated with a nearby chemical factory, and about how to proceed in the event of an accident. The *Guerra* case is also significant in demonstrating the Court's increasing willingness to examine environmental complaints. It was decided by a Grand Chamber of 20 judges, which is the forum reserved for the most important cases.

If, however, a state provides a mechanism for access to information on hazardous risks, it will not be in breach of Art. 8. The case of *McGinley and Egan v United Kingdom*[29] concerned servicemen serving on Christmas Island in the Pacific Ocean in 1957 and 1958 when the UK carried out six atmospheric tests of nuclear weapons. The

---

[24] *Khatun and 180 Others v United Kingdom* App. No.38387/97. The claimants brought a claim *inter alia* under Art. 8 of the Convention in respect of the severe levels of dust that they had suffered over three and a half years as a result of building works carried out under a government initiative to encourage regeneration of largely derelict and deprived urban areas. The European Commission of Human Rights accepted that the dust contamination severely impaired their right to enjoy their homes/private lives, but considered that the interference was justified by the importance of the regeneration.

[25] *Guerra and Others v Italy* 116/1996/735/932.

[26] See *Rayner.*

[27] This is demonstrated by the line of cases on noise from airports and the case of *Guerra v Italy.*

[28] 116/1996/735/932.

[29] Case 10/1997/794/995–996. *The Times*, June 15, 1998.

applicants suffered health problems which they attributed to the tests and they applied for a government pension. One of the bases of their action was that there had been a breach of Art. 8 in that they were not entitled to access to the documentation which would have enabled them to ascertain whether or not they were exposed to dangerous levels of radiation on Christmas Island, so that they could assess the possible consequences of the tests for their health. Their applications were rejected on the basis that documents detailing the radiation levels on the Island at the relevant time were available to the applicants under a rule of procedure in the Pension Appeals Tribunal Rules. Moreover, they had not, in fact, been exposed to dangerous levels of radiation. In its judgment, the Court held that when a state engaged in a hazardous activity, the scope of Art. 8 required that those involved in the activities should have access to all relevant information. However, the rule of procedure allowing access to the documents satisfied this requirement.[30]

It should be noted that the scope of Art. 8 appears to be confined to interference with certain types of "personal" human amenity. Thus, whilst people may suffer great distress simply because particular features of the environment are being degraded, or when this degradation affects people other than themselves, such distress is not within the ambit of Art. 8.[31] Similarly, interference with wider aspects of personal lifestyle, enjoyed outside of the home, has not generally been recognised as coming within the scope of Art. 8. In one case, however, the European Commission on Human Rights was prepared to accept that disruption to the lifestyle of a group of Laplanders (who moved around with herds of deer), which would be caused by the building of a hydro-electric plant, was a breach of their right to private and family life.[32]

(1) *A positive obligation to protect private and family life?*

Article 8 requires a public authority to refrain from *interfering* with the right to private **14–007** and family life. However, in its judgments the Court has accepted that Art. 8 may be interpreted not only as requiring abstention from interference, but also as including a positive obligation of the state to take measures to protect these rights (*e.g.* to regulate private industry, so as to prevent it from causing interference). In *Guerra v Italy*, the Court adopted this interpretation in rejecting the Italian government's argument that it had not "interfered" with the applicant's right, but had merely failed to act. In *Hatton v United Kingdom* (one of the Heathrow Airport cases), the court held that Art. 8 may apply in environmental cases whether the pollution is caused directly by an action of the state, or whether the state's role in causing it is less direct, and arises from the state's failure properly to regulate private industry. From either perspective, the principles to be applied were broadly similar—in both contexts regard must be had to the fair balance that has to be struck between the competing interests of the individual and of the community as a whole.

(2) *The "margin of appreciation"*

We have seen that para.2 of Art. 8 allows a public authority to interfere with the right **14–008** to private and family life in certain circumstances. The state or the public authority must therefore strike a fair balance between the competing interests of the community

[30] See also *LCB v United Kingdom* Case 14/1997/79/1001.
[31] See *Guerra v Italy*.
[32] *G and E v Norway*, Apps.9278/81 and 9415/135 35 Eur Com HR Dec & Rep 30, 35–6 (1984).

and the individual. The Court has tended to allow states a considerable amount of discretion (known as a "margin of appreciation") in striking this balance. In *Powell and Rayner v United Kingdom*, for example, the Court took the view that it should not substitute its own assessment for that of the UK government in formulating policy in the socially and technically difficult field of air traffic regulation.

The *Hatton* case is also illustrative of the Court's approach. The applicants in *Hatton* lived in the vicinity of Heathrow airport. They alleged that their sleep had been regularly disturbed by aircraft noise during the night, and that the noise levels in question amounted to an unjustifiable interference in their private lives. At a first hearing, in front of a Chamber of seven judges, the Court found that the UK government was in breach of Art. 8. The UK government then requested that the case be referred to the Grand Chamber, consisting of 17 judges. The Grand Chamber found that no violation of Art. 8 had occurred. The Court took the view that its role in cases involving state decisions affecting environmental issues was, as with other decisions concerning social and economic policies, essentially a subsidiary one. This was because national authorities had direct democratic legitimacy and were, in principle, better placed than an international court to evaluate local needs and conditions. In matters of general policy, on which opinions within a democratic society may reasonably differ widely, the role of the domestic policy maker should be given special weight. In this difficult social and technical sphere (the regulation of excessive aircraft noise and provision of redress for aggrieved individuals), the state must be allowed a wide margin of appreciation. The Court in *Hatton* repeated statements from the judgment in *Powell and Rayner v United Kingdom* to the effect that that it was not for the Court to substitute its own views about the formulation of policy for those of a national government.

In *Hatton*, five of the judges dissented from this approach. They saw the issue of aircraft noise as one of health, not quality of life, and therefore meriting greater protection:

> "When it comes to such intimate personal situations as the constant disturbance of sleep at night by aircraft noise, there is a positive duty on the state to ensure as far as possible that ordinary people enjoy normal sleeping conditions . . . it is significant in this respect that under Article 3 sleep deprivation may be considered as an element of inhuman and degrading treatment or even torture."

The minority therefore, could not agree with the majority's view that the role of the Court was subsidiary, and limited to reviewing whether a fair balance had been struck. The approach of the majority in *Hatton*, however, prevailed in a planning context in the case of *Buckley v United Kingdom*,[33] where the Court stated:

> "By reason of their direct and continuous contact with the vital forces of their countries, the national authorities are in principle better placed than an international court to evaluate local needs and conditions. In so far as the exercise of discretion involving a multitude of local factors is inherent in the choice and implementation of planning policies, the national authorities in principle enjoy a wide margin of appreciation."

---

[33] In a planning context, a similar approach was taken in *Buckley v United Kingdom* (1997) 23 EHRR 101.

(3) *The focus on decision-making procedures*

The approach of the Court in both *Buckley* and *Hatton* was to consider whether a fair **14–009** balance had been struck between the interests of the community and the individual by scrutinising national decision-making procedures. In *Buckley*, the Court made the point that:

> ". . . whilst Article 8 contains no explicit procedural requirements, the decision-making process leading to measures of interference must be fair and such as to afford due respect to the interests safeguarded to the individual by Article 8".

In *Hatton*, the Court noted that, in previous cases in which environmental questions had given rise to violations of the Convention, the violation was predicated on a failure by national authorities to comply with some aspect of the domestic decision-making regime. Thus, in *López Ostra*, the waste treatment plant in question was illegal because it operated without the necessary licence. In *Guerra*, the violation was also founded on a procedural irregularity, in the sense that the applicants had been unable to obtain information that the state was under a statutory obligation to provide. However, in the *Hatton* case, this element of domestic procedural irregularity was wholly absent. The UK government's policy on night flights was properly made. It had been challenged by judicial review but was found, after a certain amount of amendment, to be compatible with domestic law.

In *Hatton*, the Court accepted that the night flights scheme had affected the complainants' family life, and therefore their rights under Art. 8. It went on, however, to consider the gravity of the infringement of those rights, and whether the national authorities had overstepped their margin of appreciation by failing to strike a fair balance between protecting those rights and the wider interests of the national community. In concluding that this balance had been fairly struck, the Court was influenced by the following:

(1) it was evidentially difficult to establish whether the night flight scheme had actually led to a deterioration of the night noise climate;

(2) night flights contributed to the well-being of the economy;

(3) a number of measures had been put in place to mitigate the noise;

(4) house prices had not been affected;

(5) the UK government had implemented effective procedures for addressing the issue—it had consistently monitored the position, and had imposed restrictions on noise levels.

Article 2: The right to life

Protection of the environment is related to the right to life in the obvious sense that, to **14–010** survive, people need food free from contamination, clean water to drink, healthy air to breathe and shelter to live in. The Court has, however, tended to adopt a restrictive interpretation of the right to life, confining its role to a review of the circumstances under which states may inflict capital punishment, rather than taking a wider view of the right which might encompass protection of "quality of life".

Article 2 provides:

> "Everyone's right to life should be protected by law. No one shall be deprived of his life intentionally save in the execution of a sentence of a court following his conviction of a crime for which the penalty is provided by law.
>
> Deprivation of life shall not be regarded as inflicted in contravention of this Article when it results from the use of force which is no more than absolutely necessary:
>
> (a) in defence of any person from unlawful violence;
> (b) in order to effect a lawful arrest or to prevent the escape of a person lawfully detained;
> (c) in action lawfully taken for the purpose of quelling a riot or insurrection."

Case law under Art. 2 in relation to the environment has been sparse. However, in *Öneryildiz v Turkey*,[34] which concerned a methane explosion at a waste site, killing 39 people including nine members of the Öneryildiz family who lived in a slum underneath the site, the Court held that Turkey had violated Art. 2 in failing to take all necessary measures to prevent the loss of life. The Turkish government did not have in place sufficient safety measures, or discourage people from living in the slum. The government had also failed to warn people of the risks. The Court stated that "a violation of the right to life can be envisaged in relation to environmental issues", and that, in this regard, it should be reiterated that the recent development of European standards merely confirmed an increased awareness of the duties incumbent on national public authorities in the environmental field, particularly in relation to installations for the storage of household waste and the risks inherent in operating them.

There may be other indications that the Court is prepared to take a broader view of the right to life in the context of environmental risks. In *Guerra v Italy*, some of the judges took the view that Art. 2 guaranteed protection of the applicants' bodily integrity, and that the Court's reasoning in cases under Art. 2 should evolve[35] on the basis that protection of health and physical integrity are closely associated with the right to life. In *Guerra*, therefore, some members of the Court took the view that a government agency's withholding risks about foreseeable hazards might breach Art. 2. In *LCB v United Kingdom*,[36] another case concerning exposure of servicemen to radiation following the nuclear tests at Christmas Islands in the 1950s, the Court was prepared to concede that, had the UK authorities been in possession of information about the risks posed to the applicant, the state might have been under a duty to provide such information to the applicant as part of the protection afforded to the right to life.

---

[34] Application number 48939/99, judgment given on June 18, 2002.
[35] See the judgments of Judge Walsh and Judge Jambrek.
[36] (1998) 4 BHRC 447.

Article 1 of Protocol 1: The right to peaceful enjoyment of possessions

Article 1 of Protocol Number 1 was added to the European Convention in 1952. It **14–011** states:

> "Every natural or legal person is entitled to the peaceful enjoyment of his possessions. No one shall be deprived of his possessions except in the public interest and subject to the conditions provided for by law and by the general principles of international law.
>
> The preceding provisions shall not, however, in any way impair the right of the State to enforce such laws as it deems necessary to control the use of property in accordance with the general interest or to secure payment of taxes or other contributions or penalties."

In *Rayner v United Kingdom* the Court accepted that noise could affect the value of property, and thereby amount to a partial taking of that property. Generally, however, the Article has not provided a successful basis for challenging environmental decisions.

Protection of the environment is accepted as coming within the "general interest" referred to in the second, qualifying, paragraph of the right. This paragraph may therefore entitle the state to interfere with the enjoyment of property for environmental reasons. Thus, in *Fredin v Sweden*, the applicant had obtained a permit to exploit a gravel pit. An amendment to Swedish law on nature conservation subsequently authorised the revocation of such permits. The Court was prepared to find that nature conservation could justify state interference with the applicant's right of peaceful possession of his property.

Article 6: The right to a fair trial

Article 6 of the Convention provides: **14–012**

> "In the determination of his civil rights and obligations or of any criminal charge against him, everyone is entitled to a fair and public hearing within a reasonable time by an independent and impartial tribunal established by law."

The Convention goes on to set out certain minimum rights to be accorded (such as the right to be informed of the charges in a criminal trial).

The right to a fair trial provides procedural rather than substantive protection. In other words, it does not require a particular result to be achieved in state decisions, but simply regulates how the result is arrived at. The reference to "civil rights and obligations" has been interpreted by the Court to mean private law rights and obligations, including property rights and rights and obligations arising from commercial activities. The Court has taken a wide view of what qualifies as a "determination" of civil rights and obligations. Thus, in an environmental context, Art. 6 has been held to apply to administrative decisions about the implementation of planning controls affecting enjoyment of property,[37] and decisions about environmental licences.

---

[37] *Sporrong and Lonnorth v Sweden* (1992) 5 EHRR 35.

In *Zander v Sweden*,[38] the applicant's complaint was that he had been unable to challenge a decision of a licensing authority which allowed a company to dump waste on a tip without taking precautionary measures to avoid pollution of the applicant's drinking water. The Court found this to be a breach of Art. 6. In *Benthem v The Netherlands*,[39] the applicant applied for a licence to operate an installation for the delivery of liquid petroleum gas for motor vehicles. Such a licence was necessary to construct and operate installations that might be a source of danger or a disturbance to the surrounding area. The licence was granted by the local authorities, but was then quashed by a national decree. Article 6 was held to be applicable to the applicant's claim that his objections had not been heard by an independent and impartial tribunal.

Conversely, those who object to proposed action by the state to *protect* the environment also have the right to challenge such action before a tribunal. Thus, in *Fredin v Sweden* (considered above) where the landowner was unable to obtain judicial review of the authority's decision to prohibit him from extracting gravel, the Court held that this amounted to a breach of Art. 6.

This wide view of the application of Art. 6, however, has come into conflict with traditional boundaries between executive and judicial decision-making within domestic legal systems. In many contexts, the first line of decision-makers are administrative bodies with links to the executive. These bodies are not "independent and impartial tribunals established by law" within the meaning of Art. 6. It is a common feature of the domestic legal systems of contracting states that the grounds on which a court may review the decisions of such bodies are circumscribed in ways similar to the conventional restrictions on judicial review in English law (*i.e.* there is no full appeal on the merits before the court). The resulting tension has required the development of a compromise position in the jurisprudence of the Court of Human Rights.

The decision in *Bryan v United Kingdom*[40] reflects this compromise. Mr Bryan received an enforcement notice requiring the demolition of two brick buildings on land he had bought. The local council claimed that the buildings were erected without planning permission. Mr Bryan appealed, and an inspector was appointed to conduct an inquiry and determine the appeal. The Court noted that review by the inspector itself did not satisfy Art. 6, as the Secretary of State can at any time revoke the inspector's power to decide an appeal. However, the fact that the High Court could judicially review the procedure meant that Art. 6 was satisfied. In dealing with the problem that the High Court's powers were limited to points of law and not a rehearing of the facts, the Court stated:

> ". . . apart from the classic grounds of unlawfulness under English law (going to such issues as fairness, procedural proprietary, independence and impartiality), the inspector's decision could have been quashed by the High Court if it had been made by reference to irrelevant factors or without regard to relevant factors; or if the evidence relied on by the inspector was not capable of supporting a finding of fact; or if the decision was based on an inference from facts which was perverse or irrational in the sense that no inspector properly directing himself would have drawn such an inference."

[38] (1994) 18 EHRR 175.
[39] *Benthem v Netherlands* (1986) 8 EHRR 1.
[40] 1996 21 EHRR 342.

The Court was also influenced and reassured by the procedures adopted by the planning inspector including the quasi-judicial character of the decision-making process:

> "Such an approach by an appeal tribunal on questions of fact can reasonably be expected in specialised areas of the law such as the one at issue, particularly where the facts have already been established in the course of a quasi-judicial procedure governed by many of the safeguards required by Article 6(1). It is also frequently a feature in the systems of judicial control of administrative decisions found throughout the Council of Europe Member States. Indeed, in the instant case, the subject matter of the contested decision by the inspector was a typical example of the exercise of discretionary judgment in the regulation of citizens' conduct in the sphere of town and country planning. The scope of review of the High Court was therefore sufficient to comply with Article 6(1)."

Article 10: The right to freedom of expression

Article 10 states: **14–013**

> "Everyone has the right of freedom of expression. This right shall include freedom to hold opinions and to receive and impart information and ideas without interference by public authority and regardless of frontiers.
>
> The exercise of these freedoms, since it carries with it duties and responsibilities, may be subject to such formalities, conditions, restrictions or penalties as are prescribed by law and are necessary in a democratic society, in the interests of national security, territorial integrity or public safety, for the prevention of disorder or crime, for the protection of health or morals, for the protection of the reputational rights of others, for preventing the disclosure of information received in confidence, or for maintaining the authority and impartiality of the judiciary."

Article 10, of course, is applicable in the context of environmental protest.[41] Here, the courts seek to strike a balance between freedom of expression and the preservation of public order. *Steel v United Kingdom*[42] dealt with the cases of five protesters. The Court held that the actions of all five protesters, including the two who physically impeded the activities of which they disapproved, constituted expressions of opinion within the meaning of Art. 10. The detention of three of the protesters was deemed to be disproportionate, because their protest had been entirely peaceful.

Article 10 guarantees a right to *receive* information as well as to impart it. However, in *Guerra v Italy* (the case concerning a failure by the Italian authorities to provide the local population with information about risks from a nearby chemical factory), the state was found not to be in breach of Article 10, on the basis that the freedom to

---

[41] Note that other Convention Articles may relate to environmental protest, including Art. 5 (right to liberty and security), Art. 11 (freedom of assembly and association), and Art. 14 (prohibition on discrimination).
[42] Case 67/1997/851/1058, ECHR, *The Times*, October 1, 1998. See also *Huntingdon Life Sciences v Curtin* [1998] Env. L.R. D9, where Eady J. expressed concern about the over-wide use of the Protection from Harassment Act 1997 to prevent protest on matters of public interest.

"receive information" could not be construed as imposing on a state positive obligations to collect and disseminate information.

Article 13: the right to an effective remedy

14–014   Article 13 states:

> "Everyone whose rights and freedoms as set forth in this Convention are violated shall have an effective remedy before a national authority notwithstanding that the violation has been committed by persons acting in an official capacity."

In *Hatton v United Kingdom*, whilst the Court did not find a breach of Art. 8, it did find a breach of Art. 13. This Article can only be relied on in respect of grievances that can be regarded as "arguable" in terms of the Convention. The applicants' grievances were considered "arguable", and so the Art. 13 complaint was considered. The court held that the applicants had not been granted an effective remedy, because s.76 of the Civil Aviation Act 1982 excluded their private law rights in relation to excessive noise. Their only remaining remedy was therefore judicial review. However, at the time the applicants had sought judicial review, the Human Rights Act 1998 was not yet in force. The scope of the review process was thus limited to an application of classic English public law concepts, such as irrationality, unlawfulness and patent unreasonableness. The process did not (at the time) allow consideration of whether the claimed increase in night fights, under the 1993 scheme, represented a justifiable interference with the right to respect for private and family life of those who lived in the vicinity of Heathrow airport.

B: ENVIRONMENTAL CASES UNDER THE HUMAN RIGHTS ACT 1998

14–015   Under the Human Rights Act 1998, the European Convention on Human Rights is now directly effective within UK domestic law. This means that persons aggrieved by a breach of their Convention rights can have that breach addressed in the UK courts. In addition, the Human Rights Act 1998 has the following important implications:

- UK legislation must be interpreted so as to be compatible with the Convention;
- Public authorities must not act in a way that is incompatible with the Convention; and
- Courts and tribunals must take into account the case law of the European Court of Human Rights.

At the time of its adoption, the Act was variously described as the most significant constitutional development since the passage of the European Communities Act 1972 and, arguably, since the Bill of Rights 1689. It was acknowledged, however, that much would depend on how the courts reacted to their new power of scrutiny over public administration. During the passage of the Bill, those opposed to it expressed concern that the breadth and general nature of the European Convention would mean that the courts would be drawn more deeply into matters of public policy. The approach of the courts to environmental cases since the Act has come into force suggests that these fears are not being realised.

The following environmental cases, in which use has been made of human rights arguments, have been heard in the UK since the coming into force of the Human Rights Act in October 2000. The cases of *Marcic* and *Alconbury* are of particular importance.

Article 8: The right to respect for private and family life

(1) *Sewer flooding*

In *Marcic v Thames Water Utilities Limited*,[43] Mr Marcic alleged that Thames Water **14–016** had acted unlawfully in conducting itself in a way which was incompatible with his Convention right under Art. 8, as well as his right to peaceful enjoyment of his property under Art. 1 of the First Protocol to the Convention. The case arose out of serious and repeated foul water flooding, caused when overloaded sewers discharged effluent into his garden during heavy rain. The House of Lords was prepared to accept that direct and serious interference of this nature with a person's home was *prima facie* a violation of these Convention rights. The burden of justifying the interference which had taken place rested on Thames Water.

Their Lordships, however, were influenced by the broader picture. Between 15,000 and 20,000 properties suffered sewer flooding each year. Under the scheme of regulation for the provision of sewerage services, the costs of remedying these flooding incidents varied widely, from as little as £5,000 to more than £200,000, depending on the scale and nature of the necessary work. On average, the cost per property was between £50,000 and £70,000. In the Thames Water area alone, it would have cost £1bn to alleviate the problems of all customers whose properties were at risk of sewer flooding at least once every ten years.

The House of Lords took the view that the question whether the system adopted by a sewerage undertaker was fair was a matter inherently more suited for decision by the industry regulator than by a court. A statutory scheme, set out in the Water Industry Act 1991, provided a remedy where a system of priorities was not fair, but Mr. Marcic had not chosen to pursue this. Parliament had entrusted the relevant decisions, not to the courts, but to the regulator. The regulator had the job of balancing, on the one hand, the interests of customers of a company whose properties were prone to sewer flooding, and, on the other hand, the interests of all the other customers of the company, who would have to meet the cost of improving the drainage system. Decisions of the regulator were are subject to judicial review by the courts. In the light of these factors, Mr Marcic's claims were held to be unfounded.

(2) *Noise pollution*

Dennis v Ministry of Defence[44] concerned noise pollution from Harrier aircraft flying at **14–017** RAF Wittering, situated adjacent to the home of the Dennis family. Although no physical damage to property was sustained, the experts instructed in the case agreed

---

[43] [2003] 3 W.L.R. 1603.
[44] [2003] Env. L.R. 34.

that the noise levels were high enough to cause disturbance to the family, interfere with their normal domestic and business activities, and substantially reduce the market value of their home. Buckley J. found a breach of the claimants' Convention rights both under Art. 8 and under Art. 1 of Protocol 1. The second paragraph of Art. 8 was applicable, however, as it was in the interests of national security that the MOD should be able to fly Harrier planes at Wittering. A balance had to be struck between public and private interests, but this balance would not be fair in the absence of compensation. Accordingly, damages of £950,000 were awarded in nuisance.

(3) *Waste dumping*

14–018 In *R. (on the application of Furness) v Environment Agency and Thames Water*[45] the applicants sought judicial review of a decision to grant Thames Water an authorisation for a waste incineration dump, arguing that the conditions of authorisation would not protect their right to receive information about its effect on their homes—monitoring information about the site did not have to be made public before it was placed on a public register. Here, the court held that there was no breach of Art. 8, because there was no risk to health or property.

(4) *Travellers*

14–019 *South Bucks DC v Porter*[46] concerned the lawfulness of an injunction, under s.187B of the Town and Country Planning Act 1990, requiring travellers to move off land they occupied in mobile homes in breach of planning control. All of the travellers raised Art. 8 as a defence. It was not in dispute that there would be interference with the right to respect for private and family life, nor that this interference would be in accordance with the law, because it was for the protection of the rights of others to have the quality of the local environment preserved. What was in dispute was whether the injunctions were necessary in a democratic society, and in particular, whether they were proportionate to the legitimate aim of preserving the environment.

Before ruling on the individual cases, the Court of Appeal gave general guidance on the approach to be adopted by the courts, in the light of human rights considerations, in exercising their discretion to grant an injunction under the relevant statutory provision. Their Lordships thought that a judge should not grant an injunction unless prepared to contemplate committing the defendant to prison for breach of the injunction. Consequently, the judge must consider the question of whether the injunction would cause hardship for the defendant. Equally, the judge would need to form a broad view of the damage to the public interest that resulted from the breach of planning control, and the degree of urgency involved in bringing that breach to an end. The Court of Appeal held that, on the facts, the injunctions in question were oppressive to the travellers, and should be lifted. The House of Lords affirmed this decision and endorsed the general guidance that had been given by the Court of Appeal. Their Lordships stated that earlier decisions, pre-dating the Human Rights Act 1998, to the effect that even great hardship was irrelevant to the exercise of the court's discretion, should no longer be treated as authoritative or helpful. In the light of the Human Rights Act 1998, a different approach was required, entailing a consideration of the defendant's rights.

[45] [2002] Env. L.R. 26.
[46] [2003] 2 A.C. 558.

Article 6: The right to a fair trial

The decision of the House of Lords in *R. (on the application of Alconbury Develop-* **14–020** *ments Ltd) v Secretary of State for the Environment, Transport and the Regions*[47] concerned the same issue that had been raised in the case of *Bryan*, namely the boundary between administrative and executive decision-making. The decision can claim to be the first major constitutional decision of the House of Lords under the Human Rights Act 1998, addressing, as it does, the proper areas for decision-making by the executive and the judiciary respectively. The *Alconbury* appeals concerned planning decisions "called in" by the Secretary of State for decision by him personally, after review and report by an inspector. In each case, the essential complaint was that, when a decision was taken by the Secretary of State, the Secretary of State's role in the making of policy meant that he had such an interest in the decision that he could not be regarded as an independent and impartial tribunal. Although decisions made by the Secretary of State were subject to judicial review (or a statutory appeal to the High Court based on similar principles), there was no provision for an appeal on the facts or the merits.

The House of Lords was prepared to acknowledge that the nature of the Secretary of State's role was such that he could not himself be regarded as an independent and impartial tribunal. However, their Lordships held that the crucial question, to ensure compliance with Art. 6, was whether there was sufficient judicial control over the Secretary of State's decisions to ensure that the issues involved could *ultimately* be decided by an impartial tribunal. The ECHR's jurisprudence[48] did not require such control to entail a mechanism for rehearing cases on their merits. What was required was simply that there should be a sufficient review of the legality of the decisions and the procedures followed. The judicial review jurisdiction of the High Court provided for such a review. Accordingly, there was no breach of Art. 6. As in the case of *Bryan v UK* (see above), the court was influenced by the fact that the inspector had held an inquiry which included calling and cross-examining witnesses. Their Lordships also took account of the nature of planning decisions. Lord Nolan stated:

> ". . . the obvious unsuitability of the courts as the arbiters in planning and related matters, is that the decision to be made . . . is an administrative and not a judicial decision. In the relatively small and populous island which we occupy, the decisions made by the Secretary of State will often have acute social, economic and environmental implications. A degree of central control is essential to the orderly use and development of town and country. Parliament has entrusted the requisite degree of control to the Secretary of State, and it is to Parliament which he must account for his exercise of it. To substitute for the Secretary of State an independent and impartial body with no central electoral accountability would not only be a recipe for chaos: it would be profoundly undemocratic."

Alconbury was an important decision, because it upheld the Convention compatibility of the UK's system of planning control, which relies heavily on decision-making by the

---

[47] [2001] 2 WLR 1389.
[48] See *Albert v Belgium* (1983) 5 EHRR 533, *Byran v UK* (1995) 21 EHRR 342 and *Chapman v UK* (2001) 10 BHRC 48.

democratically accountable executive at the levels of both local government (local planning authorities) and central government (the Secretary of State). Had *Alconbury* been decided differently, a fundamental re-organisation of the planning system would have been required.

The courts have emphasised the importance of considering alleged violations of Art. 6 in the context of the whole matrix of relevant rules. In *R. (on the application of Aggregate Industries UK Ltd) v English Nature*,[49] Forbes J. considered a challenge by way of judicial review of a decision of English Nature, whereby it had confirmed the notification of certain land as a Site of Special Scientific Interest ("SSSI") pursuant to s.28 of the Wildlife and Countryside Act 1981. One of the grounds of challenge was that English Nature's decision was made in breach of Art. 6 because it had both issued the notification and confirmed the SSSI, and was therefore itself a party to the dispute which it had determined. Forbes J. disagreed. Whilst his Lordship accepted that English Nature was not itself independent and impartial, he found that the existence of an over-arching framework of legal control satisfied the requirements of Art. 6 by providing a number of procedural safeguards, such as the right to make representations, the preparation of a detailed report by English Nature, the confirmation meeting being in public with the opportunity for oral representations, and the possibility of judicial review.[50]

A similar approach dictated the outcome in *R. (on the application of Adlard) v Secretary of State for Environment, Transport and the Regions*.[51] The case concerned a planning application by Fulham Football Club for a 15,000 capacity all-seater stadium. The local planning authority resolved to grant the application. At the meeting of the planning committee, 600 people attended but oral representations were not permitted. Local residents requested that the Secretary of State call in the application for a public inquiry, but this request was refused. They then sought to challenge the planning decision on the basis that their Art. 6 rights had been breached by the failure to give them any form of oral hearing. The challenge was firmly rejected by the Court of Appeal. It was accepted that the local planning authority itself could not be regarded as an independent and impartial tribunal. This fact, however, could not be viewed in isolation. It was necessary to examine the safeguards provided by the statutory scheme as a whole. The Court of Appeal held that, because administrative decisions taken by planning authorities usually turned on questions of judgment and discretion, rather than on findings of fact, the statutory scheme did not need to provide for an oral hearing at the initial stage. The scheme was therefore compliant with Art. 6, and there was no need to resort to the Secretary of State's call in power to make it so. The remedy of judicial review enabled the court to correct any injustice it perceived in an individual case.

Obvious procedural flaw

14–021   The only cases in which the courts have been prepared to find a breach of Art. 6 have been those in which the decision-making process involved obvious procedural flaws, or excessive delay and partiality. In *R. (on the application of Anglican Water Services Ltd)*

---

[49] [2003] Env. L.R. 3
[50] Wildlife and Countryside Act 1981, s.28. See also *Langton v Secretary of State for the Environment, Food & Rural Affairs* [2002] Env. L.R. 20.
[51] [2002] 1 W.L.R. 2515.

v Environment Agency,[52] Anglian Water sought an order quashing a decision of the Environment Agency requiring it to provide a public sewer for a residential area. The Agency's decision was set aside because, among other things, the agency had failed to disclose to Anglian Water certain representations made by residents in time for Anglian Water to respond. This amounted to a procedural flaw which gave rise to a breach of Art. 6.

In *Lafarge Redland Aggregates Ltd v Scottish Ministers*[53] the applicants sought judicial review of the failure of the Scottish Ministers to determine a planning application for a quarry, and of their decision to refer to Scottish National Heritage the question of whether any part of the site should be proposed as a candidate Special Area of Conservation. The Court of Session was prepared to find a breach of Art. 6. The authorities had failed to deal with the application in an impartial manner—the Minister had referred the matter Scottish National Heritage for advice, but Scottish National Heritage had been the principal objectors to the grant of planning permission for the quarry. In addition, the excessive delay of over nine years in determining the application amounted to a breach of Art. 6.

Self-incrimination

In *Green Environmental Industries Ltd v Hertfordshire CC*,[54] a local waste regulation **14–022** authority discovered a large quantity of clinical waste on the company's land and subsequently served a request for information, pursuant to s.71(2) of the EPA 1990, asking about the source of the waste and the company's business practices. The company refused to reply without confirmation from the authority that its replies would not be used against it in a prosecution. It argued that the 1990 Act should be interpreted in accordance with Art. 6(1), which afforded a privilege against self-incrimination. The House of Lords held that the Strasbourg jurisprudence underpinning Art. 6(1) was concerned with the fairness of a trial, and not with extra-judicial enquiries. Accordingly, the authority was entitled to request factual information, even if potentially incriminating, particularly in view of the urgent need to protect public health from an environmental hazard. It was not, however, entitled to invite an admission of wrongdoing. Since none of the questions put to the company invited such an admission, it was obliged to respond to them.

Article 10: the right to freedom of expression

In *R. (Ex p. Persey and Others) v Secretary of State for the Environment, Food and Rural* **14–023** *Affairs*[55] the Court of Appeal considered the applicability of Art. 10, but found that there had been no breach. The Secretary of State had ordered an inquiry into the foot and mouth outbreak, to be held in private. A number of farmers, vets and hoteliers argued that it should be heard in public. Brown L.J. stated:

[52] [2004] Env. L.R. 15. See also *R. (on the application of Holding & Barnes Plc and Others) v Secretary of State for Environment, Transport and the Regions* [2002] Env. L.R. 12.
[53] [2001] Env. L.R. 27.
[54] [2002] 2 A.C. 412.
[55] [2003] Q.B. 794

". . . freedom of expression—whether the right to receive, or the right to impart, information—is one thing, access to information quite another. . . Article 10, whilst naturally conferring the former, does not accord the latter".[56]

His Lordship went on to say that Art. 10 imposes no positive obligation on government to provide, in addition to existing means of communication, an open forum to achieve a yet wider dissemination of views. By holding the inquiry in private, the government would not be preventing anyone from receiving information that others wished or might be willing to impart.

Some idea of the courts' approach to the applicability of Art. 10 in environmental protest cases may be gained from considering *Percy v Director of Public Prosecutions*.[57] Here, the defendant stood on an American flag at an American air base, in protest against American military policy, thereby causing distress to American service personnel. She was convicted of behaviour likely to cause distress, contrary to s.5 of the Public Order Act 1986. On appeal, it was held that her conviction was incompatible with Art. 10. The trial judge had placed too much weight on the fact that her insulting behaviour could have been avoided, and too little on "the presumption in the accused's favour of the right of freedom of expression."[58]

Article 1 of Protocol 1

14–024 In *Fisher v English Nature*[59] the court rejected a challenge to an SSSI notification based on a breach of Art. 1 of Protocol 1. The decision to confirm the notification was not a disproportionate interference with Mr Fisher's rights. Of itself, the confirmation did not interfere with the peaceful enjoyment of Mr Fisher's possessions, nor did the service of the list of operations likely to damage the site. If and when Mr Fisher wanted to carry out a potentially damaging operation, a balance could be struck between protecting the internationally important population of stone-curlew at the site and Mr Fisher's rights to carry out the operations.

C: ENVIRONMENTAL DEMOCRACY

14–025 As mentioned at the start of this chapter, the most fruitful links between human rights and environmental protection are emerging as the procedural rights granted to individuals as regards the provision of environmental information, access to effective environmental dispute resolution, and public participation in environmental decision-making. Principle 10 of the Rio Convention provides the foundation for this developing area:

"Environmental issues are best handled with participation of all concerned citizens, at the relevant level. At the national level, each individual shall have

---

[56] *ibid.*, at 822.
[57] (2002) 166 JP 93.
[58] *ibid.*, at para.28.
[59] [2004] 4 All E.R. 366.

appropriate access to information concerning the environment that is held by public authorities, including information on hazardous materials and activities in their communities, and the opportunity to participate in decision-making process. States shall facilitate and encourage public awareness and participation by making information widely available. Effective access to judicial and administrative proceedings, including redress and remedy, shall be provided."

The Aarhus Convention

The UN(ECE) Convention on Access to Information, Public Participation in Decision-making and Access to Justice in Environmental Matters (the Aarhus Convention) elaborates on Principle 10 of the Rio Declaration and aims to provide effective means for the exercise of procedural rights in an environmental context. The Convention was signed at Aarhus, Denmark, in June 1998, and came into force in October 2001. It is regional in scope, because it is a convention of the UN(ECE)—the Economic Commission for Europe of the United Nations—to which not all members of the UN belong. However, it has been described by Kofi Annan, the Secretary-General to the UN, in the following terms[60]: **14–026**

> "Although regional in scope, the significance of the Aarhus Convention is global. It is by far the most impressive elaboration of principle 10 of the Rio Declaration, which stresses the need of citizens' participation in environmental issues and for access to information on the environment held by public authorities. As such it is the most ambitious venture in the area of 'environmental democracy' so far undertaken under the auspices of the United Nations."

The Convention recognises that "adequate protection of the environment is essential to human well-being and the enjoyment of basic human rights, including the right to life itself." It also recognises the right of every person of present and future generations to live in an environment adequate for his or her health and well-being, and is the first binding international treaty to do so.

The Aarhus Convention consists of three "pillars", each of which grants different rights:

- the first pillar gives the public the right of access to environmental information;

- the second pillar gives the public the right to participate in environmental decision-making processes; and

- the third pillar ensures access to justice for the public in environmental matters.

The first pillar establishes rules and requirements for governments to disclose information about the state of the environment, and the factors, policies and activities that affect it. Citizens are entitled to obtain this information within one month of requesting it, and without having to say why they require it. In addition, the

---

[60] See Aarhus website: *www.unece.org/env/pp*.

Convention places public authorities under an obligation to actively disseminate environmental information. The second pillar requires arrangements to be made by public authorities to enable citizens and environmental organisations to comment on, for example, proposals for projects affecting the environment, and for these comments be taken into account in decision-making. The third pillar deals with the right of the public and public interest groups to seek a judicial remedy for non-compliance by governments and corporations with the legal obligations established by the first two pillars.

Environmental democracy at EC level[61]

(1) *Access to information*

14–027 Directive 2003/4/EC on public access to environmental information[62] is the main instrument which gives effect to the provisions of the Aarhus Convention on public access to environmental information. The Directive applies to any "information relating to the environment" held by "public authorities" and certain other bodies under their control. The information included under the Directive covers the "state of air, water, flora, fauna, soil and natural sites". Exemptions from the requirement to disclose include those relating to information which would affect commercial confidentially or national security, and information which relates to legal proceedings. (Member States may make these exemptions mandatory or discretionary.) A request for information must be responded to as soon as possible, or in any event within two months. Public authorities may make a reasonable charge for the supply of requested information, and provision must be made for administrative "appeal" against a refusal to disclose information. Member States must implement the Directive at the latest by February 14, 2005.

(2) *Public participation in decision making*

14–028
- Directive 2003/35/EC provides for public participation in respect of the drawing up of certain plans and programmes relating to the environment.[63]

- Directive 85/337/EEC on Environmental Impact Assessment[64] requires the environmental effects of development to be considered before planning permission is granted for projects like oil refineries, large power stations, and motorways. The purpose of the assessment is to ensure that the environmental effects of the projects are considered as early as possible in the planning process.

---

[61] The EU has put forward a "package" designed to give effect to the Aarhus Convention. This comprises a draft Directive on access to justice in environmental matters (discussed above) [2003] O.J. L41/26, a draft Regulation giving effect to all three pillars of the Convention, and a proposal for a Council decision that the EU should ratify the Convention (COM (2003) 625 final. See *www.europa.eu.int/comm/environment* (the Convention is open to ratification by regional institutions as well as by signatory states).

[62] Directive 2003/4/EC of the European Parliament and of the Council of January 28, 2003 on public access to information [2003] O.J. L41. This Directive repeals Dir.90/313/EEC.

[63] Directive 2003/35/EC of the European Parliament and of the Council of May 26, 2003 [2003] O.J. L 156.

[64] Directive 85/337/EEC on the Assessment of the Effects of Certain Public and Private Projects on the Environmental O.J. L175 July 5, 1985 p.40 as amended by Dir.97/11/EC OJL73 March 14, 1997 p.5 whose provisions came into force on March 14, 1999.

- In addition, provisions relating to public participation in environmental decision-making are to be found in a number of other environmental Directives, such as Dir.2001/42/EC of the European Parliament and of the Council of June 27, 2001 on the assessment of certain plans and programmes on the environment and Dir.2000/60/EC of the European Parliament and the Council of October 23, 2000 establishing a framework for Community action in the field of water policy.[65]

(3) *Access to justice*

The proposed Directive on access to justice contributes to implementation of the **14–029** Aarhus provisions in this field.[66] It aims to establish a framework of minimum requirements for access to judicial and administrative proceedings in environmental matters. The proposed Directive grants legal standing to certain members of the public, including certain environmental groups, provided they satisfy certain conditions. This enables them to have access to judicial or administrative proceedings to challenge actions and omissions of public authorities which contravene environmental law.

Environmental democracy in the UK

(1) *Access to information*

Directive 90/313 on access to environmental information was transposed in England **14–030** and Wales by the Environmental Information Regulations 1992.[67] These regulations place a duty on every person who holds information to which the regulations relate to make that information available to "every person who requests it".[68] This has been described as a short but significant obligation, with far-reaching implications.[69] At the time of writing, new regulations are under consideration, and have been for some time, to enable the UK to fulfil its obligations under the Aarhus Convention and under the Freedom of Information Act 2002 (see below). Access to environmental information is not currently covered by the Act, but the Act includes provision to make new regulations on public access to environmental information.

(2) *The Freedom of Information Act 2000*

The Freedom of Information Act 2000 sets out a comprehensive statutory list of public **14–031** bodies to whom the Act applies, with amendments and additions to the list being made by Order. The Act will require public authorities to adopt and maintain "publication schemes" setting out practical access arrangements, and these arrangements will be enforced by the appointment of an Information Commissioner to oversee the implementation of the Act; a code of practice setting out guidance on the implementation of the system; powers of enforcement to secure compliance; and a system of appeals for persons aggrieved.

---

[65] The "Water Framework Directive", discussed in Ch. 8.
[66] COM 2003/0246.
[67] SI 1992/3240.
[68] Regulation 3(1).
[69] House of Lords Select Committee on the European Communities, First Report 1996–1997 HL Paper 9.

(3) *Public participation in decision-making*

14–032 The Town and Country Planning Environmental Impact Assessment (England & Wales) Regulations 1999, which in essence repeat the contents of the Directive, establish two classes of project for which a formal environmental impact assessment is appropriate. Such projects include: crude oil refineries; thermal power stations; installations dealing with asbestos; installations for the intensive rearing of poultry or pigs; the construction of motorways; and glass making and paper manufacturing.

The government guidance on implementing the regulations makes clear the importance of public participation:

> "The general public's interest in a major project is often expressed as concern about the possibility of unknown or unforeseen effects. By providing a full analysis of the project's effects, an environmental statement can help to allay fears created by lack of information. At the same time it can help to inform the public on the substantive issues which the local planning authority will have to consider in reaching a decision. It is a requirement of the Regulations that the environmental statement must include a description of the project and its likely effects together with a summary in non-technical language. One of the aims of a good environmental statement should be to enable readers to understand for themselves how its conclusions have been reached, and to form their own judgments on the significance of the environmental issues raised by the project."[70]

(4) *Access to justice*

14–033 At the time of writing, access to justice in environmental matters is generating a considerable degree of debate, as the government considers whether existing arrangements are "Aarhus compliant". Environmental legislation, like planning legislation, grants a formidable array of powers to the Secretary of State and to other regulatory bodies. The primary mechanisms to challenge decisions are statutory appeals, or, once all appeal routes are exhausted, judicial review. Several problems arise in respect of these mechanisms:

- Research indicates that the appeal structure in environmental law is haphazard and complex. There are over 50 different appeal provisions under current environmental laws. In some areas, there is no right of regulatory appeal. There is concern that current appeal routes (*e.g.* to magistrates) may not provide the best expertise for resolving environmental disputes.

- Given the above-mentioned problems with appeals, judicial review is in some cases being used as the primary mechanism by which regulatory decisions are challenged by individuals and pressure groups. Judicial review, however, is limited in what it can achieve. The role of the court is confined to ensuring that

---

[70] *Environmental Assessment: A Guide to the Procedures* (HMSO, 1989), p.4.

public authorities perform their functions properly.[71] The court cannot substitute its own views on the merits of a decision for the views of a public authority. This point was emphasised by Smith J. in *R. v Secretary of State for Trade and Industry, Ex p. Duddridge*.[72] The case concerned an application for judicial review brought on behalf of three children whose parents were concerned that electric cables laid as part of the national grid would emit non-ionising radiation which would enter their homes and schools and expose them to the risk of developing leukaemia. Smith J. stated:

> "It is important to make clear at the outset that it is not the function of this court to decide whether there is in fact an increased risk of leukaemia The Court appreciates that the parents of these children are deeply concerned about these issues and it is not through any lack of sympathy with that concern that the court must decline to decide them. The only issue before the court is whether the Secretary of State acted unlawfully."

- The courts do not always display a thorough understanding of environmental issues, or of the central tenets of environmental law, such as the precautionary principle, sustainable development and "favourable conservation status".

- For both public and private law cases, the issue of costs is a significant problem. As one writer has put it:

> "Litigation through the courts is prohibitively expensive for most people unless they are either poor enough to qualify for legal aid or rich enough to be able to undertake an open-ended commitment to expenditure running into tens or hundreds of thousands of pounds."[73]

A specialist environmental tribunal or court

At the time of writing, the government is considering the effectiveness of the present **14–034** judicial system in fulfilling the access to justice provisions of the Aarhus Convention. Research has been undertaken into environmental offences, the potential use of environmental civil penalties, and on the merits of establishing a specialist environmental tribunal.[74] The establishment of a civil tribunal has been recommended. This would be all-encompassing, with jurisdiction to hear all civil environmental cases, including judicial review cases, statutory applications and appeals to the High Court, environmental claims relating to nuisance, property damage, and impairment of human rights, as well as "toxic tort" and chemical-poisoning personal injury claims.[75] A

---

[71] The courts have developed a number of such principles. They will review an exercise of power to ensure that a public body has not misinterpreted the law, that it has considered all factors relevant to its decision, that it has not taken into account any irrelevant factors, that it has acted for a purpose expressly or impliedly authorised by statute, and that it has not acted in a way that is so unreasonable that no reasonable body would so have acted. In addition, the court will ensure that the authority has observed the procedural requirements set out in the statute, that the decision taken by the authority is proportional to the problem it is trying to solve, and that the principles of fairness or natural justice have been observed.

[72] (1995) J.E.L. Vol.7(2) 224.

[73] Sir Robert Carnwath, "Environmental Litigation—A way through the maze?" (1999) J.E.L. Vol.11, No.1.

[74] See the work of Macrory, available at *www.ucl.ac.uk/laws/environment/research*.

[75] Recommended by the Environmental Justice Project. See *Environmental Justice*, Report by the Environmental Justice Project, ELF, WWF and Leigh Day & Co., 2004.

more limited model might be a single Environmental Tribunal to hear regulatory appeals (including those relating to PCC, waste, water, GM-licensing and contaminated land).[76] At the time of writing, it remains to be seen how the government will respond to these proposals.

---

[76] See Macrory and Woods, *Modernising Environmental Justice: Regulation and the Role of an Environmental Tribunal*. (available from University College London, see *www.ucl.ac.uk/laws/environment/research*).

Chapter 15

GENETICALLY MODIFIED ORGANISMS: A CASE STUDY IN POLITICS, DECISION-MAKING AND ENVIRONMENTAL LAW

"The issues thrown up by genetic modification are hugely challenging, but two facts at least seem clear. The first is that the remarkable advances in our understanding of molecular biology are here to stay. They have created the possibility of GM products of many kinds. Many of these have attracted little criticism . . . but have nonetheless given rise to intense political discussion . . . as to the terms and conditions on which they might now be developed . . . This highlights a second clear fact—that the political arrangements needed to deal legitimately with these issues in countries like the UK are immature and in immediate need of further development."[1]

Introduction

So far in this book, we have not taken a "substance-based" approach to exploring **15–001** environmental law. (We have not, for example, examined any of the specific regulations relating to asbestos, lead or mercury.) In this final chapter, however, we depart from this approach to consider regulation of genetically modified organisms. We single out these substances for special treatment because an exploration of the relevant laws, and the way they have developed, provides a useful understanding of the numerous political, social and ethical factors that define environmental decision-making processes and contribute to the formulation of policy and law.

Genetically modified organisms (GMOs) are organisms in which the genetic material (DNA) has been altered in a way that does not occur naturally.[2] The technology used to do this—genetic modification[3]—allows selected individual genes to be transferred from one organism into another, either from the same species or from a non-related species. Genetic modification is one of a number of activities that are often referred to by the term "modern biotechnology". Modern Biotechnology is

---

[1] *Crops on Trial: A Report by the Agriculture and Environment Biotechnology Commission* (now known as the Biotechnology Commission) September 2001. Available at *www.aebc.gov.uk*.
[2] "Naturally" meaning by mating or natural recombination.
[3] Sometimes also called "recombinant DNA technology" or "genetic engineering".

usually understood to refer to the application of scientific and engineering principles to biological materials to produce goods and services.

The technology of genetic modification is practised in the field of medicine. For example, animal insulin and growth hormones are modified so as to be identical to hormones produced by the human body. Genetic modification is also used with plants. This chapter is concerned with the genetic modification of plants, as opposed to the production of medicines, because the latter takes place, in the main, in contained laboratory environments, and does not therefore have the same implications for the environment as the growth of genetically modified plants in the countryside.

A scientific approach to plant breeding has been practised since the early years of the last century. Genes have long been moved into crops by cross-pollination. The use of GM technology, however, may be distinguished from conventional plant breeding in two ways:

- the technology employed is much more precise—only a few specific genes are inserted;

- the range of possible genes that may be inserted by GM techniques is much greater.

Research is ongoing, but it clear that the technology of genetic modification may be able to provide significant benefits in terms of food production and medical treatment (plants used as a source of medicines or vaccines). It may also form the basis of new, less-polluting, industrial processes, and make a significant contribution to cleaning up pollution that has already occurred. For example, GM micro-organisms might be used to remediate contaminated land.

Any new technology inevitably raises questions about the nature and likelihood of the benefits and risks it presents, requiring a decision about whether the technology should be proceeded with. This decision is not just confined to the UK. When a new technology is introduced in more than one country, each country has to make a judgment about the risks, and decide whether and how to allow the technology to proceed. The question therefore arises whether the international legal system, and, more specifically, the way that system regulates world trade, is sophisticated enough to permit different countries to react in different ways, and in particular to accommodate the needs of countries that wish to take a cautious approach.

The risks and concerns of genetic modification centre on the following:

(1) *Actual or potential adverse environmental consequences*

15–002 The behaviour of GMOs, once released into the environment, may be difficult to monitor and control, because they will multiply, adapt, evolve, and interact. As EC Council Directive 2001/18[4] puts it:

> "Living organisms, whether released into the environment in large or small amounts for experimental purposes or as commercial products, may reproduce in the environment and cross national frontiers, thereby affecting member states. The effects of such releases on the environment may be irreversible".

---

[4] Directive 2001/18/EC on the deliberate release into the environment of GMOs, [2001] O.J. L1061.

Although complex interactions are a traditional concern of environmental science, the risks presented by GMOs in this context are perhaps greater than those associated with traditional substances. The presence of GMOs in the environment may affect species diversity—they may become successful predators, competitors, parasites or pathogens of crop plants. If this happens, it may have a significant economic impact. GMOs may pose a risk to human health.[5] These consequences may not be immediately obvious, and the time-scales over which they become apparent could be lengthy.

(2) *The impact of GM crops on other systems of farming (conventional and organic)*

Widespread cultivation of GM crops will almost inevitably lead to non-GM products **15–003** containing some GM material. This will occur in a number of ways, including by cross-pollination and mixing during harvesting, transport and processing. The concern, therefore, is that GM crops may not, in the long run, be able to co-exist with existing farming in a way that continues to allow consumer choice. Under EC law, organic farmers are not currently allowed to use GM organisms and product derivatives in organic production.[6] The concern (of both farmers and consumers) is that an unwanted presence of GM material in organic crops will prevent them from being marketed as non-GM. This would have a significant economic impact on organic farmers, because their crops would lose their organic premium.

(3) *Social concerns*

The social controversy associated with GM crops has a number of different aspects:

- People have fundamentally different perceptions of, and attitudes towards, GM technology. At one end of the spectrum is the view that genetic modification of plants represents a progressive evolution of selective plant breeding, and a successful outcome of science. At the other end of the spectrum is the view that GM technology is not simply an advance in molecular biology, but a major and irreversible watershed in human intervention in nature. It may be argued that any regulatory framework must expose, respect and embrace these differences of opinion, as opposed to burying them.[7]

- Research shows that peoples' concerns about genetic technology have a significant political dimension—they can extend to a concern about the possible abuse of power by governments and multi-national companies. In relation to the latter, the fear is that the interests of society might be subordinated to the motive of profit. Lack of trust in governments has arisen from problems in the recent past like BSE.[8] The perception is that governments may not have adequate knowledge to help people take the right decisions, and that governments can be too close to producers' interests.

[5] Royal Commission on Environmental Pollution, 13th Report (1989), Cm. 720.
[6] EC Reg.2092/91. The EC has not set a threshold for the inadvertent presence of GM material in organic produce, above which the product cannot certified as organic. However, most organic certification bodies in the UK and Europe work to the limit of detection, *i.e.* a content of 0.1 per cent. Organic associations are concerned that producers will not be able to meet this standard if there is widespread cultivation of GM crops.
[7] See *Crops on Trial* (above).
[8] Bovine Spongiform Encephalopathy (commonly called "mad cow disease") caused by feeding animal by-products to cattle. It is believed that humans have contracted the fatal illness Variant Creutzfeldt-Jacob Disease (vCJD) a result of eating beef products contaminated with BSE.

This, then, is the melting pot of issues from which the current regulatory regime has emerged. An examination of how this regime has developed provides a useful case-study of the processes involved in making environmental law and policy. As mentioned in Ch. 1, the environmental policy-making process may be said to have three stages. In the first, or "ignition" stage, public opinion is raised to a temperature that stimulates action. In the second stage, the hazard is examined scientifically and objectively to establish how dangerous it is. In the third stage, that objective examination is combined with public opinion to provide a formula for political action. One of the flash points in public concern about GMOs was the failure of the pre-existing regulatory regime to take account of non-scientific concerns. We shall see how the outcome of this three-stage process has led to some accommodation of such concerns, for example through product-labelling and the introduction of mandatory public consultation.

In 1989, legal commentators writing about biotechnology and its implications for environmental law stated: "the drive to develop commercial application of biotechnology is global in sweep . . . the process of legal response has barely begun".[9] Fifteen years later, the legal picture has changed dramatically. In Europe and the UK, GMOs are subject to some of the tightest and most detailed regulation in the world. (There is, however, debate about whether this regulation appropriate.) Stringent regulation has been driven to a large extent by politics. Since 1998, the EC has had a moratorium on GM crops and products. This arose because a number of Member States made it clear they would oppose new authorisation of GM-related activities until rules on labelling and traceability were adopted. (These rules have now been put in place.) The moratorium led the US, Canada and Argentina to file a case against the EC with the World Trade Organisation (WTO). At the time of writing, this case has yet to be determined.

A: DEVELOPMENT OF THE LEGISLATIVE FRAMEWORK

Early health and safety regulation

15–004 The technology of genetic modification first came into existence in the early 1970s. From an early stage in its development, the technology was subject to a public discussion about its potential risks. This was, and is today, partly a reflection on the extraordinary nature of the science involved—a natural apprehension arising from a belief that scientists are manipulating something as fundamental as life itself, together with an awareness that the relationship between living things and their environment is imperfectly understood.[10]

In the UK, public concerns about the technology surfaced at an early stage. Public interest in the potential hazards associated with genetic engineering was first focused by a call by several distinguished scientists, in 1974, for a voluntary world-wide moratorium on genetic manipulation of certain micro-organisms because of the

[9] Stewart and Martinez, "International Aspects of Biotechnology: Implications for Environmental Law and Policy (1989) JEL.
[10] As expressed in the RCEP's 13th report.

possible danger to human health. In response to the public interest aroused by this in the UK, a research working party was set up to assess the potential benefits and hazards of the scientific techniques in question. Its report, in 1975, recommended that "because of the great benefits to which this may lead", such techniques should continue to be used, but subject to rigorous safeguards, and under conditions of appropriate containment. In 1976, a governmental advisory body was established to advise laboratories who were undertaking experiments in genetic manipulation.

Regulation was initially considered necessary only in the context of contained work in laboratories, as opposed to releases of GMOs into the environment, which were not at that time being contemplated by the scientific community. Powers under the Health and Safety at Work etc. Act 1974 were used for the protection of those engaged in laboratory work, and to protect the public against risks arising from that work. In 1978, the Health and Safety (Genetic Manipulation) Regulations were made under the Act. They required notification to the Health and Safety Executive of an intention to carry out genetic manipulation.

Concern extends to environmental impacts

In the mid-1980s, the release of genetically manipulated organisms into the environ- **15–005** ment came under scrutiny. Health and Safety Commission approved guidelines were issued, recommending that the HSE should be notified of any proposal to release GMOs, and should carry out a risk assessment of the environmental consequences of the release. Although these requirements were initially voluntary, the Genetic Manipulation Regulations 1989[11] put them on a statutory footing. In addition, other legislation provided general regulation which covered products comprising or including GMOs.[12]

Also in 1989, the Royal Commission on Environmental Pollution (RCEP) decided to undertake a study of the release of GMOs into the environment. The RCEP, presciently, took the view that an objective assessment of the issue was necessary, as genetic manipulation was likely to be of growing public concern. The RCEP wanted to contribute to the development of effective guidelines and controls, both in the UK and in the European Community. In its study, it considered the risks and benefits likely to accrue from the environmental use of genetically engineered organisms, and whether current guidelines and regulations were adequate to ensure good practice—both in relation to experimental releases and in terms of subsequent commercial use of GMOs.

The Royal Commission was clear that fresh legislation was required to provide specifically for the control of releases of GMOs into the environment. Its report concluded that, although the environment was "generally resilient, resistant to invasion by alien organisms and robust to biological perturbations," it was probable that some organisms, once released, would become established. Of these, the majority were likely to pose no hazard, but others might cause varying degrees of disturbance, which, in extreme cases, might have serious environmental consequences:

---

[11] SI 1989/1810.
[12] See *e.g.* Consumer Protection Act, 1987; Food and Environment Protection Act1985; Food Act 1984; Medicines Act 1971; Medicines Act 1968; Plant Health Act 1967.

"Advances in genetic engineering techniques and concern for the environment lead us to conclude that statutory control of releases of genetically engineered organisms to the environment must be put in place".

The Royal Commission made a series of recommendations, based around the central concept of a statutory scheme for controlling releases, including the screening of applications for release licences; the registration of companies or organisations carrying out trial releases; general public access to information on releases; a duty of care obliging those responsible for releases to take steps to protect health and the environment; and the imposition of strict statutory liability on those carrying out releases in breach of these requirements. The Report provided the impetus for legislative action, and many of its recommendations found expression in Pt VI of the Environmental Protection Act 1990. During the early stages of public debate about GM, the existence of Pt VI, and its associated regulations (discussed below) appeared not to be well recognised, even though, provided they are properly enforced, they can afford a significant level of environmental protection.

The provisions in Pt VI have been used to control deliberate release and marketing of GMOs (their *contained* use being regulated under other legislation[13]). Their purpose is to "prevent or minimise any damage to the environment which may arise from the escape or release from human control of genetically modified organisms."[14] At the same time, the government established the Advisory Committee on Releases to the Environment (ACRE) to advise as a single expert committee on both the environmental and human health risks of releases. The essential scheme of Pt VI is to require, as a minimum, that all persons proposing to import, acquire, keep, release, or market GMOs should carry out a risk assessment of possible environmental damage resulting from those acts and should, where prescribed, notify the Secretary of State of their intentions to act. Section 109 imposes a series of general duties on such persons to identify risks of environmental damage, and to cease their activities if it appears that, despite the precautions that could be taken, such risks cannot be eliminated.

The Secretary of State can enforce these duties by way of prohibition notices, and the breach of these duties entails criminal liability under s.118. Additionally, in prescribed situations, these activities require a specific consent from the Secretary of State, under s.111. Public registers of information on consents, prohibition notices, and other matters are required to be kept under s.122. In reality, the regulations made under the regime require that express consent be obtained in all cases. This means that s.111 (rather than the more minimalist, general requirements of ss.108 to 110) effectively provides the exclusive means of control.

Development of the EC legislative framework

15–006 At the same time as the UK legislation described above was evolving, the EC was developing measures to address the risks of GMOs, in terms of both their use in laboratories and their release into the environment. EC legislation on GMOs has been

[13] See Genetically Modified Organisms (Contained Use) Regulations 2000 (SI 2000/2831) (replacing the Genetically Modified Organisms (Contained Use) Regulations 1992 (SI 1992/3217).
[14] EPA 1990, s.106(1).

in place since the early 1990s, and aims to protect health and the environment while simultaneously creating a unified market for biotechnology.

Directive 92/219/EEC (the "Contained Use Directive") on the contained use of genetically modified micro-organisms (GMMs)[15] applies only to micro-organisms (organisms that are too small to be visible without the aid of the microscope).[16] It was adopted in response to the growth in biotechnology research work during the 1970s in many Member States. The Directive was originally quite rigid in its application. It adopted a system of classification entailing two different classes of GMMs and two different types of activities (basically, small-scale operations for teaching, research, and other non-commercial activities on the one hand, and all other operations on the other). Greater experience and knowledge of the risks associated with GMMs led to a revised system, set out in Dir.98/81/EC. The revised system lists four classes of risk from contained use, ranging from activities of no or negligible risk to activities of high risk, and sets out requirements for each class of activity, including some very detailed requirements (*e.g.* showers, biohazard signs, and entry to labs via airlocks).

Directive 90/220/EEC on the deliberate release into the environment of genetically modified organisms (The "Deliberate Release Directive") has proved much more controversial, as perhaps was to the expected given that public concern over GMOs has focused on their impact on the wider environment. At the time it was originally published as a proposal, national policy in Member States was relatively unformed, although guidelines and regulatory structures were beginning to be developed, in particular in Germany and Denmark. The Directive governs both the deliberate release into the environment of GMOs and their marketing, and was promoted as a measure to harmonise provisions in Member States with a view to the establishment and functioning of the internal market. The requirements of both Directives were implemented in the UK by the Contained Use Regulations 1992[17] and the Deliberate Release Regulations 1992[18] respectively, both of which have now been subject to amendment.

The tightening of regulation

During the 1990s, the Deliberate Release Directive was subject to some fine-tuning in **15–007** terms of its procedures, the information required with notification, and the introduction in 1997 of compulsory labelling of products containing GMOs.[19] However, in 1996, the European Commission published a review of the Directive after consultation with competent authorities, environmental and other interest groups, and industry. This led to the adoption, in 1997, of a proposal to amend the Directive,[20] which, in turn, opened

---

[15] Council Dir.90/219/EEC, [1990] O.J. L177, 1 (amended by Council Dir.98/81/EC, [1998] O.J. L330, 13).

[16] "Organism"is defined as any microbiological entity capable of replication or of transferring genetic material.

[17] Genetically Modified Organisms (Contained Use) Regulations 1992 (SI 1992/3217), as amended by SI 1996/967 and SI 1998/1548.

[18] Genetically Modified Organisms (Deliberate Release) Regulations 1992 (SI 1992/3280), as amended by SI 1995/304 and SI 1997/1900.

[19] See Commission Dir.97/35/EC, [1997] O.J. L169, 72; Commission Dec.94/730/EC, [1994] O.J. L292, 31; Commission Dir.94/15/EC, [1994] O.J. L103, 20; Commission Dec.92/146/EEC, [1992] O.J. L60, 19; Council Dec.91/596/EEC, [1991] O.J. L322, 1.

[20] Proposal for a European Parliament and Council Directive Amending Dir.90/220/EEC on the Deliberate Release into the Environment of Genetically Modified Organisms, COM(98)85 final.

a highly controversial debate. Experience of the Directive over the first 10 years identified the need for significant clarification, improvement and strengthening of several aspects, including:

- Co-ordinating the principles of risk assessment to ensure Member States were adopting a consistent approach to risk assessment;

- Managing the possible longer-term, indirect, delayed and cumulative effects on the environment and wildlife of releasing GMOs such as crop plants;

- The post-market monitoring of GMO products, including consideration of the length of time for which marketing consents should be valid, what should be included in monitoring plans, and measures to aid traceability and identification;

- Consultation with the public on experimental releases of GMOs, and information to the public on the release and marketing of all GMOs;

- The predictability and transparency of the procedures for reaching decisions on GMO releases, including the resolution of differences between Member States.

The proposals for amendment contemplated a much stricter regime, including more rigorous scientific consultation requirements, fixed-term consents, compulsory monitoring of environmental impact after GM products were placed on the market, and the possibility for the European Council to refuse approval of a product by a simple majority vote.

In February 2001, the new Directive (Dir.2001/18/EC) was finally approved, and replaced Dir.90/220/EC as of October 17, 2002. Its provisions—which strengthened the regime established by Dir.90/220/EC—were described by the British Labour MEP and European Parliament Rapporteur as "the tightest GM laws in the world".[21] The decision was taken to replace (rather than amend) the older Directive because of the large number of changes (and possibly the political significance associated with a new Directive). The changes included enhanced public consultation and access to information (including the establishment of registers), a revised risk assessment process, and a requirement to ensure that GMOs can be traced at all stages, to assist the regulatory authorities in protecting health and the environment. The Directive was implemented in the UK by the Genetically Modified Organisms (Deliberate Release) Regulations 2002.[22]

B: THE PRINCIPLES BEHIND GMO REGULATION

15–008 GMO regulation in the UK, and at EC level, is based on the same underlying principles, although there is some debate as to whether these are appropriate principles to apply.

---

[21] Martin Fletcher, "French Threaten to Thwart Deal on GM Crops", *The Times*, February 12, 2001.
[22] SI 2002/2443.

The precautionary principle

The precautionary principle is discussed more fully in Chs 2 and 4. Broadly, the **15–009** principle embodies the idea that legislators should err on the side of caution when taking steps to prevent environmental damage. The Cartagena Protocol, which regulates the transboundary movements of GMOs, and is discussed below, reflects the precautionary principle in stating that:

> "Lack of scientific certainty . . . regarding the extent of the potential adverse effect of a living modified organism on the . . . biological diversity in the Party of import . . . shall not prevent that Party from taking a decision . . . with regard to the import of that living modified organism."[23]

The preamble to the Deliberate Release Directive states that "the precautionary principle has been taken into account in the drafting of this Directive and must be taken into account when implementing it."

Preventive action

The preventive principle requires legislation to aim to prevent the occurrence of **15–010** damage to the environment, as opposed to cleaning up damage once caused. The scheme of regulation at both EC and UK level is to control the use of GMOs by requiring licences and risk assessments for laboratory work, releases into the environment, and marketing of GMO products.

The "step-by-step" principle

The underlying premise of regulation is that genetic modification should be allowed to **15–011** proceed, provided this will not create adverse risks to health or the environment. The preamble to the Deliberate Release Directive states that the introduction of GMOs should be carried out according to the "step-by-step" principle. This requires the containment of GMOs to be reduced, and the scale of releases increased, on a gradual basis. However, each release should be evaluated on its own merits, and releases should only be increased if an evaluation in terms of protection of human health and the environment indicates that the next step may be taken.

Scientific risk assessment

Contained use GMMs and deliberate release of GMOs are allowed to take place after **15–012** a science-based risk assessment. Ethical concerns (*e.g.* the intervention by man in nature) do not fall within the risk assessment procedure. Whilst there are provisions in the Deliberate Release Directive for consultation on the ethical implications of biotechnology, these do not affect the procedures for authorisation of releases. Indeed, it is not clear from the Directive whether or how discussion on ethical issues should be used in applying the regulatory framework.

[23] Article 10 para.6.

There has been some debate about whether science-based risk assessment addresses too narrow an area of risk. It does not address broader issues about the public acceptability of potentially irreversible environmental changes. In addition, no account can be taken of the social or economic impacts of growing GM crops, including the impacts on other farming systems and on consumer choice in the purchase of farmed products. This narrow focus is thought to have contributed to public anxieties in relation to GM. There is, however, an increasing emphasis on the need for transparency and public information in relation to scientific risk assessments. This entails open acknowledgement that such assessments do not eliminate risk—they merely attempt quantify it—and that the limits of scientific knowledge mean that scientific assessments cannot provide certainty. This is the sort of approach that was recommended in the Phillips Report on BSE, which stated: "openness requires recognition of uncertainty where it exists".

C: THE CURRENT REGULATORY FRAMEWORK

15–013 As has been said, the current EC and UK regulatory framework for GMOs has been described as the tightest in the world. A GMO will probably pass through several stages of experimental development, followed by trial release, and at each stage, these GM activities require a licence. The outcome of research may be a proposed GM product, whose suitability must be assessed again at the pre-marketing stage, and which must again be licensed for supply and use.

Contained use of GM micro-organisms in laboratories

15–014 As noted earlier, Directive 90/219/EEC, as amended by Council Directive 98/81/EC (The "Contained Use Directive") regulates the contained use of GMMs for research and industrial purposes. These Directives have been implemented in the UK by the Genetically Modified Organisms (Contained Use) Regulations 2000[24] (the "Contained Use Regulations").

Activities involving genetic modification are divided into four categories, ranging from no or negligible risk activities to activities of high risk which justify more stringent protective measures. There are no notification requirements for activities with no or negligible risk. For the other categories, however, anyone responsible for operations involving the contained use of a genetically modified micro-organism must carry out a prior assessment of the risks to health and safety and the environment, and must provide the competent authority with information about the nature of the work (including the potential hazard, scale and purpose of the work). The notification requirements are stricter for micro-organisms considered to pose a greater risk to health and the environment. Here, the competent authorities must consent to their use.

Experimental release of GMOs in the environment

15–015 The experimental release into the environment of GMOs is regulated by Dir.2001/18/ EC on the deliberate release of genetically modified organisms, discussed above. The Directive entered into force in April 2001, and Member States were required to

[24] SI 2000/2831, as amended by SI 2002/63.

implement its provisions by October 17, 2002. The Genetically Modified Organisms (Deliberate Release) Regulations 2002[25] implement the requirements of the Directive in England.

The Directive puts in place an approval process, under which a case-by-case assessment of the risks to human health and the environment is required before any GMO can be released into the environment. Member States are under a general obligation to "ensure that all appropriate measures are taken to avoid adverse effects on human health and the environment which might arise from . . . deliberate release".[26] A person must, before undertaking deliberate release of a GMO, submit a notification to the relevant competent authority, containing an environmental risk assessment of the proposed release. Before making a decision to approve or reject the request for release, the competent authority must consult with other Member States.

The requirements for the risk assessment are detailed and wide-ranging. The objective of the assessment is to identify and evaluate potential adverse effects of the GMO, either direct and indirect, immediate or delayed. Indirect effects of the GMO include its interaction with other organisms, and those which might result from changes in the way the GMO is managed and used. The assessment must also include an analysis of "cumulative long term effects", i.e. the cumulative effects of granting release consents for different GMOs. "Delayed effects" refers to effects which may not be observed when the GMO is released, but which may become apparent as a direct or indirect effect at a later stage.

One problem with the earlier system of regulation was the relatively weak requirement for public consultation, which simply stated that the Member State could, if it thought it appropriate, provide that particular groups or the public should be consulted on any aspect of the proposed release. This has now been replaced by a mandatory requirement to consult the public and, where appropriate, groups, on proposed deliberate releases.[27] An additional mandatory requirement is for Member States to make information on all deliberate releases available to the public.[28] Further, the Directive's preamble emphasises that respect of ethical principles recognised in Member States is particularly important. Member States may take into consideration ethical aspects when GMOs are deliberately released. The Directive provides for the European Commission to consult any committees it has created, with a view to obtaining advice on the ethical implications of biotechnology. However, the relevant Article goes on to indicate that this should not affect the notification and risk assessment procedures—as noted above, therefore, it is unclear how consideration of ethical principles should sit alongside the scientific risk assessment procedures if the two conflict.

Marketing of GMOs

The placing of products containing GMOs on the market is also regulated by **15–016** Dir.2001/18. The procedures are more rigorous than for experimental release because once the product has been authorised under the Directive, it may be marketed across the EC.

[25] SI 2002/2442.
[26] Council Dir.90/220/EEC, Art. 4(1).
[27] ibid., Art. 9.
[28] Article 9(2)

The manufacturer or importer must submit a notification to the competent authority when the product is to be placed on the market for the first time.[29] This must be accompanied by an environmental and human health risk assessment, details of the conditions of use and handling of the product, a plan for monitoring the GMO, and a proposal as to labelling and packaging of the product.[30]

The competent authority must either reject the application within 90 days or send the dossier to the European Commission with a favourable opinion. The Commission will forward the dossier to other Member States, which have sixty days to raise objections. If no objections are received, the competent authority is to give its consent within sixty days. If there are unresolved objections, the decision is taken by the Commission, in consultation with an expert advisory committee set up under the Directive, composed of national representatives chaired by a Commission representative. The Chairman submits a proposal on which the Committee delivers its opinion by a weighted majority: the measure is adopted if agreed to by the Committee and the Chairman; otherwise, the matter goes to the European Council for decision on a qualified majority basis.

Once consent has been given, the product may be used throughout the EC, provided that any conditions of the consent are strictly complied with. Member States may not prohibit, restrict or impede such use. Member States may, however, if there are justifiable reasons to consider that the product in question constitutes a risk to human health or the environment, *provisionally* restrict or prohibit its use or sale in their territory. If this happens, the Commission must be notified, and a decision made as to the GMOs continued marketing, within three months.

The public must be consulted about the application to market, and relevant information must be made available to the public and placed on the registers. The maximum duration of any consent for marketing and use is ten years (there are specific provisions as to renewal of consent). Labelling requirements include a requirement that the words: "This product contains genetically modified organisms" must appear either on a label or on a document accompanying the product.

Product approval

15–017 Certain products containing GMOs may require additional regulatory approval before they can be sold or supplied. Regulation 1829/2003 on "genetically modified food and feed" covers food and animal feed consisting of, or produced from, GMOs.[31] This covers human food and animal feed produced from GMOs, as well as products such as food additives, flavourings, and feed additives so produced. Genetically modified food and feed can only be authorised for placing on the EC market after a risk assessment, undertaken under the responsibility of the European Food Safety Authority. This scientific evaluation will be followed by a risk management decision by the European

[29] Article 11(1).
[30] Annex III requires the identification of potentially harmful effects associated with the GMO, including human, animal, or plant diseases, resistance to treatments or prophylactics for disease, and deleterious effects due to establishment or dissemination in the environment, or to the natural transfer of genetic material to other organisms.
[31] Regulation No. 1829/2003 of the European Parliament and of the Council of September 22, 2003 on genetically modified food and feed.

Community. When a product is likely to be used both for food and feed purposes, such a product should only be authorised when fulfilling authorisation criteria for both food and feed. GM products may also have to satisfy other non-GM regulatory procedures. For example, any new GM plant variety, like new conventional varieties, must be registered on the UK and EC seed lists. Seed lists guarantee to buyers that new varieties are distinct, uniform and stable. In addition, any use of pesticides on GM crops has to be approved by the relevant authority.

Labelling and traceability of GMOs and GM Products

The primary purpose of rules on labelling and traceability of GMOs is not environ- **15–018** mental or human health protection (although they can, of course, assist if a problem is identified, so that a product must be withdrawn from the market). Rather, such rules enable consumers to make an informed choice about products they buy. An appropriate labelling system for GM food and feed has been regarded as one of the key issues in ensuring greater acceptance of the application of gene technology in the agro-food sector. The aim has been to address the concerns of citizens, consumer organisations and economic organisations by allowing consumers and farmers to decide whether or not they wish to buy food or feed produced from GMOs.[32]

Extending the labelling regime to all food and animal feed produced from GMOs (even if no DNA or protein of GM origin is detectable in the final product) requires a *traceability* system. This is because there is frequently no detectable difference between products derived from GM and from other crops, which means that testing the actual product being sold would not tell the consumer how it had been produced. A traceability system requires each operator in the production and distribution chain to transmit to the next operator information that a product consists of, contains, or (in the case of food or feed) was produced from GMOs.

EC Regulation 1829/2003 on genetically modified food and feed, and Reg.1830/2003 concerning traceability put in place a stringent regulatory framework which closed existing gaps in the law. Regulation 1830/2003 entered into force on November 7, 2003, and applies from January 16, 2004.[33] Regulations are directly applicable in UK law, so do not require implementing legislation.

Under the Regulations:

- All GM ingredients, and products derived from them, must be labelled, whether or not GM material is actually present in a final product;

- GM products must be traceable at all stages "from farm to the supermarket shelves". Under the traceability system, business operators must, at each stage in marketing, transmit and retain information about products that contain or are produced from GMOs;

- Non-GM foodstuffs must be labelled as *containing* GM material if they have a content of GM elements of 0.9 per cent or more.

[32] See Proposal for a Regulation on GM food and feed COM (2001) 425 final.
[33] Regulation No. 1830/2003 of the European Parliament and of the Council of September 22, 2003 concerning the traceability and labelling of genetically modified organisms and the traceability of food and feed products produced from genetically modified organisms and amending Dir.2001/18/EC.

D: International Regulation: The Cartagena Protocol

15–019 International obligations on GMOs stem from the Rio Convention on Biological Diversity (discussed in Ch. 2), which entered into force in December 1993. Its objectives are to conserve biological diversity and to ensure the fair and equitable sharing of the benefits deriving from the exploitation of biotechnology. The Rio Convention required contracting parties to regulate, manage and control the environmental risks associated with the use and release of "living modified organisms" (LMOs) resulting from biotechnology, in so far as they might affect biological diversity or human health. The parties were required to consider the need for a Protocol setting out appropriate procedures, including, in particular, procedures relating to advance informed agreement, safe transfer, and safe handling of LMOs. The result has been the Cartagena Protocol on Biosafety.

The Cartagena Protocol was adopted in January 2000, and entered into force on September 11, 2003. The preamble recognises the rapid expansion of modern biotechnology and the growing public concern over its potential adverse effects on biological diversity. It also recognises that "modern biotechnology has great potential for human well-being, if developed and used with adequate safety measures". (The text refers to these factors as twin aspects of modern biotechnology, and states that they are reflected in the requirements under the Rio Convention for access to, and transfer of, technologies—including biotechnology.) The Protocol seeks to ensure the development of appropriate procedures to enhance the safety of biotechnology by regulating the transboundary movement of "living modified organisms". These are defined as any living organisms that possess a novel combination of genetic material obtained through the use of modern biotechnology. It applies to the transboundary movement, transit, handling and use of all living modified organisms, save for pharmaceuticals covered by other international agreements, and organisms destined for contained use. The preamble recognises that the Protocol is of particular benefit to developing countries—since many have limited capabilities to cope with the nature and scale of known and potential risks associated with LMOs—and aims to gives them the necessary information and the opportunity to decide which LMOs they wish to receive.

The following obligations arise under the Protocol:

- Any country exporting LMOs to another country must supply the importing country with information about the LMO, and obtain the "advance informed agreement" of that country;

- Cross-border shipments of commodities that may contain LMOs must be clearly labelled;

- Stricter procedures apply to seeds, live fish, and other LMOs for direct use as food or feed, or for use after processing. In these cases, parties to the Protocol must notify the "Biosafety Clearing House" of any domestic decisions regarding any LMO that may be subject to transboundary movement;

EC implementation of the Cartagena Protocol

The EC has implemented the Protocol by Regulation 1946/2003 on the transboundary **15–020** movement of genetically modified organisms.[34] *Imports* of GMOs into and within the EC are covered by existing EC legislation sufficient to comply with the Protocol. The Regulation therefore covers only *exports* of GMOs to countries outside the EC. The main requirements of the Regulation are:

- Exports of GMOs intended for deliberate release into the environment must be notified to the country of import, allowing it to make an informed decision about whether to import, based on a scientific risk assessment. Exporters must await the prior written express consent of the country of import before proceeding with the first transboundary movement of a GMO intended for deliberate release into the environment;

- Existing EC Rules on labelling, traceablility and identification are extended to exports of GMOs;

- Member States must take appropriate measures to prevent unintentional transboundary movements of GMOs, and appropriate steps in the event that such movements occur.

E: LIABILITY FOR ENVIRONMENTAL DAMAGE

As mentioned, the behaviour and characteristics of GMOs, once released into the **15–021** environment, cannot readily be known. Organisms which survive and become established could affect the environment in a variety of ways. Possible impacts include effects on groundwater and the effects of monoculture on soil, plants and insects.[35] Public discussion of GMOs has often raised the question of who should bear responsibility for any adverse environmental impacts which might result from growing GM crops.[36] Past experience of issues with the potential for significant environmental and/or public health consequences (such as BSE) suggests that people are concerned to have uncertainties acknowledged ahead of time, and that there should be a plan of action in case the worst does happen. A liability regime is one possible way in which responsibility can be apportioned in the event of adverse environmental consequences, although it may not be the most appropriate mechanism for resolving these consequences, given the complicated policy issues involved.

The legislation specifically regulating GMOs does not make specific provision for full compensation for environmental damage or full reinstatement of the damaged environment. Use of the common law is not a particularly attractive or effective option, because of the limited extent to which civil liability rules are able to protect

---

[34] Regulation 1946/2003 of the European Parliament and of the Council of July 15, 2003 on transboundary movements of GMOs.
[35] See *GM Crops? Co-existence and Liability: A Report by the AEBC*, November 2003 (available at *www.aebc.gov.uk*).
[36] *ibid.*

parts of the general environment that are not privately owned. In relation to habitats and biodiversity, for example, there will usually be no individual with a right protected in law who would be able to bring a successful case.

The Royal Commission on Environmental Pollution recommended, in its 1989 report on GMOs, the introduction of an environmental liability regime. The recommendation was that any person (or the directors of any company or other organisation) responsible for carrying out the release of a GMO without the necessary licence and registration should be subject to strict liability for any damage arising. Relevant provisions were originally included within the drafting for Pt VI of the Environmental Protection Act 1990, but were taken out. Liability was regarded as a wider and more complex issue than was appropriate for such regulation, and one that needed to be considered on an international basis.[37]

Instead, a more general liability regime for GMOs was included within Pt VI, which contains provisions whose purpose is ". . . preventing or minimising any damage to the environment which may arise from the escape or release from human control of genetically modified organisms".[38] The remediation provisions are expressed in rather general terms, and can only be used if the responsible party has been convicted of an offence under s.118 of the Act. Where a person is convicted of an offence under s.118, subss.(a)–(f) (the subsections dealing with actions that could directly cause environmental harm), a court may (as well as or instead of imposing a punishment) order the convicted person to take specified steps "in respect of any matters which appear to the court to be matters which it is in his power to remedy".[39] Additionally, where committing an offence under those subsections "causes any harm which it is possible to remedy", the Secretary of State may "arrange for any reasonable steps to be taken towards remedying the harm"[40] and recover the cost of those steps from the convicted person.[41]

At the time of writing, a Private Member's Bill has been introduced to Parliament,[42] the purpose of which is to create a specific liability regime for GMO releases. One of the issues being debated, however, is whether, and why, environmental consequences of GMOs should merit separate regulation on liability. At EC and international level, damage caused by GMOs is regulated under the wider umbrella of a liability regime for environmentally damaging activities (see below). It is not clear whether environmental damage caused by GMOs could be dealt with under such a general regime, or whether a specific regime in necessary to address GM-specific issues.

EC liability measures

15–022   Directive 2004/35/EC on Liability for Environmental Damage[43] is discussed in Ch. 4. It will be recalled that the Directive provides that, where environmental damage has occurred, those responsible must take all practicable steps to control, contain, remove

[37] See *Hansard* House of Lords, Vol.522 cols 704—706.
[38] EPA 1990, s.106.
[39] *ibid.*, s.210.
[40] Subject to the permission of any third party in occupation of land who might be affected by the steps taken.
[41] EPA 1990, s.121.
[42] See Genetically Modified Food and Producer Liability (No.2) Bill.
[43] Directive 2004/35/EC on environmental liability with regard to the prevention and remedying of environmental damage O.J. L143/56 30/4/2004.

or otherwise manage the relevant contaminants, and to prevent further environmental damage. This can involve restoring damaged environmental amenities or replacing them with alternative amenities.

The furore over GM crops was a driving factor behind increased political pressure on the European Commission to speed up its work programme on environmental liability. The European Parliament reluctantly agreed to abandon its call to amend the Deliberate Release Directive to provide for a specific GMO liability regime, on condition that the Commission made faster progress with the general regime. This had the desired effect. The Directive was adopted on March 12, 2001, and had to be implemented in national laws by October 17, 2002.

The prospect of environmental damage being caused by the release of GMOs is specifically recognised in the Directive, and included in the list of activities to which strict liability applies. There is a specific "reporting requirement" for GMOs imposed under Art. 18. This requires a review to be conducted of the Directive's application to environmental damage caused by GMOs, "particularly in the light of experience gained within relevant international forums and Conventions, such as the Convention on Biological Diversity and the Cartagena Protocol on Biosafety, as well as the results of any incidents of environmental damage caused by GMOs". The review must take place 10 years after adoption of the Directive.

International liability measures

International law regulating GMOs does not provide specifically for liability. However, **15–023** the Cartagena Protocol includes a provision that the parties to the Protocol should work towards formulating rules governing liability. They must adopt a "process" for achieving this at the first meeting of the parties, and must try and complete this process within four years. Although the wording of the provision seems rather vague, it does mark a step forward in diplomatic terms, by recognising the need for specific rules on GMO liability. Hitherto, the focus had been on developing general liability regimes for environmentally damaging activities. In this regard, the efforts of the international community have resulted in the Council of Europe Convention on Civil Liability for Damage Resulting from Activities Dangerous to the Environment (the "Lugano Convention"), which is not yet in force.

The purpose of the Lugano Convention is to ensure adequate compensation for environmental and other damage resulting from "dangerous activities". "Dangerous activities" are defined to include the production, handling, storage, use or discharge of any dangerous substances, genetically modified organisms or micro-organisms. Operators involved in dangerous activities are strictly liable for any damage caused by the activity as a result of incidents in the period during which they exercise control over the relevant activity. "Damage" includes loss of life and personal injury, damage to property at the site of the dangerous activity, and impairment of the environment. Direct protection of the "unowned" environment, independently of damage to property or persons, is therefore provided by the Convention. Once the Convention comes into force, the extent to which states will incorporate it into their domestic law is likely to depend upon the extent to which it becomes established as part of international law. The UK has not even signed the Convention, and so, perhaps, will not consider itself under a great obligation to give effect to its requirements.

F: WORLD TRADE ISSUES

15–024 The role of the World Trade Organisation (WTO) is discussed in Ch. 2, along with the difficult issue of reconciling international trade rules with environmental protection. One of the basic principles of the rules enforced by the WTO is that member countries may not, in their trading practices, distinguish between like products. This extends to not distinguishing between products that are substantially equivalent but have been produced differently (*e.g.* by genetic modification). However, world trade rules also recognise that countries may impose restrictions on trade in the interests of environmental protection.[44] This situation may prove problematic in relation to GMOs.

At the time of writing, no new GM crops or products have been approved in Europe since October 1998, which has created a *de facto* moratorium on GMOs within the EC. This situation arose because a number of Member States made it clear that they would oppose new environmental licensing of GMOs until rules on labelling and traceability were adopted. These new rules, which have been discussed above, came into force in April 2004. In August 2003, the US, Canada and Argentina brought a case against the EC to the World Trade Organisation. These countries claim that the unofficial EC moratorium is an illegal barrier to trade. The US estimates that it has lost $300m of agricultural sales to Europe annually since the moratorium arose. The case is expected to be decided in early 2005.

At the time of writing, although the adoption of the new EC traceability and labelling regulations should allow the moratorium to be lifted, it is unclear whether this will resolve the case. The US and Canada have expressed concerns over the new labelling and traceability regulations, suggesting they are not based on sound science and will be difficult to implement. Whereas the previous EC labelling regime was based on the physical detection of GM material in products, the new regime is based on a paper audit trail which simply *links* products to GM crops. The US has signalled that it may challenge this regime in a new case before the WTO.

The relevant world trade rules contain no specific provisions on GMOs, and it is unclear to what extent they might allow states to regulate unilaterally the importation and use of GMOs within their territories.[45] The picture is further complicated by the adoption of the Cartagena Protocol on Biosafety, which, as we have seen, provides that, as between contracting parties, no transboundary movements of GM products can take place without "advance informed agreement". The Protocol is quite clearly designed to regulate world trade in GMOs, and therefore encroaches on the world trade rules enforced by the WTO. It remains to be seen what approach will be taken by the WTO in interpreting these rules in the light of the Protocol.

---

[44] See the Sanitary and Phyto-Sanitary Agreement.
[45] Issues include whether GMO concerns might fall within the Agreement on the Application of Sanitary and Phytosanitary Measures (SPS Agreement), the Agreement on Technical Barriers to Trade (TBT Agreement), the General Agreement on Tariffs and Trade (GATT) or all three.

Index